EYEWITNESS TRAVEL GUIDES

THE
WORLD'S 200
MUST-SEE
PLACES

EYEWITNESS TRAVEL GUIDES

THE
WORLD'S 200
MUST-SEE
PLACES

DK

Château de Chambord, France

CONTENTS

INTRODUCTION *6-9*

**St Vitus's Cathedral and
Charles Bridge, Prague**

**Fresco by Giotto, Basilica of
St Francis, Assisi**

**Sydney Opera House,
Australia**

**Ruins of Machu Picchu, high in the
Peruvian Andes**

The mud-brick walls of the Djenné Mosque, Mali

INTRODUCTION

Travelers in the Classical age, whose ideas of enjoyment were probably little different from our own, had few sites to visit. It was therefore not difficult for Greek writers to list the seven best and call them the "wonders of the world." Civilizations have come a long way since then, the world has shrunk with high-speed travel, and there has been no let up in the desire to build. These days, it would be hard to pinpoint the seven most wondrous efforts in the world. But here are 200 sites that should not be missed.

Created for people of vision and flair to glorify themselves, their gods, and their power as well as their genius, these buildings are landmarks that tell us about the past, where we have come from, and what we are capable of achieving. Each one needs close inspection to appreciate its setting, structure, style, and ornament. Palaces, castles, religious houses, and places of entertainment have been handed to artists and artisans to embellish. Around and within these walls masons, carpenters, wood carvers, ceramicists, sculptors, painters, glassmakers, metalworkers, cabinet makers, embroiderers, tapestry makers, and landscape gardeners have all sought some kind of perfection. Some are well known, but most were journeymen whose names were never meant to last. In the creation of these buildings they caught the glory of their age for all the world to see, for ever.

It is astonishing that some have lasted so long. With few exceptions, such as Norway's stave churches, the palaces of Kerala, and the Todai-ji Temple in Japan, most wooden structures have not survived. Even stone buildings have frequently come to grief in earthquakes, war, fire, and flood. As a result many are like palimpsests, written over again and again. In Europe a single building can have

St Basil's Cathedral in Moscow, crowned with colorful domes

within it half a dozen cultures dating back more than 2,000 years. Their uses change: castle to palace, church to fort, and many now flourish today as museums.

UNESCO WORLD HERITAGE SITES

The Great Pyramid at Giza in Egypt is the only surviving wonder of the ancient world. In 1979 it was designated a World Heritage Site by the United Nations Educational, Scientific, and Cultural Organization (UNESCO), an agency of the United Nations set up in 1945. The idea of a fund to preserve the world's heritage was sparked in 1959 when the temples at Abu Simbel were in danger of drowning in Lake Nasser by the building of the Aswan High Dam. Following an appeal from the governments of Egypt and Sudan, UNESCO raised US$80 million to move the temples of Ramses II and Nefertari over 60 m (197 ft) out of harm's way.

Grand façade of Buckingham Palace, London

◁ **The Taj Mahal built by Shah Jahan, in memory of his wife Mumtaz**

The work was completed in 1968 and as a result of this success, UNESCO with the International Council on Monuments and Sites (ICOMOS) went on to draft a new convention to protect the world's cultural heritage. Joined by ideas from the International Union for the Conservation of Nature (IUCN), proposals for safeguarding both cultural and natural sites were formally adopted by UNESCO's General Conference in 1972.

There are some 800 UNESCO World Heritage Sites around the world today, more than 600 of them cultural, as opposed to natural, sites. Italy and Spain have the most, followed by France and Germany. Each year a dozen or more sites are added to the list. Proposals can come from any one of the signed-up member countries who give one percent of their UNESCO dues to the fund. With voluntary contributions, the Fund

Striking Gothic exterior of Cologne Cathedral, Germany

receives around US$3.5 million a year. The money goes towards preserving the sites, while some is set aside for those currently deemed at risk through man-made or natural calamities.

TOURISM

The feet of thousands of visitors also put sites at risk, and many have had to restrict access because of this. Conservation, however, is also helped by tourism which can provide funds from charging an entrance fee.

We now have a chance to see inside these buildings, to wander their corridors and squares, and our curiosity is unbounded. Today, many of these spectacular sites are only a weekend break away. Some provide exhibitions, talks, conferences, or concerts, while others are the keepers of colorful rituals and traditions.

Not all sites are so easily accessible. Religious devotees often sought remote places for their contemplations, for example in the caves of Cappadocia, or on the mountains of Metéora. Some were strategically remote, such as Macchu Pichu in Peru, so hard to find that it was lost to the world for centuries. For a traveler, perhaps the longer the journey, the greater the reward.

Many ancient and prehistoric sites were based on the movement of the sun and stars, and being there at dawn or at a solstice is to feel their potent magic. Others have their special times: when choirs and music fill the churches; when festivals recall the buildings' heydays; when a full moon hovers over the Taj Mahal, the sun sets on San Francisco's Golden Gate, or when snow is snug around St Petersburg's Winter Palace. Some museums are gratis on a particular day, while visiting any site early always tends to be best. Rainy or baking-hot seasons are to be avoided, and sometimes buildings, or parts of them, are closed for renovation. However, you might want to visit Mali in the spring to watch the renovation of Djenné Mosque when around 4,000 townspeople replaster the mud-brick building in a splendid festival.

Pyramid of the Niches, El Tajín, Mexico, once the political and religious center for the Totonac civilization

The Alhambra's Patio de los Leones, typifying the sensual architecture of the Moors

MEN AND MATERIALS

Conservation requires skilled craftspeople. A stonemason these days may be as much in demand as any in the Middle Ages. The right materials are important, too. They are not only required to be authentic, but they must work within their limitations. Stone can reach only a certain height and it wasn't until the 19th century that the 147m (482 ft) high Great Pyramid at Giza was surpassed. The secret of the new summits was cast iron, illustrated by Gustav Eiffel with his magnificent 274 m (905 ft) Parisian tower.

In the 20th century new shapes became possible through the use of reinforced concrete, notable in the structures of Brasília, New York's Guggenheim Museum, and the Sydney Opera House. These were also among the first buildings to make use of computer technology. Less than half a century later this technology helped produce marvels such as the titanium waves of Bilbao's Guggenheim Museum.

Buildings are monuments to patrons and architects – through them their names have been handed down to us. In ancient sites the archaeologists are also remembered, men driven by the desire to be the first to find treasures lost for millennia. Imagine the delight of Sir Arthur Evans when he located Crete's Palace of Knosós, or of the French team that uncovered Volubilis in Morocco.

Discoveries pepper the 19th century, a time when steam power made travel easier and artifacts from sites seemed waiting to be revealed. Ideas were revived, too, and the century saw the rebirth of many styles. The Arc de Triomphe revisited the Classical style, the parliament houses in both London and Budapest revived Gothic, while castle building was spectacularly revived in King Ludwig's Bavarian fantasy, Neuschwanstein Castle.

Ramses II, Temple of Amun, Egypt

Buildings have become emblems of whole nations: the Statue of Liberty, Buckingham Palace, St Peter's, Angkor Wat, the Taj Mahal. Romantic, exotic, seductive, the names speak volumes. By the same token churches, monasteries, mosques, temples, and shrines have become defining symbols of different faiths. More modestly, they help to conjure up the lives of a single occupant, be they homes of artists such as Rubens in Antwerp, or extraordinary figures who were irrevocably linked to a place, such as Prinsengracht 263, the house in Amsterdam where Anne Frank was hidden.

Whatever a building's form and function, and whatever its age and condition, it always has many stories to tell. Through these pages, their walls are peeled back and the layers of history are unfolded and revealed to provide the opportunity to step inside and let the imagination roam.

The Great Wall of China snakes through the landscape, a major tourist attraction and powerful symbol of China

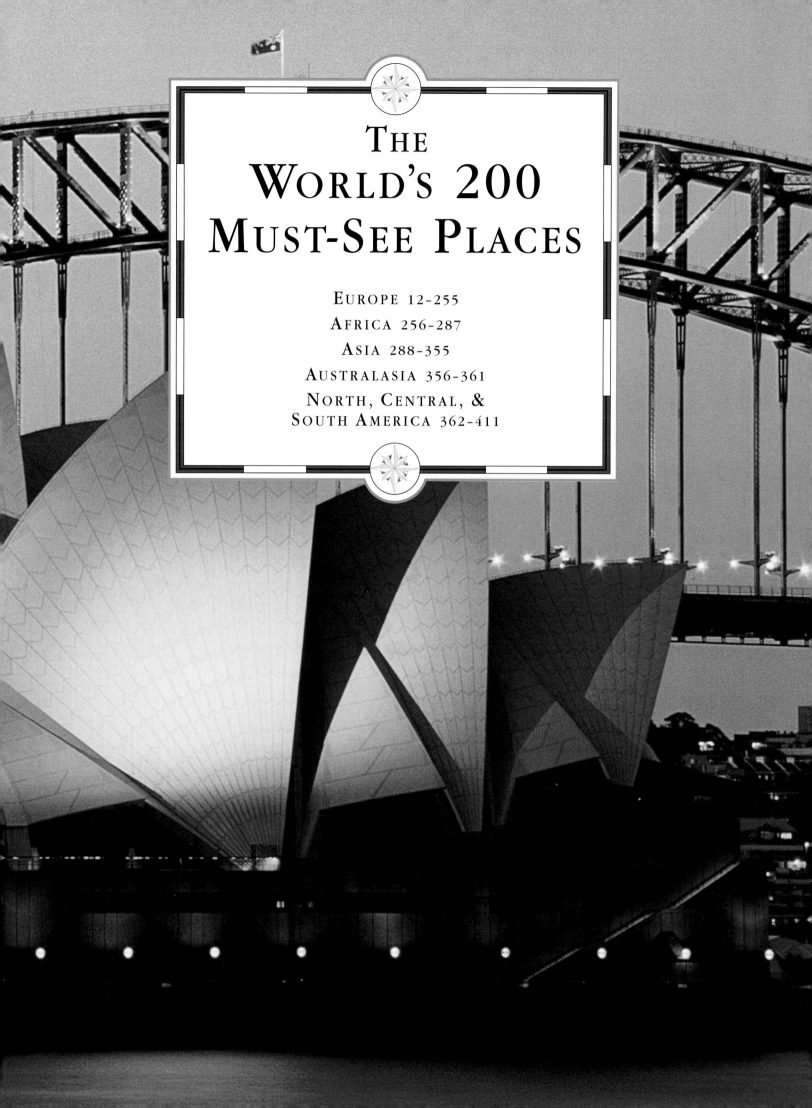

THE
WORLD'S 200
MUST-SEE PLACES

Model of old Christiana defended by the Akershus fortress

HÅKON V

King Håkon V, who reigned in Norway from 1299 to 1319, planned to create a stronger state by reducing the influence of the nobility and the church. To defend his state, he built Akershus. The location of the castle had been chosen with great care. One of the kingdom's most important roads passed nearby and the proximity to the sea was of crucial importance to military strength. Strategically, whoever controlled eastern Norway ruled the kingdom of Norway and holding Akershus was the key. Hence the battle for power became a battle for Akershus Slott. This continued after King Håkon V's death in 1319. Although the fortress has frequently been in the firing line and rebuilt several times over the centuries, King Håkon's castle still stands as testimony to his vision.

CHRISTIAN IV

When the predominantly wooden city of Oslo was burned to the ground during the great fire of 1624, it was rebuilt by Christian IV, king of Denmark and Norway from 1588 to 1648. The city was relocated within the protective walls of the fortress and named Christiania in his honor, a name it kept for 300 years (although by then it had expanded beyond the fortress walls). During this time, Christian IV converted Akershus Castle into a Renaissance palace (▷ *Renaissance Style p211*). Magnificent banqueting halls and lavish staterooms were created above well-preserved medieval dungeons (▷ *Cellars*) where outcasts were imprisoned.

Akershus Castle, Oslo

FOR 700 YEARS THE AKERSHUS FORTRESS has been standing guard over Oslo to ward off all attempts to invade the city from the sea. The castle occupies a spectacular setting on a hill at the head of Oslofjorden. King Håkon V started to build this historically grand castle in 1299, and since then the fortifications have undergone numerous improvements and reconstructions. One of the fortress's greatest moments was to resist the siege of the Swedish king, Karl XII, in 1716. In the 19th century, the castle's defensive role declined in significance and it became an administrative center for the armed forces. Today, Akershus Castle contains a variety of notable buildings, museums, and defense installations. It is also the government's principal venue for state functions.

★ Olav's Hall
The North Hall was renovated in 1976 and named after King Olav V (r.1957–91).

The Romeriks Hall
The fireplace (1634–42) with the coat-of-arms of Governor-General Christopher Urne and his wife was found in another building in 1900 and restored to the castle.

Romeriks Tower

North Wing

Scribes Rooms
The rooms known as Skrivestuene were named after a timber-framed building called the Scribes Rooms House that once stood on this site. It was used by court administrators.

STAR FEATURES

★ **Olav's Hall**

★ **Courtyard**

★ **Christian IV's Hall**

★ Courtyard
In the Middle Ages, the Courtyard (Borggården) was divided by a large tower, Vågehalsen, which was destroyed by fire in 1527. A Renaissance courtyard was created and the two towers, Romerikstårnet and Blåtårnet, were erected.

Akershus Slott in 1699

A painting by Jacob Croning, who was attached to the court of the Danish-Norwegian Christian V. The king asked Croning to paint Norwegian scenes.

Remains of Vågehalsen, the medieval tower which once divided the courtyard.

The Blue Tower (Blåtårnet)

The tapestry, *Rideskolen*, was woven by E Leyniers, c.1650, to a design by J Jordaiens.

★ Christian IV's Hall

In the 17th century this hall formed part of the Danish king and queen's private apartments. In the 19th century it became a military arsenal. Now restored, it is used by the government for receptions.

The Virgin Tower (Jomfrutårnet)

South Wing

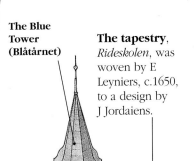

The cellars were used as dungeons from 1500–1700. One of the dungeons was known as The Witch Hole. Later, prisoners were locked up in the fortress.

Royal Mausoleum

The mausoleum contains the remains of Sigurd Jorsalfar, Håkon VII and his wife Maud, and Olav V and Martha, among others.

KEY DATES

1299 King Håkon V Magnusson commissions the building of Akershus Castle.

1624 King Christian IV refashions the building as a Renaissance palace after the great fire of 1624.

1716 The fortress survives a siege by the Swedish warrior king, Karl XII.

1942 Akershus Castle is used as a Nazi prison.

1991 King Olav V follows tradition and is buried in the chapel's mausoleum.

NORWAY'S RESISTANCE MUSEUM

During World War II, Akershus Castle was used as a Nazi prison and place of execution. On 9 April 1940, German forces invaded Norway. While a valiant attempt was made to halt their advance, Norway succumbed 62 days later. For five years the Norwegian Resistance conducted a heroic campaign against the invaders and their exploits are well-documented in Norges Hjemmefrontmuseum (Norway's Resistance Museum). Taped speeches and film clips recreate the World War II years alongside the collection of documents, posters, and memorabilia from that time. The museum is in a 200-m (656-ft) long, 17th-century stone vault in Bindingsverkshuset (Half-Timbered House) within the Akershus fortress area. It was opened on 8 May 1970, the 25th anniversary of the liberation.

Akershus Castle

Urnes Stave Church, constructed c. 1130–50

CONSTRUCTION METHODS

The earliest stave churches, built in the 11th century, had wooden wall columns which were set directly into the ground. These churches lasted no more than 100 years, as moisture in the earth caused the column bases to rot away. As construction techniques developed, it became customary to set the wooden framework on sills which rested on a stone foundation. This raised the entire wooden skeleton above ground level, protecting it from humidity. This method proved so effective that churches built in the 12th century are still standing today. Among these is Borgund Stave Church, which was built from almost 2,000 carefully crafted pieces of wood.

STAVE CHURCH DESIGN

Borgund Stave Church is one of the largest and most ornately designed of the almost 30 remaining stave churches in Norway. Commonly they were simple, relatively small structures with a ▷ *nave* and narrow chancel. Borgund's chancel also has a distinctive semicircular apse. Stave posts mark a division between the two. The interior is dark, as light can only filter through from small round openings (▷ *the windows*) under the three-tiered roof, which is crowned by a turret. An ▷ *external gallery* frequently encircles stave churches.

Borgund Stave Church

THE ONLY STAVE CHURCH to have remained unchanged since the Middle Ages is Borgund Stavkirke at Lærdal in western Norway. Dedicated to the apostle St Andrew, it dates from around 1150 and is built entirely of wood. The interior is very simple: there are no pews or decorations, and the lighting is limited to a few small openings high up on the walls. The exterior is richly decorated with carvings: dragon-like animals in life-and-death struggles, dragon-heads, and runic inscriptions. There is a free-standing belfry with a medieval bell. The pulpit dates from the 16th century.

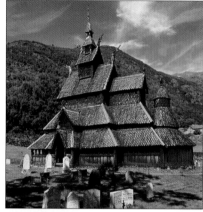

Stave Church Location
Many of the surviving stave churches are in remote locations. High, exposed sites which were noticeable and remarkable were generally chosen to create a dramatic visual effect.

Nave
Twelve posts (staves) around the central part of the nave support the roof. Disappearing into the semi-darkness of the roof, they give an increased sense of height.

Crosses decorate the gables above the doorways and apse tower.

West Door
The exterior of the church is richly adorned. The decorations on the Romanesque west door show vine-like ornamentation and dragon battles.

A spire sits at the top of the three-tiered roof.

The roofs are clad in pine shingles.

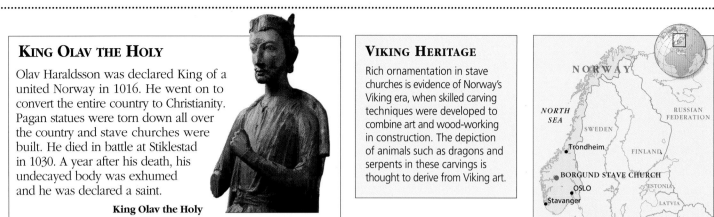

KING OLAV THE HOLY

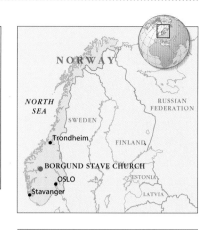

Olav Haraldsson was declared King of a united Norway in 1016. He went on to convert the entire country to Christianity. Pagan statues were torn down all over the country and stave churches were built. He died in battle at Stiklestad in 1030. A year after his death, his undecayed body was exhumed and he was declared a saint.

King Olav the Holy

VIKING HERITAGE

Rich ornamentation in stave churches is evidence of Norway's Viking era, when skilled carving techniques were developed to combine art and wood-working in construction. The depiction of animals such as dragons and serpents in these carvings is thought to derive from Viking art.

The central tower has a three-tiered roof. The first tier is decorated with dragonheads on the gables, similar to those on the main roof. These were meant to cleanse the air, purging it of the evil spirits of unlawful pagan worship.

The windows are simply circular openings in the outer walls.

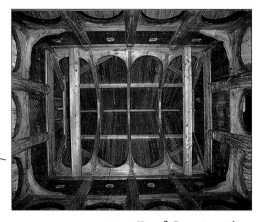

Roof Construction

Carved and constructed out of timber, this spectacular Gothic church (▷ Gothic Style p73) contains richly decorated gables, colonnades, and capitals. Seen from below, the roof is composed of an intricate framework using numerous rafters and joists.

External gallery

Altarpiece

The interior of Borgund Church contains no ornate embellishment apart from a simple pulpit and altar. This altarpiece dates from 1654.

Crosses of St Andrew, in the shape of the letter "X", border the central nave.

KEY DATES

1150 Borgund Stave Church is erected.

Late 1500s The pulpit is constructed.

Mid-1600s The altarpiece is added.

1870 The church goes out of regular service when a larger church is constructed nearby.

ORNAMENTATION

The introduction of Christianity to Norway around the year 1000 saw the merging of pagan and Christian cultures and beliefs. Most stave churches were erected on the sites of old temples which were destroyed in the wake of Christianity. The impact of this can be seen in the richly decorated carvings in stave churches, which unite pre-Christian and Christian symbolism. Pagan gods were represented in disguise alongside medieval Christian saints. The door frame designs (▷ *West Door*) are particularly elaborate, and demonstrate the skill of the carpenters who embellished them from top to bottom with intricate carvings. Wood from pine trees was commonly used as this was most readily available. Branches and bark were removed from the trees, which were then left to dry out before being chopped down. This method meant that the wood was more weather-resistant and durable.

THE GOLDEN HALL

This splendid hall is decorated with over 18 million beautifully colored mosaics, constructed from ceramic, glass, and 24 carat handmade gold leaf. Despite its large size the ▷ *Golden Hall* is very warm and intimate and is used as a banqueting hall. It was the location for the Nobel Prize festivities from 1930, until the celebrations were finally moved in 1974 to the ▷ *Blue Hall* to accommodate the large event. The hall is dominated by the *Queen of the Lake Mälaren* on the northern wall, which represents Stockholm being honored by the East and West.

**Alfred Nobel, founder
the Nobel prize**

THE NOBEL PRIZE

Alfred Nobel (1833–96) was an outstanding chemist and inventor. After his death, it was discovered that he left instructions in his will for his fortune to be used as a financial prize for individuals who had contributed to the advancement of humanity. Prizes were to be awarded for literature, chemistry, physics, and physiology or medicine by Sweden, and the prize for peace was to be awarded by Norway. The first Nobel Prize ceremony was held in 1901, at the Old Royal Academy of Music in Stockholm. One of four laureates to receive an award was Wilhelm Conrad Röntgen for the discovery of x-rays. Baroness Bertha von Suttner, one of the first female nominees, was awarded the peace prize in 1905.

City Hall, Stockholm

PROBABLY SWEDEN'S BIGGEST architectural project of the 20th century, the City Hall was completed in 1923 and has become a symbol of Stockholm. It was designed by leading Swedish architect Ragnar Östberg (1866–1945), who was inspired by the Doge's Palace in Venice. Several influential Swedish artists contributed to its rich interior, including furniture designer Carl Malmsten and textile artist Maja **Engelbrekt** Sjöström. The annual Nobel Prize festivities take place each year on 10 December in the Blue Hall.

Norra Trapptornet is crowned by a sun. Its southern counterpart features a moon.

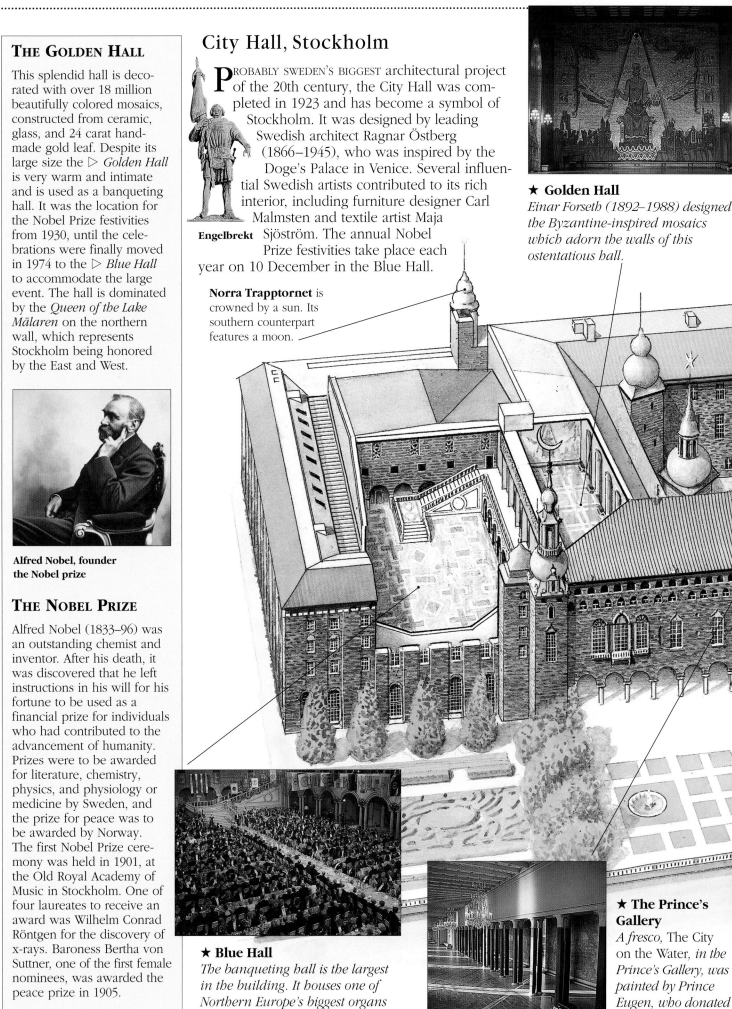

★ **Golden Hall**
Einar Forseth (1892–1988) designed the Byzantine-inspired mosaics which adorn the walls of this ostentatious hall.

★ **Blue Hall**
The banqueting hall is the largest in the building. It houses one of Northern Europe's biggest organs with over 10,000 pipes.

★ **The Prince's Gallery**
A fresco, The City on the Water, *in the Prince's Gallery, was painted by Prince Eugen, who donated to the City Hall.*

Three Crowns

Sweden's heraldic symbol, Tre Kronor, dating from the 14th century, tops the 106 m (348 ft) tower.

Borgargården Square

THE BLUE HALL'S NAME

The hall should have been painted blue, but when Östberg saw the beautiful red bricks he changed his mind. The name Blue Hall was kept as it was already on the building plans and in common use.

NORTH SEA

SWEDEN   FINLAND

NORWAY

RUSSIAN FEDERATION

CITY HALL STOCKHOLM

ESTONIA

Gothenburg

LATVIA

DENMARK   LITHUANIA

KEY DATES

1911–23 The City Hall is built under the supervision of architect and designer Ragnar Östberg.

1930 The Nobel Prize banquet is held in the City Hall for the first time.

2001 The 100th anniversary of the Nobel Prize is held in the Blue Hall at City Hall.

The Council Chamber

Stockholm's 101 councillors meet in this magnificent chamber, which contains furnishings designed by Carl Malmsten.

RAGNAR ÖSTBERG'S DESIGN

The Swedish architect Ragnar Östberg was born in Vaxholm, in 1866. He studied at the Royal Institute of Technology and at the Royal Academy of Art in Sweden. His earliest commissions were private houses, which he designed in traditional Swedish styles. His design for Stockholm's city hall erected around two squares, one covered (▷ *Blue Hall*) and the other uncovered (▷ *Borgargården Square*), is considered to be his greatest architectural work. The imposing red brick structure houses offices, banqueting halls, and the ▷ *Council Chamber* meeting room, with a roof designed to look like an overturned Viking longboat. The Ovale, antechamber to the ▷ *Blue Hall* and ▷ *Golden Hall*, displays the 17th-century Tureholm tapestries, woven in Beauvais, France. Östberg also added a tower to the east end of the building, adorned with three royal crowns, which can be seen from all over Stockholm.

Engelbrekt the Freedom Fighter

by Christian Eriksson (1858–1935).

The Dance

The steps leading to the waters of Riddarfjärden are flanked by two statues by Carl Eldh. Dansen is the figure of a woman, Sången (the Song) is that of a man.

STAR FEATURES

★ **Golden Hall**

★ **Blue Hall**

★ **The Prince's Gallery**

City Hall

Vasamuseet, designed by Marianne Dahlbäck and Göran Månsson

THE SHIP

The *Vasa* was built as a symbol of Swedish might by King Gustav II Adolf. He was steadily increasing Swedish influence over the Baltic region during the 1620s, through war with Poland. It was constructed by Dutch shipbuilder Henrik Hybertsson. *Vasa* was the largest ship in the history of the Swedish fleet and was capable of carrying 64 cannons and over 445 crew. From its high ▷ *stern* it would have been possible to fire down on smaller ships. It was equipped for both traditional close combat and artillery battles. The musketeers had shooting galleries for training, and on the upper deck were so-called "storm pieces", erected as protection against musketry fire.

LIFE ON BOARD

Vasa's destination on its maiden voyage was intended to be the Älvsnabben naval base in the southern Stockholm archipelago, where more soldiers were to embark. Each man's life on the ship would have been determined by his rank. The officers would have slept in bunks and the Admiral in his cabin. They also had better food than the crew whose meals were very basic, and consisted of beans, porridge, salted fish, and beer. The decks would have been very crowded – the small space between every two guns was the living and sleeping quarters for seven men (▷ *Gun Deck)*. There was no fresh food, so a lot of the crew would have had scurvy and died from deficiency diseases before they reached battle.

Vasa Museum, Stockholm

SWEDEN'S MOST VISITED museum enshrines the royal warship *Vasa*, which capsized on its maiden voyage of just 1,300 m (4,265 ft) in calm weather, on 10 August 1628 in Stockholm's harbor. About 50 people went down with what was supposed to be the pride of the Navy. Guns were all that were salvaged from the vessel in the 17th century and it was not until 1956 that a marine archaeologist's persistent search led to the rediscovery of the *Vasa*. After a complex salvage operation followed by a 17-year conservation program, the city's most popular museum was opened in June 1990, less than one nautical mile from the scene of the disaster.

Gun-port Lion
More than 200 carved ornaments and 500 sculpted figures decorate Vasa.

★ Lion Figurehead
King Gustav II Adolf, who commissioned the Vasa, *was known as the Lion of the North. So a springing lion was the obvious choice for the figurehead. It is 4 m (13 ft) long and weighs 450 kg (990 lb).*

The rigging has been meticulously reconstructed to reflect that of a 17th–century warship.

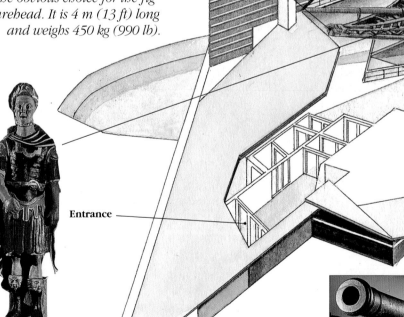

Entrance

Emperor Titus
Carvings of 20 Roman emperors stand on parade on Vasa.

Bronze Cannon
More than 50 of Vasa's *64 original cannons were salvaged already in the 17th century. Three 11 kg (24 lb) bronze cannons are on display in the museum.*

★ **Stern**
Vasa's *stern was badly damaged but has been painstakingly restored to reveal the ship's magnificent ornamentation.*

WOOD CARVINGS

The wood carvers who made the sculptures and ornaments decorating the warship came from Holland and Germany. The motifs, taken from Greek mythology, the Bible, Roman and Swedish history, were carved in oak, pine and lime, in late Renaissance and early Baroque styles.

The main mast
was originally 52 m (170 ft) high.

KEY DATES

1625 King Gustav II Adolf orders new warships including *Vasa*.

1628 *Vasa* is ready for its maiden voyage, but capsizes in Stockholm's harbour.

1956 Archaeologist Andérs Franzen locates *Vasa*.

1961 *Vasa* is raised to the surface after 333 years on the sea bed.

1962 The temporary *Vasa* museum, Wasavarvet opens.

1990 The Vasa Museum opens as a permanent museum, showing the restored *Vasa* and its treasures.

The Gun Ports
Vasa *carried more heavy cannons on its two gundecks than earlier ships of the same size. This contributed to its capsizing.*

Reconstruction of the upper gun deck

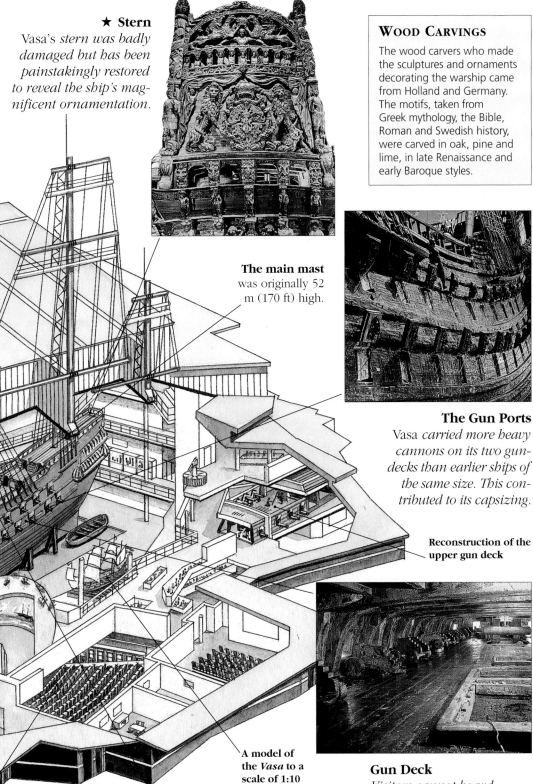

THE SALVAGE OPERATION

The marine archaeologist Andérs Franzen had been looking for *Vasa* for many years. On 25 August 1956 his patience was rewarded when he brought up a piece of blackened oak on his plumb line from *Vasa*, located 30 m (100 ft) beneath the surface. From the autumn of 1957, it took divers two years to clear tunnels under the hull for the lifting cables. The first lift with six cables was a success, after which *Vasa* was lifted in 16 stages into shallower water. Thousands of plugs were then inserted into holes left by rusted iron bolts. The final lift started on the morning of 24 April 1961, and on 4 May *Vasa* was finally towed into dry dock after 333 years under water.

A model of the *Vasa* to a scale of 1:10

Gun Deck
Visitors cannot board the ship, but there is a full-size copy of the upper gun deck with carved wooden dummies of sailors, which gives a good idea of conditions on board.

film auditorium

Upper Deck
The entrance to the cabins was towards the stern. This area was the grandest part of the ship, reserved for senior officers. Part of the original mainmast can be seen on the right.

STAR FEATURES

★ **Lion Figurehead**

★ **Stern**

PALACE APARTMENTS

Linked by a Baroque corridor, the central part of the palace is dominated by the ▷ *main staircase*, with ceiling paintings by D K Ehrenstrahl. The Green Salon marks the beginning of the main ceremonial suite, which continues with the Karl X's Gallery, the Ehrenstrahl Salon where Queen Hedvig Eleonora (1636–1715) held audiences, the ▷ *Queen Lovisa Ulrika's Library*, and the ▷ *State Bedroom* with a hidden staircase linking to the Chinese Salon above. The Oscar Room is adorned by a tapestry dating from the 1630s and leads to the General's Room, the Golden Salon, and the Queen's Room containing portraits of European queens.

The Chinese Pavilion, an exotic extravaganza

THE COURT THEATER, CHINESE PAVILION, AND PALACE PARK

The palace of Drottningholm is complemented by the Court Theater. Built in the 18th century, it was popular at the time of Gustav III, but fell into decline after his death. In 1922, it was restored to its original state under the supervision of theater historian, Agne Beijer. The Chinese Pavilion (1769) replaced a wooden structure which had been a gift to Queen Lovisa Ulrika on her 33rd birthday in 1753. Designed by architect D F Adelcrantz, the new pavilion is a mixture of Rococo and what was considered to be Chinese style, fashionable at the time. The palace includes the formal ▷ *Baroque Garden*, a water parterre with fountains, a Rococo-inspired garden, and the landscaped English-style park.

Drottningholm Palace

THE UNIQUE BAROQUE and rococo (▷ *Baroque Style p111* and *Rococo Style p118)* environment of Drottningholm – its palace, theater, park, and Chinese Pavilion – have been perfectly preserved. This royal palace on the outskirts of Stockholm emerged in its present form towards the end of the 17th century. Contemporary Italian and French architecture inspired Tessin the Elder (1615–81) in his design, which was intended to glorify royal power. The project was completed by Tessin the Younger, while 18th-century architects like Carl Hårleman and Jean Eric Rehn finished the interiors. The present Royal Family uses parts of the palace as their private residence.

Baroque Garden
The bronze statue of Hercules by the Dutch Renaissance sculptor Adrian de Vries adorns the parterre in the otherwise Baroque gardens.

The Upper South Bodyguard Room
This ante-room to the State Room, used for ceremonial occasions, was decorated with stucco works by Giovanni and Carlo Carove and ceiling paintings by Johan Sylvius.

Apartments of the Royal Family

STAR FEATURES

★ **Queen Lovisa Ulrika's Library**

★ **Main Staircase**

★ **State Bedroom**

Writing Table by Georg Haupt
Standing in the Queen's Room is this masterpiece (1770) commissioned by King Adolf Fredrik as a gift to Queen Lovisa Ulrika. Textiles for the walls and furnishings were restored in the 1970s.

★ **Queen Lovisa Ulrika's Library**

The Queen commissioned Jean Eric Rehn (1717–93) to decorate this splendid library which emphasizes her influence on art and science in Sweden in the 18th century.

COURT THEATER FESTIVAL

Every year in early September, top international artists from around the world gather to perform in 18th-century operas and ballet in the beautiful historic theater.

The Palace Church in the northern cupola was completed by Hårleman in the 1720s.

KEY DATES

1662 Queen Dowager Hedvig Eleonora builds Drottningholm Palace.

1744 Drottningholm Palace is given as a wedding present to Princess Lovisa Ulrika of Prussia, on her marriage to Swedish heir Adolf Fredrik.

1764 The Court Theater is built at the request of Queen Lovisa Ulrika.

1769 The Chinese Pavilion, designed by architect C F Adelcrantz, is erected.

1777 Gustav III moves into Drottningholm Palace, adding Neo-Classical touches and lush English-style parkland.

1991 Drottningholm Palace, the Chinese Pavilion and the surrounding park is designated a World Heritage Site.

GUSTAV III

Gustav III (1771–92) is one of the most colorful figures in Swedish history. After a bloodless revolution in 1772 he ruled with absolute power and initiated a wide-ranging program of reform. Influenced by the ideals of the Enlightenment and by French culture, he revived interest in art, literature, and theater. He made this a golden age for Swedish culture and several prestigious academies were founded at the time. But his attacks on the privileges of the nobility and his adventurous and costly foreign policy made him powerful enemies. He was shot during a masked ball in 1792.

Entrance

★ **State Bedroom**
To copy French court habits, Hedvig Eleonora held her morning receptions ("levées") in this lavish Baroque room designed by Tessin the Elder. It took about 15 years for Sweden's foremost artists and craftsmen to decorate the room, which was completed in 1683.

★ **Main Staircase**
Trompe-l'oeil paintings by Johan Sylvius adorn the walls, giving the impression that the already spacious interior stretches further into the palace.

TARA AND ITS KINGS

A site of mythical importance, Tara was the political and spiritual center of Celtic Ireland and the seat of the High Kings until the 11th century. Whoever ruled Tara could claim supremacy over Ireland. It is thought that many of Tara's kings were buried in pagan ceremonies at Newgrange. Tara's importance as a spiritual center diminished as Christianity flourished. Legend says that Tara's most famous king, Cormac Mac Art who ruled in the 3rd century, did not wish to be buried at Newgrange among pagan kings. His kinsmen, disregarding his wish, tried to cross the River Boyne to Newgrange but failed due to the huge waves and so he was buried elsewhere according to his wishes.

WINTER SOLSTICE AT NEWGRANGE

The shortest day and the longest night occurs each year on 21 December and is known as the Winter Solstice. At Newgrange, on the morning of 21 December, rays of sunlight shine into the roof box of the passage grave and light up the ▷ *passage* illuminating the north recess of the cruciform burial ▷ *chamber*. At all other times of the year the tomb is shrouded in darkness. Newgrange is the only passage grave currently excavated which has this characteristic – temples tend to be the usual locations for this type of event. Many believe that because of this, Newgrange was originally used as a place of worship, and only later as a burial ground for pagan kings.

Megalithic motifs adorning the walls of Newgrange

Newgrange

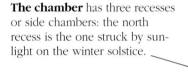

Tri-spiral carving on stone in chamber

THE ORIGINS OF Newgrange, one of the most important passage graves in Europe, are steeped in mystery. According to Celtic lore, the legendary kings of Tara were buried here, but Newgrange predates them. The grave was left untouched by all invaders except the Danish, who raided its burial chambers in the 9th century. In 1699, it was rediscovered by local landowner, Charles Campbell Scott. When it was excavated in the 1960s, archaeologist Professor M J O'Kelly discovered that on the winter solstice, 21 December, rays of sun enter the tomb and light up the burial chamber – making it the world's oldest solar observatory.

Basin Stone
The chiseled stones, found in each recess, would have once contained funerary offerings and the bones of the dead.

The chamber has three recesses or side chambers: the north recess is the one struck by sunlight on the winter solstice.

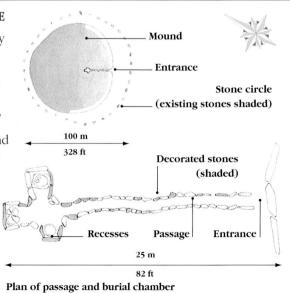

Chamber Ceiling
The burial chamber's intricate corbeled ceiling, which reaches a height of 6 m (20 ft) above the floor, has survived intact. The overlapping slabs form a conical hollow, topped by a single capstone.

CONSTRUCTION OF NEWGRANGE

The tomb at Newgrange was designed by people with clearly exceptional artistic and engineering skills, who had use of neither the wheel nor metal tools. About 200,000 tons of loose stones were transported to build the mound, or cairn, which protects the passage grave. Larger slabs were used to make the circle around the cairn (12 out of a probable 35 stones have survived), the curb, and the tomb itself. Many of the curbstones and the slabs lining the passage, the chamber, and its recesses are decorated with zigzags, spirals, and other geometric motifs. The grave's corbeled ceiling consists of smaller, unadorned slabs and has proved completely waterproof for the last 5,000 years.

Mound
Entrance
Stone circle
(existing stones shaded)
100 m
328 ft
Decorated stones
(shaded)
Recesses   Passage   Entrance
25 m
82 ft
Plan of passage and burial chamber

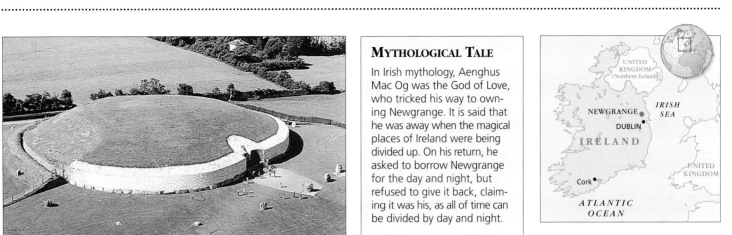

MYTHOLOGICAL TALE

In Irish mythology, Aenghus Mac Og was the God of Love, who tricked his way to owning Newgrange. It is said that he was away when the magical places of Ireland were being divided up. On his return, he asked to borrow Newgrange for the day and night, but refused to give it back, claiming it was his, as all of time can be divided by day and night.

Restoration of Newgrange

Located on a low ridge north of the river Boyne, Newgrange took more than 70 years to build. Between 1962 and 1975 the passage grave and mound were restored as closely as possible to their original state.

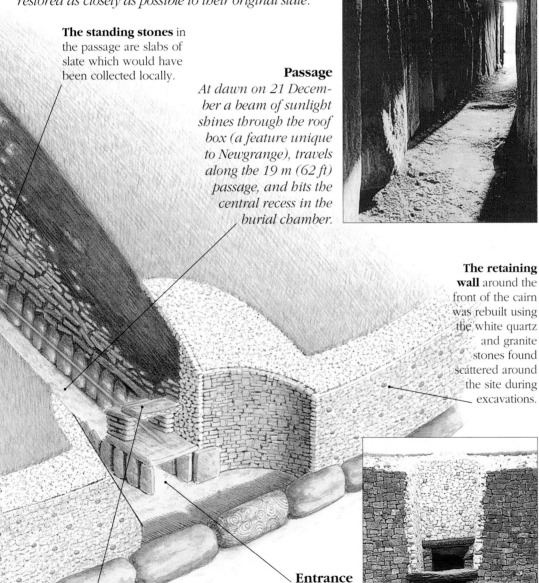

The standing stones in the passage are slabs of slate which would have been collected locally.

Passage
At dawn on 21 December a beam of sunlight shines through the roof box (a feature unique to Newgrange), travels along the 19 m (62 ft) passage, and hits the central recess in the burial chamber.

The retaining wall around the front of the cairn was rebuilt using the white quartz and granite stones found scattered around the site during excavations.

Roof box

Entrance
The opening was originally blocked by the stone standing to its right. Newgrange's most elaborately carved curbstone is in front, part of the curb of huge slabs around the cairn.

KEY DATES

c.3200 BC Construction of Newgrange.

c.860 Danish invaders raid the burial chambers of Newgrange and remove most of its treasures.

c.1140 Newgrange is used as farmland for grazing cattle until the 14th century.

1962–75 Newgrange is restored and the roof box is discovered.

1967 Archaeologists discover that rays of sun light up the burial chamber on winter solstice, 21 December.

1993 Newgrange is listed as a World Heritage Site.

DOWTH AND KNOWTH

Described as the "cradle of Irish civilization", the Boyne Valley contains two other prehistoric burial sites not far from Newgrange. The nearest is Knowth, which is only 1.5 km (1 mile) away. Excavation of this site began in 1962 and it was found to contain two tomb passages and the greatest concentration of megalithic art in Europe. Archaeologists also found evidence that the site was occupied from the Neolithic period and was used for habitation as well as for burials up until about 1400. Dowth, another passage grave 3 km (2 miles) from Newgrange, is less spectacular. Its tombs are smaller and most of its artifacts were stolen by Victorian souvenir hunters. The site has not yet been fully excavated by archaeologists.

Newgrange

THE BOOK OF KELLS

The most richly decorated of Ireland's medieval illuminated manuscripts, the *Book of Kells* may have been the work of monks from the island of Iona in Scotland, who fled to Kells in County Meath in AD 806 after a Viking raid. The book, moved to Trinity College (▷ *Treasury*) in the 17th century, contains the four gospels in Latin. The scribes who copied the texts also embellished their calligraphy with intricate interlacing spirals as well as human figures and animals. Some of the dyes used were imported from as far as the Middle East. The monogram page is the most elaborate page of the book and contains the first three words of St Matthew's account of the birth of Christ. The first word "XRI" is an abbreviation of "Christi".

Marble bust of Jonathan Swift in the Old Library

FAMOUS ALUMNI

Trinity College is Dublin's most famous seat of learning and since its foundation it has cultivated many distinguished writers and historical figures. Their time spent here had a discernible impact on their lives. Outstanding graduates include writers and dramatists such as Jonathan Swift, Oliver Goldsmith, Oscar Wilde, Bram Stoker, William Congreve, and Samuel Beckett; philosopher George Berkeley; statesman and political philosopher Edmund Burke; Nobel prizewinning physicist Ernest Walton; Ireland's first President Douglas Hyde; and Ireland's first female President Mary Robinson. Statues in tribute to its famous scholars stand throughout the college.

Trinity College, Dublin

Trinity College coat of arms

Q UEEN ELIZABETH I founded Trinity College, Dublin's oldest and most famous educational institution, in 1592. Originally a Protestant college, it only began to take Catholics in numbers after 1970, when the Catholic Church relaxed its opposition to them attending.

Among Trinity's many famous students were playwrights Oliver Goldsmith and Samuel Beckett, and political writer Edmund Burke. The college's lawns and cobbled quads provide a pleasant haven in the heart of the city. The major attractions are the Old Library and the *Book of Kells*, housed in the Treasury.

Chapel *(1798)*
This was the first university chapel in the Republic to accept all denominations. The painted window above the altar is from 1867.

Statue of Edmund Burke (1868) by John Foley

SAMUEL BECKETT (1906–89)

Nobel prizewinner Samuel Beckett was born at Foxrock, south of Dublin. In 1923 he entered Trinity, and later graduated with a first in modern languages and a gold medal. He was also an avid member of the college cricket team. Forsaking Ireland, Beckett moved to France in the early 1930s. Many of his major works such as *Waiting for Godot* (1951) were written first in French, and later translated, by Beckett, into English.

★ **Campanile**
The 30-m (98-ft) bell tower was built in 1853 by Sir Charles Lanyon, architect of Queen's University in Belfast.

Reclining Connected Forms (1969) by Henry Moore

Dining Hall (1761)

Parliament Square

Main entrance

Statue of Oliver Goldsmith (1864) by John Foley

Provost's House (c.1760)

Examination Hall
Completed in 1791 to a design by Sir William Chambers, the hall features a gilded oak chandelier and ornate ceilings by Michael Stapleton.

Library Square

The redbrick building (known as the Rubrics) on the east side of Library Square was built around 1700 and is the oldest surviving part of the college.

The Museum Building, completed in 1857, is noted for its Venetian exterior, and its magnificent multicolored hall and double-domed roof.

Sphere within Sphere (1982) was given to the college by its sculptor Arnaldo Pomodoro.

Entrance to Old Library

New Square

Berkeley Library Building by Paul Koralek (1967)

Fellows' Square

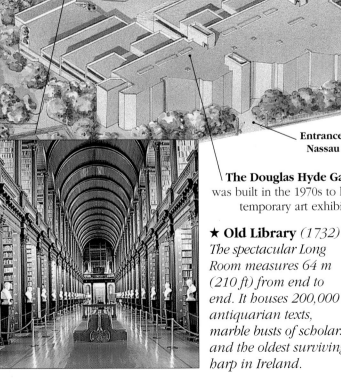

Entrance from Nassau Street

The Douglas Hyde Gallery was built in the 1970s to house temporary art exhibitions.

★ Old Library (1732)
The spectacular Long Room measures 64 m (210 ft) from end to end. It houses 200,000 antiquarian texts, marble busts of scholars, and the oldest surviving harp in Ireland.

★ Treasury
This detail is from the Book of Durrow, *one of the other magnificent illuminated manuscripts housed in the Treasury along with the celebrated* Book of Kells.

KEY DATES

1592 Trinity College is founded.

c.1661 The *Book of Kells* is given to Trinity by the Bishop of Meath.

1689 The college is turned temporarily into barracks.

1712 Work begins on the Old Library.

1793 Religious restrictions on entry are abolished.

1853 The Campanile is erected.

1987 Restoration of the Dining Hall is completed following the fire of 1984.

PARLIAMENT SQUARE

Trinity College stands on what was once part of the All Hallows Monastery grounds. The wood-tiled archway at the main entrance leads to Trinity's main quadrangle (▷ *Parliament Square*). Fine green lawns and an array of fine 18th- and 19th-century buildings characterize the cobbled square. An imposing centerpiece (▷ *Campanile*) marks the original site of All Hallows monastery. The ▷ *chapel* was designed by Sir William Chambers in 1798. Beside it is the ▷ *dining hall*, built by Richard Castle in 1742, where Trinity's students eat. This building has been considerably altered over the past 250 years, particularly after a fire caused severe damage in 1984. The walls are hung with huge portraits of college dignitaries.

STAR FEATURES

★ Campanile

★ Treasury

★ Old Library

Trinity College, Dublin

RECONSTRUCTION

Following a fire in 1684, much of Dublin Castle was left in ruins. Soon after, the castle's reconstruction was ordered by King James II. Surveyor-General Sir William Robinson was hired to plan the new building. By 1688 construction was completed and the new luxury ▷ *State Apartments* were unveiled. Further alterations were subsequently made to the castle. In 1751 a new entrance, the ▷ *Cork Hill Gate* was completed and ten years later the ▷ *Bedford Tower* was added. Having fallen into disrepair after the 1916 rebellion against English rule, the castle has been restored by repair and refurbishment to the splendid structure seen today.

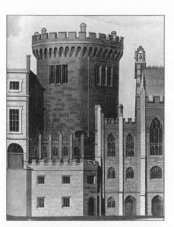

An engraving of the medieval Record Tower

CHAPEL ROYAL

Designed in the Gothic Revival style (▷ *Gothic Style p73*) by Francis Johnston, the ▷ *Chapel Royal* was built from 1807–14. Its exterior is adorned with over 100 stone heads, carved by Edward and John Smyth. The interior is also elaborately decorated with beautiful plasterwork by George Stapleton and stunning wood carvings by Richard Stewart throughout. Another notable feature of the chapel is its rich oak galleries and stained-glass windows, which display the coats of arms of the former English Justiciars, Lord Deputies, and Lord Lieutenants (the crown's representatives abroad), from 1172–1922.

Dublin Castle

FOR SEVEN CENTURIES Dublin Castle was a symbol of English rule, ever since the Anglo-Normans built a fortress here in the 13th century. Nothing remains of the original structure except the much modified Record Tower. Following a fire in 1684, the Surveyor-General, Sir William Robinson (1645–1712), laid down the plans for the Upper and Lower Castle Yards in their present form. On the first floor of the south side of the Upper Yard are the stunning State Apartments, which include St Patrick's Hall. Today the splendid rooms of the castle are used for state functions by the president.

St Patrick by Edward Smyth

Drawing Room
This beautiful and elegant room is decorated with Waterford glass, chandeliers, and Killybeg carpets.

★ **Throne Room**
Built in 1740, this room contains a throne said to have been presented by William of Orange after his victory at the Battle of the Boyne (1690).

Wedgwood Room

Portrait Gallery

The Bermingham Tower dates from the 13th century. It was turned into an elegant dining room around 1740.

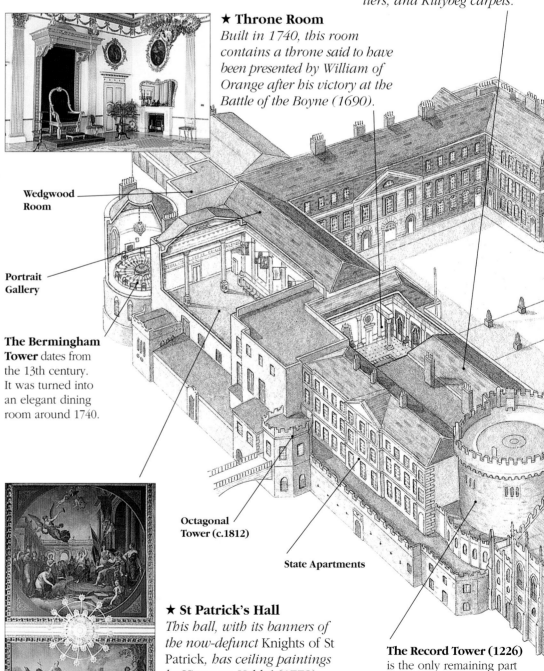

Octagonal Tower (c.1812)

State Apartments

★ **St Patrick's Hall**
This hall, with its banners of the now-defunct Knights of St Patrick, has ceiling paintings by Vincenzo Valdré (1778), symbolizing the relationship between Britain and Ireland.

The Record Tower (1226) is the only remaining part of the original medieval castle. Today it houses the Garda (police) Museum.

Bedford Tower
Completed in the mid-18th century, the building is on the site of the original Norman gate. Designed in an elegant Georgian style, it has a segmented cupola on the tower.

Figure of Justice
Facing the Upper Yard, above the main entrance from Cork Hill, this statue aroused much cynicism among Dubliners, who felt she was turning her back on the city.

Upper Yard

Cork Hill Gate

Entrance to Upper Yard

Entrance to Undercroft

Lower Yard

The Treasury Office Block

The Chapel Royal (Church of the Most Holy Trinity) was completed in 1814. It was used as the official Anglican chapel for the Lord Lieutenants of Ireland. Today the basement of the chapel is occupied by the Crypt Theatre.

ORDER OF ST PATRICK

The Illustrious Order of St Patrick was founded by King George III in 1783 to reward the most influential peers in Ireland. Their insignia, known as the "Irish Crown Jewels," were stolen in 1903 from Dublin Castle's library. The Order went into abeyance in 1922 when Ireland became a republic; the jewels were never found.

ROBERT EMMET

Considered by many as a champion of Irish liberty, Robert Emmet (1778–1803) hatched a plan to capture Dublin Castle. This was to be a signal for the country to rise up against the Act of Union, when Ireland legally became part of Britain, but he was caught and publicly hanged. However, he is remembered for his defiant, patriotic speech made from the dock, which inspired generations of freedom fighters.

STAR FEATURES

★ **Throne Room**

★ **St Patrick's Hall**

KEY DATES

1204–24 The fortress is built by Anglo-Normans.

1684–88 After a devastating fire, the Upper and Lower Yards of the castle are rebuilt.

1746 The State Apartments are renovated.

16 January 1922 Michael Collins, hero of the Irish War of Independence, is handed Dublin Castle on behalf of the new Irish Government.

CHESTER BEATTY COLLECTIONS

Some of the finest and rarest oriental artifacts, Islamic manuscripts, and papyri (including early texts of the Bible) in the world are on display in the Chester Beatty Library and Gallery of Oriental Art, located in the gardens of Dublin Castle. The fine collection of books and art were amassed by Sir Alfred Chester Beatty (1875–1968), who bequeathed them to Ireland. Burmese and Siamese art treasures include a selection of 18th- and 19th-century *Parabaiks*, books of folk tales, while jade books, paintings, and silk dragon robes are some of the fascinating Chinese displays. The Japanese exhibits are represented by paintings, woodblock prints, books, and scrolls, some with illustrations painted by Buddhist monks, from the 16th–18th centuries. In the western European room, one of the most beautiful manuscripts is the *Coëtivy Book of Hours*, a 15th-century French prayer book.

CASHEL MUSEUM

The 15th-century two-storey ▷ *Hall of the Vicars' Choral* was once the residential quarters of the cathedral choristers and today displays copies of medieval artifacts and furnishings. Its lower level houses the Cashel museum, which exhibits rare silverware, stone carvings, and the ▷ *St Patrick's Cross*, a 12th-century crutched cross with a crucifixion scene on one side and animals on the other. The cross stands on a supporting coronation stone dating from the 4th century. Tradition held that the kings of Cashel, including King Brian Boru of Munster (977–1014), were crowned at the base of the cross.

Romanesque carvings decorating the buildings of Cashel

CORMAC'S CHAPEL

The King of Munster, Cormac MacCarthy, donated this chapel to the Church in 1134, because they had helped to protect the Rock of Cashel from being invaded by the Eoghanachta clan. Romanesque in style, it was constructed in sandstone with a stone roof and two towers on either side of the nave and chancel. The interior is decorated with various motifs, some showing dragons and human heads. At the west end of the chapel there is a stone sarcophagus embellished with serpent carvings. This is thought to have once contained the body of Cormac MacCarthy. The chancel is decorated with the only surviving Romanesque frescoes in Ireland, which include a representation of the Baptism of Christ.

Rock of Cashel

A SYMBOL OF ROYAL and priestly power for more than a millennium, this is one of the most spectacular archaeological sites in Ireland. From the 5th century, it was the seat of the Kings of Munster, whose kingdom extended over much of southern Ireland. In 1101, they handed Cashel over to the Church, and it flourished as a religious center until a siege by a Cromwellian army in 1647 culminated in the massacre of its 3,000 occupants. The cathedral was finally abandoned in the late 18th century. A good proportion of the medieval complex is still standing, and Cormac's Chapel is one of the most outstanding examples of Romanesque architecture in the country (▷ *Romanesque Style p199*).

Hall of the Vicars' Choral
This hall was built in the 15th century for Cashel's most privileged choristers. The ceiling, a modern reconstruction based on medieval designs, features several decorative corbels including this painted angel.

Entrance

The museum in the undercroft contains a display of stone carvings and religious artifacts.

★ St Patrick's Cross
The carving on the east face of this cross is said to be of St Patrick, who visited Cashel in 450. The cross is a copy of the original that stood here until 1982 and is now in the museum.

Dormitory block

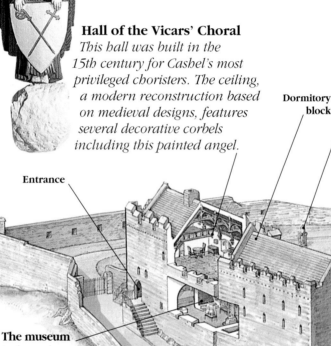

Outer wall

Limestone rock

★ Cormac's Chapel
Superb Romanesque carving adorns this chapel – the jewel of Cashel. The tympanum over the north door shows a centaur in a helmet aiming his bow and arrow at a lion.

STAR FEATURES

★ **St Patrick's Cross**

★ **Cormac's Chapel**

★ **St Patrick's Cathedral**

KEY

☐ **12th Century**
4 St Patrick's Cross (replica)
12 Cormac's Chapel
13 Round tower

☐ **13th Century**
6 Cathedral porch
7 Nave
8 Crossing
9 South transept
10 Choir
11 North transept

☐ **15th Century**
1 Ticket office
2 Hall of the Vicars' Choral (museum)
3 Dormitory
5 Castle

0 metres 50
0 yards 50

ST PATRICK AND KING AENGHUS

During the baptism ceremony of King Aenghus, St Patrick accidentally stabbed him in his foot with his crozier and the king, thinking it was part of the initiation, bore the pain without complaint.

Rock of Cashel

KEY DATES

AD 450 St Patrick visits Cashel and converts King Aenghus to Christianity.

1101 Cashel is handed over to the Church by King Muircheartach O'Brien.

1127–1134 King Cormac MacCarthy builds Cormac's Chapel as a gift for the Church.

1647 Cashel is invaded and besieged by a Cromwellian army under Lord Inchiquin.

1975 Hall of Vicars' Choral is restored.

LIFE OF ST PATRICK

Born in Wales in AD 385, St Patrick lived his early life as a pagan. When he was 16 years old, he was captured and sold as a slave to work in Ireland. During his captivity, he converted to Christianity and dedicated his life to religion. He escaped and traveled to France, where he entered St Martin's monastery to study the Scriptures, under the guidance of St Germain of Auxerre. He was appointed Bishop to Ireland in AD 432. He went on to found over 300 churches and baptized over 120,000 people, including King Aenghus, when he visited Cashel in AD 450. Today the death of St Patrick, the Patron Saint of Ireland, is celebrated on 17 March all over the world with special religious services and the wearing of shamrocks – the three-tipped clover leaf which is the national emblem of Ireland.

Round tower

Crossing

The Rock
The 28 m (92 ft) round tower, oldest and tallest building on the rock, enabled Cashel's inhabitants to scour the surrounding plain for potential attackers.

The Choir contains the 17th-century tomb of Miler Magrath, who caused a scandal by being both a Protestant and a Catholic archbishop at the same time.

Graveyard

The O'Scully Monument, an ornate memorial erected in 1870 by a local landowning family, was damaged during a storm in 1976.

★ St Patrick's Cathedral
The roofless Gothic cathedral has thick walls riddled with hidden passages; in the north transept these are seen emerging at the base of the windows.

North Transept
Panels from three 16th-century tombs in the north transept are decorated with remarkably fresh and intricate carvings. This one, against the north wall, features a vine-leaf design and strange stylized beasts.

Stirling Castle

**Engraving depicting the Battle
of Bannockburn**

THE GREAT HALL

This splendid royal hall, the
largest ever built in Scotland,
was erected by James IV
between 1501 and 1504 to
host lavish state events and
banquets. When the focus of
the monarchy shifted to
London after the Union of
the Crowns in 1603 – when
King James VI of Scotland
became King James I of
England – the ▷ *Great Hall*
was no longer required for
state occasions. Changes were
made to the hall in the 18th
century to reinforce the
castle's defenses and to create
space for military barracks.
After more than 30 years'
work the Great Hall, restored
as closely as possible to its
original condition, was
reopened by Queen Elizabeth
II on 30 November 1999.

Stirling Castle

R ISING HIGH on a rocky crag, this magnificent castle,
which dominated Scottish history for centuries, now
remains one of the finest examples of Renaissance
architecture in Scotland (▷ *Renaissance Style p211*).
Legend says that King Arthur wrested the original castle
from the Saxons, but there is no evidence of a castle at
this location before 1124. The present building dates from
the 15th and 16th centuries and was last defended in
1746 against the Jacobites, who were mainly Catholic
Highlanders wishing to restore the Stuart monarchy to the
throne. From 1881 to 1964 the castle was
used as a depot for recruits into the Argyll
and Sutherland Highlanders, though today it
serves no military function.

**Gargoyle on
castle wall**

The Prince's Tower
erected in the 16th century
is still standing today.

Robert the Bruce
*In the esplanade, this modern statue
shows Robert the Bruce sheathing
his sword after the Battle of
Bannockburn in 1314.*

Forework

Entrance

The French Spur
was an artillery spur
that formed part of a
line of defenses built
in the mid-16th
century, to improve
the defense of the
castle in an age of
modern artillery.

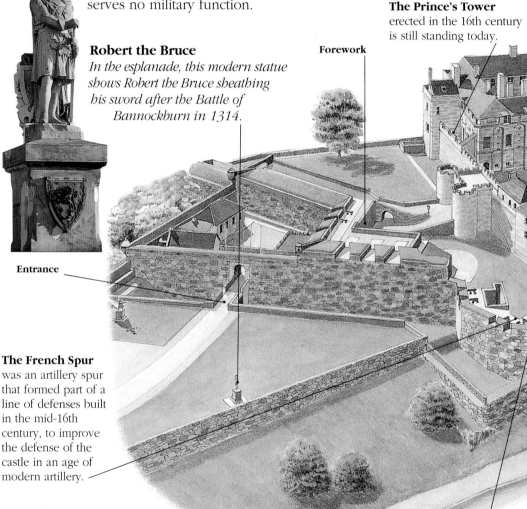

**The Elphinstone
Tower** was reduced to
half its original height to
allow it to be made into
a gun platform in 1714.

***Stirling Castle in the Time of the Stuarts*, painted by Johannes
Vorsterman (1643–99)**

★ Palace

The otherwise sparse interiors of the royal apartments contain the Stirling Heads. These Renaissance roundels depict 38 figures, thought to be contemporary members of the royal court.

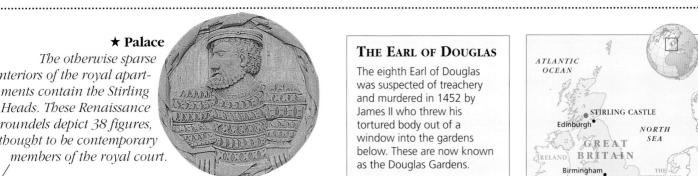

THE EARL OF DOUGLAS

The eighth Earl of Douglas was suspected of treachery and murdered in 1452 by James II who threw his tortured body out of a window into the gardens below. These are now known as the Douglas Gardens.

The King's Old Building houses the Regimental Museum of the Argyll and Sutherland Highlanders.

★ Chapel Royal

Seventeenth-century frescoes by Valentine Jenkins adorn the chapel, reconstructed in 1594.

Nether Bailey

The Great Hall, built in 1500, has been restored to its former splendor.

STAR FEATURES

★ **Palace**

★ **Chapel Royal**

Grand Battery
Seven guns stand on this parapet overlooking the town of Stirling. They were built in 1708 during a strengthening of defenses.

STIRLING BATTLES

At the highest navigable point of the Forth and holding the pass to the Highlands, Stirling occupied a key position in Scotland's struggles for independence. Seven battlefields can be seen from the castle; the 67 m (220 ft) Wallace Monument at Abbey Craig recalls William Wallace's defeat of the English at Stirling Bridge in 1297, foreshadowing Robert the Bruce's victory in 1314.

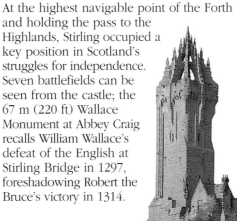

The Victorian Wallace Monument

KEY DATES

1296 Edward I captures Stirling Castle.

1297 The castle yields to the Scots after the Battle of Stirling Bridge led by William Wallace.

1314 Robert the Bruce defeats the English at the Battle of Bannockburn.

1496 James IV begins extensive construction. Work begins on the Chapel Royal.

1501 Work begins on the Great Hall.

1503 Building work starts on the Forework.

1855 The King's Old Building is badly damaged by fire.

1964 The army leaves the castle barracks.

THE KING'S OLD BUILDING

Built for James IV in 1496, the King's Old Building stands on the highest point of the castle rock. Following the completion of the palace in the 1540s, the King's Old Building was no longer the ruling monarch's residence and so was put to varied use. Additional floors and walls were added in the 1790s to provide accommodation for a military garrison. It was also rebuilt after fire damage in the mid-19th century. The building now houses the Regimental Museum of the Argyll and Sutherland Highlanders and contains a collection of memorabilia including medals, uniforms, and weapons.

Stirling Castle

Edinburgh Castle

STONE OF DESTINY

The origins of this famous stone are steeped in myth and legend. It is said to have been Jacob's pillow when he dreamt that the angels of God were descending to earth from heaven. Scottish kings, from Kenneth I in 847, sat on the stone during coronation ceremonies. It was kept in Scone, Perthshire, after which it is sometimes called The Stone of Scone. The stone was seized on Edward I's invasion of Scotland in 1296 and taken to Westminster Abbey, where it was kept for 700 years. The 1326 Treaty of Northampton promised return of the stone, but this was not honored until 1996, when a handover ceremony took place at the English-Scottish border and the stone was transported to Edinburgh Castle, where it remains today.

Edinburgh Castle viewed from Princes Street

VOLCANIC GEOLOGY

Edinburgh Castle is located in the Midland Valley of Scotland. The rocky volcanic outcrops of Arthur's Seat, measuring 251 m (823 ft) high, and Salisbury Crags, 122 m (400 ft) high, dominate the Edinburgh skyline. Salisbury Crags are igneous rocks exposed by the tilting of local rock and erosion by glaciers. Arthur's Seat is the remnant of a Carboniferous volcano, partly eroded by glacial activity. Edinburgh Castle is situated on a rock that plugs a vent of this volcano. The "crag" of basalt on which the castle stands was resistant to glacial erosion in the last ice-age. This left a "tail" of soft sedimentary rock lying behind it, which forms the main street (▷ *Royal Mile)* of Edinburgh.

Edinburgh Castle

STANDING UPON the basalt core of an extinct volcano, Edinburgh Castle is a remarkable assemblage of buildings dating from the 12th to the 20th centuries, reflecting its changing role as fortress, royal palace, military garrison and state prison. There is evidence of Bronze Age occupation of the site, which takes its name from Dun Eidin, a Celtic fortress captured by King Oswald of Northumbria in the 7th century. The castle was a favorite royal residence until the Union of Crowns in 1603, after which the king resided in England. After the Union of Parliaments in 1707, the Scottish regalia were walled up in the palace for over a hundred years. The castle is now the zealous possessor of the so-called Stone of Destiny, a relic of ancient Scottish kings which was seized by the English and not returned until 1996.

Beam support in the Great Hall

Governor's House
Complete with Flemish-style crow-stepped gables, this building was constructed for the governor in 1742 and now serves as the Officers' Mess for the castle garrison.

MONS MEG

Positioned outside St Margaret's Chapel, the siege gun (or *bombard*) Mons Meg was made in Belgium in 1449 for the Duke of Burgundy, who subsequently gave it as a present to his nephew, James II of Scotland (r.1437–60), in 1457. It was used by James IV (r.1488–1513) against Norham Castle in England in 1497. After exploding during a salute to the Duke of York in 1682, it was kept in the Tower of London until it was returned to Edinburgh in 1829, at Sir Walter Scott's request.

Scottish Crown
Now on display in the palace, the Crown was restyled by James V of Scotland in 1540.

Military Prison

Old Back Parade

Vaults
This French graffiti, dating from 1780, recalls the many prisoners who were held in the vaults during the wars with France in the 18th and 19th centuries.

STAR FEATURES

★ **Palace**

★ **Great Hall**

Argyle Battery
This fortified wall commands a spectacular view to the north of the city's New Town.

★ **Palace**
Mary, Queen of Scots (1542–87) gave birth to James VI in this 15th-century palace, where the Scottish regalia are on display.

Mons Meg

Entrance

Royal Mile →

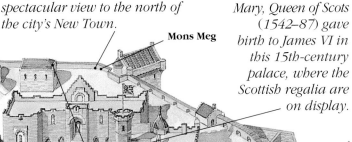

The Esplanade is the location of the Military Tattoo.

The Half Moon Battery was built in the 1570s as a platform for the artillery defending the northeastern wing of the castle.

St Margaret's Chapel
This stained-glass window depicts Malcolm III's saintly queen, to whom the chapel is dedicated. Probably built by her son, David I, in the early 12th century, the chapel is the castle's oldest existing building.

★ **Great Hall**
With its restored open-timber roof, the hall dates from the 15th century and was the meeting place of the Scottish parliament until 1639.

KEY DATES

638 King Oswald of Northumbria captures the site from the ancient Britons.

1296 Edward I takes the castle after an eight-day siege and installs a garrison of 347 men.

1496–1511 James I adds more buildings to the castle, including the Palace.

1573 After a failed siege by Mary, Queen of Scots, the castle is remodeled and the Half Moon Battery is built.

1650 The castle is fortified with barracks, officers' quarters, and storehouses.

1995 Edinburgh and its castle are inscribed a World Heritage Site.

THE MILITARY TATTOO

Since 1947, for three weeks over the summer, Edinburgh has played host to one of the world's most important arts festivals, with every available space overflowing with international artistes and performers (from theaters to street corners). It is an exciting fusion of film, music, theater, dance, comedy, and literature. The most popular event is the Edinburgh Military Tattoo, held every night on the ▷ *Esplanade.* The world's finest military bands perform with bagpipers and drummers from Scottish regiments, in full regalia. The music and marching, against the backdrop of the illuminated Edinburgh Castle, make for a marvelous spectacle.

Edinburgh Castle

STAINED GLASS

York Minster has an exceptional collection of medieval stained glass. The glass was generally colored during production, using metal oxides to produce the desired color, then worked on by craftsmen on site. When a design had been produced, the glass was first cut, then trimmed to shape. Details were painted on, using iron oxide-based paints which were fused to the glass by firing in a kiln. Individual pieces were then leaded together to form the finished window. Part of the fascination of the minster glass is its variety of subject matter. Some windows, including the ▷ *Great East Window*, were paid for by lay donors who specified a particular subject; others reflect ecclesiastical patronage.

DECORATED GOTHIC STYLE

An example of this second period of Gothic architecture from the late 13th to mid-14th century is the ▷ *Chapter House*, which radiates elegantly against the backdrop of York Minster. Delicate carvings, fine stained-glass windows, elaborate tracery, and experimental vaulting typify the Decorated Gothic style. Carvings of foliage, animals, and human figures can be viewed above the stalls inside the cathedral. Inside the ▷ *nave*, complex tracery can be seen throughout.

The Octagonal Chapter House in York Minster

York Minster

Central sunflower in rose window

T<small>HE LARGEST</small> Gothic cathedral in northern Europe (▷ *Gothic Style p73*), York Minster is 158 m (519 ft) long and 76 m (249 ft) wide across the transepts, and houses the largest collection of medieval stained glass in Britain. The word "minster" usually refers to a cathedral served by monks, but priests always served at York. The first minster began as a wooden chapel used to baptize King Edwin of Northumbria in 627. There have been several cathedrals on or near the site, including an 11th-century Norman structure. The present minster was begun in 1220 and completed 250 years later. In July 1984, the south transept roof was destroyed by fire. Restoration cost £2.25 million.

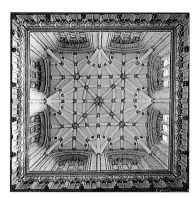

Central Tower
Reconstructed in 1420–65 (after partial collapse in 1407) from a design by the master stonemason William Colchester, its geometrical roof design has a central lantern.

East transept

★ **Great East Window**
Measuring the size of a tennis court, this is the largest expanse of surviving medieval stained glass in the world. The Bishop of Durham, Walter Shirlaw, paid glazier John Thornton four shillings a week to complete the celebration of the Creation, between 1405–8.

Five Sisters' Window

The Choir has a vaulted entrance with a 15th-century boss of the Assumption of the Virgin.

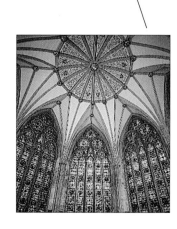

★ **Chapter House**
A Latin inscription near the entrance of the wooden-vaulted Chapter House (1260–85) reads: "As the rose is the flower of flowers, so this is the house of houses."

The Nave

Building works on the nave began in 1291 and were completed in the 1350s. It was severely damaged by fire in the late 19th century. Rebuilding costs were heavy, but it was reopened with a new peal of bells in 1844.

THE FIVE SISTERS

The north transept is adorned with the ▷ *Five Sisters' Window*. It is the largest example of grisaille glass in Britain. This 13th-century design involved creating fine patterns on clear glass and decorating it with black enamel.

West Towers

The 15th-century decorative paneling and elaborate pinnacles on the west towers contrast with the simpler design of the north transept.

Exit in south transept

16th-century rose window

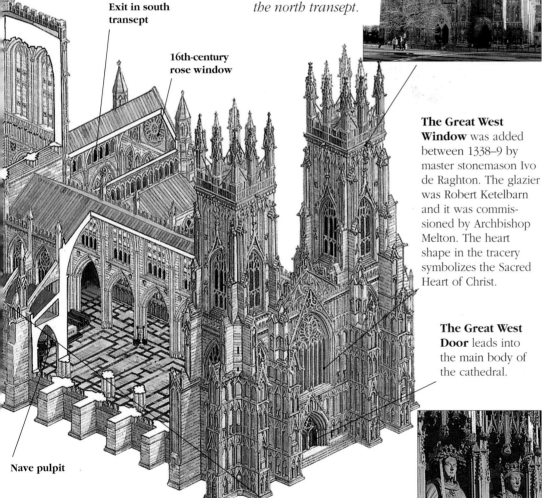

The Great West Window was added between 1338–9 by master stonemason Ivo de Raghton. The glazier was Robert Ketelbarn and it was commissioned by Archbishop Melton. The heart shape in the tracery symbolizes the Sacred Heart of Christ.

The Great West Door leads into the main body of the cathedral.

Nave pulpit

STAR FEATURES

★ **Great East Window**

★ **Chapter House**

★ **Choir Screen**

★ **Choir Screen**

Sited between the choir and the nave, this beautiful 15th-century stone screen depicts kings of England from William I to Henry VI, and has a canopy of angels.

KEY DATES

1220 Construction of the present York Minster begins.

1472 The cathedral is completed.

1730–36 The entire floor is relaid in patterned marble.

1840 Fire damages the nave.

1985 The roof in the south transept is rebuilt following a fire in 1984.

YORK MYSTERY PLAYS

These 48 medieval dramas, which relate the history of the world from the mystery of God's creation to the Last Judgment, were originally performed between the 14th and the 16th centuries for the feast of Corpus Christi. The York Mystery Plays, or cycles, are one of only four which have survived. They are divided into short episodes and performed by actors standing on a wagon. The entertainers then ride through the city streets, pausing at a number of venues to perform. It was customary for different guilds to adopt the productions which often bore a connection to their trade. For example, shipbuilders were responsible for the portrayal of Noah's Ark, bakers played the Last Supper, and butchers staged the Death of Christ. This cycle tradition was revived for the Festival of Britain in 1951 and has been performed every three to four years since. In 2000, York Minster staged a lavish millennium performance of the biblical plays in the ▷ *nave.*

THE CHAPEL

The most prominent building in the university, the chapel is thought to be Great Britain's best example of Gothic architecture (▷ *Gothic Style p73*). Building began under Henry VI whose goal was to create a chapel without equal in size or beauty. To achieve this he compelled local land-owners to sell him plots along the river, and shops and a church were pulled down to provide room for his creation. Work was halted during the Wars of the Roses (1455–85) when the monarch was taken prisoner. After Henry's murder in the Tower of London in 1471, Edward IV came to the throne. Little progress was made on the chapel until Richard III reigned. But it was under the Tudor kings, Henry VII and Henry VIII, that the building as we see it today was finished. The excellent quality of the glazing and woodwork crafted under the Tudors has made the chapel one of Europe's finest.

MASTER STONEMASONS

The awe-inspiring chapel of King's College was con-structed under four master stonemasons. Henry VI com-missioned Reginald Ely in 1444. Ely worked on the chapel during the Wars of the Roses often without pay, until work stopped altogether in 1461. When construction began again in 1476, it was under John Wolrich. He remained until Simon Clerk took over as master mason in 1477. It was Clerk who decided to fashion the stunning ▷ *Fan Vaulted Ceiling*. However, it was under John Wastell, perhaps the most brilliant stonemason, that the vaulting was created and the chapel completed.

Statue of Tudor king, Henry VIII

King's College, Cambridge

King's College Coat of Arms

HENRY VI FOUNDED this prestigious college in 1441. Work on the chapel, one of the most important examples of late medieval English archi-tecture, began five years later, and took 70 years to complete. Henry decided that it should domi-nate the city and gave specific instructions about its dimensions: 88 m (289 ft) long, 12 m (40 ft) wide and 29 m (95 ft) high. The detailed design is thought to have been the work of master stonemason Reginald Ely, although it was altered in later years.

One of four octagonal turrets

★ Fan Vaulted Ceiling
This stunning ceiling, supported by 22 buttresses, was built by master stone-mason John Wastell in 1515.

The Fellows' Building was designed in 1724 by James Gibbs, as part of an uncompleted design for a Great Court.

Side chapels

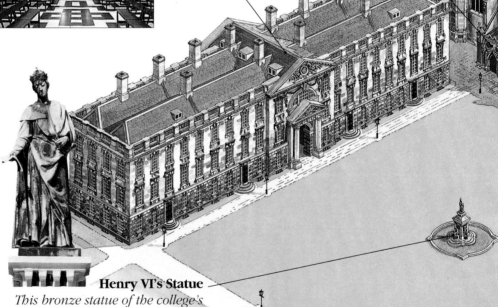

Henry VI's Statue
This bronze statue of the college's founder was erected in 1879.

KING'S COLLEGE CHOIR

When he founded the chapel, Henry VI stipulated that a choir of six lay clerks and 16 boy choristers – educated at the College school – should sing daily at services. This still happens in term time but today the choir also gives concerts all over the world. Its internationally broadcast service of carols on Christmas Eve has become a much-loved festive tradition.

Choristers in King's College Chapel

Gothic gatehouse, 19th-century

Crown and Tudor Rose

This detail of Tudor heraldry on the west door of the Chapel reflects Henry VIII's vision of English supremacy.

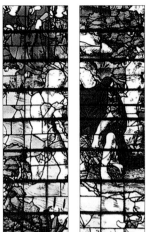

Stained-glass Windows

The 16th-century windows in the chapel all depict biblical scenes. This one shows Christ baptizing his followers.

CROMWELL AND THE CHAPEL

During the English Civil War (1642–60) King's College chapel surprisingly escaped damage, despite being used by Oliver Cromwell's parliamentary army as an exercise ground during inclement weather. It has been suggested that Cromwell himself gave orders that the chapel should be spared, having been a former student of Cambridge.

Organ

The massive 17th-century organ case above the screen is decorated with two angels playing trumpets.

The screen is a superb example of Tudor woodwork and divides the chapel into antechapel and choir.

Main entrance

★ Altarpiece

The Adoration of the Magi *was painted in 1634 by the Flemish Baroque artist Peter Paul Rubens (1577–1640) for the convent of the White Nuns in Belgium. This magnificent work was privately donated to King's College in 1961.*

STAR FEATURES

★ **Fan Vaulted Ceiling**

★ **Altarpiece**

KEY DATES

1446 The chapel's foundation stone is laid by Henry VI.

1461 Henry VI is deposed by the Yorkists and building work to the chapel is halted.

1515 Stonework completed.

1533–36 The exquisite woodwork of the choir stalls and organ screen is carved.

THE COLLEGES

King's College is one of 31 distinct colleges that form Cambridge University. The history of each college has determined their layout and individual character, much of which derives from their early connections with religious institutions. The college buildings are generally grouped around squares called courts, and the variety of architectural styles covers 600 years from the late medieval period to the present day. The oldest college is Peterhouse (1286), named after St Peter's Church next to which it was erected. The foremost English architect Sir Christopher Wren (1632–1723) designed the Classical chapels of Pembroke and Emmanuel Colleges. The latter has a Puritan tradition, and one notable graduate was clergyman John Harvard. He emigrated to America in 1636 and left all his money to a Massachusetts college that now bears his name. Other former alumni include eminent politicians, scholars, and writers, including the poet William Wordsworth, physicist Sir Isaac Newton, and naturalist Charles Darwin.

King's College, Cambridge

CHANGING OF THE GUARD

The oldest and most familiar of all royal ceremonies, the ▷ *Changing of the Guard* takes place each day in summer and every other day in winter outside the official entrance of Buckingham Palace, known as the Horse Guards. The Queen's Guard usually consists of Foot Guards in full-dress red tunics and bearskin hats. They are accompanied by a Guards band sounding the Royal Salute, as the Old Guard changes duty with the New Guard, in a spectacular 45-minute colorful ceremony. When the Queen is in residence, trumpeters parade with the ▷ *Royal Standard*, as the Guard, known as the Long Guard, changes over. When she is away from London, the Guard is reduced in size and is known as the Short Guard.

One of the Queen's Guards

ROYAL MEWS

The coach house, designed by John Nash in 1825, accommodates the horses and coaches used by the Royal Family on state occasions. Displays at the Mews show off the royal vehicles and are great for lovers of horses and royal pomp. The star exhibit is the gold State Coach, built for George III in 1761, with fine panels painted by Giovanni Cipriani. Among the other displays are the Irish state coach, bought by Queen Victoria for the annual State Opening of Parliament; the open-topped royal landau; and the glass coach used for royal weddings and transporting foreign ambassadors. The elaborate harnesses worn by the horses who pull the royal carriages are also on view.

Buckingham Palace, London

THE OFFICIAL RESIDENCE of the British monarchy, Buckingham Palace is a well-known symbol of London. Decorated with priceless works of art and fine antique furnishings, its lavish rooms are used for ceremonial occasions, including banquets for visiting heads of state. John Nash converted the original Buckingham House into a palace for King George IV (r.1820–30) in the early 19th century. Both he and his brother, William IV (r.1830–37), died before work was completed and Queen Victoria (r.1837–1901) was the first monarch to live here. Edward Blore's late 19th-century east façade, facing The Mall, was remodeled in 1913, after the original stonework began to show signs of decay.

Music Room
State guests are presented and royal christenings take place in this room, which boasts a beautiful, original parquet floor by Nash.

State Ballroom
The Georgian Baroque ballroom is used for state banquets and investitures.

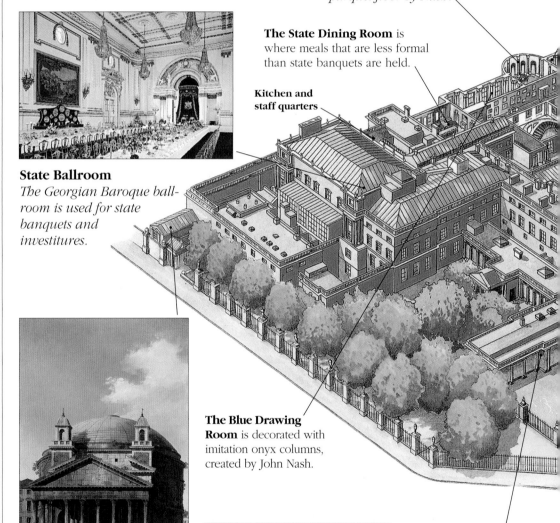

The State Dining Room is where meals that are less formal than state banquets are held.

Kitchen and staff quarters

The Blue Drawing Room is decorated with imitation onyx columns, created by John Nash.

Private post office

Queen's Gallery
Works of art from the Queen's collection, including Canaletto's Rome: The Pantheon, *are on display.*

Changing of the Guard
During the summer the palace guard is changed regularly in a colorful and musical military ceremony.

The White Drawing Room is where the Royal Family assembles before passing into the Dining Room or Ballroom.

The garden *is a haven for wildlife and is overlooked by most of the lavishly decorated state rooms at the back of the palace.*

PALACE FIRE

On the eve of the Queen's Golden Jubilee celebrations in 2002, fire broke out in the roof of the East Gallery, lasting an hour. No member of the Royal Family was present during the emergency, but musicians who were rehearsing for a concert at the palace had to be evacuated.

ATLANTIC OCEAN

Edinburgh

NORTH SEA

GREAT BRITAIN

IRELAND

Birmingham

THE NETHERLANDS

BUCKINGHAM PALACE, LONDON

BELGIUM

FRANCE

A swimming pool lies in the palace grounds as does a private cinema.

The Throne Room is illuminated by seven magnificent chandeliers.

The Green Drawing Room is the first of the state rooms entered by guests at royal functions.

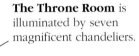

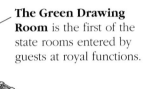

Queen's Audience Chamber
This is one of the Queen's 12 private rooms on the second floor of the palace.

The Royal Standard flies when the Queen is in residence.

KEY DATES

1703 Buckingham House is built by the Duke of Buckingham, Richard Temple.

1762 The house is bought by King George II for his wife Queen Charlotte and is renamed the Queen's House.

1820–29 King George IV hires John Nash to remodel the building. Nash is later replaced by Edward Blore.

1837 Queen Victoria resides in the newly named Buckingham Palace.

1840–47 The palace's fourth wing is built by Edward Blore.

QUEEN'S GALLERY

The Queen possesses one of the finest and most valuable collections of treasures in the world, including paintings by old masters like Vermeer and da Vinci. In 1962, she opened the ▷ *Queen's Gallery*, built on the former location of the royal chapel, bombed in World War II, to display these works to the public. In 2002 the galleries were expanded in time for the Queen's Golden Jubilee. There is now more space and an impressive new entrance gallery with a striking columned portico. Among the gallery's seven rooms, one is dedicated to a permanent display of some of the royal collection's masterworks, while the other rooms rotate an array of works, including fine art, jewels, porcelain, furniture, books, and manuscripts.

WHO LIVES IN BUCKINGHAM PALACE?

The palace is the London home of Queen Elizabeth II and her husband, Prince Phillip. Prince Edward, Prince Andrew, and the Princess Royal have private offices here. Some of the Royal Household staff who support the day-to-day activities and duties of the Royal Family also have offices.

View over The Mall
Traditionally, the Royal Family waves to eager crowds from the palace balcony.

BIG BEN

The name of the largest clock in Britain, Big Ben refers to the resonant bell on which the hours are struck. It was named for Sir Benjamin Hall, Chief Commissioner of Works, after a debate in Parliament in the 19th century. Designed by Sir Edmund Beckett, the bell was cast at Whitechapel and placed in the 96 m (316 ft) ▷ *clock tower* that rises above the Houses of Parliament. The exact time has been kept for the nation more or less continuously since the clock was first set in motion in May 1859 and its deep chimes have become a symbol of Britain worldwide.

Clock Tower

WESTMINSTER HALL

The oldest parliamentary building was originally designed by King William II and constructed between 1097–99 as part of the royal Palace of Westminster. After it was built, ▷ *Westminster Hall* was used for coronation banquets and royal entertainments. In 1393, Richard II decided to remodel the hall. He commissioned Master Mason Henry Yevele, who added new windows and cornices studded with heraldic beasts, and Hugh Herland, who designed a 21.1 m (69 ft) wide hammer-beam roof, which needed no supporting pillars. In 1512, the Palace of Westminster ceased to be a royal residence after a fire. Westminster Hall then housed the courts of law, which held many state trials, including that of Sir Thomas More in 1535, who was sentenced to death by beheading for treason. The building escaped another fire in 1834 and bombing in World War II and is now used for major public ceremonies, including the Queen's Silver Jubilee in 1977.

Houses of Parliament, London

THE PALACE OF WESTMINSTER is the most recognizable Neo-Gothic (▷ *Gothic Style p73)* parliamentary building in the world. Better known as the Houses of Parliament, it was designed by Charles Barry, assisted by A W Pugin. The building was constructed on the medieval site of the old Palace of Westminster, built by King Edward the Confessor in the middle of the 11th century. Fire in the 16th and 19th centuries destroyed most of the original palace and a new building was commissioned in 1836. Inspired by Henry VII's medieval Chapel in Westminster Abbey, Barry designed rectangular windows, carved stone motifs, and octagonal turrets for the external façades. He also added a steep pitched cast-iron roof, covered with interlocking cast-iron plates. The finest materials were sought and used in the building's construction. The Neo-Gothic detailing on the palace's exterior continues inside, which is decorated in stained glass, carved wood panels, gilded carvings, tiles, and brass railings.

★ Commons' Chamber
The room is upholstered in green. The Government sits on the left, the Opposition on the right, and the Speaker presides from a chair between them.

Commons Court

Speaker's Court

Clock Tower, originally designed to provide ventilation for the Houses of Parliament.

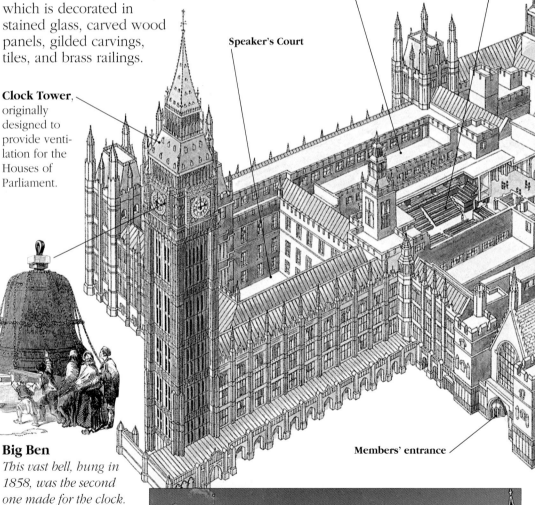

Members' entrance

Big Ben
This vast bell, hung in 1858, was the second one made for the clock. The first was cracked during a test ringing in the Palace Yard at Westminster.

The Neo-Gothic building was designed to assert the power and prestige of the monarchy, the Lords, the Commons, and the people of the United Kingdom to the rest of the world.

Central Lobby
People who come to meet their MP wait here under a ceiling of rich mosaics.

Peers are members of the House of Lords – many receive their titles for services to their country. This is their lobby.

GUNPOWDER PLOT

Catholic conspirator Guy Fawkes planned to blow up the Houses of Parliament during the State Opening on 5 November 1605. His plot was discovered and he was hanged for treason. Today fireworks displays around the country mark the date of the plot.

ATLANTIC OCEAN

NORTH SEA

Edinburgh

GREAT BRITAIN

IRELAND

Birmingham

THE NETHERLANDS

HOUSES OF PARLIAMENT, LONDON

BELGIUM

FRANCE

Victoria Tower houses the House of Lords' Records Office where over 1.5 million Acts of Parliament passed have been kept since 1497.

KEY DATES

1042 Work starts on the Palace of Westminster.

1836–68 After a second fire destroyed most of its buildings, the new Palace of Westminster is built.

1941 The House of Commons is bombed in World War II.

1950 The damaged building is restored.

1987 The Palace of Westminster is designated a UNESCO World Heritage Site.

HOUSE OF COMMONS AND HOUSE OF LORDS

Since 1512, the Palace of Westminster has been the seat of the two houses of Parliament called the Commons and the Lords. The Commons is made up of elected Members of Parliament (MPs) from different political parties; the party with the most MPs forms the Government and its leader becomes Prime Minister. MPs from other parties make up the Opposition. Commons' debates can become heated and are impartially chaired by an MP designated as Speaker. The role of the House of Lords is to debate and revise important legislation. Its members are not elected by the public and they do not become involved in financial and tax issues. The Lords is also the final court of law for civil cases in the United Kingdom, and for criminal cases in England, Wales and Northern Ireland.

Royal Gallery
The Queen passes through here at the State Opening. It is lined with peers' desks.

St Stephen's entrance

★ **Lords' Chamber**
At the State Opening of Parliament the Queen delivers a speech from the throne of the House of Lords, which outlines the Government's plans.

★ **Westminster Hall**
The only surviving part of the original Palace of Westminster, it dates from 1097; its hammer-beam roof is from the 14th century.

STAR FEATURES

★ **Commons' Chamber**

★ **Lords' Chamber**

★ **Westminster Hall**

Houses of Parliament

Lady Nightingale's Memorial by Roubiliac (1761), North Transept

FAMOUS TOMBS AND MONUMENTS

Many sovereigns and their consorts are buried in Westminster Abbey. Some tombs are deliberately plain, while others are lavishly decorated. The shrine of the Saxon king Edward the Confessor and various tombs of medieval monarchs are located at the heart of the abbey (▷ *St Edward's Chapel*). The *Grave of the Unknown Warrior* in the ▷ *Nave* commemorates those killed in World War I who had no formal resting place. One un-named soldier is buried here. Monuments to a number of Britain's greatest public figures – from politicians to poets – crowd the aisles. Memorials to countless literary giants such as Chaucer, Shakespeare, and Dickens can be found in the South Transept (▷ *Poets' Corner*).

HENRY VII CHAPEL

Work on the chapel began in 1503, on the orders of King Henry VII. It was intended to enshrine Henry VI, but it was Henry VII himself who was finally laid to rest here in an elaborate tomb. The highlight of this chapel, completed in 1519, is the vaulted roof, a glorious example of Perpendicular architecture. The undersides of the choir stalls (1512) are beautifully carved with exotic and fantastic creatures. Inside the chapel is the fine tomb of Elizabeth I, who reigned 1558–1603, also containing the body of her half-sister, Mary I, who ruled 1553–8.

Westminster Abbey, London

S INCE THE 13TH CENTURY, Westminster Abbey has been the burial place of Britain's monarchs and the setting for many coronations and royal weddings. It is one of the most beautiful buildings in London, with an exceptionally diverse array of architectural styles, ranging from the austere French Gothic of the nave to the astonishing complexity of Henry VII's Chapel. Half national church, half national museum, the abbey aisles and transepts are crammed with an extraordinary collection of tombs and monuments honoring some of Britain's greatest public figures, ranging from politicians to poets.

★ **Nave**
At a height of 31 m (102 ft), the nave is the highest in England. The ratio of height to width is 3:1.

CORONATION

The coronation ceremony is over 1,000 years old. The last occupant of the Coronation Chair was the present monarch, Queen Elizabeth II. She was crowned on 2 June 1953 by the Archbishop of Canterbury in the first televised coronation.

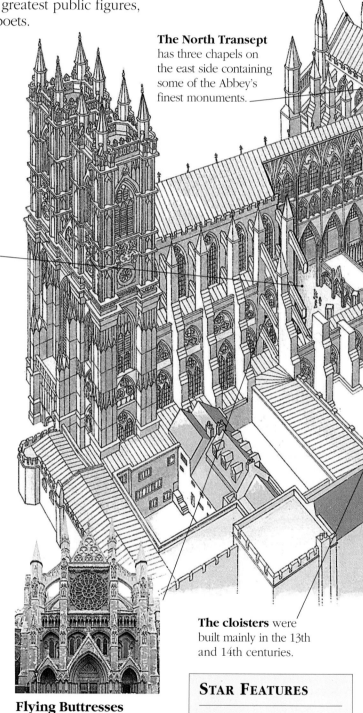

North Entrance
The mock-medieval stonework is Victorian.

The North Transept has three chapels on the east side containing some of the Abbey's finest monuments.

Flying Buttresses
The abbey's enormous flying buttresses help to redistribute the great weight of the soaring nave roof.

The cloisters were built mainly in the 13th and 14th centuries.

STAR FEATURES

★ **Nave**

★ **Henry VII Chapel**

★ **Chapter House**

Westminster Abbey

★ Henry VII Chapel

The chapel, built in 1503–12, has superb late Perpendicular vaultings and choir stalls dating from 1512.

The Sanctuary, built by Henry III, has been the scene of 38 coronations.

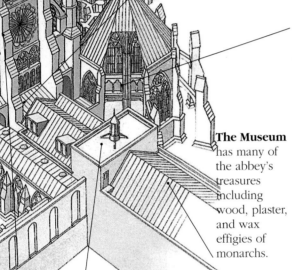

THE CORONATION CHAIR

This magnificent chair, used for all coronations since 1308, used to hold the supposedly biblical Stone of Destiny that Edward I seized from Scotland in 1296. It can now be seen at Edinburgh Castle. The chair remains in the abbey (▷ *St Edward's Chapel*).

Poets' Corner

A host of great poets are honored here, including Shakespeare, Chaucer, and T S Eliot.

The Museum has many of the abbey's treasures including wood, plaster, and wax effigies of monarchs.

★ Chapter House

A beautiful octagonal room, remarkable for its 13th-century tile floor. It is lit by six huge stained-glass windows showing scenes from the abbey's history.

The Pyx Chamber is where the coinage was tested in medieval times.

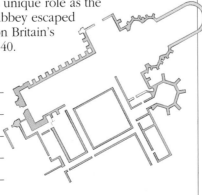

St Edward's Chapel

The shrine of Edward the Confessor is housed here, along with the Coronation Chair and many tombs.

HISTORICAL PLAN OF THE ABBEY

The first abbey church was established as early as the 10th century, but the present French-influenced Gothic structure (▷ *Gothic Style p73*) was begun in 1245 at the behest of Henry III. Because of its unique role as the coronation church, the abbey escaped Henry VIII's onslaught on Britain's monastic buildings in 1540.

KEY

■	Built before 1500
■	Built in 1500–20
■	Completed by 1745
□	Remodeled after 1850

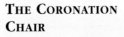

ATLANTIC OCEAN

NORTH SEA

Edinburgh

GREAT BRITAIN

IRELAND

Birmingham

THE NETHERLANDS

WESTMINSTER ABBEY, LONDON

BELGIUM

FRANCE

KEY DATES

1065 Edward the Confessor founds the original abbey.

1245 Henry III demolishes the old abbey and begins work on Westminster Abbey as we know it today.

1503 Work commences on the stunning Henry VII Chapel.

1734 Construction of the west towers begins.

1953 Queen Elizabeth II's coronation is the most recent in the abbey's history.

THE CORONATION CEREMONY

Every monarch since William the Conqueror, except Edward V and Edward VIII, has been crowned in Westminster Abbey. Many elements in this solemn and mystical ceremony date from the reign of Edward the Confessor (1042–66). The king or queen proceeds to the abbey and is accompanied by some of the crowns, scepters, orbs, and swords that form the royal regalia. The jeweled State Sword, one of the most valuable in the world, represents the monarch's own sword. He or she is anointed with holy oil, to signify divine approval, and invested with ornaments and royal robes. The climax of the ceremony is when St Edward's Crown is placed on the sovereign's head; there is a cry of "God Save the King" (or Queen), the trumpets sound, and guns at the Tower of London are fired.

Westminster Abbey

Admiral Lord Nelson's tomb in the crypt

FAMOUS TOMBS

St Paul's Cathedral is the final resting place of Sir Christopher Wren whose tomb is marked by a slab. The inscription states: "Reader, if you seek a monument look around you." Around 200 tombs of famous figures and popular heroes can be found in the crypt, such as Nelson, naval hero of the Battle of Trafalgar (1805), and the Duke of Wellington, hero of the Battle of Waterloo (1815). Other tombs and memorials include those of Sir Arthur Sullivan the composer, Sir Henry Moore the sculptor, and the artists Sir John Everett Millais and Sir Joshua Reynolds. Florence Nightingale, famous for her pioneering work in nursing standards and the first woman to receive the Order of Merit, is also buried here, as well as Alexander Fleming who discovered penicillin.

THE INTERIOR

St Paul's cool, beautifully ordered, ornate and spacious interior is instantly striking. The nave, transepts, and choir are arranged in the shape of a cross, as in a medieval cathedral, but Wren's Classical vision shines through this conservative floor plan, forced on him by the cathedral authorities. The interior is dominated by the vast cupola (▷ *Dome*) which is decorated with monochrome frescoes by Sir James Thornhill. Master woodcarver Grinling Gibbons produced intricate carvings of cherubs, fruits, and garlands (▷ *Choir Stalls*), while wrought ironwork genius Jean Tijou created the sanctuary gates.

St Paul's Cathedral, London

THE GREAT FIRE OF LONDON in 1666 left the medieval cathedral of St Paul's in ruins. Wren was commissioned to rebuild it, but his design for a church on a Greek Cross plan (where all four arms are equal) met with considerable resistance. The authorities insisted on a conventional Latin cross, with a long nave and short transepts, to focus the congregation's attention on the altar. Despite the compromises, Wren created a magnificent, world-renowned Baroque cathedral which was built between 1675 and 1710 and has since formed the lavish setting for many state ceremonies.

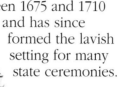

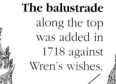

★ **Dome**
At 113 m (370 ft), the elaborate dome is one of the highest in the world.

The balustrade along the top was added in 1718 against Wren's wishes.

★ **West Front and Towers**
The towers were added by Wren in 1707. Their design was inspired by the Italian Baroque architect, Boromini.

The West Portico consists of two stories of coupled Corinthian columns, topped by a pediment carved with reliefs showing the Conversion of St Paul.

The Nave
An imposing succession of massive arches and saucer domes open out into the vast space below the cathedral's main dome.

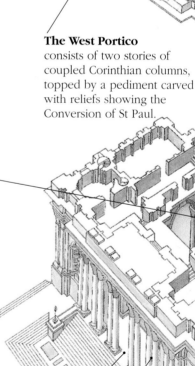

West Porch

Main entrance approached from Ludgate Hill

CHRISTOPHER WREN

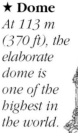

Trained as a scientist, Sir Christopher Wren (1632–1723) began his impressive architectural career at the age of 31. He became a leading figure in the rebuilding of London after the Great Fire of 1666, building a total of 52 new churches. Although Wren never visited Italy, his work was influenced by Roman, Baroque, and Renaissance architecture, as is apparent in his masterwork, St Paul's Cathedral.

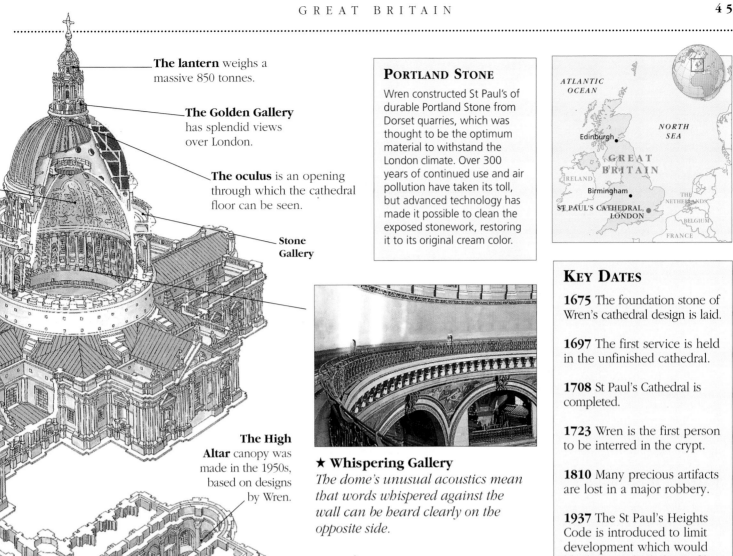

The **lantern** weighs a massive 850 tonnes.

The Golden Gallery has splendid views over London.

The oculus is an opening through which the cathedral floor can be seen.

Stone Gallery

The **High Altar** canopy was made in the 1950s, based on designs by Wren.

Entrance to crypt, which has many memorials to the famous.

Entrance to Golden, Whispering, and Stone galleries

The South Portico was inspired by the porch of Santa Maria della Pace in Rome. Wren absorbed the detail by studying a friend's collection of architectural engravings.

PORTLAND STONE

Wren constructed St Paul's of durable Portland Stone from Dorset quarries, which was thought to be the optimum material to withstand the London climate. Over 300 years of continued use and air pollution have taken its toll, but advanced technology has made it possible to clean the exposed stonework, restoring it to its original cream color.

★ **Whispering Gallery**

The dome's unusual acoustics mean that words whispered against the wall can be heard clearly on the opposite side.

Choir

Jean Tijou, a Huguenot refugee, created much of the fine wrought ironwork in Wren's time, including these choir screens.

STAR FEATURES

★ **Dome**

★ **West Front and Towers**

★ **Whispering Gallery**

Choir Stalls

The 17th-century choir stalls and organ case were made by Grinling Gibbons (1648–1721), a wood-carver from Rotterdam. He and his team of craftsmen worked on these intricate carvings for two years.

KEY DATES

1675 The foundation stone of Wren's cathedral design is laid.

1697 The first service is held in the unfinished cathedral.

1708 St Paul's Cathedral is completed.

1723 Wren is the first person to be interred in the crypt.

1810 Many precious artifacts are lost in a major robbery.

1937 The St Paul's Heights Code is introduced to limit development which would block the cathedral's profile on the London skyline.

1940–1 Slight bomb damage occurs during World War II when the cathedral is targeted in the Blitz.

SPECIAL EVENTS

Aided by some of the finest craftsmen of his day, Sir Christopher Wren created an interior of grand majesty and Baroque splendor (▷ *Baroque Style p111)*, a worthy setting for the many great ceremonial events that have taken place here. These include the funerals of Admiral Lord Nelson (1806), the Duke of Wellington (1852), and Sir Winston Churchill (1965). Celebrated royal occasions have included the wedding of Prince Charles and Lady Diana Spencer (1981), and the Queen's Golden Jubilee (2002). The cathedral also provided the venue for a special service to mark the 11 September 2001 attacks in America.

THE LEGEND OF THE RAVENS

The Tower's most celebrated residents are a colony of eight ravens. It is not known when they first settled here, but these scavenger birds would have arrived soon after the castle was constructed to feed off the abundant refuse. Their presence has been protected by the legend that should the birds desert the Tower, the kingdom will fall. In fact they have their wings clipped on one side, making flight impossible. Unfortunately, as the ravens court in flight, this also makes breeding difficult. The Ravenmaster, one of the Yeoman Warders (▷ *"Beefeaters"*), looks after the birds. A memorial in the moat commemorates some of the ravens who have died at the Tower since the 1950s.

FAMOUS PRISONERS

The Tower has been prison to kings and notorious characters throughout its history. One of the first monarchs to be held here was Henry VI, who was murdered while at prayer in 1471. The Duke of Clarence, brother of Edward IV, was convicted of treason and assassinated in 1478 by drowning in a cask of wine. Two of Henry VIII's wives and his former chancellor Sir Thomas More were beheaded here. Even Elizabeth I was held in the tower for two months, and on her death in 1603 her favorite explorer Sir Walter Raleigh was imprisoned and later executed. The last prisoner, held in the ▷ *Queen's House* in 1941, was deputy leader of the Nazi party, Rudolf Hess.

The 19th-century Tower Bridge overlooking the Tower

The Tower of London

SOON AFTER HE BECAME KING in 1066, William the Conqueror built a castle here to guard the entrance to London from the Thames Estuary. In 1097 the White Tower, standing today at the center of the complex, was completed in sturdy stone; other fine buildings were added over the centuries to create one of the most powerful and formidable fortresses in Europe. The Tower has served as a royal residence, armory, treasury, and most famously as a prison for enemies of the Crown. Many were tortured and among those who met their death here were the "Princes in the Tower", the sons and heirs of Edward IV. Today the Tower is a popular attraction, housing the Crown Jewels and other priceless exhibits which remain powerful reminders of royal might and wealth.

"Beefeaters"
Thirty-seven Yeoman Warders guard the Tower and live here. Their uniforms hark back to Tudor times.

Queen's House
This Tudor building is the sovereign's official residence at the Tower.

Beauchamp Tower
Many high-ranking prisoners were held here, often with their own retinues of servants. The tower was built by Edward I around 1281.

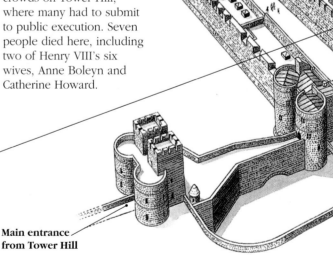

Two 13th-century curtain walls protect the tower.

Tower Green was the execution site for favored prisoners, away from crowds on Tower Hill, where many had to submit to public execution. Seven people died here, including two of Henry VIII's six wives, Anne Boleyn and Catherine Howard.

Main entrance from Tower Hill

THE CROWN JEWELS

The world's best-known collection of precious objects, now displayed in a splendid exhibition room, includes the gorgeous regalia of crowns, scepters, orbs, and swords used at coronations and other state occasions. Most date from 1661, when Charles II commissioned replacements for regalia destroyed by Parliament after the execution of Charles I (r.1625–49). Only a few older pieces survived, hidden by royalist clergymen until the restoration of the monarchy in 1660 – notably, Edward the Confessor's (r.1327–77) sapphire ring, now incorporated into the Imperial State Crown. The crown was made for Queen Victoria in 1837 and has been used at every coronation since.

The Sovereign's Ring (1831)

The Sovereign's Orb (1661), a hollow gold sphere encrusted with jewels

★ Jewel House

Among the magnificent Crown Jewels is the Scepter with the Cross (1660), which contains the world's biggest diamond.

★ White Tower

When the tower was finished in 1097, it was the tallest building in London at 27 m (90 ft) high.

TORTURE AND DEATH

Early prisoners in the Tower, who were sentenced to execution, could look forward to a drawn-out death. In the 14th and 15th centuries many would have been hung, drawn, and quartered or burnt at the stake, although some may have been stretched on a rack first. Others were disemboweled or hacked to pieces.

The Salt Tower, built in 1238, contains two residential rooms which were used as prison cells during Tudor times.

KEY DATES

1078 Work begins on building the White Tower.

1533 Henry VIII marries Anne Boleyn at the Tower.

1601 Last victim of the axe is beheaded on Tower Green.

1841 Fire destroys part of the White Tower.

THE WHITE TOWER

Begun by William I in 1078, the ▷ *White Tower* is the oldest surviving building in the Tower of London. It was designed as a palace-fortress to accommodate the king and the Constable of the Tower, the garrison commander. Each had self-contained rooms including a hall, for public occasions, a partitioned chamber, and a chapel. When the fortress was enlarged a century later, both king and constable moved to new residences. On the upper two stories, the monarch's elegant Royal Suite was used to hold distinguished prisoners. The ceremonial chambers would have been twice their present height; a pitched roof was removed in 1490 so that extra floors could be built on top. Rising through two floors is the ▷ *Chapel of St John,* an exquisite example of an early Norman church. Originally this would have been decorated with rich furnishings, painted stonework, and stained-glass windows. These were removed in 1550 during the English Reformation. By the 1600s, the tower was used as a storehouse and armory.

★ Chapel of St John

This austerely beautiful Romanesque chapel is a particularly fine example of Norman architecture.

Traitors' Gate

The infamous entrance was used for prisoners brought from trial in Westminster Hall.

Bloody Tower

Edward IV's two sons were put here by their uncle, Richard of Gloucester (subsequently Richard III), after their father died in 1483. The princes, depicted here by John Millais (1829–96), disappeared mysteriously and Richard was crowned later that year. In 1674 the skeletons of two children were found nearby.

STAR FEATURES

★ Jewel House

★ White Tower

★ Chapel of St John

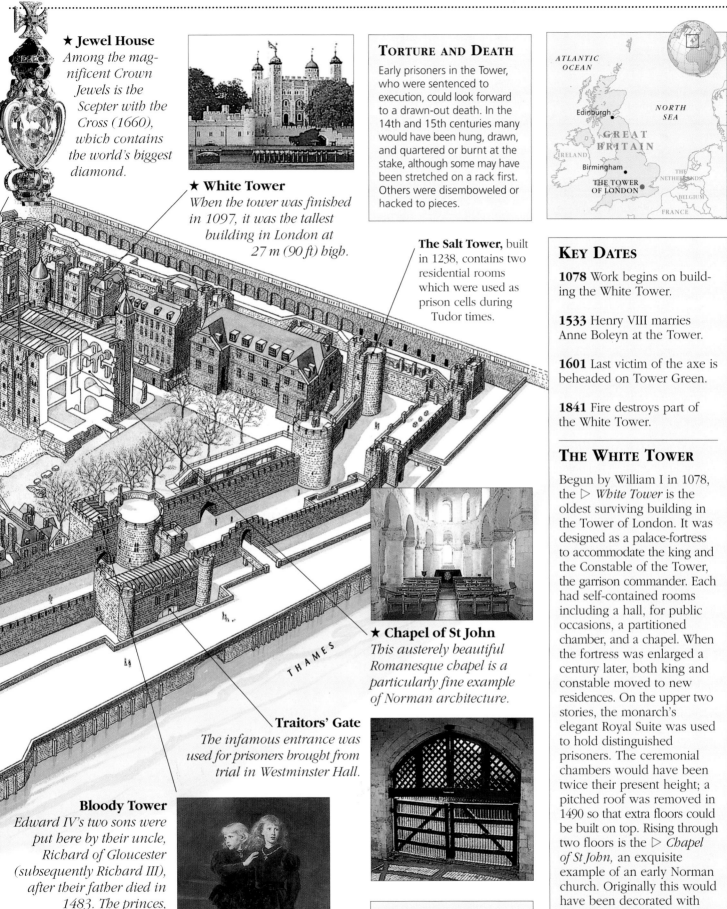

THE ROYAL COLLECTION

Paintings, drawings, textiles, jewelry, and furniture are some of the items included in the vast Royal Collection. The objects have mostly been acquired since 1660 when Charles II regained the throne following the Civil War. Additions made by subsequent rulers reflect their personal artistic preferences. This has shaped the variety and richness of this historic collection on display at the official royal households. Exhibits in the splendid ▷ *State Apartments* include paintings by Holbein, Canaletto, Leonardo da Vinci, Rembrandt, Rubens, and Van Dyck, sculpture, ceramics, fine tapestries, a 17th-century silver furniture set, and an impressive armor collection.

ST GEORGE'S CHAPEL

Edward IV started to build the sumptuous ▷ *St George's Chapel* in 1475 and it was completed in 1528 by Henry VIII. This grand Perpendicular structure has slender columns soaring up to the fan-vaulted roof and rich decoration. It is the second most important royal burial ground after Westminster Abbey in London. Ten monarchs are buried here including Edward IV, Henry VIII and his third wife Jane Seymour, Charles I, George V and Queen Mary, and George VI. Following Henry VI's death in 1471, visitors to his tomb, located near the high altar, experienced curious visions and reported incredible cures. The chapel consequently became a major center of pilgrimage.

Henry II's imposing Round Tower

Windsor Castle

Henry II (r.1154–89)

THE OLDEST CONTINUOUSLY inhabited royal residence in Britain, the imposing Windsor Castle creates a spectacular skyline. Originally made of wood, it was built by William the Conqueror in 1070 to guard the western approaches to London. He chose the site as it was on high ground and just a day's journey from London. Successive monarchs have made alterations that render it a remarkable monument to royalty's changing tastes. King George V's affection for it was shown when he chose Windsor for his family surname in 1917. The castle is an official residence of the Queen and her family.

Albert Memorial Chapel
First built in 1240, it was rebuilt in 1485 and finally converted into a memorial for Prince Albert in 1863.

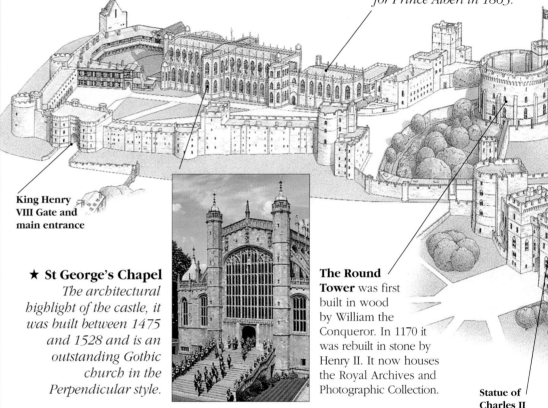

King Henry VIII Gate and main entrance

★ St George's Chapel
The architectural highlight of the castle, it was built between 1475 and 1528 and is an outstanding Gothic church in the Perpendicular style.

The Round Tower was first built in wood by William the Conqueror. In 1170 it was rebuilt in stone by Henry II. It now houses the Royal Archives and Photographic Collection.

Statue of Charles II

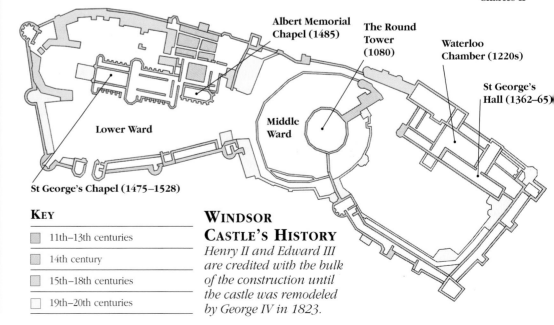

Albert Memorial Chapel (1485)

The Round Tower (1080)

Waterloo Chamber (1220s)

St George's Hall (1362–65)

Lower Ward

Middle Ward

St George's Chapel (1475–1528)

KEY

▢	11th–13th centuries
▢	14th century
▢	15th–18th centuries
▢	19th–20th centuries

WINDSOR CASTLE'S HISTORY

Henry II and Edward III are credited with the bulk of the construction until the castle was remodeled by George IV in 1823.

Drawings Gallery
This black chalk etching of Christ by Michelangelo is part of the Royal Collection. The great size of this collection means that the exhibition changes frequently and works are often loaned to other museums.

The Audience Chamber is where the Queen greets her guests.

The Queen's Ballroom

Queen Mary's Dolls' House, designed by Sir Edwin Lutyens, was given to Queen Mary in 1924. The wine cellar contains valuable vintage wine.

THE FIRE OF 1992
It took 250 firefighters 15 hours and 1.5 million gallons of water to extinguish the fire of 20 November which severely damaged 100 rooms. The £40m restoration was largely financed by the Queen.

Waterloo Chamber
The walls of this banqueting hall, first built in the 13th century, are lined with portraits of the leaders who played a part in Napoleon's defeat in 1815.

Brunswick Tower

The East Terrace Garden was created by Sir Jeffry Wyatville for King George IV in the 1820s.

KEY DATES

1070 Windsor Castle is founded.

1170s King Henry II makes fortification improvements to the castle which include rebuilding the round tower in stone.

1475 Work begins on St George's Chapel.

1997 Restoration of the Castle following severe fire damage in 1992 is completed.

THE ORDER OF THE GARTER

▷ *St George's Chapel* is home to the sovereign's highest order of chivalry, the Order of the Garter, founded in 1348 by Edward III. The name refers to the symbol of the garter worn by its member knights. From the 18th century to 1946, the government recommended admissions to the Order. Today, the Queen makes appointments as a mark of royal favor. This follows the original custom of the Middle Ages. Traditionally Garter Knights were associated with nobility, however today there is increasing diversity between those who are appointed. New appointments are announced on St George's Day, 23 April, each year to honor the Order's patron saint. The knights gather at Windsor Castle in June and new knights swear an oath. Their banners and engraved plates bearing their coats of arms are added to the display in St George's Chapel. This has resulted in an unrivaled collection of heraldry.

★ **State Apartments**
These rooms contain many treasures, such as this 18th-century bed in the King's State Bedchamber, hung in its present splendor for the visit in 1855 of Napoleon III.

STAR FEATURES

★ St George's Chapel

★ State Apartments

St George's Hall
A devastating blaze began during maintenance work in 1992. St George's Hall was destroyed but has been rebuilt.

Windsor Castle

ROYAL TENNIS COURT AND THE MAZE

Henry VIII had the ▷ *royal tennis court* built in the 16th century, as he was very fond of the game. Legend says that he was playing tennis at Hampton Court while his second wife Anne Boleyn was being executed. When William III moved into the palace in 1689, he had the gardens and the buildings remodeled. Wren's design for the gardens included the ▷ *Fountain Garden* and the ▷ *Maze*. The Maze was planted with hornbeams until the 18th century, when they were replaced with yews and hollies.

The Chapel Royal decorated with carved pendants and royal arms

THE CHAPEL ROYAL AND THE GREAT HALL

Cardinal Wolsey had the ▷ *Chapel Royal* built during his time at Hampton Court. As soon as King Henry VIII moved in, he refurbished the chapel and installed its impressive vaulted ceiling in 1535–6. The chapel subsequently became the location for many decisive moments in Henry's life – he learnt of his fifth wife Katherine Howard's infidelity and married his last wife Catherine Parr here. The ▷ *Great Hall*, with its delightful hammerbeam roof and Gothic fireplaces, was also part of Henry's rebuilding of Hampton Court. Stained-glass windows were added to the beautiful hall, showing him flanked by the coats of arms of his six wives.

Hampton Court Palace

Ceiling decoration from the Queen's Drawing Room

CARDINAL WOLSEY, influential Archbishop of York to Henry VIII, began building Hampton Court in the early 16th century. Originally it was not a royal palace, but was intended as Wolsey's riverside country house. Later, in 1528, Hampton Court was seized by the king when Wolsey fell from royal favor. The buildings and gardens were then twice rebuilt and extended into a grand palace, first by Henry himself and then, in the 1690s, by William III and Mary II, who employed Christopher Wren as architect. There is a striking contrast between Wren's Classical royal apartments and the Tudor turrets, gables, and chimneys elsewhere. The inspiration for the gardens as they are today comes largely from the time of William and Mary, for whom Wren created a vast formal Baroque landscape, radiating avenues of majestic limes and many collections of exotic plants.

★ Clock Court
The so-called Anne Boleyn's Gateway is at the entrance to Clock Court. Henry VIII's Astronomical Clock, created in 1540 by Nicholas Oursian, is also located here.

The Pond Garden
This sunken water garden was part of Henry VIII's elaborate designs.

★ The Maze
Its yew and holly hedges are approximately 2 m (7 ft) high and 0.9 m (3 ft) wide.

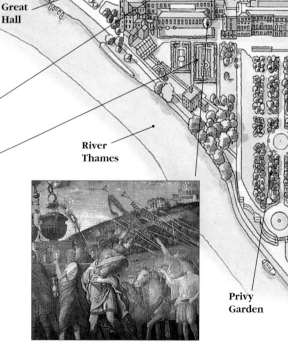

Royal tennis court

Chapel Royal

Great Hall

River Thames

Privy Garden

★ The Mantegna Gallery
Andrea Mantegna's nine canvases depicting The Triumphs of Caesar *(1490s) are housed here.*

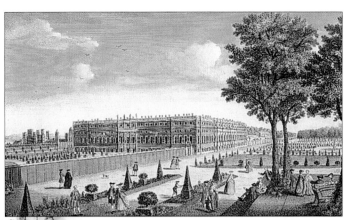

Broad Walk
A contemporary print shows the East Front and the Broad Walk during the reign of George II (1727–60).

HAMPTON COURT FLOWER SHOW

The large ornamental gardens at Hampton Court host one of Britain's most popular horticultural events each summer. Some of the best gardeners from all over the country showcase their garden designs, surrounded by flowers and exotic plants. Creators of the most captivating gardens are awarded medals.

Long Water
A man-made lake runs almost parallel to the Thames, from the Fountain Garden across the Home Park.

Fountain Garden
A few of the clipped yews here were planted in the reign of William and Mary.

The East Front
The windows of the Queen's Drawing Room, designed by Wren, overlook the central avenue of the Fountain Garden.

STAR FEATURES

★ **The Maze**

★ **Clock Court**

★ **The Mantegna Gallery**

KEY DATES

c.1236 The Knights Hospitalers of St John of Jerusalem acquire the manor of Hampton and begin to use the site as a grange.

1514 Cardinal Thomas Wolsey obtains the lease of Hampton Court from the Knights Hospitalers.

1532 As part of Henry VIII's rebuilding of Hampton Court, work on the Great Hall begins.

1838 Hampton Court Palace opens to the public for the first time.

CARDINAL WOLSEY AND HENRY VIII

The English statesman and Cardinal, Thomas Wolsey (c.1475–1530), was considered the most powerful person in England after the king. During Henry VIII's reign from 1509, Wolsey was given the role of managing England's foreign affairs, as well as being the king's advisor. This important position earned Wolsey a lot of wealth, but he also had enemies. His downfall came when Henry wanted a church annulment from his first wife Catherine of Aragon so he could marry Anne Boleyn. Wolsey, aware that his life would be in danger if he did not achieve Henry's demand, proceeded slowly with a request to the Pope. This angered the king and also Anne who used her influence to remove Wolsey from court. A few years later, Wolsey died suddenly on his way to face trial for treason.

THE BELL BEAKER CULTURE

It is believed that the Beaker people emerged in Britain around 2200 BC. Their name derives from the distinctive bell-shaped pottery cups found in their burial mounds. They are credited with building ▷ *the Bluestone Circle* at Stonehenge because concentric circles were typical of their culture and much of their pottery was unearthed in the vicinity. Their advanced construction technique suggests that the Beaker Folk were sun worshipers as well as highly organized and skilled craftsmen. They created ▷ *the Avenue* which runs directly toward the midsummer sun, and widened the entrance to the henge, aligning it more precisely with the sunrise of the summer solstice.

THE SITE

Despite centuries of archaeological, religious, and mystical interest in Stonehenge, the site's original purpose remains unknown. The building of this inscrutable prehistoric megalith has been attributed to Druids, Greeks, Phoenicians, and Atlanteans. Theories on the reason it was built range from sacrificial ceremonies to astronomical calendars. Unearthed evidence of burials suggests that human sacrifices took place here and most experts agree that Stonehenge has religious foundations. The arrangement of the stones fuels beliefs in an astronomical purpose. The significance of this site must have been great as the stones used were not quarried locally but brought from as far away as Wales (▷ *the Bluestone Circle*).

An impression of the completed prehistoric monument

Stonehenge

BUILT IN SEVERAL STAGES from about 3000 BC, Stonehenge is Europe's most famous prehistoric monument. We can only guess at the rituals that took place here, but the alignment of the stones leaves little doubt that the circle is connected with the sun and the passing of the seasons, and that its builders possessed a sophisticated understanding of both arithmetic and astronomy. Despite popular belief, the circle was not built by the Druids; this Iron Age priestly cult flourished in Britain from around 250 BC, more than 1,000 years after Stonehenge was completed.

The Winter Solstice
There are many lunar and solar alignments. The inner horseshoe faces the winter solstice sunrise.

The Heel Stone, a large sarsen stone quarried in the Marlborough Downs, stands at the entrance to the site. It casts a long shadow straight to the heart of the inner circle on Midsummer's Day.

The Avenue is a dirt path built by the Beaker Folk which forms a ceremonial approach to the site.

The Slaughter Stone, named by 17th-century antiquarians who believed Stonehenge to be a place of human sacrifice, was in fact one of a pair forming a doorway.

The Prehistoric Site
This was possibly a ceremonial area for fertility, birth, and death rituals. Evidence of burials and cremations exists nearby and inside the circle.

The Outer Bank, dug around 3000 BC, is the oldest part of the historic Stonehenge site.

RECONSTRUCTION OF STONEHENGE

This illustration shows what Stonehenge probably looked like about 4,000 years ago. The stones remaining today create a strong impression of how incredible the original site would have been to see.

BUILDING OF STONEHENGE

Stonehenge's monumental scale is more impressive given that the only tools available were made of stone, wood, and bone. The labour involved in quarrying, transporting, and erecting the huge stones was such that its builders must have been able to command immense resources and vast numbers of people. One method is explained here.

A sarsen stone *was moved on rollers and levered down into an awaiting pit.*

With levers *supported by timber packing, it was gradually raised by 200 men.*

Stonehenge as it is Today

The ruins of Stonehenge reflect the grand structure that existed 4,000 years ago. Only half of the original stones remain due to natural weathering and human destruction.

PREHISTORIC WILTSHIRE

Ringing the horizon around Stonehenge are scores of circular barrows, or burial mounds, where ruling class members were honored with burial close to the temple site. Ceremonial bronze weapons, jewelry, and other finds excavated around Stonehenge can be seen in the museums at Salisbury and Devizes.

Stonehenge

KEY DATES

3000–1000 BC Stonehenge is constructed in three phases.

1648 The site is recognized as a prehistoric religious base.

1900 Two stones on the site fall down.

1978 The government prohibits visitors from walking within the stone circle.

1984 Stonehenge is added to UNESCO's World Heritage Site list.

The Bluestone Circle was built around 2000 BC out of some 80 slabs quarried in south Wales. It was never completed.

The Horseshoe of Sarsen Trilithons was built around 2300 BC out of sandstone from the Marlborough Downs.

Finds

From a burial mound near Stonehenge, these prehistoric finds are now part of Devizes museum's exceptional collection.

The Horseshoe of Bluestones is likely to have been transported from Wales on a combination of sledges and rafts.

The Sarsen Circle was erected around 2300 BC and is capped by lintel stones held in place by mortice and tenon joints.

Restoration

Formal excavation and restoration work on the site only began during the 20th century.

THE DRUIDS

Archaeologists initially claimed that Stonehenge was built by Druids, priests of a pre-Christian, Celtic society, who performed ritualistic ceremonies and sacrifices here. Although the site is still associated with Druids, radiocarbon dating has proved that it was raised over a thousand years before Druids were established in the region, and they may have used the existing site as a temple of worship. Today Stonehenge is famous for the Druid ceremonies and festivals. English Heritage, who control the site, permit Druid gatherings in the inner circle each year for the solstices and equinoxes, however the site itself is cordoned off to protect against damage caused by an increasing number of tourists. Many Druids associate Stonehenge with the magician Merlin. Said to have been a Druid master, legend claims he taught and advised the fabled King Arthur of Britain.

The pit *round the base was packed tightly with stones and chalk.*

Alternate ends *of the lintel were levered up.*

The weight *of the lintel was supported by a timber platform.*

The lintel *was then levered sideways onto the uprights.*

Sculpture of a seated Jesus on Christ Church Gate

ST THOMAS BECKET

When Archbishop Theobold died in 1161, King Henry II saw the opportunity to increase his power over the Church by consecrating his faithful adviser, Thomas Becket, as the Archbishop of Canterbury – the most prominent ecclesiastical role in the kingdom. The king mistakenly believed that this would allow him to exert pressure on the Church. Becket's loyalty shifted and the struggle between Church and monarch for ultimate control of the realm culminated in the murder of Becket in 1170 by four knights attempting to gain the king's favor. People flocked to mourn him and three days later, a series of miracles took place which were attributed to Becket. After Becket's canonization in 1173, Canterbury became a major center of pilgrimage.

THE REFORMATION

In 1534, Henry VIII broke with the Church of Rome when the Pope refused to divorce him from Catherine of Aragon. The Archbishop of Canterbury, Thomas Cranmer, was made to do so instead. The Church of England was created, with Henry as its supreme head and the Archbishop of Canterbury its ecclesiastical guide. The *Book of Common Prayer*, compiled by Cranmer, became the cornerstone of the Church of England.

Canterbury Cathedral

THIS GLORIOUS HIGH-VAULTED cathedral was designed in the French Gothic style (▷ *Gothic Style p73*) by William of Sens in 1070 and became the first Gothic church in England. It was built to reflect the city's growing ecclesiastical rank as a major centre of Christianity by the first Norman archbishop, Lanfranc, on the ruins of an Anglo-Saxon cathedral. Enlarged and rebuilt many times it remains, however, an exceptional example of the different styles of medieval architecture. The most significant moment in its history came in 1170 when Archbishop Thomas Becket was murdered here. In 1220 Becket's body was moved to a new shrine in Trinity Chapel which, until Henry VIII destroyed it, soon became one of Christendom's chief pilgrimage sites.

The nave seen today was rebuilt by Henry Yevele in the Perpendicular style from 1377–1405.

★ Medieval Stained Glass

This depiction of the 1,000-year-old Methuselah is a detail from the southwest transept window. The cathedral's unique collection of stained glass gives a precious glimpse into medieval thoughts and practises.

THE CANTERBURY TALES

Considered to be the first great English poet, Geoffrey Chaucer (c.1345–1400) is chiefly remembered for his rumbustious and witty saga of a group of pilgrims who travel from London to Becket's shrine in 1387, called *The Canterbury Tales*. Chaucer's pilgrims represent a cross-section of 14th-century English society and the tales remain one of the greatest and most entertaining works of early English literature.

Wife of Bath, *The Canterbury Tales*

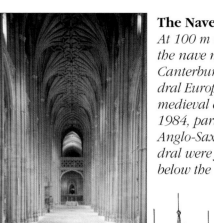

The Nave
At 100 m (328 ft), the nave makes Canterbury Cathedral Europe's longest medieval church. In 1984, parts of an Anglo-Saxon cathedral were found below the nave.

Main entrance

The South Porch (1426) may have been built to commemorate the victory at Agincourt. The statues date from the 19th century.

STAR FEATURES

★ **Medieval Stained Glass**

★ **Site of the Shrine of St Thomas Becket**

★ **Black Prince's Tomb**

Canterbury Cathedral

Bell Harry Tower

The central tower was built in 1496 to house a bell donated by Prior Henry (Harry) of Eastry. The present Bell Harry was cast in 1635. The fan vaulting is a superb example of this late Gothic style.

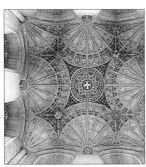

St Augustine

In 597, Pope Gregory the Great sent Augustine on a mission to convert the English to Christianity. Augustine founded a church on the present-day site of Canterbury Cathedral and became its first Archbishop.

★ Site of the Shrine of St Thomas Becket

This Victorian illustration (anon) portrays Becket's canonization. The Trinity Chapel was built to house his tomb which stood here until 1538. The spot is now marked by a lighted candle.

Great Cloister

Chapter House

★ Black Prince's Tomb

This copper effigy is on the tomb of Edward, Prince of Wales, who died in 1376.

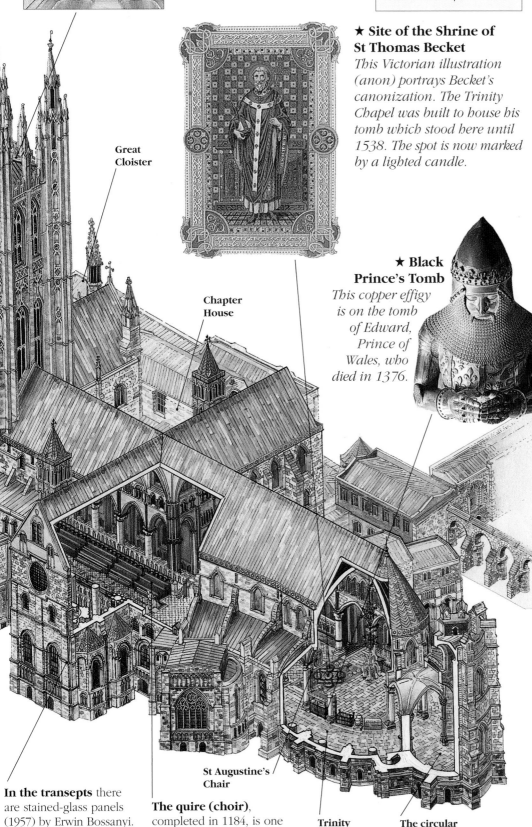

In the transepts there are stained-glass panels (1957) by Erwin Bossanyi.

The quire (choir), completed in 1184, is one of the longest in England.

St Augustine's Chair

Trinity Chapel

The circular Corona Chapel

Key Dates

597 St Augustine founds the first cathedral at Canterbury.

1070 The cathedral is rebuilt by Archbishop Lanfranc.

1170 Archbishop Thomas Becket is murdered at the altar and canonized in 1173.

1534 Henry VIII splits from the Church of Rome and forms the Church of England.

1538 St Thomas Becket's shrine is destroyed by Henry VIII.

1982 Pope John Paul II and Archbishop Robert Runcie pray at Thomas Becket's tomb.

The Black Prince

Edward, Prince of Wales (1330–76), known as "The Black Prince", gained popularity as leader of the English at the Battle of Crécy in 1346. He again emerged victorious in 1356 at the Battle of Poitiers when the French King, John the Good, was captured and brought to Canterbury Cathedral to worship at St Thomas' tomb. As heir to the throne, the prince wished to be buried in the crypt but it was throught appropriate that this hero be laid to rest alongside the tomb of St Thomas in the ▷ *Trinity Chapel*. The copper effigy in the ▷ *Black Prince's Tomb* is one of the most impressive in the cathedral. Edward was outlived by his father Edward III but the Prince's son was crowned Richard II in 1377.

Canterbury Cathedral

PIETER PAUL RUBENS (1577–1640)

Rubens had apprenticeships with prominent Antwerp artists from an early age and was inspired to visit Italy in 1600 to study the work of the Italian Renaissance masters. It was here that his majestic style was largely founded. On returning to Antwerp in 1608, his reputation earned him his appointment as court painter to Archduke Albert and his wife, the Infanta Isabella. He became the most renowned Baroque painter in Europe, combining Flemish realism with the classical imagery of Italian Renaissance art. After 1626, he was assigned diplomatic missions, nominated to the courts of Charles I in England, Marie de' Medici in France, and Felipe IV in Spain. Having helped to conclude a treaty between England and Spain in 1629, he was knighted by Charles I for his peacemaking efforts. Rubens spent the later years of his life distancing himself from diplomatic duties and focusing once again on his painting.

Baroque portico of the inner courtyard, Rubens' House

RUBENS IN ANTWERP

On his return to Antwerp in 1608, Rubens was swamped by commissions from the nobility, Church, and state. He was asked to paint pictures for church altar pieces, to etch, engrave, design tapestries, and plan entire pageants. His well-run ▷ *studio*, modeled on those in Italy, was able to meet the demand. Under his guidance, a school of superior artists flourished. His most significant undertaking was for the decoration of the Jesuit church in Antwerp. Sadly, most of his work there was destroyed by a fire in 1718.

Rubens' House, Antwerp

Statue of Neptune

PIETER PAUL RUBENS' home and studio for the last thirty years of his life, from 1610 to 1640, is found on Wapper Square in Antwerp. The city bought the premises just before World War II, but the house had fallen into ruin, and what can be seen today is the result of careful restoration and is a fascinating insight to how the artist lived and worked. Rubenshuis is divided into two sections. To the left of the entrance are the narrow rooms of the artist's living quarters, equipped with period furniture. Behind this part of the house is the *kunstkamer*, or art gallery, where Rubens exhibited both his own and other artists' work, and entertained his friends and wealthy patrons, such as the Archduke Albert and the Infanta Isabella. To the right of the entrance lies the main studio, a spacious salon where Rubens worked on – and showed – his works.

Façade of Rubens' House
The older Flemish part of the house sits next to the later house, whose elegant early Baroque façade was designed by Rubens.

Formal Gardens
The small garden is laid out formally and its charming pavilion dates from Rubens' time. He was influenced by such architects of the Italian Renaissance as Vitruvius when he built the Italian Baroque addition to his house in the 1620s.

★ Rubens' Studio
It is estimated that Rubens produced some 2,500 paintings in this large, high-ceilinged room. In the Renaissance manner, Rubens designed the work which was usually completed by a team of other artists employed in his studio.

STAR FEATURES

★ Rubens' Studio

★ Kunstkamer

Rubens' House

Bedroom

The Rubens family lived in the Flemish section of the house, with its small rooms and narrow passages. The portrait by the bed is said to be of Rubens' second wife, Helena Fourment.

The Familia Kamer, or

family sitting room, is cozy and has a pretty tiled floor. It overlooks Wapper Square.

Dining Room

Intricately fashioned leather panels line the walls of this room, which also displays a noted work by Frans Snyders.

RELIGIOUS WORKS

Rubens was a fervent Roman Catholic prompting magnificent religious and allegorical masterpieces, some of which can be seen in Antwerp's cathedral.

★ Kunstkamer

This art gallery contains a series of painted sketches by Rubens. At the far end is a semi-circular dome, modeled on Rome's Pantheon, displaying a number of marble busts.

Checkered mosaic tiled floor

Baroque Portico

One of the few remaining original features, this portico was designed by Rubens, and links the older house with the Baroque section. It is adorned with a frieze showing scenes from Greek mythology.

KEY DATES

1610 Rubens buys a house on Wapper Square, Antwerp.

1614 The studio is enlarged to satisfy growing demand for Rubens' work.

1629 Rubens is knighted by English king Charles I.

1640 Rubens dies in his house.

1937 Rubens' House is bought and renovated by the city of Antwerp and opened to the public in 1946.

RUBENS' HOUSE DESIGN

Rubens' sojourn in Italy (1600–08) influenced his views on architecture as well as painting. Rubens' House was embellished to reflect his love of Italian Renaissance forms, incorporating Classical arches and sculpture (▷ *Renaissance Style p211*). His style boldly contrasted with the architectural traditions of the day and bears witness to the artist's voracious creativity. It was here that Rubens received prominent guests throughout his career. The house is entered as Rubens intended: through the main gate leading to the inner courtyard which created an imposing impression of the surrounding features. The opulent Baroque portico (▷ *Baroque Style p111*) between the courtyard and the ▷ *Formal Gardens* was designed by Rubens. The renovations completed in 1946 were based on the artist's original sketches.

Rubens' House

THE WINDOWS

One of the most notable features of the cathedral is its stained-glass windows from the Renaissance period. The dramatic ▷ *Last Judgment window* (1528) is at the front of the building above the main doors. Windows from the same period illuminate the ▷ *transept*. Designed in 1537 by the Brussels artist Bernard van Orley, and donated by the royal family, one scene shows Charles V and his wife, Isabelle of Portugal, beneath a triumphal arch being presented to God. Another depicts Charles's sister Marie and her husband, King Louis of Hungary. The Chapelle de Notre Dame has later windows by Jean de la Bear and T van Thulden (1656) illustrating scenes from the life of the Virgin Mary.

HENRY I, DUKE OF BRABANT

In the Middle Ages Brabant was an independent duchy centered on Louvain to the east of Brussels. It came into being when the Counts of Louvain acquired Lower Lorraine in 1100. Henry I was the fourth duke, ruling from 1190. He governed the region by involving himself in town planning and building. His second marriage, in 1213, to Princess Marie, daughter of Philip II of France, increased his standing and in 1226 he embarked on the ambitious rebuilding of the church. Henry died in 1235.

Henry I, fourth Duke of Brabant, initiator of the cathedral

Cathedral of St Michael and St Gudule, Brussels

THE NATIONAL CHURCH OF Belgium, this cathedral is the finest surviving example of Brabant Gothic architecture (▷ *Gothic Style p73*). There has been a church on this site since at least the 11th century. Work began on the cathedral in 1226 under Henry I, Duke of Brabant and continued for more than 300 years. It was finally completed with the construction of two front towers at the beginning of the 16th century under Charles V. The interior is very bare; this is a result of ransacking by iconoclasts in the 16th century and looting by French soldiers in 1783. The cathedral is made of a sandy limestone, which was brought from local quarries, and today, fully restored and cleaned for the royal wedding between Crown Prince Philippe and Princess Mathilde in 1999, it again shows its original splendor.

Detail of Confessional

Façade
The huge square towers were not completed until the 16th century.

This pair of towers soars above the city. Unusually, they were designed together in the 15th century; Brabant architecture typically has only one.

★ Last Judgment Window
At the front of the cathedral, facing the altar, is a magnificent stained-glass window depicting Christ awaiting saved souls. The designer's vivid use of reds, blues, and yellows places it in the 16th-century style. The Renaissance panes are surrounded by later additions of Baroque garlands of flowers.

Romanesque remains of the first church here, dating from 1047, were discovered during renovation work. They are on display in the crypt.

St Gudule
Although she is buried in her home town of Hamme, Gudule's relics were placed in this church in 1047. They were lost completely after the church was ransacked by Calvinists in 1579.

STAR FEATURES

★ Last Judgment Window

★ Baroque Pulpit

Millennial Organ

In 2000 this splendid modern organ was installed. It is situated on the north side of the nave. There are frequent organ recitals by internationally acclaimed musicians.

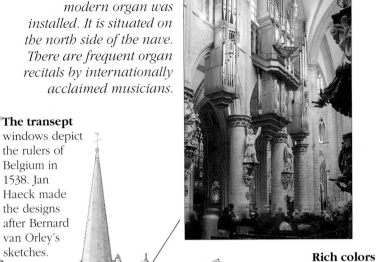

The transept

windows depict the rulers of Belgium in 1538. Jan Haeck made the designs after Bernard van Orley's sketches.

St Gudule

One of the two patron saints of Brussels (the other is Michael), Gudule was born in Brabant in the 7th century. She was raised in a convent and noted for her piety. Legend has it that when she arrived one early morning at church, the devil blew out her lantern, but it relit miraculously. Every dawn following, the devil tried, unsuccessfully, to extinguish her light. For this reason, Gudule is usually depicted holding a lantern.

Rich colors

were used in this stained-glass window

The Statue of St Michael

depicts the male patron saint of the cathedral and of Brussels. While the gilded plaster statue is not itself historically exceptional, its long heritage is. Here the Archangel St Michael is shown killing the dragon, symbolic of his protection of the city.

The Lectern

In the shape of an eagle with outspread wings, the lectern symbolizes St John the Evangelist. It was carved in 1975 by Simon Lewi, a Polish Jewish artist.

★ Baroque Pulpit

The carved pulpit in the central aisle is the work of an Antwerp-born sculptor, Henri-François Verbruggen. Designed in 1699, it was given to the church by the Jesuits of Louvain and installed in 1776.

Key Dates

1047 The relics of St Gudule are moved to the Church of St Michael.

1226 Henry I of Brabant lays the cornerstone of the new structure.

1516 Charles V is proclaimed King of Spain in the building.

1962 The collegiate church becomes a cathedral.

1999 Renovation is completed for the marriage of the Belgian Crown Prince.

Brabant Gothic

From the 12th to the 14th centuries, the Duchy of Brabant was the wealthiest region of the Low Countries and large sums were devoted to church building. This cathedral embraced four styles of architecture over its 300-year building period – the Romanesque (▷ *Romanesque Style p199*), Gothic, Renaissance (▷ *Renaissance Style p211),* and Baroque (▷ *Baroque Style p111) –* but overwhelmingly the Brabant Gothic dominates. In this style, the pillars were rounded and crowned with capitals embellished with cabbage leaves; single towers had blind arches and niches. Here, the fine rounded columns of the nave supporting statues of the 12 Apostles were added in the 17th century. In less wealthy areas of Brabant, churches were built in brick with towers having decorative layers of brick and stone.

AROUND THE GRAND PLACE

This cobblestone square is still Brussels' civic and historical hub, bustling centuries after its creation, and offering fine examples of Belgium's ornate 17th-century architecture. As now, open-air markets were held on or near this site as early as the 11th century. By the end of the 14th century the city's town hall, the Hôtel de Ville, was built and tradesmen added individual guildhalls in a medley of styles. In 1695 almost two days of cannon fire by the French destroyed all but the town hall and two façades. The guilds had to rebuild the halls in approved styles, and this created the unified effect seen today.

The colorful morning flower market in the Grand Place

A SYMBOL OF POWER

Some of Belgium's civic buildings, which were erected to demonstrate its wealth, power, and autonomy, rival its finest churches in lavish decoration. The Cloth Halls of Ypres and Bruges are dazzling examples, while the town halls of Brussels, Bruges, and especially Louvain and Oudenaarde represent a triumphant flourishing of the Gothic style in Belgium. Brussels' Hôtel de Ville is the architectural star performer of the Grand Place. Its façade, liberally decorated with rich Late Gothic tracery, features scores of statues, with the Dukes and Duchesses of Brabant, who ruled the region from 580–1564, dominating.

Hôtel de Ville, Brussels

Stone gargoyle

WHEN THIS architectural masterwork was finally completed in 1459, it was considered the finest civic building in the country, a position it still enjoys. The idea of having a town hall that would reflect Brussels' growth as a major European trading center had been mooted since the end of the 13th century but it was not until 1401 that the first foundation stone was laid. T Jacques van Thienen was commissioned to design the left wing of the building, where he used a multitude of columns, sculptures, turrets, and arcades. The skyscraping belfry and spire begun in 1449 by Jan van Ruysbroeck helped seal its reputation. To top it all off, there is a dinky 1455 statue (with weather-vane duties) of the city's patron saint, Michael, on the tower. Few fail to be impressed by the ornate Late Gothic façade (▷ *Gothic Style p73),* towering turrets and a grand interior with tapestries.

A part of the delicately carved façade with stone statues of the nobility

Ornate stone carvings decorate the spire and turrets.

There are 137 statues adorning the walls and many mullioned windows.

The Grand Staircase
The 19th-century staircase is lined with paintings depicting the history of Brussels. The busts show city governors since 1830.

Gothic Hall
This room is decorated with Gothic panels and eight 19th-century tapestries made in Mechelen illustrating the different trades of Brussels. It is still used for official functions.

STAR FEATURES

★ **Conference Room Council Chamber**

★ **Aldermen's Room**

The belfry was built by architect Jan van Ruysbroeck. A statue of St Michael tops the 96 m (315 ft) spire.

★ Conference Room Council Chamber

In the most splendid of all the public rooms, ancient tapestries and gilt mirrors line the walls above an inlaid floor.

The gabled roof, like much of the town hall, was fully restored in 1837, and cleaned in the 1990s.

THE OMMEGANG PAGEANT

Originally a religious festival, this colorful medieval event, which takes place annually in July in the Grand Place, has been celebrated in Brussels since 1549, and now draws huge crowds from all over the world. Over 2,000 participants dressed in Renaissance costume parade as jesters, courtiers, nobles, and soldiers.

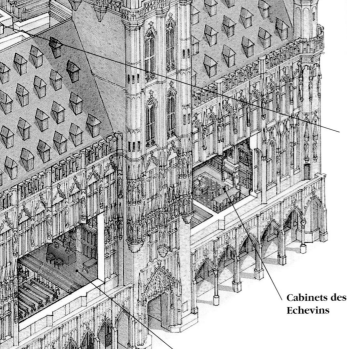

Ornamental stone balcony staircase

Cabinets des Echevins

Wedding Room

A Neo-Gothic style dominates this office, which is used for civil weddings, with its ornate carved timbers, including ebony and mahogany.

★ Aldermen's Room

Still in use today for the meetings of the aldermen and mayor of Brussels, this council chamber contains a series of 18th-century tapestries depicting the history of 6th-century King Clovis.

KEY DATES

1401 Building work begins on the Hôtel de Ville.

1695 French troops attack the Grand Place and much of the square is left in ruins.

1695–1700 The guilds rebuild the houses around the square.

1998 The Hôtel de Ville and the Grand Place join the UNESCO list of World Heritage sites.

TAPESTRIES IN THE HÔTEL DE VILLE

For over six centuries, Belgian tapestry and lace have been highly prized luxury products. Tapestry originated in Flanders in the 12th century, and has since been handmade in Tournai, Brussels, Arras, Mechelen, and Oudenaarde. Brussels was also known for its delicate lace, as was Bruges. Since fine tapestry and lace were status symbols of the nobility, the makers often had aristocratic patrons. From the 15th to the 18th centuries both tapestry and lace were staple exports throughout Europe. Within the Hôtel de Ville some of the council chambers, including the
▷ *Conference Room Council Chamber* and the
▷ *Aldermen's Room*, contain rich Brussels-made tapestries dating from the 15th to the 19th centuries. The themes depicted are grand historical episodes, including scenes from the life of Clovis, King of the Franks, and activities of the Dukes of Brabant.

Hôtel de Ville

THE ALTERATION

In the 16th century, Spain's Habsburg rulers tried to halt the Protestant Reformation which was sweeping across northern Europe. Amsterdam had initially sided with Spain but switched loyalties in 1578 – an event known as the Alteration – to become the fiercely Protestant capital of an infant Dutch Republic. After this, Calvinists took civil power and Amsterdam officially became a Protestant city. The Old Church was converted to Protestant worship and looted of all its Roman Catholic adornments. Religious imagery, altars, and sculptures were removed and demolished in preparation for Protestant worship. Even today, the sparse interior of the Old Church bears witness to the violations of this period in time.

CHURCH HISTORY

A small wooden church stood on this site in the early 13th century. This was replaced in 1300 when construction of the Old Church began. Its spacious, "hall church" plan with a nave and two similar aisles is thought to have been the first of its kind in The Netherlands. It was gradually enlarged to hold the growing congregation. Transepts were added to form a cross shape. The north transept dates from 1380 and the south transept from 1460. Work may have been interrupted by fires in 1421 and 1452 which razed two-thirds of the city. Various additions were made after this time, notably the ▷ *Lady Chapel* in 1552 and the ▷ *Great Organ* in 1724. To avert the danger of collapse, the church was closed in 1951 for emergency restoration work which took place between 1955 and 1979.

Stained-glass coats of arms in the Lady Chapel

Old Church, Amsterdam

Carving on 15th-century choir misericord

THE ORIGINS of the Old Church, the oldest building in Amsterdam, date from the early 13th century, when a wooden church was built in a burial ground on a sand bank. The present Gothic structure (▷ *Gothic Style p73*) is 14th-century and it has grown from a single-aisled church into a basilica. As it expanded, it became a gathering place for traders and a refuge for the poor. Its paintings and statuary were destroyed after the Alteration in 1578, but the gilded ceiling and stained-glass windows were undamaged. The stark interior has changed little since the Great Organ was added in 1724.

The spire of the bell tower was built by Joost Bilhamer in 1565. François Hemony added the 47-bell carillon in 1658.

Tomb of Saskia, first wife of Rembrandt (1612–42)

The Old Church Today

Located on Oudekerks-plein, the Old Church is surrounded by shops, cafés, and houses. It remains a calm and peaceful haven at the heart of the frenetic red light district.

Christening Chapel

Tomb of Admiral Abraham van der Hulst (1619–66)

Stone slabs mark the graves of Amsterdam's elite, including artists and naval heroes. There are more than 2,500 in total.

The wooden aisles are in their original medieval condition.

17th- and 18th-century houses

★ **Great Organ** (1724)
This well-known oak-encased organ has eight bellows and 54 gilded pipes. Marbled-wood statues of biblical figures surround it. Christian Vater started to construct the organ in 1724 and it was restored and added to in 1738 by Johan Müller. It is nowadays used for concerts.

★ Gilded Ceiling

The delicate 15th-century vault paintings have a gilded background. They were hidden with layers of blue paint in 1755 and not revealed until 1955.

THE CHOIR

In 1681 the choir was closed off with a brass rood screen. The text above this reads "The false practises gradually introduced into God's church were here undone again in the year seventy eight (XV)" – a reference to the Alteration in 1578.

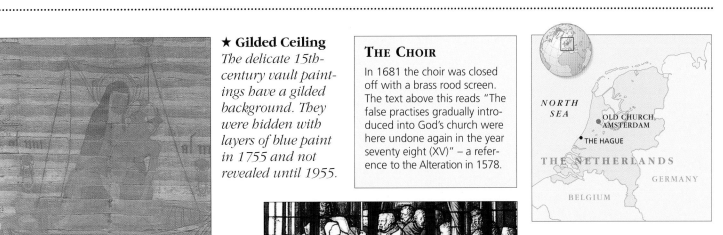

NORTH SEA

OLD CHURCH, AMSTERDAM

● THE HAGUE

THE NETHERLANDS

GERMANY

BELGIUM

★ Lady Chapel *(1552)*

The Death of the Virgin Mary *by Dirk Crabeth is one of three restored stained-glass windows in the Lady Chapel.*

Tomb of Admiral Jacob van Heemskerk (1567–1607)

KEY DATES

1300 Construction begins on a small stone church.

1330 The church is consecrated to St Nicholas.

1552 Lady Chapel is added.

1566 The spire is added to the 13th-century bell tower.

1578 Calvinists triumph in the Alteration and the Old Church is stripped of its Roman Catholic decoration.

1979 The church reopens to the public after 24 years of restoration work.

THE MIRACLE OF AMSTERDAM

A few days before Palm Sunday in 1345, legend says that a dying man sent for a priest to administer his last rites. He was given the Sacrament but later vomited on the fire, expelling the Sacred Host which was miraculously unburned. The priest brought this back to the Old Church but it returned itself twice to the sick man's side. This miracle was soon acknowledged and in 1347, a chapel was erected on the site where the extraordinary event had taken place. In commemoration, the Host was conveyed from the chapel to the Old Church in an annual procession which is likely to have taken place until the Alteration of 1578, when the Host vanished. Each March, a nocturnal procession, the *Stille Omgang,* which terminates at the Old Church still recalls the miracle.

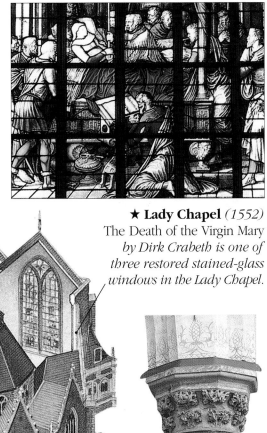

Brocaded Pillars
Decorative pillars originally formed niches holding a series of statues of the Apostles, all destroyed by the iconoclasts in 1578.

Former sacristy

The Red Door

The inscription on the lintel above the door into the former sacristy warns those about to enter: "Marry in haste, repent at leisure."

STAR FEATURES

★ **Great Organ**

★ **Gilded Ceiling**

★ **Lady Chapel**

Old Church

ANNE FRANK

Anne Frank was born in Germany in 1929 but was forced to flee with her family to The Netherlands in 1933 when the National Socialist Party led by Hitler came to power and anti-Jewish decrees made their lives increasingly difficult. The Franks spent the following years in relative peace until The Netherlands was invaded by Germany in 1940. In 1942, Jews began to receive call-up notices to report for the work camps. These deportations soon had an impact on the Frank family when Anne's sister Margot received her call-up notice. They promptly went into hiding in the secret ▷ *annex* of the building which housed her father's business. It was here that the 13-year-old Anne wrote her now-famous diary, first published in 1947 as *Het Achterhuis* (The Annex). It gives a unique account of life in confinement and of growing up under persecution. When the annex was eventually discovered, Anne was taken to Bergen-Belsen concentration camp where she contracted typhus and died in March 1945.

IN HIDING

On 13 July 1942, another Jewish family joined the Franks in hiding. The Van Pels had known the Frank family since 1937 when Mr Van Pels became involved in Otto Frank's spice business. Anne calls them the Van Daans. Dentist Fritz Pfeffer, who is known as Albert Dussel in the diary, arrived in November 1942. For over two years these eight people lived in the secret annex, forced to remain silent during office hours for fear of being discovered. They were visited only by ▷ *the helpers* who brought basic provisions and news of the outside world. In 1944, they were betrayed and deported to concentration camps in Holland, Poland, and Germany where they all perished with the exception of Anne's father, Otto.

Anne Frank House, Amsterdam

Star of David

ON 6 JULY 1942, to avoid their German persecutors, the Jewish Frank family moved to the rear annex of the house at Prinsengracht 263 in Amsterdam. Anne; her mother, Edith; her father, Otto; and her older sister, Margot, lived here, along with the Van Pels family and Fritz Pfeffer. It was in this historic house, now visited by thousands each year, that Anne wrote her world-famous diary. On 4 August 1944, the annex was raided by the Gestapo. All those hiding here were taken to German concentration camps.

The Secret Entrance
Behind the hinged bookcase was a small suite of rooms where the eight hideaways lived.

Anne in May 1942
This photograph was taken in 1942, when Anne started writing in the now-famous diary that she had been given on 12 June 1942, her 13th birthday. Less than one month later, the Frank family went into hiding.

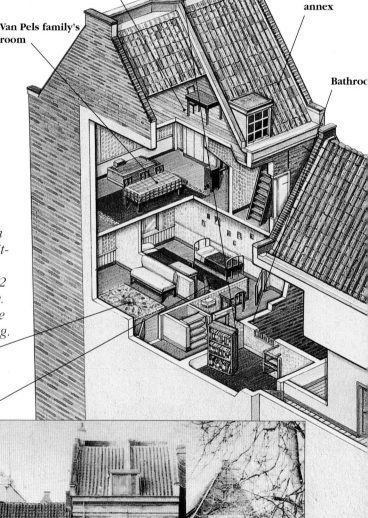

Attic

Van Pels family's room

The annex

Bathroo

Frank family bedroom

Anne's bedroom still has her movie star pin-ups on the walls. She shared the room with her sister and Fritz Pfeffer due to limited space.

View of the Annex
The rear annex of the house adjoined the main building, which housed the offices of Otto Frank's herb and spice business. Those in hiding had to keep quiet during office hours for fear of being captured.

Anne and Margot's Bedroom

Anne and Margot slept on the first floor of the annex. On the bedroom walls were photos of movie stars, which Anne collected. Anne wrote most of her diary at the table here.

WAR DIARIES

In March 1944, Anne listened to a radio broadcast asking citizens to keep their diaries after the war as a historical record. She realized that her diary may be of interest to others and started to revise it. *"Just imagine how interesting it would be if I was to publish a novel about the Secret Annex."*

The Helpers

The people in hiding were wholly dependent on their helpers, all of whom were close colleagues of Anne's father, Otto Frank. From left to right: Miep Gies, Johannes Kleiman, Otto Frank, Victor Kugler, and Bep Voskuijl.

NORTH SEA

ANNE FRANK HOUSE, AMSTERDAM

THE HAGUE

THE NETHERLANDS

BELGIUM   GERMANY

Anne Frank House

KEY DATES

1940 Otto Frank's company moves into the premises at 263 Prinsengracht.

1942 The Franks, Van Pels, and Fritz Pfeffer go into hiding in the rear annex of 263 Prinsengracht. Anne begins writing her diary.

1944 The annex is raided and all those in hiding are deported to concentration camps.

1945 Anne Frank dies.

1947 Anne's diary which was discovered in the annex is published.

1960 Anne Frankhuis opens.

THE MAIN BUILDING

Like so many canal-side houses in Amsterdam, Anne Frank House has a front and back section. The front part is where ▷ *the helpers* worked in Otto Frank's former office. Visitors can get a real sense of the events which took place here, as the rooms have been restored to capture the atmosphere of the period when the Frank family was hiding in ▷ *the annex*. Original items from their time here are exhibited alongside photographs, and films are shown to inform people about the era. Quotes from Anne Frank's diary are used as a tool to educate visitors about the Holocaust. Next door at Prinsengracht 265, information is given about the diary and its historical importance. The original diary is permanently on display here.

Façade of Prinsengracht 263

Main building housing offices

MUSEUM GUIDE

The rear annex is accessible via the reconstructed offices of Otto Frank. Its rooms are now empty except for Anne's pictures and a model of the annex. The building at Prinsengracht 265, beside Anne Frank House, holds various exhibitions.

THE DIARY OF ANNE FRANK

Otto Frank returned to Amsterdam in 1945 to discover that his entire family had perished: his wife, Edith, in Auschwitz and his daughters, Anne and Margot, in Bergen-Belsen. Miep Gies, one of the family's helpers while they were in hiding, had kept Anne's diary. First published in 1947, it has since been translated into 55 languages, with some 20 million copies sold. For many, Anne symbolizes the six million Jews murdered by the Nazis in World War II. The diary is a moving portrait of a little girl growing up in times of oppression.

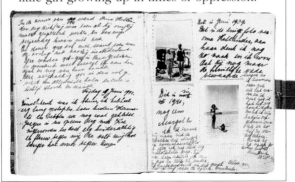

Engraving of William III of Orange (1650–1702)

THE HOUSE OF ORANGE-NASSAU

The marriage of Hendrik III of Nassau-Breda to Claudia of Chalon-Orange established the House of Orange-Nassau in 1515. Since that time the family has played a central role in governing the Netherlands. The House of Orange is also important in British history. In 1677, William III of Orange married the English princess Mary Stuart. William and Mary became king and queen of England in 1689 when Mary's father James II went into exile in France, and the couple ruled as joint monarchs.

THE HET LOO PALACE INTERIOR

The Orange-Nassau family continued to use Het Loo Palace as a royal summer house until 1975. The palace is now a museum, and painstaking restoration has recreated its 17th-century look. The interior, sumptuously decorated with rich materials, is laid out symmetrically, with the royal apartments to the east and west of the Great Hall. The wings of the palace contain exhibitions of court costumes, as well as documents, paintings, silver, and china relating to the House of Orange-Nassau over three centuries.

Het Loo Palace, Apeldoorn

STADTHOLDER WILLIAM III, the future king of England, built the magnificent Het Loo Palace, regarded as the "Versailles of the Netherlands," as a royal hunting lodge in the 17th century. Generations of the House of Orange used the lodge as a summer palace. The main architect was Jacob Roman (1640–1716); the interior decoration and layout of the gardens were the responsibility of Daniel Marot. The building's Classical façade belies the opulence of its lavish interior; extensive restoration work was completed on both in 1984.

★ **Royal Bedroom** *(1713)*
The wall coverings and draperies in this luxuriously furnished bedroom are of rich orange damask and purple silk.

Stadtholder William III's Closet *(1690)*
The walls of William's private study are covered in embossed scarlet damask. His favorite paintings and Delftware pieces are exhibited here.

Coat of arms (1690) of William and Mary, future king and queen of England.

King William III's bedroom

King's Garden

Classic Cars
This 1925 Bentley, nicknamed Minerva, was owned by Prince Hendrik, husband of Queen Wilhelmina. It is one of the Dutch royal family's vintage cars on display in the stable block (1910).

STAR FEATURES

★ **Royal Bedroom**

★ **Old Dining Room**

★ **Formal Gardens**

Het Loo Palace

QUEEN WILHELMINA

After the death of the Dutch King William III (r.1848–90), his daughter Wilhelmina was the first female to rule the country as Queen (r.1890–1948). During her reign she used the Het Loo Palace as her summer retreat.

★ **Old Dining Room** *(1686)*
In 1984, six layers of paint were removed from the marbled walls, now hung with tapestries depicting scenes from Ovid's poems.

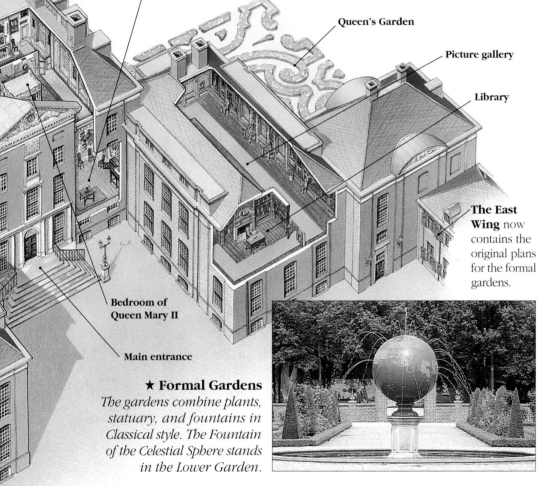

Queen's Garden

Picture gallery

Library

The East Wing now contains the original plans for the formal gardens.

Bedroom of Queen Mary II

Main entrance

★ **Formal Gardens**
The gardens combine plants, statuary, and fountains in Classical style. The Fountain of the Celestial Sphere stands in the Lower Garden.

Het Loo Palace

(vertical tab) Het Loo Palace

KEY DATES

1684–6 Building of the Het Loo Palace, for Prince William III and Princess Mary.

1691–4 King William III commissions new building works on the palace.

1814 Het Loo becomes the property of the Dutch state.

1984 Restoration of the house and garden comes to an end; Het Loo reopens.

THE GARDENS AND FOUNTAINS

In 1686 the ▷ *formal gardens* surrounding Het Loo Palace were laid and quickly became celebrated. The designer was Daniel Marot (1661–1752), who added a host of small details such as wrought-iron railings and garden urns. The gardens, which include the ▷ *Queen's Garden* and ▷ *King's Garden*, were designed to be strictly geometrical. They were decorated with formal flower beds and embellished with fountains, borders, topiary, and cascades. Statues were also placed throughout. Today, the King's Garden features clipped box trees and pyramid-shaped juniper trees. At the center stands an octagonal white marble basin with a spouting triton and gilt sea dragons. The slightly raised ▷ *Upper Garden* is home to the impressive King's Fountain, which is fed by a natural spring and operates 24 hours a day. It is a classic, eye-catching feature in a royal garden.

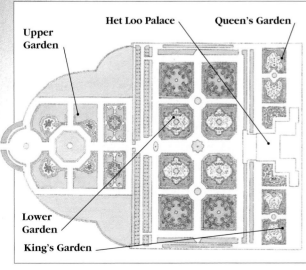

Upper Garden

Het Loo Palace   Queen's Garden

Lower Garden

King's Garden

THE FORMAL GARDENS

Old prints, records, and plans were used as the guidelines for recreating Het Loo's formal gardens, which lie in the vast acres behind the palace. Grass was planted over the original walled and knot gardens in the 18th century, and this was cleared in 1975. By 1983, the intricate floral patterns had been re-established, replanting had begun, the Classical fountains were renovated and the water supply fully restored. The garden reflects the late 17th-century belief that art and nature should operate in harmony.

Layout of the formal section of the gardens

Illustration of the façade of Amiens cathedral

GOTHIC ORNAMENTATION

Like all Gothic churches, Amiens' cathedral is richly decorated. Sculpture served to detract attention from structural features, making a virtue out of a necessity, as with grotesque gargoyles that disguise waterspouts, or natural forms decorating columns. Even where the carvings would not be seen at close hand, they were still produced with tremendous skill and care. The ▷ *choir stalls* alone are decorated with over 4,000 wooden carvings of figures, many representing local trades of the day, residents of Amiens and biblical figures.

VIOLLET-LE-DUC

The renowned theorist and designer Eugène Emmanuel Viollet-le-Duc (1814–79) worked on the restoration of the cathedral in the 1850s. Trained in both architecture and medieval archaeology, he was a leading figure in France's Commission for Historical Monuments, which undertook early restoration work on many architectural landmarks, including Notre-Dame in Paris. Today, he is best known for his encyclopedic writings on French architecture and design, especially the *Analytical Dictionary of French Architecture from the 11th–16th Centuries* (1854–68).

Amiens Cathedral

Amiens Cathedral

A MASTERPIECE OF ENGINEERING and Gothic architecture (▷ *Gothic Style p73*) carried to a bold extreme, Amiens' Notre-Dame Cathedral is also the largest cathedral in France. It was begun around 1220 and took only fifty years to build, financed by profits from the cultivation of woad, a plant valued for its blue dye. Built to house the head of St John the Baptist brought back from the Crusades, which is still displayed, the cathedral became a magnet for pilgrims. After restoration by Viollet-le-Duc, and miraculously surviving two World Wars, the cathedral is famous for its wealth of statues and reliefs, which inspired John Ruskin's *The Bible of Amiens* in 1884.

★ West Front
The King's Gallery, a row of 22 colossal statues representing the kings of France, spans the west front. They are also thought to symbolize the Kings of Judah.

Weeping Angel
Sculpted by Nicolas Blasset in 1628, this sentimental statue in the ambulatory became a popular image during World War I.

St Firmin Portal is decorated with figures and scenes from the life of St Firmin, the martyr who brought Christianity to Picardy and became the first bishop of Amiens.

The Calendar shows signs from the Zodiac, with the corresponding monthly labors below. It depicts everyday life in the 13th century.

North Tower

Central Portal
Above the doors are scenes from the Last Judgment and there is a statue of Christ between the doors.

STAR FEATURES

★ **West Front**

★ **Nave**

★ **Choir Stalls**

★ **Choir Screens**

Towers

Two towers of unequal height frame the west front. The south tower was completed in 1366; the north in 1402. The spire was replaced twice, in 1627 and 1887.

St Firmin

The patron saint of Amiens, St Firmin was born in Pamplona, Spain c.272. After ordination, he was sent to northern France, where he pursued his mission boldly, unafraid of persecution, and soon settled in Amiens. Because of his persuasive preaching, he was beheaded by the Romans in c.303.

The flamboyant tracery of the rose window was created in the 16th century.

A double row comprising 22 elegant flying buttresses supports the construction.

★ Nave

Soaring 42 m (138 ft) high, with support from 126 slender pillars, the brightly illuminated interior of Notre-Dame is a hymn to the vertical.

Key Dates

1220 Work begins on the foundations of the cathedral.

1279 The relics of St Firmin and St Ulphe are presented, attended by the kings of France and England.

1849 Restoration of the cathedral under the direction of Viollet-le-Duc.

1981 Amiens Cathedral joins the list of UNESCO World Heritage Sites.

Building Amiens Cathedral

The cathedral was designed by the French architect Robert de Luzarches, and inspired by the Gothic cathedral at Reims. Work began in 1220 and by 1236 the façade, rose window, and portals were complete. By this stage the architect Thomas de Cormont had taken over from de Luzarches, who had died prematurely in about 1222. De Cormont directed the building of the choir and apse. The cathedral was finished by 1270 and this speed of execution perhaps explains the building's coherence and purity of style. Research has shown that the figures on the beautiful west portal would originally have been brightly painted. Modern laser technology has now enabled experts to assess the original coloring of the sculptures, and a light show is put on periodically to illuminate the portal, recreating the look of over 700 years ago.

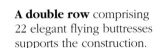

★ Choir Stalls

The 110 oak choir stalls (1508–19) are delicately carved with over 4,000 biblical, mythical, and real life figures.

The flooring was laid down in 1288 and reassembled in the late 19th century. The faithful followed its labyrinthine path on their knees.

★ Choir Screens

Vivid scenes from the lives of St Firmin and St John, carved in the 15th–16th centuries, adorn the walkway.

Amiens Cathedral

Mont-St-Michel

St Michael

SHROUDED BY MIST and encircled by sea, the enchanting silhouette of Mont-St-Michel soars proudly above glistening sands. Now linked to the mainland by a causeway, the island of Mont-Tombe (Tomb on the Hill) stands at the mouth of the river Couesnon, crowned by an abbey that almost doubles its height. This superb example of a fortified abbey ranks as one of the most significant sites of pilgrimage in Christendom. Lying strategically on the frontier between Brittany and Normandy, Mont-St-Michel grew from a humble 8th-century oratory to become a Benedictine monastery of great influence. Pilgrims known as *miquelots* journeyed from afar to honor the cult of St Michael, and the monastery was a renowned center of medieval learning. After the Revolution the abbey became a prison. It is now a national monument that draws one million visitors a year.

★ **Ramparts**
Fortified walls with imposing towers were build to withstand English attacks during the Hundred Years' War (1337–1453).

BISHOP AUBERT

For centuries, the Mont was recognised as a sacred site of devotion, where both Druids and Romans worshiped. In 708 Aubert, Bishop of the nearby town of Avranches, had a vision in which the Archangel Michael commanded that a chapel be built in his honor on Mont-St-Michel. In response, Bishop Aubert had an oratory erected on the summit, his belief inspiring one of Christianity's most spectacular holy sites. The faithful came to appeal for the archangel's protection and Mont-St-Michel soon became an important place of pilgrimage. Although nothing remains of Bishop Aubert's original oratory, it is thought to have been situated on the west side of the rock, on the ground where ▷ *St Aubert's Chapel* now stands.

Early 13th-century Anglo-Norman style cloisters

THE ABBEY

The three levels of the abbey reflect the monastic hierarchy. The monks lived at the highest level, in an enclosed world of the church, refectory, and the elegant columns of the cloister. In 1776, three bays in the church's nave were pulled down to create the West Terrace which has fine views of the coastline. Monks ate in the long, narrow refectory which is flooded with light through tall windows. On the middle level, the abbot entertained his noble guests. Soldiers and pilgrims further down on the social scale were received at the lowest level of the abbey, in the almonry. The three-story complex of La Merveille (The Miracle), added to the north side in the early 13th century, is a Gothic masterwork (▷ *Gothic Style p73*).

OVER THE CENTURIES

The 10th-century abbey
Richard I, Duke of Normandy, founded this great Benedictine abbey in 966.

The 11th-century abbey
The Romanesque abbey church was built between 1017 and 1144. (▷ Romanesque Style p199).

The 18th-century abbey
Few monks remained in the abbey by the end of the 18th century when it became a political prison.

Gabriel Tower
was built in 1524 by military engineer, Gabriel du Puy.

Entrance

St Aubert's Chapel
A small 15th-century chapel built on an outcrop of rock is dedicated to St Aubert, the founder of Mont-St-Michel.

Mont-St-Michel

Tides of Mont-St-Michel
Extremely strong tides in the Baie du Mont-St-Michel act as a natural defense. They rise and fall with the lunar calendar and can reach speeds of 10 km/h (6 mph) in spring.

★ Abbey
Protected by high walls, the abbey and its church occupy an impregnable position on the island.

King's Tower

The Arcade Tower provided lodgings for the abbot's soldiers.

Église St Pierre

Liberty Tower

★ Grande Rue
Now crowded with restaurants, the pilgrims' route, followed since the 12th century, climbs up past Église St-Pierre to the abbey gates.

STAR FEATURES

★ **Ramparts**

★ **Abbey**

★ **Grande Rue**

THE FORTIFICATIONS

Mont-St-Michel became a symbol of national identity when its defensive 15th-century walls protected it against fierce cannon attacks in the Hundred Years' War. All of Normandy was conquered by the English except this well-fortified island.

Gautier's Leap
At the top of the Inner Staircase, this terrace is named after a prisoner who leaped to his death.

KEY DATES

708 St Aubert builds an oratory on Mont-Tombe, dedicated to St Michael.

966 Duke Richard I founds the Benedictine abbey.

1446–1521 The late Gothic choir is built.

1874 The abbey is declared a national monument.

1877–9 A causeway is built, linking Mont-St-Michel to mainland France.

1895–7 The Belfry, spire, and statue of St Michael are added.

1922 Services are again held in the abbey church.

1979 Mont-St-Michel is added to UNESCO's World Heritage Site list.

THE MONT PRISON

The monastery first served as a prison in the 15th century under the reign of Louis XI whose political opponents were kept here in famously severe conditions. During the French Revolution, the monks were dismissed and the abbey once again functioned as a penitentiary with aristocrats, priests, and political adversaries imprisoned within its walls. Recognized figures, including writers such as Chateaubriand and Victor Hugo, protested against this practise but Mont-St-Michel remained a state prison for 73 years until 20 October, 1863 when a decree was passed, returning the abbey to divine worship.

Mont-St-Michel

**The buttressed apse of
Notre-Dame**

THE HUNCHBACK OF NOTRE-DAME

The novel *Notre-Dame de Paris*, published in English as *The Hunchback of Notre-Dame*, was the work of the Romantic French novelist Victor Hugo (1802–85) and was published in 1831. The hunchback of the title is the bell-ringer Quasimodo, ward of the cathedral, and the novel tells the story of his doomed love for the dancer Esmeralda. The cathedral features strongly in the work and Hugo used his book to rail against its neglect, declaring that medieval cathedrals were "books in stone" and should be deeply treasured. The novel aroused widespread interest in the restoration of Notre-Dame.

THE INTERIOR

Notre-Dame's interior grandeur is strikingly apparent in its high-vaulted central nave. This is bisected by a huge ▷ *transept*, at either end of which is a medieval ▷ *rose window*, 13 m (43 ft) in diameter. Works by famous sculptors adorn the cathedral. Among them are Jean Ravy's choir-screen carvings, Nicolas Coustou's *Pietà*, which stands on a gilded base sculpted by François Girardon, and Antoine Coysevox's statue of Louis XIV. The 13th-century stained-glass North Rose Window depicts the Virgin encircled by figures from the Old Testament. Against the southeast pillar of the transept stands a 14th-century statue of the Virgin and Child.

Notre-Dame, Paris

N O OTHER BUILDING is so associated with the history of Paris as Notre-Dame. It stands majestically on the Ile de la Cité, in the heart of the city. When the first stone was laid in 1163, it marked the start of 170 years of toil by armies of Gothic architects and medieval craftsmen. Since then, a series of coronations and royal marriages have passed through its doors. Built on the site of a Roman temple, the cathedral is a masterpiece of Gothic architecture. When it was finished, in about 1330, it was 130 m (430 ft) long and featured flying buttresses, a large transept, a deep choir, and 69-m (228-ft) high towers.

★ **Galerie des Chimères**
The cathedral's legendary gargoyles (chimères) *hide behind a large upper gallery between the towers.*

★ **West Rose Window**
This window depicts the Virgin in a medallion of rich reds and blues.

STAR FEATURES

★ **West Façade and Portals**

★ **Galerie des Chimères**

★ **West Rose Window**

★ **Flying Buttresses**

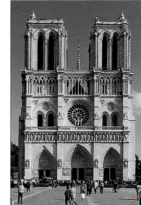

★ **West Façade and Portals**
Two huge towers, three main doors, superb statuary, a central rose window, and an openwork gallery are impressive features of the west façade.

The south tower houses the cathedral's famous Emmanuel bell.

The Kings' Gallery features 28 Kings of Judah.

Portal of the Virgin
The Virgin surrounded by saints and kings is a fine composition of 13th-century statues.

★ Flying Buttresses
Jean Ravy's spectacular flying buttresses at the east end of the cathedral have a span of 15 m (50 ft).

The spire, designed by Viollet-le-Duc, soars to a height of 90 m (295 ft).

The transept was built at the start of Philippe-Auguste's reign, in the 13th century.

The treasury houses the cathedral's religious treasures, including ancient manuscripts and reliquaries.

The "May" Paintings
These religious paintings, by Charles Le Brun and Le Sueur among others, were presented by the Paris guilds every 1 May from 1630 to 1707.

CORONATIONS

Notre-Dame has seen a number of coronations in its long history. Henry VI of England was crowned here in 1430, and Mary Stuart became Queen of France after her marriage to François II in the same year. In 1804 Napoleon became Emperor of France, crowning first himself and then his wife Josephine here.

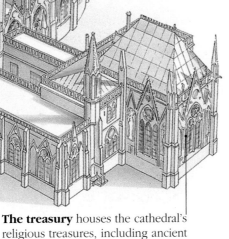

View of Interior
From the main entrance the high-vaulted central nave, choir, and high altar give an impression of great height and grandeur.

South Rose Window
This south façade window, with its central depiction of Christ, is an impressive 13 m (43 ft) high.

KEY DATES

1163 Work begins when Pope Alexander III lays the foundation stone.

1793 Revolutionaries loot the cathedral and rename it the Temple of Reason.

1845 Architect Viollet-le-Duc undertakes restoration work of the cathedral.

1991 Notre-Dame becomes a UNESCO World Heritage Site.

GOTHIC STYLE

The Gothic style emerged in France around the end of the 12th century, with the Basilica of St-Denis (1137–1281), north of Paris, where most of the French monarchs are buried. The pointed arch, the ribbed vault, tracery, and the rose window were all used to great effect there and were important features of the Gothic style. The desire to build ever taller, more magnificent light-filled ecclesiastical buildings grew. Another key feature emerged with the use of flying buttresses, which provided support for high walls and helped redistribute their weight. With its soaring interior and stained-glass filtered light from the large ▷ *rose windows*, the Notre-Dame Cathedral is one of the best known and most impressive examples of the Gothic style. Across Europe in many countries, including Italy, Germany, Belgium, Switzerland, and Great Britain, architects took to the style with enthusiasm.

Notre-Dame

HISTORY OF THE BUILDING

The Louvre dates back to the 12th century when King Philippe-Auguste built what is now part of the ▷ *Sully Wing*, to protect Paris from constant raids. It was not until the reign of Charles V (1338–80) that it became the official royal residence and further additions and improvements were made by him. Future French kings and emperors also added to the Louvre, including François I who hired the architect Pierre Lescot and Catherine de' Medici who commissioned the Palais des Tuileries in 1564. She also began construction on the Galerie du Bord de l'Eau (The Waterside Gallery), which was eventually completed by King Henri IV.

The Louvre viewed from the River Seine

THE COLLECTIONS

The museum collections can be traced to François I who acquired many Italian paintings including Leonardo da Vinci's *Mona Lisa (La Gioconda, 1504)*. In Louis XIV's reign there were a mere 200 works, but donations and purchases have augmented the collection ever since. The antiquities include priceless works of art from the Neolithic period (c.6000 BC) to the fall of the Roman empire, including Egyptian funerary portraits, Etruscan sarcophagi, and Greek sculpture such as *Venus de Milo* (2nd century BC). The stunning collection of European art covers the 14th century to 1848, including works by Giotto, El Greco, Holbein, Caravaggio, Michelangelo, Watteau, J L David, Ingres, and Corot.

Louvre Museum, Paris

ONCE THE LARGEST and most impressive palace in Europe, the Louvre contains one of the most important art collections in the world and has a history extending back to medieval times. First constructed as a fortress in 1190 by King Philippe-Auguste, it lost its imposing keep in the reign of François I, who replaced it with a Renaissance-style (▷ *Renaissance Style p211*) building. Thereafter, four centuries of French kings and emperors improved and enlarged it.

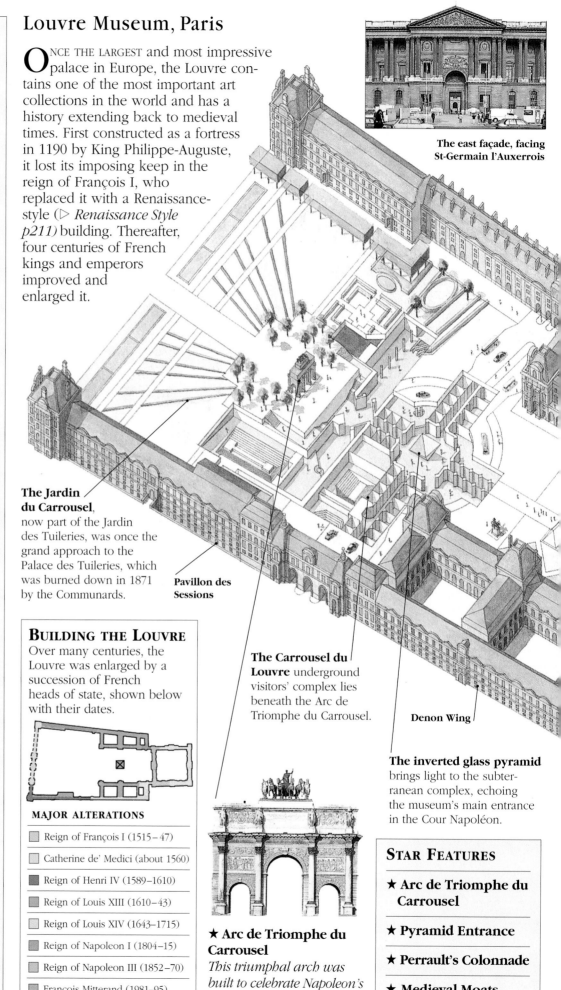

The east façade, facing St-Germain l'Auxerrois

The Jardin du Carrousel, now part of the Jardin des Tuileries, was once the grand approach to the Palace des Tuileries, which was burned down in 1871 by the Communards.

Pavillon des Sessions

The Carrousel du Louvre underground visitors' complex lies beneath the Arc de Triomphe du Carrousel.

Denon Wing

The inverted glass pyramid brings light to the subterranean complex, echoing the museum's main entrance in the Cour Napoléon.

BUILDING THE LOUVRE

Over many centuries, the Louvre was enlarged by a succession of French heads of state, shown below with their dates.

MAJOR ALTERATIONS

▢	Reign of François I (1515–47)
▢	Catherine de' Medici (about 1560)
▢	Reign of Henri IV (1589–1610)
▢	Reign of Louis XIII (1610–43)
▢	Reign of Louis XIV (1643–1715)
▢	Reign of Napoleon I (1804–15)
▢	Reign of Napoleon III (1852–70)
▢	François Mitterand (1981–95)

★ **Arc de Triomphe du Carrousel**
This triumphal arch was built to celebrate Napoleon's victories in 1805.

STAR FEATURES

★ **Arc de Triomphe du Carrousel**

★ **Pyramid Entrance**

★ **Perrault's Colonnade**

★ **Medieval Moats**

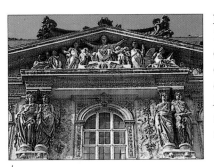

Pavillon Richelieu
This imposing 19th-century pavilion is part of the Richelieu Wing, once home to the Ministry of Finance but now converted into magnificent galleries.

Cour Marly is the glass-roofed courtyard that now houses the 19th-century Marly Horses by Guillaume Coustou.

★ Pyramid Entrance
The popular new main entrance, designed by the architect I M Pei, was opened in 1989.

Richelieu Wing

Cour Puget

Cour Khorsabad

Sully Wing

Cour Carrée

★ Perrault's Colonnade
The east façade with its majestic rows of columns was built by Claude Perrault, who worked on the Louvre with Louis Le Vau in the mid-17th century.

Cour Napoléon

The Salle des Caryatides takes its name from the statues of women created by Jean Goujon in 1550 to support the upper gallery.

The Louvre of Charles V
In about 1360, Charles V transformed Philippe-Auguste's old fortress into a royal residence.

★ Medieval Moats
The base of the twin towers and the drawbridge support of Philippe-Auguste's fortress can be seen in the excavated area.

KEY DATES
1190 The first parts of the Louvre built by King Philippe-Auguste.

1793 In the aftermath of the 1789 Revolution and the execution of Louis XVI, the Louvre opens to the public for the first time.

1848 The Louvre becomes the property of the state.

1871 The Palais des Tuileries is torched during the Paris Commune uprising.

1993 The Louvre celebrates its 200th anniversary.

1999 Restoration of the buildings (started in 1981) is completed, providing space for 12,000 works of art.

ARC DE TRIOMPHE DU CARROUSEL
Designed by architects Charles Percier and Pierre Léonard Fontaine, the arch was built between 1806–08 to commemorate Napoleon's 1805 victories. Its three arches, the middle arch measuring 6.4 m (21 ft) high and 2.74 m (9 ft) wide and the ones either side, measuring 4.27 m (14 ft) high and 2.74 m (9 ft) wide, are richly decorated in rose marble on the columns and with bas-reliefs depicting Napoleon's battles and treaties. It is crowned with soldiers of the Grande Armée, which replaced the bronze horses Napoleon looted from St Mark's in Venice, later returned there after the Battle of Waterloo.

Louvre Museum

BUILDING THE EIFFEL TOWER

Gustave Eiffel was awarded the contract to build the Eiffel Tower in January 1887. He had two years to complete the project and so started the construction work within a few weeks. He kept on schedule by partially fabricating over 18,000 of the tower's cast-iron pieces in his workshop (▷ *Ironwork Pattern)*, then numbered and delivered them to the site by barge. Each piece was then lifted into place and riveted with no need for further drilling. This revolution in design helped with the speedy progress of the project. Eiffel also introduced new work practices on the site. He employed a limited amount of skilled men, paying them very well and provided a canteen nearby. This was great for morale and ensured that the Eiffel Tower was completed in time for the Exposition Universelle.

THE TOWER'S CRITICS

Several artists and authors, including Alexandre Dumas Jr, Guy de Maupassant, and Charles Gounod, objected to the Eiffel Tower's construction. A protest letter was even published in *Le Temps* newspaper in 1887, addressed to the Exposition's director of works. It condemned the tower as "monstrous" and an "ink stain" on the Parisian skyline. The critics were quickly hushed, however, when over two million paying visitors flocked to the tower on the first day it opened.

The Eiffel Tower illuminated by over 20,000 light bulbs

Eiffel Tower, Paris

Eiffel Tower seen from the Trocadéro

THE WORLD'S TALLEST structure until 1931, the Eiffel Tower (Tour Eiffel) was originally built to impress visitors attending the Exposition Universelle of 1889. Designed by Gustave Eiffel, the striking tower was meant to be a temporary addition to the Paris skyline. After the exhibition, however, it was used as a weather station, a radio broadcasting station from 1898, a radiotelegraphy center in World War I, and a television broadcasting site from 1936. Initially criticized by leading authors of the day, including Oscar Wilde, the tower is now a symbol of Paris.

Elevator Engine Room
Eiffel emphasized safety over speed in choosing elevators for the tower.

STAR FEATURES

★ **Cinémax**

★ **Hydraulic Elevator Mechanism**

★ **Viewing Gallery**

★ **Eiffel Bust**

THE DARING AND THE DELUDED

The tower has inspired many crazy stunts. It has been climbed by mountaineers, cycled down by a journalist, and used as a launch pad by parachutists and as a setting by trapeze artists. In 1912 a Parisian tailor, Reichelt, attempted to fly from the parapet with only a modified cape for wings. He plunged to his death in front of a large crowd. According to the autopsy, he died of a heart attack before even touching the ground.

Birdman Reichelt

Ironwork Pattern
According to Eiffel, he chose the complex pattern of pig-iron girders to stabilize the tower in strong winds. But Eiffel's design also quickly won admirers for its pleasing symmetry.

★ **Cinémax**
This small museum tells the history of the tower through a short film. It includes footage of famous personalities who have visited the tower, including Charlie Chaplin, Josephine Baker, and Adolf Hitler.

★ **Hydraulic Elevator Mechanism**
Still in working order, this part of the original 1900 mechanism was automated in 1986.

The third level, 274 m (905 ft) above the ground, can hold 800 people at a time.

★ **Viewing Gallery**
On a clear day it is possible to see for 72 km (45 miles), including a distant view of Chartres Cathedral.

Double-Decker Elevators
During the tourist season, the limited capacity of the elevators means that it can take up to two hours to reach the top.

The second level is at 115 m (376 ft), separated from the first level by 359 steps, or a few minutes in the elevator.

Jules Verne Restaurant is one of the best restaurants in Paris, offering superb food and panoramic views.

The first level, at 57 m (187 ft) high, can be reached by elevator or by 360 steps. There is a post office here.

LIGHTING DISPLAYS

French automobile maker Citroën was one of the first to install a lighting display on the tower, which lasted from 1926 to 1936. It was such a success that more displays followed. In 2001 Paris's mayor, Jean Tiberi, commissioned a 10-year display which sparkles for ten minutes every hour from dusk until one in the morning.

THE TOWER IN FIGURES

• the top (including the antennae) is 324 m (1,063 ft) high
• when heated, the top can move in a curve of 18 cm (7 in)
• there are 1,665 steps to the third level
• 2.5 million rivets hold the tower together
• never sways more than 7 cm (2.5 in)
• 10,100 tons in weight
• 60 tons of paint are used every seven years

Workman building the Tower

★ **Eiffel Bust**
Eiffel's (1832–1923) achievement was crowned with the Légion d'Honneur in 1889. Another honor was the bust by Antoine Bourdelle, placed beneath the tower in 1929.

EIFFEL TOWER, PARIS

KEY DATES

1887–89 The Eiffel Tower is constructed.

1900 The second level of the tower is remodeled.

1957 Due to a fire on the Eiffel Tower, the top is reconstructed and additional levels and antennae are added above the third level.

1991 The banks of the River Seine, incorporating the Eiffel Tower, are inscribed a UNESCO World Heritage Site.

LIFE OF GUSTAVE EIFFEL

One of the most influential French architects and engineers of the 19th century, Gustave Eiffel studied chemistry for over five years before joining Nepveu & Cie in 1856 as an engineer. His first major commission was to design railway stations for the French Western Railway in 1857, including Toulouse station and the Garabit Viaduct in France. His lightweight iron design saved time and money and helped establish his reputation as a brilliant engineer. Eiffel set up his own company in 1864, designing viaducts and "portable" bridges, shipped in "kits" around the world. In 1885, he designed the wrought-iron lattice interior for the Statue of Liberty and his great masterwork, the Eiffel Tower, soon after. He spent his later life pioneering the field of aerodynamics and designed one of the first wind tunnels around 1903.

Eiffel Tower

Arc de Triomphe, Paris

CARVED RELIEFS

The west façade of the arch is adorned with colossal reliefs. *The Resistance of the French in 1814* is depicted on the right. Here, a soldier defends his family and is encouraged by the embodiment of the future. *The Peace of 1815* on the left shows a man, protected by Minerva, Goddess of Wisdom, returning his sword to its scabbard. These reliefs are by the sculptor Antoine Étex. Above this are two bas-reliefs. The left frame depicts the *Capture of Alexandria* (1798) as General Kléber urges his troops forward. The right-hand panel shows the *Passage of the Bridge of Arcola* (1796) with Napoleon advancing against the Austrians. The south façade details the Battle of Jemmapes in 1792.

THE BATTLE OF AUSTERLITZ

Napoleon commissioned the arch in 1806 to honor his soldiers who achieved a masterful victory at the Battle of Austerlitz in 1805. Heavily outnumbered, Napoleon led the Allies to believe that his army was weak and successfully lured them into a vulnerable position. Fierce battle ensued, forcing the Allies to retreat across frozen Lake Satschan. It is believed that Napoleon's army fired on the ice in an attempt to drown the fleeing enemy. The armies of Russia and Austria, members of the Third Coalition alliance against France in the Napoleonic Wars, were destroyed. The French had 9,000 casualties whereas the Allies suffered three times as many.

Arc de Triomphe viewed from the west

The east façade of the Arc de Triomphe

AFTER HIS greatest victory, the Battle of Austerlitz in 1805, Napoleon promised his men, "You shall go home beneath triumphal arches." The first stone of what was to become the world's most famous and largest triumphal arch was laid the following year. But disruptions to architect Jean Chalgrin's plans and the demise of Napoleonic power delayed the completion of this monumental building until 1836. Standing 50 m (164 ft) high, the arch is now the customary starting point for victory celebrations and parades.

The Battle of Aboukir, a bas-relief by Seurre the Elder, depicts a scene of Napoleon's victory over the Turkish army in 1799.

Triumph of Napoleon
J P Cortot's high-relief celebrates the Treaty of Vienna peace agreement of 1810. Victory, History, and Fame surround Napoleon in this relief.

★ Tomb of the Unknown Soldier
An unknown French soldier from World War I is buried here.

Place Charles de Gaulle
Twelve avenues radiate from the triumphal arch at the center. Some bear the names of important French military leaders. Baron Haussman, in charge of urban planning under Napoleon III, created the star-shaped configuration.

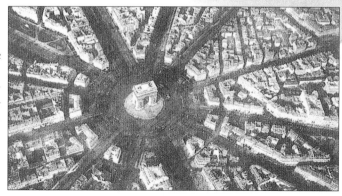

Thirty shields just below the arch's roof each bear the name of a victorious Napoleonic battle fought in either Europe or Africa.

The frieze was executed by Rude, Brun, Jacquet, Laitié, Caillouette, and Seurre the Elder. This east façade shows the departure of the French armies for new campaigns. The west side shows their return.

East façade

NAPOLEON'S NUPTIAL PARADE

Napoleon divorced Josephine in 1809 because she was unable to bear him children. A diplomatic marriage was arranged in 1810 with Marie-Louise, daughter of the Austrian emperor. Napoleon was determined to impress his bride by going through the Arc on their way to the wedding at the Louvre, but work had barely been started. So Chalgrin built a full-scale model of the arch on the site for the couple to pass beneath.

THE BATTLE OF VERDUN

On the day this battle started in 1916, the sword carried by the figure representing France broke off from ▷ *Departure of the Volunteers in 1792.* The relief was covered up so that the public would not interpret it as a sign of misfortune.

The viewing platform affords one of the best views in Paris, overlooking the grand Champs-Élysées on one side. Beyond the other side is La Défense.

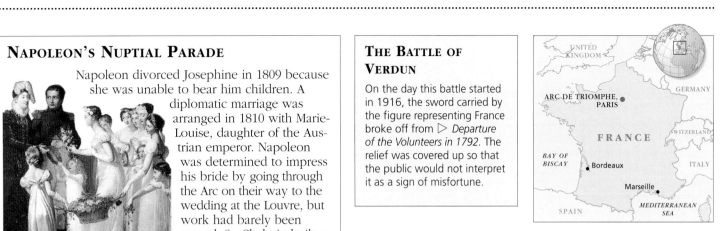

KEY DATES

1806 Napoleon commissions Jean Chalgrin to build the triumphal arch.

1815 With Napoleon's downfall, work ceases.

1836 The arch is completed.

1885 The body of French poet and novelist Victor Hugo is laid in state beneath the Arc.

1920 An unknown World War I soldier is buried here.

NEO-CLASSICAL STYLE

The power, might, and learning of Western Europe was represented in the 18th and the first half of the 19th centuries by architecture inspired by that of ancient Greece and Rome. The traditional principles of the Classical style were extended and adapted as the culture of the ancient world was increasingly revealed, documented, and disseminated. This new Classicism was seen as an ideal match for the ambition of the powerful European states, whether autocratic or witnessing the birth pangs of democracy, and of the young United States of America for which it symbolized a connection with the Republican ideals of pre-Augustan Rome and the democracy of Athens and the Greek states. The Neo-Classical style is defined by elaborate details and a refined sense of proportion, hallmarks of ancient Classical architecture, which could be adapted to every conceivable purpose.

General Marceau's Funeral
Marceau defeated the Austrians in 1795, only to be killed in fighting them the next year.

The Battle of Austerlitz by Gechter shows Napoleon's army breaking up the ice on the Satschan lake in Austria to drown thousands of enemy troops who were marching across.

Officers of the Imperial Army are listed on the walls of the smaller arches.

Entrance to museum

★ **Departure of the Volunteers in 1792**
François Rude's work shows citizens leaving to defend the nation. This patriotic relief is commonly known as "La Marseillaise".

STAR FEATURES

★ **Tomb of the Unknown Soldier**

★ **Departure of the Volunteers in 1792**

Arc de Triomphe

RESIDENTS OF VERSAILLES

In 1682, Louis XIV declared Versailles the official seat of the government and court. During his reign, life in this sumptuous Baroque palace (▷ *Baroque Style p111*) was ordered by rigid etiquette. Under Louis XV (1715–74), it became increasingly opulent with the help of Madame de Pompadour, the king's mistress, who set a taste for elegance which soon spread across Europe. In 1789, Louis XVI was forced to leave Versailles when it was invaded by the Revolutionary Parisian mob. It was subsequently looted and left until the reign of Louis-Philippe (1830–48), who converted part of it into a museum of French history.

Madame de Pompadour, a renowned patron of the arts

THE GARDENS

André Le Nôtre (1613–1700), the greatest French landscape gardener, created a number of magnificent château gardens. His superb architectural orchestration, Classical vision, and sense of symmetry are seen in the sweeping vistas of Versailles, his greatest triumph. The gardens are styled into regular patterns of flowerbeds and box hedges, paths and groves, ornate pools of water, and fountains. The Water Parterre's vast pools of water are decorated with fine bronze statues. Geometric paths and shrubberies are features of the formal gardens. The Petit Trianon, a small château built in 1762 as a retreat for Louis XV, is found in the gardens. This became a favorite of Marie-Antoinette.

Château de Versailles

A MAGNIFICENT palace with sumptuous interiors and splendid gardens, Versailles represents the glory of Louis XIV's reign. Starting in 1668 with his father's modest hunting lodge, he commissioned the largest palace in Europe, with 700 rooms, 67 staircases and 730 ha (1,800 acres) of landscaped parkland. Architect Louis Le Vau built a series of wings that expanded into an enlarged courtyard. They were decorated with marble busts, antique trophies, and gilded roofs. Jules Hardouin-Mansart took over in 1678 and added the two immense north and south wings. He also designed the chapel, which was finished in 1710. Charles le Brun planned the interiors and André Le Nôtre redesigned the gardens.

Gold crest from the Petit Trianon

Louis XIV's statue, erected by Louis-Philippe in 1837, stands where a gilded gateway once marked the beginning of the Royal Courtyard.

STAR FEATURES

★ **Marble Courtyard**

★ **L'Opéra**

★ **Chapelle Royale**

South Wing
The wing's original apartments for great nobles were replaced by Louis-Philippe's museum of French history.

Ministers' Courtyard

Main Gate
Mansart's original gateway grille, surmounted by the royal arms, is the entrance to the Ministers' Courtyard.

★ Marble Courtyard
The courtyard is decorated with marble paving, urns, busts, and a gilded balcony.

PURSUIT OF QUEEN MARIE-ANTOINETTE

On 6 October 1789, a Parisian mob invaded Versailles seeking the despised Marie-Antoinette, whose frivolous behavior had earned her fierce public criticism. The queen fled through the anteroom known as the ▷ *Oeil-de-Boeuf* to the king's rooms. She and the king, Louis XVI, were later removed to Paris by the cheering and triumphant mob.

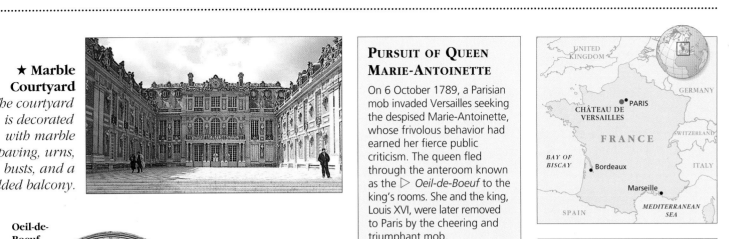

KEY DATES

1668 Le Vau starts construction of the château.

1671 The interior decoration is begun by Le Brun.

1833 Louis-Philippe turns the château into a museum.

1919 The Treaty of Versailles is signed in the Hall of Mirrors, ending World War I.

Oeil-de-Boeuf

The Clock
Hercules and Mars flank the clock overlooking the Marble Courtyard.

Hall of Mirrors

Salon d'Apollon

Salon d'Hercule

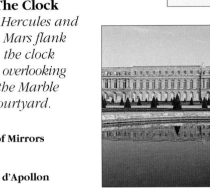

North Wing
The chapel, opera, and picture galleries occupy this wing, which originally housed royal apartments. Masses, concerts, and operas are still held in this extravagant setting.

INSIDE THE CHÂTEAU

The lavish main apartments are on the first floor of the vast château complex. Around the ▷ *marble courtyard* are the private apartments of the king and the queen. On the garden side are the state apartments where official court life took place. These were richly decorated by Charles Le Brun with colored marbles, stone and wood carvings, murals, velvet, silver, and gilded furniture. Starting with the ▷ *Salon d'Hercule*, each state room is dedicated to an Olympian deity. The ▷ *Salon d'Apollon*, dedicated to the god Apollo, was Louis XIV's throne room. A copy of Hyacinthe Rigaud's famous portrait of the king (1701) hangs here. The climax is the ▷ *Hall of Mirrors* stretching 70 m (230 ft) along the west façade. Great state occasions were held in this room where 17 mirrors face tall arched windows. Another highlight is the ▷ *Chapelle Royale*, with the second floor reserved for the royal family and the first floor for the court. The chapel's interior is richly decorated in white marble, gilding, and Baroque murals.

★ L'Opéra
The Opéra was completed in 1770, in time for the marriage of the future Louis XVI and Marie Antoinette. It was intended for lavish spectacles.

★ Chapelle Royale
Mansart's last great work, this two-story Baroque chapel, was Louis XIV's last addition to Versailles.

The Royal Courtyard was separated from the Ministers' Courtyard by elaborate grillwork during Louis XIV's reign. It was accessible only to royal carriages.

Chartres Cathedral label (vertical, left margin)

THE ROYAL PORTAL

Following the devastating fire of 1194, a decision was taken to retain the magnificent, still-standing west entrance (▷ *Royal Portal*), which was a survivor of the earlier Romanesque church (▷ *Romanesque Style p199*). Although this created a variation in architectural styles, it was an astute decision which resulted in the survival of some of the finest sculpture of the early Middle Ages. The Royal Portal, carved between 1145 and 1155, is the most ornamental of the cathedral's three entrances. The features of the statues in the portal are lengthened in typical Romanesque style (▷ *Elongated Statues*) and depict figures from the Old Testament. The portal represents the glory of Christ.

Stained-glass panels of the Blue Virgin Window

THE STAINED GLASS OF CHARTRES

Donated by aristocracy, the merchant brotherhoods, and royalty between 1210 and 1240, this glorious array of ▷ *stained-glass windows* is world-renowned. Over 150 windows illustrate biblical stories and daily life in the 13th century. Each window is divided into panels, usually read from left to right, bottom to top (earth to heaven). The bottom panel of the Blue Virgin window depicts Christ's conversion of water into wine. During both World Wars the windows were dismantled piece by piece and removed for safety. There is an on-going program, begun in the 1970s, to restore the windows.

Chartres Cathedral

Part of the Vendôme Window

THE EPITOME OF EARLY GOTHIC architecture (▷ *Gothic Style p73*), Chartres Cathedral established a style which soon spread throughout Christendom. It was built around the remains of an earlier Romanesque church which had been partly destroyed by fire. The result is a blend of styles, with the original north and south towers, south steeple, west portal, and crypt enhanced by lofty Gothic additions. Peasant and lord alike helped to rebuild the church in just 25 years. Few alterations were made after 1250, and fortunately Chartres was unscathed by the Wars of Religion and the French Revolution.

STAR FEATURES

★ **Royal Portal**

★ **Stained-glass Windows**

★ **South Porch**

Gothic Nave
As wide as the Romanesque crypt below it, the nave reaches a soaring height of 37 m (121 ft).

★ Royal Portal
The central tympanum of the Royal Portal (1145–55) shows Christ in Majesty.

Elongated Statues
These statues on the Royal Portal represent Old Testament figures.

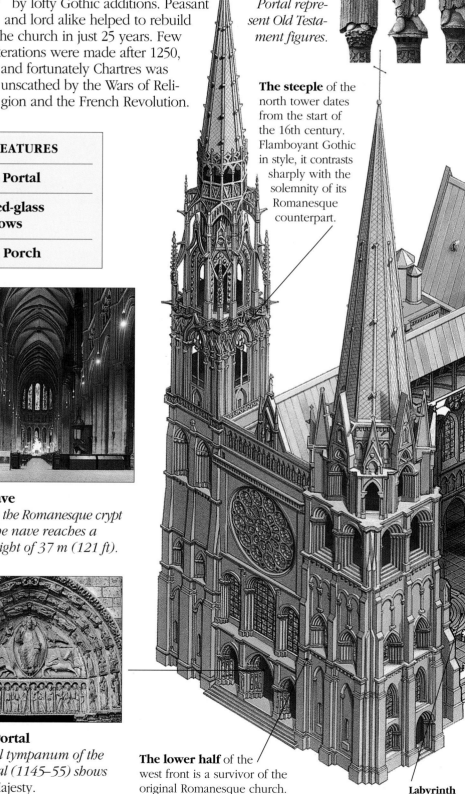

The steeple of the north tower dates from the start of the 16th century. Flamboyant Gothic in style, it contrasts sharply with the solemnity of its Romanesque counterpart.

The lower half of the west front is a survivor of the original Romanesque church.

Labyrinth

THE LABYRINTH

The 13th-century labyrinth, inlaid in the nave floor, was a feature of most medieval cathedrals. As a penance, pilgrims used to follow the tortuous route on their knees, echoing the Way of the Cross. The journey of 262 m (859 ft), around 11 bands of broken concentric circles, took at least one hour to complete.

VEIL OF THE VIRGIN

The miraculous survival of this relic after the fire of 1194 made Chartres a holy pilgrimage site and attracted generous donations. The veil is said to have been worn by the Virgin Mary when she gave birth to Jesus.

KEY DATES

1020 Romanesque cathedral is begun.

1194 A fire partly destroys the Romanesque cathedral.

1220s The cathedral is rebuilt, with new parts in the early Gothic style.

1260 The cathedral is formally consecrated.

1507 A Flamboyant Gothic steeple is added to the north tower.

1836 The cathedral's wooden roof is damaged by fire.

1974 The cathedral is added to UNESCO's World Heritage Site list.

GOTHIC STATUARY

There are approximately 4,000 statues at Chartres Cathedral. Fortunately, having remained virtually untouched since being sculpted in the 13th century, they are in a remarkable state of preservation. Incredible examples, tracing the evolution of Gothic sculpture, are clustered around the north and south portals. The north porch is devoted to representations of such Old Testament figures as Joseph, Solomon, the Queen of Sheba, Isaiah, and Jeremiah. Scenes from Christ's childhood and the Creation of the World are also illustrated. The ▷ *South Porch* portrays the Last Judgment, and episodes in the lives of the Saints. The hundreds of figures decorating both portals were originally painted in bright colors.

Apsidal Chapel
This chapel houses the oldest cathedral treasure, the Veil of the Virgin *relic, which miraculously survived the fire of 1194. More artifacts can be found in the St Piat Chapel.*

Vaulted Ceiling
A network of ribs supports the vaulted ceiling.

★ Stained-glass Windows
The windows cover a surface area of over 2,600 sq m (28,000 sq ft).

★ South Porch
Sculpture on the South Porch (1197–1209) reflects New Testament teaching.

The Crypt
This is the largest crypt in France, most of it dating from the early 11th century. It comprises two parallel galleries, a series of chapels, and the 9th-century St Lubin's vault.

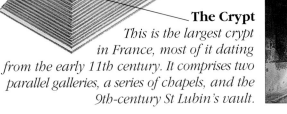

Château de Chambord

The Château de Chambord with the Cosson, a tributary of the Loire, in the foreground

THE STAIRCASE

One of Chambord's most striking architectural features is the ▷ *grand staircase,* reputedly adapted from a design by Leonardo da Vinci. Vaulted halls arranged in the shape of a cross intersect at this magnificent double spiral staircase. It is supported by eight square pillars and consists of two separate flights of stairs. The double helix structure allows people to use it simultaneously without ever crossing paths. This allowed the king to ascend and descend without meeting his servants and may also have been useful for the king's mistresses who could have avoided using the same staircase as the Queen. The staircase leads to the unique ▷ *roof terraces.*

ROYAL HUNTING

Under the influence of François I, hunting was a popular pastime of the court during the 16th century. The king rode out at dawn to his vast oak forests to await the red deer tracked by his beaters. The quarry flushed, he would ride at full tilt in pursuit. For ladies of the court, Chambord's ▷ *roof terraces* offered matchless views of these exertions. François's son Henri II and grandson Charles IX were also keen and practised hunters, sometimes pursuing quarry on foot. Louis XIV favored the English sport of following packs of hounds but falconry was preferred by Louis XV. The court regarded hunting as an art, so horns, weapons, and costumes were exquisitely designed and crafted.

An engraving of the northwest façade

Statue of Diana in the Salle de Diane

THE DAZZLING AND extravagant Château de Chambord, with its 440 rooms, 84 staircases, and 365 sculpted chimneys, is the largest and most impressive château in the Loire region. It began life as a hunting lodge in the Boulogne forest until 1519 when the original building was razed and a grand edifice begun, to a design probably initiated by Leonardo da Vinci. By 1537 the keep, built for King François I, with its towers and terraces, had been completed by 1,800 men and two master masons. In 1538, a private royal pavilion with a connecting two-story gallery was added. François's son, Henri II, continued the west wing with the chapel, and Louis XIV completed the splendor in 1685.

★ Skyline
Chambord's roof is its most astonishing feature – said to represent the skyline of a small city built to enliven the ladies' walks.

Salamander
François I's emblem appears more than 700 times in the château. It symbolizes patronage of the good and destruction of the bad.

The roof terraces include miniature spires, stair turrets, sculpted gables, and cupolas.

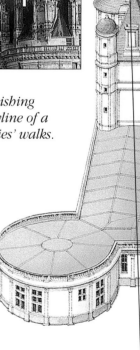

The central keep, with its four circular towers, forms the nucleus of the château.

Chapel
Begun by François I shortly before his death in 1547, the chapel was given a second story by his son Henri II. Later, Louis XIV embellished the roof.

STAR FEATURES

★ **Skyline**

★ **Grand Staircase**

François I Staircase
The external spiral staircase located in the northeastern courtyard was added at the same time as the galleries, starting in 1538.

The lantern tower, 32 m (105 ft) high, is supported by flying buttresses.

The guardrooms, which were once the setting for royal balls and plays, have ornate, vaulted ceilings.

François I's bedchamber in the east wing, has remained unchanged since his death in 1547.

THE GROUNDS

The château is situated in a vast park covering 53.5 sq km (20.65 sq miles), a large area of which is a protected zone for wildlife. Its surrounding wall, the longest in France, runs for nearly 32 km (20 miles). At one point, François I suggested diverting the Loire to flow in front of his château but instead settled for redirecting the nearer Cosson stream to fill his moat.

Cabinet de François I
The king's barrel-vaulted study (cabinet) *in the outer north tower was turned into an oratory in the 18th century by Queen Catherine Opalinska, wife of Stanislas Leszcynski (Louis XV's father-in-law and the deposed king of Poland).*

KEY DATES

1519–47 The original hunting lodge is demolished by François I and the château created.

1547–59 Henry II adds the west wing and second story of the chapel.

1685 Louis XIV finishes the building.

1840 Chambord is declared a *Monument Historique*.

1970s The château is restored and refurnished and the moats re-dug.

1981 The château is added to UNESCO's World Heritage list.

KING FRANÇOIS I

As a result of the French invasion of Italy in 1494, the ideals and aesthetics of the Italian Renaissance (▷ *Renaissance Style p211*) spread to France, reaching their height during the reign of François I (r.1515–47). Born in Cognac in 1494 to Charles of Orléans and Louise of Savoy, François I was a true supporter of Renaissance ideals. He was also skilled in letters and art, as well as sport and battle. As a major patron of the arts the French king invited Italian artists, such as Leonardo and Cellini, to his court. His magnificent castles across France (including the Louvre, Chambord, and Fontainebleau) were built at the expense of the nation's economy, which struggled to meet his extravagant tastes.

★ Grand Staircase
Seen here from the guardrooms, this innovative double staircase was supposedly designed by Leonardo da Vinci. Two flights of stairs spiral around each other.

Louis XIV's Bedchamber
The Sun King's state apartments are the grandest in the château.

Château de Chambord

The gardens' current design, dating from the 19th century

THE FORMAL GARDENS

As the mistress of Henri II, Diane de Poitiers wanted a surrounding fit for a king and set about creating her grand garden along the banks of the River Cher. Divided into four triangles and kept from flooding by elevated stone terraces, it was planted with an extensive selection of flowers, vegetables, and fruit trees. When Catherine de' Medici arrived at Chenonceau, she created her own garden from a design by Bernard Palissy in his *Drawings of a Delectable Garden*. Today, over 4,000 flowers are planted in the gardens each year.

THE CREATION OF CHENONCEAU

Catherine Briçonnet, wife of the royal chamberlain, was the first of many females who added their feminine touches to Chenonceau. During King Henri II's reign (1547–59) he gave the castle to his mistress Diane de Poitiers, who went on to dramatically transform it. She redecorated its interiors, built a bridge over the River Cher, and constructed a ▷ *formal garden*. When the king died, his wife Catherine de' Medici reclaimed the château from Diane and set about erasing her presence. She redesigned the castle and built a ▷ *Grande Galerie* on the bridge above the Cher. Over the centuries other ladies have shaped Chenonceau's destiny and design, including Louise de Lorraine who was bequeathed the castle in 1589, the enlightened Louise Dupin, friend of Voltaire and Rousseau, in the 18th century, and Madame Pelouze in the 19th century.

Château de Chenonceau

S TRETCHING ROMANTICALLY across the River Cher, this Renaissance château (▷ *Renaissance Style p211*) was the residence for queens and royal mistresses, including Catherine de' Medici and Diane de Poitiers. Transformed over the centuries from a modest manor and water mill into a castle designed solely for pleasure, it is surrounded by elegant formal gardens and wooded grounds. The interior rooms have been restored to their original style and a small waxworks museum illustrates the building's history. The site also includes a stable with a miniature train ride down the lovely tree-lined drive, and a restaurant.

★ Cabinet Vert
The walls of Catherine de' Medici's study were originally covered with green velvet.

Chapelle
The chapel has a vaulted ceiling and pilasters sculpted with acanthus leaves and cockle shells. The stained glass, ruined by a bomb in 1944, was replaced in 1953.

To Formal Gardens

The Tour des Marques survives from the 15th-century castle of the Marques family.

Louise de Lorraine's room was painted black and decorated with monograms, tears, and knots in white after the death of her husband Henri III in 1589.

The Three Graces
Painted by Charles-André Van Loo (1705–65), The Three Graces *depicts the pretty Mailly-Nesle sisters, all royal mistresses.*

STAR FEATURES

★ Cabinet Vert

★ Tapestries

★ Grande Galerie

★ Tapestries

As was the practise in the 16th century, Chenonceau is hung with Flemish tapestries that both warm and decorate its well-furnished rooms.

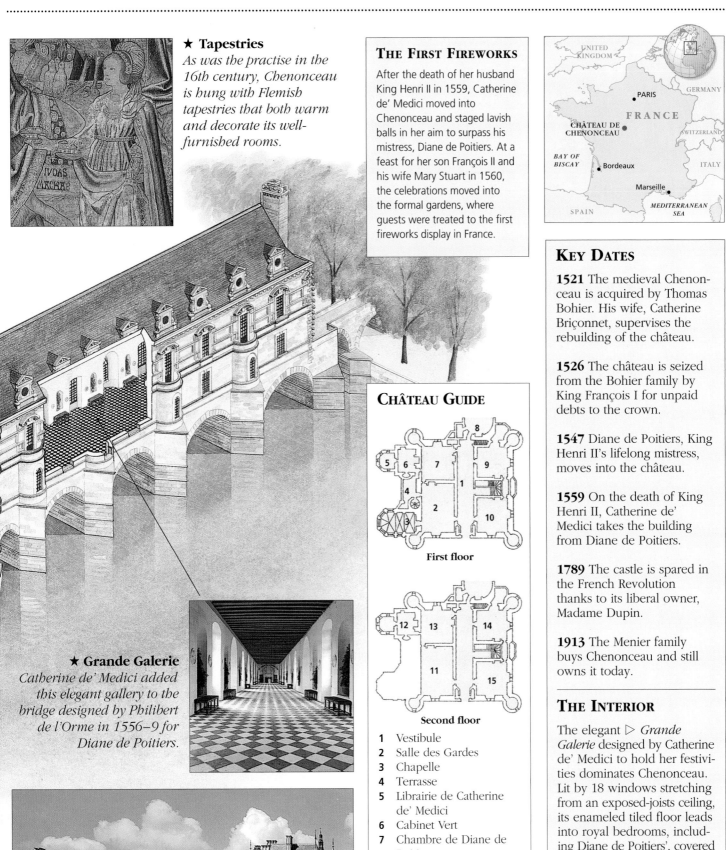

THE FIRST FIREWORKS

After the death of her husband King Henri II in 1559, Catherine de' Medici moved into Chenonceau and staged lavish balls in her aim to surpass his mistress, Diane de Poitiers. At a feast for her son François II and his wife Mary Stuart in 1560, the celebrations moved into the formal gardens, where guests were treated to the first fireworks display in France.

CHÂTEAU GUIDE

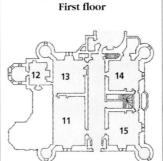

First floor

Second floor

1 Vestibule
2 Salle des Gardes
3 Chapelle
4 Terrasse
5 Librairie de Catherine de' Medici
6 Cabinet Vert
7 Chambre de Diane de Poitiers
8 Grande Galerie
9 Chambre de François I
10 Salon Louis XIV
11 Chambre des Cinq Reines
12 Cabinet des Estampes
13 Chambre de Catherine de' Medici
14 Chambre de Vendôme
15 Chambre de Gabrielle d'Estrées

★ Grande Galerie

Catherine de' Medici added this elegant gallery to the bridge designed by Philibert de l'Orme in 1556–9 for Diane de Poitiers.

Chenonceau's Florentine-style Grande Galerie, which stretches across the River Cher for 60 m (197 ft)

KEY DATES

1521 The medieval Chenonceau is acquired by Thomas Bohier. His wife, Catherine Briçonnet, supervises the rebuilding of the château.

1526 The château is seized from the Bohier family by King François I for unpaid debts to the crown.

1547 Diane de Poitiers, King Henri II's lifelong mistress, moves into the château.

1559 On the death of King Henri II, Catherine de' Medici takes the building from Diane de Poitiers.

1789 The castle is spared in the French Revolution thanks to its liberal owner, Madame Dupin.

1913 The Menier family buys Chenonceau and still owns it today.

THE INTERIOR

The elegant ▷ *Grande Galerie* designed by Catherine de' Medici to hold her festivities dominates Chenonceau. Lit by 18 windows stretching from an exposed-joists ceiling, its enameled tiled floor leads into royal bedrooms, including Diane de Poitiers', covered in Flemish ▷ *tapestries*. The tiles in the second floor hall are stamped with fleurs de lys crossed by a dagger. Marble medallions brought from Italy by Catherine de' Medici hang above the doors, including those in her bedroom, which is full of 16th-century furnishings and tapestries depicting biblical scenes.

Atmospheric cloister, Abbey of Fontenay

CISTERCIAN STYLE

The Middle Ages saw the building of some of the finest monasteries in Europe, and perhaps the greatest of all were created by the monks of the Cistercian order. Brought together by the conviction that religion had become too bound up with lavish ostentation, Cistercian monks desired reform and a return to simplicity in religious rituals as well as in architecture and personal embellishment. Decoration in churches was felt to be unnecessary and distracting to the spiritual endeavor, so Cistercian interiors were free of stained glass and works of art, and high altars were kept bare. The result was a monastery of austere but beautiful simplicity.

THE FORGE

The Abbey of Fontenay housed a range of facilities to serve the community, including a ▷ chapter house, ▷ infirmary, and ▷ visitors' hostel as well as an ▷ abbey church and ▷ cloisters. There was also a ▷ forge, one of the oldest for working metal known in Europe. The imposing 12th-century building, 53 m (174 ft) long, was where the monks used to make metal tools. The iron ore was mined locally and the charcoal for the furnace came from the nearby Châtillonnais forests in Burgundy. The mill race, which was used to drive a number of heavy metal-working hammers in the forge, was a technological innovation in its time. The great furnace can still be seen today.

Abbey of Fontenay

THE TRANQUIL ABBEY of Fontenay is the oldest surviving Cistercian foundation in France and offers a rare insight into the Cistercian monks' way of life. With its Romanesque (▷ *Romanesque Style p199*) church, 12th-century cloisters, and plain but elegant interiors in early Gothic style (▷ *Gothic Style p73*), Fontenay reflects the true spirit of the order. Founded in 1118 by St Bernard and established deep within a forest, the abbey provided the peace and seclusion the monks sought. Support from the local nobility enabled the abbey to thrive until the French Revolution, after which it was sold and converted into a mill. Recent owners have restored it to its original appearance.

The bakehouse is no longer intact but the 13th-century oven and chimney have survived.

The visitors' hostel is where weary wanderers and pilgrims were offered board and lodging by the monks.

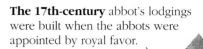

Dovecot
A magnificent circular dovecot, built in the 13th century, is situated next to the kennel where the precious hunting dogs of the dukes of Burgundy were guarded by servants.

The 17th-century abbot's lodgings were built when the abbots were appointed by royal favor.

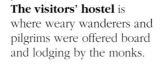

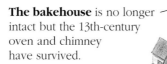

★ Cloisters
For a 12th-century monk a walk through the cloisters was an opportunity for meditation and provided shelter from the weather.

Warming Room

In the forge monks produced their own tools and hardware.

Fontenay "Prison"
This 15th-century building may not have actually been used to lock away local miscreants but was possibly a way of protecting important abbey archives from damage by rats.

Scriptorium
Manuscripts were copied here. The adjacent Warming Room was used to warm chilled hands.

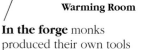

★ Abbey Church
Rich decoration has no place in this church from the 1140s. But the severe architectural forms, the warm color of the stone and the diffused light convey grandeur and tranquility.

Dormitory
Monks slept in long rows on straw mattresses in this large, unheated room. The timberwork roof is from the late 15th century.

The herb garden was skillfully cultivated by the monks who grew healing herbs for medicines and potions.

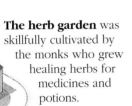

Infirmary

CISTERCIANS ABROAD
The order spread to Spain, Italy and Germany as well as north to Britain and Ireland. Interesting abbey ruins survive in England: Tintern, Kirkstall, Fountains, and Rievaulx.

STAR FEATURES
★ **Cloisters**

★ **Abbey Church**

Chapter house
Once a day, the abbot and the monks assembled in this room to discuss matters concerning the community. It derives much of its charm from the elegant 12th-century piers and the rib-vaults.

PARIS · GERMANY
ABBEY OF FONTENAY ·
SWITZERLAND
FRANCE
BAY OF BISCAY
Bordeaux ·
ITALY
Marseille ·
SPAIN
MEDITERRANEAN SEA
UNITED KINGDOM

KEY DATES

1118 St Bernard of Clairvaux founds Fontenay on a former hermitage site.

1791 The monastery, secularized during the French Revolution, is sold and becomes a paper mill.

1906–11 The Ayard family restores the complex.

1981 UNESCO adds the Abbey of Fontenay to the World Heritage Sites list.

LIFE IN A CISTERCIAN MONASTERY

The rules of the Cistercian Order were based on the principles of austerity and simplicity. Abbeys were divided into two communities, which did not mix. Lay brothers, not bound by holy vows, ensured the self-sufficiency of the abbey by managing the barns, tilling the fields, milling corn, and welcoming guests. The full, or choir, monks were the only ones allowed into the cloister, at the heart of the complex, and could not leave the abbey without the permission of the abbot. The monks' days started at 2am and ended at 7pm, and were regularly punctuated by religious devotions, which included prayers, confession, meditation, and mass. The strict rule of silence was broken only to read from the Bible or from the Rules of the Order. Many monks were literate, and monasteries played a leading role in copying manuscripts.

ST BERNARD AND THE CISTERCIANS

When Bernard, a young Burgundian nobleman, joined the Cistercians in 1112 the order was still obscure. It had been founded only 14 years earlier by a group of monks who wanted to turn their backs on an elaborate lifestyle, renouncing the world and espousing poverty and simplicity. During Bernard's lifetime the Cistercians became one of the largest and most famous orders of its time. Part of this success was clearly due to Bernard's powerful personality and his skills as a writer, theologian, and statesman. He reinforced the poverty rule, rejecting all forms of embellishment. In 1174, only 21 years after his death, he was canonized.

The Virgin Protecting the Cistercian Order, by Jean Bellegambe

JEAN, DUC DE BERRY

The marble tomb of the 14th-century Duc de Berry is located in the ▷ crypt. He was the son of King Jean II (reigned 1350–64), brother of King Charles V (r.1364–80), and uncle of King Charles VI (r.1364–80). In appanage, he received the province of Berry and under his lavish and resourceful patronage its capital, Bourges, flourished and became a distinguished artistic platform. He was a passionate sponsor of the arts and an ostentatious collector, investing large sums and initiating works ranging from grandiose buildings to richly illuminated manuscripts and precious jewels. He is most renowned for commissioning the famous 15th-century illuminated prayer book, *Les Très Riches Heures*. Jean, Duc de Berry bestowed the grand window of the west façade (▷ *The Grand Housteau*).

WESTERN PORTALS

The west façade is dominated by five sculpted 13th-century portals. Saints, angels, cherubs, and prophets can be seen in the remarkable carvings. The ornamental doorways are an original feature and are in a fine state of preservation. The central portal is a majestic feat of medieval sculpture (▷ *Last Judgment*). The two doorways to its left were restored in the 16th century after damage caused by the collapse of the north tower in 1506. The first shows scenes from the life of the Virgin Mary and retains some 13th-century elements. The second is devoted to the life of St William, Archbishop of Bourges, 1200–1209. The mid-13th-century doorways to the right of the central portal are dedicated to St Stephen, patron saint of St-Étienne cathedral, and to St Ursin who was the first Bishop of Bourges.

Stained-glass window

Cathedral of St-Étienne, Bourges

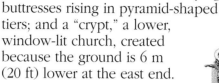

Stained-glass window detail

THIS MASTERPIECE OF French Gothic architecture was built mainly between 1195 and 1260 (▷ *Gothic Style p73*). The unknown architect designed St-Étienne without transepts which, combined with the interior's unusual height and width, makes it much lighter than most Gothic cathedrals. This effect is beautifully enhanced by the brilliant hues of the medieval stained glass. Also unusual is the asymmetrical west front; the double row of flying buttresses rising in pyramid-shaped tiers; and a "crypt," a lower, window-lit church, created because the ground is 6 m (20 ft) lower at the east end.

Vast Interior
The interior is 124 m (400 ft) long and 37 m (120 ft) high.

North Tower

The Tour Sourde
(Deaf Tower) is so called because it has no bell.

★ **Astrological Clock**
Dating from the 1420s, this fascinating clock was designed by Canon Jean Fusoris, a mathematician.

Entrance

THE LAST JUDGMENT

The tympanum on the central portal of the west façade depicts Archangel Michael weighing souls. Those found wanting are hustled by devils into the mouth of Hell, while the elect are gathered into the bosom of Abraham. The youthful, naked dead lift up their tombstones in a dramatic Resurrection scene.

The Last Judgment portal of the Cathédrale St-Étienne

The Grand Housteau
is a striking rose window, donated by the renowned patron of the arts Jean, Duc de Berry.

The five portals of the west front are surrounded by carved scenes. The doorways vary in size and shape, adding to the asymmetry of the façade.

★ Stained-glass Windows

The medieval stained glass in the choir was sponsored by local guilds, whose members are depicted practising their crafts at the bottom of each window.

The Chapelle Jacques-Cœur has a glorious Annunciation window.

THE ASTROLOGICAL CLOCK

This imposing astrological clock, in the second aisle on the right from the entrance, is the oldest in France. It shows the hour, day, and month and chimes every 15 minutes. Canon Fusoris' original 15th-century mechanism has been well preserved.

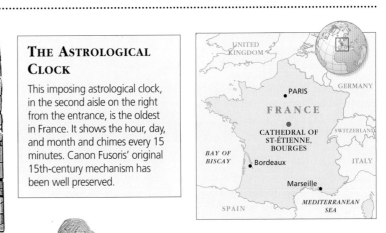

Praying Figures
In the crypt are statues of the Duc and Duchesse de Berry. During the French Revolution, the statues were decapitated and the existing heads are copies.

KEY DATES

1195 Construction of the cathedral begins.

1214 The choir is added.

1225–50 Construction of the nave is completed.

1542 The north tower is rebuilt after collapsing in 1506.

1562 Protestants destroy statues on the west façade during the Wars of Religion.

1992 The cathedral is added to UNESCO's World Heritage Site list.

THE INTERIOR

St-Étienne's ▷ *vast interior* is simple yet tremendously grand. The triple-tiered exterior evokes the idea of a partitioned interior. However, it is the flying buttresses which support the soaring nave, creating a spectacular effect of spaciousness within the cathedral. Double aisles and the omission of transepts broaden the vista and as a result, the many grandiose pillars appear slender. This arrangement affords visitors an unobstructed view through the cathedral's entire length to the choir's magnificent 13th-century ▷ *stained-glass windows*. The bold design has been admired by many writers including Stendhal (1783–1842) who declared, "this vast cathedral fulfills its purpose perfectly. The traveler wandering among its immense columns is filled with awe: he senses the nullity of man in the presence of the Divinity."

The crypt, or lower church, was built in the earlier Gallo-Roman moat.

The Romanesque portal on the cathedral's south side is decorated with a *Christ in Majesty* and the 12 apostles.

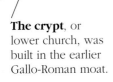

★ St Sépulcre

This dramatic sculpture of the Entombment of Christ *was placed at the far end of the lower church in 1540.*

STAR FEATURES

★ **Astrological Clock**

★ **Stained-glass Windows**

★ **St Sépulcre**

Jean, Duc de Berry
The recumbent marble effigy of Jean, Duc de Berry, his feet resting on a bear, was originally part of his tomb.

ST AMADOUR

There are various stories about the life of St Amadour. One legend claims that he was Zaccheus of Jericho, who knew and conversed with Jesus during his time on earth. His wife, St Veronica, gave Jesus a cloth to wipe his face during his journey to Calvary. After Jesus's crucifixion, Zaccheus and his wife fled from Palestine to escape religious persecution. On their travels, they met the Bishop St Martial, another disciple of Jesus in Aquitaine, France, who was preaching the Gospel, but continued to Rome. While in Rome they witnessed the martyrdoms of St Peter and St Paul. The death of his wife led Zaccheus back to France and the place later named after him, where he stayed until he died in 70 AD.

CHAPEL OF NOTRE-DAME

This Romanesque chapel (▷ *Romanesque Style p199*) was built in the 15th century near the site where St Amadour's body was found. It houses the statue of the Black Virgin and Child. Pilgrims who heard about the statue flocked to the shrine, climbing the ▷ *Grand Stairway* on their knees as they prayed for the forgiveness of their sins. A 9th-century bell hangs in the chapel's vault and is thought to ring when a miracle occurs. Saints and kings also visited the chapel, including England's King Henry II. Legend says that he was cured of his ailment when he prayed before the Black Virgin and Child.

Rocamadour, both a place of pilgrimage and a tourist sight

Rocamadour

PILGRIMS HAVE FLOCKED to Rocamadour since the discovery in 1166 of an ancient grave and sepulchre containing an undecayed body, said to be that of the early Christian hermit St Amadour. King Louis IX, St Bernard and St Dominic were among many who visited the site as a spate of miracles were heralded, it is claimed, by the bell above the Black Virgin and Child in the Chapel of Notre-Dame. Although the town suffered with the decline of pilgrimages in the 17th and 18th centuries, it was heavily restored in the 19th century. Still a holy shrine, as well as a popular tourist destination, the site above the Alzou valley is phenomenal. The best views of the town can be had from the hamlet of L'Hospitalet.

Black Virgin and Child

The Château stands on the site of a fort which protected the sanctuary from the west.

St Michael's Chapel contains well-preserved 12th-century frescoes.

General View
Rocamadour is at its most breathtaking in the sunlight of early morning: the cluster of medieval houses, towers, and battlements seems to sprout from the base of the cliff.

The Tomb of St Amadour once held the body of the hermit from whom the town took its name (Rock of Amadour).

Museum of Sacred Art

Grand Stairway
Pilgrims would climb this broad flight of steps on their knees as they said their rosaries. The stairway leads to a square on the next level, around which the main pilgrim chapels are grouped.

The Chapel of St John the Baptist faces the fine Gothic portal of the Basilica of St-Sauveur.

Ramparts

The Basilica of St-Sauveur, a late 12th-century sanctuary, backs on to the bare rock face.

St Anne's Chapel dates from the 13th century, and contains a 17th-century gilded altar screen.

Cross of Jerusalem

THE SPORTELL

Crafted in either lead, bronze, tin, silver or gold, the Sportell or medal displays the Virgin Mary and Child. It is worn by pilgrims who have visited Rocamadour and was once used as a pass to cross war-torn countries.

Chapel of St Blaise

Stations of the Cross
Pilgrims encounter the Cross of Jerusalem and 14 stations marking Jesus's journey to the Cross on their way up the hillside to the château.

Rocamadour Town
Now a pedestrian precinct, its main street is lined with souvenir shops to tempt the throngs of pilgrims.

Chapel of Notre-Dame
A statue of the 12th-century Black Virgin and Child, made of walnut wood and covered in blackened silver, stands on the altar.

KEY DATES

1166 The preserved body of Zaccheus, later named St Amadour, is discovered.

1172 The *Book of Miracles* is drafted with the testimonies of miracles granted to pilgrims.

1193–1317 Over 30,000 pilgrims flock to the religious site.

1479 The Chapel of Notre-Dame is constructed.

1562 The chapels are plundered by Protestants.

1858–72 Rocamadour's restoration is supervised by abbot Jean-Baptiste Chevalt.

ROCAMADOUR'S MUSEUM

The ▷ *Museum of Sacred Art* is housed in the Bishop's Palace, which was constructed by the abbots of Tulle in the 13th century. The museum was restored in 1996 and is dedicated to the French music composer Francis Poulenc (1899–1963), who was inspired to compose *Litanies to the Black Virgin* after he visited Rocamadour. The museum's collection of statues, paintings, and religious artifacts has been assembled from different sites around Rocamadour. Particularly interesting is the 17th-century statue of the prophet Jonah, carved in wood, and the fine lanterns, vases, and chalices, which are still used in various religious ceremonies at Rocamadour.

Rocamadour

EMPEROR AUGUSTUS

Orange was an ancient settlement called Arausio, founded around 40 BC by veterans of Julius Caesar's second regiment. The region flourished impressively under the reign of Emperor Augustus (27 BC–AD 14), during which time the theater at Orange was built. The Romans not only viewed it as a way of spreading their culture but also wished to distract citizens from uprisings by providing them with dazzling spectacles. A further reason was to make the Roman soldiers feel at home, being surrounded by familiar classical Roman architecture (▷ *Classical Style p231*). The theater thus represents the might of Roman colonization and of Emperor Augustus.

Modern production in Orange's ancient theater

LES CHORÉGIES D'ORANGE

The theater's first modern performance was held in 1869. Audiences were enthralled by the atmospheric setting and incredible acoustics. From 1902, a festival has been held yearly and is referred to as "Les Chorégies d'Orange" (▷ *Night Concerts*). All of the leading names of the French classical genre have honored the theater's stage at some point. Until 1969, the festival showcased plays, musical compositions, opera productions, and symphonies. Thereafter, the focus shifted toward operatic works. Classic pieces such as *Tosca, Carmen, Aida*, and *La Traviata* performed by leading vocalists including Placido Domingo and Montserrat Caballé have brought the festival international acclaim.

Roman Theater, Orange

ORANGE'S ROMAN THEATER is one of the best preserved of the entire Roman empire in Europe. It was constructed in the first century AD against the natural height of the Colline-St-Eutrope. Its stage doors were hollow so that actors could stand in front and amplify their voices; today other acoustic touches make it ideal for concerts. In Roman times the theater was also used for meetings and lectures. The *cavea*, or tiered semicircle, held up to 7,000 spectators, seated according to their social status. From the 16th to 19th centuries, the theater was filled with squalid housing, traces of which can still be seen.

ROMAN THEATER

This reconstruction shows the theater as it would have looked in Roman times. Today it owes its reputation to the excellent state of the *frons scaenae*, the stage wall.

A canvas awning, known as a *velum*, protected the theatergoers from sun or rain.

Main entrance

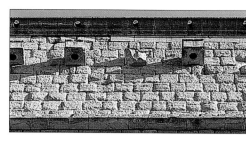

Awning Supports
Still visible on the exterior walls are corbels which held the huge velum-*bearing masts.*

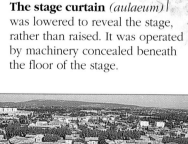

The stage curtain (*aulaeum*) was lowered to reveal the stage, rather than raised. It was operated by machinery concealed beneath the floor of the stage.

Night Concerts
Cultural events such as Les Chorégies d'Orange, *a festival of opera, drama, and ballet, once frequented by Sarah Bernhardt, have been held here since 1860. The theater is also a popular rock concert venue.*

Frons Scaenae
Built of red limestone, this great stage wall is 103 m (338 ft) long, 36 m (117 ft) high and over 1.8 m (5 ft) thick.

Emperor Augustus

This 3.5-m (11-ft) statue, with a hand raised in greeting, dominates the stage at the third level. At its base kneels a figure in breeches, possibly a defeated enemy. Other statues have been destroyed, but this copy was returned to the niche in 1951.

Side rooms, or *parascaenia*, were where actors could rest, and props be stored, when not required on stage.

The Inner Face

The inner face of the frons scaenae *(stage wall) still bears fragments of marble friezes and mosaics. A frieze of centaurs framed the royal doorway in the centre.*

Each strip of *velum* awning could be rolled individually to suit the direction of the sunlight.

Marble Columns

The stage wall had three levels, the two upper levels with 76 marble columns, of which only two remain. The wall's many surfaces broke up sound waves, so that the actors could speak without their voices having an echo.

Winched capstans held and tightened the ropes supporting the *velum*.

The Great Roman Temple

From 1925–37, excavations took place to the west of the theater, where 22 houses had been pulled down. They unearthed a vast semicircle and ruins of a temple. Together with the theater, they would have formed an Augusteum, *an architectural unit devoted to the worship of Roman emperors.*

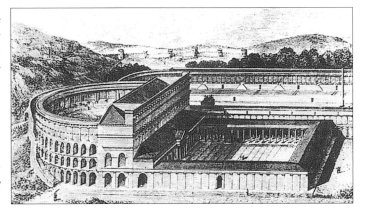

KEY DATES

c.40 BC Colony of Arausio is founded.

1st century AD The theater is constructed.

391 The theater is closed due to opposition from the Church to pagan shows. With the fall of the Roman Empire, the theater is abandoned.

16th century The theater is used as a refuge and fills with dwellings during the Wars of Religion (1562–93).

1981 The theater is added to UNESCO's World Heritage Site list.

THE STRUCTURE

Mimes, pantomimes, poetry, and farcical comedies were among the favored public spectacles performed in the Roman theater. The semi-circular three-tiered area, molded into the surrounding hillside, comprised terraced rows of seating divided into sections by walkways. The theater was the only venue where men and women could mix freely although different social classes were kept apart by these walkways. Marble seats were reserved for guests of honor, senators, and others of high social standing. The stage was separated from the auditorium by the miraculously intact ▷ *frons scaenae,* considered by Louis XIV to be the most beautiful wall in his kingdom. The niches, pillars, and blocks adorning the ▷ *inner face* of this wall contribute to the great acoustics.

Roman Theater

THE PALACE

This fortress-like complex is overwhelming in size. Entrance is by means of the ▷ *Champeaux gate*, beneath the twin pencil-shaped turrets of the flamboyant Palais Neuf, built by Clement VI (1342–52). This extends south from the plain Palais Vieux, erected by Pope Benedict XII (1334–42), centered around ▷ *Benedict XII's cloister*, with its two defense towers, ▷ *Trouillas tower* (1347) and ▷ *Belltower* (1340). Ten fortified towers were erected in total, with high walls and powerful ramparts reinforcing the entire southern and eastern sides. These give an idea of the grand life of the ruling Popes who built this miniature Vatican to convey an image of defensive strength.

ARCHITECTURE

Differing architectural styles characterize the palace. Pope Benedict XII commissioned architect Pierre Poisson to design the austere and solemn Palais Vieux. The Pope was a member of the Cistercian Order and so did not approve of frivolity. The principal room of Poisson's Palais Vieux is the ▷ *Consistory Hall*. Clement VI later sought to double the building's surface area and entrusted this construction to architect Jean de Louvres whose lavish and decorative Palais Neuf is a stark contrast to its predecessor. The rich embellishment of this style culminates in de Louvres' masterpiece, the ▷ *Great Audience Hall* with its splendid two-nave hall.

The Pont St-Bénézet and the Palais des Papes in Avignon

Palais des Papes, Avignon

Pope Clement VI (1342–52)

CONFRONTED WITH FACTIONAL STRIFE in Rome and encouraged by the scheming of Philippe IV of France, Pope Clement V moved the papal court to Avignon in 1309. Here it remained until 1377, during which time his successors transformed the modest episcopal building into this grand example of 14th-century Gothic architecture (▷ *Gothic Style p73*). Its heavy fortification was vital for defense against rogue mercenaries. Today it is empty of the luxurious trappings of 14th-century court life, as virtually all the furnishings and artwork were destroyed or looted over the centuries.

Benedict XII's cloister incorporates the guest and staff wings, and the Benedictine chapel.

Trouillas tower

Belltower

Corner tower

La Gache tower

Champeaux gate

Military Architecture
The palace and its ten towers were designed as an impregnable fortress. It eventually covered an area of 15,000 sq m (160,000 sq ft).

THE AVIGNON POPES

Seven "official" popes reigned in Avignon until 1376. They were followed by two "anti-popes," the last of whom, Benedict XIII, fled in 1403. Popes or anti-popes, few were known for their sanctity. Clement V died eating powdered emeralds, prescribed as an indigestion cure; Clement VI (1342–52) thought that the best way to honor God was through luxury. Petrarch was shocked by "the filth of the universe" at court. In 1367, Urban V tried to return the Curia (papal court) to Rome, a move that became permanent in 1377.

Benedict XII (1334–42)

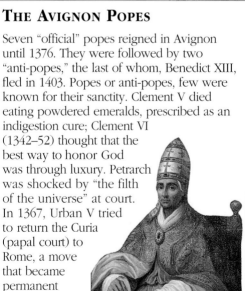

Consistory Hall
Simone Martini's exquisite frescoes (1340) replaced works destroyed by fire in the papal reception hall in 1413.

Papal Power
More like a warlord's citadel than a papal palace, the building's heavy fortification reflects the insecure religious climate of the 14th century.

FESTIVAL D'AVIGNON
The great courtyard is the setting for France's largest arts festival. Theater, movie, music, and dance productions are staged between July and early August each year, attracting over 250,000 visitors.

★ Grand Tinel
A series of fine 17th- and 19th-century Gobelin tapestries now hang in this vast banqueting hall, where cardinals gathered to elect a new pope.

★ Stag Room
Fourteenth-century hunting frescoes and ceramic tiles make Clement VI's study the palace's most lovely room.

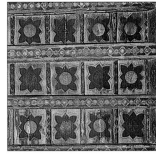

Angels' tower

Pope's chamber

Great courtyard

The Great Chapel is 20 m (66 ft) high and covers an area of 780 sq m (8,400 sq ft).

The Great Audience Hall is divided into two naves by five columns with bestiary sculpture on their capitals.

STAR FEATURES

★ Grand Tinel

★ Stag Room

BUILDING THE PALACE

The palace comprises the simple Palais Vieux of Benedict XII (1334–42) and the flamboyant Palais Neuf of Clement VI (1342–52). Ten towers, some of which are over 50 m (164 ft) high, are set in the walls to protect its four wings.

KEY

☐ By Benedict XII (1334–42)

☐ By Clement VI (1342–52)

KEY DATES

1334–42 Benedict XII begins work on the Palais Vieux.

1342–52 Clement VI expands the complex, adding the Palais Neuf.

1413 Works of art are destroyed by a fire in the Consistory Hall.

1791 The French National Assembly ransacks the palace and many of the rooms are left empty.

1947 The annual Festival d'Avignon is first held in the great courtyard.

SIMONE MARTINI

When the Papal See moved to Avignon in the early 14th century, an artistic momentum ensued, bringing the city European recognition as paintings, artists, and studios abounded. The maze of corridors and rooms in the Palais des Papes was richly decorated by skilled artists and craftsmen introduced from Italy. Pope Benedict XII wished to encourage artistic development and invited Simone Martini, a notable painter of the Sienese School, to Avignon in 1339. Martini's focus was on realism and the innovative use of 3-dimensional space. Several examples of his masterful fresco painting can be seen in the ▷ *Consistory Hall*. A fusion of styles resulted and Martini's delicate and accurate compositions influenced the emerging Gothic style of art in Italy which valued attention to detail.

Palais des Papes

THE COURT ARCHITECT

Georg Adolph Demmler (1804–86) was appointed court architect to the Dukes of Schwerin while still a young man. Many of the city of Schwerin's grander buildings can be attributed to him, among them the town hall with its Tudor-style façade, which he designed in 1835. Demmler's other works include the Marstall (1838–43), the College Buildings (1825–34) that now house the state chancellery, and his own private residence at Mecklenburgstrasse 1 (1842). The fortress-like arsenal and barracks on the south shore of the Pfaffenteich lake (1840–44) is also Demmler's work, although his greatest achievement is undoubtedly Schwerin Palace. He became a celebrated figure in Schwerin and was elected onto the Citizens' Committee in 1845.

PREVIOUS CASTLES ON THE SITE

The Slavic Obotrite princes had built themselves a castle on an island between Lake Schwerin and the Castle Lake. This, however, was destroyed in 1160 by Prince Niklot (▷ *Gateway*), the last of the Obotrite princes, who wanted to prevent the castle falling into the hands of the advancing troops of Henry the Lion. Unperturbed, Henry promptly ordered the castle to be rebuilt. The oldest building in today's complex is the ▷ *New Palace*, erected by Duke Magnus II (1477–1503). The ▷ *Palace Church* was added between 1560 and 1563 and miraculously survived the fires that in the late 16th century destroyed much of the old palace. It housed the first Protestant church in Mecklenburg. In 1616, Duke Adolf Friedrich I (1606–58) commissioned two new wings to the south-east and north, both of which were rebuilt almost beyond recognition in the 19th century.

Schwerin Palace

THE DUCAL PALACE of Schwerin, with its cupola-topped turrets and fairytale location on an island on Lake Schwerin, is probably the most beautiful example of Neo-Renaissance architecture (▷*Renaissance Style p211*) to be found in northern Germany. It was built in 1843–57 to a design by Georg Adolph Demmler and Friedrich August Stüler, who were inspired by the Château de Chambord on the Loire (▷*pp84–5*), and incorporates 16th- and 17th-century buildings on the site. Today, the palace houses the Mecklenburg-Western Pomeranian state assembly.

Garden sculpture

Fountain
The fountain at one end of the garden is surrounded by a horseshoe-shaped colonnade.

Palace Garden
The garden on three sides of the palace contains a number of rare trees and plants.

Grotto
The artificial grotto, built in 1850, is composed of roughly hewn granite blocks and supports a viewing platform overlooking the water.

★ **Throne Room**
The opulent Throne Room is decorated with coats-of-arms, statues and paintings depicting the history of the state of Mecklenburg-Schwerin and the dukes who once ruled it.

New Palace

★ **Palace Church**
The Renaissance church in the north wing was designed by the architect Johann Batista Parra. It is noted for its star-like ribbed vaulting, Neo-Gothic choir and stained-glass windows.

★ Ancestral Gallery

Portraits of the dukes of Mecklenburg from the 14th–18th centuries line the walls of this ornate gallery.

"PETERMÄNNCHEN"

According to legend, the palace's vaulted cellar is home to the Petermännchen – or "Little Peter." Clad in 17th-century attire, this benevolent if rather grumpy-looking gnome is said to protect the palace from intruders.

Castle Lake Wing

This view of the Castle Lake Wing, which was rebuilt after a devastating fire in 1913, is strongly reminiscent of the palace's French model.

Schwerin Palace

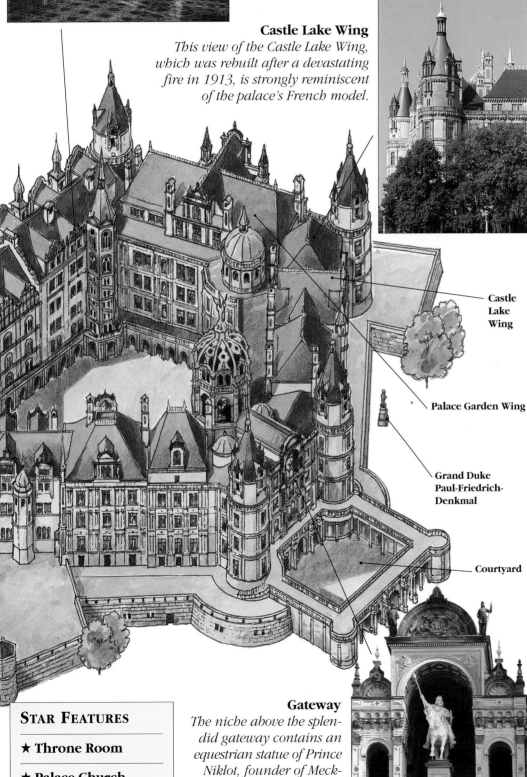

Castle Lake Wing

Palace Garden Wing

Grand Duke Paul-Friedrich-Denkmal

Courtyard

Gateway

The niche above the splendid gateway contains an equestrian statue of Prince Niklot, founder of Mecklenburg's ducal dynasty, which lived at Schwerin from 1318–1918.

KEY DATES

c.970 The first mention of a castle on this site appears in the diary of Ibrahim ibn Yakub, an Arabian traveler.

mid-1300s The Mecklenburg family takes up residence.

1553–5 Duke Johann Albrecht I has the castle rebuilt in Renaissance style and the inner courtyard richly decorated in terracotta.

1748–56 The architect Jean Laurent Legeay adds the palace garden.

1913 One-third of the palace is destroyed by fire.

1918 The Mecklenburg family abdicates and moves out of the Ducal Palace.

1990 The palace becomes the seat of the Mecklenburg-Western Pomeranian state assembly.

THE MODEL CHATEAU

Schwerin Palace is modeled on the Château de Chambord in France, built in the Renaissance style between 1519 and 1547. Designed as a hunting lodge for François I, and later used as a retreat for French kings, including Louis XIV, Chambord bristles with turrets, chimneys, oriel windows, and ramparts. It was this effect that the dukes of Mecklenburg wanted for their residence. Schwerin Palace is an artful reconstruction of the Chambord style and is a masterpiece of late 19th-century Neo-Renaissance architecture.

STAR FEATURES

★ **Throne Room**

★ **Palace Church**

★ **Ancestral Gallery**

Bremen Town Hall

Roland (right) on the Market Square in Bremen

THE STATUE OF ROLAND

This 10-m (33-ft) high statue of Roland has been a fixture of Bremen's Market Square for 600 years. A Christian knight and nephew of Charlemagne, the Holy Roman Emperor (r.800–814), Roland symbolizes a town's independence. His gaze is directed towards the cathedral, the residence of the bishop, who often sought to restrict Bremen's autonomy. Roland's sword of justice symbolizes the judiciary's independence, and the engraved motto confirms the emperor's edict, conferring town rights on Bremen. The statue was carved in 1404 by a member of the Parléř family, a well-known clan of architects and sculptors. It was the prototype for 35 similar statues in other German towns.

WESER RENAISSANCE

Bremen's Gothic Town Hall owes much of its splendor to its magnificent ▷ *façade*. Having been completely reworked by the architect Lüder von Bentheim in 1595–1612, this façade is considered an outstanding example of Weser Renaissance architecture, the style that predominated throughout the Weser region of northern Germany between 1520 and 1630. Nobles who had toured Italy returned home inspired by the Renaissance architecture they had seen and attempted to replicate it in their own designs. The ▷ *ornamental gables* and frieze along the arcade are both typical of this style, as are the richly sculptured projecting oriels.

THE BRICK FAÇADE IN THE STYLE of the Weser Renaissance makes Bremen Town Hall one of the northernmost Renaissance masterpieces to be found in mainland Europe (▷ *Renaissance Style p211*). Behind the façade lies a magnificent late-Gothic manifestation of civic pride (▷ *Gothic Style p73*). The rectangular building is decorated with medieval statuary, including life-size sandstone sculptures of Emperor Charlemagne and the seven Electors, four prophets, and four wise men. The frieze above the arcade represents an allegory of human history.

Façade
The original Gothic building was clad with a magnificent Weser Renaissance façade designed by Lüder von Bentheim in 1595–1612.

Fireplace Room
Adjoining the Gobelin Room, the Fireplace Room owes its name to a high, French marble fireplace.

★ Upper Hall
New laws were passed in the splendid Upper Hall, which occupies the entire second floor. Model sailing ships suspended from the ceiling are reminiscent of Bremen's role as a major port.

Main entrance

★ Ratskeller
The Gothic Ratskeller stores hundreds of different wines. Murals by Max Slevogt (1927) decorate the walls.

Gobelin Room

This room derives its charm from a large, exquisitely wrought tapestry produced by the 17th-century Gobelin workshop in Paris.

MUSICIANS OF BREMEN

On the north side of the Town Hall is a bronze statue of the four animals – a donkey, dog, cat, and cockerel – immortalized in the Grimm Brothers' fairytale of *The Musicians of Bremen*. It was cast by Gerhard Marcks in 1951.

★ Ornamental Gable

The architect Lüder von Bentheim gave the Town Hall façade a local touch by adding a decorative Flemish-style stepped gable that is five storys high.

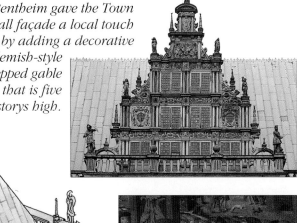

Bremen Town Hall

KEY DATES

1251 Inauguration of Bremen's first civic building, the *domus consulum*.

1405–10 The dilapidated town hall is replaced by a new Gothic structure.

1491 The plaque bearing the "12 Cautions" for the benefit of councillors is mounted in the Upper Hall.

1620 The Bacchus and what is now the Hauff Room for the storage of wine are built.

1905 Completion of the Jugendstil Room.

1909–13 Addition of the New Town Hall on the east side of the building.

1927 Completion of the murals in the Hauff Room.

THE RATSKELLER

To the west side of the Town Hall is the entrance to the ▷ *Ratskeller*, which has been serving wine since 1405. Today, more than 650 different wines can be sampled here, all of which are from German wine-growing regions and some of which are stored in decoratively carved wine casks. The atmosphere in the Ratskeller is known to have inspired many an artist. Wilhelm Hauff, for example, wrote his *Fantasies in the Bremer Ratskeller* in 1827 and these later inspired the German Impressionist painter, Max Slevogt, to paint the humorous frescoes that now decorate the Hauff Room.

The Judgment of Solomon
The mural (1532) of Solomon's court in the Upper Hall is a reference to the room's dual function as a council chamber and courtroom.

STAR FEATURES

★ **Upper Hall**

★ **Ratskeller**

★ **Ornamental Gable**

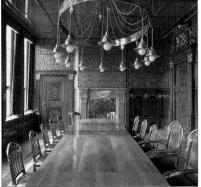

Jugendstil Room

The lower room of the two-story Gülden-kammer owes its 1905 Jugendstil makeover to the artist Heinrich Vogeler. The gilded leather wallpaper dates from the 17th century.

PREVIOUS CATHEDRALS

In 1465, Pope Paul II accorded the chapel of St Erasmus the status of a cathedral chapter. The chapel was part of the elector's new palace in Cölln on the River Spree – a town that would later merge with Berlin. In 1536, Elector Joachim II moved the chapter to the basilica of a dissolved Dominican monastery just south of his palace, and three years later it became a Lutheran church. After Elector Johann Sigismund's conversion to Calvinism in 1613, the cathedral changed denominations and became a Reformed church to both the royal court and the parish of Berlin. Between 1747 and 1750, Friedrich II (Frederick the Great) had the old church demolished and replaced with a Baroque cathedral to the north of the royal palace. In 1817, to mark the union of Prussia's Lutheran and Reformed churches, King Friedrich Wilhelm III asked the architect Karl Friedrich Schinkel to redesign the cathedral in the Neo-Classical style (▷ *Neo-Classical Style p79*). The work was completed in 1822.

THE SAUER ORGAN

When Raschdorff's cathedral was consecrated in 1905, the congregation was able to admire not only the new building, but also the sound of the ▷ *Sauer Organ*, which, for a time, was the largest in Germany. The organ-builder, Wilhelm Sauer, had made organs for the church of St Thomas, Leipzig, and the cathedral in Bremen. But while the Berlin organ was the highpoint of his career, it also marked the end of "orchestral organs" that tried to reproduce the volume and range of a symphony orchestra. This Sauer organ is known for its full and rather dark sound. Badly damaged at the end of the World War II, it was painstakingly restored and reinaugurated in 1993.

Berlin Cathedral

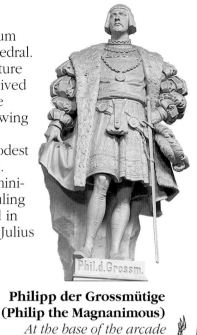

At the northern point of Berlin's Museum Island stands the city's imposing cathedral. It is a remarkable Neo-Baroque structure (▷ *Baroque Style p111*) that has survived the architectural whims of successive rulers and extensive restoration following its destruction in World War II. The original cathedral was based on a modest Baroque design by Johann Boumann. Built between 1747 and 1750 on the site of a Dominican church, it included the original crypt of the ruling Hohenzollern family, one of the largest of its kind in Europe. The present Neo-Baroque structure is by Julius Raschdorff and dates from 1894 to 1905. It has a central copper dome, 98 m (321 ft) high.

Frederick III's coat of arms

Figures of the Apostles

Philipp der Grossmütige (Philip the Magnanimous)

At the base of the arcade stand the statues of church reformers and those who supported the Reformation. The statue of Prince Philip the Magnanimous is the work of Walter Schott.

★ Church Interior

The impressive and richly-decorated interior was designed by Julius Raschdorff at the start of the 20th century.

Sauer's Organ

The organ, the work of Wilhelm Sauer, has an exquisitely carved case. The instrument contains some 7,200 pipes.

Main entrance

★ The Elector's Tomb

This tomb is the oldest relic to be found in the cathedral, dating from c.1530. It was commissioned from the Vischers' studio in Nuremberg by Joachim I for his grandfather, Johann Cicero.

The Four Evangelists

Mosaics depicting the Four Evangelists decorate the ceilings of smaller niches in the cathedral. They were designed by Woldemar Friedrich.

The Ascension

The stained glass in the windows of the apses depicts scenes from the life of Jesus. They are the work of Anton von Werner.

The main altar, saved from the previous cathedral, is the work of Friedrich August Stüler. It dates from 1820.

KEY DATES

1894–1905 Building of the new cathedral by Raschdorff.

1951 Having been largely destroyed during World War II, the cathedral's dome is temporarily roofed over.

1975–83 The cathedral is rebuilt in simplified form, without the Memorial Chapel.

1984–93 Restoration of the interior, including the Imperial Staircase (1989) and Sermon Chapel (1993).

1999 Berlin's Museum Island, on which the cathedral is situated, becomes a UNESCO World Heritage Site.

2002 Completion of the final reconstructed mosaic inside the dome.

HOHENZOLLERN CRYPT

Within Berlin Cathedral is one of Europe's most important royal burial sites. The Hohenzollern Crypt contains 94 sarcophagi and tombstones from the 16th to the early 20th century, some of which were taken from family vaults inside previous buildings on the site. The tombs include those of Great Elector Friedrich Wilhelm (1620–88) and King Friedrich I of Prussia (1657–1713) and his wife, Sophie Charlotte (▷ *Sarcophagi of Friedrich I and his Wife*). After the devastation of World War II, the crypt, complete with its tombstones and ornate sarcophagi made of wood, metal, and stone, was restored and finally reopened to the public in 1999.

The Pulpit

The elaborate Neo-Baroque pulpit was originally part of the cathedral's ornate decor in the early 20th century.

★ Sarcophagi of Friedrich I and his Wife

Both tombs were designed by Andreas Schlüter. The sculpture on Sophie Charlotte's sarcophagus depicts death.

STAR FEATURES
★ **Church Interior**
★ **The Elector's Tomb**
★ **Sarcophagi of Friedrich I and his Wife**

Frederick the Great of Prussia

THE OWNER

Frederick II of Prussia (r.1740–86), whose victory in the Second Silesian War (1744–45) earned him the appendage "the Great", was born in 1712. Unlike his father, the "Soldier King", Frederick II was an enlightened absolutist. Not only did he invite the French author Voltaire to visit the court in Berlin (between 1750 and 1753, Voltaire was a frequent guest at Sanssouci), but he also instituted important educational reforms as well as initiating a large-scale building project in Potsdam. As a man of talent with an artistic temperament, Frederick wanted Sanssouci to be a pleasure palace, far removed from the cares of state. He was a prolific writer on the military, governmental issues, and history.

FREDERICIAN ROCOCO

The Palace of Sanssouci is a classic example of Frederician Rococo. Prevalent throughout Prussia during the early part of Frederick the Great's reign in the 18th century, this style combined elements of Classicism (▷ *Classical Style p78*) with those of Baroque (▷ *Baroque Style p111*) and Rococo (▷ *Rococo Style p118*). Unlike the highly decorative Rococo architecture of southern Germany, France, and Italy, however, Frederician Rococo is much less "cluttered" and the buildings are remarkable for their clarity of design.

Sanssouci Palace, Potsdam

THE NAME SANSSOUCI is French for "without a care" and gives a good indication of the flamboyant character of this enchanting Rococo palace, built in 1745. The original sketches, made by Friedrich II (Frederick the Great) himself, were finalized by Georg Wenzeslaus von Knobelsdorff. The glorious interiors were designed by Knobelsdorff and Johann August Nahl. The king so loved this palace that he asked to be buried here, near the tomb of his Italian greyhounds. He was actually interred in the Garnisonkirche, Potsdam, but his final wishes were carried out in 1991.

Bacchanalian Figures
The carved male and female bacchanalian figures on the pilasters are the work of Friedrich Christian Glume.

The colonnade frames the view of the artificial ruins on the hill.

The wings were added to the building between 1841 and 1842.

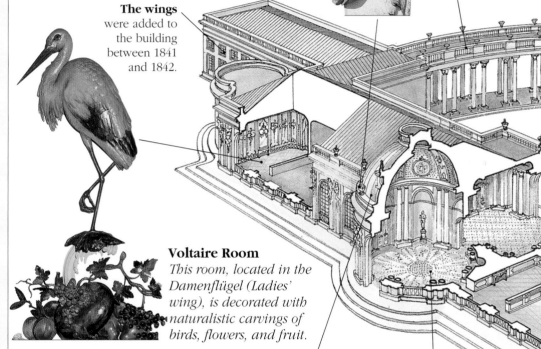

Voltaire Room
This room, located in the Damenflügel (Ladies' wing), is decorated with naturalistic carvings of birds, flowers, and fruit.

Domed Roof
The oxidized green dome covers the Marble Hall. It is embellished with Baroque sculptures.

STAR FEATURES

★ **Fêtes Galantes**

★ **Recital Room**

Marble Hall
The imposing marble Hall is decorated with pairs of columns made from Carrara marble. Frederick the Great wanted this room to be loosely based on the Pantheon in Rome.

Arbour
The palace design is complemented by picturesque arbors and pergolas decorated with sun motifs.

Between 1755 and 1764, Frederick the Great had a building erected for no other purpose than to house his collection of paintings (which included works by both Rubens and Caravaggio). This is Germany's oldest purpose-built art gallery.

★ Fêtes Galantes (c.1715)
The real jewels in the palace are the enchanting paintings by Antoine Watteau. He was one of Frederick II's favorite artists.

Weimar Urn (1785)
This Neo-Classical urn from the Berlin company KPM is a copy of the original urn, which was presented to the Duchess of Weimar.

KEY DATES

1745–7 Building of Sanssouci Palace.

1748 Frederick II has artificial ruins erected in the park of Sanssouci.

1754–64 Building of the Chinese Pagoda under Johann Gottfried Büring.

1841–2 Two new wings are added to Sanssouci.

1990 Sanssouci becomes a UNESCO World Heritage Site.

THE ARCHITECT

Georg Wenzeslaus von Knobelsdorff (1699–1753) is the main proponent of Frederician Rococo. Originally an army man, Knobelsdorff decided in 1729 to take up both architecture and painting and began having lessons with Antoine Pesne (▷ *Recital Room*). Frederick II took a liking to Knobelsdorff and while Crown Prince, commissioned him to build a small temple of Apollo in Neuruppin, north of Potsdam, and to enlarge his nearby palace of Rheinsberg (1737). On Frederick's accession in 1740, he appointed Knobelsdorff superintendent of the royal palaces and gardens and the buildings of the royal provinces. The architect went on to build both the Stadtschloss in Potsdam (1744–51), which has since been destroyed, and Berlin's Staatsoper unter den Linden (1741–43). He also designed the park of Sanssouci.

★ Recital Room
The walls of the salon are lined with paintings by Antoine Pesne, based on Greek mythology.

Library
Frederick the Great's library contains 2,100 books. The walls are lined with cedar to create a contemplative atmosphere.

Sanssouci Palace

Hildesheim Cathedral

Thanks to bishops Bernward and Hezilo, Hildesheim's majestic St Mary's Cathedral contains an exceptionally rich collection of Romanesque works of art. While the diocese itself was founded in 815, the first church was built on the site in the 11th century, but was added to and reworked in the 12th and 14th centuries (▷ *Romanesque Style p199*). The cathedral suffered such severe bomb damage in World War II that it had to be almost entirely rebuilt. Its museum contains countless medieval treasures, including ancient gospels, reliquaries, crosses, and vestments.

Illustrated book of gospels in the Cathedral Museum

THREE GREAT BISHOPS

The 11th century saw a tremendous flowering of arts and culture in Hildesheim thanks mainly to three bishops, Bernward (993–1022), Godehard (1022–38), and Hezilo (1054–79). Bishop Bernward was an especially important patron of the arts who attracted craftsmen to the town from far and wide. Many of the cathedral's Romanesque treasures were commissioned by him (▷ *Pillar of Christ,* ▷ *Bernward Doors*). He is buried in the crypt of Hildesheim's St Michael's Church, which he founded in 1010. Bishop Godehard (▷ *Crypt*), who like Bernward was also canonized, gave his name to the town's Church of St Godehard (1133–72). Bishop Hezilo, founder of St Maurice's Church, played a key role in having work on the cathedral continued.

THE CATHEDRAL MUSEUM

The main highlights of the museum are the treasures belonging to the Cathedral Chapter. The oldest exhibit, the cathedral's founding reliquary, dates from the 9th century, although the collection also includes medieval manuscripts and costly utensils and vestments for liturgical use, many of which are thought to have belonged to Bishop Bernward, as did both the Large Cross and the Silver Bernward Cross.

New Paradise
Built onto the transept, the New Paradise features a Gothic six-paned window and is decorated with statues of the Virgin Mary and Bishops Bernward and Godehard.

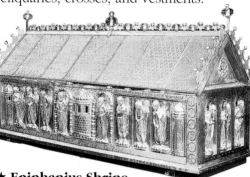

★ Epiphanius Shrine
This splendid shrine (c.1140) is made of silver- and gold-plated sheet copper and contains relics of the cathedral's patrons.

★ Bernward Doors
The Romanesque bronze doors were a gift from Bishop Bernward in 1015. The panels show scenes from the Old and New Testaments.

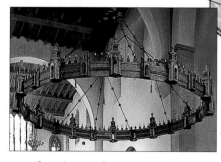

Hezilo Chandelier
This copper chandelier dates from 1060. More than 6 m (20 ft) in diameter, it symbolizes the Holy City of Jerusalem.

★ Pillar of Christ
The bronze Pillar of Christ (c.1020), commissioned by Bishop Bernward, is decorated with a spiral relief showing 24 scenes from the life of Jesus.

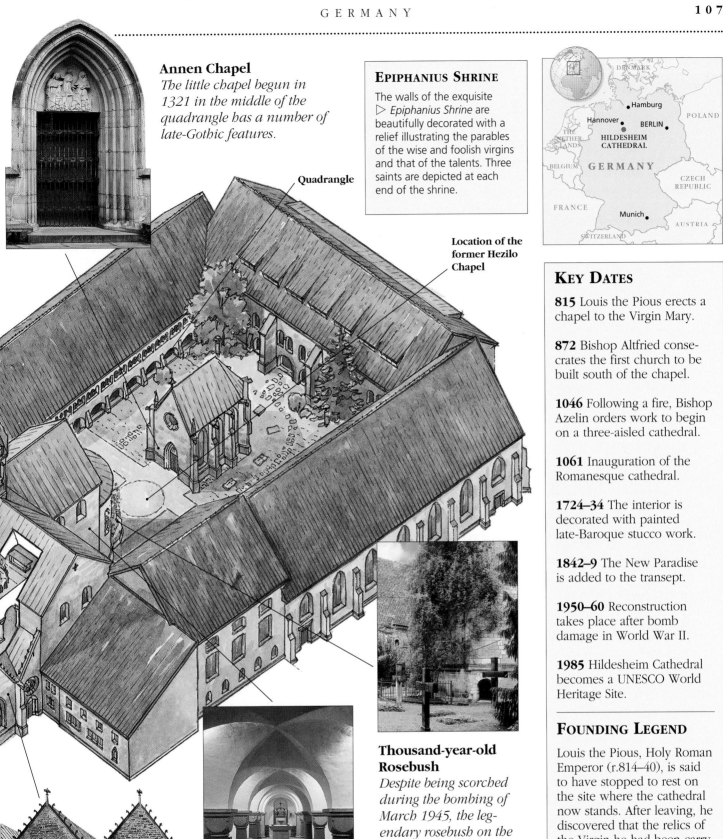

Annen Chapel
The little chapel begun in 1321 in the middle of the quadrangle has a number of late-Gothic features.

Quadrangle

EPIPHANIUS SHRINE

The walls of the exquisite ▷ *Epiphanius Shrine* are beautifully decorated with a relief illustrating the parables of the wise and foolish virgins and that of the talents. Three saints are depicted at each end of the shrine.

Location of the former Hezilo Chapel

Hildesheim Cathedral

KEY DATES

815 Louis the Pious erects a chapel to the Virgin Mary.

872 Bishop Altfried consecrates the first church to be built south of the chapel.

1046 Following a fire, Bishop Azelin orders work to begin on a three-aisled cathedral.

1061 Inauguration of the Romanesque cathedral.

1724–34 The interior is decorated with painted late-Baroque stucco work.

1842–9 The New Paradise is added to the transept.

1950–60 Reconstruction takes place after bomb damage in World War II.

1985 Hildesheim Cathedral becomes a UNESCO World Heritage Site.

FOUNDING LEGEND

Louis the Pious, Holy Roman Emperor (r.814–40), is said to have stopped to rest on the site where the cathedral now stands. After leaving, he discovered that the relics of the Virgin he had been carrying – allegedly now contained in the reliquary in the Cathedral Museum – had been left behind and sent his chaplain to fetch them. The man was unable to extricate them from the bush (▷ *Thousand-year-old Rosebush*) on which they had been hung for safe-keeping. Louis took this to be a sign from God that he should build a chapel on the site.

Thousand-year-old Rosebush
Despite being scorched during the bombing of March 1945, the legendary rosebush on the apse of the cathedral flowered again in May of that year and has continued doing so ever since.

Crypt
Beneath the choir, the crypt contains the Godehard Shrine created after the canonization of Bishop Godehard in 1131, one of the cathedral's early patrons.

STAR FEATURES

★ **Epiphanius Shrine**

★ **Bernward Doors**

★ **Pillar of Christ**

Side Chapels
The many chapels that line the side aisles of the nave were added to the cathedral in the 14th century.

Altarpiece of the Crucifixion

EKKEHARD'S CHURCH

Count Ekkehard I is said to have founded the city of Naumburg with the building of a castle *(Nuwenburg)*. In 1028, his sons, Ekkehard II and Hermann (▷ *Founders' Statues)* were successful in having the seat of the bishop moved from Zeitz to Naumburg and as they themselves were childless, bequeathed all their property to the church. The construction of an early-Romanesque church, the Stiftskirche der Ekkehardinger (some remains of which can still be seen in today's cathedral), began just a few years later.

STATUES OF EKKEHARD AND UTA

Ekkehard II and his wife, Uta, are the best known of the 12 ▷ *Founders' Statues* inside the choir. Together with a second couple, Ekkehard's brother Hermann and his wife Reglindis, they form the center of a group of eight men and four women, the others being the Counts Dietmar, Syzzo, Wilhelm, Thimo, Konrad, and Dietrich and the Countesses Gerburg and Gepa. While it was highly unusual to place images of lay men and women in the choir, it was doubtless felt to be justified in this case, given the sums these nobles had contributed towards the new cathedral. Carved in limestone some 150–200 years after the subjects had died, what makes these life-size statues so exceptional is the realism of the portraiture seen in each individual's pose and facial expression. The 13th-century statues' clothing was given a coat of paint in the 16th century.

Naumburg Cathedral

THE IMPRESSIVE Cathedral of Saints Peter and Paul in Naumburg is one of the finest Gothic structures in Germany (▷ *Gothic Style p73)*. The present cathedral is the second to be built on the site; only a section of the eastern crypt of the earlier Romanesque church has survived (▷ *Romanesque Style p199)*. Construction started before 1210, with the earliest parts including the late-Romanesque east choir, the transept, and the main body. The early-Gothic west choir was built in the mid-13th century. The northeast towers date from the 15th century, the southwest towers from 1894.

Stained-glass Windows in the Presbytery
The stained-glass windows depict scenes of the apostles of virtue and sin. Some sections are original 13th-century work, but two were completed in the 19th century.

West choir

★ Founders' Statues
The statues of Ekkehard II and his wife, Uta, are true masterpieces – the artist succeeded marvelously in capturing the beauty and sensitivity of his subjects.

STAR FEATURES

★ **Founders' Statues**

★ **Portal of the West Reading Room**

★ **Main Portal**

★ Portal of the West Reading Room
The Gothic twin portal depicts the Crucifixion, a moving and highly expressive group sculpture by the brilliant "Naumburg Master" whose identity remains unknown.

Pulpit

The richly ornamented pulpit basket, from 1466, and the adjoining stairs have recently been renovated.

THE WEST ROOD SCREEN

The purpose of the rood screen in medieval churches was to separate the chancel from the rest of the church. The West Rood Screen in Naumburg Cathedral is a work of consummate artistry.

★ Main Portal

The late-Romanesque, 13th-century portal is decorated on the left side with eagles. The tympanum features Christ in a mandorla (almond-shaped area) supported by angels.

Sarcophagus of Bishop Dietrich II

East choir

East Choir Altar

This Gothic altar features the Virgin Mary with the Infant Jesus, surrounded by the figures of the saints.

The Main Altar, built in the mid-14th-century, is a stone retable depicting the Crucifixion and the saints, which was transferred from another altar.

St Mary's Altar

This late-Gothic triptych (c.1510) depicts the Virgin Mary with the Infant, framed by Saints Barbara and Catherine, with the Apostles in the wings.

KEY DATES

1042 The first early-Romanesque church is consecrated.

c.1170 Building of the crypt beneath the east choir.

c.1210 Various additions to the cathedral (the nave and transept, east choir, and east towers) are consecrated.

1250 Building of the west choir containing a rood screen showing the Crucifixion of Christ.

c.1330 Extension of the east choir.

c.1500 Raising of the Romanesque east towers.

1711–13 Copper domes are added to the east towers.

THE NAUMBURG MASTER

We do not know his name or where he came from, yet the Naumburg Master is one of the greatest artists of the Middle Ages. His most outstanding works, namely the ▷ *Founders' Statues* and the West Rood Screen, can be seen in Naumburg Cathedral, which is why he is known as the "Naumburg Master". He is thought to have belonged to a team of masons at Reims Cathedral and to have created a rood screen in Mainz Cathedral. He worked in Naumburg in the mid-13th century. The individuality and expressiveness of his statues is remarkable among medieval sculptures.

Naumburg Cathedral

Hofkirche (1738–51), Dresden's Baroque Catholic cathedral

OLD MASTERS

The collection of old masters now housed in the ▷ *Old Masters' Gallery* of the Zwinger was begun in 1560. However, it was not until the first half of the 18th century, under Augustus the Strong and his son, Augustus III, that in the space of just 60 years it became one of Europe's most important collections of paintings. The main focus is on Italian Renaissance and Baroque painting and on the Flemish and Dutch masters of the 17th century. The architect Gottfried Semper later built a gallery adjoining the Zwinger to house the collection, which today numbers more than 760 paintings.

AUGUSTUS THE STRONG

As the greatest promoter of Dresden Baroque, Frederick Augustus I, Elector of Saxony (r.1694–1733) and King of Poland (r.1697–1706, 1709–33), commissioned a number of important buildings, including the Zwinger in Dresden and the Residence in Warsaw. Inspired by the Château de Versailles, his magnificent projects earned Dresden the nickname "Florence on the Elbe", and reflect the image Augustus had of himself as an absolutist ruler in the style of Louis XIV of France.

The Zwinger, Dresden

THE MOST FAMOUS building in Dresden is the Zwinger, a beautiful Baroque structure. Its name means "intermural", and it was built in the space between the former town fortifications. Commissioned by Augustus the Strong, it was constructed in 1709–32 to a design by Matthäus Daniel Pöppelmann, with the help of the sculptor Balthasar Permoser. Its spacious courtyard, once used to stage tournaments, festivals, and fireworks displays, is completely surrounded by galleries into which are set pavilions and gates. Today it houses several museums.

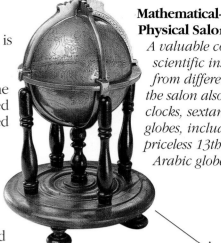

Mathematical-Physical Salon
A valuable collection of scientific instruments from different ages, the salon also features clocks, sextants, and globes, including a priceless 13th-century Arabic globe of the sky.

Crown Gate
This gate owes its name to the crown positioned on top of its dome.

Main entrance

Allegorical figures crown the balustrades.

★ Porcelain Collection
The Porcelain Collection holds Japanese and Chinese pieces, but its centerpiece is a collection of Meissen porcelain, including parts of the stunning Swan Service made for Heinrich Brühl, to a design by Joachim Kändler.

Carillon Pavilion
Once known as Town Pavilion (Stadtpavillon), the building's name was changed to Carillon Pavilion (Glockenspielpavillon) when it acquired a set of Meissen porcelain bells, in 1924–36.

Wall Pavilion

A stunning marriage of architecture and sculpture, this Baroque pavilion is crowned by a statue of Hercules, symbolizing the Elector, Augustus the Strong.

WHAT'S IN A NAME?

The word "Zwinger" originally meant the space between two fortifying walls. Dresden's Zwinger occupies what was once a walled garden and was intended not just as a residence, but as a fairground, too.

★ Nymph Fountain
This fountain features tritons and nymphs, sculptures, and grottoes, which were popular in the Baroque era.

Courtyard

Old Masters Gallery
Occupying the wing built by Gottfried Semper in 1847–55, the gallery contains works by Raphael, Titian, and Vermeer, among others.

★ Armory
Exhibited in the armory are magnificent arms, with the best examples dating from the 16th century, such as a suit of armor made for Erik XIV by Eliseus Libaerts in 1562–4.

STAR FEATURES

★ **Porcelain Collection**

★ **Nymph Fountain**

★ **Armory**

The Zwinger

KEY DATES

1709 Augustus the Strong commissions the palace.

1711 Work commences on the Nymphs' Fountain.

1716–19 The Wall Pavilion is built.

1719 The Zwinger is inaugurated as the venue for the wedding of Frederick Augustus I, Elector of Saxony.

1728 Completion of the palace complex.

1746 Installation of the Mathematical-Physical Salon.

1820–30 Gardens and a pond are created in the inner courtyard.

1945–63 Reconstruction of the bomb-damaged palace.

BAROQUE STYLE

Baroque was the style that predominated for much of the 17th and early 18th centuries. Whereas in Italy the golden age of Baroque was the High Baroque of 1630–80, Germany saw a flourishing of Late Baroque well beyond 1700. The hallmarks of Baroque architecture are its preference for dynamic, curvaceous forms and broken gables, as exemplified by the ▷ *Wall Pavilion*; its *Gesamtkunstwerk*, or fusion of the arts to create an exuberant whole; and its liberal use of ornamentation and sculpture (▷ *Nymphs' Fountain*). Also typical of this style is the picturesque splendor of the Zwinger's interior.

Cologne Cathedral at night

THE CATHEDRAL BELLS

The 3.4-tonne bell cast in 1418 in honor of the Three Kings was tuned to the note B. It hung in a belfry adjacent to the cathedral, but in 1437 was moved to the south tower. Eleven years later, it was joined by Europe's largest bell, the 10-tonne "Pretiosa" ("Precious One"), tuned to G. When rung together, the bells produced a G-major chord. In 1449, the 4.3-tonne "Speciosa" ("Beautiful One") was added. It is tuned to A so that Cologne Cathedral became the first church to have its bells tuned to a melody rather than a chord. The first bell has since been replaced.

THE CHOIR

About 30 years after the cathedral's foundation stone was laid, the pillars of the choir were decorated with early-Gothic statues of Christ, the Virgin Mary, and the 12 Apostles. These larger-than-life figures are clad in splendid robes. Above them there is a choir of angels playing musical instruments, symbolizing the heavenly music played to celebrate the celestial coronation of Mary the Virgin. The coronation itself is depicted in the figures of Christ and Mary. A similar interpretation, dating from 1248, can be seen in the church of Sainte-Chapelle in Paris. There, too, 12 of the pillars supporting the building symbolize the 12 Apostles as the most important pillars of the Christian church.

Cologne Cathedral

10th-century Gero Cross

THE MOST FAMOUS Gothic structure in Germany, Cologne Cathedral is also unusually complex, whether in terms of its splendor, its size or even simply the date of its construction. The foundation stone of the current cathedral was laid on 15 August 1248 and the presbytery consecrated in 1322. The cathedral was built gradually until c.1520, but remained unfinished until the 19th century. The building was finally completed in 1842–80, according to the rediscovered, original Gothic designs (▷ *Gothic Style p 73*).

Cathedral Interior
The presbytery, the ambulatory and the chapels retain a large number of Gothic, mainly early-14th-century, stained-glass windows.

Engelbert Reliquary (c.1630)
The cathedral treasury is famous for its large collection of golden objects, vestments, and the fine ornamentation of its liturgical books.

Pinnacles
Elaborately decorated pinnacles top the supporting pillars.

Main entrance

Petrusportal, or the portal of St Peter, the only one built in the second half of the 14th century, has five Gothic figures.

STAR FEATURES

★ **Gothic Stalls**

★ **Shrine of the Three Kings**

★ **Altar of the Magi**

★ Gothic Stalls
The massive oak stalls, built in 1308–11, were the largest that have ever been made in Germany.

Buttresses support the entire bulk of the cathedral.

Semicircular arches transfer the thrust of the vaults onto the buttresses.

EARLIER CHURCHES
Several churches had come and gone on the site by the time the first cathedral was completed in 870. Today's larger Gothic cathedral became necessary owing to the numbers of pilgrims wanting to see the Shrine of the Three Kings.

Cologne Cathedral

KEY DATES

1248 The cathedral's foundation stone is laid.

1265 The outer walls of the choir and adjacent chapels are completed.

c.1530 Work on the cathedral halts with the south tower at 58 m (190 ft) high.

1794 French troops use the cathedral as a warehouse.

1801 The cathedral is reconsecrated.

1842–80 Completion of the cathedral according to historical plans.

1996 Cologne Cathedral becomes a UNESCO World Heritage Site.

SHRINE OF THE THREE KINGS

The ▷ *Shrine of the Three Kings*, the largest reliquary in the western world, is located near the ▷ *High Altar*. Studded with precious and semi-precious stones, this shrine is a masterpiece of medieval goldsmithery. Its sides are decorated with images of the prophets and apostles, the adoration of the Kings, and the baptism of Christ. The rear depicts a portrait of Rainald von Dassel, Archbishop of Cologne (1159–67). As chancellor to Emperor Barbarossa (r.1152–90), he is said to have brought the mortal remains of the Three Kings from Milan to Cologne in 1164. On 6 January every year, the front of the shrine is opened to reveal the skulls.

High Altar
The Gothic altar slab, which dates back to the consecration of the presbytery, depicts the Coronation of the Virgin Mary, flanked by the 12 Apostles.

★ Shrine of the Three Kings
This huge Romanesque reliquary was made by Nikolaus von Verdun in 1181–1220 to hold the relics of the Three Kings. These relics were brought to Cologne in 1164 for Emperor Friedrich I Barbarossa.

★ Altar of the Magi
This splendid altar (c.1445), the work of Stephan Lochner, is dedicated to the Three Kings, the patrons of Cologne.

Mailänder Madonna
This fine early-Gothic carving of the Milan Madonna and Child dates from around 1290. It is currently displayed in the Marienkapelle.

On 18 and 19 October 1817, the Jenaische Burschenschaft, a group of students from Jena in eastern Thuringia, organized a convention at Wartburg Castle to commemorate both the beginning of the Reformation in 1517 and the Battle of Leipzig in 1813. This convention formed the high point of the student reform movement calling for the political, economic and religious unity of Germany.

THE REFORMER

Martin Luther publicized his criticisms of the Catholic Church by nailing 95 theses to the door of Wittenberg Church on 31 October 1517. It was this action that led to his excommunication in December 1520, although he continued to defend his position, even when summoned before the Diet of Worms less than a year later. While on his way home from Worms, Luther was captured on the orders of Frederick the Wise of Saxony and for his own safety taken to Wartburg Castle (▷ *Luther's Study*). He remained at Wartburg from May 1521 to March 1522 and while there, in just 11 weeks, translated the entire New Testament into the German vernacular. Published in 1522 as the *September Testament*, this translation was of seminal importance to the development of written High German.

Martin Luther (1483–1546)

Wartburg Castle, Eisenach

THE MIGHTY FORTRESS towering above Eisenach, in Thuringia, is the legendary castle probably founded by Ludwig the Leaper in the 11th century. Reputedly, it was the setting for the singing contest immortalized by Richard Wagner in his opera *Tannhäuser*. Between 1211 and 1228 the castle was the home of St Elizabeth of Thuringia, and from May 1521 to March 1522 the reformer Martin Luther found refuge here while he translated the New Testament into German. Major reconstruction in the 19th century gave the castle its old-time romantic character.

Singing Hall
The hall in its present form is the result of restoration work. It was said to have been the scene of the famous Minnesänger *(minstrels') contest, in Richard Wagner's opera* Tannhäuser *(1842–5).*

★ St Elizabeth's Rooms
The mosaics adorning the walls of St Elizabeth's rooms illustrate the story of the saint's life. They were designed by August Oetken and placed in 1902–06.

The Palas (Great Hall)

Landgraves' Chambers
In 1854 the Landgraves' Chambers in the oldest part of the castle, the Palas, were decorated with paintings depicting the castle's history, by Moritz von Schwind.

STAR FEATURES

★ **St Elizabeth's Rooms**

★ **Luther's Study**

Bergfried
This vast square tower is the work of 19th-century restorers. Its base partially includes foundations of its medieval predecessor and it is crowned with a 4-m (13-ft) tall Latin cross.

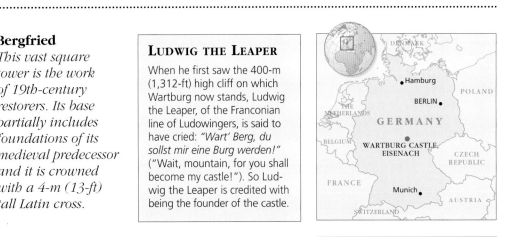

The Torhalle (gate house) erected in 1865, forms the entrance to the main castle.

The Dirnitz (heated hall) was constructed in the 19th century.

Margareth Wartburg

★ Luther's Study
The room where Martin Luther lived and worked for ten months is very plainly furnished and has simple wood paneling on the walls.

Vogtei
In 1872 this building acquired an original oriel window (c.1475), brought here from the Harsdörffersches House in Nuremberg.

Entrance gate

New Chambers
These chambers were added during the mid-19th century. Today they house an art collection with sculptures from the workshop of Tilman Riemenschneider (c.1460–1531).

KEY DATES

1067 Wartburg Castle is founded.

1172–1217 Landgraves Ludwig III and Hermann I have the castle enlarged in late-Romanesque style (▷ *Romanesque Style p199).*

1190–1220 Addition of the Romanesque Palace.

1838–90 Reconstruction of the ruined Wartburg.

1980 Further restoration work begins.

1999 The castle becomes a UNESCO World Heritage Site.

SINGING CONTEST

The legend of the Minstrels' Contest (▷ *Singing Hall),* reputed to have taken place in Wartburg Castle, has its origin in an anthology of poetry collected in Thuringia between 1260 and 1270. One poem, *In Praise of the Prince,* describes a singing competition at the court of Hermann I of Thuringia, in which Heinrich von Ofterdingen was outperformed by his rivals, Walther von der Vogelweide, Biterolf, Reinmar von Zweten, and Wolfram von Eschenbach. The poem *Riddle* describes a singing duel between two brothers. Some 600 years later, the story of the contest inspired Richard Wagner (1813–83) to compose his opera *Tannhäuser.* The tonal language of this work was unlike anything heard before and was to prove a challenge to the singers of the day.

Wartburg Castle

Mainz Cathedral

MARTIN OF TOURS

Martin of Tours is thought to have become the patron saint of Mainz Cathedral in the mid-6th century, although the earliest documentary evidence of his patronage dates from the mid-8th century. Since then, St Martin has been revered as the patron saint of the Franks and there are numerous references to this in the cathedral. The most splendid of these are the sculptures of St Martin on various tombs, the depiction of the saint with two beggars in the choir stalls, and the relief decorating the font. ▷ *St Martin's Choir* was named for him.

Half-timbered houses in Mainz

CORONATION CHURCH

In Germany, the coronation of the monarch was an extremely solemn and highly symbolic act, usually involving the king's anointment by the Church. Until the 11th century, the ceremony was performed by the Archbishop of Mainz and several regents were crowned in the cathedral. The service was based on that used by the Pope to crown the Holy Roman Emperor. In 1024, the office of coronation bishop passed to the Archbishop of Cologne and in the centuries following, most German rulers were crowned in the chapels of the imperial palaces or in Aachen Cathedral. In the 16th century, Mainz Cathedral once again became the venue for the coronation ceremony in Germany.

Mainz Cathedral

Crucifix in the St Gotthard Chapel

THE GREATEST ATTRACTION of the Rhineland city of Mainz is its superb cathedral, gleaming red in the sunshine. Together with those of Speyer and Worms it is one of the only three Romanesque imperial cathedrals to have survived almost intact to this day (▷ *Romanesque Style p199*). Its framework was laid out in 1081–1137 and 1183–1239, but its oldest parts date from the early 11th century, with the rows of Gothic side chapels added during the 13th and 14th centuries. Although neither the Gothic altars nor the magnificent choir screen have survived to this day, it is still possible to see the large group of bishops' monuments dating from the 13th to 19th centuries.

Pulpit
This Neo-Gothic pulpit was made by Joseph Scholl, 1834 (▷ Gothic Style p73).

Two large and two small towers are symmetrically positioned on the ends of the cathedral.

Portal of the "Memorie" Burial Chapel
The late-Gothic portal, leading to the Romanesque burial chapel of the cathedral canons, was made by Madern Gerthener, after 1425.

St Stephen's Choir
The Romanesque eastern choir, one of the first parts to be built, is simpler in style than other parts of the cathedral.

Round staircase towers are from the previous building, built in the early 11th century.

★ **Monument of Heinrich Ferdinand von der Leyen**
This Baroque monument of the cathedral rector, by Johann Mauritz Gröninger, was erected in 1706.

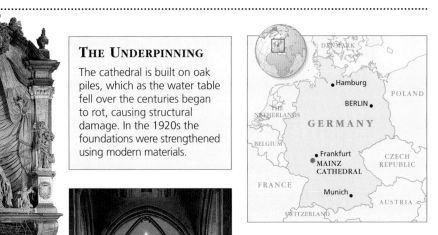

THE UNDERPINNING

The cathedral is built on oak piles, which as the water table fell over the centuries began to rot, causing structural damage. In the 1920s the foundations were strengthened using modern materials.

DENMARK

• Hamburg
THE NETHERLANDS
BERLIN •
POLAND
GERMANY
BELGIUM
• Frankfurt
FRANCE
MAINZ CATHEDRAL
CZECH REPUBLIC
Munich •
AUSTRIA
SWITZERLAND

St Martin's Choir
The late-Romanesque western choir with its trefoil closing is an early 13th-century addition.

KEY DATES

975 Building work commences.

1009 A fire destroys much of the building.

1036 Consecration of the rebuilt cathedral.

1081 The cathedral is again ravaged by fire.

1239 Completion of the Romanesque cathedral.

1769 The west tower is rebuilt with a stone steeple.

1924–28 The rotten foundations are repaired.

TOMBS INSIDE THE CATHEDRAL

The most impressive tombs in the cathedral are those of 45 bishops of Mainz from the 13th–18th centuries. These are located in the nave, as well as in the walls of the transept and side altars. Among the most beautiful are those dating from the transition from late Gothic to Renaissance style, such as the tombs of the Archbishops Berthold von Henneberg (1504), ▷ *Jakob von Liebenstein*, and Uriel von Gemmingen (1514). These are all the work of Hans Backoffen, a mason employed by the archbishops and electors of the city. The tombs of the later bishops of Mainz can be seen in the crypt beneath the west choir (▷ *St Martin's Choir*). They are more modest in design.

★ **Stalls**
The superb Rococo oak stalls encircling almost the entire presbytery were created by Franz Anton Hermann in 1767 (▷ Rococo Style p118).

Main entrance

Tomb of Jakob von Liebenstein
The late-Gothic tomb of the archbishop von Liebenstein, who died in 1508, is the work of Hans Backoffen. It depicts the deceased in draped robes, lying under an ornate canopy.

STAR FEATURES

★ **Monument of Heinrich Ferdinand von der Leyen**

★ **Stalls**

Mainz Cathedral

TIEPOLO

Born in Venice, the Italian painter, Giovanni Battista Tiepolo (1696–1770) is considered the last great master of Venetian art. He created numerous altarpieces and frescoes for churches, castles, palaces, and villas in Italy and Germany. His ceiling in the ▷ *Treppenhaus* is an allegorical depiction of the four continents and an outstanding example of fresco painting.

ROCOCO STYLE

The Würzburg Residence is such a fine example of German Rococo that it had a style named after it, Würzburg Rococo. Typical of this style are the vast *trompe-l'oeil* painted ceilings and large, domed rooms. Rococo derives from the French word *rocaille*, meaning "rock-work", a decorative trend for both interiors and façades featuring abstract, shell-like forms and curves. Trees, flowers, and Chinese scenes were among the most popular motifs. Stucco craftsmen and wood-carvers became just as revered as architects and painters for the quality and splendor of their work.

An example of the decorative stucco work typical of Rococo

Würzburg Residence

Sculpture in the Residence garden

A MASTERPIECE OF GERMAN ROCOCO, the Residence was commissioned by two prince-bishops, the brothers Johann Philipp Franz and Friedrich Karl von Schönborn, as an episcopal palace. Its construction between 1720 and 1744 was supervised by several architects, including Johann Lukas von Hildebrandt and Maximilian von Welsch. However, the Residence is mainly associated with the name of Balthasar Neumann, the creator of its remarkable Baroque staircase (▷ *Baroque Style p111*).

★ Treppenhaus
The work of the Venetian artist Giovanni Battista Tiepolo, the largest fresco in the world adorns the vault of the stairwell.

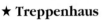
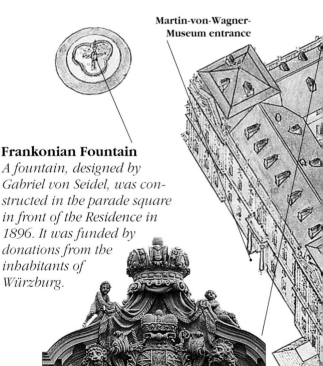

Napoleon's bedroom

Main entrance

Martin-von-Wagner-Museum entrance

Frankonian Fountain
A fountain, designed by Gabriel von Seidel, was constructed in the parade square in front of the Residence in 1896. It was funded by donations from the inhabitants of Würzburg.

The Arms of the Patron
The richly decorated façade by Johann Wolfgang von der Auwery bears the personal arms of Friedrich Karl von Schönborn, Prince-Bishop of Bamberg and Würzburg.

★ Emperor's Chamber

The centerpiece of the palace, the sumptuous Kaisersaal testifies to the close relationship between Würzburg and the Holy Roman Empire.

Garden Chamber

This vast, low hall has Rococo stucco work by Antonio Bossi, dating from 1749. There is also a painting on the vaulting by Johan Zick, dating from 1750, depicting The Feast of the Gods and Diana Resting.

Venetian Room

This room is named after a tapestry depicting the Venetian Carnival. Further ornaments include decorative panels with paintings by Johann Thalhofer, a pupil of Rudolph Byss.

★ Hofkirche

The church interior is richly decorated with paintings, sculptures, and stucco ornaments. The side altars were designed by the architect Johann Lukas von Hildebrandt and feature paintings by Giovanni Battista Tiepolo.

STAR FEATURES

★ Treppenhaus

★ Emperor's Chamber

★ Hofkirche

KEY DATES

1720–44 Building of the Würzburg Residence.

1732–92 The Residence garden is landscaped.

1751–53 Decoration of the Residence with ceiling frescoes by Tiepolo.

1765 Ludovico Bossi oversees the decorative stucco work in the stairwell.

1945 The palace is damaged in a bombing raid.

1981 The Residence becomes a UNESCO World Heritage Site.

1987 The completion of the Mirror Cabinet marks the end of the reconstruction work.

2003 The restoration of the stairwell frescoes begins.

THE PATRONS

Many of the people who were involved in the building of the Residence were members of the Schönborn family, a powerful 18th-century dynasty of princes and electors on the Main, Rhine, and Moselle. Among them was Johann Philipp von Schönborn, who became Prince Bishop of Würzburg in 1719. He was succeeded by his brother, Friedrich Karl, one of the chief instigators of the Residence project. They engaged architects and painters of international renown, such as Tiepolo, for what was to become a truly unique *Gesamtkunstwerk*, combining all the arts.

Würzburg Residence

HEIDELBERG ROMANTICISM

Heidelberg is widely held to be Germany's most romantic city and Heidelberg Castle was a favorite target of early 19th-century revisionism, with poets such as Achim von Arnim, Clemens Brentano, Joseph von Eichendorff, and Ludwig Görres recasting it as the cradle of German Romanticism. The ruins came to symbolize the artistic, intellectual, and political return to Germany's national roots that the poets so much wanted to see. It was at this period that Count Charles de Graimberg acted to prevent further looting of stone from the site in an attempt to preserve the ruins. Even today, the sprawling castle complex provides an extraordinarily majestic scene. Since being destroyed by the French in the 17th century, this once important residence has been° regarded as Germany's most palatial ruin.

Heidelberg's Church of the Holy Ghost housing the electors' tombs

RUPRECHT III

One of the most important figures in the history of Heidelberg Castle was Elector Ruprecht III, a member of the Wittelsbach dynasty. Born in Amberg in 1352, he became Elector of the Palatinate in 1398 and spearheaded a successful campaign to depose Wenceslas, the Holy Roman Emperor, in 1400. Ruprecht was elected emperor in his place, although his election was not universally recognized. He died in Oppenheim in 1410, having failed to restore the crown to its former glory.

Heidelberg Castle

Ruprecht's coat of arms

Towering over the town, the majestic Heidelberg Castle is a vast residential complex that was built between the 12th and 17th centuries. Originally a supremely well-fortified Gothic castle (▷ *Gothic Style p73*), but now mostly in ruins, this was the seat of the House of Wittelsbach palatines. After remodeling in the 16th century, the castle became one of Germany's most beautiful Renaissance residences (▷ *Renaissance Style p211*). Its splendor was extinguished by the Thirty Years' War (1618–48) and the 1689 war with France, when most of the structure was destroyed.

★ **Ottheinrich's Palace**
The German Pharmacy Museum is housed within the shell of this Renaissance building. It features Baroque and Rococo workshops and a traveling pharmacy.

★ **Friedrich's Palace**
One of the latest parts of the castle is Friedrich's Palace, which dates from 1601–07. Inside are statues of members of the Wittelsbach dynasty, including Charles the Great.

The bell tower, which was erected in the early 15th century, was remodeled frequently in subsequent years.

Castle moat

English Palace
These imposing ruins in the castle complex are the remains of a 17th-century building that Friedrich V built for his wife Elizabeth Stuart.

Gunpowder Tower

Built during the reign of the Elector Ruprecht, this 14th-century tower once formed part of the castle defenses. It was damaged by lightning in 1764, after which the townspeople took its stone for building.

Fountain Hall

This Gothic loggia features early-Romanesque columns taken from the palace of Charles the Great in Ingelheim.

Panoramic View

Heidelberg Castle has survived as a picturesque ruin, and its imposing structure occupies a commanding position above the town. From its terrace there is a beautiful view of the medieval old town of Heidelberg.

Gate Tower

Main entrance

★ Ruprecht's Palace

Built around 1400 by a master builder from Frankfurt, this is the oldest surviving part of the castle.

STAR FEATURES

★ **Ottheinrich's Palace**

★ **Friedrich's Palace**

★ **Ruprecht's Palace**

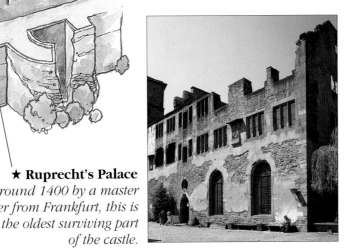

KEY DATES

Mid-12th century
Construction begins under Count Palatine Conrad.

1400 Ruprecht's Palace is built.

1556–9 Ottheinrich builds his Renaissance-style palace.

1614–19 The castle garden is landscaped.

1689–93 The castle is destroyed in the War of the Palatine Succession.

1742–64 Reconstruction takes place under Elector Karl Theodor.

1810 Attempts are made to preserve the ruins.

STYLISTIC ACCRETIONS

Inside the Gothic-style ▷ *Ruprecht's Palace*, there are two models of the castle showing the various additions over the ages. In 1524, Ludwig V added a residential building known as Ludwig's Palace. The Glazed Palace (1549), named after its mirrored hall, symbolizes the architectural transition from Gothic to Renaissance style. ▷ *Ottheinrich's Palace* is a splendid example of German early-Renaissance architecture, while ▷ *Friedrich's Palace* has a typical late-Renaissance façade. This was followed by the ▷ *English Palace*. The jewel in the crown was undoubtedly the castle garden of Friedrich V (r.1613–19), once described as the eighth wonder of the world.

Heidelberg Castle

The Tapestry Room in Linderhof

LUDWIG'S BUILDINGS

Today, Ludwig II of Bavaria (1845–86) is known above all for his extravagant building projects, including Linderhof, near Neuschwanstein, and the palace at Herrenchiemsee in eastern Bavaria. While Neuschwanstein was an attempt to recreate the Middle Ages (▷ *Castle Building)*, Herrenchiemsee was inspired by the Château de Versailles. Linderhof was originally a hunting lodge that from 1869 onward was repeatedly rebuilt, its interior shaped largely by Ludwig's fantasy world. The main inspiration here, as at Herrenchiemsee, was the French Rococo style of Louis XIV, as is evident from the Gobelin tapestries that adorn the Tapestry Room (▷ *Rococo Style p118)*.

A MODERN CASTLE

The medieval character of Neuschwanstein is purely illusory, for hidden behind the façade is what, for the 19th century, was state-of-the-art technology. The royal chambers, for example, all have central heating and there is running water on every floor with both hot and cold water in the kitchens. There is a dumb-waiter linking the kitchens and the ▷*dining room*. The fourth and fifth floors of the castle even have telephone jacks and an electric bell system, which Ludwig II could use to summon his servants and adjutants.

Neuschwanstein Castle

S ET AMIDST MAGNIFICENT mountain scenery on the shores of the Schwansee (Swan Lake), the fairy-tale Neuschwanstein Castle was built in 1869–91 for the eccentric Bavarian king, Ludwig II, to a design by the theater designer Christian Jank. When deciding to build this imposing residence, the king was undoubtedly inspired by Wartburg Castle in Thuringia, which he visited in 1867. But Neuschwanstein is no ordinary castle: behind the pale gray granite exterior, which draws on a variety of styles, the interior is fitted with the latest 19th-century comforts. The castle offers spectacular views of the surrounding landscape.

Vestibule
The walls of the vestibule and of other rooms in the castle are lavishly covered with paintings depicting scenes from old German myths and legends.

★ Throne Room
The gilded interior of the throne room reminds one of Byzantine temples and the palace church of All Saints in the Residence in Munich.

★ Singing Room
The Sängersaal was modeled on the singing room at Wartburg Castle in Eisenach.

Study

Dining Room
Like other rooms in the palace, the dining room includes fabulous pictures, intricately carved panels, and beautifully decorated furniture, all bearing witness to the skill and artistry of the 19th-century craftsmen.

Neuschwanstein Castle

★ Castle Building
Neuschwanstein Castle is the archetypal fairy-tale castle and has provided the inspiration for countless toy models, book illustrations, and movie sets.

THE SWAN MOTIF

Ludwig was fascinated by swans (hence his early identification with Lohengrin, the Knight of the Swan) and not just as a symbol of purity, but also because he regarded himself as successor to the Lords of Schwangau, whose heraldic beast was the swan. Not surprisingly, the swan motif dominates the interior décor.

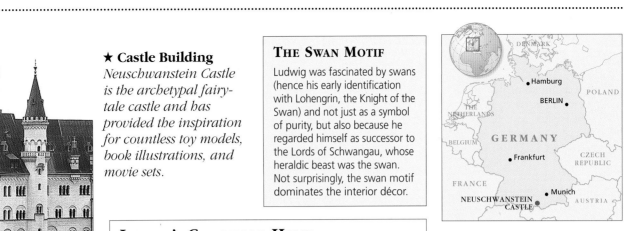

The Kemanate was completed after Ludwig's death and was planned to feature statues of female saints.

LUDWIG'S CHILDHOOD HOME

The skyline of Schwangau is dominated by another castle, the majestic Hohenschwangau Castle. Ludwig's father, Maximilian II, acquired the castle when he was crown prince and had it rebuilt in 1832 in a Neo-Gothic style (▷ *Gothic Style p73*). As a child, Ludwig was captivated by its frescoes depicting various legends.

Hohenschwangau Castle

Two-story arcades surround the castle courtyard.

The Knight's House connects the gatehouse with the main building.

Courtyard
The heart of the castle was supposed to have been a mighty 90-m (295-ft) high tower with a Gothic castle church. It was never built, but in 1988 its planned position was marked in white stone.

The Gatehouse, completed in 1872, served as temporary accommodation for the king. He had an apartment on the second floor.

Main entrance

STAR FEATURES

★ **Singing Room**

★ **Throne Room**

★ **Castle Building**

KEY DATES

1868 Ludwig makes known his plans to build a new castle.

1869 The foundation stone is laid.

1873 Completion of the gatehouse.

1880 A ceremony marks the completion of all five floors.

1884 The castle is occupied.

1886 Seven weeks after Ludwig II drowns, the castle is opened to visitors.

1891 Completion of the castle.

PICTURE CYCLE

Ludwig II's choice of interior decoration was inspired by the operas of Richard Wagner (1813–83). Yet although Ludwig commissioned set painter Christian Jank with the interior design, most of the murals depict scenes taken not from operas, but from the same medieval sagas that Wagner himself used as a source. They feature Tannhäuser the poet, Lohengrin, the Knight of the Swan, and his father, Parsifal, King of the Holy Grail. Murals in the ▷ *Singing Room* show one of the legendary singing contests held at Wartburg Castle in the 13th century. Scenes from Wagner's *Lohengrin* (1846–48) decorate the King's Chambers. Among the artists employed were Josef Aigner, Wilhelm Hauschild, and Ferdinand Piloty.

THE CRYPT

Several calamitous fires destroyed much of the Romanesque Episcopal church erected in 830–37 on the site where the Cathedral of St Gall now stands. The only part of the building to survive the ravages of time is the 9th–10th century ▷ *crypt*, which became an integral part of the Baroque cathedral. The bishops of St Gall have long found their final resting place here – a tradition that has continued to the present day. Among those buried in the cathedral are Abbot Otmar, who founded the abbey and who, ten years after his death in 769, was interred in St Otmar's Crypt beneath what is now the west gallery, and Bishop Otmar Mäder, who died in 2003.

THE ABBEY LIBRARY

Built in the second half of the 18th century according to plans drawn up by Peter Thumb, the Abbey Library is richly decorated with ceiling frescoes, intricate stuccowork, wood carving, and intarsia. The two-story reading room, containing walnut and cherry bookcases reaching to the ceiling, is especially impressive. Around 130,000 leather-bound volumes and 2,000 manuscripts are housed here. These include such biblio-philic treasures as a copy of the *Song of the Nibelungen* and *Codex Abrogans* (790), a dictionary of synonyms presumed to be one of the oldest existing written documents in German. The liturgical collection is renowned for its *Psalterium Aureum*, a psalter composed c.900. The best-known item in the collection is the *St Gallener Klosterplan*, showing the layout of an ideal Benedictine monastery. Copied from an earlier manuscript by the monks of Reichenau on Lake Constance in the early 9th century, this document is thought to have been the blueprint for the St Gallen Monastery.

St Gallen Monastery

THE BENEDICTINE ABBEY in St Gallen, established in 720, was one of the most important monasteries in Europe as well as being a foremost center for the arts, letters, and sciences. A priceless library was gathered and monks came from far and wide to copy manuscripts, many of which still exist. Only the crypt remains of the early Romanesque church and monastery built in the 9th century. The present Baroque cathedral and abbey (▷ *Baroque Style p111*) by architects Peter Thumb and Johann Michael Beer, were completed in 1766 and feature exquisite Rococo decorations (▷ *Rococo Style p118*).

★ **Ceiling Frescoes**
The ceiling is decorated with frescoes by Joseph Wannenmacher.

Main Altarpiece
The painting on the high altar of the Assumption of the Virgin *is by Francesco Romanelli. Dating from 1645, it was later heavily retouched.*

High altar

Thrones
Two thrones by Franz Joseph Anton Feucht-mayer and decorated with paintings by Franz Joseph Stälzer stand in the choir stalls.

STAR FEATURES

★ **Ceiling Frescoes**

★ **Choir Stalls**

Confessional

The 11 Baroque confessionals in the nave are crowned with medallions featuring reliefs by Franz Joseph Anton Feuchtmayer and Anton Dirr dating from 1761–3.

ST GALL

According to the *Gallus-Vita* (835) by Walahfrid Strabo, the Abbey of St Otmar was founded on the site where a monk named Gallus (c.560–650) – later canonized as St Gall – built a hermit's shelter for himself in 612.

Crypt

Beneath the cathedral is the crypt of the earlier church (▷ Romanesque Style p199).

Pulpit

The fine Rococo pulpit, decorated with figures of the Evangelists and of angels, was made by Anton Dirr in 1786.

Main entrance

★ Choir Stalls

The Baroque choir stalls (1763–70), made of walnut and decorated with painting and gilding, are by Franz Joseph Anton Feuchtmayer and Franz Joseph Stälzer.

KEY DATES

c.720 An abbey is founded by a priest named Otmar.

816–37 A Benedictine abbey with basilica is built.

937 The abbey is severely damaged by fire.

1529 The people of St Gallen expel the monks.

1532 The monks return.

1755–67 The Baroque Episcopal church is built.

1758–67 The Abbey Library is constructed.

1805 Dissolution of the monastery.

1824 The Episcopal church is elevated to the status of a cathedral.

1983 St Gallen Monastery becomes a UNESCO World Heritage Site.

THE CHOIR STALLS

Among the most striking interior features of the Cathedral of St Gall are the highly ornate, three-tiered ▷ *choir stalls*. Carved in walnut, they are a masterpiece of Rococo woodcarving. The sides and backrests of the stalls feature detailed gilded reliefs showing scenes from the life of St Benedict. Franz Joseph Anton Feuchtmayer (1696–1779), the German sculptor and stucco craftsman, who also designed the ▷ *confessional*, worked mainly in the Lake Constance region.

St Gallen Monastery

RUDOLF THE FOUNDER

In 1359, Duke Rudolf IV of Austria, later known as Rudolf the Founder, laid the foundation stone for the Gothic enlargement of what was then a Romanesque church (▷ *Romanesque Style p199*). Born in 1339, Rudolf became a duke in 1358 and campaigned tirelessly to have St Stephen's Church granted its independence from the Bishop of Passau and elevated to the status of a cathedral. But it was not until 1469 that Vienna, under Friedrich III, became a diocese in its own right. On Rudolf's death in 1365 a monument to him was placed in front of the ▷ *High Altar*. In 1945, it was moved to the Ladies' Choir. Rudolf is buried in the ducal vault next to his wife, Katharina.

The catacombs

CATACOMBS

The extensive ▷ *catacombs* beneath St Stephen's Cathedral were excavated around 1470 to relieve pressure on Vienna's main cemetery. For the next 300 years, the people of Vienna were interred here and by the time Emperor Joseph II put a stop to the practise in 1783, some 10,000 people had been laid to rest in the catacombs. At the heart of the complex is the Habsburg Vault built by Rudolf IV in 1363. This houses 15 sarcophagi belonging to the early Habsburgs and 56 urns, which contain the entrails of the later Habsburgs who, from 1633 onward, were buried in the imperial vault of the Capuchin Monastery Church. Vienna's archbishops are interred beneath the Apostles' Choir in the Episcopal vault, completed in 1953.

St Stephen's Cathedral, Vienna

SITUATED IN THE medieval center of Vienna, St Stephen's Cathedral is the soul of the city itself; it is no coincidence that the urns containing the entrails of some of the Habsburgs lie in a vault beneath its main altar. A church has stood on the site for more than 800 years, but all that remains of the original 13th-century Romanesque structure are the Giants' Doorway and Heathen Towers. The Gothic nave, choir, and side chapels are the result of a major rebuilding program in the 14th and 15th centuries (▷ *Gothic Style p73*). The lofty vaulted interior contains an impressive collection of works of art spanning several centuries.

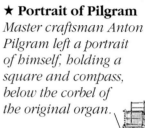

Carving of Rudolf IV

★ Portrait of Pilgram
Master craftsman Anton Pilgram left a portrait of himself, holding a square and compass, below the corbel of the original organ.

The Heathen Towers and Giant's Doorway stand on the site of an earlier heathen shrine.

STAR FEATURES

★ **Portrait of Pilgram**

★ **Singer Gate**

★ **Steffl or Spire**

★ **Tiled Roof**

The symbolic number "O5" of the Austrian Resistance Movement was carved here in 1945.

The North Tower, according to legend, was never completed because its master builder, Hans Puchsbaum, broke a pact he had made with the devil, by pronouncing a holy name. The devil then caused him to fall to his death.

Entrance to the catacombs

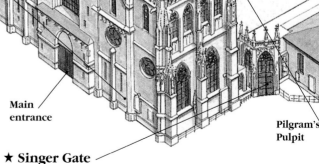

Main entrance

Pilgram's Pulpit

Lower Vestry

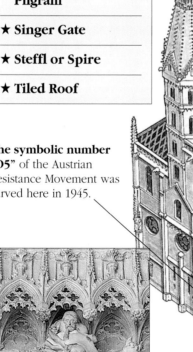

★ Singer Gate
This was once the entrance for male visitors. A sculpted relief above the door depicts scenes from the life of St Paul.

★ Steffl or Spire

The 137-m high (450-ft) Gothic spire is a famous landmark. From the Sexton's Lodge, it is possible to climb the stairs as far as a viewing platform.

TOOTHACHE FIGURE

According to legend, the "Zahnwehherrgott", a sculpture of a man in agony, punished those who ridiculed him by inflicting them with toothache. Only when they atoned for their sins did the pain subside. The figure is located beneath the ▷ *North Tower*.

KEY DATES

1137–47 The first Romanesque church is built.

1304 Work begins on a Gothic choir.

1433 The south tower is completed.

1556–78 The dome is added to the north tower.

1722 The church is elevated to cathedral status.

1945–60 Reconstruction of the cathedral after it was severely damaged during World War II.

2001 The historic center of Vienna, including St Stephen's Cathedral, becomes a UNESCO World Heritage Site.

ANTON PILGRAM

One of the cathedral's foremost craftsmen was Anton Pilgram, a master-builder from Brünn (c.1460–1515). His sandstone ▷ *pulpit* (1514–15) inside the nave contains portraits of the Four Fathers of the Church (theologians representing four physiognomic temperaments) and is considered a masterwork of late-Gothic stone sculpture. Pilgram even included a portrait of himself as a "watcher at the window" beneath the pulpit steps. There is another ▷ *portrait of Pilgram* in the cathedral. Here, the builder and sculptor is shown peeping through a window into the church. Pilgram signed this work with the monogram "MAP 1513".

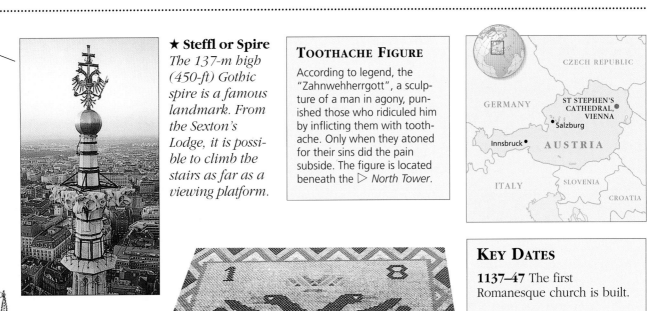

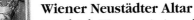

★ Tiled Roof

Almost a quarter of a million glazed tiles cover the roof; they were meticulously restored after the damage caused in the last days of World War II.

Wiener Neustädter Altar

Friedrich III commissioned the elaborate altarpiece in 1447. Painted panels open out to reveal an earlier carved interior of the life of Christ. This panel shows the Adoration of the Magi *(1420).*

The High Altar is adorned with an altarpiece by Tobias Pock showing the martyrdom of St Stephen.

JOHANNES CAPISTRANO

On the exterior northeastern wall of the choir is a pulpit built after the victory over the Turks at Belgrade in 1456. It was from here that the Italian Franciscan, Johannes Capistrano (1386–1456), is said to have preached against the Turkish invasion while on a visit to Austria in 1451. Capistrano had trained as a lawyer. He was appointed governor of Perugia, but while on a peace mission to the neighboring state of Malatesta he was imprisoned. After some soul-searching and the appearance of St Francis in a dream, he joined the Franciscans and became a priest in 1425. In 1454 he assembled troops for the successful crusade against the Turks. This event is depicted in the 18th-century statue above the pulpit showing Capistrano trampling on a Turkish invader. He was canonized in 1690.

Baroque statue of St Johannes Capistrano

St Stephen's Cathedral

VIENNA BOYS' CHOIR

Vienna's Hofmusikkapelle, the ensemble that gave rise to the famous Wiener Sänger-knaben (Vienna Boys' Choir), was founded in 1498 by Emperor Maximilian I (r.1493–1519), a great patron of the arts. The choir sang exclusively for the Viennese Court. Both Joseph Haydn and Franz Schubert were choristers, and eminent musicians such as Christoph Willibald Gluck, Wolfgang Amadeus Mozart, Antonio Salieri, and Anton Bruckner performed with the choir over the centuries. In 1922, four years after the demise of the monarchy, the rector of ▷ *the Burg-kapelle* reformed the choir at his own expense. In 1926, their first concerts outside the Burgkapelle were widely acclaimed. Today, there are some 100 boys in the choir.

THE SPANISH RIDING SCHOOL

The Spanish Riding School has been cultivating the classic skills of horsemanship for more than 430 years. Emperor Maximilian II (r.1564–76) brought the first of the school's original stallions from Spain to Austria in 1562 and began a program of breeding and training that continues today. Lipizzaner horses take their name from the original stud at Lipizza near Trieste, founded by Archduke Karl in 1580. They perform their intricate maneuvers in the ▷ *Winter Riding School*, built by Joseph Emanuel Fischer von Erlach, 1729–35.

Lipizzaner stallion and rider

The Hofburg Complex, Vienna

FROM MODEST CITY FORTRESS to vast and glorious palace, the Hofburg was the grand imperial residence of the Habsburgs from 1279 until they fell from power in 1918. Successive rulers, all anxious to make their mark, have left a legacy of seven centuries of architectural development. The complex contains the former imperial apartments, several museums, a chapel, a church, the Winter Riding School, the Austrian National Library, and the President of Austria's offices.

Burggarten

Albertina

Augustiner-kirche

★ Prunksaal
The showpiece of the Austrian National Library (1722–35) is the flamboyant, wood-paneled Prunksaal, or Hall of Honor.

A Statue of Joseph II (1806) by Franz Anton Zauner stands in the center of the Josefsplatz.

The Burgkapelle contains Gothic statuary in canopied niches and a bronze crucifix (1720) by Johann Känischbauer.

Alte Burg

Redoute Wing

Winter Riding School

Michaelertor

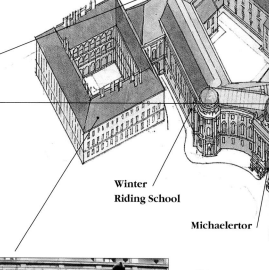

★ Michaelertrakt (1893)
The splendid curved façade of the Michaelertrakt is surmounted by an imposing dome.

Stallburg
Built in the 16th century, the Stallburg was later converted into the stables ranged around a large courtyard with arcades on three stories.

Mozart Memorial *(1896)*
Viktor Tilgner's statue of the composer stands just inside the Ringstrasse entrance.

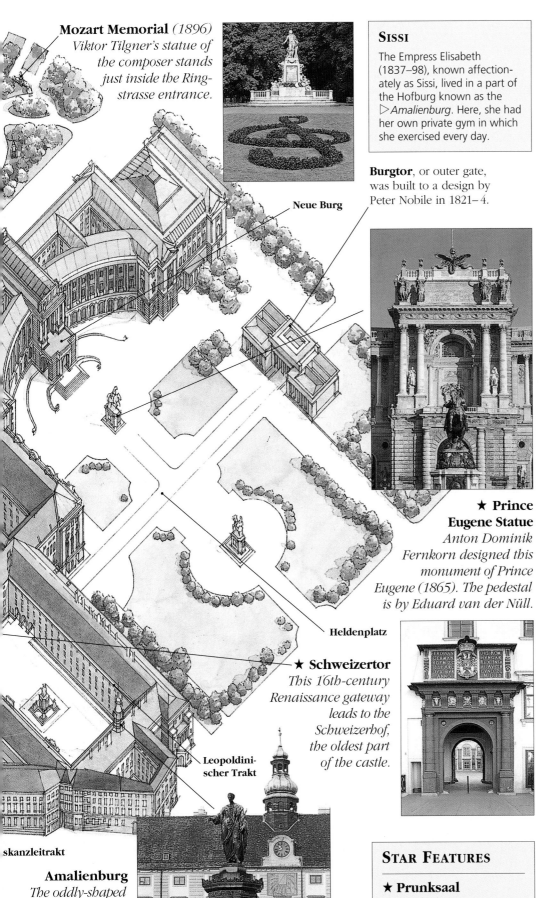

Burgtor, or outer gate, was built to a design by Peter Nobile in 1821–4.

Neue Burg

★ Prince Eugene Statue
Anton Dominik Fernkorn designed this monument of Prince Eugene (1865). The pedestal is by Eduard van der Nüll.

Heldenplatz

★ Schweizertor
This 16th-century Renaissance gateway leads to the Schweizerhof, the oldest part of the castle.

Leopoldinischer Trakt

skanzleitrakt

Amalienburg
The oddly-shaped Amalienburg, built in 1575 for emperor Maximilian's son Rudolf, has a Renaissance façade and an attractive Baroque clock tower.

KEY DATES

1275 The castle is built by Otakar II, King of Bohemia.

1279 The Habsburgs capture the castle.

1447–9 Emperor Frederick III redesigns the Burgkapelle.

1559 The Stallburg is built by Emperor Maximilian II.

1575 Emperor Rudolf II builds the Amalienburg.

1668–80 Emperor Leopold I constructs the Leopoldinischer Trakt.

1730 The Imperial Chancellery is completed under Emperor Charles VI.

1881–1913 Emperor Franz Joseph I adds the Neue Burg to the Hofburg Complex.

THE TREASURIES

The Hofburg Treasuries contain countless priceless items amassed during centuries of Habsburg rule. At the heart of the collection are the jewels and insignia of the Holy Roman Empire, such as the exquisite 10th-century imperial crown set with enamel plaques and cabochons, and a coronation robe dating from 1134. Magnificent artifacts also include treasures from the Order of the Golden Fleece, a dynastic order of the Habsburgs; the splendid armor made in 1517 is on show. Among the sacred objects in the collection are liturgical utensils, ivory carvings, reliquaries, and 12th-century vestments.

STAR FEATURES

★ **Prunksaal**

★ **Michaelertrakt**

★ **Prince Eugene Statue**

★ **Schweizertor**

The Hofburg Complex

Schönbrunn Palace, Vienna

THE FORMER SUMMER RESIDENCE of the imperial Habsburg family takes its name from a beautiful spring found on the site. Leopold I asked Johann Bernhard Fischer von Erlach to design a grand residence here in 1695, but it was not until Empress Maria Theresa employed the Rococo architect Nikolaus Pacassi in the mid-18th century that it was completed (▷*Rococo Style p118*). Glorious gardens complement the architecture.

**Empress
Maria Theresa**

MARIA THERESA

The daughter of Emperor Charles VI, Maria Theresa (1717–80) became Arch-duchess of Austria and Queen of Hungary and Bohemia on her father's death in 1740. Five years later her husband, Duke Francis Stephen of Lorraine, was recognized as Holy Roman Emperor. Maria Theresa instigated numerous reforms in the spirit of the Enlightenment. She initiated state-supported elementary schools, introduced a new penal code, and reduced taxation. She also worked toward unifying Habsburg lands by centralizing control over the empire. Among her 16 children was Marie Antoinette, who married Louis XVI of France.

PREVIOUS PALACES

Schönbrunn stands on the site of the Katterburg, a 14th-century castle that belonged to the Neuburg Convent. By the time Emperor Maximilian II bought the property in 1569, it included a mansion, mill, and stables. Maximilian intended to turn it into a pleasure palace and zoo, and indeed a palace was finally built in the mid-17th century by the widow of Emperor Ferdinand II. She named it "Schönbrunn" after the "Schönen Brunnen" ("beautiful spring"), discovered by Emperor Matthew II, while hunting on the estate in 1612. This first palace was destroyed by the Turks during the siege of Vienna in 1683. Emperor Leopold I acquired the estate in 1686 and commissioned today's palace.

Round Chinese Cabinet
Maria Theresa used this white and gold room for private discussions with her State Chancellor, Prince Kaunitz. The walls are adorned with lacquered panels.

★ **Great Gallery**
Used for imperial banquets, the gallery has a lovely ceiling fresco by Gregorio Guglielmi.

A hidden staircase leads to the apartment of the State Chancellor, above which he had secret conferences with the Empress.

Chapel

Blue Chinese Salon
The last Austrian emperor, Karl I, signed his abdication in 1918 in this Rococo room with its Chinese scenes.

Napoleon Room

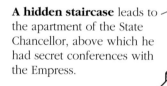

The Millions' Room, featuring superb Rococo decor, was Maria Theresa's conference room.

★ **Vieux-Lacque Room**
During her widowhood Maria Theresa lived in this room, which is decorated with exquisite oriental lacquered panels.

Main entrance

Breakfast Room

The imperial family's breakfast room has white wood paneling inlaid with appliqué floral designs worked by Maria Theresa and her daughters.

A MILITARY MAN

When visiting Schönbrunn, Emperor Franz Joseph I would sleep in a simple, iron-framed bed, as befit a man who felt more at home in the field. He died at the palace in 1916, after nearly 68 years on the throne.

Large Rosa Room

This is one of three rooms decorated with monumental Swiss and Italian landscape paintings by Josef Rosa, after whom the room is named.

PALACE GUIDE

On the second floor, the suite of rooms to the right of the Blue Staircase was occupied by Franz Joseph I and Elisabeth. The rooms in the east wing include Maria Theresa's bedroom and rooms used by Grand Duke Karl.

The Billiard Room is the first of a suite of rooms that provide a glimpse of Emperor Franz Joseph's life at the palace.

The Blue Staircase is so-called because of its original decorative scheme.

STAR FEATURES

★ **Great Gallery**

★ **Vieux-Lacque Room**

KEY

	Franz Joseph I's apartments
	Empress Elisabeth's apartments
	Ceremonial and reception rooms
	Maria Theresa's rooms
	Grand Duke Karl's rooms
	Closed to visitors

THE COACH MUSEUM

One wing of Schönbrunn Palace, formerly housing the Winter Riding School, now contains a marvelous collection of coaches – one of the most interesting in the world. It includes more than 60 carriages dating back to the 17th century, as well as riding uniforms, horse tack, saddles, coachmen's liveries, and paintings and drawings of horses and carriages. The pride of the collection is the coronation coach of Emperor Charles VI. Exhibits include sleighs and sedan chairs belonging to Maria Theresa, among others.

Coronation coach of Charles VI

Schönbrunn Palace

KEY DATES

1696 Work begins on Emperor Leopold I's residence.

1728 Emperor Charles VI purchases Schönbrunn and later makes a gift of it to his daughter, Maria Theresa.

1743–63 Nikolaus Pacassi enlarges the palace in the Rococo style.

1775–80 Johann Ferdinand Hetzendorf von Hohenberg redesigns the park.

1880–82 The Palm House is created.

1904 The Sundial House is built.

1996 Schönbrunn becomes a UNESCO World Heritage Site.

CEREMONIAL STATE ROOMS

As architect to the court of Empress Maria Theresa, Nikolaus Pacassi oversaw the enlargement and redesigning of Schönbrunn. Together with Rococo artists and craftsmen such as Albert Bolla, Gregorio Guglielmi, Isidor Canevale, and Thaddaeus Adam Karner, Pacassi was responsible for creating the interiors of both the state rooms and the private quarters. The ▷ *Large Rosa Room* and the ▷ *Millions' Room*, for example, feature frescoes and stuccowork in the Rococo style commissioned by Maria Theresa herself. The palace is renowned for its intricate gilded stuccowork, elegant mirrored galleries, and exotic chinoiserie.

Front view of the Stiftskirche

BERTHOLD DIETMAYR

Appointed abbot of Melk Abbey in 1700, Berthold Dietmayr (1670–1739), whose real name was Karl Josef Dietmayr, was to oversee the Benedictine monastery's transformation into a Baroque masterwork during his 40-year term of office. As a member of the Lower Austrian Council of Prelates and councillor to Emperors Leopold I, Joseph I, and Charles VI, he held a position of considerable influence and power. Convinced that a splendid new building was needed to reflect the abbey's religious, scientific, and political importance, he entrusted the task of planning the new complex to the architect Jakob Prandtauer, who was succeeded by his nephew, Joseph Munggenast.

JAKOB PRANDTAUER

As the architect of choice for Austria's prelates, Jakob Prandtauer was involved in the building of chapels and churches in both Lower and Upper Austria. Born the son of a miner in Tyrol in 1660, Prandtauer's magnum opus was undoubtedly Melk Abbey, on which he continued to work until his death in 1726. Prandtauer's concept for making the best possible use of the rocky promontory, high up above the Danube, envisaged a series of courtyards (▷ *Prelates' Courtyard*), surrounded on all sides by the various buildings, which were to be linked harmoniously. The dominant feature is the ▷ *Stiftskirche*, which has a central dome and two towers flanking the main portal.

Melk Abbey

THE TOWN AND ABBEY OF MELK, the original seat of the Babenbergs, are a spectacular sight towering above the Danube, 60 km (37 miles) west of Vienna. In the 11th century, Leopold II invited the Benedictines from Lambach to Melk, and granted them land and the castle which the monks turned into a fortified abbey. Destroyed by fire in 1297, the abbey has subsequently been rebuilt many times. In the 16th century, it had to withstand a Turkish invasion. In 1702, Abbot Berthold Dietmayr began to remodel the complex. Jakob Prandtauer, von Erlach, Joseph Munggenast, and other architects helped to give the present abbey its magnificent Baroque form (▷ *Baroque Style p111*).

Stairwell
A spiral staircase with ornamental balustrade connects the library with the Stiftskirche, the monastery church of St Peter and St Paul.

★ Library
The impressive library holds over 100,000 volumes, including 2,000 manuscripts and 750 incunabula. It is decorated with a beautiful ceiling fresco by Paul Troger.

Crowning with the Crown of Thorns
This powerful painting by Jörg Breu (1502) is exhibited in the Abbey Museum.

Marble Hall
This glorious room, decorated with a painting by Paul Troger, was once used for receptions and ceremonies.

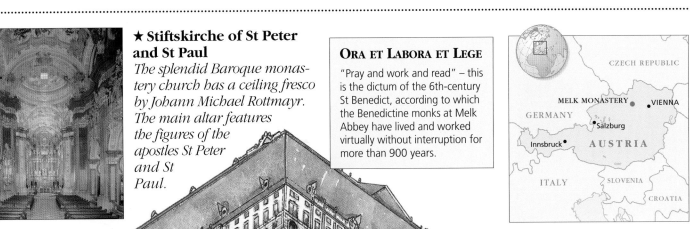

★ Stiftskirche of St Peter and St Paul
The splendid Baroque monastery church has a ceiling fresco by Johann Michael Rottmayr. The main altar features the figures of the apostles St Peter and St Paul.

ORA ET LABORA ET LEGE
"Pray and work and read" – this is the dictum of the 6th-century St Benedict, according to which the Benedictine monks at Melk Abbey have lived and worked virtually without interruption for more than 900 years.

Melk Abbey

Convent courtyard

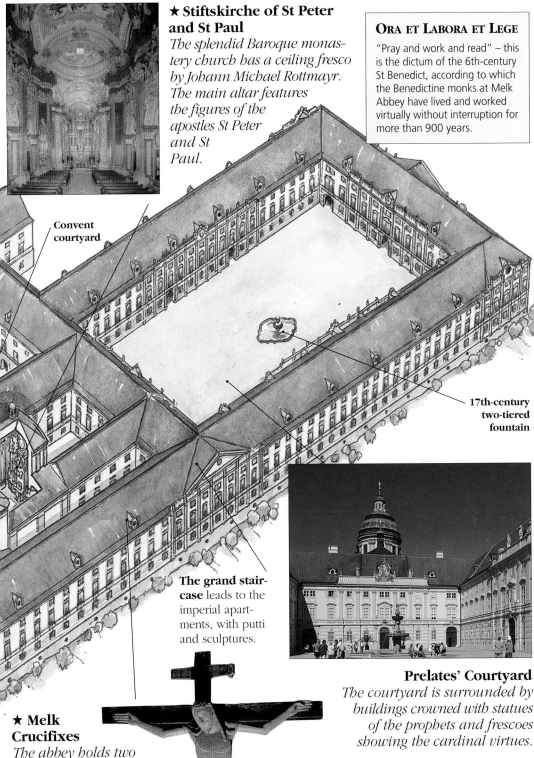

17th-century two-tiered fountain

The grand staircase leads to the imperial apartments, with putti and sculptures.

Prelates' Courtyard
The courtyard is surrounded by buildings crowned with statues of the prophets and frescoes showing the cardinal virtues.

★ Melk Crucifixes
The abbey holds two important crucifixes – one is Romanesque (c.1200, shown here), the other from the 14th century, containing gems and a piece of Christ's cross.

STAR FEATURES

★ **Library**

★ **Stiftskirche of St Peter and St Paul**

★ **Melk Crucifixes**

The view
The magnificent Baroque monastery, Melk Abbey, is a vast yellow building perched dramatically on a high bluff overlooking the Danube.

KEY DATES

976 Leopold I becomes margrave and makes Melk castle his official residence.

1089 Leopold II hands the castle to the Order of St Benedict.

1140 The monastic school is founded.

1418 After the Council of Constance, Melk spearheads a monastic reform movement that spreads throughout Austria and southern Germany.

1429 Consecration of the new church in Melk.

1702–36 Baroque expansion of the abbey.

1738 The roof is destroyed by fire.

1978–2000 The abbey undergoes extensive renovation.

THE ABBEY LIBRARY

Although many of the abbey's collection of early manuscripts were lost in the fire of 1297, the ▷ *library* still houses some 1,800 manuscripts, the oldest of which date from the early 9th century. Melk was an important center of Middle High German literature and the library possesses a fragment of a copy of the *Song of the Nibelungen* dating from 1300. Other treasures include 750 incunabula (books printed before 1500), 1,700 works from the 16th century, 4,500 from the 17th, and 18,000 from the 18th, as well as 100,000 later works.

Hohensalzburg Castle

THE SIEGE

The teachings of Martin Luther and the other reformers spread to Salzburg and the surrounding region around 1525. In the same year a peasants' revolt laid siege to Hohensalzburg Castle, the seat of the archbishop, for 14 weeks. This was the only occasion in its 900-year history that the castle was besieged. Hohensalzburg, however, proved unassailable and the peasants eventually gave up.

THE SALZBURG STEER

The famous "Salzburg Steer," Austria's oldest freestanding organ, is to be found in the Hohen Stock, a palace within the castle. The organ owes its name to the raucous F-A-C chord it produces when being warmed up. The resulting "shriek" was likened by the people of Salzburg to the bellowing of a bull. The organ was built in 1502 and has 200 pipes. From Palm Sunday to 31 October each year, it is played three times a day after the carillon of the New Palace has sounded, at 7am, 11am, and 6pm. There was a time when the Salzburg Steer was played just twice a day: once to get people out of bed at 4am and again in the evening, after the Ave bells had been rung. In the mid-16th century, a barrel organ was added that at first could play only one chorale. Since then, its repertoire has been expanded to include melodies by Leopold and Wolfgang Amadeus Mozart, both of whom spent at least part of their working lives in Salzburg in the late 18th century.

Hohensalzburg Castle

Perched on the rocky peak of Festungsberg, overlooking Salzburg, the mighty Hohensalzburg Castle was built in the 11th century, during the wars between the Holy Roman Empire and the Papacy, and was gradually extended. The castle served as a refuge for Salzburg's archbishops whenever they felt threatened. Archbishop Leonhard von Keutschach gave it its present look in the 16th century; Archbishop Paris Lodron introduced further changes in the 17th century. A military barracks in the 19th century, today it is a major tourist attraction.

An interesting feature in the fortress courtyard is a well dating from 1539.

Early Cannons
Aimed at the town, many cannons can be seen among the numerous bastions, bulwarks, and walkways.

The Glockenturm, through which the castle's residential quarters can be reached, has a bell case created by Hans Reichert in 1505.

Salzburg Coat of Arms
This coat of arms is placed above the wicket leading to the inner courtyard in front of the old castle.

Archbishop Johann Jakob Khuen-Belasy
This portrait of the archbishop (1560–86), who carried out the final remodeling of the old fortress, hangs in a room in the old castle.

STAR FEATURES

★ Golden Chamber

★ Torture Chamber

Schoolhouse and Cake Tower

These buildings are the remains of fortifications built outside the castle in the 16th century during a revolt against the all-powerful archbishops.

★ Golden Chamber

The richly ornamented Golden Chamber, with its large tiled stove in Gothic style, is one of the loveliest rooms in the castle.

Small Courtyard

In a small square on the castle ramparts stand an old salt warehouse (former stables), and two towers, Hasenturm (Hares' Tower) and Schwefelturm (Sulphur Tower).

★ Torture Chamber

Reckturm, the corner tower, was once a prison and torture chamber. Prisoners were tortured at Hohensalzburg as recently as 1893.

KEY DATES

1077 Building work starts under Archbishop Gebhard.

1461–66 Archbishop Burkhard von Weisspriach builds four round towers.

1495–1519 Archbishop Leonhard von Keutschach expands the residential palace.

1619–35 Archbishop Paris Lodron rebuilds the castle in Baroque style with further fortifications.

1681 Completion of the Kuenburg Bastion marks the end of the expansion.

1816 The castle begins to be used as a barracks and prison.

1861 Hohensalzburg is abandoned.

c.1890 A funicular is built leading up to the castle.

THE PRINCE'S CHAMBERS

The late-Gothic Prince's Chambers, renowned for their painted wood paneling, are situated on the fourth floor of the Old Palace (▷ *Gothic Style p73*). The walls and ceiling of the ▷ *Golden Chamber*, which contains an exquisite majolica stove, are decorated with Gothic tendrils, a motif that is repeated in the wrought-iron fittings on the doors. The Golden Hall is noted for its splendid blue ceiling, studded with golden bosses, and its red marble pillars. Both rooms are used for concerts.

Hohensalzburg Castle

TREASURED OBJECTS

There are 31 chapels in the Church of St Mary, each displaying precious examples of Medieval and Baroque art. Among the most treasured items is the 15th-century figure of the Virgin and the Child, known as the *Madonna of Gdańsk*, in the Chapel of St Anne. According to legend, the artist was a local man who had been accused of murder. The story tells how he carved the Madonna in just one night in 1410 and the magistrates were so taken with its beauty that they pardoned him. The Chapel of St Reinhold contains a copy of an altarpiece by Hans Memling of the *The Last Judgement*. The original (1467–73) is in the National Museum in Gdańsk. It was commissioned by the Florentine manager of the Medici bank in Bruges but the ship transporting the work to Italy was raided in the Anglo-Hanseatic War and the painting taken to Gdańsk.

The Madonna of Gdańsk

TIME MACHINE

One of the highlights of the Church of St Mary is the remarkable ▷ *Astronomical Clock*, designed by Hans Dürunger in the 15th century. The clock is renowned for its time-keeping – the bell is struck by figures of Adam and Eve. It also maintains a calendar of the saints, and complex dials show the position of the sun and moon in relation to the zodiac signs. The clock was removed during World War II, then returned after the church's reconstruction. Legend has it that the town's mayor ordered the clock-maker to be blinded so that he could never make a more beautiful clock.

Church of St Mary, Gdańsk

THE CHURCH OF ST MARY (Kościół Mariacki) rises dramatically above the narrow cobbled streets of Old Gdańsk. Its plain brick exterior conceals a stark but impressive Gothic interior (▷ *Gothic Style p73*) with a three-aisled choir and soaring vaulted ceilings. The church was designed to accommodate 25,000 worshipers. Construction of Europe's largest brick church began in 1343 with a three-aisled basilica, and took more than 150 years to complete. The transept and apse were based on designs by Heinrich Ungeradin. Later the height of the tower was increased to 80 m (262 ft). This was followed by additions to the nave, with rows of chapels placed between the buttresses that had previously been erected in the interior. In the final restructuring, completed under the supervision of Heinrich Hetzel in 1502, a vaulted roof was added to the church.

View of the church in 1945 after its destruction in World War II

★ **Bell Tower**
This architectural element dominates the silhouette of the church. The tower is 82 m (269 ft) tall and offers a spectacular view over the historical city of Gdańsk.

★ **St George Slaying the Dragon**
This 15th-century depiction of St George and the dragon combines mural painting and sculptural elements.

Bell tower entrance

Astronomical Clock
Made by Hans Dürunger in 1464–70, the clock shows the hour and also the days of the week, dates of movable feasts, and phases of the moon. At noon a procession of figures representing Adam and Eve, the Apostles, the Three Kings, and Death appears.

Tablet of the Ten Commandments
This panel dating from around 1480–90 illustrates obedience to and disregard of the laws.

Contemporary Window
This gorgeous, colorful stained-glass window is situated in the apse.

Tower at intersection of nave and transept

STREET FESTIVAL

For four days in mid-August every year the Old Town of Gdańsk is the setting for the International Street and Open-Air Festival. Theater groups, dancers, musicians, and acrobats from all over the world bring an extraordinary variety of performances to the streets.

★ Vaulted Ceilings
The elaborate decoration of the vaulted stone ceilings of the aisles is an innovation of late Gothic architecture.

The South Transept
This engraving, by Johann Carl Schultz, depicts the South transept as it was before World War II.

Chancellor's Gate
This double stone gateway is decorated with tracery. It highlights the complex shape of the arches above the doors.

STAR FEATURES

★ **Bell Tower**

★ **St George Slaying the Dragon**

★ **Vaulted Ceilings**

KEY DATES

1343 The church's foundation stone is laid.

1470 The Astronomical Clock is completed.

1473 Hans Memling's altarpiece *The Last Judgement* is given to St Mary's.

1502 The Church of St Mary is completed.

1945 St Mary's is destroyed during World War II.

1956 The reconstruction of the Church of St Mary is completed.

INSIDE ST MARY'S

From 1529 to 1945 St Mary's was renowned for its sumptuous decoration and furnishings. After World War II some pieces were saved; however, the reconstructed interior is far less lavishly embellished, although it does contain Gothic and Baroque furnishings (▷ *Baroque Style p111*). The high altar is adorned with a triptych (1511–17) by Michael Schwarz of Augsburg, a disciple of the German Renaissance artist Albrecht Dürer. It features a relief carving showing the coronation of the Virgin in the central panel. Paintings decorate the wings. Another winged altarpiece, brought from Antwerp in 1510, forms the focal point of the Chapel of the Holy Cross. An exquisite stone *Pietá*, carved in 1410 by the same local artist that created the *Madonna of Gdańsk*, is situated in one of the side chapels.

THE TEUTONIC ORDER

In 1190, during the Third Crusade of the Holy Land, some German nobles founded a military religious fraternity. This order went on to play a major role in Eastern Europe in the late Middle Ages, helping convert heathens to Christianity and to increase the holdings of the Christian Church. In the early 13th century the knights helped to subjugate the pagan East Prussians. Their victory awarded them control over a large area of what is today part of northern Poland. They built a large stronghold at Malbork which became their headquarters. By 1410 their fortunes began to fade with defeat in a battle at Tannenberg against Lithuania and Poland. In 1457 they were ousted from Prussia and their power gradually began to decrease. In 1525 they ceased to be a crusading order when their Grand Master became a Lutheran, and today they are a charitable organization.

THE UPPER CASTLE

The oldest structure of the complex, the ▷ *Upper Castle* is rectangular in plan with a central courtyard and impressive fortifications. A Gothic doorway (▷ *Golden Gate*) leads to the ▷ *Church St Mary* which was completed by 1280. Nearby, underneath the presbytery, is the ▷ *Chapel of St Anne*. Decisions on how the knights should function as a religious order were made in the Chapter House, while part of the second floor housed the residential quarters of the order's dignitaries.

The imposing bulk of the Upper Castle, part of Malbork Castle

Malbork

THE FORMER MAIN seat of the Teutonic Knights, Malbork is a wonderful example of a brick Gothic castle (▷ *Gothic Style p73*). In 1309 it was made the capital of an independent state established by the order. The first major phase of building was the fortified monastery, later known as the Upper Castle. The Middle Castle was built sometime after 1310, and the Palace of the Grand Master was constructed in 1382–99 by Konrad Zöllner von Rotenstein. In 1457 the castle was taken by Poland and used as a fortress. It was restored in the 19th century and again after World War II.

The well in the courtyard of the High Tower

★ Palace of the Grand Master
The grandeur of the four-story palace was almost without equal in medieval Europe.

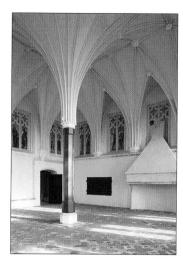

Summer Refectory
This beautiful room has double rows of windows and late Gothic palm vaulting, supported on a central column. The Winter Refectory adjoins it on its eastern side.

★ Golden Gate
Built in the late 13th century, this is enclosed by a porch. The keystone in the vaulting is carved with the figure of Christ.

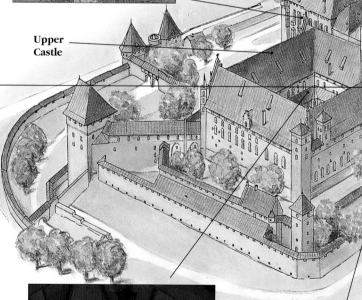

Upper Castle

Church of St Mary
contains an exhibition of decorative elements from the church and other items from the era of the Teutonic Knights.

Cloistered Courtyard
The inner courtyard of the Upper Castle is surrounded by slender Gothic arches with triangular vaulting.

STAR FEATURES

★ Palace of the Grand Master

★ Golden Gate

Lower Castle

These partly reconstructed farm buildings, abutting the former Chapel of St Lawrence, have been converted into a hotel.

LOWER CASTLE

Surrounded by moats and curtain walls with numerous towers, the Lower Castle was built to provide extra defense for the Teutonic Knights. A large armory was stored here in addition to there being a riverside granary, stables, and a brewery. St Lawrence's Chapel nearby was set aside for the use of the castle's servants.

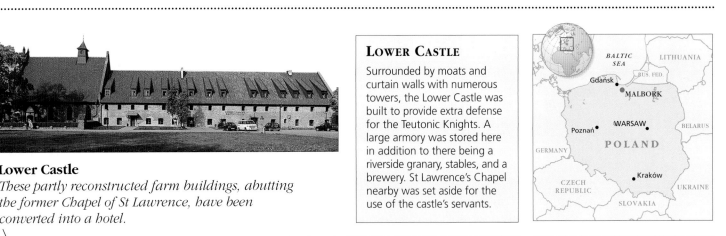

Battlements
A good view of the towers and walls surrounding the castle can be had from the east side.

Malbork

KEY DATES

1274 Construction work on the castle begins. The castle is enlarged and reconstructed throughout the 14th and early 15th centuries.

1457 The castle is seized by the Poles.

1772 Malbork is captured by the Prussians who turn it into a barracks, partially destroying it.

1817 Restoration work begins.

1945 Artillery bombardment damages part of the castle.

Early 1970's Most of the castle is restored.

1997 Malbork is declared a UNESCO World Heritage Site.

PALACE OF THE GRAND MASTERS

As the strength and power of the Teutonic Knights increased in the 14th century, Malbork underwent a period of restructuring. In the 1380s, construction began on the impressive ▷ *Palace of the Grand Masters*, which forms part of the Middle Castle on the western side. The imposing external features of this building appear to be of a defensive nature with watchtowers, crenelations, and turrets; however these are more decorative than functional. Inside, the ▷ *Summer Refectory* contains the original Gothic decorative elements. The basement housed the Grand Masters' offices, and the Order's postal chamber.

Teutonic Knight
The Teutonic Knights, or the Knights of the Teutonic Order of the Hospital of St Mary in Jerusalem, had a strict monastic code. In battle they were distinguished by the black crosses on their white cloaks.

Chapel of St Anne
Built in 1331–44 beneath the choir of the Church of St Mary, this contains the tombs of eleven Grand Masters.

Tombs of prominent Polish citizens in the cathedral crypt

INSIDE THE CATHEDRAL

Partly ruined at the start of World War II in 1939, St John's Cathedral came under attack again during the Warsaw Uprising in 1944 when a tank filled with explosives destroyed the southern section. In the reconstruction that took place after the war, the building was restored to its Gothic shape. The ornate embellishments of the 1830s however, were not reinstated and as a result the cathedral's interior is surprisingly austere. The plain white walls and brick vaulting give added prominence to the roof, which is decorated with stars, and to the exquisite stained-glass windows. Using documentation, copies were made of lost furnishings, such as the 17th-century wooden ▷ stalls.

HEROES AT REST

The cathedral is the resting place of many famous Poles. Cardinals, ▷ Mazovian dukes, and statesmen are buried in the crypt and a number of their tombs and memorials survived the war in various states of disrepair. Among them is the last king of Poland, Stanisław August Poniatowski, who was laid to rest here in 1798. Henryk Sienkiewicz (1846–1916), author of Quo Vadis? and the 1905 Nobel prize-winner for literature, is also buried here. So, too, is the former Polish president Gabriel Narutowicz (1865–1922), assassinated only a few days after taking office, as well as the Polish prelate and cardinal Stefan Wyszyński. The tomb of pianist and prime minister Ignacy Paderewski (1860–1941) also resides here.

St John's Cathedral, Warsaw

COMPLETED IN THE EARLY 15th century, the astounding St John's Cathedral (katedra św Jana) was once a parish church and is the oldest of Warsaw's churches. Gaining collegiate status in 1406, it was not until 1798 that St John's became a cathedral. Among the important events held here was the coronation of Stanisław August Poniatowski in 1764, and the swearing of an oath by the deputies of the *Sejm* (Parliament) to uphold the 1791 Constitution. After World War II, 19th-century additions were removed from the façade, and the cathedral was restored to its original Gothic design (▷ *Gothic Style p73*). The interior contains tombs and religious art.

★ Crypt of Gabriel Narutowicz
Poland's first president, assassinated two days after taking the presidential oath, is buried here, as is the Nobel prize-winning novelist Henryk Sienkiewicz.

Tomb of the Mazovian Dukes
This marble tomb commemorates the last two Mazovian dukes, after whose death the dukedom was incorporated into the Polish crown.

Bell tower

The towering red-brick façade was rebuilt after World War II in the Gothic style.

Chapel of the Holy Sacrament

Main entrance

PRIMATE OF THE MILLENNIUM

Cardinal Stefan Wyszyński (1901–81) became Primate of Poland in October 1948. Committed to defending the nation's Christian identity, he was arrested in 1953 and not released until 1956. Until his death he was the spiritual leader of Polish Catholics, which frequently brought him into conflict with the communist leaders. In 1980–81 he was a mediator between Solidarity and government.

St John's Cathedral

★ **Baryczka Crucifix**
Hanging in Baryczka Chapel, this 16th-century crucifix is credited with several miracles. Human hair was used on the head of Christ.

ORGAN FESTIVAL

Every year, from July to September, the "Organs of the Cathedral" festival fills St John's with music. Virtuosos from around the world are invited to play on the cathedral's historic collection of organs, which includes an acclaimed, modern German Eule organ, built in 1987.

Stalls
The existing stalls are copies of those commissioned by King Jan III Sobieski in gratitude for his 1683 victory over the Turks.

Chapel of the Men of Letters

Gallery
leading to the Royal Castle.

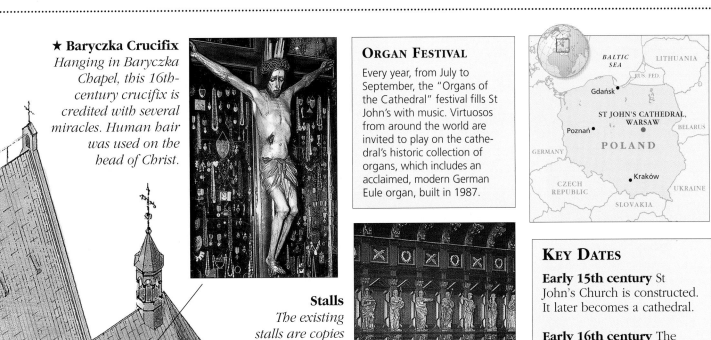

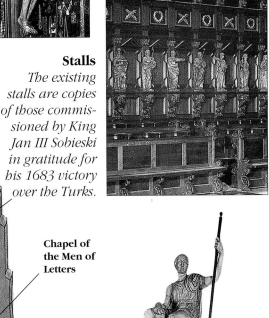

Memorial to Stanisław Małachowski
This marble sculpture is from a design by the Danish Neo-Classicist Bertel Thorwaldsen.

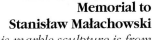

Caterpillar Track
Mounted on the wall, this track is from a Nazi radio-controlled tank that destroyed part of the cathedral during the Warsaw Uprising in 1944.

St John's Cathedral

KEY DATES

Early 15th century St John's Church is constructed. It later becomes a cathedral.

Early 16th century The building is badly damaged by fire.

1836–40 Architect Adam Idźkowski refurbishes the cathedral's façade.

1944 The cathedral is almost totally destroyed in the Warsaw Uprising.

1947–56 Rebuilding of the cathedral takes place.

1980 The rebuilt Old Town of Warsaw, including St John's Cathedral, is designated a UNESCO World Heritage Site.

CEREMONIAL EVENTS

St John's Cathedral has been the setting for some of Poland's major ceremonies. Kings crowned here include Władyslaw IV Vasa (1632–48) and Stanisław Leszczyński (1704–9, 1733–36). The coronation of Poland's last king, Stanisław August Poniatowski, took place in the cathedral on 25 November 1764. During his reign, the Polish constitution – the first in Europe – was passed on 3 May 1791 and crowds gathered at St John's to witness the king's oath to uphold the constitution and the swearing in of the *Sejm* (the Polish parliament). In the 16th century, when the capital moved from Cracow to Warsaw, the church became a focal point for music.

STAR FEATURES

★ **Crypt of Gabriel Narutowicz**

★ **Baryczka Crucifix**

INSIDE THE CASTLE

The Royal Castle's fascinating interiors are the result of its dual role: both as a royal residence and as the seat of the *Sejm* (Parliament). A tour of the castle features lavish royal apartments as well as the ▷ *Deputies' Chamber* and the Senate. Throughout it has been meticulously reconstructed in the style of the 18th century, and many of the furnishings and *objets d'art* are original to the castle. These include statues, paintings, and even fragments of woodwork and stucco, notably used in the New Audience Room, which were rescued from the building and hidden during World War II. The ▷ *Canaletto Room* displays 18th-century paintings of Warsaw by the Italian artist that were used as source material for the rebuilding of the Old Town of Warsaw and the castle.

THE GALLERIES

Among the many permanent exhibitions in the castle, two galleries are of particular interest. The Gallery of Decorative Arts, opened in 1998, is a showcase for 17th- and 18th-century ceramics, glass, furniture, textiles, bronzes, silverware, and jewelry. Around 200 pieces are on display including an Etruscan vase saved from the original castle. In the ▷ *Lanckoroński Gallery* there are paintings from the former royal gallery of King Stanisław August Poniatowski, donated by the Lanckoroński family in 1994. The collection includes works by Rembrandt, Teniers the Younger, and Anton von Maron.

The New Audience Room featuring original stucco-work

Royal Castle, Warsaw

Tabletop from 1777

A GRAND EXAMPLE of Baroque architecture, the original Royal Castle (Zamek Królewski) was planned on the site of a Mazovian fortress when Zygmunt III Vasa decided to move the capital from Cracow to Warsaw in 1596. It was designed in the early Baroque manner (▷ *Baroque Style p111*) by the Italian architects Giovanni Trevano, Giacomo Rodondo, and Matteo Castelli between 1598 and 1619. Successive rulers remodeled the castle many times. Following its destruction during World War II, the castle was rebuilt between 1971 and 1984, and many of the original furnishings were returned. This massive undertaking was funded largely by donations from the Polish people.

STAR FEATURES

★ **Ballroom**

★ **Marble Room**

★ **Canaletto Room**

★ **Ballroom**
Decorated with 17 pairs of golden columns, the ballroom is one of the castle's most elaborate interiors.

Royal Princes' Rooms
Historical paintings by Jan Matejko are displayed here.

Deputies' Chamber
In this room, the Constitution of 3 May was formally adopted in 1791. The coats of arms of all the administrative regions and territories of the Republic are depicted on the walls. A reconstructed royal throne is also on show.

Main entrance

Zygmunt Tower
This tower, 60 m (197 ft) high, was built in 1619. It is crowned by a cupola with a spire. It is also known as the Clock Tower (Zegarowa), since a clock was installed in 1622.

★ **Marble Room**
The interior dates from the time of Władysław IV
Vasa (r.1632–48). The magnificent portraits
of Polish rulers by Marcello Bacciarelli are
the only later additions.

The Lanckoroński Gallery on the
third floor contains two paintings by
Rembrandt: *Portrait of a Young*
Woman and *Scholar at his Desk.*

Knights' Hall
The finest piece in this
beautiful interior is
the Neo-Classical
sculpture of Chronos
by le Brun and
Monaldi.

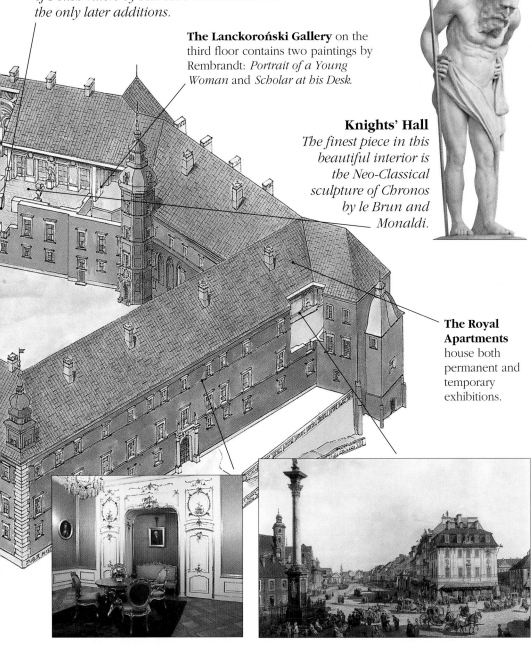

The Royal
Apartments
house both
permanent and
temporary
exhibitions.

CONSTITUTION

The Constitution of 3 May
was an experiment in
democratic reform – the first
of its kind in Europe. Members
of the *Sejm* (parliament) had
to swear an oath of allegiance
to it in St John's Cathedral.

KEY DATES

Early 1300s The dukes of
Mazovia build a fortress on
the site of the Royal Castle.

1598 Construction begins on
the Baroque addition.

1939–44 The Royal Castle is
destroyed in World War II.

1980 The rebuilt Old Town
of Warsaw, including the
Royal Castle, is designated a
UNESCO World Heritage Site.

1984 The restored Royal
Castle opens to the public.

POLAND'S LAST KING

Born in 1732, King Stanisław
August Poniatowski (r.1764–
95) was the son of the
palatine of Mazovia. He spent
his early life in St Petersburg
where he was introduced to
the future empress, Catherine
the Great, who took him as
her lover. Russia was keen to
add Poland to its empire and
perhaps to this end, Catherine
promised the Polish crown
to Poniatowski. When he fell
out of favor and was sent
back to Warsaw she was true
to her word and in 1764
engineered his election as
king of Poland. As king he
notably introduced economic
reforms, promoted the arts
and sciences. and presided
over the adoption of the
Constitution of 3 May 1791.
But he was unable to repel
his mighty neighbors: the
country was partitioned
between Russia, Prussia, and
Austria and by 1795 Poland
had lost its statehood. The
king abdicated and died in
St Petersburg in 1798.

Apartment of Prince
Stanisław Poniatowski
The Rococo paneling, thought to be by
Juste-Aurèle Meissonier, was taken from
the former Tarnowski Palace.

★ **Canaletto Room**
The walls of this room are decorated
with scenes of Warsaw by Canaletto, the
Venetian painter who was one of the most
commercially successful artists of his day.

Royal Castle

THE INTERIOR

This Gothic hall, with its distinctive crenelated gable, has been a house of prayer for over 700 years. Its twin-nave has a ribbed, vaulted ceiling. To avoid the sign of the cross, a fifth rib was added (▷ *five-rib vaulting*) and decorated with vine leaves, symbolizing the fertility of the land, and ivy. In a two-story building the women's gallery would be upstairs, but here it is located in the vestibule. The number 12 recurs in features throughout the synagogue, probably a reference to the 12 tribes of Israel.

The Old-New Synagogue and the Jewish Town Hall

THE JEWISH GHETTO

The Old-New Synagogue stands in Josefov, once Prague's Jewish Ghetto. The area is named after Emperor Josef II, who partially relaxed the discrimination against Jews during his reign in the 18th century. For centuries Prague's Jews had suffered from oppressive laws – in the 16th century they had to wear a yellow circle as a mark of shame. In the 1890s the ghetto slums were razed, but a handful of buildings survived, including the Jewish Town Hall and a number of synagogues. During World War II the Nazis occupied Prague and almost two-thirds of the city's Jewish population perished in the Holocaust, mainly in Terezín concentration camp, situated northwest of Prague.

Old-New Synagogue, Prague

Star of David in Červená Street

BUILT AROUND 1270, this is the oldest surviving synagogue in Europe and one of the earliest Gothic buildings in Prague (▷ *Gothic Style p73*). The synagogue has survived fires, slum clearances in the 19th century, and several Jewish pogroms. Residents of the city's Jewish Quarter (Josefov) have often had to seek refuge within its walls and today it is the religious center for Prague's Jewish community. It was originally called the New Synagogue until another synagogue was built nearby – this was later destroyed.

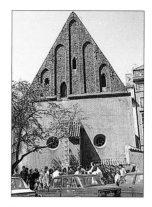

The synagogue's eastern side

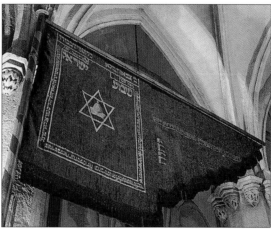

★ Jewish Standard
The historic banner of Prague's Jews is decorated with a Star of David and within it the hat that had to be worn by Jews in the 14th century.

These windows formed part of the 18th-century extensions built to allow women a view of the service.

14th-century stepped brick gable

Candlestick holder

RABBI LÖW AND THE GOLEM

The scholar and philosophical writer Rabbi Löw, director of the Talmudic school (which studied the Torah) in the late 16th century,

was also thought to possess magical powers. He was supposed to have created a figure, the Golem, from clay and then brought it to life by placing a magic stone tablet in its mouth. The Golem went berserk and the Rabbi had to remove the tablet. He hid the creature among the Old-New Synagogue's rafters.

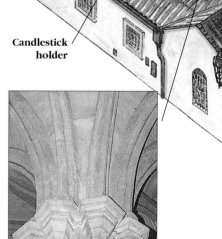

★ Five-rib Vaulting
Two massive octagonal pillars inside the hall support the five-rib vaults.

Right-hand Nave
The glow from the bronze chandeliers provides light for worshipers using the seats lining the walls.

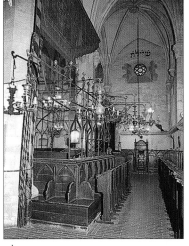

OLD JEWISH CEMETERY
Near the Old-New Synagogue is the Old Jewish Cemetery. For over 300 years, this was the only burial ground permitted for Jews. Over 100,000 people are estimated to be buried here. The oldest gravestone dates from 1439, and the last burial was in 1787.

The tympanum above the Ark is decorated with 13th-century leaf carvings.

★ **Rabbi Löw's Chair**
A Star of David marks the chair of the Chief Rabbi, placed where the distinguished 16th-century scholar used to sit.

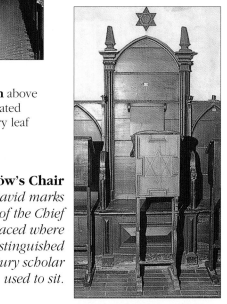

The cantor's platform and its lectern are surrounded by a wrought-iron Gothic grille.

Entrance to the Synagogue

The Ark
This shrine is the holiest place in the synagogue and holds the sacred scrolls of the Torah.

Entrance Portal
The tympanum above the door in the south vestibule is decorated with clusters of grapes and vine leaves growing on twisted branches.

STAR FEATURES

★ **Jewish Standard**

★ **Five-rib Vaulting**

★ **Rabbi Löw's Chair**

KEY DATES

Mid- to late 13th century
Work starts on building the New Synagogue.

18th century Construction of the women's gallery on the western and northern sides of the synagogue.

1883 The architect Joseph Mocker begins renovation work on the building.

1992 The Historic Center of Prague becomes a UNESCO World Heritage Site.

WORSHIPING IN THE SYNAGOGUE

The Old-New Synagogue is one of three synagogues in Prague where services are held today. Admonishing worshipers on their way into the synagogue are the following words inscribed on the ▷ *entrance portal*: "Revere God and observe his commandments! For this applies to all mankind". Inside, men and women are segregated for religious rituals. Services are held in the main prayer hall and are reserved for men only; those attending must keep their heads covered. Women may follow the rituals from the adjacent women's gallery, where they can stand and watch through small slot ▷ *windows*. In the center of the hall is the *bima*, similar to a wrought-iron cage, with a lectern from which the Torah is read daily (▷ *the cantor's platform*). Above this is a red ▷ *Jewish Standard*, which is a copy of the 1716 original.

Old-New Synagogue

PETER PARLÉŘ

The innovative 23-year-old builder, Peter Parléř (1330–99), began construction on St Vitus's Cathedral in 1359 after the original architect Matthew of Arras died in 1352. Under Parléř's supervision work on the cathedral continued based on Arras's designs and drawings, completing his planned sacristy and the Holy Cross chapel. Parléř then added his own plans to the cathedral in Gothic design (▷ *Gothic Style p73*). In the late 1300's he completed the choir, the ▷ *chancel*, the magnificent ▷ *Gothic vaulting*, the ▷ *Chapel of St Wenceslas*, and the south porch. Two years before his death, Parléř handed over construction of St Vitus's to his talented sons and nephews.

The Royal Mausoleum in St Vitus's Cathedral

THE ROYAL MAU-SOLEUM AND CRYPT

The white marble Royal Mausoleum is situated in front of the cathedral's high altar. It was designed and sculpted by Alexander Collin from Mecheln and built between 1566–89. The tombstone is adorned with sculpted figures. Steps lead down from the ground floor of the cathedral to the crypt, which contains the bodies of several Czech monarchs. These include King Charles IV (1316–78) and his four wives and Emperor Ferdinand I who died in 1564, as well as his beloved wife Anne and his son Maximilian II.

St Vitus's Cathedral, Prague

WORK BEGAN ON the city's most distinctive landmark in 1344 on the site of two previous churches, a 10th-century rotunda and an 11th-century basilica. The first architect was the French Matthew of Arras. After his death, Swabian Peter Parléř took over. His masons' lodge continued to work on the building until the early 15th century. The cathedral was finally completed by mid-19th- and 20th-century architects and artists. The cathedral houses the crown jewels and numerous tombs including saints such as "Good King" Wenceslas and King Rudolf II (1552–1612).

The Triforium was added between 1374–85 by master builder Peter Parléř. It is one of the most beautiful aspects of the cathedral.

The twin west spires were added during construction in the mid-19th to early 20th centuries.

Rose Window
Designed by František Kysela in 1925–7, this beautifully colored window above the portals depicts scenes from the biblical story of the creation.

The stained-glass windows in the cathedral contain many superb examples of 20th-century Czech glass designs.

Nave

St Vitus's Cathedral
This 19th-century engraving shows how the cathedral looked before the additions made in 1872–1929.

The main entrance's bronze doors are decorated with scenes from the cathedral's history.

Gargoyles
On the ornate west façade of St Vitus's, these gutter spouts are given their tradi-tional expressive disguise. The gargoyles are also meant to represent the fight between good and evil.

★ Flying Buttresses

The slender buttresses that surround the exterior of the nave and chancel, supporting the vaulted interior, are richly decorated like the rest of the cathedral.

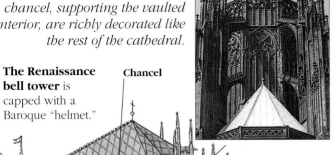

The Renaissance bell tower is capped with a Baroque "helmet."

Chancel

LIFE AND DEATH OF ST WENCESLAS

When the Christian Prince Wenceslas (c.907–929) came to power in 921 he tried to convert his pagan nobles and he swore allegiance to the German king, Henry I. This outraged some of his citizens as well as his brother Boleslav, who helped to assassinate him.

ST VITUS'S CATHEDRAL, PRAGUE

★ Chapel of St Wenceslas

The bronze ring on the chapel's north portal was thought to be the one to which St Wenceslas clung as he was murdered by his brother Boleslav.

KEY DATES

c.925 The rotunda of St Vitus's is constructed by St Wenceslas.

1060 Work on the triple-naved basilica begins.

1861–1929 The Gothic cathedral begun in 1344 is restored.

1929 St Vitus's is consecrated nearly 1,000 years after the death of St Wenceslas.

1992 The Historical Center of Prague, which includes St Vitus's, is inscribed a UNESCO World Heritage Site.

THE FOUR ERAS OF ST VITUS'S CATHEDRAL

Excavations of St Vitus's have revealed four different stages of the construction of the cathedral. The earliest building on the site was St Wenceslas' rotunda. Archaeologists also unearthed sections of the architectural and sculptural remains of the later basilica. Work on the cathedral was halted due to the Hussite wars in the early 15th century. At the time, construction had begun on the 96-m (315-ft) high south tower. When work eventually resumed, architectural fashion had moved into the Renaissance (▷ *Renaissance Style p211*) and the cathedral's designs were altered accordingly. In the 19th and 20th centuries final additions were made, which included ▷ *the twin west spires*, the western-side entrance and the gigantic ▷ *Rose Window*.

To Royal Palace

The tomb of St Wenceslas is connected to an altar, decorated with semi-precious stones.

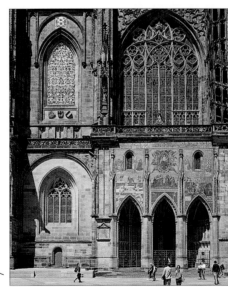

★ Golden Portal

Until the 19th century this was the main cathedral entrance, and it is still used on special occasions. Above it is a mosaic of The Last Judgment *by 14th-century Venetian craftsmen.*

Gothic Vaulting

The skills of architect Peter Parléř are never more clearly seen than in the delicate fans of ribbing that support the three Gothic arches of the Golden Portal.

STAR FEATURES

★ Flying Buttresses

★ Chapel of St Wenceslas

★ Golden Portal

St Vitus's Cathedral

THE SCULPTORS

Matthias Braun (1684–1738), who was born near Innsbruck and learned his craft in Austria and Italy, came to Prague in 1710. His first work, the statue of ▷ *St Luitgard*, was produced when he was only 26. Other sculptors were Johann Brokoff (1652–1718), of German origin, and his sons Michael and Ferdinand. The latter produced some of the bridge's most dynamic figures, such as ▷ *St Adalbert*, and his statue of ▷ *St Francis Xavier* which shows the Jesuit missionary supported by three Moorish and two Oriental converts.

EMULATING ROME

Charles Bridge was named after Charles IV, crowned Holy Roman Emperor in 1355, who wanted the bridge to echo the ancient Rome of the Caesars. However, it was not until the late 17th century that statues inspired by Roman sculptures were placed on the bridge. The statues mainly depict saints including ▷ *St Vitus*, the bridge's patron saint. Cherubs, dice, and a centurion's gauntlet form part of the statue of the ▷ *Madonna and St Bernard*. Nearby, the Dominicans are shown with the Madonna and their emblem, a dog (▷ *The Madonna, St Dominic, and St Thomas*).

Detail from the statue of St John de Matha, St Felix de Valois, and the Blessed Ivan

Charles Bridge, Prague

Prague's most familiar monument, connecting the city's Old Town with the Little Quarter, was the city's only crossing over the Vltava river until 1741. It is 520 m (1,706 ft) long and built of sandstone blocks. Now pedestrianized, at one time it could take four carriages abreast. Today, due to wear and tear, many of the statues are copies. The Gothic Old Town Bridge Tower (▷ *Gothic Style p73*) is one of the finest buildings of its kind.

View from Little Quarter Bridge Tower
The tall pinnacled wedge tower gives a superb view of the city of 100 spires.

LITTLE QUARTER SIDE

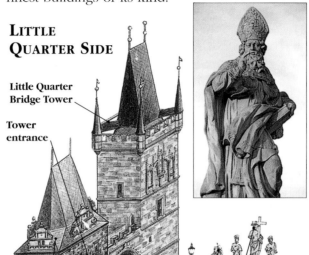

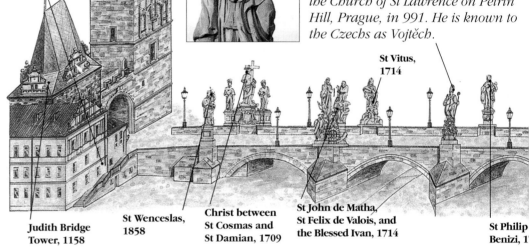

Little Quarter Bridge Tower

Tower entrance

Judith Bridge Tower, 1158

St Wenceslas, 1858

Christ between St Cosmas and St Damian, 1709

St Vitus, 1714

St John de Matha, St Felix de Valois, and the Blessed Ivan, 1714

St Philip Benizi, 1

St Adalbert, 1709
Adalbert, Bishop of Prague, founded the Church of St Lawrence on Petřín Hill, Prague, in 991. He is known to the Czechs as Vojtěch.

OLD TOWN SIDE

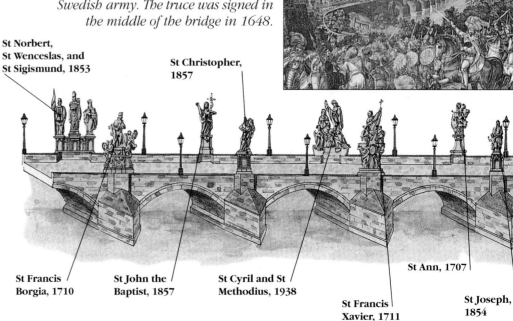

Thirty Years' War
In the last hours of this war, the Old Town was saved from the invading Swedish army. The truce was signed in the middle of the bridge in 1648.

St Norbert, St Wenceslas, and St Sigismund, 1853

St Christopher, 1857

St Francis Borgia, 1710

St John the Baptist, 1857

St Cyril and St Methodius, 1938

St Francis Xavier, 1711

St Ann, 1707

St Joseph, 1854

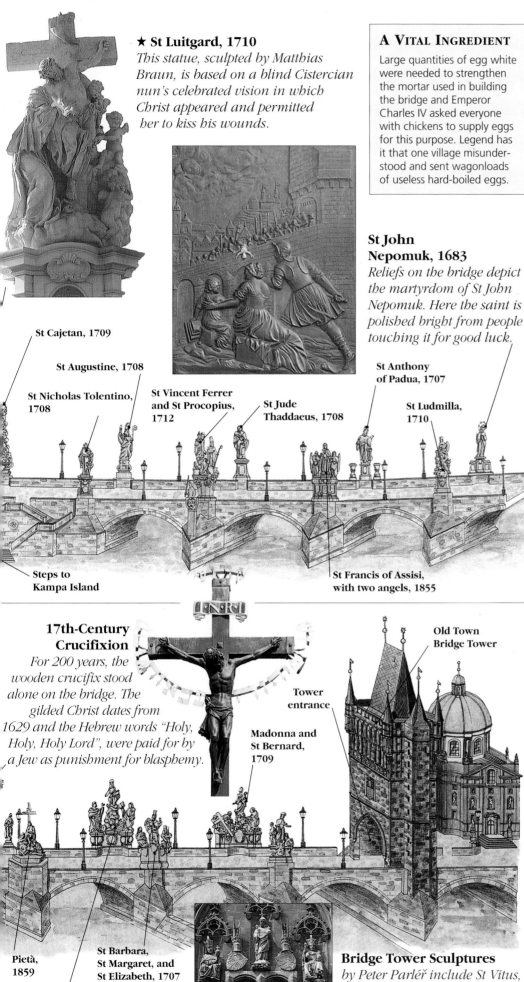

★ St Luitgard, 1710

This statue, sculpted by Matthias Braun, is based on a blind Cistercian nun's celebrated vision in which Christ appeared and permitted her to kiss his wounds.

A Vital Ingredient

Large quantities of egg white were needed to strengthen the mortar used in building the bridge and Emperor Charles IV asked everyone with chickens to supply eggs for this purpose. Legend has it that one village misunderstood and sent wagonloads of useless hard-boiled eggs.

St John Nepomuk, 1683

Reliefs on the bridge depict the martyrdom of St John Nepomuk. Here the saint is polished bright from people touching it for good luck.

St Cajetan, 1709

St Augustine, 1708

St Nicholas Tolentino, 1708

St Vincent Ferrer and St Procopius, 1712

St Jude Thaddaeus, 1708

St Anthony of Padua, 1707

St Ludmilla, 1710

Steps to Kampa Island

St Francis of Assisi, with two angels, 1855

17th-Century Crucifixion

For 200 years, the wooden crucifix stood alone on the bridge. The gilded Christ dates from 1629 and the Hebrew words "Holy, Holy, Holy Lord", were paid for by a Jew as punishment for blasphemy.

Tower entrance

Madonna and St Bernard, 1709

Old Town Bridge Tower

Pietà, 1859

St Barbara, St Margaret, and St Elizabeth, 1707

The Madonna, St Dominic, and St Thomas, 1708

Bridge Tower Sculptures

by Peter Parléř include St Vitus, the bridge's patron saint, Charles IV (left), and Wenceslas IV.

KEY DATES

1357 Charles IV commissions Peter Parléř to construct a new bridge, replacing the Judith Bridge.

1683 The first statue, of St John Nepomuk, is placed at the center of the bridge.

1683–1720 Statues by the Brokoffs and Braun are erected along the bridge.

1974 The bridge becomes a pedestrian area.

1992 The Historic Center of Prague joins the UNESCO list of World Heritage Sites.

THE LIFE OF ST JOHN NEPOMUK

The cult of St John Nepomuk, who was canonized in 1729, was promoted by the Jesuits to rival the revered Czech martyr Jan Hus, whose reformist preaching earned him a huge following in the early 15th century. Jan Nepomucký, vicar-general of the Archdiocese of Prague, was arrested in 1393 by Wenceslas IV along with others who had displeased the king over the election of an abbot. John died under torture and his body was bound and thrown off Charles Bridge. He is commemorated by a statue (▷ *St John Nepomuk*) and bronze relief depicting him being thrown off the bridge. St John Nepomuk is a popular figure and statues modeled on this one can be seen throughout central Europe, especially on bridges.

Charles Bridge

GERMANY

POLAND

CHARLES BRIDGE PRAGUE

Plzeň

CZECH REPUBLIC

Brno

AUSTRIA

SLOVAKIA

MÁTYÁS CHURCH CORONATIONS

Hungarian rulers had to be crowned in a church before they were officially accepted by their subjects. One of the first kings to be crowned in Mátyás Church was Charles I Robert of Anjou (1307), who ruled Hungary for 35 years, followed by Sigismund of Luxemburg in 1387. Mátyás Corvinus was also crowned here in the 15th century. In 1867 the coronation of Habsburg Emperor Franz Joseph I and his wife Elizabeth as king and queen of Hungary took place in the church. A splendid *Coronation Mass* was composed by Franz Liszt especially for the occasion. The last king of Hungary, Charles IV, was crowned in Mátyás Church in 1916.

RESTORING MÁTYÁS CHURCH

During the Turkish occupation of Hungary in the 16th century, Mátyás Church was turned into a mosque and many of its internal furnishings were stripped out. The ornate Christian frescoes adorning the walls of the building were whitewashed. When the Turks were expelled in 1686, the building was reclaimed by the Church and attempts were made to restore it. However, it was not until the late 19th century, under the direction of architect Frigyes Schulek, that the church regained its former glory. He uncovered past architectural features from the 13th century and reconstructed the early Gothic motifs. New ▷ *stained-glass windows* were designed for the church and the glazed tile ▷ *roof* was added.

White stone-laced Gothic tower

Mátyás Church, Budapest

THE PARISH CHURCH of Our Lady Mary is one of the oldest coronation churches in Hungary. Some of the Gothic features (▷ *Gothic Style p73*) date from the reign of Sigismund of Luxemburg but the church is named after King Mátyás Corvinus, who greatly enlarged and embellished the church. Much of its original details were lost when the invading Turks converted the church into the Great Mosque in 1541. After the liberation of Buda, the church was rebuilt with a Baroque interior (▷ *Baroque Style p111*) by Franciscan Friars. The church suffered more damage in 1723 and was restored in the Neo-Gothic style by Frigyes Schulek in 1873–96.

Rose Window
Frigyes Schulek faithfully reproduced the medieval stained-glass window that was located here during the early Gothic era.

★ Baroque Madonna
According to legend, the original statue was set into a wall of the church during the Turkish occupation. When the church was virtually destroyed in 1686, the Madonna made a miraculous appearance. The Turks took this as an omen of defeat.

Béla Tower
This tower is named after the church's founder, King Béla IV (r.1235–70). It has retained several of its original Gothic features.

Main Portal
Above the arched west entrance is a 19th-century bas-relief of the Madonna and Child, seated between two angels. The work is by Lajos Lantai.

STAR FEATURES

★ **Baroque Madonna**

★ **Tomb of King Béla III and Anne de Châtillon**

★ **Mary Portal**

★ Tomb of King Béla III and Anne de Châtillon
The remains of this royal couple were transferred from Székesfehérvár Cathedral to Mátyás Church in 1860. They lie beneath an ornamental stone canopy in the Trinity Chapel.

MUSEUM OF ECCLESIASTICAL ART

Beneath the crypt of Mátyás Church is a museum displaying replicas of the Hungarian royal crown. There are also old chalices and vestments, as well as the remains of medieval stonework.

The roof is decorated with multicolored glazed tiles.

Pulpit
The richly decorated pulpit, in the south side of the church, includes the carved stone figures of the four Fathers of the Church and the four Evangelists.

The main altar was created by Frigyes Schulek and based on Gothic triptychs.

Stained-Glass Windows
Three arched windows on the south elevation have beautiful 19th-century stained glass which were designed by Frigyes Schulek, Bertalan Székely, and Károly Lotz.

The interior was painted by Károly Lotz and Bertalan Székely in geometric patterns and adorned with frescoes in the 19th century.

★ Mary Portal
This depiction of the Assumption of the Blessed Virgin Mary is the most magnificent example of Gothic stone carving in Hungary. Frigyes Schulek reconstructed the portal using fragments that remained after World War II.

KEY DATES

1255 The Mátyás Church is founded by King Béla IV.

1300s Sigismund of Luxemburg redesigns the church in the Gothic style.

1945 The church is badly damaged by the German and Russian armies.

KING MÁTYÁS CORVINUS

The greatest Hungarian king, Mátyás Corvinus (1440–90), was crowned in 1458. He was the first Hungarian on the throne since the 14th century, as Hungary had been subsequently ruled by foreign kings. During his reign Corvinus introduced new reforms, which raised the nation's social, economic, and cultural standards. These lifted the tax burdens off the poor and eliminated tax exemptions for high-ranking nobles. A centralized court system, overseen by Corvinus and his chosen judges, ensured equal rights for all citizens. The king was a generous patron of the Church and he encouraged art and literature. However, as the country flourished, bloody battles were being fought abroad with the Holy Roman Emperor Frederick III, who challenged the king for the Hungarian crown. Corvinus later sought and won the right to rule Bohemia where he was crowned king in 1469. Crusades against the Turks were also fought, which ended in 1483 after a victorious campaign by Hungary.

Mátyás Church

IMRE STEINDL

Professor of architecture at Hungary's Technical University, Imre Steindl (1839–1902) won the competition to design Hungary's Parliament. The building was to symbolize the country's thriving democracy. Steindl drew inspiration from Charles Barry and A W Pugin's Neo-Gothic Houses of Parliament in London. However, for the internal spaces, including the superb ▷ *Dome Hall*, he used references from Baroque (▷ *Baroque Style p111*) and Renaissance (▷ *Renaissance Style p211*) styles as well.

Parliament building's exterior adorned with lace-like pinnacles

SACRED CROWN OF ST STEPHEN I

The first Hungarian king, St Stephen I (c.975–1038), received the royal crown from Pope Sylvester II in the year 1000. The crown became a symbol of Christianity and all Hungarian kings who followed after Stephen I were crowned with the sacred diadem. Many today believe that the crown bears little resemblance to the original crown, because over the centuries it has been lost and stolen. Battles and wars have also been fought for possession of the crown. At the end of World War II it was taken to America for safekeeping and returned to Hungary with much fanfare in 1978. The crown now resides in Hungary's Parliament.

Parliament, Budapest

I MRE STEINDL's rich Neo-Gothic Parliament (▷ *Gothic Style p73*) is Hungary's largest building and a symbol of Budapest. Hungarian materials, techniques, and master craftsmen were used in its construction. The building is 268 m (880 ft) long and 96 m (315 ft) high. The north wing houses the offices of Hungary's Prime Minister, while the south wing contains those of the President of the Republic.

One of the pair of lions at the main entrance

Aerial View
The magnificent dome marks the central point of the Parliament building. Although the façade is elaborately Neo-Gothic, the ground plan follows Baroque conventions.

★ Dome Hall
Adorning the massive pillars that support Parliament's central dome are figures of some of the rulers of Hungary.

★ National Assembly Hall
Formerly the upper house, this hall is now where the National Assembly convenes. Two paintings by Zsigmond Vajada hang on either side of the Speaker's lectern. These were especially commissioned for the building.

Façade facing River Danube

South wing

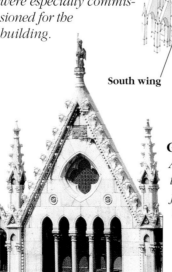

Gables
Almost every corner of the Parliament building features gables with pinnacles based on Gothic sculptures.

Lobby
Lobbies, the venues for political discussions, line the corridors lit by stained-glass windows.

Dome
The ceiling of the 96-m (315-ft) high dome is covered in an intricate design of Neo-Gothic gilding combined with heraldic decoration.

PARLIAMENT VASE
In 1954, the Herend Porcelain Manufacturers made the first Parliament Vase. It stood in the ▷ *Dome Hall* for ten years and was then moved to the Herend Museum. A new vase was created in 2000 to mark Hungary's 1000 years of statehood.

Gobelin Hall
This hall is decorated with a Gobelin tapestry illustrating Prince Árpád, with seven Magyar leaders under his command, signing a peace treaty and blood oath.

North wing

Main Entrance

The Royal Insignia, excluding the Coronation Mantle, are kept in the Dome Hall.

STAR FEATURES

★ **Dome Hall**

★ **National Assembly Hall**

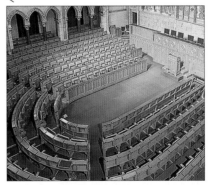

Congress Hall
This vast hall is virtually a mirror image of the National Assembly Hall. Both halls have public galleries running around a horseshoe-shaped interior.

Main Staircase
The best contemporary artists were invited to decorate the interior. The sumptuous main staircase features ceiling frescoes by Károly Lotz and sculptures by György Kiss.

KEY DATES

1882 Imre Steindl wins the competition for the design of the Parliament building.

1885 The first foundation stone is laid as construction of the Parliament building begins.

1902 Work on the Parliament building is completed.

1987 The historical area of Budapest, which includes the Parliament building, is inscribed a UNESCO World Heritage Site.

PARLIAMENT'S STATUES

Surrounding the external façade of Parliament are 90 statues, which include some of Hungary's past monarchs, writers, revolutionaries, and Prime Ministers. A statue of the Transylvanian prince, Ferenc Rákóczi II (1676–1735), who fought the Habsburgs for Hungary's freedom, is at the southern end. Nearby is a seated statue of the Hungarian writer József Attila (1905–37). His first collection of poems was published at the age of 17. Adorning the ▷ *north wing* is the statue of Lajos Kossuth (1802–94), who fought for Hungary's independence for six months in 1849 before being driven into exile. Next to Kossuth's statue is that of the democratic Prime Minister and revolutionary, Mihály Károlyi (1875–1955). He ruled Hungary for five months in 1919 until he was forced into exile, after the government was overthrown by the Communists.

Parliament

AUGUSTE DE MONTFERRAND

Tsar Alexander I awarded the young architect Auguste de Montferrand (1786–1858) the commission to design and build the present-day St Isaac's Cathedral, dedicated to Saint Isaac of Dalmatia. The foundations were laid in 1818 but it took a further 40 years before the cathedral was completed. During that time Montferrand supervised St Isaac's construction, while he took on other works. He designed the Alexander Column (1830–32), a memorial celebrating Russia's victory over Napoleon, which is erected in St Petersburg's Palace Square, and restored parts of the Winter Palace for Tsar Nicholas I. St Isaac's was finally inaugurated in 1858 and Montferrand died that same year.

ST ISAAC'S BUILDING MATERIALS

Constructed from over 40 different minerals, granites, and marbles, the magnificent St Isaac's, nicknamed "museum of Russian geology", dominates the St Petersburg skyline. Materials used in the construction of the cathedral came from Siberia, Finland, and Italy among other places. The external steps made from large blocks of granite lead to entrances under porticoes, which are supported by ▷ *red granite columns,* decorated in bronze bas-reliefs. Inside, the cathedral floor is crafted from marble in different colors, shades, and patterns.

St Isaac's dome, gilded with over 100 kg (220 lb) of pure gold.

St Isaac's Cathedral, St Petersburg

ONE OF THE WORLD'S largest cathedrals, St Isaac's was designed by the then unknown architect Auguste de Montferrand. It was the fourth and final St Isaac's to be built in St Petersburg. Previous versions ordered by Russian rulers over the centuries were either destroyed or remodeled. Construction of Montferrand's vast building was a major engineering feat. Thousands of wooden piles were sunk into the ground to support its weight of 300,000 tonnes and 48 columns were hauled into place. The cathedral opened in 1858, but was designated a museum from the time of the Soviet era.

The Dome
From the dome there are panoramic views over the city which include the Admiralty and the Hermitage. Adorning the dome are angels sculpted by Josef Hermann.

The mosaic icons on the iconostasis are by Bryullov, Neff, and Zhivago.

Angels with Torch
Ivan Vitali created many of the cathedral's sculptures, including the pairs of angels supporting gas torches which crown the four attic corners.

This chapel honors Alexander Nevsky who defeated the Swedes in 1240.

★ Iconostasis
Three rows of icons surround the royal doors through which a stained-glass window (1843) is visible. Above the doors is Peter Klodt's gilded sculpture, Christ in Majesty *(1859).*

The north pediment is decorated with a bronze relief (1842–44) of the Resurrection designed by François Lemaire.

Malachite and lapis lazuli columns frame the iconostasis. About 16,000 kg (35,280 lbs) of malachite decorate the cathedral.

Exit

St Catherine's Chapel has an exquisite white marble iconostasis, crowned by a sculpted Resurrection (1850–54) by Nikolay Pimenov.

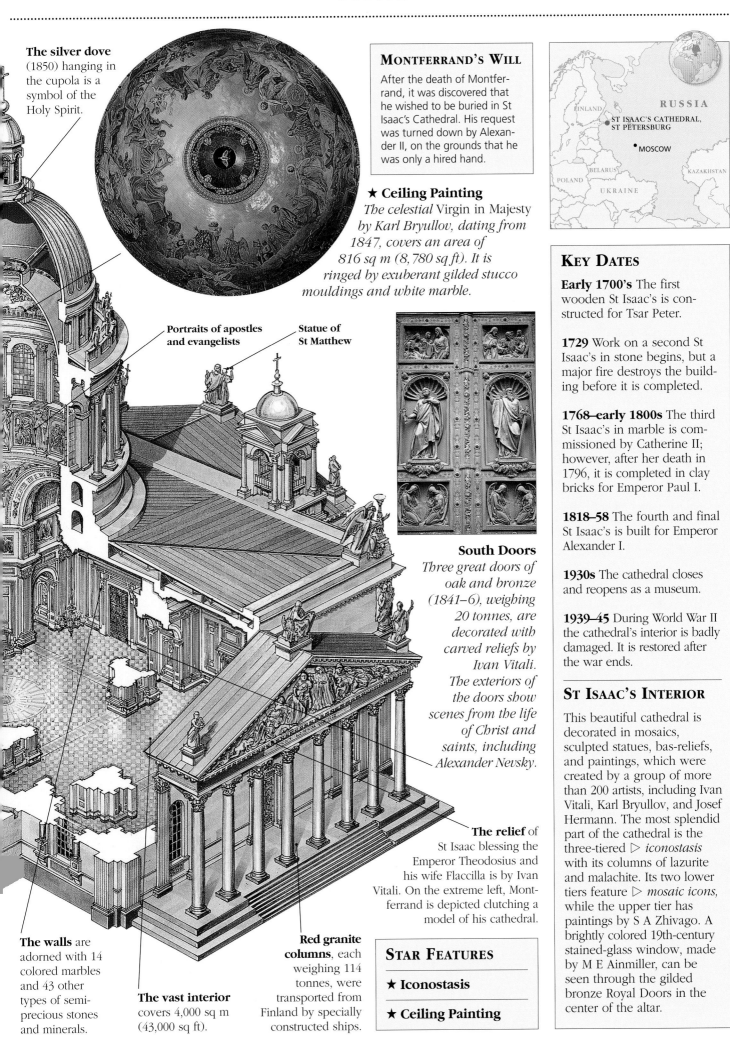

The silver dove (1850) hanging in the cupola is a symbol of the Holy Spirit.

Portraits of apostles and evangelists

Statue of St Matthew

The walls are adorned with 14 colored marbles and 43 other types of semi-precious stones and minerals.

The vast interior covers 4,000 sq m (43,000 sq ft).

Red granite columns, each weighing 114 tonnes, were transported from Finland by specially constructed ships.

RUSSIA

ST ISAAC'S CATHEDRAL,
ST PETERSBURG

• MOSCOW

FINLAND

POLAND   BELARUS
         UKRAINE   KAZAKHSTAN

MONTFERRAND'S WILL

After the death of Montfer-rand, it was discovered that he wished to be buried in St Isaac's Cathedral. His request was turned down by Alexander II, on the grounds that he was only a hired hand.

★ Ceiling Painting

The celestial Virgin in Majesty by Karl Bryullov, dating from 1847, covers an area of 816 sq m (8,780 sq ft). It is ringed by exuberant gilded stucco mouldings and white marble.

South Doors

Three great doors of oak and bronze (1841–6), weighing 20 tonnes, are decorated with carved reliefs by Ivan Vitali. The exteriors of the doors show scenes from the life of Christ and saints, including Alexander Nevsky.

The relief of St Isaac blessing the Emperor Theodosius and his wife Flaccilla is by Ivan Vitali. On the extreme left, Mont-ferrand is depicted clutching a model of his cathedral.

STAR FEATURES

★ **Iconostasis**

★ **Ceiling Painting**

KEY DATES

Early 1700's The first wooden St Isaac's is con-structed for Tsar Peter.

1729 Work on a second St Isaac's in stone begins, but a major fire destroys the build-ing before it is completed.

1768–early 1800s The third St Isaac's in marble is com-missioned by Catherine II; however, after her death in 1796, it is completed in clay bricks for Emperor Paul I.

1818–58 The fourth and final St Isaac's is built for Emperor Alexander I.

1930s The cathedral closes and reopens as a museum.

1939–45 During World War II the cathedral's interior is badly damaged. It is restored after the war ends.

ST ISAAC'S INTERIOR

This beautiful cathedral is decorated in mosaics, sculpted statues, bas-reliefs, and paintings, which were created by a group of more than 200 artists, including Ivan Vitali, Karl Bryullov, and Josef Hermann. The most splendid part of the cathedral is the three-tiered ▷ *iconostasis* with its columns of lazurite and malachite. Its two lower tiers feature ▷ *mosaic icons*, while the upper tier has paintings by S A Zhivago. A brightly colored 19th-century stained-glass window, made by M E Ainmiller, can be seen through the gilded bronze Royal Doors in the center of the altar.

St Isaac's Cathedral

THE SMALL AND LARGE HERMITAGE

Catherine hired architect Yuriy Velten to erect the Small Hermitage so she could privately entertain her chosen friends at court. The building was designed in the Late Baroque style with Early Classical features to blend alongside Rastrelli's Baroque Winter Palace. After the Small Hermitage was constructed, Catherine decided to house her newly acquired collection of over 255 paintings in the building as well. The Large Hermitage was built a few years later to accommodate the tsarina's vast library and works of art. Over the centuries, Catherine's original collection has been added to. There are now over 3 million pieces of art displayed in the Small and Large Hermitage, as well as in an ensemble of buildings, which includes the Winter Palace. There are exhibits from the Stone Age up to the 20th century, including works by Matisse, Rembrandt, and Cézanne.

BARTOLOMEO RASTRELLI

The Italian architect Rastrelli (1700–71) studied under his father and assisted him during his appointment as architect for Tsar Peter I. In 1722 Rastrelli took on his own commissions in Moscow and St Petersburg, which established him as a brilliant Baroque architect. During Elizabeth's reign, he was appointed Chief Court Architect and went on to design several buildings, including the grandiose Winter Palace. When Catherine the Great ascended the throne, Rastrelli retired from court as she preferred a stricter Classical design.

Rastrelli, court architect until 1763

The Winter Palace, St Petersburg

THIS SUPERB EXAMPLE of Baroque architecture (▷ *Baroque Style p111*) was the home of the Russian tsars and tsarinas from the late 18th century, including Catherine the Great. Built for Tsarina Elizabeth (r.1741–62), this opulent winter residence was the finest achievement of Italian architect Bartolomeo Rastrelli. Though the exterior has changed little, the interiors were altered by a number of architects and then largely restored after a fire gutted the palace in 1837. After the assassination of Alexander II in 1881, the imperial family rarely lived here. In July 1917, the Provisional Government took the palace as its headquarters, which led to its storming by the Bolsheviks.

The 1812 Gallery (1826) has portraits of Russian military heroes of the Napoleonic War, most by English artist George Dawe.

The Armorial Hall (1839), with its vast gilded columns, covers over 800 sq m (8,600 sq ft). It now houses the European silver collection and a restored imperial carriage.

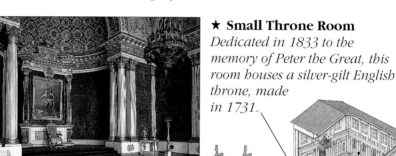

★ **Small Throne Room**
Dedicated in 1833 to the memory of Peter the Great, this room houses a silver-gilt English throne, made in 1731.

The Field Marshals' Hall (1833) was the reception room where the devastating fire of 1837 broke out.

To Large Hermitage

The Hall of St George (1795) has monolithic columns and wall facings of Italian Carrara marble.

The Nicholas Hall, the largest room in the palace, was always used for the first ball of the season.

North façade overlooking the River Neva

★ **Jordan Staircase**
This vast, sweeping staircase (1762) was Rastrelli's masterpiece. It was from here that the imperial family watched the Epiphany ceremony of baptism in the Neva, which celebrated Christ's baptism in the Jordan.

★ **Malachite Room**
Over two tonnes of ornamental stone were used in this sumptuous room (1839) which is decorated with malachite columns and vases, gilded doors and rich parquet flooring.

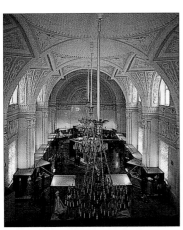

Alexander Hall
Architect Aleksandr Bryullov employed a mixture of Gothic vaulting and Neo-Classical stucco bas-reliefs of military themes in this reception room of 1837.

STORMING THE PALACE

On the evening of 25 October 1917, the Bolsheviks fired some blank shots at the Winter Palace, storming it soon after to arrest the Provisional Government who resided there. The communists took over power and the Revolution was a fact.

RUSSIA

THE WINTER PALACE, ST PETERSBURG

FINLAND

• MOSCOW

POLAND   BELARUS   KAZAKHSTAN

UKRAINE

The White Hall
was decorated for the wedding of the future Alexander II in 1841.

The French Rooms,
designed by Bryullov in 1839, house a collection of 18th-century French art.

South façade on Palace Square

Dark Corridor
The French and Flemish tapestries here include The Marriage of Emperor Constantine, *made in Paris in the 17th century to designs by Rubens.*

The Rotunda
(1830) connected the private apartments in the west with the state apartments on the palace's north side.

West wing

The Gothic Library
and other rooms in the northwest part of the palace were adapted to suit Nicholas II's bourgeois lifestyle. This wood-paneled library was created by Meltzer in 1894.

The Gold Drawing Room
Created in the 1850s, this room was extravagantly decorated in the 1870s with all-over gilding of walls and ceiling. It houses a display of Western European carved gems.

STAR FEATURES

★ **Small Throne Room**

★ **Jordan Staircase**

★ **Malachite Room**

KEY DATES

1754–62 The Winter Palace is constructed.

1764–75 The Small Hermitage by Yuriy Velten is built for Catherine II's art collection.

1771–87 The Large Hermitage, also by Yuriy Velten, is added.

1917 Anatoly Lunacharsky of the Soviet Government declares the Winter Palace and the Hermitage state museums.

1990 The historical city of St Petersburg, which includes the Winter Palace and the Hermitage, is inscribed a UNESCO World Heritage Site.

CATHERINE II

Tsarina Elizabeth chose the German-born princess Catherine (1729–96), the future Catherine the Great, as a wife for her successor Peter III. When he ascended the throne in 1762, Catherine had resided in Russia for 18 years and had fully immersed herself in the Russian culture. She was also widely read and corresponded with French intellectuals such as Voltaire and Diderot. Six months into Peter's reign, Catherine and her allies at the Imperial Guard had the tsar killed. She was then crowned ruler of Russia in 1763. During her reign she implemented many reforms and expanded the Russian territory. Art and trade flourished and new academies were built, including the Russian Academy of Sciences and the Academy of Fine Art.

The Winter Palace

AGATE ROOMS AND CAMERON GALLERY

Charles Cameron (1740–1812), an expert on Roman bath architecture, was employed to translate Catherine the Great's ideas for the estate into reality. The ▷ *Agate Rooms*, part of the imperial baths, are among his most impressive work. The heavily rusticated lower story of this sumptuous pavilion contrasts with the upper tier, which was modeled on a Renaissance villa. Its name derives from the interior's decoration of agate, malachite, and other semiprecious stones. The ▷ *Cameron Gallery* has a rusticated stone first floor, surmounted by a Neo-Classical peristyle of 44 Ionic columns. The colonnade features bronze busts of ancient poets, rulers, and philosophers. In 1792–4 Cameron added a ramp to facilitate access to the gardens for his aging patron.

THE GARDENS

The gardens of Catherine Park illustrate the two dominant schools of 18th-century landscape gardening – formal and naturalistic. In front of the palace are the ▷ *formal gardens* laid out geometrically with radiating avenues, terraces, parterres, hedges, elegant pavilions, and Classical statuary. The naturalistic landscaped area of the lower park was created by gardeners such as the Englishman John Bush. This romantic garden contains canals, cascades, and ponds where Catherine the Great would float on gilded gondolas to music.

Formal gardens in front of the palace at Tsarskoe Selo

Tsarskoe Selo

THE LAVISH imperial palace at Tsarskoe Selo was designed by the Italian architect Bartolomeo Rastrelli (1700–71) in 1752 for Tsarina Elizabeth. Over the next two centuries the palace became the summer residence of the tsars, and craftsmen ensured that the opulence and splendor found here were supreme. Elizabeth named the building the Catherine Palace in honor of her mother, Catherine I, who originally owned the estate. During the subsequent reign of Catherine the Great (1762–96), the Scotsman Charles Cameron redesigned the Baroque interiors for her more Neo-Classical taste (▷ *Neo-Classical Style p79*). The opulence of the palace is matched by a magnificent landscaped park, one of the first in Russia.

Atlantes
The stunning 300-m (980-ft) long Baroque façade is adorned with a profusion of atlantes, columns, pilasters, and ornamented window framings.

| 0 meters | 25 |
| 0 yards | 25 |

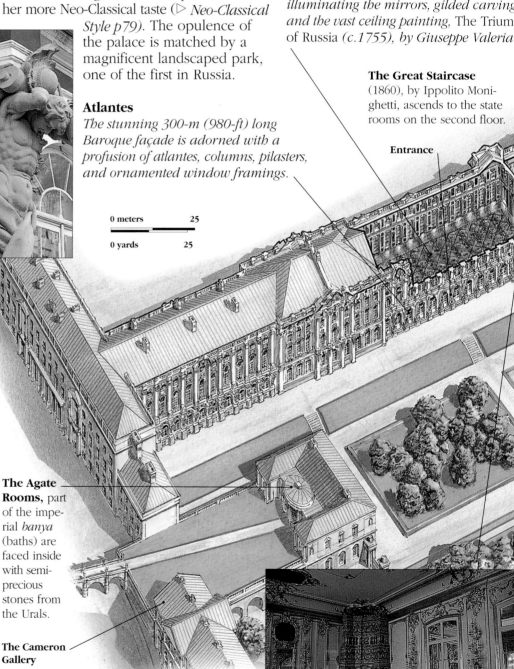

★ **The Great Hall**
Light streams into Rastrelli's glittering hall illuminating the mirrors, gilded carvings and the vast ceiling painting, The Triumph of Russia *(c.1755), by Giuseppe Valeriani.*

The Great Staircase
(1860), by Ippolito Monighetti, ascends to the state rooms on the second floor.

Entrance

The Agate Rooms, part of the imperial *banya* (baths) are faced inside with semiprecious stones from the Urals.

The Cameron Gallery

The Cavaliers' Dining Room
The table is laid for Tsarina Elizabeth's gentlemen-in-waiting, in the refined gold and white room created by Rastrelli.

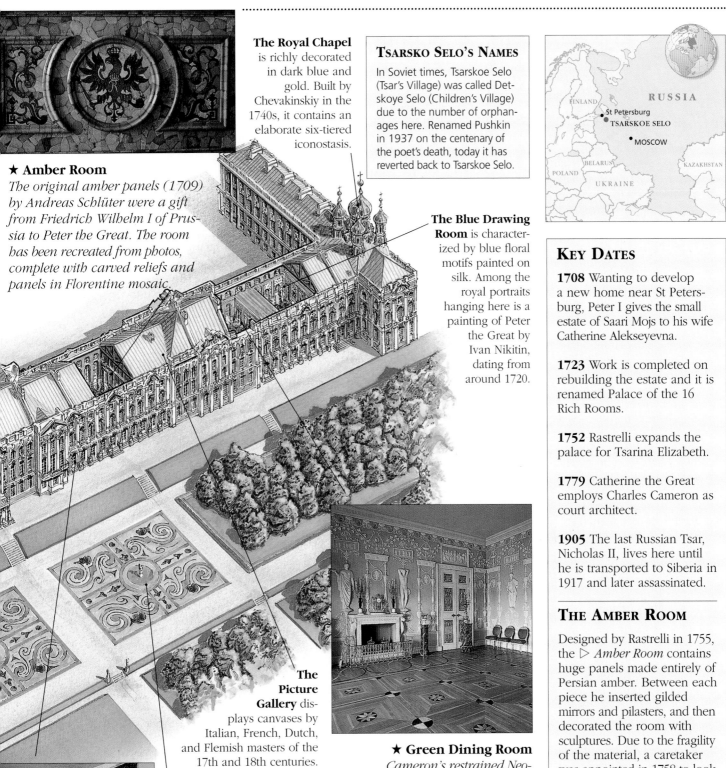

The Royal Chapel is richly decorated in dark blue and gold. Built by Chevakinskiy in the 1740s, it contains an elaborate six-tiered iconostasis.

★ **Amber Room**
The original amber panels (1709) by Andreas Schlüter were a gift from Friedrich Wilhelm I of Prus-sia to Peter the Great. The room has been recreated from photos, complete with carved reliefs and panels in Florentine mosaic.

The Blue Drawing Room is character-ized by blue floral motifs painted on silk. Among the royal portraits hanging here is a painting of Peter the Great by Ivan Nikitin, dating from around 1720.

KEY DATES

1708 Wanting to develop a new home near St Peters-burg, Peter I gives the small estate of Saari Mojs to his wife Catherine Alekseyevna.

1723 Work is completed on rebuilding the estate and it is renamed Palace of the 16 Rich Rooms.

1752 Rastrelli expands the palace for Tsarina Elizabeth.

1779 Catherine the Great employs Charles Cameron as court architect.

1905 The last Russian Tsar, Nicholas II, lives here until he is transported to Siberia in 1917 and later assassinated.

THE AMBER ROOM

Designed by Rastrelli in 1755, the ▷ *Amber Room* contains huge panels made entirely of Persian amber. Between each piece he inserted gilded mirrors and pilasters, and then decorated the room with sculptures. Due to the fragility of the material, a caretaker was appointed in 1758 to look after the precious fossil. Extra panels were commissioned for the lower tiers, and the room was completed in 1770. Considered the most beautiful room in the palace, the Amber Room symbolizes the huge loss of Russian art treasures during World War II. All of the original panels disappeared during the German occupation and were never recovered. The room has been pains-takingly reconstructed using old photos and documents, and was completed in 2003.

The Picture Gallery dis-plays canvases by Italian, French, Dutch, and Flemish masters of the 17th and 18th centuries.

The French-style formal gardens were laid out in the 1740s. Their formality and symmetry contrasts with the naturalistic English-style landscaping of the park, created in 1768.

★ **Green Dining Room**
Cameron's restrained Neo-Classical style contrasts with the Baroque flamboyance of Rastrelli's work. The exquisite stucco bas-reliefs, sculpted by Ivan Martos, were based on motifs from frescoes discovered in Pompeii.

Small Enfilade
A varied selection of furniture and objets d'art make up the exhibition in these unrestored rooms. Chinese lacquer furniture and Oriental rugs were among the treasures used to furnish the palace in the 19th century.

STAR FEATURES

★ **The Great Hall**

★ **Amber Room**

★ **Green Dining Room**

Tsarskoe Selo

Two-headed eagle, adopted from Byzantium by Ivan III

IVAN THE GREAT

Under the reign of Ivan III, "the Great" (1462–1505), Moscow came to rule a kingdom which stretched from the Arctic Ocean in the north to the Urals in the east. To underscore the city's position and to raise its status further, Ivan the Great undertook an ambitious building programme which saw the aggrandisement of the Kremlin. He started the tradition of importing foreign architects to design his buildings, especially Italians, who built the present Kremlin walls. To help secure Moscow's claim to being the last defender of the true Eastern Orthodox Church, and to strengthen his dynastic position, Ivan married the niece of the last Byzantine emperor. In 1480 his rule became absolute when he freed Muscovy from Mongol rule.

FRESCOES

The cathedral's spacious and light interior is entirely covered with frescoes. Originally created by the icon painter Dionysius, most have been replaced by later masters (▷ Frescoes), yet the effect is still impressive. Following the tradition of Russian Orthodox churches, there is a depiction of the The Last Judgment on the west wall showing sinners being delivered to Hell with Christ towering above. The upper tiers of the north and south walls are beautifully illustrated with stories from the life of the Virgin. The painted ▷ pillars are also one of the building's highlights. All the works are highly schematized with lucid compositions, and are of excellent quality.

Cathedral of the Assumption, Moscow

FROM THE EARLY 14TH CENTURY, the Cathedral of the Assumption was the most important church in Moscow. It was here that princes were crowned and the metropolitans and patriarchs of the Orthodox Church were buried. In the 1470s Ivan the Great decided to build a more imposing cathedral, to reflect the growing might of the nation during his reign. When the first version collapsed, possibly in an earthquake, Ivan summoned the Italian architect Aristotele Fioravanti to Moscow. He designed a light and spacious masterpiece in the spirit of the Renaissance.

The golden domes stand on towers inset with windows which allow light to flood into the interior of the cathedral.

Scenes from the Life of Metropolitan Peter
Attributed to the great icon painter Dionysius, this 15th-century work is located on the cathedral's south wall. It depicts different events in the life of this religious and political leader.

Orthodox cross

★ Frescoes
In 1642–4, a team of artists headed by Sidor Pospeev and Ivan and Boris Paisein painted these frescoes. The walls of the cathedral were first gilded to give the look of an illuminated manuscript.

Metropolitans' and patriarchs' tombs line the walls of the nave and the crypt. Almost all of the leaders of the Russian Orthodox Church are buried in the cathedral.

The Tsarina's Throne (17th–19th centuries) is gilded and has a double-headed eagle crest.

STAR FEATURES
★ **Frescoes**
★ **Iconostasis**

Western door and main entrance

The Tabernacle contains holy relics including the remains of Patriarch Hermogen, who starved to death in 1612 during the Polish invasion of the Kremlin.

★ Iconostasis

The haunting 14th-century Icon of the Saviour Not Made With Hands is one of several icons forming part of the cathedral's iconostasis. The iconostasis itself dates from 1652.

Frescoes in the central dome

The pillars that stand in the centre of the cathedral are painted with over 100 figures of canonized martyrs and warriors.

Royal Gate

STALIN'S SECRET

It is believed that in the winter of 1941, when the Nazis had reached Greater Moscow, Stalin secretly ordered a service to be held here to pray for the country's salvation from the invading Germans.

South Portal

This splendid arched portal, decorated with 17th-century frescoes, was the entrance used for royal processions. Brought to Moscow from Suzdal in 1401, the door's reverse side is engraved with scenes from the Bible.

THE MONOMAKH THRONE

The royal seat of Ivan the Terrible is decorated with carvings relating the exploits of Prince Vladimir Mono-makh. The panels depict his 11th-century military campaigns and one shows him receiving the crown from the Byzantine emperor Constantine Mono-machus. This legend was used to confer legitimacy on the idea that the Russian monarchs were the heirs to Byzantium.

Inscribed legend of Prince Vladimir

Panels depicting scenes from Vladimir's life

Monomakh Throne

The Patriarch's Seat was carved from white stone in 1653 for use by the head of the Russian Orthodox Church.

The Harvest Chandelier contains silver recovered from the French after their occupation of the city in 1812.

KEY DATES

1326 Moscow's first stone church is built during the reign of Ivan Kalita.

1474 A second church, erected in 1472, is destroyed by an earthquake.

1475 Building work begins on the Cathedral of the Assumption which takes only four years to complete.

1611–12 Poles occupy the Kremlin and the cathedral.

1918 Under Communism services are prohibited in Kremlin cathedrals.

1990 The Cathedral becomes the property of the Church and, as part of the Kremlin and Red Square, is declared a World Heritage Site.

THE ICONOSTASIS

Separating the sanctuary from the main body of the church, the ▷ *iconostasis* symbolizes the boundary between the spiritual and temporal worlds. The icons are arranged in five tiers. The lowest, or "local", tier contains icons of saints with strong links to the Church. Above this is the second, or "*deis-usny*" tier, depicting saints, apostles, and archangels surrounding a central icon portraying an enthroned Christ flanked by the Virgin. The third, "festival," tier illustrates various festivals of the Orthodox Church, while the fourth tier contains images of the prophets. The final tier is adorned with images of the biblical forefathers.

Cathedral of the Assumption

Main façade of the Bolshoy Theater on Theater Square

THE BOLSHOY'S DESIGN

Having preserved the layout and size of Bove and Mikhaylov's Neo-Classical building (▷ *Neo-Classical Style p79*), Kavos changed its proportions and revised the architectural decor. In particular, he erected cast-iron passageways with lamps on the building's sides and reconstructed ▷ *the auditorium*. The 1853 fire destroyed the sculpture of Apollo, the god of music, that had adorned the building. Sculptor Pyotr Klodt (1805–67) created a new piece. This splendid work, ▷ *Apollo in the Chariot of the Sun*, is 6.5 m high, over 1.5 m higher than the original. Except for small changes to the magnificent interior and exterior, the theater looks the same today as it did over a century ago.

FAMOUS DANCERS

Maya Plisetskaya (b.1925) is one of the Bolshoy's best known dancers. She became a soloist with the theater after graduating from its school in 1943. Soon recognized as one of the world's foremost ballerinas, she combined a perfected technique with a sensitivity to emotional nuances. Under the excellent choreography of Yuri Grigorovich, Ekaterina Maximova and Maris Liepa have also both had successful Bolshoy careers. Liepa was awarded the title of "People's Artist of the USSR" in 1976, while Maximova enjoyed 20 years of dancing at the theater, primarily with her on- and off-stage partner Vladimir Vasiliev. She also toured with foreign companies which was rare among Soviet-period artists.

Bolshoy Theater, Moscow

HOME TO ONE OF THE OLDEST, and probably the most famous, ballet companies in the world, the Bolshoy Theater is also one of Moscow's major landmarks. The first Bolshoy Theater opened in 1780 and presented masquerades, comedies, and comic operas. It burned down in 1805, but its successor was completed in 1825 to a design by Osip Bove and Andrey Mikhaylov. This building too was destroyed by fire, in 1853, but the essentials of its highly praised design were retained in Albert Kavos' reconstruction of 1856. The opening of this third theater was rushed to coincide with the coronation of Alexander II. Today the theater still provides a truly magnificent setting for performances of ballet and opera.

Neo-Classical Pediment
The relief on the Neo-Classical pediment was an addition by Albert Kavos during his reconstruction of the theater. It depicts a pair of angels bearing aloft the lyre of Apollo, the Greek god of music and light.

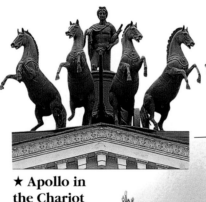

★ Apollo in the Chariot of the Sun
This sculpture by Pyotr Klodt, based on the original 1825 building, was recommissioned by Albert Kavos. It depicts Apollo driving the chariot on which he carried the sun across the sky.

★ Royal Box
Situated at the center of the gallery, the royal box, hung with crimson velvet, is one of over 120 boxes. The imperial crown on its pediment was removed in the Soviet era but has now been restored.

Entrance

Vestibule
Patrons entering the theater find themselves in this grand, black and white tiled vestibule. Magnificent staircases, lined with white marble, lead up from either side of the vestibule to the spacious main foyer.

Eight-columned portico

Beethoven Hall
This ornately decorated room was formerly known as the Imperial Foyer. It is now used for occasional chamber concerts and lectures. The stuccoed decoration on the ceiling includes approximately 3,000 rosettes and the walls are adorned with delicately embroidered panels of crimson silk.

Main stage

The backstage area provides jobs for over 700 workers, including crafts-men and women making ballet shoes, costumes and stage props.

Apollo and the Muses
The ten painted panels decorating the auditorium's ceiling are by Pyotr Titov. They depict Apollo dancing with the nine muses of Greek myth, each of which is connected with a different branch of the arts or sciences.

THE UNESCO/BOL-SHOY PARTNERSHIP

This scheme was launched in 1993 to help the theater remain a leading center for performing arts. Renovations, identifying sponsors and consulting other theaters are on the agenda.

RUSSIA

St Petersburg

BOLSHOY THEATRE, MOSCOW

FINLAND

BELARUS
POLAND
UKRAINE
KAZAKHSTAN

KEY DATES

1780 The first Bolshoy Theater, the Petrovskiy, opens but is destroyed by a fire in 1805.

1825 Bove and Mikhaylov's theater is erected but is also burned down in 1853.

1856 Albert Kavos recon-structs the theater.

1877 Tchaikovsky's *Swan Lake* premieres here.

1920 Beethoven Hall opens on the 150th anniversary of the composer's birth.

BALLETS, MUSICIANS AND COMPOSERS

The Bolshoy Theater has been home and host to some of the world's most important musicians and composers. These have included the famous Russian composer Glinka (1804–57), whose opera *A Life for the Tsar* opened here in 1842. Russia's national anthem is sung to a melody from this work. Mussorgsky, composer of the opera *Boris Godunov,* starred here as did Tchaikovsky, who premiered his *Swan Lake* at the theater. Rachmaninov, Borodin and Prokofiev also worked at the Bolshoy during the course of its history. Richard Wagner left a mark after his concerts in 1863. Before he performed here it was custom for conductors to stand in the first row of the orchestra facing the audience. He was the first in Moscow to face the orchestra with his back to the audience.

STAR FEATURES

★ **Royal Box**

★ **Apollo in the Chariot of the Sun**

Artists' dressing room

The auditorium has six tiers and a seating capacity of 2,500. When Kavos rebuilt it he modified its shape to improve the acoustics.

The main foyer extends around the whole of the front of the build-ing on the second floor. Its vaulted ceiling is decorated with paintings and elaborate stucco work.

THE BOLSHOY BALLET IN THE SOVIET ERA

In the 1920s and 1930s new ballets conforming to Revolutionary ideals were created for the Bolshoy, but the company's heyday was in the 1950s and 1960s. Ballets such as *Spartacus* were produced and the dancers toured abroad for the first time, to widespread acclaim. Yet a number of dancers also defected to the West in this period, in protest at the company's harsh management and a lack of artistic freedom.

A production of *Spartacus* (1954), by Aram Khachaturian, at the Bolshoy

Bolshoy Theater

BASIL, THE "HOLY FOOL"

Born in 1464 into a peasant family in the village of Yelo-khovoe, Basil worked as an apprentice in a shoemaker's. His skill at divining the future soon became apparent and at the age of 16 he left for Moscow. There he undertook the ascetic challenge of walking the city's streets bare-footed, educating Muscovites in piety. Although he was often derided and beaten for his sermonizing, his fortune changed in 1547 when he foresaw the fire of Moscow and was credited with pre-venting it from destroying the entire city. On Basil's death, at the age of 88, Tsar Ivan the Terrible carried his body to the cathedral for burial. He was canonized in 1579.

Colorful, onion-shaped dome, part of the façade of St Basil's

CATHEDRAL DESIGN

St Basil's Cathedral consists of nine churches dedicated to different saints. Each of these, except the ▷ *Central Chapel of the Intercession*, symbolizes the eight assaults on Kazan and is topped by a multi-colored ▷ *dome*. All of the churches are uniquely decorated and different in size from each other, giving the structure an all-round balance. The building is designed to be viewed from every angle, hence there is no single main façade. In plan the eight churches form an eight-pointed star. The four larger domes form the endpoints of an imaginary cross with the Central Chapel in the middle, and the smaller churches between the larger ones.

St Basil's Cathedral, Moscow

Detail, Chapel of the Entry of Christ into Jerusalem

REGARDED AS ONE OF THE MOST beautiful monuments to the Russian Orthodox Church, St Basil's has come to represent Moscow and Russia to the outside world. Commissioned by Ivan the Terrible to celebrate the capture of the Mongol stronghold of Kazan in 1552, the cathedral was completed in 1561. It is reputed to have been designed by the architect Postnik Yakovlev. According to legend, Ivan was so amazed at the beauty of Postnik's work that he had him blinded so that he could never design anything as exquisite again. The church was officially called the Cathedral of the Intercession because the final siege of Kazan began on the Feast of the Intercession of the Virgin. However, it is more usually known as St Basil's after the "holy fool" Basil the Blessed whose remains are interred here in the cathedral's ninth chapel.

MININ AND POZHARSKIY

A bronze statue by Ivan Martos depicts two heroes from the Time of Troubles (1598–1613), the butcher Kuzma Minin and Prince Dmitriy Pozharskiy. They raised a volunteer force to fight the invading Poles and, in 1612, led their army to victory when they drove the Poles out of the Kremlin. The statue was erected in 1818, in the triumphal afterglow of the Napoleonic Wars. Originally placed in the center of Red Square facing the Kremlin, it was moved to its present site in front of St Basil's during the Soviet era.

Monument to Minin and Prince Pozharskiy

Bell tower

Chapel of the Trinity

★ **Domes**
Following a fire in 1583 the original helmet-shaped cupolas were replaced by ribbed or faceted onion domes. It is only since 1670 that the domes have been painted many colors; at one time St Basil's was white with golden domes.

Chapel of St Cyprian
This is one of eight main chapels commemorating the campaigns of Ivan the Terrible against the town of Kazan, to the east of Moscow. It is dedicated to St Cyprian, whose feast is on 2 October, the day after the last attack.

Chapel of the Three Patriarchs

The Chapel of St Basil, the ninth chapel to be added to the cathedral, was built in 1588 to house the remains of the "holy fool," Basil the Blessed.

The entrance to the cathedral contains an exhibition on its history, armor and weapons dating from the time of Ivan the Terrible.

Tent roof on the Central Chapel

Central Chapel of the Intercession

Light floods in through the windows of the tent-roofed central church, which soars to a height of 61 m (200 ft).

Chapel of St Nicholas

★ Main Iconostasis

The Baroque-style iconostasis in the Central Chapel of the Intercession dates from the 19th century. However, some of the icons contained in it were painted much earlier.

Chapel of St Varlaam of Khutynskiy

Tiered gables

Chapel of Bishop Gregory

★ Gallery

Running around the outside of the Central Chapel, the gallery connects it to the other eight chapels. It was roofed over at the end of the 17th century and the walls and ceilings were decorated with floral tiles in the late 18th century.

RED SQUARE

St Basil's Cathedral is located in Red Square in the heart of Moscow. The name of the square derives from the Russian word *krasnyy*, which originally meant "beautiful" but later came to denote "red".

STAR FEATURES

★ **Domes**

★ **Main Iconostasis**

★ **Gallery**

The Chapel of the Entry of Christ into Jerusalem was used as a ceremonial entrance during the annual Palm Sunday procession. On this day the patriarch rode from the Kremlin to St Basil's Cathedral on a horse disguised to look like a donkey.

FINLAND
RUSSIA
St Petersburg
BELARUS
ST BASIL'S CATHEDRAL, MOSCOW
KAZAKHSTAN
POLAND
UKRAINE

KEY DATES

1555 Building work commences, and St Basil's is completed six years later.

1583 Onion-shaped domes are built to replace the original cupolas destroyed by fire.

1812 Napoleon's cavalry stable their horses in St Basil's during his invasion of Russia.

1918 Communist authorities close the cathedral down.

1923 St Basil's reopens as a museum.

1990s St Basil's Cathedral is declared a World Heritage Site in 1990, and returned to the Orthodox Church in 1991.

THE ART OF ICON PAINTING IN RUSSIA

The Russian Orthodox Church uses icons for both worship and teaching and there are strict rules for creating each image. Iconography is a symbolic art, expressing in line and color the theological teaching of the Church. Icons are thought to be imbued with power from the saint they depict and are often invoked for protection during wars. The first icons were brought to Russia from Byzantium. Kiev, today the capital of Ukraine, was Russia's main icon painting center until the Mongols conquered it in 1240. The Moscow school was born in the late 15th century when Ivan the Terrible decreed that artists must live in the Kremlin. Dionysius and Andrey Rublev were members of this renowned school.

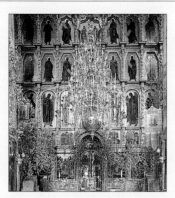

Beautiful iconostasis in the Cathedral of the Assumption

THE CHURCHES

The exquisite white ▷ *Trinity Cathedral* is the oldest stone building in the monastery. It is decorated with traditional semicircular shaped *kokoshniki* gables above a triple-banded frieze. The ▷ *Church of St Sergius* has a magnificent iconostasis brought from Moscow's Church of St Nicholas near Red Square in 1688. The delicate fretwork seems to be metal but is actually made of wood. The lovely ▷ *Cathedral of the Assumption* has a central golden cupola surrounded by four blue, star-spangled domes. Inside, beneath a fresco of the Last Judgment, are the names of the artists who took just 100 days to decorate the interior in 1684.

BORIS GODUNOV

When Ivan the Terrible died in 1584, the throne passed to his retarded son Fyodor, whose inability to govern demanded that a regent be appointed. Godunov had already gained Ivan's favor, having helped him to organize the social and administrative system. Furthermore, Fyodor's marriage to Godunov's sister lent support to Godunov's appointment as regent. He became tsar following Fyodor's death in 1598, ushering in the Time of Troubles, a period of unrest and power struggles for the throne. Godunov's reign was blighted by accusations of murdering Fyodor's brother, the heir to the throne, and dogged by pretenders seeking to usurp him. He died in 1605.

Trinity Monastery of St Sergius

FOUNDED AROUND 1345 by Sergius of Radonezh, the Trinity Monastery of St Sergius in the town of Sergiev-Possad is one of Russia's most important religious centers and places of pilgrimage. In 1608–10, during the Time of Troubles, the monks survived a siege by the Polish army. In 1682, Peter the Great and his half-brother Ivan V found refuge here during the Streltsy Rebellion, a revolt due to rivalry over the succession. The monastery was closed down by the Communists in 1919 but was reopened again in 1946, when it became headquarters of the Russian Orthodox Church until 1988. The churches, grouped around the spectacular Cathedral of the Assumption, are among the most beautiful in Russia.

★ **Trinity Cathedral**
Built in 1422–3 over the grave of St Sergius, this splendid church contains an iconostasis painted by a team led by the monk-artist Andrey Rublev.

Palace of the Metropolitans
This grand palace was completed in 1778. It was the residence of the metropolitans and patriarchs in 1946–88.

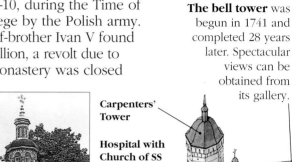

Chapel Over the Well
This delightful, Moscow-Baroque chapel was built in the late 17th century to mark the site of a holy spring.

Sacristy

Water Tower

Church of the Holy Spirit

The Church of the Virgin of Smolensk was built in 1745 to house the Icon of the Smolensk Virgin.

The bell tower was begun in 1741 and completed 28 years later. Spectacular views can be obtained from its gallery.

Carpenters' Tower

Hospital with Church of SS Zosima and Savvatiy

Obelisk

Treasury

★ **Church of St Sergius and Refectory**
The monks' refectory was built in 1686–92 with the Church of St Sergius at its eastern end. The colorful façade features pillars with vine-leaf decoration and checkered walls. The interior is equally lavish.

Tsars' Apartments

These apartments were built in the late 17th century for Tsar Alexis Mikhailovich. He often visited the monastery with a retinue of over 500 courtiers. The building now houses a theological college.

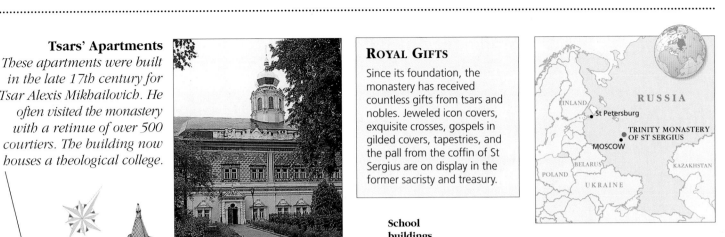

ROYAL GIFTS

Since its foundation, the monastery has received countless gifts from tsars and nobles. Jeweled icon covers, exquisite crosses, gospels in gilded covers, tapestries, and the pall from the coffin of St Sergius are on display in the former sacristy and treasury.

RUSSIA

FINLAND

St Petersburg

TRINITY MONASTERY
OF ST SERGIUS

MOSCOW

BELARUS

KAZAKHSTAN

POLAND

UKRAINE

KEY DATES

c.1345 Monastery is founded by Sergius of Radonezh.

1422 Trinity Cathedral is built over the remains of St Sergius.

1559 Cathedral of the Assumption is commissioned by Ivan the Terrible.

1745 Church of the Virgin of Smolensk is the last of the churches to be constructed.

1919 Communists close down the monastery.

1946 Patriarchs and metropolitans are allowed to return to the monastery.

1993 Trinity Monastery is added to UNESCO's World Heritage Site list.

THE HOLIEST MONK

Sergius of Radonezh was born into a noble family in the early 14th century. Along with his brother, he withdrew from the world to live as a hermit in the forests north of Moscow, where he built a wooden church consecrated to the Holy Trinity. Pilgrims were attracted by reports of Sergius' piety. He organized them into a community, thus founding the monastery. Sergius was instrumental in encouraging Russia's princes to unite against the Mongol invaders. In 1380, Prince Dmitriy Donskoy, commander of the Russian army, asked for his blessing before attacking the Mongols at Kulikovo. The victory along with Sergius' religious fervor determined his canonization in 1422.

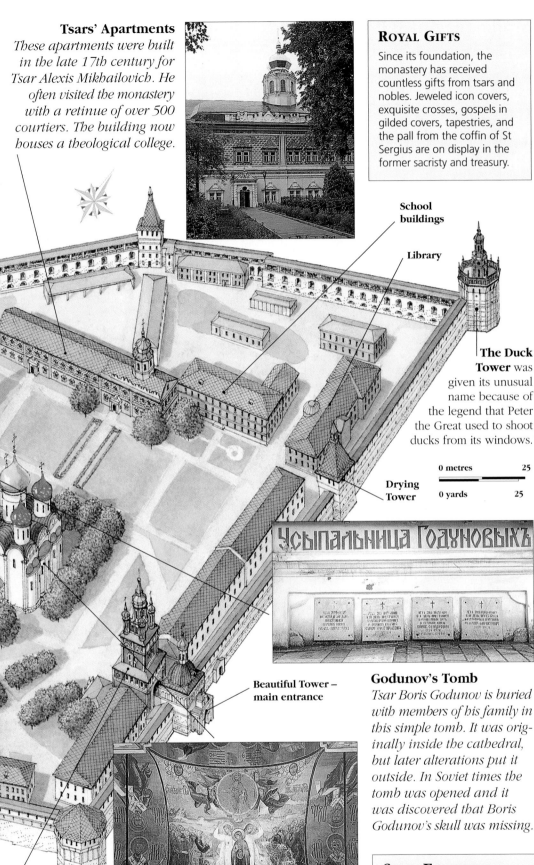

School buildings

Library

The Duck Tower was given its unusual name because of the legend that Peter the Great used to shoot ducks from its windows.

| 0 metres | 25 |
| 0 yards | 25 |

Drying Tower

Godunov's Tomb

Tsar Boris Godunov is buried with members of his family in this simple tomb. It was originally inside the cathedral, but later alterations put it outside. In Soviet times the tomb was opened and it was discovered that Boris Godunov's skull was missing.

Beautiful Tower – main entrance

The Gate Church of St John the Baptist stands over the main entrance. It was built in 1692–99 by the wealthy Stroganov family.

★ Cathedral of the Assumption

Commissioned in 1559 by Ivan the Terrible to commemorate the capture of Kazan, this is the monastery's main cathedral. Its sumptuous interior was decorated by artists from Yaroslavl over a century later.

STAR FEATURES

★ **Trinity Cathedral**

★ **Church of St Sergius and Refectory**

★ **Cathedral of the Assumption**

JOÃO I

João's succession to the throne had been a bloody affair. His half-brother Fernando's widow, Queen Leonor, allied with Castile in order to help establish her daughter as monarch. But the populace was outraged and a national revolt spread led by João, which ended with ▷ *the Battle of Aljubarrota*. A major contribution to this crushing victory was João's friendship with the Englishman John of Gaunt, who sent archers to the battle. This union was further strengthened when João married John's daughter Philippa of Lancaster. A treaty was signed with England, forming the oldest alliance in European history. João's reign was characterized by administrative reforms and colonial expansion, which heightened his popularity.

HENRY THE NAVIGATOR

Although he did not sail himself, Henry (1394–1460), the third surviving son of João I, laid the foundations for Portugal's maritime expansion that were later built upon by João II and consolidated by Manuel I. As Master of the wealthy Order of Christ and Governor of the Algarve, Henry was able to finance expeditions along the African coast. He also founded a great school of navigation at Sagres, on the southwesternmost point of Portugal. The institute included a research and development facility with libraries, an astronomical observatory, provisions for shipbuilding, accommodations, and a chapel. Henry is buried in the ▷ *Founder's Chapel.*

Lateen-rigged caravel, favored by the first Portuguese explorers

Monastery of Batalha

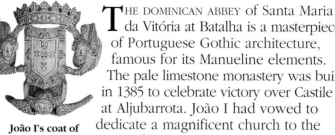

João I's coat of arms on portal

THE DOMINICAN ABBEY of Santa Maria da Vitória at Batalha is a masterpiece of Portuguese Gothic architecture, famous for its Manueline elements. The pale limestone monastery was built in 1385 to celebrate victory over Castile at Aljubarrota. João I had vowed to dedicate a magnificent church to the Virgin if he won the battle. The abbey was begun in 1388 under master builder Afonso Domingues, succeeded in 1402 by David Huguet. Over the next two centuries successive kings left their mark on the monastery: João's son, King Duarte, ordered a royal pantheon behind the apse, and Manueline additions include the Unfinished Chapels and much of the decoration of the abbey buildings. Today, two unknown soldiers from World War I lie in the chapter house.

★ Royal Cloister
Gothic arches by Afonso Domingues and David Huguet around the cloister are embellished by Manueline tracery to achieve a harmony of form and decoration.

The lavabo, where monks washed their hands before and after meals, contains a fountain built around 1450.

Chapter house
Guards keep watch by the Tomb of the Unknown Soldiers beneath David Huguet's striking star-vaulted ceiling.

Refectory

Main entrance

Portal
The portal was decorated by Huguet with religious motifs and statues of the apostles in intricate late Gothic style.

STAR FEATURES

★ **Royal Cloister**

★ **Unfinished Chapels**

★ **Founder's Chapel**

★ Unfinished Chapels

Begun under King Duarte, the octagonal mausoleum was abandoned by Manuel I in favour of the Jerónimos monastery in Lisbon.

THE CHAPTER HOUSE

The incredible vaulted ceiling is remarkably unsupported. Convinced that it would collapse at any moment, the Church authorites employed criminals already condemned to death to build it.

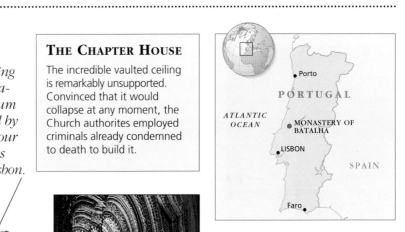

• Porto

PORTUGAL

ATLANTIC OCEAN

• MONASTERY OF BATALHA

• LISBON

SPAIN

• Faro

The stained-glass window behind the choir dates from 1514.

Lofty nave by Afonso Domingues

Manueline Portal

Most of the decoration of the Unfinished Chapels dates from the reign of Manuel I. This delicate portal was carved in 1509 by Mateus Fernandes.

★ Founder's Chapel

The tomb of João I and his English wife Philippa of Lancaster, lying hand in hand, was begun in 1426 by Huguet. Their son, Henry the Navigator, is also buried here.

The chapel is topped by an octagonal lantern.

João I's motto, *Por bem* (for good), is inscribed on his tomb.

THE BATTLE OF ALJUBARROTA

In 1383 Portugal's direct male line of descent ended with the death of Fernando I (r.1367–83). Dom João, the illegitimate son of Fernando's father, was proclaimed king, but his claim was opposed by Juan of Castile. On 14 August 1385 João I's greatly outnumbered forces, commanded by Nuno Álvares Pereira, faced the Castilians on a small plateau near Aljubarrota, 15 km (9 miles) south of Batalha. João's spectacular victory ensured 200 years of independence from Spain. The monastery now stands as a symbol of Portuguese sovereignty and the power of the house of Avis.

Commander Nuno Álvares Pereira

KEY DATES

1386 The Treaty of Windsor is signed, which allies Portugal and England.

1388 Work on the abbey commences, to celebrate Portugal's victory over Castile.

1435 The Unfinished Chapels are built.

1983 Mosteiro da Batalha is inscribed as a UNESCO World Heritage Site.

MANUELINE STYLE

This style of architecture that flourished during the reign of Manuel I (r.1495–1521) is a Portuguese variant of Late Gothic (▷ *Gothic Style p73*). It is typified by maritime motifs inspired by Portugal's Age of Discovery, and by elaborate "all-over" decoration. This exuberant style is also associated with exotic plants and animals of the Orient, discovered on overseas expeditions. This is evident in the entwined blossom, branch, and vegetation motifs in the ▷ *Royal Cloister*. Significant decorative details include the armillary sphere, the Cross of the Order of Christ, the twisted rope, and anchors. The sphere was a navigational device that was the emblem of Manuel I, and the Cross was the symbol of a military order that helped to finance early voyages – it often emblazoned flags and sails. Naturalistic and fantastic forms evoking the Orient were typically used, as well as finely crafted designs such as the portal leading to the ▷ *Unfinished Chapels*.

Entrance to the chapterhouse, Mosteiro de Alcobaça

AFONSO HENRIQUES

Afonso was born in 1109 and succeeded his father as Count of Portugal in 1112. Since Afonso was too young to rule, his power passed to his mother instead. Opposing political views put strain on their relations and in 1120, Afonso was exiled on his mother's orders. Three years later, he defeated his mother's troops and seized control of the land. Successful battles against the Moors followed and Afonso was proclaimed king by his soldiers in 1139, making him the first king of Portugal after independence from Castile. After a decisive victory in 1147, Afonso vowed to build this fine monastery for the Cistercians. He died during its construction, in 1185.

THE CLOISTER AND SALA DOS REIS

Traceried stonework characterizes the fine ▷ *Cloister of Dom Dinis*. An upper level of twisted pillars and Manueline arches (▷ *Manueline Style p169*) was added in the 16th century. The picturesque cloister garden is framed by galleries supported by Gothic arches (▷ *Gothic Style p73*). Statues of nearly all the Portuguese kings up to Dom José I (r.1750–77) rest on Baroque consoles around the ▷ *Sala dos Reis*. Depictions of the siege of Santarém, King Afonso Henriques' vow, and the foundation of the monastery are shown on the 18th-century blue *azulejo* (tile) panels on the walls.

Monastery of Alcobaça

RENOWNED FOR ITS simple medieval architecture, the Mosteiro de Santa Maria de Alcobaça was founded in 1153. The monastery is closely linked to the arrival of the Cistercian order in Portugal in 1138 and to the birth of Gothic art and architecture in Portugal. In 1147, Afonso Henriques conquered the Moorish stronghold of Santarém. To commemorate the victory, he fulfilled his vow to build a mighty church for the Cistercians. This task was completed in 1223. The monarchy continued to endow the monastery, notably King Dinis (r.1279–1325) who built the main cloister. Among those buried here are King Pedro (r.1357–67) and his murdered mistress Inês de Castro.

The chapter house was where the monks met to elect the abbot and discuss issues regarding the monastery.

Sacristy Doorway
Exotic foliage and elaborate pinnacles adorn the Manueline doorway, attributed to João de Castilho.

Tomb of Inês de Castro

Dormitory

Refectory and Kitchen
Stairs lead up to the pulpit where one of the monks read from the Bible as the others ate in silence. In the vast kitchen next door, oxen could be roasted on the spit inside the chimney and a specially diverted stream provided a constant water supply.

The kitchen's huge chimney

The octagonal lavabo was where the monks washed their hands.

★ Cloister of Dom Dinis
Also known as the Cloister of Silence, this exquisite cloister was ordered by King Dinis in 1308. The austere galleries and double arches are in keeping with the Cistercian regard for simplicity.

STAR FEATURES

★ Cloister of Dom Dinis

★ Tombs of Pedro I and Inês de Castro

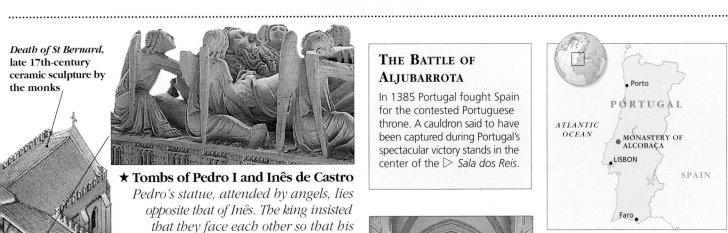

Death of St Bernard,
late 17th-century
ceramic sculpture by
the monks

★ Tombs of Pedro I and Inês de Castro
Pedro's statue, attended by angels, lies
opposite that of Inês. The king insisted
that they face each other so that his
first sight on Judgment Day would
be of his beloved.

Central Nave
The vaulted roof and
soaring columns of the
central nave create an
impression of harmony
and austere simplicity.

The façade is a richly
decorated 18th-century
addition. Marble statues of
St Benedict and St Bernard
flank the main doorway.

Main
entrance

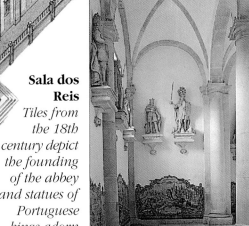

Sala dos
Reis
Tiles from
the 18th
century depict
the founding
of the abbey
and statues of
Portuguese
kings adorn
the walls.

THE BATTLE OF ALJUBARROTA

In 1385 Portugal fought Spain
for the contested Portuguese
throne. A cauldron said to have
been captured during Portugal's
spectacular victory stands in the
center of the ▷ *Sala dos Reis.*

KEY DATES

1223 Work on the monastery
is completed.

1810 The tombs of King
Pedro I and Inês de Castro
are damaged by pillaging
French troops.

1834 Monks are expelled
from the monastery when all
religious orders in Portugal
are dissolved.

1989 The monastery is
added to UNESCO's World
Heritage Site list.

CISTERCIAN STYLE

The Cistercians were a
puritanical order who broke
away from the Benedictines in
1098, wishing to return to a
more ascetic observance of
Benedictine standards. The
austerity and purity that the
Cistercian monks sought to
revive in their monastic life is
symbolized in their undyed,
white robes and reflected in
their style of architecture.
Their buildings became
renowned for an exquisite
simplicity through an absence
of stained glass, sculpture, or
decoration. It is this severe
Cistercian beauty that marks
the vast space, devoid of
ornamentation, on entering
the Monastery of Alcobaça.
The imposing style of the
100-m (327-ft) ▷ *Central*
Nave is accentuated by the
great girth of the columns and
the narrowness of the spaces
between them. The design is
modeled on the Cistercian
church of Cîteaux in the
Burgundy region of France
where the Cistercian monks
first founded a monastery.

THE MURDER OF INÊS DE CASTRO

Reasons of state obliged
Pedro, son and heir of
Afonso IV (r.1325–57), to
marry Costanza, Infanta
of Castile, despite the
fact he was in love
with a lady at court,
Inês de Castro. When
Costanza died, Pedro
went to live with Inês.
Persuaded that her fam-
ily's increasing political
influence could threaten the independence
of the Portuguese crown, Afonso IV had
Inês murdered on 7 January 1355. On
Afonso's death, Pedro took revenge on
two of the killers by having their hearts torn
out. Declaring that he had been married to
Inês, Pedro had her corpse exhumed and
crowned. He compelled his court to kneel
before Inês and kiss her decomposed hand.

BARON VON ESCHWEGE

In 1839, Ferdinand of Saxe-Coburg-Gotha acquired the well-positioned land of a former monastery and appointed German architect Baron von Eschwege (1777–1855) to construct his fabulous summer palace. Von Eschwege turned the king's extravagant dreams into reality and, over the following decade, he erected a fantasy palace around the restored ruins of the monastery. On a nearby crag stands the statue of a warrior-knight which supposedly guards the palace. It is an enormous stone sculpture whose base bears an engraving of the Baron's coat of arms.

DESIGN

Ferdinand's passion for the arts and for scientific progress resulted in an eclectic mix of architectural styles with Gothic (▷ *Gothic Style p73*), Renaissance (▷ *Renaissance Style p211*), and Manueline (▷ *Manueline Style p169*) elements. Painted in shades of pink, blue, and yellow, the exterior of the building is lavishly carved or covered with *azulejo* tile arrangements, with golden domes, crenelated turrets, and gargoyles. Inside the palace, highlights include the Renaissance retable by sculptor Nicolau Chanterène (▷ *Chapel Altarpiece*) and the exotic furniture which contribute to the prevailing air of decadence.

Parque da Pena overlooked by the Palace of Pena

Palace of Pena, Sintra

Triton Arch

ON THE HIGHEST PEAKS of the Serra de Sintra stands the spectacular Palace of Pena. This eclectic medley of architectural styles was built in the 19th century for the husband of the young Queen Maria II (r.1834–53), Ferdinand of Saxe-Coburg-Gotha – King Dom Fernando II of Portugal. It stands over the ruins of a Hieronymite monastery founded here in the 15th century on the site of the chapel of Nossa Senhora da Pena. The outlandish rooms of the enchanting summer palace are filled with oddities from all over the world. The monarchy was overthrown in 1910 and with the declaration of the Republic, the palace became a museum, preserved as it was when the royal family lived here.

Entrance Arch
A studded archway with crenelated turrets greets the visitor at the entrance to the palace. The palace buildings are painted the original daffodil yellow and strawberry pink.

Manuel II's Bedroom
The oval-shaped room is decorated with bright red walls and a stuccoed ceiling. A portrait of Manuel II, the last king of Portugal, hangs above the fireplace.

In the kitchen the copper pots and utensils still hang around the iron stove. The dinner service bears the coat of arms of Ferdinand II.

★ Ballroom
The spacious ballroom is sumptuously furnished with German stained-glass windows, precious Oriental porcelain, and four life-size turbaned torch-bearers holding giant candelabra.

★ Arab Room
Marvelous trompe-l'oeil frescoes cover the walls and ceiling of the Arab Room, one of the loveliest in the palace. The Orient was a great inspiration to Romanticism.

ENTERTAINMENT
The palace hosts a number of live events throughout the year. These include concerts of classical music, exhibitions, ballets, and historical plays performed by internationally acclaimed artistes.

The Triton Arch is encrusted with Neo-Manueline decoration and is guarded by a fierce sea monster.

★ Chapel Altarpiece
The impressive 16th-century alabaster and marble retable was sculpted by Nicolau Chanterène. Each niche portrays a scene of the life of Christ, from the manger to the Ascension.

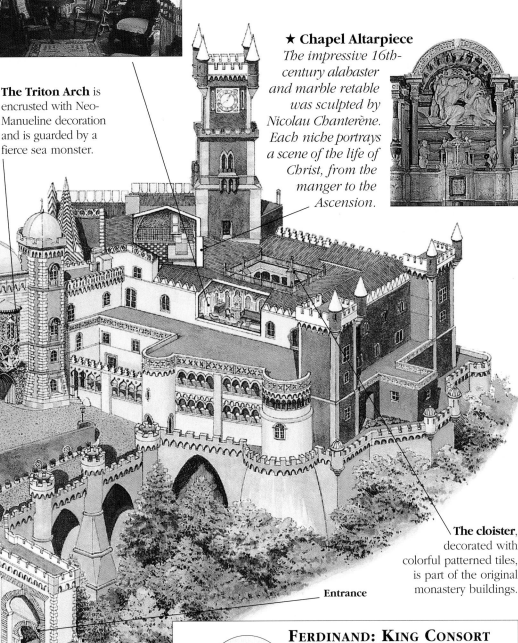

The cloister, decorated with colorful patterned tiles, is part of the original monastery buildings.

Entrance

KEY DATES

15th century A Hieronymite monastery is founded here.

1839 Ferdinand of Saxe-Coburg-Gotha buys the ruins of the monastery.

1840s Baron von Eschwege puts the king's ideas into effect and transforms the site into a palace residence, preserving the original monastery cloister and chapel.

1910 The palace opens to the public as a museum.

1995 The city of Sintra is added to UNESCO's World Heritage list.

ROMANTICISM

Sintra has long been recognized as an enchanting place of outstanding beauty, internationally revered by kings, noblemen and artists. In 1809 the English poet Lord Byron described its verdant beauty as "glorious Eden" and further praise was given in *Os Lusíadas*, Portugal's celebrated 16th-century epic poem by Luís Vaz de Camões. The Palace of Pena's garish union of styles including exotic Gothic traces made it a forerunner of European Romanticism. Largely inspired by Bavarian palaces, Arab, Portuguese, German, Classical, and Romantic influences are combined to create a unique and at times bizarre effect. The surrounding grounds of Pena park are also of striking romantic beauty, comprising thousands of delicately arranged trees imported from all over the world.

Palace of Pena

STAR FEATURES

★ Ballroom

★ Arab Room

★ Chapel Altarpiece

FERDINAND: KING CONSORT

Ferdinand was known in Portugal as Dom Fernando II, the "artist" king. Like his cousin Prince Albert, who married the English Queen Victoria, he loved art, nature, and the new inventions of the time. He was himself a watercolor painter. Ferdinand enthusiastically adopted his new country and devoted his life to patronizing the arts. In 1869, 16 years after the death of Maria II, Ferdinand married his mistress, the opera singer Countess Edla. His lifelong dream of building the extravagant palace at Pena was completed in 1885, the year he died.

VASCO DA GAMA

The real breakthrough for Portuguese imperialism occurred in 1498 when Vasco da Gama sailed around the Cape of Good Hope and opened the sea route to India. Although the Hindu ruler of Calicut, who received him wearing diamond and ruby rings, was not impressed by his humble offerings of cloth and wash basins, da Gama returned to Portugal with a cargo of spices. Trade routes were established and Portugal assumed control of the Indian Ocean and the spice trade. These foundations led the kingdom to became a mercantile super-power. King João III appointed da Gama Viceroy of India in 1524, but he died of a fever soon after. In 1880, da Gama's huge influence was honored and he was eventually laid to rest in the choir beside the rulers of Portugal (▷ *Tomb of Vasco da Gama*).

MANUEL I

Manuel I's reign (1495–1521) marked the peak in Portugal's golden age of discovery and conquest. A tax levied on trade with new territories brought the affluence of the Indies pouring into Portugal, establishing it as the foremost commercial nation in the western world. Manuel I also strove to unite the great wealths of Spain and Portugal through marriage. He used his prosperity to commission a number of majestic buildings, built to command admiration and respect for the king and country. The incredibly lavish Jerónimos Monastery reflects the king's power and taste for opulence.

Vaulted arcades decorate the Manueline cloister

Jerónimos Monastery, Lisbon

Armillary sphere in the cloister

AMONUMENT TO THE WEALTH of Portugal's Age of Discovery, the monastery is the epitome of Manueline architecture (▷ *Manueline Style p169*). Commissioned by Manuel I in around 1501, after Vasco da Gama's return from his historic voyage, it was financed largely by "pepper money," a tax levied on spices, precious stones, and gold.

Various masterbuilders worked on the building. The most notable was Diogo Boitac, replaced by João de Castilho in 1517. The monastery was cared for by the Order of St Jerome (Hieronymites) until 1834, when all religious orders were disbanded.

Tomb of Vasco da Gama
The 19th-century tomb of the explorer is carved with ropes, armillary spheres, and other seafaring symbols.

The fountain is in the shape of a lion, the heraldic animal of St Jerome.

Refectory
The walls of the refectory are tiled with 18th-century azulejos. *The panel at the northern end depicts the Feeding of the Five Thousand.*

The modern wing, built in 1850 in Neo-Manueline style, houses the Museu Nacional de Arqueologia.

The west portal was designed by the French sculptor Nicolau Chanterène.

Entrance to church and cloister

Gallery

View of the Monastery
This 17th-century scene by Felipe Lobo shows women at a fountain in front of the Jerónimos Monastery.

STAR FEATURES

★ **Cloister**

★ **South Portal**

★ Cloister
João de Castilho's pure Manueline creation was completed in 1544. Delicate tracery and richly carved images decorate the arches and balustrades.

MARITIME IMAGERY

Carved symbols of life at sea such as fish, rope, anchors, and shells decorate the monastery. It was customary for seafarers to pray in the chapel for a safe journey before their departure.

Nave
The spectacular vaulting in the church of Santa Maria is held aloft by slender octagonal pillars. These rise like palm trees to the roof creating a feeling of space and harmony.

The chapter house holds the tomb of Alexandre Herculano (1810–77), historian and first mayor of Belém.

The chancel was commissioned in 1572 by Dona Catarina, wife of João III.

The tombs of Manuel I, his wife Dona Maria, João III, and Catarina are supported by elephants.

★ South Portal
The strict geometrical architecture of the portal is almost obscured by the exuberant decoration. João de Castilho unites religious themes, such as this image of St Jerome, with the secular, exalting the kings of Portugal.

Tomb of King Sebastião
The young King Sebastião never returned from battle in Morocco in 1578. His tomb stands empty.

KEY DATES

1501 Diogo Boitac begins work on the monastery.

1517–20 Construction of the sacristy.

1544 The vaulted roof of the cloister is completed.

1564 The chancel is built.

1880 Vasco da Gama's bones are laid to rest in a tomb in the lower choir.

1907 The monastery is declared a National Historic Monument.

1984 The site is added to UNESCO's World Heritage list.

MUSEU NACIONAL DE ARQUEOLOGIA

The long west wing of the monastery (▷ *the modern wing)*, formerly the monks' dormitory, has housed Portugal's main archaeological museum and research center since 1893. Exhibits, from sites all over the country, include a gold Iron Age bracelet found in the Alentejo, Visigothic jewelry from Beja, Roman ornaments, and early 8th-century Moorish artifacts. The main Egyptian and Greco-Roman section is strong on funerary art, featuring figurines, tombstones, masks, terracotta amulets, and funeral cones inscribed with hieroglyphics alluding to the solar system. The dimly-lit Room of Treasures has an exquisite collection of coins, necklaces, bracelets, and other jewelry dating from 1800–500 BC.

ARCHITECTURAL ELEMENTS

When Manuel I came to power in 1495 he reaped the profits of the Age of Discovery, building grandiose monuments and churches that mirrored the spirit of the time. The Tower of Belém is a fine example of the exuberant, exotic Manueline style of architecture, essentially a Portuguese variant of Gothic architecture (▷ *Gothic Style p73*), incorporating a range of motifs including twisted ropes, armillary spheres, square crosses of the Order of Christ, and naturalistic elements in the form of animals such as rhinoceroses.

THE AGE OF DISCOVERY

Set at the mouth of the River Tagus, from where the caravels set sail on voyages of discovery, the Lisbon suburb of Belém is inextricably linked with Portugal's Golden Age. This great period of conquest and exploration began in 1415 with the capture of the North African city of Ceuta. Maritime expeditions into the Atlantic and along the West African coast followed, motivated by a desire for commercial gain. Diogo Cão made the first (failed) attempt to find a sea route to India in 1482, and planted a *padrão* (stone cross) at every stop he made. Great fortunes were made from the gold and slaves taken from the Guinea coast but the real breakthrough for Portuguese imperialism came in 1498, when Vasco da Gama reached India. Portugal soon controlled the Indian Ocean and the spice trade, and set up an eastern trading post at Goa. When a Portuguese explorer "discovered" Brazil, the country became a mercantile power rivaled only by Spain.

A Portuguese *padrão* (stone cross)

Tower of Belém, Lisbon

Arms of Manuel I

THIS OFFSHORE FORTRESS is one of the world's most decorated fortified buildings. Commissioned by Manuel I in the 16th century to guard Lisbon from attack, it is adorned with ropes carved in stone and boasts openwork balconies, Moorish-style domes, and distinctive battlements in the shape of shields. This Manueline gem (▷ *Manueline Style p169*) was built by architect Francisco de Arruda and permanently armed. Having set off from the suburb of Belém back in 1497, navigator Vasco da Gama discovered India. It is fitting, therefore, that Belém and its grand fortress should become a symbol of Portugal's great era of overseas expansion and discovery.

Staircase
Spiral stairs lead up to great views from the top of the tower.

Virgin and Child
A statue of Our Lady of Safe Homecoming *faces the sea so that sailors could ask for her protection on their sea voyages.*

Armillary spheres are symbols of Portugal's seafaring prowess.

Royal coat of arms of Manuel I

Battlements
These are in the shape of shields and are decorated with the cross of the Order of Christ.

Sentry posts

STAR FEATURES

★ **Interior**

★ **Entrance**

★ **Decorated Loggia**

The Tower of Belém in 1811
This painting by J T Serres, of a British ship navigating the Tagus, shows the tower much further from the shore than it is today. In the 19th century land on the north bank was reclaimed, making the river narrower.

The Tower

The tower is made from a special stone, pedra calçaria de Lioz, *in a variety of colors – red, yellow, and gray.*

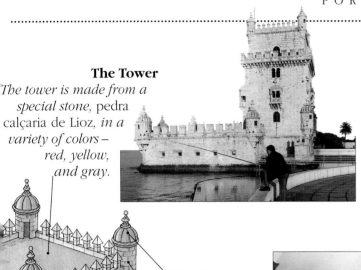

THE SPICE TRADE

In 1498 Vasco da Gama sailed around the Cape of Good Hope, opening the sea route to India. He returned with a cargo of spices, initiating Portuguese monopoly of the spice trade in the Indian Ocean. Spices such as nutmeg, pepper, cinnamon, and cloves were worth their weight in gold to Portugal.

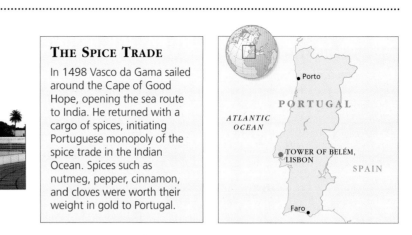

KEY DATES

1514–20 The Tower of Belém is constructed.

1580 The tower is enlarged and the dungeons are used as State prisons.

1983 UNESCO declares the Tower of Belém a World Heritage Site.

FRANCISCO DE ARRUDA

The Tower of Belém was a fundamental part of the fortifications built to defend the mouth of the River Tagus and Lisbon. The designer of the tower was Francisco de Arruda, one of the most representative architects of Manueline style. Having made a name for himself in North Africa, where he built numerous fortresses, Arruda was appointed Master Builder of the Tower of Belém upon his return from Africa. The architect's contribution to the tower is clearly visible in the architectural form and the delicate proportions of the building. He was also responsible for the Moorish and Oriental decorative elements, such as the segmented domes and striking pepper pot-shaped cupolas which top the ▷ *sentry posts.* Construction of the Tower of Belém was completed in 1520 and with its carved stone balustrades, terraces, openwork balconies, and statues, Francisco de Arruda created a structure that is both exotic and yet distinctively Portuguese – a fitting national monument.

Cupolas are Moorish in style.

Sentry posts

Twisted rope decoration

★ Interior

The Gothic interior (▷ Gothic Style p73) is austere. It was used as a prison until the 19th century by King Dom Miquel (r.1828–34) who kept political prisoners in the dungeons.

Gangway to shore

Vaulted dungeon

★ Entrance

With its decorated arched doorway and wooden drawbridge the fortress resembles a medieval castle.

★ Decorated Loggia

Inspired by Italian architecture, the elegant arcaded loggia with its finely carved balustrades brings a light touch to the defensive battlements.

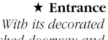

Tower of Belém

JAMES THE GREAT

According to legend, having spent time preaching in Spain, James returned to Jerusalem and was the first apostle to be martyred. His body is thought to have been translated, some claim miraculously, to a burial site in Galicia. A bishop is said to have discovered the relics some 800 years later in 813, guided by a divine vision. A cathedral was erected in St James' honor on the sacred spot. Invading Moors devastated Santiago in 997 yet fortunately the saint's tomb was spared (▷ *Crypt)*. This and subsequent Christian victories led to St James becoming Spain's patron saint and forged the cathedral's reputation as one of Christendom's major pilgrimage sites.

THE ROAD TO SANTIAGO

In the Middle Ages, half a million pilgrims a year flocked to Santiago Cathedral from all over Europe. Several pilgrimage roads converge on Santiago. The main road from the Pyrenees is known as the French Route. The various routes, marked by the cathedrals, churches, and inns built along them, are still used by travelers today. To qualify for a certificate, pilgrims must produce a stamped and dated pilgrim passport and have covered the final 100 km (62 miles) on foot or horseback, or have cycled the final 200 km (125 miles). They must also declare a spiritual or religious motivation. A crucial medieval manuscript on St James' life and miracles, the 12th-century *Codex Calixtinus*, is kept in the cathedral library. Named in Pope Calixtus II's honor, it includes a practical guide for pilgrims en route to Santiago.

A certificate awarded to pilgrims

Santiago Cathedral

The gigantic *botafumeiro*

As BEFITS ONE OF THE GREAT SHRINES of Christendom, this monument to St James is a majestic sight, dominated by its soaring twin Baroque towers (▷ *Baroque Style p111*). The rest of the cathedral dates from the 11th–13th centuries although it stands on the site of Alfonso II's 9th-century basilica. Through the famous Pórtico da Gloria is the same interior that met pilgrims in medieval times. The choir, designed by Maestro Mateo, has been completely restored.

"Passport" – proof of a pilgrim's journey

★ **West Façade**
The richly sculpted Baroque Obradoiro façade was added in the 18th century.

★ **Pórtico da Gloria**
Statues of apostles and prophets decorate the 12th-century Doorway of Glory.

STAR FEATURES

★ **West Façade**

★ **Pórtico da Gloria**

★ **Porta das Praterias**

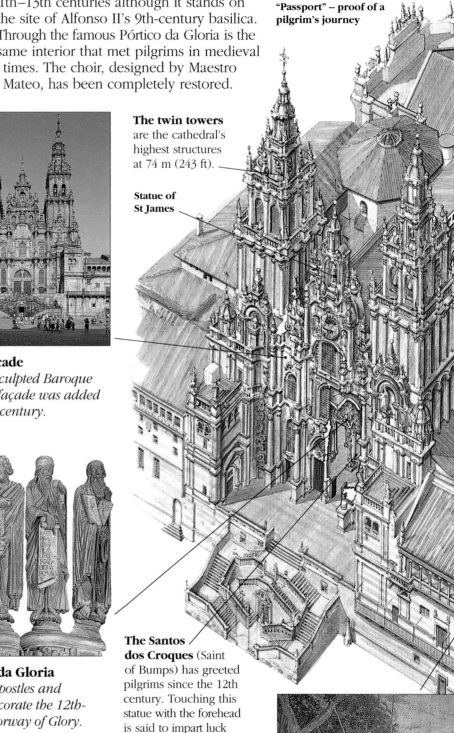

The twin towers are the cathedral's highest structures at 74 m (243 ft).

Statue of St James

The Santos dos Croques (Saint of Bumps) has greeted pilgrims since the 12th century. Touching this statue with the forehead is said to impart luck and wisdom.

Tapestry Museum
Tapestries dating from the early 16th century are on display in a museum above the chapter house and library. Some later tapestries are based on Goya's works.

The *botafumeiro*, a giant censer, is swung high above the altar by eight men during important services.

Mondragon Chapel (1521) contains fine wrought-iron grilles and vaulting.

THE SCALLOP SHELL

As the symbol of St James, scallop shells were worn by pilgrims in the Middle Ages to show that they had journeyed to his shrine. Houses willing to accept passing pilgrims en route hung shells over their doors.

Clock Tower

High Altar
Visitors can pass behind the ornate high altar to embrace the silver mantle of the 13th-century statue of St James.

★ Porta das Praterias
The 12th-century Goldsmiths' Doorway is rich in bas-relief sculptures of biblical scenes.

Cloisters

Crypt
The relics of St James and two disciples are said to lie in a tomb in the crypt, under the altar, in the original 9th-century foundations.

Chapter house

KEY DATES

1075 Construction of the present building begins.

1128 The cathedral is consecrated.

1750 The west façade of the building is completed.

1985 The Old Town of Santiago is added to UNESCO's World Heritage Site list.

PÓRTICO DA GLORIA

The Romanesque pillars, pointed arches, and ribbed vaulting (▷ *Romanesque Style p199*) of this doorway were carved in part by Maestro Mateo. The lintel of the central arch bears his signature and the date 1188. This was the original entrance to the cathedral. Its three arches are carved with almost 200 expressive biblical figures. Christ sits at the center baring his wounds, flanked by his apostles and the 24 Elders of the Apocalypse who are carrying musical instruments. St James is seated below Christ, perched serenely before the richly sculpted central column. Several indentations are visible on this column which also depicts the Tree of Jesse. These have been created by the millions of pilgrims who have touched this spot with their hands as a gesture of thanks for their safe journey. On the other side, pilgrims bend to rest their heads on the statue of the ▷ *Santos dos Croques* hoping to gain inspiration from his wisdom.

Santiago Cathedral

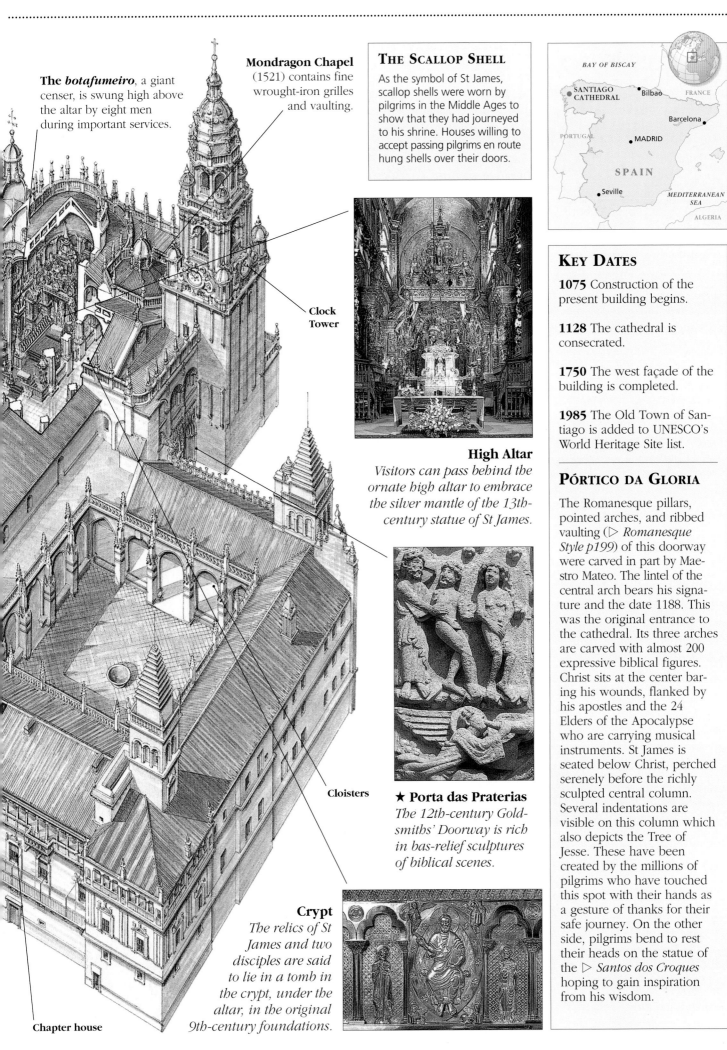

FRANK O GEHRY

Architect Frank O Gehry

Canadian-born architect Frank O Gehry designed the extraordinary Guggenheim museum in Bilbao. He studied architecture at the University of Southern California and then Urban Planning at Harvard before setting up his own firm in 1962. His early work was notable for its unusual materials including chain-link and corrugated metal. More recent works have possessed an almost sculptural quality, made possible by computer design, creating distinctly unique modern landmarks. In the course of his career, Gehry has been awarded large-scale public and private commissions in America, Japan, and Europe. His impressive work has received worldwide praise and numerous awards.

THE BUILDING

The edifice is a breathtaking combination of curling fragmented shapes, limestone blocks, glass walls, and panels which beam light into the building. The central space (▷ *Atrium*), one of the most pioneering design features, is crowned by a metal dome and skylight. Framing this vast area is a futuristic vision of suspended curved walkways, glass elevators and soaring staircases that lead to the 19 galleries. Ten of these have a classic rectangular form and are recognized from the outside by their stone finish. The other rooms are erratically shaped and identified by their exterior titanium paneling (▷ *Titanium façade*). Volumes and perspectives have been manipulated throughout to blend the overall sculpted design with the surrounding landscape, embracing Bilbao's industrial identity.

Guggenheim Museum, Bilbao

THE JEWEL IN BILBAO's development program, the Museo Guggenheim unites art and architecture. The building itself is a star attraction: a mind-boggling array of silvery curves by the architect Frank O Gehry, which are alleged to resemble a ship or flower. The Guggenheim's collection represents an intriguingly broad spectrum of modern and contemporary art, and includes works by Abstract Impressionists such as Willem de Kooning and Mark Rothko. Most of the art shown here is displayed as part of an ongoing series of temporary exhibitions and major retrospectives. Some of these are also staged at the Guggenheim museums in New York, Venice, and Berlin.

Roofscape
The Guggenheim's prow-like points and metallic material make it comparable to a ship.

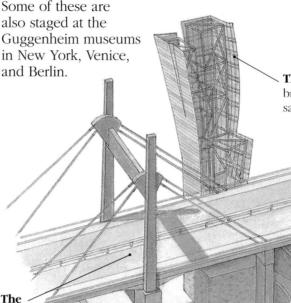

The tower, on the far side of the bridge, was designed to resemble a sail. It is not an exhibition space.

The Puente de la Salve was incorporated into the design of the building, which extends underneath it.

★ Titanium Façade
Rare in buildings, titanium is more commonly used for aircraft parts. In total 60 tonnes were used, but the layer is only 3 mm (0.1 inch) thick.

The Snake, by Richard Serra, was created in hot-rolled steel. It is over 30 m (100 ft) long.

Fish Gallery
Dominated by Richard Serra's Snake, *this gallery is the museum's largest. The fish motif, seen in the flowing shape, is one of architect Frank O Gehry's favorites.*

Guggenheim Museum

★ **Atrium**
The space in which visitors to the museum first find themselves is the extraordinary 60-m (197-ft) high atrium. It serves as an orientation point and its height makes it a dramatic setting for exhibiting large pieces.

Third-floor balcony

SYMBOLISM

Built to rescue the city from economic decline, the museum uses materials and shapes to convey Bilbao's industrial past of steel and shipbuilding while simultaneously symbolizing the city's commitment to its future.

Puppy, by American artist Jeff Koons, has a coat of flowers irrigated by an internal system. Originally a temporary feature, the sculpture's popularity with Bilbao's residents earned it a permanent spot.

BAY OF BISCAY
GUGGENHEIM MUSEUM, BILBAO   FRANCE
Barcelona
PORTUGAL   MADRID
SPAIN
Seville   MEDITERRANEAN SEA
ALGERIA

KEY DATES

1991 Plans to build the museum are approved.

1993 Frank O Gehry presents his museum design model.

1994 Work begins on the museum building.

1997 The museum is opened to the public.

THE COLLECTION

The collection is arranged over three levels around the ▷ *atrium* with Mark Rothko's *Untitled* (1952) marking the chronological start. The collection comprises works by significant artists of the late 20th century, ranging from the earliest avant-garde movements to present-day genres. Prominent artists featured include Eduardo Chillida, Yves Klein, Willem de Kooning, Robert Motherwell, Clyfford Still, Antoni Tàpies, and Andy Warhol. There are also a number of works by emerging Basque and Spanish artists. The museum's own permanent collection is supplemented by important artworks from the extensive collection of the Solomon R Guggenheim Museum in New York and the Peggy Guggenheim Collection in Venice. These include significant examples of Pop Art, Minimalism, Arte Povera, Conceptual Art, Abstract Expressionism, and Surrealism. This sharing of works allows the collection to assume a constantly evolving, versatile role as it presents different aspects of contemporary art.

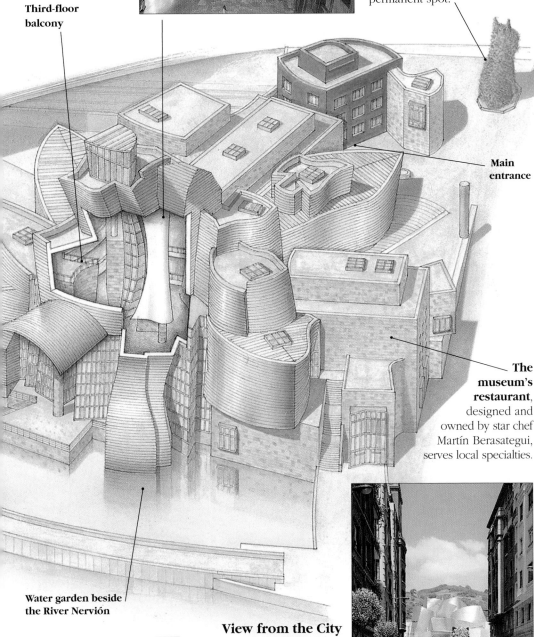

Main entrance

The museum's restaurant, designed and owned by star chef Martín Berasategui, serves local specialties.

Water garden beside the River Nervión

STAR FEATURES

★ **Titanium Façade**

★ **Atrium**

View from the City
Approaching along the Calle de Iparraguirre, the "Guggen," as the museum has been nicknamed by locals, stands out amid traditional buildings.

Guggenheim Museum

INTERIOR DECORATIONS

The inside of Burgos' cathedral is enriched with beautiful furnishings and architectural features. Among its treasures are Renaissance and Baroque paintings, sculptures, and Flemish and Hispanic tapestries. Several Gothic and Renaissance tombs, including those designed by Diego de Siloé, are on view. Some of the most striking parts of the cathedral are the 16th-century ▷ *Golden Staircase*, the ▷ *Crossing,* and the Chancel. A superb marble stairway leads from the Chancel toward a sculpted reredos at the end of the Presbytery. Dedicated to St Mary, these impressive panels are decorated with elegant reliefs and sculptures.

Baroque biblical fresco covering the domed ceiling of the sacristy

CONSTABLE'S CHAPEL

Burgos' cathedral boasts 13 chapels and its most impressive is the Chapel of Purification, otherwise known as ▷ *Constable's Chapel*. This funerary chapel was built by Simon of Cologne for the Countess Doña Mencía and her husband, Pedro Fernández de Velasco, High Constable (chief commander of the royal army) of Castile. Construction began in 1842, but the High Constable died before the chapel was completed. His sepulcher and that of his wife who died later are in the center of the chapel. The main altarpiece near their tombs is decorated with sculptures by Diego de Siloé and Philippe de Bigarny.

Burgos Cathedral

SPAIN'S THIRD-LARGEST CATHEDRAL was founded in 1221 by Bishop Mauricio under Fernando III. The ground-plan – a Latin cross – measures 84 m (276 ft) by 59 m (194 ft). Its construction was carried out in several stages over three centuries and involved many of the greatest artists and architects in Europe. The style is almost entirely Gothic (▷ *Gothic Style p73)* and shows influences from Germany and France as well as the Low Countries. First to be built were the nave and cloisters, while the intricate, crocketed spires and richly decorated side chapels are mostly later work. The architects skillfully adapted the cathedral to its sloping site, adding stairways inside and out.

Christ at the Column, by Diego de Siloé

West Front
The lacy, steel-gray spires soar above a sculpted balustrade depicting Castile's early kings.

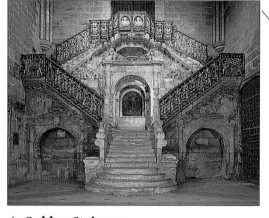

★ Golden Staircase
This elegant Renaissance staircase by Diego de Siloé (1523) links the nave with a tall door at street level.

STAR FEATURES

★ Golden Staircase

★ Constable's Chapel

★ The Crossing

Lantern

Tomb of El Cid

Capilla de Santa Tecla

Puerta de Santa María (main entrance)

Capilla de Santa Ana
The altarpiece (1490) in this chapel is by the sculptor Gil de Siloé. The central panel shows the Virgin with St Joachim.

Capilla de la Presentación (1519–24) is a funerary chapel with a star-shaped, traceried vault.

Retrochoir
Several reliefs around the chancel were carved by Philippe de Bigarny. This expressive scene, which was completed in 1499, depicts the road to Calvary.

Capilla de San Juan Bautista and museum

★ Constable's Chapel
The tomb of the High Constable of Castile and his wife lies beneath the openwork vault of this chapel of 1496.

Sacristy *(1765)*
The sacristy was rebuilt in Baroque style, with an exuberant plasterwork vault and rococo altars.

Capilla de la Visitación

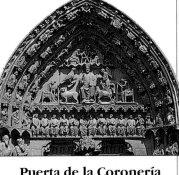

Puerta de la Coronería
The tympanum of this portal of 1240 shows Christ flanked by the Evangelists. Statues of the apostles sit below.

Capilla del Santísimo Cristo

★ The Crossing
The magnificent star-ribbed central dome, begun in 1539, rises on four huge pillars. It is decorated with effigies of prophets and saints. Beneath it is the tomb of El Cid and his wife.

KEY DATES

1221 Construction begins on Burgos' cathedral. The first brick is laid by King Fernando III.

1250 The transept, adjoining walls and the central part of the nave are completed.

1260 The cathedral is consecrated.

1539 The lantern tower collapses.

1540–68 The lantern tower is rebuilt by Juan de Vallejo and Francisco Colonia.

1984 Burgos Cathedral is inscribed a UNESCO World Heritage Site.

EL CID

Rodrigo Díaz de Vivar was born into a noble family in Vivar del Cid, north of Burgos, in 1043. He served King Fernando I, but was banished from Castile after becoming embroiled in the fratricidal squabbles of the king's sons, Sancho II and Alfonso VI. He switched allegiance to fight for the Moors, then changed sides again, capturing Valencia for the Christians in 1094, ruling the city until his death at the end of the 11th century. For his heroism he was named El Cid, from the Arabic *sidi* (Lord). He was a charismatic man of great courage, but it was an anonymous poem, *El Cantar del Mio Cid*, in 1180, that immortalized him as a romantic hero of the Reconquest. The ▷ *tomb of El Cid* and his wife, Jimena, are in Burgos cathedral.

Burgos Cathedral

MODERNISME

Towards the end of the 19th century a new style of art and architecture, a variant of Art Nouveau, was born in Barcelona. It became a means of expression for Catalan nationalism and attempted to re-establish a local identity that had waned under the rule of Castilian Madrid. It is characterized by curved lines, a profusive use of colored tiles and tiled mosaics. Modernisme counted Josep Puig i Cadafalch, Lluís Domènech i Montaner, and, above all, Antoni Gaudí among its major exponents, and its radical style is one of the principal attractions of Barcelona today.

ANTONI GAUDÍ

Born into a family of artisans, Antoni Gaudí (1852–1926) was the leading exponent of Modernisme. Following a stint as a blacksmith's apprentice, he studied at Barcelona's School of Architecture. Inspired by a nationalistic search for a romantic medieval past, his work was supremely original. His most celebrated building is the extravagant church of the Sagrada Família, to which he devoted his life from 1883. He gave all his money to the project and often went from house to house begging for more, until his death a few days after being run over by a tram. Gaudí designed, or collaborated on designs, for almost every known medium. He combined bare, undecorated materials – wood, rough-hewn stone, rubble, and brickwork – with meticulous craftwork in wrought iron and stained glass.

Stained-glass window in the Sagrada Família

Sagrada Família, Barcelona

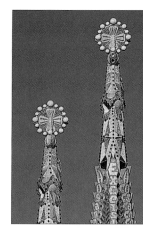

A carved whelk

Europe's most unconventional church, the Temple Expiatori de la Sagrada Família is an emblem of a city that likes to think of itself as individualistic. Crammed with symbolism inspired by nature, and striving for originality, it is Antoni Gaudí's greatest work. In 1883, a year after work had begun on a Neo-Gothic church on the site (▷ *Gothic Style p73*), the task of completing it was given to Gaudí who changed everything, extemporizing as he went along. It became his life's work; he lived like a recluse on the site for 16 years and is buried in the crypt. At his death only one tower on the Nativity façade had been completed, but work continued after the Spanish Civil War and several more have since been finished to his original plans. Work continues today, financed by public subscription.

Bell Towers
Eight of the 12 spires, on for each apostle, have been built. Each is topped by Venetian mosaics.

THE FINISHED CHURCH

Gaudí's initial ambitions have been scaled down over the years, but the design for the completion of the building remains impressive. Still to come is the central tower, which is to be encircled by four large towers representing the Evangelists. Four towers on the Glory (south) façade will match the existing four on the Passion (west) and Nativity (east) façades. An ambulatory – like an inside-out cloister – will run round the outside of the building.

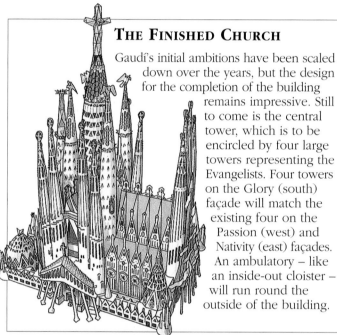

Tower with elevator

The apse was the first part of the church Gaudí completed. Stairs lead down from here to the crypt below.

The altar canopy, designed by Gaudí, is still waiting for the altar.

★ **Passion Façade**
This bleak façade was completed in the late 1980s by artist Josep Maria Subirachs. A controversial work, its sculpted figures are angular and often sinister.

Entrance to Crypt Museum

Spiral Staircases
Viewed from the top, the spiral of stone steps is reminiscent of a snail or a sea shell. The steps allow access to the towers and upper galleries.

Sagrada Família

BAY OF BISCAY

Bilbao

FRANCE

SAGRADA FAMÍLIA, BARCELONA

PORTUGAL

MADRID

SPAIN

Seville

MEDITERRANEAN SEA

ALGERIA

★ Nativity Façade
The most complete part of Gaudí's church, finished in 1904, has doorways representing Faith, Hope, and Charity. Scenes of the Nativity and Christ's childhood are embellished with symbolism, such as doves representing the congregation.

Tower with elevator

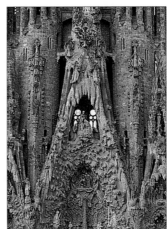

KEY DATES

1882 The foundation stone of the Sagrada Família is laid.

1885 The church is inaugurated.

1893 Work on the Nativity façade begins.

1954 Work resumes on the church after it was halted during the Spanish Civil War (1936–39). The church is still incomplete.

★ Crypt
The crypt, where Gaudí is buried, was built by the original architect, Francesc de Paula Villar i Lozano, in 1882. On the lower floor a museum traces the careers of both architects and the church's history.

SYMBOLISM

Gaudí united nature and religion in his symbolic vision of the Sagrada Família. The church has three monumental façades. The east front (▷ *Nativity Façade*) is directed toward the rising sun and dedicated to the birth of Christ. Flora and fauna, spring and summer symbols, fruits, birds, and flowers adorn this façade. The west front (▷ *Passion Façade*) represents Christ's Passion and death, with columns eerily reminiscent of bones combined with a somber lack of decoration to reflect the loss which death brings. The Glory façade to the south has not yet been constructed, but is projected to be the largest of all. It will depict the Christian virtues and show that ascension to heaven can only be attained through prayer and sacraments. Gaudí intended the interior of the church to evoke the idea of a forest (▷ *nave*). Columns are "planted" symbolically like tree trunks, and dappled light filters in through the skylights.

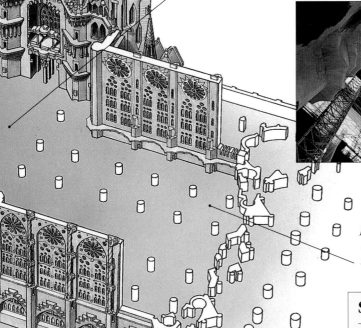

Nave
In the nave, which is still under construction, fluted pillars will support four galleries above the aisles, while skylights let in natural light.

Main entrance

STAR FEATURES

★ **Passion Façade**

★ **Nativity Façade**

★ **Crypt**

View of the Monestir de Santes Creus near Poblet

CISTERCIAN TRIANGLE

Three monasteries form the so-called Cistercian triangle in Catalonia: Poblet, Vallbona de les Monges, and Santes Creus. Traditionally, Cistercian monasteries were built in isolated spots usually by springs or running water. The monastery of Santa Maria de Poblet lies at the foot of the northern slopes of the Prades mountains. Vallbona de les Monges, founded in 1153, is the most important female Cistercian monastery in Catalonia. Its main entrance is adorned with one of the first reliefs of St Mary found on a tympanum in Catalonia. Santes Creus was founded in 1168. Its Gothic cloisters are decorated with figurative sculptures, while the austere interior of the church is relieved by a splendid rose window.

THE RULE OF RAMÓN BERENGUER IV

The history of Poblet goes back to 1151 when Ramón Berenguer IV, Count of Barcelona, gave the land to the Abbey of Fontfreda (near Narbonne in France) so that a Cistercian abbey could be founded. Berenguer was a powerful figure in 12th-century Spain, a position reinforced by his marriage to the two-year-old Petronila, daughter of the King of Aragón, in 1137. As well as uniting the regions of Catalonia and neighboring Aragón, it was a turning point in the fortunes of Catalonia. This new power and status enabled Berenguer to expand his kingdom. For the next three centuries Aragón-Catalonia prospered.

Poblet Monastery

THE MONASTERY OF SANTA MARIA DE POBLET is a haven of tranquillity and a resting place of kings. Built in the simple but beautiful early Gothic style (▷ *Gothic Style p73*), this large site is the first and most important of three monasteries in the area known as the Cistercian triangle that were established by Ramón Berenguer IV. It was inhabited until 1835 when, during political upheavals, it was plundered and damaged by fire. Restoration of the ruins during the 20th century enabled the monks to return.

The dormitory is reached by stairs from the church. The vast 87-m (285-ft) gallery dates from the 13th century. Half of it is still in use by the monks.

View of Poblet
The abbey, its buildings enclosed by fortified walls that have hardly changed since the Middle Ages, is in an isolated valley near the Riu Francolí's source.

The 12th-century refectory is a vaulted hall with an octagonal fountain and a pulpit.

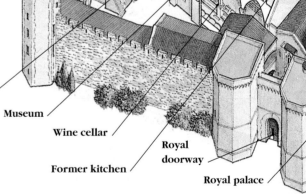

Museum

Wine cellar

Former kitchen

Royal doorway

Royal palace

Library
The Gothic scriptorium was converted into a library in the 17th century, when the Duke of Cardona donated his book collection.

Church Façade
The entrance to the abbey church, this façade has sculptures of St Mary (center), patroness of the Abbey, with SS Benito and Bernardo on either side.

Chapter house
This perfectly square room, with slender columns, has tiers of benches for the monks. It is paved with the tombstones of 11 abbots who died between 1393 and 1693.

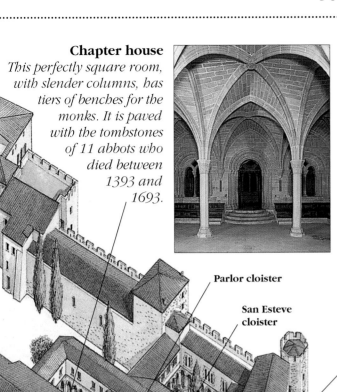

Parlor cloister

San Esteve cloister

New sacristy

The Abbey Church, large and unadorned with three naves, is a typical Cistercian building.

★ Cloisters
The evocative, vaulted cloisters were built in the 12th and 13th centuries and were the center of monastic life. The beautiful capitals are decorated with carved scrollwork.

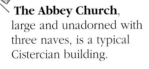

FIT FOR ROYALTY
The first Cistercian monks came to Poblet in 1153. Despite the order's ascetic beliefs, the community grew, acquiring wealth and power. Poblet enjoyed royal protection and in the 14th century it was chosen as a royal mausoleum by Pedro III.

★ High Altar Reredos
Behind the stone altar, supported by Romanesque columns, an impressive alabaster reredos fills the apse. It was carved by Damià Forment in 1527.

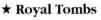

★ Royal Tombs
The tombs in the pantheon of kings were begun in 1359. In 1950 the sculptures were restored by Federico Marès.

STAR FEATURES

★ **High Altar Reredos**

★ **Royal Tombs**

★ **Cloisters**

KEY DATES

1151 Ramón Berenguer IV founds Poblet monastery.

1835 The monastery is looted and the monks abandon it.

1921 Poblet is declared a National Monument.

1930 Restoration starts.

1940 Cistercian monks return to the monastery to live.

1991 UNESCO declares Poblet Monastery a World Heritage Site.

THE ABBEY CHURCH

At the heart of the monastery complex, in the Plaça Major, stands the lovely ▷ *Abbey Church*. Built by King Alfonso I between 1166 and 1198, the church of Santa Maria is an outstanding example of Cistercian architecture (▷ *Cistercian Style p171*), with its clean, elegant lines and harmonious proportions. It is built on a plain basilica plan with three aisles separated by pillars. The nave has a pointed vault and there is a central apse at the end. A huge and strikingly ornate ▷ *high altar reredos* occupies the apse. The church is also the royal mausoleum, and high up on either side of the altar are the beautiful ▷ *royal tombs* of the monarchs of Catalonia and Aragón, including Jaume I, Alfonso I, and Juan II, the last king of Aragón. The exquisite sculptures were restored in the 20th century.

THE LIBRARY

Established by Felipe II (r.1556–98), this was Spain's first public library. In 1619, a decree was issued demanding that a copy of each new publication in the empire be sent here. At its zenith, it contained some 40,000 books and manuscripts, mainly from the 15th and 16th centuries. The long Print Room has a marble floor and a glorious vaulted ceiling. The ceiling frescoes by Pellegrino Tibaldi (1527–96) depict Philosophy, Grammar, Rhetoric, Dialectics, Music, Geometry, Astrology, and Theology. The wooden shelving was designed by Juan de Herrera (1530–97). On the four main pillars hang portraits of the royal House of Habsburg – Carlos I (Roman Emperor Charles V), Felipe II, Felipe III, and Carlos II.

Marble sarcophagi in El Escorial's octagonal Royal Pantheon

THE PANTHEONS

Directly beneath the high altar of the basilica is the ▷ *Royal Pantheon*, where almost all Spanish monarchs since Carlos I are laid to rest. This pantheon, with Spanish black marble, red jasper, and Italian gilt bronze decorations, was finished in 1654. Kings lie on the left of the altar and queens on the right. The most recent addition to the pantheon was the mother of Juan Carlos I in 2000. Of the eight other pantheons, one of the most notable is that of Juan de Austria, Felipe II's half-brother, who became a hero after defeating the Turks at the Battle of Lepanto in 1571. Also worth seeing is La Tarta, a white marble polygonal tomb that resembles a cake, where royal children are buried.

El Escorial, Madrid

Fresco by Luca Giordano

FELIPE II'S IMPOSING GRAY PALACE of San Lorenzo de El Escorial stands out against the foothills of the Sierra de Guadarrama to the northwest of Madrid. It was built between 1563 and 1584 in honor of St Lawrence, and its unornamented severity set a new architectural style which became one of the most influential in Spain. The interior was conceived as a mausoleum and contemplative retreat rather than a splendid residence. Its artistic wealth, which includes some of the most important works of art of the royal Habsburg collections, is concentrated in the museums, chapter houses, church, royal pantheon, and library. In contrast, the royal apartments are remarkably humble.

★ **Royal Pantheon**
The funerary urns of Spanish monarchs line the marble mausoleum.

Basilica
The highlight of this huge decorated church is the lavish altarpiece. The chapel houses a superb marble sculpture of the Crucifixion by Cellini.

The Alfonso XII College was founded by monks in 1875 as a boarding school.

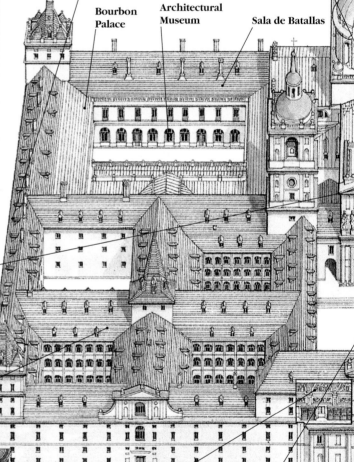

Main entrance

Bourbon Palace

Architectural Museum

Sala de Batallas

Patio de los Reyes

Entrance to Basilica only

★ **Library**
This impressive array of 40,000 books incorporates King Felipe II's personal collection. On display are precious manuscripts, including a poem by Alfonso X the Learned. The 16th-century ceiling frescoes are by Tibaldi.

STAR FEATURES

★ **Royal Pantheon**

★ **Library**

★ **Museum of Art**

The royal apartments, on the third floor of the palace, consist of Felipe II's modestly decorated living quarters. His bedroom opens directly on to the high altar of the basilica.

★ **Museum of Art**
Flemish, Italian, and Spanish paintings hang in the museum, located on the second floor. One of the highlights is The Calvary, *by 15th-century Flemish artist Rogier van der Weyden.*

The Patio de los Evangelistas has a magnificent pavilion by Juan de Herrera at its center.

ST LAWRENCE
On 10 August 1557 – St Lawrence's Day – King Felipe II defeated the French in battle, immediately vowing to build a monastery in the saint's honor. El Escorial's gridiron plan is said to recall the instrument of St Lawrence's martyrdom.

Chapter houses
On display here is Charles V's portable altar. The ceiling frescoes depict monarchs and angels.

The monastery was founded in 1567, and has been run by Augustinian monks since 1885.

BAY OF BISCAY
Bilbao
FRANCE
Barcelona
PORTUGAL
EL ESCORIAL
MADRID
SPAIN
Seville
MEDITERRANEAN SEA
ALGERIA

KEY DATES

1563 The foundation stone of the monastery is laid.

1581 Work on the Basilica is finished.

1654 The Royal Pantheon is completed.

1984 El Escorial is added to UNESCO's World Heritage Site list.

THE BASILICA

Historically, only the aristocracy were permitted to enter the ▷ *Basilica*, and the townspeople were confined to the vestibule at the entrance. The basilica contains 45 altars. Among its highlights are the exquisite statue of Christ Crucified (1562) in Carrara marble by Benvenuto Cellini. It is found in the chapel to the left of the entrance, with steps leading up to it. Either side of the high altar, above the doors leading to the ▷ *royal apartments,* are fine gilded bronze cenotaphs of Charles V and Felipe II worshiping with their families. The enormous altarpiece was designed by Juan de Herrera with colored marble, jasper, gilt-bronze sculptures, and paintings. The central tabernacle, backlit by a window, took Italian silversmith Jacoppo da Trezzo (1515–89) seven years to craft. The paintings are by Federico Zuccaro (1542–1609) and Pellegrino Tibaldi, who also executed the fresco above. The wood for the cross (also used for Felipe II's coffin) came from a Spanish ship, the *Cinco Llagas* (Five Wounds).

The Glory of the Spanish Monarchy by Luca Giordano
This beautiful fresco, above the main staircase, depicts Charles V and Felipe II, and scenes of the building of the monastery.

The Building of El Escorial
When chief architect Juan Bautista de Toledo died in 1567 he was replaced by Juan de Herrera, royal inspector of monuments. The plain architectural style of El Escorial is called desornamentado, *literally "unadorned".*

El Escorial

FERNANDO III

In 1217, King Enrique of Castile was killed and his sister, Fernando III's mother, renounced her right to the crown in her son's favour. In 1230 Fernando III (1199–1252) inherited León from his father and promptly united the two kingdoms. He devoted his reign to the crusade against the invading Moors and recaptured the greater part of Andalusia, taking Córdoba in 1236, Murcia in 1243, Jaén in 1246, and Seville in 1248. Only Granada remained under Moorish rule. Fernando's death in 1252 bequeathed the task of completing the conquest to his son, Alfonso X. Known as El Santo or "the Saint," Fernando was canonized by the Roman Catholic Church in 1671. He was buried in Seville cathedral in the habit of St Francis.

PRECIOUS WORKS OF ART

An enormous gilded screen with highly detailed polychrome wood carvings, typical of the late Gothic, dominates the monumental altarpiece (▷ *High Altar Reredos*). Scenes of the Nativity and the Assumption are portrayed in the upper sections. Located in the ▷ *Sacristy* is El Greco's exceptional *The Denuding of Christ*. This dignified and emotional scene shows followers crowding Christ at the base of the cross as he awaits crucifixion. His striking luminous red robe highlights El Greco's original and powerful use of color.

The belfry rising above Toledo's rooftops

Toledo Cathedral

THE SPLENDOR OF TOLEDO's massive cathedral reflects its history as the spiritual heart of the Spanish Church and the seat of the Primate of all Spain. The 6th-century Mozarabic Mass is still said here. The present cathedral was built on the site of a 7th-century church. Work began in 1226 and continued until the last vaults were completed in 1493. This long construction period explains the mixture of styles: French Gothic on the exterior (▷ *Gothic Style p73*); with Spanish decorative styles, such as Mudéjar (▷ *Mudéjar Style p194*) and Plateresque, an ornate style popular here during the early Renaissance, used in the interior.

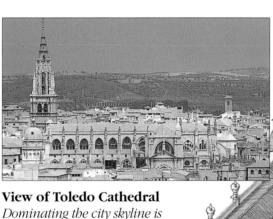

View of Toledo Cathedral
Dominating the city skyline is the cathedral's Gothic north tower, begun in 1380. The tower's lantern and spire, with a symbolic Crown of Thorns, were added in 1492.

The belfry in the tower contains a heavy bell known as *La Gorda* ("the Fat One").

The Puerta del Mollete, on the west façade, is the main entrance to the cathedral. From this door, *mollete,* or soft bread, was distributed to the poor.

Monstrance
In the Treasury is the 16th-century Gothic silver and gold monstrance. It is carried through the streets of Toledo during the Corpus Christi celebrations.

★ **Sacristy**
El Greco's The Denuding of Christ, *above the marble altar, was painted especially for the cathedral. Also here are works by Titian, Van Dyck, and Goya.*

The Cloister, on two floors, was built in the 14th century on the site of the old Jewish market.

STAR FEATURES

★ **Sacristy**

★ **Transparente**

★ **High Altar Reredos**

★ **Choir**

★ **Transparente**
Narciso Tomé's extraordinary Baroque altar-piece (▷ Baroque Style p111) made of colored marble, jasper, and bronze is illuminated by an ornate skylight.

ROMAN VS MOZARABIC
Legend says that Alfonso VI (1040–1109) devised a series of tests to determine whether the Roman or Mozarabic liturgy was more valuable. Several trials by battle took place, each with differing outcomes. However, influenced by the pope, Alfonso favored the Roman rite.

Capilla de Santiago

The Capilla de San Ildefonso contains the superb Plateresque tomb of Cardinal Alonso Carrillo de Albornoz.

Chapter house
Above 16th-century frescoes by Juan de Borgoña is this multicolored Mudéjar ceiling, unique in the city.

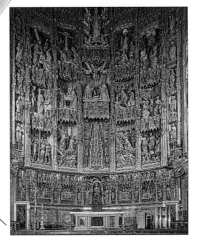

★ **High Altar Reredos**
The polychrome reredos, one of the most beautiful in Spain, depicts scenes from Christ's life.

Puerta de los Leones

Puerta Llana

The Puerta del Perdón, or Door of Mercy, has a tympanum decorated with religious characters.

The Capilla Mozárabe has a beautiful Renaissance ironwork grille, carved by Juan Francés in 1524.

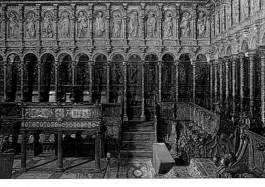

★ **Choir**
The carvings on the wooden lower stalls depict scenes of the fall of Granada. The alabaster upper ones show figures from the Old Testament.

Toledo Cathedral

KEY DATES

1226 The first stone of the cathedral is laid.

1418 Work begins on the west façade.

1498–1504 The High Altar is constructed.

1986 The city of Toledo is inscribed on UNESCO's World Heritage Site list.

CAPILLA MOZÁRABE

The Mozarabs were Christians practicing their religion under Moorish rule. Built in 1504 by Enrique de Egas, the ▷ *Capilla Mozárabe* still has a daily morning service of the Mozarabic liturgy, the original national liturgy of the Spanish church. This chant dates back to the 6th-century conversion to Catholicism during the Visigothic period, although little evidence remains of its content prior to 711 when the Moors first invaded Spain. Several attempts were made over the centuries to abolish this rite and to use the Roman liturgy instead, however the practise continued in certain dominions, enabling its survival to this day. Today the rite only exists in Toledo and Salamanca. Francisco Jiménez de Cisneros, appointed Archbishop of Toledo in 1495, set up a number of initiatives to preserve the rite from extinction. He employed masters of the liturgical tradition to prepare two editions of the chant which were published in 1500 and 1502 respectively. He also established the Mozarabic service here.

THE OMAYYAD RULERS

The first Arab-Islamic dynasty of Caliphs, which was founded in 660 in Damascus by Muawiya Ibn Abi Sufian, ended in 750 with the assassination of all the family members except one, Abd al Rahman I. He fled to Spain and founded another Omayyad dynasty to rule in Córdoba from 756 to 1031. The Omayyad court was one of splendor, a haven for poets, artists, and intellectuals. It was also a period of production and prosperity. During the gradual Reconquest of Andalucia by the Spanish, the Moors retreated and Córdoba fell to Ferdinand III of Castile in 1236

THE BUILDING

The stunning and gigantic Mezquita covers a total area of 24,000 sq m (258,333 sq ft). It was originally constructed by Abd al Rahman over the Visigoth Christian church of San Vicente. However, additions were made to the building over the centuries in both the Islamic and Christian eras. One of the most distinctive features of the building are the rows of ▷ *arches and pillars*, some of which were added by al Hakam II between 961–76, which support the roof. Equally striking is the ▷ *mihrab*, believed to have been carved from a single block of marble, which was added around 965. Surrounded by high arched windows, it is beautifully decorated with colorful mosaics.

The Mezquita walls, hiding a vast Mosque and a cathedral within

The Mezquita, Córdoba

CÓRDOBA'S GREAT MOSQUE, dating back 12 centuries, is the largest mosque in the western world. The original mosque was constructed by the city's Moorish ruler in AD 785–7. The structure expanded over the centuries with more columns and additions, including, in the 10th century, the elaborate *mihrab* (prayer niche) and *maqsura* (caliph's enclosure). During the 16th century, an area was destroyed to make space for a cathedral in its heart. The result is a fascinating mix of religions, cultures, and architectural styles.

Patio de los Naranjos
Orange trees grow in the courtyard where the faithful once washed before prayer.

Torre del Alminar
This bell tower, 93 m (305 ft) high, is built on the site of the original minaret. Steep steps lead to the top for a fine view of the city.

The Puerta del Perdón is a Mudéjar-style entrance gate, built during Christian rule in 1377. Penitents were pardoned here.

Puerta de San Esteban is set in a section of wall from an earlier Visigothic church.

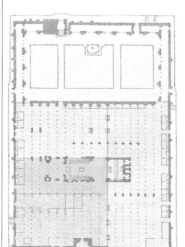

EXPANSION OF THE MEZQUITA

Abd al Rahman I built the original mosque. Extensions were added by successive rulers Abd al Rahman II, al Hakam II, and al Mansur.

KEY TO ADDITIONS

- ☐ Mosque of Abd al Rahman I
- ☐ Extension by Abd al Rahman II
- ☐ Extension by al Hakam II
- ☐ Extension by al Mansur
- ☐ Patio de los Naranjos

STAR FEATURES

★ **Arches and Pillars**

★ **Mihrab**

★ **Capilla de Villaviciosa**

Cathedral Dome
The Capilla Mayor (Main Cathedral), which was designed chiefly by members of the Hernán Ruiz family, features an elaborate Italianate dome.

DYNASTIC AMBITIONS
The building of the Mezquita was intended to rival the grandeur of such monuments as the Dome of the Rock in Jerusalem and the Great Mosque at Damascus, which were in the hands of the Abbasids, longtime enemies of the Omayyads.

BAY OF BISCAY
Bilbao
FRANCE
Barcelona
PORTUGAL
MADRID
SPAIN
Seville
THE MEZQUITA, CÓRDOBA
MEDITERRANEAN SEA
ALGERIA

The cathedral choir has stalls carved by Pedro Duque Cornejo in 1758.

Capilla Mayor

Capilla Real

★ **Arches and Pillars**
Hundreds of columns of granite, jasper, and marble support the roof, and the striped double-tier arches create a dazzling visual effect.

★ **Mihrab**
This richly ornamented prayer niche once held a gilt copy of the Koran. The worn flagstones show where many pilgrims circled it seven times on their knees.

★ **Capilla de Villaviciosa**
The first Christian chapel was built in the mosque in 1257 by Moorish craftsmen who added stunning arches.

KEY DATES

584 Construction of Visigothic church on a pagan site.

785–7 The Mezquita is built by Abd al Rahman I.

821–976 Naves and rows of columns are added.

1523 Construction of the cathedral inside the Mezquita.

THE CATHEDRAL

The site of the Mezquita has been a significant one in its history due to its proximity to the Guadalquivir river. This can be seen in the constant construction, reconstruction, and additions to the site. First a pagan temple, then a Visigothic church, and finally a mosque under the Moors were built. The Spanish regained Córdoba in the 13th century and promptly consecrated the Mezquita as a church but left much of the superb Moorish architecture intact. It was Moorish craftsmen who built the first Christian chapel, ▷ *Capilla de Villaviciosa*, in 1257 with beautiful Mudéjar details (▷ *Mudéjar Style p194*). The ▷ *Capilla Real* (Royal Chapel) was begun in 1258. In the 16th century, the center of the Mezquita was removed and a domed cathedral, ▷ *Capilla Mayor*, was erected within. The doors were blocked and stained-glass windows added. The story goes that on seeing the gloomy interior, Emperor Charles V instantly regretted agreeing to the alterations, lamenting the loss of "something unique".

The Mezquita

Real Alcázar

THE ALMOHAD RULERS

In the mid-12th century, the ruling Almoravids from North Africa were ousted by the Almohads from Morocco. Seville accepted their rule in 1147 and was designated the capital of their expanding empire. Andalusia was governed from the Real Alcázar which became a citadel at the center of the city's fortifications. The Almohads sustained power until the crushing defeat in 1212 by the Christians at Las Navas de Tolosa in nearby Jaén. The Almohads created the oldest features within the palace complex that can be seen today. The ▷ *Patio del Yeso* survives from this period.

MUDÉJAR STYLE

The *Mudéjares* – Muslims who remained in territories under Christian occupation – created a distinctive architectural style recognized by its ornamental work in brick, plaster, and ceramics. Mudéjar literally means "those permitted to stay." Spectacular designs resulted from this hybrid Christian Islamic style. Islamic grandeur blended with the Romanesque (▷ *Romanesque Style p199*), Gothic (▷ *Gothic Style p73*), and Renaissance (▷ *Renaissance Style p211*) features prevalent in Europe from the 12th to the 16th centuries. The Palacio Pedro I, with its exquisitely harmonious collection of patios and halls, is considered to be the most complete example of Mudéjar architecture in Spain.

Mudéjar tiles in Patio de las Doncellas

Real Alcázar, Seville

Mudéjar stucco

IN 1364 PEDRO I ordered the construction of a royal residence within the palaces which had been built by the city's Almohad rulers. Within two years, craftsmen from Granada and Toledo had created an exquisite jewel box of Mudéjar patios and halls at the heart of Seville's Real Alcázar, the Palacio Pedro I. Later monarchs added their own distinct marks: Isabel I (1451–1504) dispatched navigators to explore the New World from her Casa de la Contratación, while grandiose, richly decorated apartments were built during the reign of Carlos I (1516–56) – the Holy Roman Emperor Charles V.

Gardens of the Alcázar
Laid out with terraces, fountains, and pavilions, these gardens provide a delightful refuge from the heat and bustle of Seville.

Jardín de Troya

★ Charles V Rooms
Vast tapestries and lively 16th-century azulejos (tiles) decorate the vaulted halls of the apartments and chapel of Charles V.

Patio del Crucero lies above the old baths.

PLAN OF THE REAL ALCÁZAR

The complex has been a residence of Spanish kings for almost seven centuries. The palace's upper floor is used by the royal family today.

KEY

▢ Area illustrated above

▢ Gardens

★ Patio de las Doncellas
The Patio of the Maidens boasts plasterwork by the top craftsmen of Granada.

★ **Salón de Embajadores**
Built in 1427, the dazzling dome of the Ambassadors' Hall is of carved and gilded, interlaced wood.

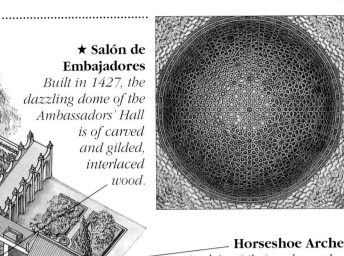

Horseshoe Arches
Azulejos (tiles) and complex plasterwork decorate the Ambassadors' Hall, which has three symmetrically arranged, ornate archways, each with three horse-shoe arches.

Casa de la Contratación

PUERTA DEL LEÓN
Azulejos (tiles) depicting a cross and a crowned lion adorn the arch above the ▷ Puerta del León. These images represent the Christians' victory over the Moors. It is alleged that wild lions were once chained here to protect the royal occupants.

Patio de las Muñecas
The Patio of the Dolls and its surrounding bedrooms formed the domestic heart of the palace. It derives its name from two tiny faces on one of its arches.

The façade of the Palacio Pedro I is a prime example of Mudéjar style.

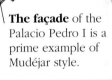

Puerta del León (entrance)

The Patio de la Montería was where the court met before hunting expeditions.

Patio del Yeso
The Patio of Plaster, a garden with flower beds and a water channel, retains features of the earlier, 12th-century Almohad Alcázar.

KEY DATES

712 Construction of the original fortress begins.

1364–6 Palacio Pedro I is built by Mudéjares on the site of the Moorish fortress.

1503 Isabel I of Castile erects the Casa de la Contratación.

1890 The Almohad Patio del Yeso is discovered.

1988 The Real Alcázar is added to UNESCO's World Heritage Site list.

THE GARDENS

The palace grounds boast a number of unique gardens that are a virtual paradise with concealed statues, fountains, rippling pools, and carved archways. Many of the trees and plants were brought back from the New World by Columbus and later explorers. The exotic flora includes palm, cypress, myrtle, mulberry, magnolia, orange, and lemon trees. The gardens again highlight the contrast between Mudéjar and European influences. Decorative tiles, a geometric maze-like structure and the varied use of water are characteristic of Mudéjar design. There is also an "English" garden modeled on 18th-century examples. The ▷ Patio del Crucero is a stylized garden divided into the shape of a cross. This was the palace's private garden. The bath here is dedicated to Maria de Padilla, Pedro I's mistress. It was believed that those who drank from her bath would be guaranteed her favor.

STAR FEATURES

★ **Charles V Rooms**

★ **Patio de las Doncellas**

★ **Salón de Embajadores**

Real Alcázar

Patio de la Acequia, Generalife

THE GENERALIFE

Located west of the Alhambra, the Generalife was the country estate of the Nasrid kings. Here, they could escape the intrigues of the palace and enjoy tranquility high above the city, a little closer to heaven. The name Generalife, or Yannat al Arif, has various interpretations, perhaps the most pleasing being "the garden of lofty paradise". The gardens, begun in the 13th century, have been modified over the years. They originally contained orchards and pastures for animals.

THE NASRID DYNASTY

The wars of the Reconquest of land lost to the Moors since 711 started in northern Spain, arriving in Andalusia with a landmark Christian victory at Las Navas de Tolosa in 1212. As the Christians infiltrated the Muslim empire, Granada became the principal Arab stronghold in Spain. The Nasrids came to power in the Kingdom of Granada in 1236, bringing a prolonged period of peace and prosperity. Muhammad I, founder of the Nasrid Dynasty, undertook the construction of the Alhambra and Generalife in 1238, building a fortified complex of singular beauty that became the official residence of the Nasrid sultans. Granada finally fell in 1492 to Fernando and Isabel of Aragón and Castilla, the Catholic Monarchs. According to legend, Boabdil, the last Moorish ruler, wept as he was expelled from the kingdom.

The Alhambra, Granada

AMAGICAL USE of space, light, water and decoration characterizes this most sensual piece of Moorish architecture. The Moors first arrived in Spain in 710. By the late 13th century only the Nasrid kingdom of Granada remained under Muslim control, and the Alhambra is one of the most remarkable structures that remains from this period. Seeking to belie an image of waning power, they created their idea of paradise on Earth. Modest materials were used, but they were superbly worked. Restored after suffering from pillage and decay, the Alhambra's delicate craftsmanship still dazzles the eye.

★ Patio de Arrayanes
This pool, set amid myrtle hedges and graceful arcades, reflects light into the surrounding halls.

★ Salón de Embajadores
The ceiling of this sumptuous throne room, built from 1334 to 1354, represents the seven heavens of the Muslim cosmos.

Sala de la Barca

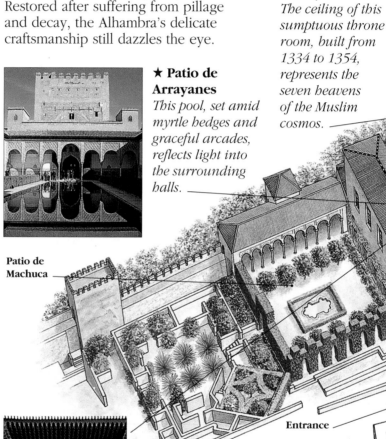

Patio de Machuca

Entrance

Patio del Mexuar
This council chamber, completed in 1365, was where the reigning sultan listened to the petitions of his subjects and held meetings with his ministers.

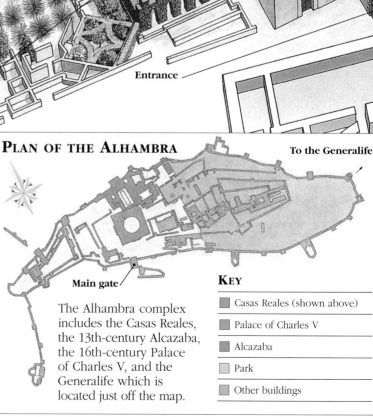

PLAN OF THE ALHAMBRA

To the Generalife

Main gate

The Alhambra complex includes the Casas Reales, the 13th-century Alcazaba, the 16th-century Palace of Charles V, and the Generalife which is located just off the map.

KEY

▪ Casas Reales (shown above)

▪ Palace of Charles V

▪ Alcazaba

▪ Park

▪ Other buildings

The Alhambra

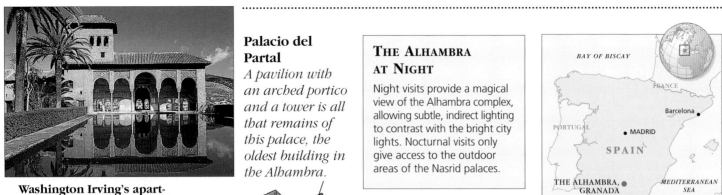

Palacio del Partal
A pavilion with an arched portico and a tower is all that remains of this palace, the oldest building in the Alhambra.

Washington Irving's apartments, where the celebrated author wrote *Tales of the Alhambra.*

Baños Reales

Jardín de Lindaraja

Sala de las Dos Hermanas, with its honeycomb dome, is regarded as the ultimate example of Spanish Islamic architecture.

Sala de los Reyes
This great banqueting hall was used to hold extravagant parties and feasts. Beautiful ceiling paintings on leather, from the 14th century, depict tales of hunting and chivalry.

Puerta de la Rawda

★ Sala de los Abencerrajes
This hall takes its name from a noble family, who were rivals of Boabdil. According to legend, he had them massacred while they attended a banquet here. The geometrical ceiling pattern was inspired by Pythagoras' theorem.

The Palace of Charles V (1526) houses a collection of Spanish-Islamic art, whose highlight is the Alhambra vase.

★ Patio de los Leones
Built by Muhammad V (1354–91), this patio is lined with arcades supported by 124 slender marble columns. At its center, a fountain rests on 12 marble lions.

STAR FEATURES

- **★ Salón de Embajadores**
- **★ Patio de Arrayanes**
- **★ Sala de los Abencerrajes**
- **★ Patio de los Leones**

BAY OF BISCAY
FRANCE
Barcelona
PORTUGAL
MADRID
SPAIN
THE ALHAMBRA, GRANADA
MEDITERRANEAN SEA
ALGERIA

KEY DATES

1236 The Nasrid Dynasty comes to power in the sole remaining Islamic state in Spain, the Kingdom of Granada.

1238 Construction of the Alhambra complex begins.

1492 The Nasrid Dynasty falls to the Catholic Monarchs.

1984 Alhambra is added to UNESCO's World Heritage list.

MOORISH ARCHITECTURE

The palaces of the Moors were designed with gracious living, culture, and learning in mind. Space, light, water, and ornamentation were combined to harmonious effect. The superbly crafted Alhambra possesses all the enduring features of Moorish architecture: arches, stucco work, and ornamental use of calligraphy. The elaborate stucco work (▷ *Sala de los Abencerrajes*) typifies the Nasrid style. Reflections in water combined with an overall play of light are another central feature. Water cooled the Moors' elegant courtyards and served a contemplative purpose. Often water had to be pumped from a source far below (▷ *Patio de los Leones*). The Moors introduced techniques for making fantastic mosaics of tiles in sophisticated geometric patterns to decorate their palace walls. The word *azulejo* derives from the Arabic *az-zulayj* or "little stone". Exquisite Moorish *azulejos* made of unicolored stones can be seen throughout the Alhambra complex.

The Alhambra

San Zeno Maggiore

St Zeno and His Church

The well-educated eighth Bishop of Verona, St Zeno, governed the church with great zeal between 362–80. A native of North Africa, he was a fine speaker and increasingly championed Christianity against those who had not yet converted. He died in 380 and a small chapel was erected in his memory. Little remains of the original chapel as it has been destroyed and rebuilt on numerous occasions. The final building was completed in the 12th century. Its colonnaded ▷ *crypt*, decorated with mythical animals and monsters, sculpted by Adamino da San Giorgio (1225), houses the body of St Zeno.

San Zeno's porch supported by pillars and marble lions

Frescoes and Paintings

Towards the presbytery is an impressive series of frescoes, often placed one above the other. They are thought to date from the 13th to 15th centuries but their painter is unknown. The most interesting frescoes date from the 14th century and are attributed to two Veronese artists known as the First and Second Masters of San Zeno. Inside the church is the beautiful ▷ *altarpiece by Mantegna*, commissioned by Gregorio Correr, abbot of San Zeno, in 1457. The painting was completed in the mid-15th century and is a real gem of the early Renaissance in the Veneto region.

San Zeno Maggiore, Verona

Detail from San Zeno's façade

T HE MOST ornate Romanesque church in northern Italy, San Zeno was built to house the shrine of Verona's patron saint. The present mid-12th century church replaced a late-10th century version, which was destroyed by an earthquake in 1137. The façade is adorned with an impressive rose window, marble reliefs, and a graceful porch canopy. The highlight, however, is the fascinating 11th- and 12th-century bronze door panels.

Nave Ceiling
The nave has a magnificent example of a ship's keel ceiling, so called because it resembles the inside of an upturned boat. This ceiling was constructed in 1386 when the apse was rebuilt.

The bell tower, started in 1045, reached its present height of 72 m (236 ft) in 1173.

Altarpiece by Mantegna
The Madonna's halo in Andrea Mantegna's altarpiece of the Virgin and Child with saints (1457–59) echoes the shape of the church's rose window.

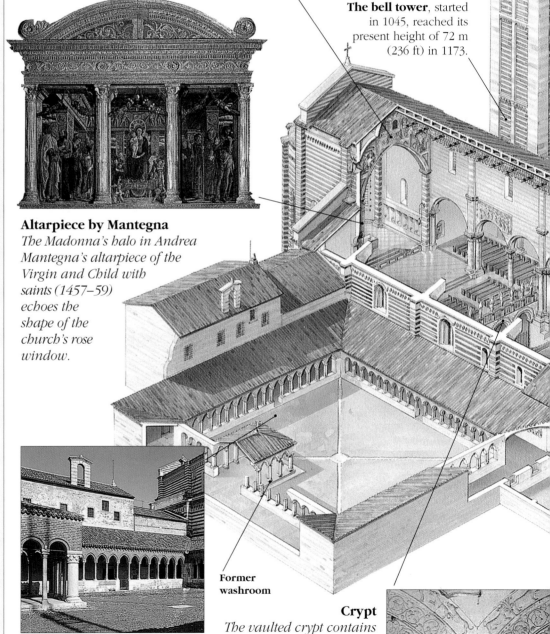

Former washroom

★ Cloister (1293–1313)
The arches are rounded Romanesque on one side, pointed Gothic on another.

Crypt
The vaulted crypt contains the tomb of San Zeno, patron saint of Verona and children learning to walk and speak.

Nave and Main Altar

The plan of the church is modeled on an ancient Roman basilica, the Hall of Justice. The main altar is situated in the raised sanctuary where the judge's throne would have stood.

Striped brickwork is typical of Romanesque buildings in Verona. Courses of local pink brick are alternated with ivory-colored tufa.

The rose window, dating from the early 12th century, symbolizes the Wheel of Fortune: figures on the rim show the rise and fall of human luck.

SAN ZENO'S CHAPELS

Since the 4th century, there have been different buildings on the site of San Zeno Maggiore in Verona. These were constructed in the 5th, 9th, 10th, and 12th centuries after the first three were destroyed by invaders or natural disasters.

BRONZE DOOR PANELS

The 48 bronze panels of the west doors are primitive, but forceful in their depiction of biblical stories and scenes from the life of San Zeno. Those on the left date from 1030 and survive from an earlier church on the site; those on the right were made after the earthquake in the mid-12th century. The panels, decorated with masks, are the work of three separate craftsmen. Huge staring eyes and Ottoman-style hats, armor, and architecture feature prominently. Among the scenes, some of which are unclear, are Adam and Eve, Salome dancing for the head of John the Baptist, and a startling Descent into Limbo.

Descent into limbo

Christ in Glory

Human head

The Romanesque porch is one of the finest examples of the style in northern Italy. Since 1138 it has shielded biblical bas-reliefs, above the west doors, from the elements.

Marble side panels, which were carved in 1140, illustrate events from the life of Christ (to the left of the doors) and scenes from the Book of Genesis (to the right).

★ West Doors

Each of the wooden doors has 24 bronze plates nailed on to make the doors look like solid metal. A multi-colored bas-relief above them depicts San Zeno, flanked by the people of Verona, vanquishing the devil.

STAR FEATURES

★ **Cloister**

★ **West Doors**

FRANCE
SWITZ.
AUSTRIA
Venice
SAN ZENO MAGGIORE,
VERONA
ITALY
ROME
Naples
TYRRHENIAN
SEA
MEDITERRANEAN SEA
IONIAN
SEA

KEY DATES

1120–38 The present San Zeno Maggiore is constructed

2000 The City of Verona is inscribed a UNESCO World Heritage Site.

ROMANESQUE STYLE

When Charlemagne was crowned head of the Holy Roman Empire in AD 800, he encouraged a wave of ambitious church building throughout Western Europe. Massive Roman vaults and arches, characteristic of the ancient Roman Empire, fused with elements from Byzantium and the Middle East, and from the Germans, Celts, and other northern tribes in Western Europe. These combinations created a number of local styles known as Romanesque, meaning "in the manner of the Roman". Romanesque structures are characterized by their vast size, huge piers and round arches, which are distinct from the pointed arch that was typical of the later Gothic style (▷ *Gothic Style, p73*). Decorations in Romanesque architecture are also carved into the structural fabric rather than painted on. An outstanding achievement of the Romanesque architects was the development of stone vaulted buildings. The nave is usually higher and narrower than in earlier structures to make room for windows in the walls below the vaults. These vaults, being heavier than the pre-Romanesque wooden roofs, are supported by massive columns.

San Zeno Maggiore

St Mark's Basilica, Venice

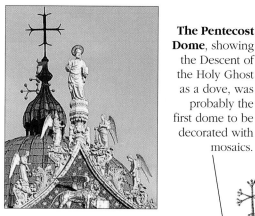

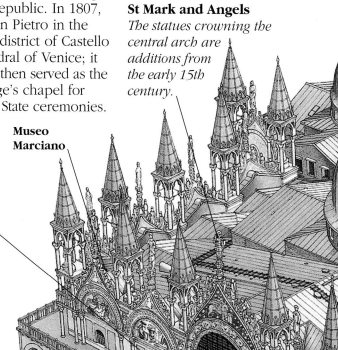

One of the ornate, jeweled
panels from the Pala d'Oro

PALA D'ORO

The most valuable treasure
held in the St Mark's Basilica
is the Pala d'Oro (Golden
Altar Screen). This jewel-
spangled altarpiece is
situated behind the high
altar, beyond the chapel of
St Clement. The Pala consists
of 250 enamel paintings on
gold foil, enclosed within a
gilded silver Gothic frame.
The subjects include
scenes from the life of
Christ and the life of St
Mark. Originally begun in
Byzantium in 976, the
altarpiece was enlarged
and embellished over the
centuries. Following the fall
of the Republic in 1797,
Napoleon removed some of
the precious stones, but the
screen still gleams with
jewels such as pearls, rubies,
sapphires, and amethysts.

ST MARK'S TREASURY

Although the treasury was
plundered after the French
invasion in the late 18th
century, and much depleted
by a fund-raising sale of
jewels in the early 19th
century, it nevertheless
possesses a precious
collection of Byzantine silver,
gold, and glasswork. Today,
the treasures, 283 pieces in
all, are mostly housed in a
room whose remarkably
thick walls are believed to
have been a 9th-century
tower of the Doges' Palace.
A dazzling array of exhibits
by Byzantine and Venetian
craftsmen includes chalices,
goblets, reliquaries, two
intricate icons of the
archangel Michael, and an
11th-century silver-gilt
reliquary made in the form
of a five-domed basilica.

THIS STUNNING BASILICA, built on a Greek
cross plan and crowned with five huge
domes, clearly shows the influence of
Byzantine architecture (▷ *Byzantine Style
p247*) which had been brought to Venice
through the city's extensive links with
the East. Today's basilica is the third
church to stand on this site. The first, built
to enshrine the body of St Mark, was
destroyed by fire. The second was pulled
down in the 11th century in order to make
way for a more spectacular
edifice, reflecting the escalating
power of the Republic. In 1807,
it succeeded San Pietro in the
administrative district of Castello
as the cathedral of Venice; it
had until then served as the
Doge's chapel for
State ceremonies.

**The Pentecost
Dome**, showing
the Descent of
the Holy Ghost
as a dove, was
probably the
first dome to be
decorated with
mosaics.

St Mark and Angels
*The statues crowning the
central arch are
additions from
the early 15th
century.*

**Museo
Marciano**

★ Horses of St Mark
*The four horses are
replicas of the gilded
bronze originals, now
protected inside the
Basilica.*

**★ Central Doorway
Carvings**
*The central arch features
13th-century carvings of
the* Labors of the Month.
*The grape harvester
represents
September.*

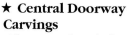

★ Façade Mosaics
*A 17th-century mosaic
shows the smuggling out
of Alexandria of St
Mark's body, reputedly
under slices of pork to
deter prying Muslims.*

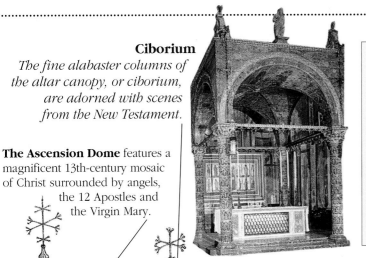

Ciborium

The fine alabaster columns of the altar canopy, or ciborium, are adorned with scenes from the New Testament.

The Ascension Dome features a magnificent 13th-century mosaic of Christ surrounded by angels, the 12 Apostles and the Virgin Mary.

St Mark's body, believed lost in the fire of AD 976, supposedly reappeared when the new church was consecrated in 1094. The remains are housed in the altar.

Allegorical mosaics

St Mark's Treasury

Baptistry

Baptistry Mosaics

Herod's Banquet *(1343–54) is one of the mosaics in a cycle of scenes from the life of St John the Baptist.*

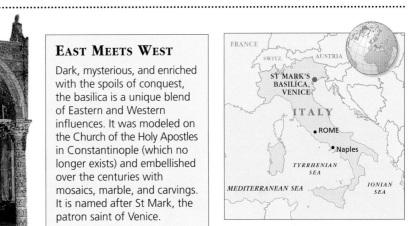

EAST MEETS WEST

Dark, mysterious, and enriched with the spoils of conquest, the basilica is a unique blend of Eastern and Western influences. It was modeled on the Church of the Holy Apostles in Constantinople (which no longer exists) and embellished over the centuries with mosaics, marble, and carvings. It is named after St Mark, the patron saint of Venice.

★ The Tetrarchs

This charming sculptured group in porphyry (4th-century Egyptian) is thought to represent Diocletian, Maximian, Valerian, and Constance. Collectively they were the tetrarchs, appointed by Diocletian to help rule the Roman Empire.

The so-called Pilasters of Acre in fact came from a 6th-century church in Constantinople.

STAR FEATURES

★ **Horses of St Mark**

★ **Central Doorway Carvings**

★ **Façade Mosaics**

★ **The Tetrarchs**

KEY DATES

832 A shrine is built to house the body of St Mark the Evangelist, brought from its tomb in Alexandria.

1063–94 The third church is built on the site, much as it is seen today.

1345 Pala d'Oro is finally completed. It was first commissioned in 976.

1987 The city of Venice and its Lagoon are added to UNESCO's World Heritage list.

ST MARK'S MUSEUM

A stairway from the atrium of the basilica leads up to the ▷ *Museo Marciano*, or church museum. There are splendid views into the basilica interior from the gallery, and from the exterior loggia the Piazza San Marco can be seen. Doges and dignitaries once looked down on ceremonies in the square from this vantage point. Four replica chariot horses stand here. The original ▷ *Horses of St Mark* are housed at the far end of the museum. They were stolen from the Hippodrome (ancient race-course) in Constantinople (now Istanbul) in 1204 but their origin, either Roman or Hellenistic, remains a mystery. The same room contains Paolo Veneziano's 14th-century *Pala Feriale*, painted with stories from the life of St Mark, which once covered the Pala d'Oro. Also on display are medieval illuminated manuscripts, fragments of ancient mosaics, and antique tapestries.

St Mark's Basilica

Doge's Palace

SALA DEL CONSIGLIO DEI DIECI

This was the meeting room of the awesomely powerful Council of Ten, founded in 1310 to investigate and prosecute people for crimes concerning the security of the State. Napoleon pilfered some of the Veronese paintings from the ceiling but two of the finest found their way back in 1920: *Age and Youth* and *Juno Offering the Ducal Crown to Venice* (both 1553–54). Offenders awaited sentence in the next room, the ▷ *Sala della Bussola*. In the same room is a *bocca di leone* (lion's mouth), used to post secret denunciations, one of several in the palace. Convicts were sent across ▷ *the Bridge of Sighs* for incarceration.

THE BRIDGE OF SIGHS

According to legend, the Bridge of Sighs, built in 1600 to link the Doge's Palace with the new prisons, takes its name from the lamentations of the prisoners as they made their way over to the offices of the feared State Inquisitors. Just below the leaded roof of the Doge's Palace are the *piombi* cells. Prisoners here were more comfortable than those in the *pozzi* in the dungeons at ground level. One of the more famous inmates was the Venetian libertine Casanova, incarcerated here in 1755. He made a daring escape from his cell in the *piombi* through a hole in the roof.

The Bridge of Sighs, with the Ponte della Paglia beyond

Doge's Palace, Venice

AT THE HEART of the powerful Venetian Republic, the magnificent Doge's Palace was the official residence of the Doge (ruler). Originally built in the 9th century, the present palace dates from the 14th and early 15th centuries and is adorned with glorious paintings and sculptures. To create their airy Gothic masterpiece (▷ *Gothic Style p73*), the Venetians perched the bulk of the palace (built in pink Veronese marble) on top of an apparent fretwork of loggias and arcades (built from white Istrian stone).

Mars by Sansovino

★ **Giants' Staircase**
This 15th-century staircase is crowned by Sansovino's statues of Mars and Neptune, symbols of Venice's power.

Sala del Senato

Sala del Collegio

Anticollegio

The Arco Foscari
has copies of Antonio Rizzo's 15th-century Adam and Eve.

Main entrance

★ **Porta della Carta**
This 15th-century Gothic gate is the principal entrance to the palace. From it, a vaulted passageway leads to the Arco Foscari and the internal courtyard.

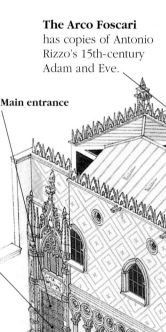

Courtyard

★ **Sala del Maggior Consiglio**
This vast hall was used as a meeting place for members of Venice's Great Council. Tintoretto's huge Paradise *(1590) fills the end wall.*

Sala dello Scudo
The walls of this room, once part of the doge's private apartments, are covered with maps of the world. In the center of the room are two giant 18th-century globes.

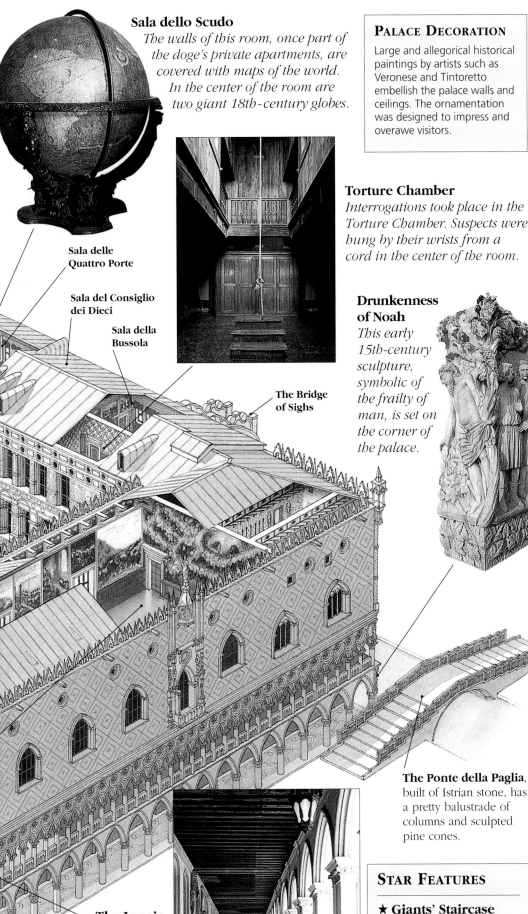

Sala delle
Quattro Porte

Sala del Consiglio
dei Dieci

Sala della
Bussola

The Bridge
of Sighs

PALACE DECORATION
Large and allegorical historical paintings by artists such as Veronese and Tintoretto embellish the palace walls and ceilings. The ornamentation was designed to impress and overawe visitors.

Torture Chamber
Interrogations took place in the Torture Chamber. Suspects were hung by their wrists from a cord in the center of the room.

Drunkenness of Noah
This early 15th-century sculpture, symbolic of the frailty of man, is set on the corner of the palace.

The Ponte della Paglia, built of Istrian stone, has a pretty balustrade of columns and sculpted pine cones.

The Loggia
Each arch of the ground level portico supports two arches of the loggia, which commands fine views of the lagoon.

KEY DATES

Early 9th century Square fortress is built on the site, but destroyed by fire in 976.

1106 Another fire destroys replacement building.

1340–1424 Building of Gothic palace to house the Great Council.

1419 Inauguration of Sala del Maggior Consiglio.

1600 Bridge of Sighs is built.

CHOOSING A DOGE

The Doge's Palace was the Republic's seat of power and home to its rulers. New doges were nominated in the Sala dello Scrutinio and were chosen from the members of the Maggior Consiglio, Venice's Great Council. A lengthy and convoluted system was used to count votes during dogal elections; a method designed to prevent candidates bribing their way to power. Once elected, the doge occupied the post for the rest of his lifetime, but numerous restrictions were placed on him in an attempt to prevent him from exploiting his position. Despite the precautions, numerous doges met their deaths in office or were sent into exile for activities such as conspiring against the state. One of the most famous was Doge Marin Falier, beheaded in 1355 for conspiring to overthrow the councils of Venice. Others survived in office for many years: the diplomat Doge Leonardo Loredan ruled for 20 years.

STAR FEATURES

★ **Giants' Staircase**

★ **Porta della Carta**

★ **Sala del Maggior Consiglio**

NICOLA AND GIOVANNI PISANO

The Italian sculptors and architects Nicola and Giovanni Pisano were father and son, and their work left a distinctive stamp on the religious and secular buildings of Tuscany and Umbria in the 13th century. Although they often worked in tandem, different styles can be discerned in their work. The ▷ *Baptistry Pulpit* in Pisa (1259) is one of Nicola Pisano's first works and is adorned with a narrative in stone of great power and dramatic effect, a radical new adaptation of Classical forms. This work was followed by a more complex pulpit for the cathedral in Siena. Nicola's son Giovanni worked with him on his last important project, the Fontana Maggiore in Perugia (1278).

Detail from the Duomo pulpit by Giovanni Pisano

CARRARA MARBLE

The pure white marble of Massa Carrara is world-famous and was the stone of choice for many sculptors and architects. During the Renaissance it was a great favorite with Michelangelo and many of his most famous works are sculpted from Carrara marble. The 300 or so quarries near Carrara date back to Roman times, making this the oldest industrial site in continuous use in the world. In Carrara itself today there are showrooms and workshops where the marble is worked into sheets or made into ornaments. The town also contains the house where Michelangelo used to stay when buying marble. It is marked by a plaque.

Campo dei Miracoli, Pisa

Cemetery memorial

P ISA'S WORLD-FAMOUS Leaning Tower is just one of the splendid buildings rising from the lawns of the "Field of Miracles". It is joined by the Duomo, a triumph of marble decorations; Italy's largest Baptistry, with an acoustically perfect interior; and the Campo Santo cemetery, containing Roman sarcophagi. The buildings combine Moorish elements, such as inlaid marble in geometric patterns (arabesques), with delicate Romanesque colonnading and spiky Gothic niches and pinnacles.

The Triumph of Death
These late 14th-century frescoes depict various allegorical scenes such as this of a knight and lady overwhelmed by the stench of an open grave.

Campo Santo
The cemetery contains earth from the Holy Land and carved Roman sarcophagi.

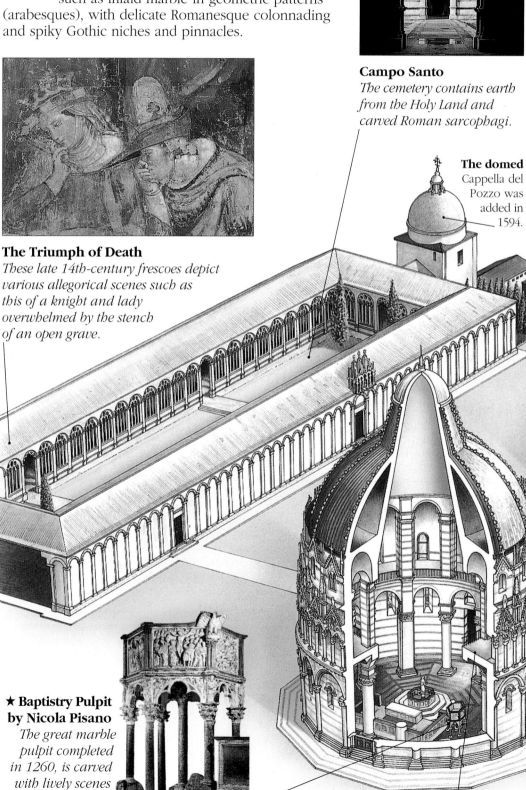

The domed Cappella del Pozzo was added in 1594.

★ **Baptistry Pulpit by Nicola Pisano**
The great marble pulpit completed in 1260, is carved with lively scenes from the life of Christ.

Upper gallery

★ **Portale di San Ranieri**
Bonanno Pisano's bronze panels for the south transept doors depict the life of Christ. Palm trees and Moorish buildings show Arabic influence.

Frescoes were added to the dome's interior after a fire in 1595.

Fragments of the 11th-century marble floor survive beneath the dome.

PISAN ARCHITECTURE
The Romanesque architecture of Pisa (▷ *Romanesque Style p199*) with its tiers of open colonnades on a background of marble and arcaded themes, was to spread widely and examples can be found throughout Italy and as far as Zadar in Croatia.

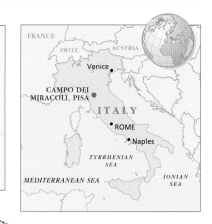

The Leaning Tower was completed in 1350, when its seven bells were hung.

A frieze shows that work began in 1173.

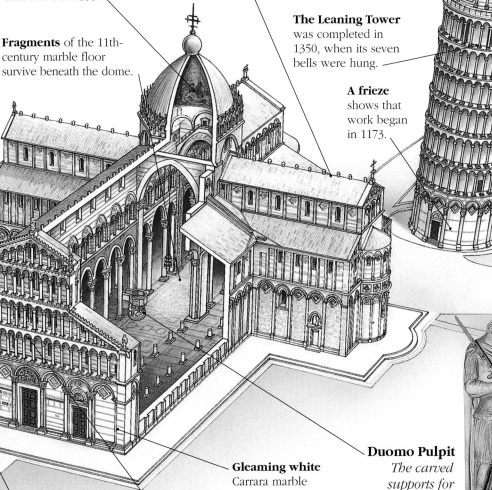

KEY DATES

1063 Work starts on the Duomo.

1152 Building work on the Baptistry begins.

1173 Construction starts on the Leaning Tower.

1260 Nicola Pisano completes the marble Baptistry pulpit.

1311 Giovanni Pisano finishes sculpting the Duomo pulpit.

1987 Campo dei Miracoli buildings are declared a UNESCO World Heritage Site.

THE LEANING TOWER OF PISA

The tower is not the only leaning building on this site; the shallow foundations and sandy silt subsoil also create problems for all of the surrounding structures. However none tilts so famously as the *Torre Pendente* or ▷ *Leaning Tower*. The tower began to tip sideways even before the third story was completed. Despite this, construction continued until its completion in 1350, when the addition of the bell chamber at the top of the tower brought its total height to 54.5 m (179 ft). Recent engineering interventions have corrected the tilt by 38 cm (15 in). Measures adopted include excavations at below soil level, the removal of soil on the north side, the use of counterweights (1993–4), and the introduction of ten anchors (1994–5). The tower was reopened to visitors in December 2001.

Gleaming white Carrara marble decorates the walls.

Duomo Pulpit
The carved supports for Giovanni Pisano's pulpit (1302–11) symbolize the Arts and Virtues.

This 12th-century wall tomb is for Buscheto, the Duomo's original architect.

★ **Duomo Façade**
Colored sandstone, glass, and majolica plates decorate the Lombard-style 12th-century façade. Its patterned surface includes knots, flowers, and animals in inlaid marble.

STAR FEATURES

★ **Baptistry Pulpit by Nicola Pisano**

★ **Portale di San Ranieri**

★ **Duomo Façade**

Campo dei Miracoli

THE CATHEDRAL WORKS MUSEUM

This highly informative museum consists of a series of rooms dedicated to the history of the cathedral. The main first floor room holds statues from Arnolfo di Cambio's workshop, which once occupied the cathedral's niches. Nearby is Donatello's *St John* and Michelangelo's *Pietà* can be seen on the staircase. The upper floor contains two choir lofts from the 1430s by Luca della Robbia and Donatello. The haunting statue of *La Maddalena* is also by Donatello.

THE EAST DOORS

Lorenzo Ghiberti's famous bronze Baptistry doors were commissioned in 1401 to mark the city's deliverance from the plague. Ghiberti was chosen for the project after a competition involving seven leading artists of the day including Donatello, Jacopo della Quercia, and Brunelleschi. The trial panels by Ghiberti and Brunelleschi are so different from the Florentine Gothic art of the time, notably in the use of perspective and individuality of figures, that they are often regarded as the first works of the Renaissance. The great Michelangelo enthusiastically dubbed the East Doors the "Gate of Paradise." Ghiberti worked on them from 1424 to 1452, after spending 21 years on the ▷ *North Doors*. The original ten relief panels are now on display in the Museo dell'Opera del Duomo.

Door panel depicting Abraham and the Sacrifice of Isaac

Cathedral and Baptistry, Florence

Sir John Hawkwood by Paolo Uccello, in the Duomo

R ISING ABOVE THE heart of the city, the richly-decorated cathedral (Santa Maria del Fiore) and its massive dome have become Florence's most famous symbols. Typical of the Florentine determination to lead in all things, the cathedral is Europe's fourth-largest church, and is still the Tuscan city's tallest building. The Baptistry, with its celebrated bronze doors and host of mosaic panels inside, is one of Florence's oldest buildings. The Campanile, designed by Giotto in 1334, was finally completed in 1359, 22 years after his death.

Campanile
At 85 m (278 ft), the Campanile is 6 m (20 ft) shorter than the dome. It is clad in white, green and pink Tuscan marble.

★ Baptistry
Colorful 13th-century mosaics illustrating the Last Judgment *decorate the ceiling above the octagonal font, where many famous Florentines, including Dante, were baptized. The doors are by Andrea Pisano (south) and Lorenzo Ghiberti (north, east).*

Gothic windows

The Neo-Gothic marble façade echoes the style of Giotto's Campanile, but was only added in 1871–87.

North Doors

East Doors

Main entrance

South Doors

Campanile Reliefs

Copies of reliefs by Andrea Pisano on the Campanile's first level depict the Creation of Man, and the Arts and the Industries. The originals are kept in the Museo dell'Opera del Duomo.

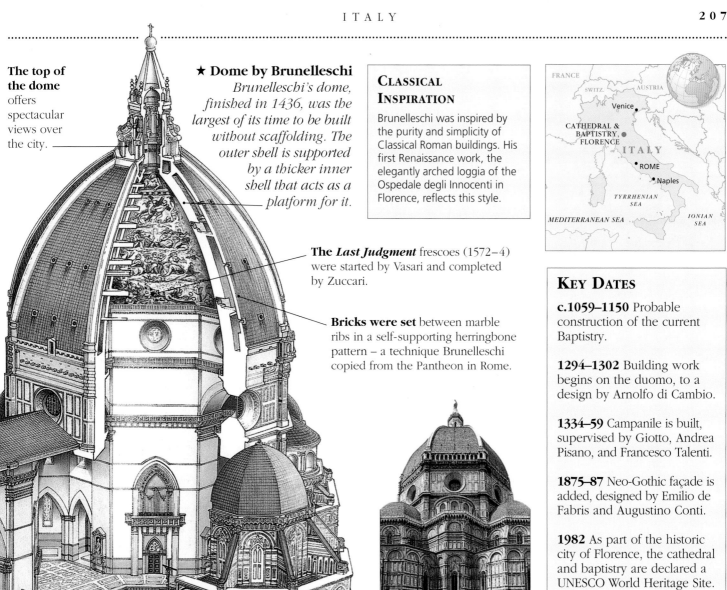

The top of the dome offers spectacular views over the city.

★ **Dome by Brunelleschi**
Brunelleschi's dome, finished in 1436, was the largest of its time to be built without scaffolding. The outer shell is supported by a thicker inner shell that acts as a platform for it.

The *Last Judgment* frescoes (1572–4) were started by Vasari and completed by Zuccari.

Bricks were set between marble ribs in a self-supporting herringbone pattern – a technique Brunelleschi copied from the Pantheon in Rome.

Entrance leading to the dome

The marble sanctuary around the High Altar was created by Baccio Bandinelli in 1555.

Marble Floor
The colorful, intricately inlaid floor (16th century) was designed in part by Baccio d'Agnolo and Francesco da Sangallo.

Dante Explaining the Divine Comedy *(1465)*
This painting by Michelino shows the poet outside Florence against a backdrop of Purgatory, Hell, and Paradise.

CLASSICAL INSPIRATION
Brunelleschi was inspired by the purity and simplicity of Classical Roman buildings. His first Renaissance work, the elegantly arched loggia of the Ospedale degli Innocenti in Florence, reflects this style.

Chapels at the East End
The three apses, crowned by smaller copies of the dome, have five chapels each. The 15th-century stained glass is by Ghiberti.

STAR FEATURES

★ **Baptistry**

★ **Dome by Brunelleschi**

KEY DATES

c.1059–1150 Probable construction of the current Baptistry.

1294–1302 Building work begins on the duomo, to a design by Arnolfo di Cambio.

1334–59 Campanile is built, supervised by Giotto, Andrea Pisano, and Francesco Talenti.

1875–87 Neo-Gothic façade is added, designed by Emilio de Fabris and Augustino Conti.

1982 As part of the historic city of Florence, the cathedral and baptistry are declared a UNESCO World Heritage Site.

BRUNELLESCHI'S DOME

A stunning feat of technical as well as artistic skill, Brunelleschi's ▷ *Dome* was unprecedented for its time and epitomizes Florentine Renaissance architecture (▷ *Renaissance Style p211*). Construction took over 14 years and only began after a lengthy period of planning and model building, during which Brunelleschi worked hard to convince the skeptics that the project was feasible. At one point he even built a large-scale model by the river to demonstrate that the dome was technically achievable. The dome spans 43 m (140 ft) and is not buttressed; instead, a double wall of spirally laid bricks has been strengthened by the use of stone chains. Despite his brilliance as an engineer and architect, Brunelleschi was not made Chief Architect until 1445, a year before his death.

Cathedral and Baptistry, Florence

Ponte Vecchio, Florence

THE OLDEST BRIDGE in Florence, the Ponte Vecchio or Old Bridge, was built in 1345. It was the only bridge in the city to escape being blown up during World War II. There have always been workshops on the bridge, but the butchers, tanners, and blacksmiths who were here originally (and who used the river as a convenient rubbish tip) were evicted by Duke Ferdinando I in 1593 because of the noise and stench they created. The workshops were rebuilt and let to the more decorous goldsmiths, and the shops lining and overhanging the bridge continue to specialize in new and antique jewelry to this day.

The sculpted head and shoulders of Grand Duke Cosimo de' Medici

THE DUKES OF MEDICI

The Medici family held power in Florence almost continuously from 1434 until 1743. Their rule began with Cosimo il Vecchio, son of a self-made man, Giovanni di Bicci. For years, Cosimo and his descendants directed policy with popular support, but without ever being voted into office. Later generations gained titles and power but ruled by force. In 1532 the decadent Alessandro took the title Duke of Florence. From him control passed to Cosimo I, who was crowned Grand Duke of Tuscany. Ruling a strong and prosperous Tuscany, Cosimo I also established efficient government in the region. The Medici dukes were important patrons of the arts; the Vasari Corridor is among numerous works commissioned by Cosimo I.

BENVENUTO CELLINI

Much is known about the life of the Florentine sculptor, goldsmith, and metal worker thanks to his famous autobiography, first published in 1728. He spent his early career in Rome but from 1540–45 he worked for François I in France, creating exquisite gold and enamel work. The rest of his life was spent in the employ of Cosimo I in Florence, for whom he sculpted a famous bronze statue of *Perseus*. Cellini's work can be seen in Piazza della Signoria and the Bargello museum in Florence.

Private Corridor
The aerial corridor built by Vasari along the eastern side of the bridge is hung with the self-portraits of many great artists, including Rembrandt, Rubens, and Hogarth.

Medieval Workshops
Some of the oldest workshops have rear extensions overhanging the river, supported by timber brackets called sporti.

The three-arched medieval bridge rests on two stout piers with boat-shaped cutwaters.

VASARI'S CORRIDOR

The Corridoio Vasariano was built in 1565 by Giorgio Vasari, court architect to the Medici dukes. The elevated corridor links the Palazzo Vecchio to the Palazzo Pitti, via the Uffizi. This private walkway allowed members of the Medici family to move about between their various residences, admiring the paintings on the corridor's walls, without having to step into the street below and mix with the crowds.

Palazzo Vecchio

The Uffizi

Ponte Vecchio

Arno

Palazzo Pitti

Bust of Cellini
A Bust of Benvenuto Cellini (1500–71), the famous Florentine goldsmith and sculptor, was placed in the middle of the bridge in 1900.

★ Bridge at Sunset
The Ponte Vecchio is especially attractive when viewed in the setting sun from Ponte Santa Trinità, or from one of the river embankments.

★ Jewelers' Shops
The shops sell everything from affordable modern earrings to precious antique rings.

Mannelli Tower
This medieval tower was built to defend the bridge. The Mannelli family stubbornly refused to demolish it to make way for the Vasari Corridor.

The Vasari Corridor, supported on brackets, circumvents the Mannelli tower.

Circular windows called *oculi* (eyes) light the corridor.

Viewpoint
There are few better places for enjoying the river views; buskers, portrait painters, and street traders congregate on the bridge, adding to the color and bustle.

WORKING WITH GOLD
By the 15th century, Florence was famous for its skilled gold work and trade flourished. Many well-known artists, including Ghiberti, were apprentices in the workshops of Florentine goldsmiths.

KEY DATES

1345 Ponte Vecchio is built.

1565 Vasari designs and builds a corridor over the Ponte Vecchio.

1966 Floods devastate Florence and the Ponte Vecchio is badly damaged.

1982 Historic center of Florence becomes a UNESCO World Heritage Site.

GIORGIO VASARI

The Italian painter, architect, and writer was accomplished in a number of artistic skills but is perhaps best known for his biographical work. His book about his fellow artists, *The Lives of the Most Eminent Italian Architects, Painters, and Sculptors*, was first published in 1550, and is still a key source of detailed information about Italian Renaissance art. Vasari's view was that art had reached a peak in Classical antiquity and did not revive until the era of Giotto. The book traces the development of art in Tuscany from Giotto and Cimabue to Leonardo, Raphael, and Michelangelo. Giorgio Vasari was born in the Tuscan town of Arezzo in 1511 but worked mainly in Rome and Florence. He produced works of art in both cities but is generally held in higher esteem for his architecture. In 1560 he was commissioned by Cosimo I to design the Uffizi palace in Florence, now home to the world-famous art galleries. The layout included offices (*Uffizi*) on the ground floor.

STAR FEATURES

★ Bridge at Sunset

★ Jewelers' Shops

Ponte Vecchio

FEDERICO DA MONTEFELTRO

In the 15th century, Federico da Montefeltro (1420–82) transformed his capital city into a delightful Renaissance town and gathered around him one of the most cultured courts to be found anywhere in Europe. As a child, he received a broad humanist education in astronomy, Latin, athletics, geometry, music, and mathematics. Having accumulated immense wealth through his military career, he devoted the latter half of his reign to study and patronage of the arts, commissioning work from artists such as Piero della Francesca. Federico's palace in Urbino is spacious and light, and a model of Renaissance harmony.

Frieze on the chimney in the Sala degli Angeli, Ducal Palace

TREASURES IN THE DUCAL PALACE

The Galleria Nazionale delle Marche houses a comprehensive collection of works by the region's artists, and paintings commissioned by the various Dukes of Urbino. The chief treasures are Piero della Francesca's enigmatic ▷ *The Flagellation* and the *Madonna of Senigallia*, and the celebrated ▷ *La Muta* by Raphael. There are also works by Luca Signorelli, Andrea del Verrocchio, Paolo Uccello, and Titian *(Last Supper)*. Other rooms in the Ducal apartments include the spacious Salone del Trono (Throne Hall) full of 17th-century tapestries, and the ▷ *Sala degli Angeli* (Room of Angels), named for the friezes decorating the fireplace, created by Domenico Rosselli.

Ducal Palace, Urbino

ITALY'S MOST BEAUTIFUL Renaissance palace was built for Duke Federico da Montefeltro, ruler of Urbino (1444–82). He was a soldier but also a man of the arts, and his palace with its library, paintings, and refined architecture is a tribute to courtly life and to the artistic and intellectual ideals of the Renaissance. The Ducal Palace houses the Galleria Nazionale delle Marche.

The palace rising above Urbino

★ **The Flagellation**
The dramatic perspective creates an unsettling effect in this 15th-century painting of the scourging of Christ by Piero della Francesca.

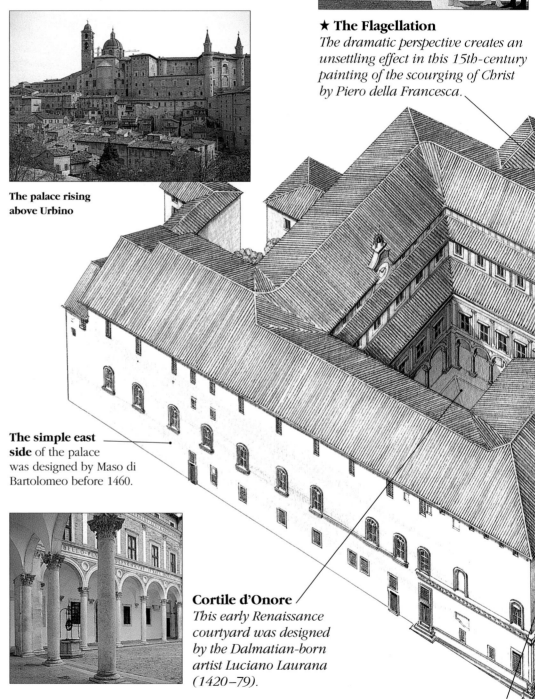

The simple east side of the palace was designed by Maso di Bartolomeo before 1460.

Cortile d'Onore
This early Renaissance courtyard was designed by the Dalmatian-born artist Luciano Laurana (1420–79).

Ideal City
Attributed to Luciano Laurana, this 15th-century painting of an imaginary Renaissance city is notable for its measured perspective and lack of people.

★ Studiolo
The former study of Federico da Montefeltro is decorated with intarsia (inlaid wood), some of it designed by Botticelli. Federico's armor, books, and musical and scientific instruments are depicted in the paneling.

RENAISSANCE COURTS

The Italian courts played a vital role in the development of Renaissance culture. Florence, Rome, and Venice were all powerful but the smaller regional courts, including Urbino, Ferrara, and Mantua, were also wealthy, prestigious centers of arts patronage. Federico's court attracted nobles, intellectuals, diplomats, and artists.

KEY DATES

1440–60s The Ducal Palace is built in Urbino.

1998 Historic Center of Urbino joins the UNESCO World Heritage Site list.

RENAISSANCE STYLE

Brunelleschi's design for the Ospedale degli Innocenti (1419–24) in Florence ushered in a new era of architecture in Italy with its Classically-inspired slender columns and semi-circular arches. In the following decades the Renaissance style spread to the other urban centers in Italy. The vanguard of the movement relocated to Rome in the late 15th and early 16th centuries. By this point, Renaissance styles had reached most of Europe even as far as Moscow, via Venice. The Renaissance (or "rebirth") in building design was intended to be rational and humane. Taking inspirations from the principal elements of architecture – square, cube, circle, and sphere – architects began to plan buildings according to mathematical proportions. Homes were constructed around a central courtyard (▷ *Cortile d'Onore*) as fortification became an integral part of the layout. Churches were no longer designed according to the shape of crosses, but were instead based around the circle. City landscapes also changed as rational principles were applied to urban designs. Streets were widened and planning led to a focus on monuments and fountains.

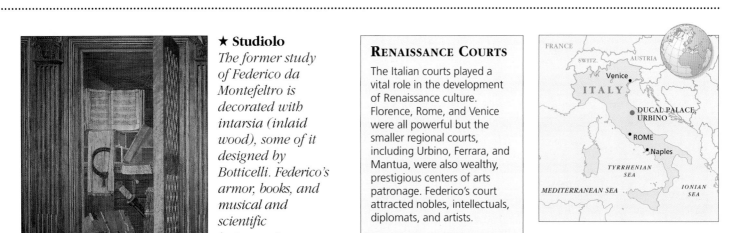

Towers attributed to Laurana

Duke Federico
The duke, shown here with his son in this 15th-century painting by Pedro Berruguete, was always portrayed in left profile after an injury to his face.

Hanging garden

The rooms in this wing are known as the Appartamento della Duchessa.

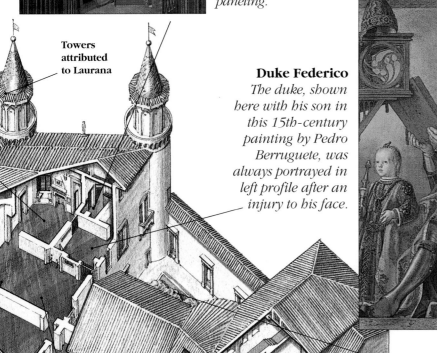

Main entrance

Sala degli Angeli

The Library was one of Europe's largest in its day.

STAR FEATURES

★ **The Flagellation**

★ **Studiolo**

★ **La Muta**

★ La Muta
The Mute Woman *may be a portrait of Maddalena Doni, a Florentine noblewoman. It was painted by the great Renaissance artist Raphael, who was born in Urbino in 1483, the year after Federico's death.*

Ducal Palace

The ornate Gothic façade of Siena's Cathedral

THE BAPTISTRY OF ST JOHN

Underneath part of the cathedral is a rectangular baptistry, dedicated to St John (San Giovanni). Some of the best-known figures of the Renaissance contributed to its decorative features, including the Florentine artists Donatello and Ghiberti. The focal point is an impressive monumental baptismal font (1417–30), decorated with relief panels and crowned with a statue of John the Baptist. The bronze reliefs depict scenes from the life of John the Baptist by Jacopo della Quercia, Donatello (a fine *Herod's Feast*), and Ghiberti.

THE PICCOLOMINI LIBRARY

Halfway along the nave of the cathedral is the entrance to the ▷ *Piccolomini Library*, built by Cardinal Francesco Piccolomini, the future Pope Pius III, to honor his uncle Aeneas Piccolomini, Pope Pius II. The library contains wonderfully exuberant frescoes by Pinturicchio (1454–1513) and his school which depict ten episodes from the life of Pius II. The frescoes (1502–8) were carried out half a century after the events shown, and indeed after the death of Pius III himself in 1503. He was a noted published author in his lifetime and the library houses his personal collection of books and papers.

Siena Cathedral

O NE OF THE the most spectacular cathedrals in Italy, Siena's Cathedral (1136–1382) is also one of the few to have been built south of the Alps in full Gothic style (▷ *Gothic Style p73*). Many ordinary citizens helped to cart the black and white stone used in its construction from nearby quarries. In 1339, the Sienese decided to build a new nave to the south with the aim of making it the biggest church in Christendom. This plan came to nothing when plague hit the city soon afterwards, killing off much of the population. The uncompleted nave now contains a museum and gallery.

★ Pulpit Panels
Carved by Nicola Pisano in 1265–8, the panels on the octagonal pulpit depict scenes from the life of Christ.

★ Inlaid Marble Floor
The Massacre of the Innocents *is one of a series of scenes in the inlaid marble floor. The marble is usually uncovered during September each year.*

Nave
Black and white marble pillars support the vault.

Chapel of St John the Baptist

STAR FEATURES

★ Pulpit Panels

★ Inlaid Marble Floor

★ Piccolomini Library

★ Piccolomini Library
Pinturicchio's frescoes (1502–8) portray the life of Pope Pius II. Here he presides at the betrothal of Frederick III to Eleonora of Portugal.

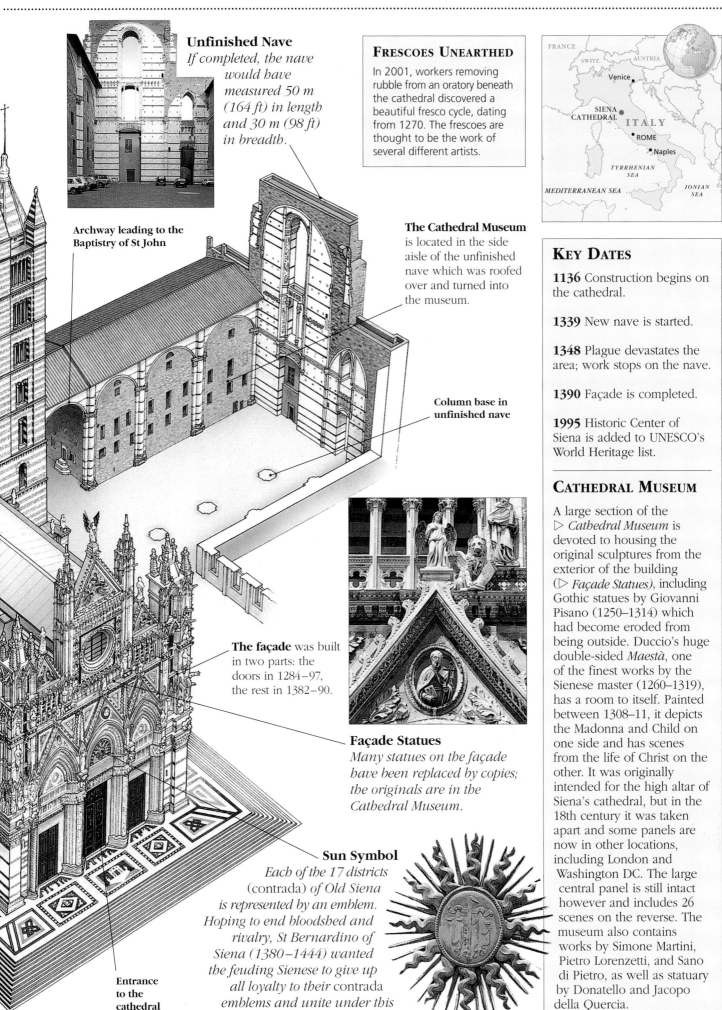

Unfinished Nave
If completed, the nave would have measured 50 m (164 ft) in length and 30 m (98 ft) in breadth.

Archway leading to the Baptistry of St John

The Cathedral Museum is located in the side aisle of the unfinished nave which was roofed over and turned into the museum.

Column base in unfinished nave

KEY DATES

1136 Construction begins on the cathedral.

1339 New nave is started.

1348 Plague devastates the area; work stops on the nave.

1390 Façade is completed.

1995 Historic Center of Siena is added to UNESCO's World Heritage list.

CATHEDRAL MUSEUM

A large section of the ▷ *Cathedral Museum* is devoted to housing the original sculptures from the exterior of the building (▷ *Façade Statues*), including Gothic statues by Giovanni Pisano (1250–1314) which had become eroded from being outside. Duccio's huge double-sided *Maestà*, one of the finest works by the Sienese master (1260–1319), has a room to itself. Painted between 1308–11, it depicts the Madonna and Child on one side and has scenes from the life of Christ on the other. It was originally intended for the high altar of Siena's cathedral, but in the 18th century it was taken apart and some panels are now in other locations, including London and Washington DC. The large central panel is still intact however and includes 26 scenes on the reverse. The museum also contains works by Simone Martini, Pietro Lorenzetti, and Sano di Pietro, as well as statuary by Donatello and Jacopo della Quercia.

The façade was built in two parts: the doors in 1284–97, the rest in 1382–90.

Façade Statues
Many statues on the façade have been replaced by copies; the originals are in the Cathedral Museum.

Sun Symbol
Each of the 17 districts (contrada) of Old Siena is represented by an emblem. Hoping to end bloodshed and rivalry, St Bernardino of Siena (1380–1444) wanted the feuding Sienese to give up all loyalty to their contrada *emblems and unite under this symbol of the risen Christ.*

Entrance to the cathedral

Engraving of the Basilica of St Francis in Assisi

St Francis

A highly revered and loved Christian saint, St Francis was born in 1182 in Assisi to a rich family. During his mid-20s he decided to reject the family's wealth and embrace a life of poverty, chastity, meditation, and prayer. He looked after the sick and extended his care to birds and animals. His humble spirituality soon attracted numerous followers and he established a religious order, the Friars Minor, in 1209. This new order was orally recognized by Pope Innocent III the same year, and in 1223 it was officially confirmed by Pope Honorius III. A Franciscan order of nuns, the Poor Clares, was founded in 1215. St Francis died in Assisi in 1226 and was canonized two years later. He became the patron saint of Italy in 1939.

The Earthquakes of 1997

The earthquakes that hit Umbria in September and October 1997 killed 11 people and left tens of thousands homeless. A large number of centuries-old buildings were also badly damaged. The eastern part of Umbria was the most affected, with the basilica in Assisi suffering the worst structural upheaval. In the ▷ Upper Church the vaults in the two bays collapsed, shattering ancient frescoes by Cimabue and others attributed to Giotto. However, the great St Francis cycle (▷ frescoes by Giotto) survived, as did the stained-glass windows. Painstaking restoration followed, and the church reopened to the public in November 1999.

Basilica of St Francis, Assisi

ONE OF THE GREATEST Christian shrines in the world, the Basilica of St Francis is visited by a vast number of pilgrims throughout the year. It is the burial place of St Francis, and building work began two years after the saint's death in 1226. Over the next century its Upper and Lower Churches were decorated by the foremost artists of their day, among them Cimabue, Simone Martini, Pietro Lorenzetti, and Giotto, whose frescoes on the *Life of St Francis* are among the most renowned in Italy.

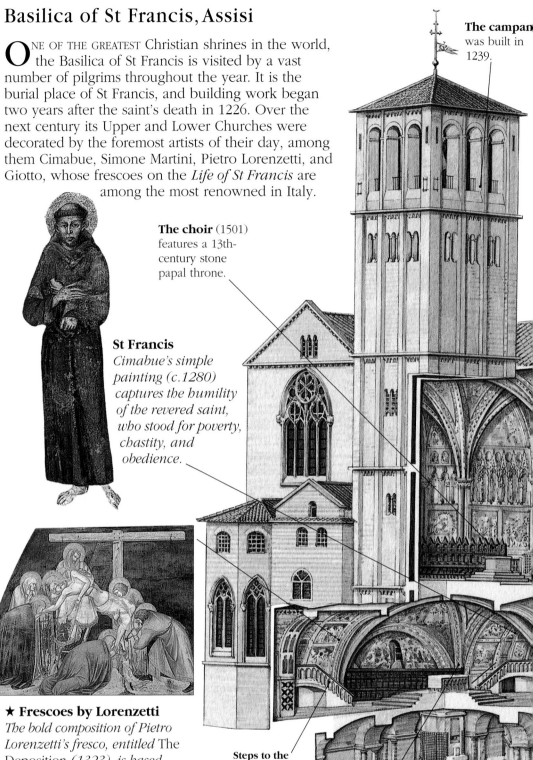

The campan was built in 1239.

The choir (1501) features a 13th-century stone papal throne.

St Francis
Cimabue's simple painting (c.1280) captures the humility of the revered saint, who stood for poverty, chastity, and obedience.

Steps to the Treasury

The crypt contains the tomb of St Francis.

★ **Frescoes by Lorenzetti**
The bold composition of Pietro Lorenzetti's fresco, entitled The Deposition *(1323), is based around the truncated Cross, focusing attention on the twisted figure of Christ.*

STAR FEATURES

★ **Frescoes by Lorenzetti**

★ **Capella di San Martino**

★ **Frescoes by Giotto**

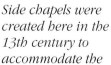

Lower Church
Side chapels were created here in the 13th century to accommodate the growing number of pilgrims.

Upper Church

The soaring Gothic lines (▷ Gothic Style p73) of the 13th-century Upper Church symbolize the heavenly glory of St Francis. This style also influenced later Franciscan churches.

THE POETRY OF ST FRANCIS

In order to reach a wide audience, St Francis preached and wrote in his native tongue, instead of using the Latin texts of the Church of Rome. He wrote simple, lyrical hymns that everyone could understand. In the *Laudes Creaturarum* (1224), a milestone in Italian vernacular poetry, he praised all of God's creation.

KEY DATES

1228 Building begins on the Basilica of St Francis.

September 1997 An earthquake damages the basilica; the vault collapses and many frescoes are shattered.

October 1997 Restoration work on the basilica begins.

2000 The Basilica of St Francis is added to UNESCO's list of World Heritage Sites.

GIOTTO'S FRESCOES

The work of the great Tuscan architect and artist Giotto di Bondone (1267–1337) is often seen as the inspirational starting point for Western painting. He broke away from the ornate but highly formulated Byzantine style to visualize naturalness and human emotions, placing three-dimensional figures in convincing settings. The Assisi cycle (▷ *Frescoes by Giotto*) was painted "al fresco" by spreading paint onto a thin layer of damp, freshly laid plaster. Pigments were drawn into the plaster by surface tension and the color became fixed as the plaster dried. The pigments reacted with the lime in the plaster to produce strong, rich colors. The technique is not suited to damp climates but was widely used in hot, dry Italy and had been for centuries. Many of the frescoes found buried in Pompeii after the eruption of Mount Vesuvius in 79 AD were produced by adopting the same methods.

Faded paintings by Roman artists line the walls above Giotto's *Life of St Francis.*

The façade and its rose window are early examples of Italian Gothic.

Entrance to Upper Church

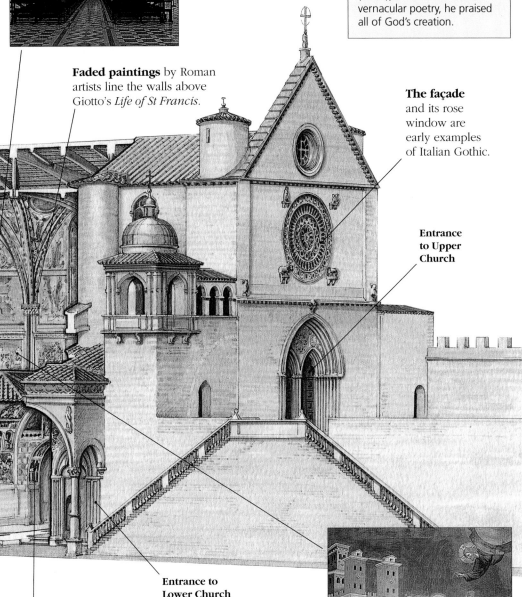

Entrance to Lower Church

★ Cappella di San Martino

The frescoes in this chapel on the Life of St Martin (1315) are by the Sienese painter Simone Martini. This panel shows the Death of the Saint. Martini was also responsible for the fine stained glass in the chapel.

★ Frescoes by Giotto

The Ecstasy of St Francis *is one of 28 panels that make up Giotto's cycle on the* Life of St Francis *(c.1290–95).*

Basilica of St Francis

GLADIATORIAL FIGHTS IN THE ARENA

The emperors of Rome held impressive shows which often began with animals performing circus tricks. Then on came the gladiators, who fought each other to the death. Gladiators were usually slaves, prisoners of war, or condemned criminals. When one was killed, attendants dressed as Charon, the mythical ferryman of the dead, carried his body off on a stretcher, and sand was raked over the blood in preparation for the next bout. A badly wounded gladiator would surrender his fate to the crowd. The "thumbs-up" sign from the emperor meant he could live, while "thumbs-down" meant that he would die. The victor became an instant hero and was some-times rewarded with freedom.

EMPEROR VESPASIAN

Titus Flavius Vespasianus (▷ *Founder of the Colosseum*) was Roman emperor for a decade from AD 69. At that time Rome was in total disarray, the legacy of Emperor Nero. Vespasian's rule is noted for the stability and relative peace he brought to the empire. He instigated a number of building projects, including a temple dedicated to Claudius on the Celian Hill, a Temple of Peace near the Forum, and most famously, the Colosseum. At the time of his death in AD 79 the amphitheater was still incomplete, and it was left to his sons and successors, Titus and Domitian, to finish the work.

Looking across the ancient Forum to the Colosseum in Rome

Colosseum, Rome

ROME'S GREATEST amphitheater was commissioned by the Emperor Vespasian in AD 72 on the marshy site of a lake in the grounds of Nero's palace, the Domus Aurea. Deadly gladiatorial combats and wild animal fights were staged free of charge by the emperor and wealthy citizens for public viewing. The Colosseum was built to a practical design, with its 80 arched entrances allowing easy access to 55,000 spectators, but it is also a building of great Classical beauty (▷ *Classical Style p231*). The drawing here shows how it looked at the time of its inauguration in AD 80. It was one of several similar amphitheaters built in the Roman Empire, and some survive – at El Djem in North Africa, Nîmes and Arles in France, and Verona in northern Italy. Despite being damaged over the years by neglect and theft, it remains a majestic sight.

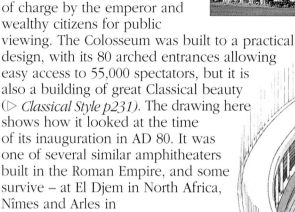

Founder of the Colosseum
Vespasian was a professional soldier who became emperor in AD 69, founding the Flavian dynasty.

Outer Wall of the Colosseum
Stone plundered from the façade in the Renaissance was used to build several palaces, bridges, and parts of St Peter's.

The outer walls are made of travertine.

FLORA OF THE COLOSSEUM

By the 19th century the Colosseum was heavily overgrown. Different microclimates in various parts of the ruin had created an impressive variety of herbs, grasses, and wild flowers. Several botanists were inspired to study and catalog them and two books were published, one listing 420 different species.

Borage, a herb

The bollards anchored the velarium.

The velarium was a huge awning which shaded spectators from the sun. Supported on poles fixed to the upper story of the building, it was then hoisted into position with ropes anchored to bollards outside the stadium.

Internal Corridors

These were designed to allow the large and often unruly crowd to move freely and to be seated within ten minutes of arriving at the Colosseum.

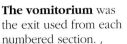

The vomitorium was the exit used from each numbered section.

A GLADIATOR'S LIFE

Gladiator fights were not mere brawls but were professional affairs between trained men. Gladiators lived and trained in barracks and a range of different fighting styles was practiced, each with its own expert coach. Larger barracks had a training arena where men could get used to fighting in front of noisy spectators.

KEY DATES

AD 72 The Colosseum is commissioned by Vespasian.

81–96 Amphitheater is completed during the reign of Emperor Domitian.

248 Games are held to mark the thousandth anniversary of Rome's founding.

1980 Historic Center of Rome is added to UNESCO's World Heritage list.

INSIDE THE COLOSSEUM

The stadium was built in the form of an ellipse, with tiers of seats around a vast central arena. The different social classes were segregated and the consul and emperor had their own separate entrances and boxes. A complex of rooms, passages, and lifts lay in the subterranean area (▷ *Beneath the Arena)*, and this was where animals, men, and scenery were moved around. Cages for the animals were found at the lowest level beneath the wooden arena floor. When the animals were needed, the cages were moved upwards to the arena by means of winches and the animals were released. A system of ramps and trap doors enabled them to reach the arena. Animals were brought here from as far away as North Africa and the Middle East. The games held in AD 248 to mark the thousandth anniversary of Rome's founding saw the death of hundreds of lions, elephants, hippos, and zebras.

Colossus of Nero
The Colosseum may have acquired its name from this huge gilt bronze statue that stood near the amphitheater.

Entry routes to take the spectators to their seats were reached by means of staircases to the various levels of the amphitheater.

Brick formed the inner walls.

Corinthian columns

Ionic columns

Doric columns

The podium was a large terrace where the emperor and the wealthy upper classes had their seats.

rched entrances, 0 in total, were all umbered to let in ne vast crowds that ttended the fights. ach spectator had *tessera* (small quare tile) with an ntrance number amped on it.

Beneath the Arena
Late 19th-century excavations exposed the network of underground rooms where the animals were kept.

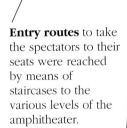

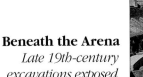

Colosseum

The interior of St Peter's, looking towards the great Baldacchino

St Peter's, Rome

CATHOLICISM'S most sacred shrine, the sumptuous, marble-clad Basilica of St Peter, draws pilgrims and tourists from all over the world. It holds hundreds of precious works of art, some salvaged from the original 4th-century basilica built by Constantine, others commissioned from Renaissance and Baroque artists. The dominant tone is set by Bernini, who created the baldacchino twisting up below Michelangelo's huge dome. He also created the Cathedra in the apse, with four saints supporting a throne that contains fragments once thought to be relics of the chair from which St Peter delivered his first sermon.

Baldacchino
Commissioned by Pope Urban VIII in 1624, Bernini's extravagant Baroque canopy stands above St Peter's tomb.

The church is 186 m (610 ft) long.

MICHELANGELO

The great Florentine artist, sculptor, architect, and poet Michelangelo Buonarroti (1475–1564) was one of the towering figures of the Renaissance. One of his very early works, the ▷ *Pietà*, a technically accomplished masterwork, produced when the artist was only 25, is in St Peter's. Michelangelo felt that he was primarily a sculptor, but in 1508 he accepted Pope Julius II's commission to paint the ceiling of the Sistine Chapel in the Vatican. When it was completed in 1512 it was immediately hailed as a masterwork of the age. In 1546 he was appointed chief architect of St Peter's and devoted the last decades of his life to completing the building.

GIANLORENZO BERNINI

The Italian sculptor, architect, set designer, and painter was the outstanding figure of the Baroque age in Italy. Born in Naples in 1598, the son of a sculptor, the young Bernini was quickly acknowledged to have a precocious talent for marble. He became the favorite architect, sculptor, and town planner to three successive popes, and transformed the look of Rome with his churches, palaces, piazzas (he designed the colonnaded ▷ *Piazza San Pietro* in front of St Peter's), statues, and fountains. He worked on various parts of St Peter's for over 57 years.

HISTORICAL PLAN OF THE BASILICA OF ST PETER

St Peter was buried in AD 64 in a necropolis near his crucifixion site at the Circus of Nero. Constantine built a basilica on the burial site in AD 324. In the 15th century, the old church was found to be unsafe and had to be demolished. It was rebuilt in the 16th and 17th centuries. By 1614 the façade was ready and in 1626 the new church was consecrated.

KEY

- Circus of Nero
- Constantinian
- Renaissance
- Baroque

Dome of St Peter's
The 136.5 m (448 ft) high Renaissance dome (▷ Renaissance Style p211), designed by Michelangelo, was not completed in his lifetime.

A staircase of 537 steps leads to the summit of the dome.

Entrance to Historical Artistic Museum and Sacristy

The Papal Altar stands over the crypt where St Peter is reputedly buried.

Monument to Pope Alexander VII
Bernini's last work in St Peter's was finished in 1678 and shows the Chigi pope among the allegorical figures of Truth, Justice, Charity, and Prudence.

The Grottoes

A fragment of this 13th-century mosaic by Giotto, salvaged from the old basilica, can be found in the Grottoes, where many popes are buried.

ST PETER

One of the most important and popular saints, Peter was one of the first two disciples of Christ. Peter's apostolate brought him to Rome in the year AD 44 where he established the Church of Rome. The saint is traditionally associated with two keys, one for earth and one for heaven.

KEY DATES

AD 64 St Peter is buried in Rome.

324 Emperor Constantine builds a basilica over St Peter's tomb.

1506 Pope Julius II lays first stone of new basilica.

1546 Michelangelo is appointed chief architect.

1980 Properties of the Holy See join the list of UNESCO World Heritage Sites.

THE MONUMENTS IN ST PETER'S

The vast basilica's long, marble-crusted interior contains 11 chapels and 45 altars in addition to a wealth of precious works of art. Much of the elaborate decoration is owed to Bernini's work in the mid-17th century. As well as the extravagant ▷ *Baldacchino* and the ▷ *Monument to Pope Alexander VII*, there is also a monument to Pope Urban VIII in the apse. Above is Bernini's Baroque sculpture of 1656–65, depicting the Holy Spirit, shown as a dove amid clouds, rays of sunlight, and flights of angels. Works by other artists include a marble *Monument to Leo XI* (1650) by Alessandro Algardi and a statue of St Peter by Arnolfo di Cambio (13th century), sculpted in bronze. Near the entrance is Filippo Barigioni's sentimentally expressive 18th-century monument to Maria Clementina, wife of James Stuart, the Old Pretender.

Two minor cupolas by Vignola (1507–73)

The foot of St Peter by Arnolfo di Cambio, 13th century, has worn thin from the touch of pilgrims over the centuries.

Michelangelo's Pietà

Protected by glass since an attack in 1972, this famous marble sculpture was created in 1499.

Filarete Doors

These bronze doors from the old basilica were decorated with biblical reliefs by Filarete between 1439 and 1445.

Façade by Carlo Maderno (1614)

The Holy Door is used only in Holy Years.

Entrance

Markings on the floor of the nave show how other churches compare in length.

Atrium by Carlo Maderno

Piazza San Pietro

On Sundays, religious festivals and special occasions such as canonizations, the pope blesses the crowds from a balcony.

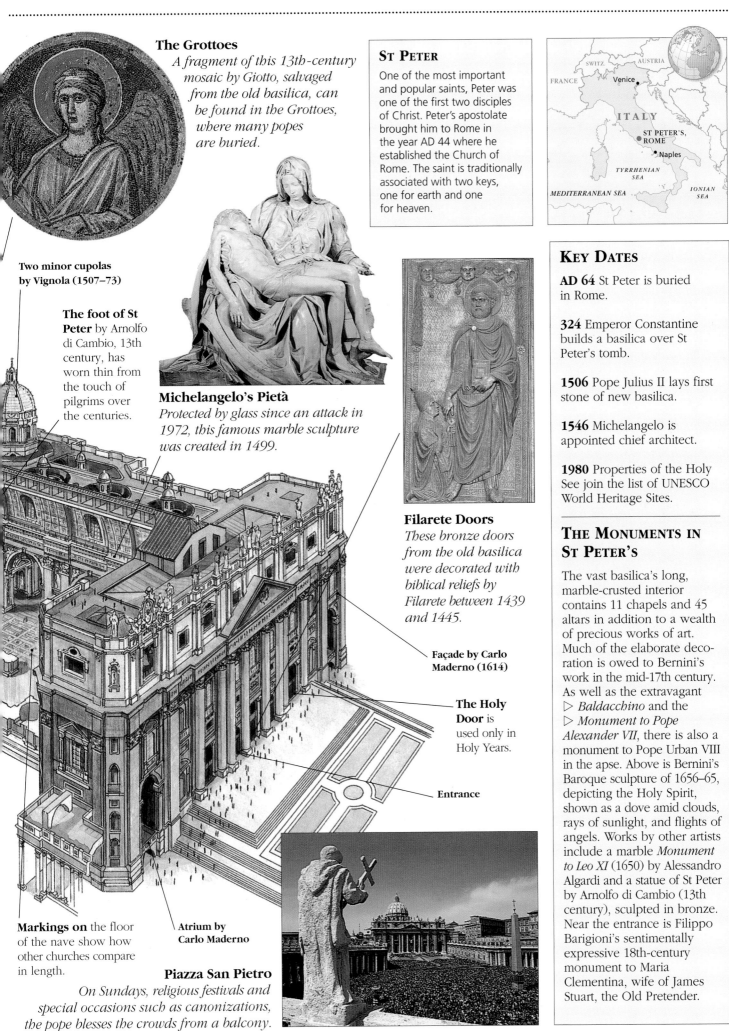

St Peter's

VILLA OF THE MYSTERIES

This large villa outside the city walls on Via dei Sepolcri was built in the early 2nd century BC. First designed as an urban dwelling, it was extended into an elegant country house. The villa is famous for its interior decoration and contains a series of well-preserved fresco cycles. The most famous is in the salon and features 29 brightly colored, life-size figures against a red background. They represent a bride's initiation into the Dionysian mysteries or a postulant's initiation into the Orphic mysteries. Some scholars say this subject was depicted because the owner was a priestess of the Dionysian cult, which was widespread in southern Italy.

Scene from the famous fresco cycle in the Villa of the Mysteries

VIA DELL'ABBONDANZA AND VIA STABIANA

Once the liveliest, busiest street in Pompeii, ▷ *Via dell'Abbondanza* was lined with private homes and shops selling a wide range of goods. Felt and tanned hide were sold at the shop of Verecundus and further along there is also a well-preserved laundry. Among the inns, the most famous belonged to Asellina, whose obliging foreign waitresses are depicted in graffiti on the wall. The inn (*thermopolium*) still has the record of the proceeds of that fateful day in AD 79: 683 sesterces. The Via Stabiana was a major thoroughfare, used by carriages traveling between Pompeii and the port and coastal districts. On the west side stood the Stabian Baths.

Pompeii

WHEN MOUNT VESUVIUS erupted in AD 79, the entire town of Pompeii was buried in 6 m (20 ft) of pumice and ash. It was discovered in the 16th century, but serious excavation only began in 1748. This amazing find revealed an entire city petrified in time. Houses, temples, works of art, and everyday objects have been unearthed, all remarkably preserved, providing a unique insight to how people lived at this moment in history.

★ **House of the Faun**
This famous villa of the wealthy patrician Casii is named after its bronze statuette. The mosaic Battle of Alexander, *in the Museo Archeologico Nazionale in Naples, originated here.*

| 0 metres | 100 |
| 0 yards | 100 |

Sacrarium of the Lares
Close to the Temple of Vespasian, this building housed the statues of Pompeii's guardian deities, the Lares Publici.

★ **House of the Vettii**
This partly reconstructed patrician villa of the wealthy merchants Aulus Vettius Conviva and Aulus Vettius Restitutus contains wonderful frescoes.

Villa of the Mysteries

Forum Baths

Forum

In the bakery
of Modesto, carbonized loaves of bread were found.

Macellum
Pompeii's market place was fronted by a portico with two money-changers' kiosks.

STAR SIGHTS
★ **House of the Vettii**
★ **House of the Faun**

PLAN OF POMPEII

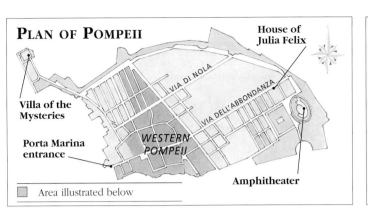

House of Julia Felix

VIA DI NOLA

VIA DELL'ABBONDANZA

Villa of the Mysteries

Porta Marina entrance

WESTERN POMPEII

Amphitheater

☐ Area illustrated below

THE ART OF POMPEII

Villas and public areas such as theaters were richly decorated with lively wall frescoes, mosaics, and statues, some of which miraculously survived the eruption. Designs and themes were strongly influenced by late Classical and Hellenistic art and clients often commissioned close copies of Greek originals.

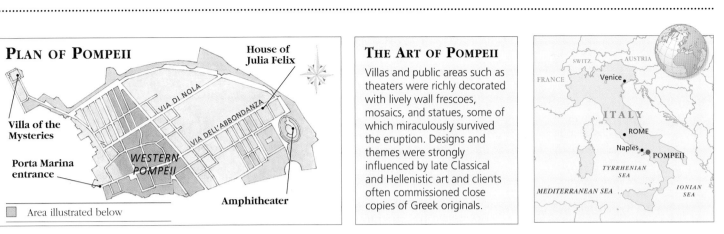

SWITZ.   AUSTRIA

FRANCE

Venice

ITALY

ROME

Naples   POMPEII

TYRRHENIAN SEA

MEDITERRANEAN SEA

IONIAN SEA

Pompeii

WESTERN POMPEII

This illustration shows part of the western area of Pompeii, where the most impressive and intact Roman ruins are located (▷ *Classical Style p231*). There are several large patrician villas in the eastern area where some wealthy residents built their homes; however much of eastern Pompeii still awaits excavation.

Amphitheater and sports ground

Teatro Grande

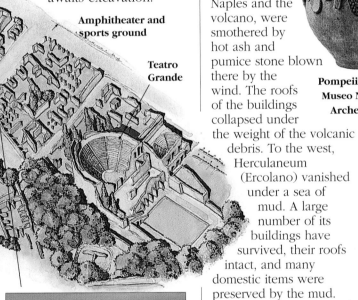

Via dell'Abbondanza
This was one of the original and most important roads through ancient Pompeii. Many inns lined the route.

VESUVIUS AND THE CAMPANIAN TOWNS

Nearly 2,000 years after the eruption of Mount Vesuvius, the Roman towns in its shadow are still being released from the petrification that engulfed them. Both Pompeii and Stabiae (Castellam-mare di Stabia), to the southeast of Naples and the volcano, were smothered by hot ash and pumice stone blown there by the wind. The roofs of the buildings collapsed under the weight of the volcanic debris. To the west, Herculaneum (Ercolano) vanished under a sea of mud. A large number of its buildings have survived, their roofs intact, and many domestic items were preserved by the mud. About 2,000 Pompeiians perished but few, if any, of the residents of Herculaneum died.

In AD 79 Pliny the Elder, the Roman soldier, writer, and naturalist, was the commander of a fleet stationed off Misenum (present-day Miseno, west of Naples) and with his nephew Pliny the Younger observed the ongoing eruption from afar. Eager to see this natural catastrophe closer to hand, Pliny the Elder

Pompeiian vase in Museo Nazionale Archeologico

proceeded to Stabiae, but was overcome by fumes and died. Based on reports by survivors, Pliny the Younger related the first hours of the eruption and his uncle's death in detail in two letters to the Roman historian Tacitus.

Much of our knowledge of the daily lives of the ancient Romans derives from the excavations of Pompeii and Herculaneum. Most of the objects from them as well as Stabiae are now in Naples' Museo Archeologico Nazionale, creating an outstanding and fascinating archaeological collection.

Although Mount Vesuvius has not erupted since 1944, it rumbles occasionally, causing minor earthquakes.

Casts of a dying mother and child in the museum in Naples

KEY DATES

c.8th century BC Building of early Pompeii.

August, AD 79 Vesuvius erupts and Pompeii and Stabiae are showered with debris and completely buried for centuries.

1594 Workers digging a trench discover traces of the ancient town.

1860 Giuseppe Fiorelli becomes director of excavations; the town is gradually uncovered by archaeologists.

1997 The Archaeological Area of Pompeii is added to UNESCO's World Heritage list.

LIFE IN POMPEII

In the 1st century AD, Pompeii was a prosperous commercial town. Once Etruscan, and later Greek, by AD 79 it was a thriving Roman town with baths, amphitheaters, temples, and luxurious villas for the wealthy. The ▷ *House of Julia Felix* occupies an entire block, divided into the owner's quarters and rented dwellings and shops. The house also had baths that were open to the public. On the highest spot in Pompeii was the rectangular, paved ▷ *Forum*, formerly the market place. This was the center of public life and the focus for the most important civic functions, both political and religious. The ▷ *Amphitheater* (80 BC) was used for gladiatorial combat and is the oldest one of its kind.

A BLEND OF STYLES

By the time Norman control of Sicily was complete in 1091, the island had seen all kinds of occupation. Part of Greece from the 1st century BC, Sicily then became part of the Roman Empire. By 535 it belonged to Byzantium. From 831 the Arabs controlled Palermo but by 1091 the island was in Norman hands. However, a deliberate policy of assimilation of these diverse influences led to an exhilarating blend of styles and motifs in the Norman era. The palace of La Zisa in Palermo, for example, features Islamic domes, Byzantine mosaics, interwoven Norman arches, and Classical columns.

THE MOSAICS OF MONREALE

The art of using mosaic patterns goes back to the Romans and was first used in flooring. The interior of Monreale is plainly laid out and an effective background for the scores of golden and colored mosaics gleaming on the walls, above the nave, in the crossing, in the transepts, and in the aisles. The story of the life of Christ is narrated in the crossing and the transepts, while the Genesis cycle runs on two levels above the nave arcade. Gazing down from the apse is the huge figure of ▷ *Christ Pantocrator*, depicted in the traditional Byzantine way with his court of archangels, angels, prophets, and evangelists. The images are an astonishing blend of Byzantine, Arab, and Norman figurative elements, but the identities of the master mosaicists remains unknown.

The apse mosaics dominated by the figure of Christ Pantocrator

Monreale Cathedral

Capital from cloister column

Oₙₑ ᴏғ ᴛʜᴇ wonders of the medieval world, Sicily's Monreale Cathedral was founded in 1172 by the Norman King William II, and marks the pinnacle of achievement of Arab-Norman art. Its interior glitters with mosaics designed by Sicilian and Byzantine artists – the inspiration of a king who wanted to rival the power of the Archbishop of Palermo. The cloister has pointed Arab arches with geometric motifs, and scenes from the Bible are sculpted on the capitals of the 228 white marble twin columns.

Apse Exterior
With their rich multi-colored ornamentation in tufa and marble, the three apses represent the apogee of Norman decoration.

Entrance to Cappella del Crocifisso and Treasury

The royal tomb of William II, in white marble, flanks the porphyry tomb of William I in the corner of the transept.

★ Christ Pantocrator
The cathedral's Latin-cross plan focuses on the imposing mosaic of the all-powerful Christ (12th–13th century).

Nave and aisles separated by Roman columns

Magnificent gilded wood ceiling

Original Cosmati floor in choir

Barisano da Trani's bronze door (1179) on the north side is shielded by a portico designed by Gian Domenico and Fazio Gagini (1547–69).

★ Mosaic Cycle
Completed in c.1182, the rich mosaics show scenes from the Old Testament (nave), Teachings of Christ (aisles, choir, and transepts), and the Gospels (side apses). The story of Noah's Ark is depicted here.

★ **Cloisters**
A masterpiece of Norman artistic expression from the time of William II, the columns – plain, carved, or inlaid with richly lustred tiles – support elaborate capitals from which spring Arabic-style arches.

NORMAN SICILY

Sicily was ruled by Norman kings for not much more than a century, yet Norman rule left an enduring stamp on the island. Palermo's sumptuous Cappella Palatina and the cathedral at Cefalù were the lasting achievements of Roger II, crowned king in 1130.

The south wall and cloisters survive as elements from the Benedictine monastery.

Small Oriental-inspired fountain

Column Detail
Craftsmen from Campania, Apulia, Lombardy, and Sicily worked on the cloister columns. The detail here shows Adam and Eve.

The 18th-century porch is surrounded by two squat towers.

Northern Tower

Bronze Door Panel
Bonanno Pisano's fine bronze door (1185), signed by him, depicts 42 scenes from the Bible set within elaborate borders. The lion and griffin are symbols of the Norman kingdom.

STAR FEATURES

★ **Christ Pantocrator**

★ **Mosaic Cycle**

★ **Cloisters**

KEY DATES

1060–90 Norman conquest of Sicily from the Arabs. Kingdom of the Two Sicilies established.

1172–89 Benedictine abbey and cloister are built.

1172–c.1183 Monreale Cathedral is constructed.

c.1182–90 Mosaic decoration is carried out.

17th century Baroque chapel of the Crucifix (Cappella del Crocifisso) is added.

KING WILLIAM II

During the reign of William II, church authority in Sicily became centered around Monreale, which developed into a rich and powerful monastic establishment. The young king (a teenager when William I died in 1166) was determined that the cathedral should not only be a monument to his reign but also a center for the dissemination of Christian culture in western Sicily. William's grandfather, Roger II, had been appointed Apostolic Legate by the Pope and as a result Norman Sicilian monarchs had a great deal of freedom in Church affairs. When William died in 1189, aged only 36, the ▷ *northern tower* was still incomplete, as was the exterior of the ▷ *nave* and much of the floor. In his lifetime William built a number of palaces and was known as "William the Good". His sarcophagus (▷ *royal tomb*) is in the transept of Monreale.

Monreale Cathedral

Basilica of Euphrasius, Poreč

ST MAURUS AND BISHOP EUPHRASIUS

Little is known about the early life of St Maurus, the first Bishop of Poreč and Bishop Euphrasius. In the 4th century St Maurus built an oratory which was used by early Christians for secret worship. Legend says that he endured a martyr's death during the Roman Emperor Diocletian's persecution of Christians. In the 6th century his body was transferred from a cemetery near the basilica and placed in the ▷ Votive Chapel. The influential 6th-century Bishop Euphrasius sought the best craftsmen for the construction of the basilica, and created one of the greatest architectural complexes of the period.

BYZANTINE MOSAIC TECHNIQUE

The art of mosaics, especially in churches, reached its peak during the Byzantine period. Small colored glass pieces were inlaid onto the walls while more hard-wearing natural stones and marbles were encrusted into the floors. In the 6th century, mosaicists began to use gold and silver glass tesserae in their designs to help reflect the maximum amount of light. Most mosaics exclusively depicted Christian biblical scenes or saints and a few also included images of the builders. Bishop Euphrasius commissioned marvelous Byzantine designs for his basilica. The most impressive is that of the Virgin and Child in the apse, flanked by images of St Maurus and Euphrasius (▷ apse mosaics).

Virgin and Child mosaic in the apse

A mosaic in the apse

THIS 6TH-CENTURY CHURCH, a Byzantine masterwork (▷ Byzantine Style p247), is decorated with splendid mosaics on a gold background. The Basilica of Euphrasius was constructed for Bishop Euphrasius between 539 and 553 by enlarging the existing 4th-century Oratory of St Maurus, one of the earliest Christian religious sites in the world. Over the centuries the building has undergone several alterations. Some of the original floor mosaics still survive, many of which were rediscovered during the 19th-century restoration.

★ **Ciborium**
Dominating the presbytery is a beautiful 13th-century ciborium, supported by four marble columns. The canopy is decorated with mosaics.

★ **Apse Mosaics**
Mosaics from the 6th century cover the apse. On the triumphal arch are Christ and the Apostles (above), on the vault, the Virgin enthroned with Child and two Angels, to the left St Maurus, Bishop Euphrasius with a model of the basilica and Deacon Claud with his son.

Remains of a 4th-century mosaic floor from the Oratory of St Maurus are in the garden.

Sacristy and the Votive Chapel
Past the sacristy's left wall is a triple-apsed chapel with a mosaic floor from the 6th century. Here lie the remains of the saints Maurus and Eleuterius.

STAR FEATURES

★ Ciborium

★ Apse Mosaics

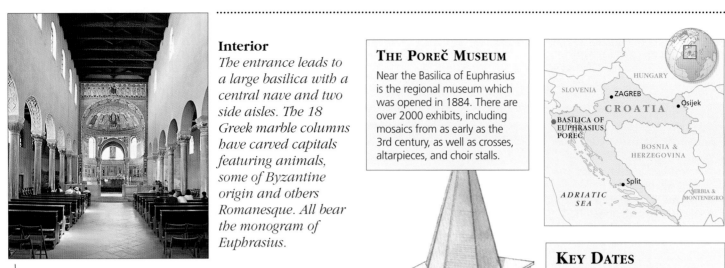

Interior
The entrance leads to a large basilica with a central nave and two side aisles. The 18 Greek marble columns have carved capitals featuring animals, some of Byzantine origin and others Romanesque. All bear the monogram of Euphrasius.

THE POREČ MUSEUM
Near the Basilica of Euphrasius is the regional museum which was opened in 1884. There are over 2000 exhibits, including mosaics from as early as the 3rd century, as well as crosses, altarpieces, and choir stalls.

KEY DATES

Mid-6th century The Basilica of Euphrasius is built.

1277 The ciborium is constructed.

19th century The building undergoes extensive restoration work.

1997 The Basilica of Euphrasius is inscribed a UNESCO World Heritage Site.

THE INTERIOR

The basilica is entered through the ▷ *atrium*, which contains small traces of Byzantine mosaics that were restored in the 19th century. Nearby is the ▷ *Baptistry*, built with a wooden roof in the 5th century and remodeled during the construction of Euphrasius's basilica. Early Christian converts were baptized in the central font until the 15th century. Inside the basilica beautiful mosaics, partly made of semi-precious stones and mother-of-pearl, are still visible especially in the apse (▷ *apse mosaics*) and the ▷ *ciborium*. Several fires and earthquakes over the centuries have altered the shape of the building; the southern wall of the central nave was destroyed in the 15th century and later rebuilt with Gothic windows (▷ *Gothic Style p73*). On the western side of the basilica is the Holy Cross Chapel, adorned with a polyptych created in the 15th century by Antonio Vivarini, as well as an oil painting of *The Last Supper* by Jacobo Palma Junior.

Baptistry
This octagonal building dates from the 6th century. In the center is a baptismal font and there are also fragments of mosaics; to the rear rises a 16th-century bell tower.

The Bishop's Palace, a triple-aisled building dating from the 6th century, now houses several paintings by Antonio da Bassano, a polyptych by Antonio Vivarini, and a painting by Palma il Giovane.

Atrium
This has a roughly square portico with two columns on each side. Tombstones and a variety of archaeological finds dating from the medieval period are displayed in this area.

Basilica of Euphrasius

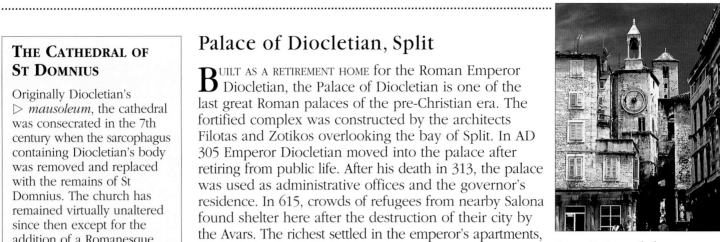

Palace of Diocletian, Split

BUILT AS A RETIREMENT HOME for the Roman Emperor Diocletian, the Palace of Diocletian is one of the last great Roman palaces of the pre-Christian era. The fortified complex was constructed by the architects Filotas and Zotikos overlooking the bay of Split. In AD 305 Emperor Diocletian moved into the palace after retiring from public life. After his death in 313, the palace was used as administrative offices and the governor's residence. In 615, crowds of refugees from nearby Salona found shelter here after the destruction of their city by the Avars. The richest settled in the emperor's apartments, the poorer in the towers and above the gates, and the people of Split have continued to inhabit the grounds of the palace since then. It has been much altered over the years, and few of the original Roman structures are still visible; much of the medieval building work incorporated blocks and columns removed from them.

Iron Gate and the Clock Tower
This is the best preserved gate: beyond is the church of Our Lady of the Belfry with a 12th-century tower next to it.

THE CATHEDRAL OF ST DOMNIUS

Originally Diocletian's ▷ *mausoleum*, the cathedral was consecrated in the 7th century when the sarcophagus containing Diocletian's body was removed and replaced with the remains of St Domnius. The church has remained virtually unaltered since then except for the addition of a Romanesque bell tower (12th–16th centuries) and the 13th-century choir inside. An ancient granite sphinx rests at the base of the bell tower. Inside the octagonal cathedral is a double order of Corinthian columns, most of them Roman originals (▷ *Classical style, p231*). Above them is a decorated frieze supporting medallions with portraits of Diocletian and his wife Prisca. The 13th-century pulpit is held aloft by thin columns with carved capitals. The Altar of St Domnius is the work of Bonino of Milan (1427).

THE PAPALIĆ PALACE

The old center of Split has been established in and around the vast Roman Palace of Diocletian. After two centuries of Byzantine rule and the establishment of Croat communities, Split became part of the Venetian territories in 1409. Under the Venetians, new walls and a fort were built and the arts flourished. The Venetian Gothic Papalić Palace (▷ *Gothic Style p73*) is one of the most interesting of the 15th–16th-century buildings constructed in the abandoned parts of the palace complex. It is now the ▷ *Museum of Split* (Musez Grada Splita), which has areas displaying art and artifacts, including 16th-century works and paintings, as well as books illustrating the history of Split from the 12th to the 18th centuries.

Temple of Jupiter
The body of the building had a coffered vault and rested on an underground crypt. There was also an atrium with six columns. In the early Middle Ages it was turned into the Baptistry of St John.

Detail of the Papalić Palace in Split

The temples of Venus and Cybele were circular outside and had a hexagonal ground-plan inside. A colonnaded corridor ran around the outside.

Peristyle
Near the crossroads of the Cardo and Decumanus, the peristyle gave access to the sacred area. On one side were the temples of Venus and Cybele and, further back, that of Jupiter (now the Baptistry of St John); on the other side was the mausoleum, now the cathedral.

The Golden Gate

This was the grandest entrance to the palace and is well preserved. Arched niches once contained statues. The 2th-century St Martin's Chapel, which contains a Black Madonna icon, is built into the gate.

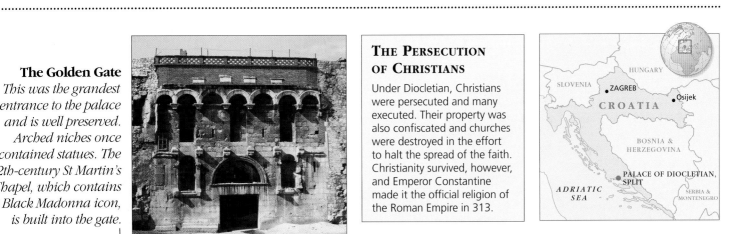

THE PERSECUTION OF CHRISTIANS

Under Diocletian, Christians were persecuted and many executed. Their property was also confiscated and churches were destroyed in the effort to halt the spread of the faith. Christianity survived, however, and Emperor Constantine made it the official religion of the Roman Empire in 313.

Bust of Diocletian

After reorganizing the empire, the emperor sought the spiritual unification of its citizens. The state religion, personified by the emperor, gained in importance, and temples were constructed bearing his image. Christians were subject to extremely violent persecution.

The Museum of Split is housed in a Gothic mansion built over this part of the complex.

The Mausoleum of Diocletian, now the Cathedral of St Domnius.

The outer walls were a necessary fortification against the threat of uprisings and gave the palace a military air.

RECONSTRUCTION OF DIOCLETIAN'S PALACE

The palace, shown here in its original form, was like a typical Roman military camp. It was 215 m (705 ft) long and 180 m (590 ft) wide, enclosed by very thick walls, at times 28 m (92 ft) high. The four-sided stronghold was reinforced with towers on the north, east, and west sides. There is a gate on each side, connected by two roads corresponding to the Roman *Cardo* and *Decumanus*.

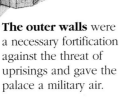

The Silver Gate

Located on the eastern side of the palace, the gate was unearthed to its original Roman level in the 19th century.

KEY DATES

c. late 3rd–early 4th century AD The Palace of Diocletian is constructed.

1757 Architect Robert Adams and his draftsmen conduct the first study of the palace.

1979 UNESCO declares Historic Split, including the Palace of Diocletian, to be a World Heritage Site.

EMPEROR DIOCLETIAN

Born in the ancient town of Salona, near modern-day Split, in 245, Diocletian was the son of slaves. His rapid rise to power was the result of military ability rather than connections or birth. He was appointed Roman emperor in 284 at the age of 39 and quickly set out to reorganize the immense Roman Empire. He reformed the economy, the army, and the administrative structures by devising a system of government known as the Tetrarchy, or rule by four. This involved dividing power over the empire into east and west sectors; he controlled the east as Caesar, and another ruler controlled the west as Augustus. To ensure that new leaders were appointed without a possible civil war, two "juniors" were named as their successors. The pagan Diocletian was also renowned for his persecution of Christians. In 303 he issued an edict forbidding the religion, the last of the persecutions. Exhausted and in poor health, Diocletian abdicated the throne in 305 and lived in the palace until his death in 313.

ROCK FORMATIONS

The name Metéora simply means "suspended rocks". There are many theories on how the rocks of Metéora were formed, but none has so far been proven. The most dominant theory is that of a German geologist, who studied rock formations in Thessaly and Epirus in Greece at the end of the 19th century. He argued that the rocks emerged from the delta region of a large river. The river flowed over 25–30 million years ago into the small but deep sector of the sea covering what is today Thessaly. Waste matter and stones settled forming huge rocks which were then left exposed once the sea had retreated. The rocks were further shaped by wind and rain.

The interior of Rousánou, decorated with beautiful wall frescoes

MONK ATHANÁSIOS

The famous monk of Metéora, Athanásios, was born in 1310 in Greece. Both of his parents died when he was young and he was raised by his uncle. He studied theology and philosophy in Thessaloniki and traveled around the Greek Islands. He came upon Mount Athos (the holy mountain where numerous monks lived and worshiped) and realized that he wanted to become a monk. While Athanásios lived on Mount Athos the monasteries were constantly raided by invaders, so he and a small group of monks set out to find a safer fortress. Athanásios came upon Metéora, which provided a natural haven from invaders, and founded one of the first monasteries on the site. He then lived here until his death in 1383.

Metéora

Icon of Our Lord, Varlaám

THE LARGEST AND MOST important group of monasteries in Greece can be found on Metéora. The rocks were first used as a religious retreat when, in AD 985, a hermit named Barnabas occupied a cave here. In the mid-14th century Neílos, the Prior of Stagai convent, built a small church. Then in 1382 the monk Athanásios founded the huge monastery of Megálo Metéora, later completed by monk Joseph. Twenty-three monasteries followed, though most had fallen into ruin by the 19th century. In the 1920s stairs were cut to make the monasteries more accessible and today a religious revival has seen the return of many monks and nuns.

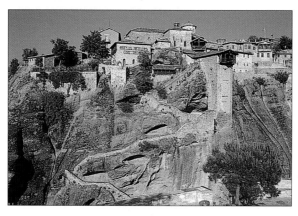

LOCATION OF MONASTERIES OF METÉORA

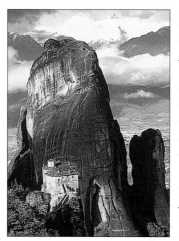

Rousánou

Moní Rousánou, perched precariously on the very tip of a narrow spire of rock, is the most spectacularly located of all the monasteries. Its church of the Metamórfosis (1545) is renowned for its harrowing frescoes, painted in 1560 by the iconographers of the Cretan school.

Monastic cells

Outer walls

VARLAÁM

Founded in 1518, the monastery of Varlaám is named after the first hermit to live on this rock in 1350. The *katholikón* was built in 1542 and contains some frescoes by the Theban iconographer Frágkos Katelános.

Megálo Metéoro

Also known as the Great Meteoron, this was the first and, at 623 m (2,045 ft), highest monastery to be founded. By the entrance is a cave in which Athanásios first lived. His body is buried in the main church.

Katholikón

Dedicated to Agioi Pántes (All Saints), the church is adorned with frescoes, including one of Theofánis (right) and Nektários, its founders.

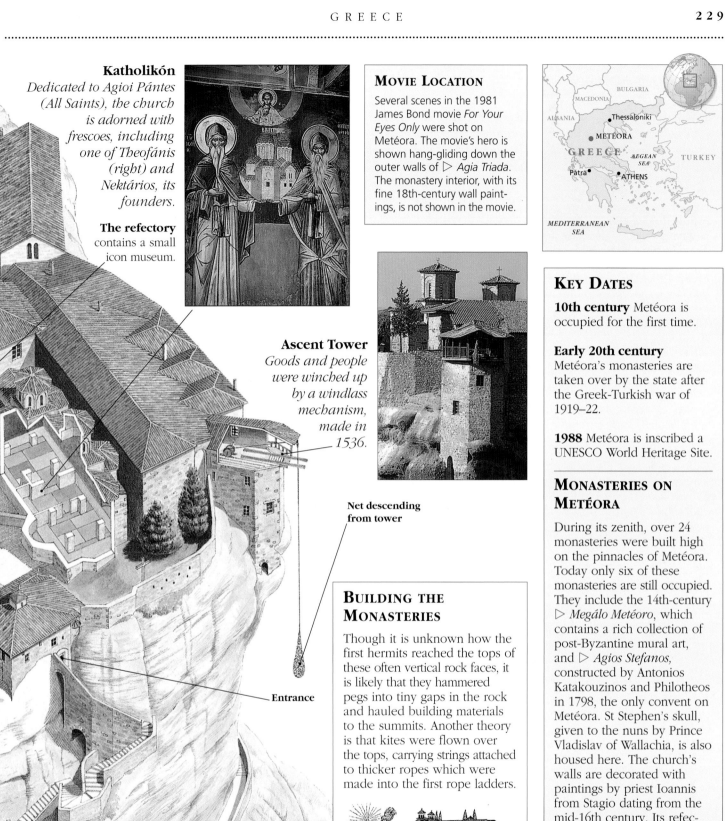

The refectory contains a small icon museum.

MOVIE LOCATION

Several scenes in the 1981 James Bond movie *For Your Eyes Only* were shot on Metéora. The movie's hero is shown hang-gliding down the outer walls of ▷ *Agia Triada*. The monastery interior, with its fine 18th-century wall paintings, is not shown in the movie.

Ascent Tower

Goods and people were winched up by a windlass mechanism, made in 1536.

Net descending from tower

Entrance

BUILDING THE MONASTERIES

Though it is unknown how the first hermits reached the tops of these often vertical rock faces, it is likely that they hammered pegs into tiny gaps in the rock and hauled building materials to the summits. Another theory is that kites were flown over the tops, carrying strings attached to thicker ropes which were made into the first rope ladders.

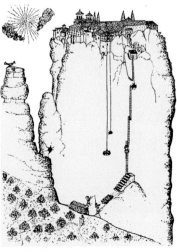

KEY DATES

10th century Metéora is occupied for the first time.

Early 20th century Metéora's monasteries are taken over by the state after the Greek-Turkish war of 1919–22.

1988 Metéora is inscribed a UNESCO World Heritage Site.

MONASTERIES ON METÉORA

During its zenith, over 24 monasteries were built high on the pinnacles of Metéora. Today only six of these monasteries are still occupied. They include the 14th-century ▷ *Megálo Metéoro*, which contains a rich collection of post-Byzantine mural art, and ▷ *Agios Stefanos,* constructed by Antonios Katakouzinos and Philotheos in 1798, the only convent on Metéora. St Stephen's skull, given to the nuns by Prince Vladislav of Wallachia, is also housed here. The church's walls are decorated with paintings by priest Ioannis from Stagio dating from the mid-16th century. Its refectory also contains a museum showcasing religious artifacts. Other monasteries of note are ▷ *Agia Triada* founded in the 15th century by monk Dometius, which is decorated with beautiful frescoes by Nikolaos and Antonios, and ▷ *Agios Nikolaos* built in the 16th century by Dionysious. Its walls are adorned with paintings by the Cretan iconographer Theophanis Bathas-Strelitzas.

Metéora

ACROPOLIS MUSEUM

Opened in 1878, the Acropolis Museum is located on the southeast corner of the site, and contains exhibits devoted to finds from the Acropolis. Divided chronologically, the collection begins with 6th-century BC works which include fragments of painted pedimental statues such as *Moschophoros*, or Calf-Bearer, a young man carrying a calf on his shoulders (c.570 BC). Two rooms in the museum house a unique collection of *korai* from c.500 BC. These were votive statues of maidens offered to Athena. Together they represent the development of ancient Greek art – moving from the formal bearing of *Peplos Kore* to the more natural body movement of the *Almond-Eyed Kore*. Elsewhere, a well-preserved *metope* from the ▷ *Parthenon* shows the battle between the Lapiths and centaurs. The collection ends with the original four caryatids from the south porch of Erechtheion (▷ *Porch of the Caryatids*).

THE PARTHENON

Built as an expression of the glory of ancient Athens, this temple (▷ *Parthenon)* was designed by Kallikrates and Iktinos to house the 12-m (40-ft) high statue of Athena Parthenos (Maiden) sculpted by Pheidias. Taking nine years to complete, the building was finally dedicated to the goddess in 438 BC. This peripteral temple was 70 m (230 ft) long and 30 m (100 ft) wide with a striking red, blue and gold entablature. Every aspect of the Parthenon was built on a 9:4 ratio. The sculptors used every visual trickery to counteract the laws of perspective to make the building completely symmetrical. Over the centuries the temple has served as a church, a mosque, and an arsenal.

**Moschophoros,
Acropolis Museum**

Acropolis, Athens

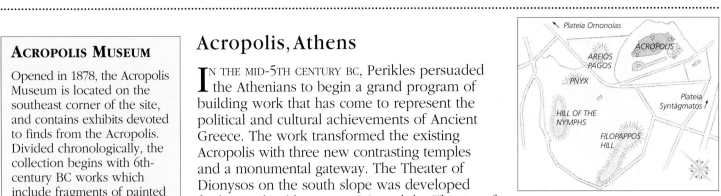

IN THE MID-5TH CENTURY BC, Perikles persuaded the Athenians to begin a grand program of building work that has come to represent the political and cultural achievements of Ancient Greece. The work transformed the existing Acropolis with three new contrasting temples and a monumental gateway. The Theater of Dionysos on the south slope was developed further in the 4th century BC, and the Theater of Herodes Atticus was added in the 2nd century AD.

LOCATOR MAP
☐ Area illustrated below

★ Porch of the Caryatids
These statues of women were used in place of columns on the south porch of the Erechtheion. The originals, four of which are now in the Acropolis Museum, have been replaced by casts.

An olive tree now grows where Athena first planted her tree in a competition against Poseidon.

The Propylaia was built in 437–432 BC to form a new entrance to the Acropolis.

★ Temple of Athena Nike
This temple to Athena of Victory is on the west side of the Propylaia. It was built in 426–421 BC.

The Beulé Gate was the first entrance to the Acropolis.

STAR FEATURES

★ **Porch of the Caryatids**

★ **Temple of Athena Nike**

★ **Parthenon**

Theater of Herodes Atticus
Also known as the Odeion of Herodes Atticus, this superb theater was originally built in AD 161. It was restored in 1955 and is used today for outdoor concerts.

★ Parthenon

Although few sculptures are left on this famous temple to Athena, some can still be admired, such as this one on the east pediment.

THE ELGIN MARBLES

Lord Elgin acquired the famous ▷ *Parthenon* marbles in 1801–3 and sold them to the British in 1816. Controversy surrounds the sculptures, now in London's British Museum, as many believe they belong in Athens.

The Acropolis Museum exhibits stone sculptures from the Acropolis monuments and artifacts from on-site excavations.

Two Corinthian columns are the remains of monuments erected by sponsors of successful dramatic performances.

Panagía Spiliótissa is a chapel set in a cave in the Acropolis rock.

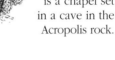

Theatre of Dionysos

This figure of the comic satyr, Silenus, can be seen here. The theater visible today was built by Lykourgos in 342–326 BC.

Shrine of Asklepios

Stoa of Eumenes

The Acropolis rock was an easily defended site. It has been populated for nearly 5,000 years.

The Acropolis today

The Acropolis provides a stunning backdrop to the modern city of Athens and is Greece's single most visited site. Having survived earthquakes, fires, and wars for over 2,500 years, today its monuments are under threat from the atmospheric pollution which is slowly softening their marble.

KEY DATES

3000 BC First of the settlements on the Acropolis.

510 BC The Delphic Oracle declares the Acropolis a holy place of the gods.

451–429 BC Lavish building program is begun under Perikles.

AD 267 Much of the Acropolis is destroyed by the Germanic Heruli tribe.

1987 UNESCO declares the Acropolis a World Heritage Site.

CLASSICAL STYLE

At the heart of Greek architecture were the Classical "orders" – the types and styles of columns, and the forms of structures and decoration that followed on from them. Of these, Doric is the earliest; the column has no base, a fluted shaft, and a plain capital. The Ionic column is a lighter development from the Doric; the fluted shaft has a base and a volute capital. The Corinthian, with its plinth and fluted shaft, is a variant of the Ionic, and distinctive in its ornate capital. The capitals of these columns were representations of natural forms, as in the rams' horns of the Ionic or the stylized acanthus leaves of the Corinthian. Other architectural features included pediments (triangular structures crowning the front of the temples), caryatids (sculptures used as columns), and friezes of relief sculptures, used to adorn exteriors.

Acropolis

The entrance to the Treasury of Atreus, with a gap over its lintel

TOMBS OF MYCENAE

Mycenae's nobles were entombed in shaft graves, such as ▷ *Grave Circle A* or, later, in *tholos* ("beehive") tombs, like the ▷ *Treasury of Atreus*, which dates from the 14th century BC. The *tholos* tombs, found outside the palace walls, were built using successive circles of masonry, each level nudged steadily inward to narrow the diameter until the top could be closed with a single stone. The entire structure was then buried, save for an entrance approached by a *dromos* or open-air corridor.

HEINRICH SCHLIEMANN

The German born archaeologist Heinrich Schliemann (1822–90) was self-educated and by the age of 47 had become a millionaire, expressly to fund his own archaeological digs. Having discovered Troy and proved the factual basis of the Greek poet Homer's epics, Schliemann came to Mycenae in 1874 and commenced digging in ▷ *Grave Circle A*. On discovering a gold death mask, which had preserved the skin of a royal skull, he proclaimed: "I have gazed upon the face of Agamemnon!" Although archaeologists have since dated the mask to 300 years earlier than any historical Trojan warrior, the discovery corroborated Homer's description of "well-built Mycenae, rich in gold."

Mycenae

THE FORTIFIED PALACE complex of Mycenae, uncovered by the archaeologist Heinrich Schliemann in the late 19th century, is one of the earliest examples of sophisticated citadel architecture. The term "Mycenaean," more properly late Bronze Age, applies to an entire culture spanning the years 1700–1100 BC. Only the ruling class inhabited this hilltop palace, with artisans and merchants living just outside the city walls. It was abandoned in 1100 BC after a period of great disruption in the region.

Secret Stairway
A flight of 99 steps drops to a cistern deep beneath the citadel. Connected by pipes to a spring outside, the cistern was added to protect the water supply in times of siege.

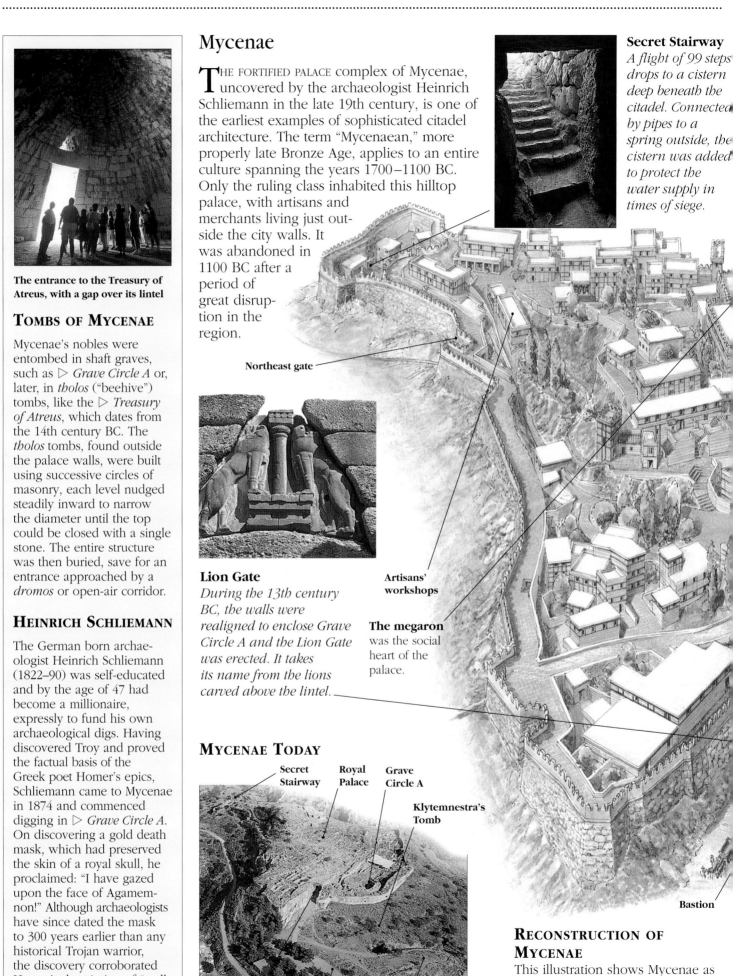

Northeast gate

Lion Gate
During the 13th century BC, the walls were realigned to enclose Grave Circle A and the Lion Gate was erected. It takes its name from the lions carved above the lintel.

Artisans' workshops

The megaron was the social heart of the palace.

MYCENAE TODAY

Secret Stairway — Royal Palace — Grave Circle A

Klytemnestra's Tomb

Lion Gate — Path to the Treasury of Atreus — Grave Circle B

Bastion

RECONSTRUCTION OF MYCENAE

This illustration shows Mycenae as it was in the time of the House of Atreus and the 1250 BC Trojan War. Most tombs lie outside the walls.

Royal Palace
Situated at the acropolis summit, only the floors remain of this structure. Burn-marks dating to its destruction in 1200 BC are still visible on the stone.

TREASURY OF ATREUS

Unlike their Greek contemporaries who would cremate their dead, the Mycenaeans buried their deceased in tombs. In the Treasury of Atreus, one of only two double-chambered tombs in Greece, a Mycenaean king was buried with his weapons and enough food and drink for his journey through the Underworld.

The "Cyclopean" walls, up to 14 m (46 ft) wide, were unbreachable. Later Greeks imagined that they had been built by giants.

The houses of Mycenae yielded a number of tablets inscribed with an archaic script, known as Linear B, deciphered by Michaïl Ventrís in 1952.

The House of Tsoúntas, named after its discoverer, was a minor palace.

Great ramp

Grave Circle A
This housed six royal family shaft-graves containing 19 bodies. The 14 kg (31 lb) of gold funerary goods are on display in Athens.

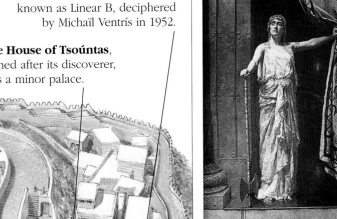

Klytemnestra, after murdering her husband, Agamemnon

THE CURSE OF THE HOUSE OF ATREUS

King Atreus slaughtered most of his brother Thyestes's children and fed them to him; for this outrage the gods laid a curse on Atreus and his descendants. Thyestes's surviving daughter, Pelopia, bore her own father a son, Aigisthos, who murdered Atreus and restored Thyestes to the throne of Mycenae. But Atreus also had an heir, the energetic Agamemnon, who seized power. Agamemnon raised a fleet to punish the Trojan Paris, who had stolen his brother's wife, Helen. He sacrificed his daughter to obtain a favorable wind. When he returned he was murdered by his wife, Klytemnestra, and her lover Aigisthos. The murderous pair were in turn disposed of by Agamemnon's children, Orestes and Elektra.

KEY DATES

1874 The Mycenae ruins are rediscovered by Heinrich Schliemann.

1999 The archaeological site of Mycenae is inscribed on the UNESCO World Heritage list.

NATIONAL ARCHAE-OLOGICAL MUSEUM

Located in central Athens is the National Archaeological Museum. Its most popular attraction is the Hall of Mycenaean Antiquities, with its dazzling array of 16th-century BC gold treasures. Other exhibits in the collection include frescoes, ivory sculptures and seal rings made out of precious stones. From the famous shaft graves, including ▷ *Grave Circle A* and ▷ *Grave Circle B*, came a procession of cups, as well as a number of regal death masks like the famous *Mask of Agamemnon* dating from the mid-1600s BC. A selection of daggers including a superb gold and silver bronze dagger is on view. It is inlaid in bands of niello and decorated with a lion-hunting scene on one side of the blade and a lion seizing antelopes on the other. Two superb *rhytons*, or wine jugs, are also on display: one in the shape of a bull's head, made in silver with gold horns, and one in gold shaped like a lion's head. A rock crystal oval bowl with an open spout and a handle in the design of a duck's head is another of the museum's sumptuous pieces.

ZEUS

Chief and most powerful of the ancient Greek gods, Zeus lived on Mount Olympos along with the other immortals and was thought to be responsible for the destinies of men. He was also god of weather and thunderstorms. Ancient Greek myths tell of Zeus's amorous liaisons and his numerous children, some of whom were gods or goddesses and some heroes. He was worshipped at Olympia and at Dodóni in Epirus, site of the oldest oracle of Greece.

5th-century Zeus and Ganymede

OLYMPIA ARCHAEOLOGICAL MUSEUM

Officially opened in 1982, the Olympia archaeological museum was built opposite the excavation site. It has many treasures on display and is one of the richest museums in Greece. The central hall is devoted solely to the pediment and metope sculptures from the ▷ *Temple of Zeus*. In a corner room of the museum are the Olympic galleries housing a 5th-century BC bronze statuette of a runner at the starting point, dedicated to Zeus. A 9th-century BC bronze horse, a bronze tripod, and elongated male figures upholding cauldron handles can be found in the Prehistoric, Geometric, and Archaic galleries. Finds dating from 475–350 BC are displayed in the Classical galleries. They include helmets and weapons made as offerings to Zeus and a 5th-century BC Corinthian terracotta of *Zeus and Ganymede*. The Roman galleries showcase a series of statues of Roman emperors and generals and a marble bull dedicated by Regilla, wife of Herodes Atticus.

Ancient Olympia

THE SANCTUARY OF Olympia enjoyed over 1,000 years of esteem as a religious site and the world's first athletics centre. Though the sanctuary flourished in Mycenaean times, its historic importance dates to the coming of the Dorians and their worship of Zeus, after whose abode on Mount Olympos the site was named. More elaborate temples and secular buildings were erected as the sanctuary acquired a more Hellenic character, a process completed by 300 BC. By the end of the reign of Roman emperor Hadrian (AD 117–38), the sanctuary had begun to have less religious and political significance.

Aerial view south over the Olympia site today

The Temple of Hera, begun in the 7th century BC, is one of the oldest temples in Greece.

The Philippeion, commissioned by Philip II, honors the dynasty of Macedonian kings.

Main entrance

Olympia Archaeological Museum

Pheidias's Workshop
A huge statue of Zeus was made here. The ruins include those of a 5th-century AD basilica.

The Heroön housed an altar dedicated to an unknown hero.

0 meters   50

0 yards   50

Palaestra
This was a training center for wrestlers, boxers, and long-jumpers. Much of the colonnade which surrounded the central court has been reconstructed.

Stadium Entrance
Late in the 3rd century BC, the stadium entrance acquired a vaulted ceiling, part of which survives. The existing stadium was the third laid out at Olympia.

THE ANCIENT PENTATHLON

Sprinting, boxing, wrestling, javelin and discus-throwing, and the long jump (using swinging weights) made up the ancient pentathlon games in Olympia. From 720 BC, male athletes competed naked and women were excluded from attending.

The Treasuries, which stored votive offerings from their donor city-states, looked like miniature temples.

The Metroön was a Doric shrine to the pre-Olympian goddess Rhea.

South Hall

Altar of Oaths

The Bouleuterion, or council house, was the seat of the Olympic Senate.

Sanctuary entrance

The Leonidaion, with its clover-shaped water-garden, accommodated distinguished guests.

RECONSTRUCTION OF OLYMPIA (AD 100)

This shows Olympia as it was under the Romans. The worship of Zeus still predominated; the games were dedicated to him, and his temple (containing a huge statue of the god) was at the heart of the Olympian enclosure (▷ *Classical Style p231*).

Temple of Zeus
Though only column bases and tumbled sections remain, they clearly indicate the grandeur of this 5th-century BC Doric temple.

KEY DATES

3rd millennium BC Site of Olympia is inhabited for the first time.

776 BC The first recorded Olympic Games take place at Olympia.

AD 551 Earthquake destroys most of Olympia.

AD 600 Alfeiós River begins to bury the site in silt.

1766–1870 German archaeologists excavate the Olympia site.

1989 Olympia is inscribed a UNESCO World Heritage Site.

THE ORIGIN OF THE OLYMPIC GAMES

The establishment of the Olympic Games in 776 BC is traditionally treated as the first certain event in Greek history. Originally, men's sprinting was the only event and competitors were local men; the first recorded victor was Koroivos, a cook from nearby Elis. During the 8th and 7th centuries BC, wrestling, boxing, equestrian events, and boys' competitions were added. The elite of many cities came to compete although, until the Romans took charge in 146 BC, entry was restricted to Greeks. Local cities disputed control of the games, but a truce guaranteed safe conduct to spectators and competitors. As the games were part of a pagan festival, the Christians did not approve of them and they were banned in AD 393. The games were revived in 1896.

**Holy Cave of the Apocalypse
where St John lived and worked**

ST JOHN AND THE HOLY CAVE

Inside the church of Agía Anna, near the Monastery of St John, is the Holy Cave of the Apocalypse. It is here that St John saw his vision of fire and brimstone inspiring the *Book of Revelation,* which he dictated to his disciple, Próchoros. Inside the cave is the rock where the *Book of Revelation* was written and the indentation where St John is said to have rested his head. There are 12th-century wall paintings and icons from 1596 of St John and the Blessed Christodoulos by the Cretan painter Thomás Vathás. St John is said to have heard the voice of God coming from a cleft in the rock, still visible today.

CHRISTODOULOS

Christian monk Christodolous (slave of Christ) was born in the early 11th century in Asia Minor. He spent much of his life building monasteries on several Greek islands. He was given permission by the Byzantine Emperor Alexios I Comnenos (r.1081–1118) to build a temple on Pátmos, in honor of the Apostles. Christodolous laid the first foundation stone for the Monastery of St John, but died in 1093 before it was completed. His remembrance celebrations are held each year in Pátmos on 16 March and 21 October.

Monastery of St John, Pátmos

THE MONASTERY OF ST JOHN is one of the most important places of worship among Orthodox and Western Christian faithful alike. It was founded in 1088 by a monk, the Blessed Christodoulos, in honor of St John the Divine, author of the *Book of Revelation*. One of the richest and most influential monasteries in Greece, its towers and buttresses make it look like a fairy-tale castle, but were built to protect its religious treasures, which are now the star attraction for the thousands of pilgrims and tourists.

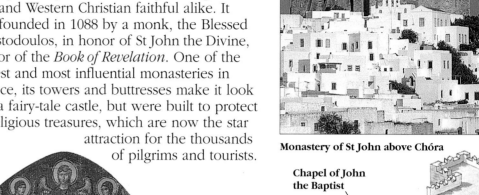

Monastery of St John above Chóra

The Hospitality of Abraham
This is one of the most important of the 12th-century frescoes that were found in the chapel of the Panagía. They had been painted over but were revealed after an earthquake in 1956.

The monks' refectory has two tables made of marble taken from the Temple of Artemis, which originally occupied the site.

Kitchens

Inner courtyard

Chapel of John the Baptist

The Chapel of Christodoulos contains the tomb and silver reliquary of the Blessed Christodoulos.

★ Icon of St John
This 12th-century icon is the most revered in the monastery and is housed in the katholikón, *the monastery's main church.*

STAR FEATURES

★ **Icon of St John**

★ **Main Courtyard**

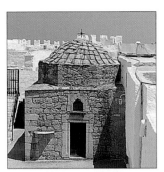

Chapel of the Holy Cross

This is one of the monastery's ten chapels built because church law forbade Mass being heard more than once a day in the same chapel.

SHIP OF STONE

Close to Pátmos is a rock which resembles an upturned ship. Legend says that Christodoulos, discovering that a pirate ship was on its way to Pátmos, seized an icon of John the Evangelist and pointed it at the ship, turning it to stone.

Chrysobull

This scroll of 1088 in the treasury is the monastery's foundation deed, sealed in gold by the Byzantine Emperor Alexios I Comnenos.

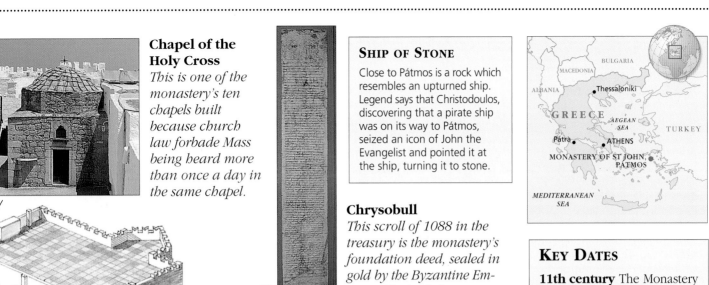

The treasury houses over 200 icons, 300 pieces of silverware and a dazzling collection of jewels.

★ Main Courtyard

Frescoes of St John from the 18th century adorn the outer narthex of the katholikón, *whose arcades form an integral part of the courtyard.*

The Chapel of the Holy Apostles lies just outside the gate of the monastery.

KEY DATES

11th century The Monastery of St John is constructed.

1999 The Monastery of St John and the Cave of the Apocalypse are inscribed a UNESCO World Heritage Site.

THE LIBRARY

The ▷ *treasury*, also known as the library, contains a vast and important collection of theological and Byzantine works. There is a central room, decorated with stone columns supporting plastered arches, off which are other rooms displaying religious artifacts. Priceless icons and sacred art, such as vestments, chalices, and Benediction crosses, are on view. Floor-to-ceiling bookcases, built into the walls, store religious manuscripts and biographical materials, many written on parchment. Manuscripts of important note include the *Book of Job*, sermons by St George the Theologue, the Purple Code, and a volume containing images of the Evangelists, dating from the 14th century, entitled *Gospel of Four*. The library also possesses 15th- to 18th-century embroidered stools and mosaics, as well as beautiful 17th-century furnishings. There are also garments worn by past bishops, some woven in gold thread. Patriarchal seals from Byzantine emperors and princes can be found in the library, along with the foundation deed (▷ *Chrysobull*) donated by Emperor Alexios I Comnenos.

NIPTIR CEREMONY

The Orthodox Easter celebrations on Pátmos are some of the most important in Greece. Hundreds of people visit Chóra to watch the *Niptír* (washing) ceremony on Maundy Thursday. The abbot of the Monastery of St John publicly washes the feet of 12 monks, re-enacting Christ's washing of His disciples' feet before the Last Supper. The rite was once performed by the Byzantine emperors as an act of humility.

Embroidery of Christ washing the disciples' feet

The main entrance has slits for pouring boiling oil over marauders. This 17th-century gateway leads up to the cobbled main courtyard.

Palace of the Grand Masters

MOSAIC FLOORS AND STATUES FROM KOS

During the restoration of the Palace of the Grand Masters, beautiful early Christian, Hellenistic, and Roman mosaics were brought in from the nearby island of Kos. These were used to rebuild the floors throughout the palace, including those of the ▷ *Chamber with Colonnades* and the ▷ *Medusa Chamber*. The magnificent statues displayed in the ▷ *Central Courtyard* were also taken from Kos; they date from the Hellenistic and Roman periods.

THE KNIGHTS OF RHODES

Founded in the 11th century by merchants from Amalfi, the Order of Knights Hospitalers of St John guarded the Holy Sepulcher and defended Christian pilgrims in Jerusalem. They became a military order after the First Crusade (1096–9), but took refuge in Cyprus when Jerusalem fell in 1291 to the Mamelukes. They then bought Rhodes from the Genoese and conquered the Rhodians in 1309. A Grand Master was elected for life to govern the Order, which was divided into seven Tongues, or nationalities: France, Italy, England, Germany, Spain, Provence, and Auvergne. Each Tongue protected an area of the city wall known as a Curtain. The Knights fortified the Dodecanese with around 30 castles and their defenses are some of the finest examples of medieval military architecture.

Odos Ippotón – ancient street used by the Knights of Rhodes

Palace of the Grand Masters, Rhodes

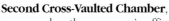

A FORTRESS WITHIN a fortress, this was the seat of 19 Grand Masters, the nerve centre of the Collachium, or Knights' Quarter, and last refuge for the Rhodians in times of danger. Built in the 14th century, it survived earthquake and siege, but was blown up by an accidental explosion in the mid-19th century. It was restored by the Italians in the early 20th century for Mussolini and King Victor Emmanuel III. The palace has some priceless mosaics from sites in Kos, after which some of the rooms are named. It also houses two exhibitions: Medieval Rhodes and Ancient Rhodes.

Gilded angel candleholder

Chamber with Colonnades
An early Christian mosaic from the 5th century AD decorates the floor. Two elegant colonnades support the roof.

Thyrsus Chamber

Second Cross-Vaulted Chamber, once used as the governor's office, is paved with an intricately decorated early Christian mosaic from Kos dating from the 5th century AD.

First Cross-Vaulted Chamber

★ Medusa Chamber
The mythical Gorgon Medusa, with hair of writhing serpents, forms the centerpiece of this important late Hellenistic mosaic. The chamber also features Chinese and Islamic vases.

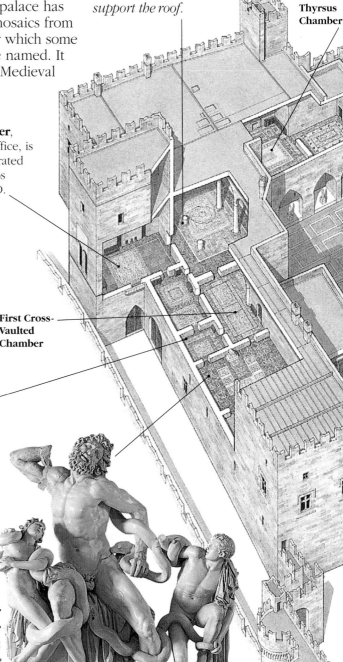

Laocoön Chamber
A copy of the sculpture of the death of the Trojan Laocoön and his sons dominates the hall. The 1st-century BC original by Rhodian masters Athenodoros, Agesandros, and Polydoros is in the Vatican.

The battle-ments and heavy fortifications of the palace were to be the last line of defense in the event of the city walls being breached.

THE MEN OF THE ORDER

Men were drawn from noble Roman Catholic families all over Europe to join the Order of the Knights of St John; however, there were never more than 600 knights at one time. Those who entered the Order swore vows of chastity, obedience, and poverty.

KEY DATES

14th century The Palace of the Grand Masters is constructed.

1856 The palace is accidentally demolished by a gunpowder explosion.

1937–40 The building is restored by Italian architect Vittorio Mesturino.

1988 The Medieval City of Rhodes, which includes the Palace of the Grand Masters, is inscribed a UNESCO World Heritage Site.

EXHIBITIONS

In the south and west wings of the Palace of the Grand Masters is the splendid Medieval Rhodes exhibition. Covering the 4th century AD to the Turkish Conquest (1522), it gives an insight into trade and everyday life in Byzantine and medieval times, with Byzantine icons, Italian and Spanish ceramics, armor, and military memorabilia. The Ancient Rhodes exhibition is situated off the ▷ *central courtyard* in the north wing. It details 45 years of archaeological investigations on the island with a marvelous collection of finds. Some of the exhibits include vases and figurines from the prehistoric period up to 408–7 BC, excavated from the Minoan site at Trianda. There are also grave stelae, jewelry, and pottery from the tombs of Kamiros, Lindos, and Ialysos, which date from the 8th and 9th centuries BC.

★ **Central Courtyard**
Hellenistic statues taken from the Odeion in Kos line the central courtyard. Its north side is paved with geometric marble tiles.

Entrance to Ancient Rhodes exhibition

Chamber of the Nine Muses has a late Hellenistic mosaic featuring busts of the Nine Muses of Greek myth.

★ **Main Gate**
This imposing entrance, built by the Knights, has twin horseshoe-shaped towers with swallowtail turrets. The coat of arms is that of Grand Master del Villeneuve, who ruled from 1319–46.

Entrance

First Chamber, with its 16th-century choir stalls, features a late Hellenistic mosaic.

Grand staircase

Entrance to Medieval Rhodes exhibition

Second Chamber has a late Hellenistic mosaic and carved choir stalls.

THE FIRST GRAND MASTER

The first Grand Master, or Magnus Magister of the Knights, was Foulkes de Villaret (1305–19), a French knight. He negotiated to buy Rhodes from the Lord of the Dodecanese, Admiral Vignolo de Vignoli, in 1306. This left the Knights with the task of conquering the island's inhabitants. The Knights of Rhodes, as they became known, remained here until their expulsion in 1522. The Villaret name lives on in Villaré, one of the island's white wines.

Foulkes de Villaret

MAGNUS MAGISTER
FRATER FULCUS DEVILLARET
1305 1319

STAR FEATURES

★ **Medusa Chamber**

★ **Central Courtyard**

★ **Main Gate**

Palace of the Grand Masters

Palace of Knosós

RESTORED AREAS

Shield motif, Knosós

Parts of the Palace of Knosós were imaginatively restored by Sir Arthur Evans in the early 20th century. His interpretation is the subject of academic controversy, but his reconstruction of the palace gives a brilliant impression of life in Minoan Crete. Some noteworthy areas include the ▷ *West Magazines*, which contained storage jars or ▷ *giant pithoi*, the ▷ *Throne Room*, where ritual bathing is thought to have taken place, and the ▷ *Grand Staircase* made of gypsum, which provided access from the colonnaded courtyard up to the ▷ *Royal Apartments* decorated with frescoes of floral and animal motifs.

THE MINOAN DOUBLE AX AND LABYRINTH

The Minoan double ax served both as a common tool used by carpenters, masons, and shipbuilders, and as an extremely powerful sacred symbol thought to have been a cult object connected with the Mother Goddess. Evidence of the importance of the ax for the Minoans is clear from the many vases, *larnakes* (clay coffins), seals, frescoes, and pillars that were inscribed or painted with the ceremonial double ax, including the walls of the Palace of Knosós. The ceremonial ax is often depicted between sacred horns or in the hands of a priest. Votive *azes* (ritual offerings) were highly decorated and made of gold, silver, copper, or bronze. According to myth, the Labyrinth (maze) at Knosós was designed by Daedalus as the "dwelling place of the double ax" and the Minotaur. Daedalus was later imprisoned in the maze by King Minos, who was angry with him for disclosing the secret of the Labyrinth to Ariadne.

Palace of Knosós, Crete

BUILT AROUND 1900 BC, the first palace of Knosós was destroyed by an earthquake in about 1700 BC and was soon completely rebuilt. The restored ruins visible today are almost entirely from this second palace. The focal point of the site is its vast north–south aligned Central Court, off which lie many of the palace's most important areas. The original frescoes are in the National Archaeological Museum of Irákleio.

View across the Central Court towards the northeast

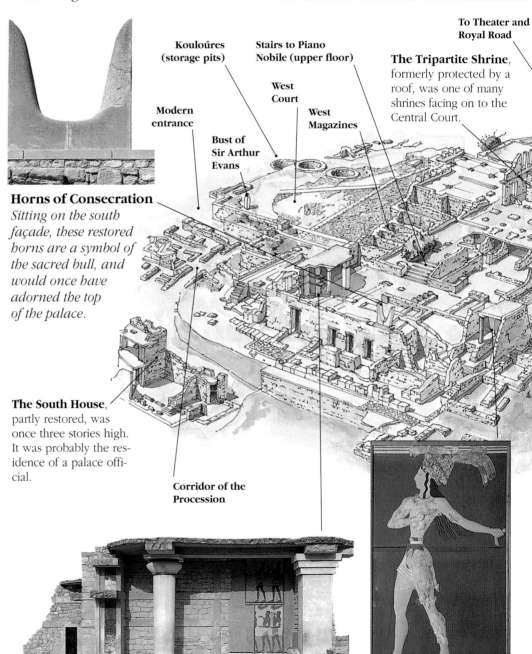

Kouloúres (storage pits)

Stairs to Piano Nobile (upper floor)

West Court

West Magazines

Modern entrance

Bust of Sir Arthur Evans

To Theater and Royal Road

The Tripartite Shrine, formerly protected by a roof, was one of many shrines facing on to the Central Court.

Horns of Consecration
Sitting on the south façade, these restored horns are a symbol of the sacred bull, and would once have adorned the top of the palace.

The South House, partly restored, was once three stories high. It was probably the residence of a palace official.

Corridor of the Procession

South Propylon
Entrance to the palace was through this monumental, pillared gateway, decorated with a replica of the Cup-Bearer figure, a detail from the Procession fresco.

★ Priest-King Fresco
This replica of the Priest-King *fresco, also known as the* Prince of the Lilies, *is a detail from the* Procession *fresco and depicts a figure wearing a crown of lilies and feathers.*

THE MINOTAUR

In legend, Knosós was believed to be the site of an underground Labyrinth designed to imprison the Minotaur. This half-man, half-bull was born of King Minos's wife, Pasiphaë. The Minotaur was slain by Theseus, who was aided by his lover Ariadne.

★ Throne Room

With its adjoining antechamber and lustral basin, the Throne Room is believed to have served as a shrine. The original stone throne, thought to be that of a priestess, is guarded by a restored fresco of griffins, sacred symbols in Minoan times.

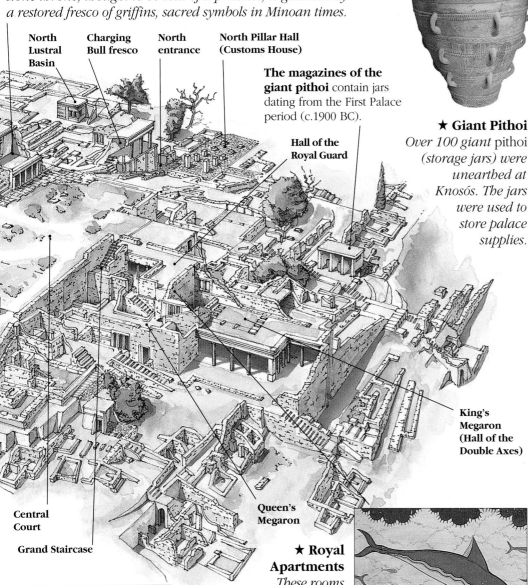

North Lustral Basin

Charging Bull fresco

North entrance

North Pillar Hall (Customs House)

The magazines of the giant pithoi contain jars dating from the First Palace period (c.1900 BC).

Hall of the Royal Guard

★ Giant Pithoi
Over 100 giant pithoi (storage jars) were unearthed at Knosós. The jars were used to store palace supplies.

King's Megaron (Hall of the Double Axes)

Central Court

Grand Staircase

Queen's Megaron

★ Royal Apartments
These rooms include the King's Megaron, also known as the Hall of the Double Axes; the Queen's Megaron, which is decorated with a copy of the famous dolphin fresco and has an en suite bathroom; and the Grand Staircase.

STAR FEATURES

★ **Priest-King Fresco**

★ **Throne Room**

★ **Giant Pithoi**

★ **Royal Apartments**

KEY DATES

c.1900 BC The first Palace of Knosós is constructed.

c.1700 BC The palace is destroyed by an earthquake and a second palace is built.

c.1370 BC The second palace is destroyed by fire.

1818 Archaeologist Mínos Kalokairinós begins excavation of the site.

1900–29 Sir Arthur Evans partly restores the Palace of Knosós site.

NATIONAL ARCHAEO-LOGICAL MUSEUM

The world's most important collection of Minoan artifacts is housed in the National Archaeological Museum in Irákleio. The collection gives a unique insight into the highly sophisticated civilization that existed on Crete over 3,000 years ago. Treasures amassed from Knosós include frescoes, stone vessels, figurines, and ceramics. These impressive finds include a 16th-century Bull's Head *rhyton* (vessel) used for the pouring of ritual wines. It is carved from steatite, a black stone, with inset rock crystal eyes and a mother-of-pearl snout. There are also two 1600 BC bare-breasted figurines, which are thought to represent the snake goddess or a priestess performing religious rituals. On view in the Hall of Frescoes is an elaborate frescoed Agía Triáda sarcophagus, dating from around 1400 BC.

ISLAMIC ARTS MUSEUM

The Museum of Turkish and Islamic Arts *(Türk ve Islam Eserleri Müzesi)* is located in the *medrese* (college) of the Selimiye Mosque. The museum's first room is devoted to the local sport of grease-wrestling. It includes enlarged reproductions of historic miniatures depicting 600 years of the sport. These show the wrestling stars resplendent in their leather shorts, their skin glistening with olive oil. Other objects on display in the museum include the original doors of the Beyazit II Mosque, built in 1484–8 on the northern bank of the Tunca River, 1.5 km (1 mile) from the center of Edirne. Korans and calligraphic art can be seen, too. There are also military exhibits. Among them are some beautiful 18th-century Ottoman shields, with woven silk exteriors, and an imperial tent used during military campaigns.

IMPERIAL ARCHITECT

In 1512, during the annual roundup of Christian youths for the sultan's army, a stonemason and carpenter named Joseph was brought from Anatolia to Istanbul. Converted to Islam and given the name Sinan, he was educated at an elite palace school. Sinan became a military engineer, building bridges and fortifications, but won the eye of Süleyman the Magnificent, who made him imperial architect in 1538. Mimar Koca Sinan ("Great Architect Sinan") created spectacular masterworks for his patron, such as the Süleymaniye (1550–57), Istanbul's most important mosque. In his lifetime he built 131 mosques and 200 other buildings, including palaces, schools, and tombs. He died aged 97.

**Mimar Koca Sinan
(c.1491–1588)**

Selimiye Mosque, Edirne

THE GREATEST OF ALL the Ottoman mosque complexes, the Selimiye is the apogee of an art form and the symbol of Edirne. Built on a slight hill, the mosque is a prominent landmark. Its complex includes a *medrese*, now housing the Museum of Turkish and Islamic Arts, a school, and the Kavaflar Arasta, a covered bazaar. Selim II commissioned the mosque which took 6 years to build and was completed in 1575. It was the culmination of a life's ambition for its architect, Sinan, who designed a unique octagonal supporting system, dispersing the weight of the grand dome across a symmetrical network of walls and pillars. The use of more windows casts abundant light into the interior creating an illusion of breathtaking spaciousness beneath the dome. As is customary in Sinan's works, design elements are exposed on the exterior, revealing ornate domes and marble columns.

STAR FEATURES

* ★ **Minarets**
* ★ **Dome**
* ★ **Minbar**

★ Minarets
The mosque's four slender minarets tower to a height of 84 m (275 ft). Each one has three balconies. The two northern minarets contain three intertwining staircases, each one leading to a different balcony.

Ablutions Fountain
Intricate, pierced carving decorates the top of the 16-sided open şadırvan (ablutions fountain), which stands in the centre of the courtyard. The absence of a canopy helps to retain the uncluttered aspect.

The columns supporting the arches of the courtyard are made of marble blocks plundered from Byzantine architecture.

Courtyard Portals
Alternating red and honey-colored slabs of stone were used to build the striking arches above the courtyard portals. This echoes the decoration of the magnificent arches running around the mosque courtyard itself.

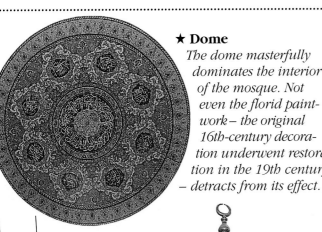

★ Dome
The dome masterfully dominates the interior of the mosque. Not even the florid paint-work – the original 16th-century decoration underwent restoration in the 19th century – detracts from its effect.

CALL TO PRAYER

Only imperial mosques such as Selimiye have more than one minaret. Formerly made by the *muezzin* (mosque official) from the minaret's balcony, the call to prayer is now broadcast over loudspeakers.

KEY DATES

1413–58 Prior to Constantinople, Edirne is the capital of the Ottoman Empire.

1538 Sinan becomes chief architect to Süleyman I, the Magnificent.

1569 Selim II succeeds Süleyman I and commissions Sinan to build a mosque at Edirne, the Selimiye.

1574 Selim II dies a year before his mosque is completed.

★ Minbar
Many experts claim that the Selimiye's minbar, with its conical tiled cap, is the finest in Turkey. Its lace-like side panels are exquisitely carved.

Mihrab, cut from Marmara marble

The Interior
The mosque is the supreme achievement of Islamic architecture. Its octagonal plan allows for a reduction in the size of the buttresses supporting the dome. This permitted extra windows to be incorporated, making the interior exceptionally light.

The *muezzin mahfili* still retains original, intricate 16th-century paintwork on its underside. Beneath it is a small fountain.

INSIDE A MOSQUE

A typical mosque is a charitable foundation as well as a place of worship. Around its periphery are a *ban* or *caravanserai* to provide accommodations for travelers, a kitchen, hospital, theological colleges, and baths. In the courtyard there is an ▷ *ablutions fountain* or row of taps for the washing of the head, hands, and feet before worship. Inside the often exquisitely decorated prayer hall (▷ *the interior*), men and women pray separately – the women often using a screened-off area. A central ▷ *muezzin mahfili* provides a platform for the *muezzin* (mosque official) to chant his responses to the prayers of the *imam* (head of the mosque). The *imam* delivers his sermon from a lofty ▷ *minbar* (pulpit). Next to the pulpit is the ▷ *mihrab*, an ornate niche in the wall, which marks the direction of Mecca. The ▷ *sultan's loge* is a screened balcony for the sultan to pray in safety.

Entrance from Kavaflar Arasta

Sultan's Loge
The imperial loge is supported by green marble columns. They are connected by pointed arches, whose surrounds are adorned with floral İznik tiles. Unusually, its ornately decorated mihrab contains a shuttered window, which opened on to countryside when the mosque was built.

Main entrance

LIFE IN THE HAREM

The word *harem* derives from the Arabic for "forbidden." It was the residence of the sultan's wives, concubines, children, and mother (the most powerful woman), who were guarded by black slave eunuchs. The sultan and his sons were the only other men allowed into the harem. The concubines were slaves, gathered from the farthest corners of the Ottoman Empire and beyond. Their aim was to become a favorite of the sultan and bear him a son. Competition was stiff, for at its height the harem had more than 1,000 women. Topkapı's harem was laid out by Murat III in the 16th century. The last women eventually left in 1909.

The harem's Imperial Hall, used for staging entertainments

MEHMET II

Blowing apart the mighty city walls and capturing the strategically-important Constantinople from the Byzantines in 1453 was one of Mehmet II's greatest achievements. It marked a turning point in the development of the Ottoman Empire. Mehmet (1432–81) was the son of Murat II and a slave girl. He became known as "the Conqueror", not only for taking Constantinople, but for successful campaigns abroad in the Balkans, Hungary, Crimea, and elsewhere, which enlarged his empire. In his 30 years as sultan, he rebuilt his new capital, reorganized government, codified the law, and set up colleges which excelled in mathematics and astronomy.

Topkapı Palace, Istanbul

Süleyman I's *tuğra* (monogram)

THE OFFICIAL RESIDENCE of the Ottoman Sultans for more than 400 years, the splendid Topkapı Palace was built by Mehmet II between 1459 and 1465, shortly after his conquest of Constantinople. Rather than a single building, it was conceived as a series of pavilions contained by four enormous courtyards, a stone version of the tented encampments from which the nomadic Ottomans had emerged. Initially, the palace served as the seat of government and contained a school in which civil servants and soldiers were trained. However, the government was moved to the Sublime Porte in Istanbul in the 16th century. Sultan Abdül Mecid I left Topkapı in 1853 in favour of Dolmabahçe Palace. In 1924, two years after the sultanate was abolished, it was opened to the public as a museum.

★ **Harem**
This was a labyrinth of exquisite rooms where the sultan's wives and concubines lived.

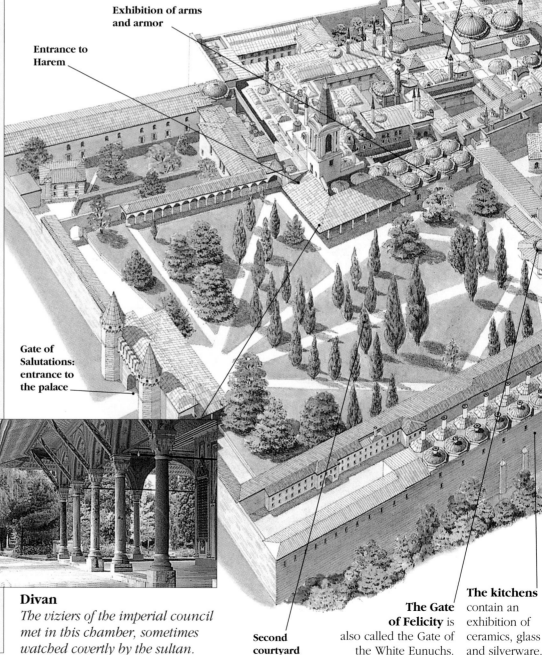

Exhibition of arms and armor

Entrance to Harem

Gate of Salutations: entrance to the palace

Divan
The viziers of the imperial council met in this chamber, sometimes watched covertly by the sultan.

Second courtyard

The Gate of Felicity is also called the Gate of the White Eunuchs.

The kitchens contain an exhibition of ceramics, glass and silverware.

İftariye Pavilion

Under the pavilion's golden roof, Sultan Ahmed III awarded gold coins to those who entertained him during a festival honoring the circumcision of his sons in 1720.

THE CAGE

A new sultan would order the execution of his brothers to avoid succession contests. From the 17th century, brothers were spared, but incarcerated in the notorious "Cage," a set of rooms in the harem.

Baghdad Pavilion

In 1639 Murat IV built this pavilion to celebrate his capture of Baghdad. It has exquisite blue-and-white tilework.

Circumcision Pavilion

Exhibition of clocks

vilion of the ly Mantle

Exhibition of miniatures and manuscripts

The fourth courtyard is a series of gardens dotted with pavilions.

Third courtyard

Library of Ahmet III

Erected in 1719, the library is an elegant marble building. This ornamental fountain is set into the wall below its main entrance.

one m

Hall of the Campaign Pages

★ **Treasury**
This 17th-century jewel-encrusted jug is one of the precious objects exhibited in the former treasury.

STAR FEATURES

★ **Harem**

★ **Treasury**

KEY DATES

1465 The palace is finished.

1574 Grand rebuilding to house Murat III's vast harem.

1640s The Circumcision Pavilion is built.

1665 A fire destroys parts of the Harem and Divan.

PALACE COLLECTIONS

During their 470-year reign, the Ottoman sultans amassed a glittering collection of treasures, which are on display in Topkapı Palace. As well as diplomatic gifts and articles commissioned from palace craftsmen, many items were booty brought back from military campaigns. ▷ *The kitchens* contain cauldrons and utensils used to prepare food for the 12,000 residents, and Chinese porcelain carried along the Silk Route. The ▷ *Treasury* holds thousands of precious and semi-precious stones: highlights include the bejeweled Topkapı dagger (1741), commissioned by the sultan as a gift for the Shah of Persia, and the 86-carat Spoonmaker's diamond said to have been found on an Istanbul rubbish heap in the 17th century. Mehmet II's sumptuous silk kaftan is among the imperial costumes in the ▷ *Hall of the Campaign Pages*. In the ▷ *Pavilion of the Holy Mantle* are some of the holiest relics of Islam, such as the mantle once worn by the Prophet Mohammed. Manuscripts and exquisite copies of the Koran are on display throughout the palace.

Topkapı Palace

Imposing calligraphic roundels from the 19th century

THE FIRST FLOOR

The interior of Haghia Sophia succeeds in imparting a truly celestial feel. Highlights include the fine Byzantine ▷ *Mosaics,* mostly dating from the 9th century or later. The most conspicuous features at ground level are those added by the Ottoman Sultans after the conquest of Istanbul in 1453, when the church was converted into a mosque. These comprise the *mihrab,* a niche indicating the direction of Mecca; the *minbar,* a platform used by the *imam* to deliver sermons; the ▷ *Sultan's loge,* a safe place in which the sultan could pray; and the ▷ *Kürsü,* a throne used by the *imam* while reading from the Koran.

UPPER WALLS AND DOME MOSAICS

The apse is dominated by a large and striking mosaic showing the Virgin with the infant Jesus on her lap. Two other mosaics, unveiled in 867, depict the archangels Gabriel and Michael, yet only fragments of the latter now remain. Portraits of the saints Ignatius the Younger, John Chrysostom, and Ignatius Theophorus adorn niches in the north tympanum. In the concave areas at the base of the dome are mosaics of the six-winged seraphim. The dome itself is decorated with Koranic inscriptions (▷ *Calligraphic roundels*). It was once covered in golden mosaic.

Haghia Sophia, Istanbul

THE "CHURCH OF HOLY WISDOM", Haghia Sophia is among the world's greatest architectural achievements. More than 1,400 years old, it stands as a testament to the sophistication of the 6th-century Byzantine capital and had a great influence on architecture in the following centuries. The vast edifice was built over two earlier churches and inaugurated by Emperor Justinian in 537. In the 15th century the Ottomans converted it into a mosque: the minarets, tombs, and fountains date from this period. To help support the structure's great weight, the exterior has been buttressed on numerous occasions, which has partly obscured its original shape.

Print of Haghia Sophia from the mid-19th century

Byzantine Frieze
Among the ruins of the monumental entrance to the earlier Haghia Sophia (dedicated in AD 415) is this frieze of sheep.

Seraphim adorn the pendentives at the base of the dome.

Calligraphic roundel

Kürsü

Buttress

Imperial Gate

Entrance

Outer narthex

Inner narthex

The galleries were originally used by women during services.

HISTORICAL PLAN OF HAGHIA SOPHIA

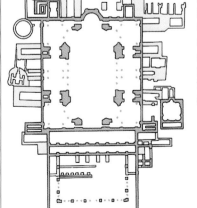

Nothing remains of the first 4th-century church on this spot, but there are traces of the second one from the 5th century, which burned down in AD 532. Earthquakes have taken their toll on the third structure, strengthened and added to many times.

KEY

☐ 5th-century church

▨ 6th-century church

☐ Ottoman additions

STAR FEATURES

★ **Nave**

★ **Mosaics**

★ **Ablutions Fountain**

★ Nave
Visitors cannot fail to be staggered by this vast space which is covered by a huge dome reaching to a height of 56 m (184 ft).

WEEPING PILLAR
Crowds often gather around the pillar of St Gregory the Miracle-Worker in the north-west corner of the ground floor. Moisture seeping from this brass-clad column is believed to have healing powers.

Brick minaret

★ Mosaics
The church's splendid Byzantine mosaics include this one at the end of the south gallery. It depicts Christ flanked by Emperor Constantine IX and his wife, the Empress Zoe.

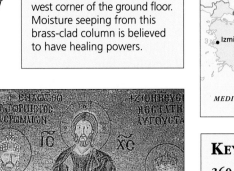

Sultan's loge

Muezzin mahfili

The Coronation Square served for the crowning of emperors.

Mausoleum of Mehmet III

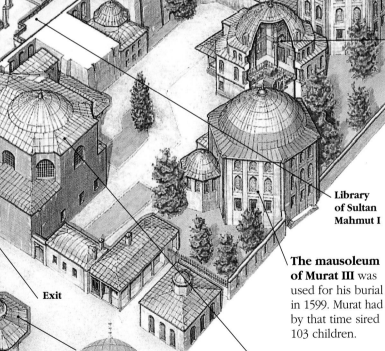

Exit

Library of Sultan Mahmut I

The mausoleum of Murat III was used for his burial in 1599. Murat had by that time sired 103 children.

The Baptistry, part of the 6th-century church, now serves as the tomb of two sultans.

★ Ablutions Fountain
Built around 1740, this fountain is an exquisite example of Turkish Rococo style. Its projecting roof is painted with floral reliefs.

Mausoleum of Selim II
The oldest of the three mausoleums was completed in 1577 to the plans of Sinan, Süleyman I's imperial architect. Its interior is entirely decorated with İznik tiles.

KEY DATES

360 Inauguration of the first church on the site.

532 Architects Anthemius of Tralles and Isidore of Miletus are commissioned to build Haghia Sophia.

1453 Ottomans convert the church into a mosque.

1934 Haghia Sophia opens as a museum.

BYZANTINE STYLE

When Emperor Constantine I (r.306–337) chose Byzantium for his capital and renamed it Constantinople, he amassed artists, architects, and craftsmen to build his new imperial city. They came mainly from Rome, bringing with them an early Christian style. To this were added eastern influences and a distinctive Byzantine style evolved. Churches once based on a longitudinal design became centralized, such as Haghia Sophia, with an eastern apse and three aisles. Mosaics covered the interiors, depicting angels, archangels, and saints in strict hierarchy. The Virgin Mary would be pictured in one of the domes. Figures were front-on, with large, penetrating eyes, and set against a gold background. Individual features were flattened to give a spiritual look. Sculpture took the form of small relief carving and frescoes rather than figures. The Byzantines were also sophisticated metalworkers, producing great bronze doors inlaid with silver for their churches.

Haghia Sophia

İZNIK CERAMICS

At the peak of its production in the late 16th century, the lakeside town of İznik in southern Marmara had more than 300 kilns producing the finest ceramics in the Ottoman world. Sultan Mehmet I brought potters from Persia to İznik in the early 15th century. They made vessels, plates, and tiles glazed in brilliant blue and white with floral patterns and animal motifs. The designs were inspired by Chinese porcelain imported into Turkey. In the 16th century the "tomato red" color was developed. At that time, wall tiles began to be made in quantity, such as those for the Süleymaniye Mosque in Istanbul. The last major commission was for the 21,043 tiles featuring some 50 different designs for the Blue Mosque in 1609.

İznik tiled wall panel in cobalt blue

VAKIFLAR CARPET MUSEUM

A ramp to the left of the main doorway into the Blue Mosque leads up to the Vakıflar Carpet Museum. It has been installed in what was formerly the mosque's ▷ *Imperial Pavilion*. Built by Ahmet I, the pavilion was used by him and his successors when they attended Friday prayers. The carpets are hidden from potentially destructive sunlight by stained-glass windows. They date from the 16th to the 19th centuries and are mostly from the Anatolian regions of Uşak, Bergama, and Konya. For many years mosques have played a vital role in the preservation of early rugs: all the carpets in this museum lay inside mosques until recently.

Blue Mosque, Istanbul

THE BLUE MOSQUE, which takes its name from the mainly blue İznik tilework decorating its interior, is one of the most famous religious buildings in the world. Serene at any time, it is at its most magical when floodlit at night, its minarets circled by keening seagulls. Sultan Ahmet I commissioned the mosque during a period of declining Ottoman fortunes, and it was built between 1609–16 by Mehmet Ağa, the imperial architect. The splendor of the plans provoked great hostility at the time, because a mosque with six minarets was considered a sacrilegious attempt to rival the architecture of Mecca.

A 19th-century engraving showing the Blue Mosque viewed from the Hippodrome

Thick piers support the weight of the dome.

The loge accommodated the sultan and his entourage during mosque services.

Mihrab

The Imperial Pavilion now houses the Vakıflar Carpet Museum.

Minbar
The 17th-century minbar is intricately carved in white marble. It is used by the imam *during prayers on Friday.*

Prayer hall

Muezzin mahfili

Entrance to courtyard

★ İznik Tiles
No cost was spared in the decoration. The tiles were made at the peak of tile production in İznik.

STAR FEATURES

★ **İznik Tiles**

★ **Inside of the Dome**

★ **View of the Domes**

★ **Inside of the Dome**
Mesmeric designs employing flowing arabesques are painted onto the interior of the mosque's domes and semidomes. The windows which pierce the domes no longer have their original 17th-century stained glass.

SULTAN AHMET I

For the inauguration of the Blue Mosque in 1616, Ahmet I (r.1603–17) wore a turban in the shape of the Prophet's foot as a sign of his humility. He died of typhus in 1617 and was buried near the mosque.

Over 250 windows allow light to flood into the mosque.

Entrance

★ **View of the Domes**
The graceful cascade of domes and semidomes makes a striking sight when viewed from the courtyard below.

Ablutions Fountain
The hexagonal şadırvan is now purely ornamental since ritual ablutions are no longer carried out at this fountain.

Each minaret has two or three balconies.

Exit to Hippodrome

The courtyard covers an area the same size as the prayer hall, balancing the whole building.

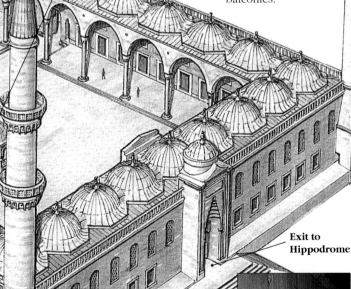

Washing the Feet
The Muslim's ritual ablutions conclude with the washing of the feet. Taps outside the mosque are used by the faithful for this purpose.

KEY DATES

1453 The Ottomans capture Constantinople from the Byzantines and start building mosques.

1616 The Blue Mosque is completed after eight years of construction work.

1617 Sultan Ahmet I dies. He is buried in a marble tomb on the periphery of the Blue Mosque.

MEHMET AĞA

The architect of the Blue Mosque, Mehmet Ağa (1553–1625), arrived in Istanbul as a child in 1563. Five years later he was awarded a scholarship to study at the city's academy of architecture. He was taught by no fewer than three imperial architects, including the Ottoman Empire's greatest, Mimar Koca Sinan, who designed both the Süleymaniye and Selimiye mosques. In the 1570s Murat III sent Mehmet on an extensive tour of Arabia, Egypt, and Europe. He wrote in great detail to the sultan about what he had seen. Under Mehmet III he was made master architect, and then Ahmet I appointed him imperial architect in 1606, commissioning him to build a truly magnificent mosque. Plans were drawn up and in 1609 Ahmet broke the earth for the Blue Mosque using a golden shovel (now on show in the Topkapı Palace). Mehmet supervised the construction of his masterwork, and his name is inscribed on a fountain in the outer courtyard.

Blue Mosque

Rock-cut church entrances, Göreme

CHURCHES OF GÖREME

Of the valley's numerous churches, ▷ *Tokalı Church* ("Church with the Buckle") contains some of the best examples of 10th-century Byzantine wall paintings. The single-nave Old Church, entirely covered with scenes from the Gospels, leads into the barrel-vaulted New Church. This, too, is ornately decorated, showing scenes from the life of Christ. In close proximity to each other are ▷ *Çarıklı Church* ("Church of the Sandals") and the 11th-century Karanlik Church (▷ *Dark Church*). Inside the latter, the ravishing azurite blue used in the frescoes predominates. The ▷ *Barbara Church* is built on the plan of a Greek cross while frescoes in ▷ *Yılanlı Church* ("Church of the Snake") show St George and St Theodore in battle with a serpent.

ST GEORGE

St George is thought to have lived in the 3rd century and died a Christian martyr. Legends dating from the 6th century describe him as a warrior-saint who saved a Libyan king's daughter from a dragon, which he then killed on the understanding that the kingdom would convert to Christianity. A cult grew around him, especially in England during the Crusades, and by the late Middle Ages he was the patron saint of many other locations, including Venice, Portugal, and Catalonia.

Göreme Open-air Museum

THE GÖREME VALLEY HOLDS the greatest concentration of rock-cut chapels and monasteries in Cappadocia. Dating largely from the 9th century onwards, the valley's 30 or more churches were built by cutting rooms out of the soft volcanic tuff. Many of the churches contain superb Byzantine frescoes depicting scenes from the Old and New Testaments, often focusing on the life of Christ and the deeds of the saints. The cultural importance of the valley has been recognized by the Turkish government which has restored and preserved the many caves to create the Göreme Open-air Museum.

Tokalı Church
The Tokalı Church contains some of the most beautiful frescoes in the Göreme Valley. Indigo backgrounds dominate the main chamber frescoes in the New Church.

Fairy chimneys are eroded rock formations, often elongated or in the shape of a cone or pedestal.

★ **Kızlar Monastery**
Monks lived and worked in this hollowed-out formation. Ladders or scaffolding were probably used to reach the upper levels.

STAR FEATURES

★ **Kızlar Monastery**

★ **Dark Church**

★ **Elmalı Church**

Camel Tours
Portions of the Göreme Valley and surrounding area can be viewed from atop a camel on guided tours.

★ **Dark Church**
A pillared church, built around a small courtyard, the Dark Church contains frescoes depicting the Ascension of Christ.

UNDERGROUND CITIES

Not only churches but entire cities with living quarters, stables, wells, and ventilation systems were concealed underground. Derinkuyu, south of Göreme, is thought to have been home to 20,000 people.

Çarıklı Church

Katherina Church

Dining Hall

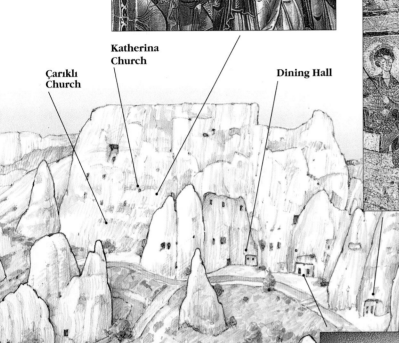

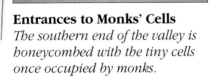

Yılanlı Church
The barrel-vaulted church has painted panels devoted to a number of saints.

KEY DATES

1st century St Paul introduces Christianity to the Cappadocia region.

7th–8th century The arrival of Arab raiding parties drives the local Christian community underground where they form Göreme's underground cities.

1907 A French priest rediscovers the underground cities.

1985 The Göreme Valley is declared a UNESCO World Heritage Site.

VOLCANIC LANDSCAPE

The extraordinary landscape of Cappadocia, as seen in the Göreme Valley, was created around 30 million years ago, when erupting volcanoes blanketed the region with ash. The ash solidified into an easily eroded material called tuff, overlain in places by layers of the hard volcanic rock (basalt). The bewitching natural formations for which the region is celebrated are partly the result of erosion by water, wind, and changes in temperature. Rainfall and rivers wear down the tuff and, like the wind, carry away loose material. During winter, extreme temperature changes cause the rocks to expand and contract and eventually to disintegrate. ▷ *Fairy chimneys*, some up to 40 m (130 ft) high, are an extraordinary example of erosion. Today, these rocks are peppered with openings denoting the churches, dwellings, and even entire cities that have been sculpted within. The volcanoes are now extinct.

Entrances to Monks' Cells
The southern end of the valley is honeycombed with the tiny cells once occupied by monks.

★ **Elmalı Church**
Noted for the sophistication of its frescoes, this church dates from the 11th century.

Barbara Church
The church takes its name from a fresco on the west wall, which is thought to depict St Barbara. A seated figure of Christ occupies the central apse. St George and St Theodore are depicted killing the dragon.

Ephesus

Restored Mural
Murals in the houses opposite the Temple of Hadrian indicate that these were the homes of wealthy people.

O NE OF THE GREATEST ruined cities in the western world, Ephesus defines Classical architecture (▷ *Classical Style p231)*. A Greek city was first settled here in about 1000 BC and it soon rose to fame as a center for the worship of Cybele, the Anatolian Mother Goddess. The city we see today was built by Alexander the Great's successor, Lysimachus, in the 4th century BC. But it was under the Romans that Ephesus became the chief port on the Aegean. Most of the surviving structures date from this period. As the harbor silted up the city declined, but it played an important role in the spread of Christianity. Two great Councils of the early Church were held here in AD 431 and 449. It is said that the Virgin Mary spent her last days nearby and that St John the Evangelist came to care for her.

Statue of Artemis

CHURCH OF ST MARY

Occupying a place of particular significance in the development of Christianity, the Church of St Mary is said to be the first church dedicated to the Blessed Virgin. It was here in AD 431 that the Council of the Church accepted that Jesus, son of the Virgin Mary, was indeed the son of God. Once a Roman warehouse, the long and narrow building has been altered over time and was at one point used for training priests. In the 4th century it was converted into a basilica with a central nave and two aisles. Later, an apse was created on the eastern wall and, to the western side of the church, a circular baptistry with a central pool was built. Additions dating from the 6th century include a domed chapel between the apse and the entrance of the original church. Geometric patterns feature in the balustrading panels between the columns of the nave and in the floor mosaics.

EPHESUS MUSEUM

The Archaeological Museum at Selçuk, 3 km (2 miles) from the excavations, is one of the most important in Turkey. It contains many of the remarkable artifacts uncovered at Ephesus. The museum displays items which have been excavated since World War II. An entire hall is devoted to Artemis, the Greek goddess of chastity, hunting, and the Moon. Other exhibits feature marble and bronze statues, ancient frescoes, and wall paintings, jewels, Mycenean vases, gold and silver coins, Corinthian column heads, tombs, bronze and ivory friezes, and the altar from the ▷ *Temple of Domitian.*

A statue of the goddess Artemis, Ephesus Museum

★ Library of Celsus
Built in AD 114–117 by Consul Gaius Julius Aquila for his father, the library was damaged first by the Goths and then by an earthquake in AD 1000. The statues occupying the niches in front are Sophia (wisdom), Arete (virtue), Ennoia (intellect), and Episteme (knowledge).

THE HOUSE OF MARY

According to the Bible, Jesus asked St John the Evangelist to look after his mother Mary after his death. John brought Mary with him to Ephesus in AD 37, and she spent the last years of her life here in a modest stone house. The house

The house of the Blessed Virgin

of the Blessed Virgin is located at Meryemana, 8 km (5 miles) from the center of Ephesus. The shrine, known as the Meryemana Kultur Parkı, is revered by both Christians and Muslims. Pilgrims visit the shrine, especially on 15 August (Assumption) every year.

The Commercial Agora was the main marketplace of the city.

The brothel was adorned with a statue of Priapus, the Greek god of fertility.

Private houses featured murals and mosaics.

Temple of Domitian

| 0 metres | 200 |
| 0 yards | 200 |

STAR FEATURES

★ **Library of Celsus**

★ **Theater**

★ **Temple of Hadrian**

★ **Theater**
Carved into the flank of Mount Pion during the Hellenistic period, the theater was later renovated by the Romans.

A FISH AND A BOAR

Androklos asked the oracle at Delphi where he should build his city. He was told, "A fish and a boar will show you the place." When he crossed the Aegean and went ashore to cook a fish, a bush caught fire and a boar ran out. Ephesus was founded on that spot.

The skene
(stage building) featured elaborate ornamentation.

Marble Street was paved with blocks of marble.

★ **Temple of Hadrian**
Built to honor a visit by Hadrian in AD 123, the relief marble work on the façade portrays mythical gods and goddesses.

KEY DATES

1000 BC The city of Ephesus is founded by Androklos, son of Kodros, King of Athens.

133 BC Ephesus comes under the rule of Rome. It is made capital of Asia Province.

4th century The harbor silts up, trade decreases, and the city starts to decline.

1869 The first excavations of the city begin.

GENERAL LYSIMACHUS

On the death of Alexander the Great in 323 BC, the Macedonian empire – including Ephesus – was divided among his generals. Lysimachus (360–281 BC) was entrusted with Thrace. He soon added Asia Minor and in 286 BC took Ephesus, heralding a new era for the city. It was a strategic trading port, but the receding coastline and silt-filled harbor threatened its livelihood. Lysimachus dredged the harbor. Then he moved the city to its present site, fortified it with huge walls and renamed it (for a brief time) Arsinoe, after his third wife. The city was soon densely populated and began to prosper. Meanwhile, Arsinoe, eager to ensure that her son and not the son of Lysimachus's first wife would succeed him, persuaded her husband to execute the elder boy on the grounds that he was plotting to kill his father. During the ensuing furore, Asia Minor was attacked by King Seleucus of Syria. Lysimachus was killed in battle.

Gate of Hercules
The gate at the entrance to Curetes Street takes its name from two reliefs showing Hercules draped in a lion skin. Originally a two-story structure, and believed to date from the 4th century AD, it had a large central arch with winged victories on the upper corners of the archway. Curetes Street was lined by statues of civic notables.

The Odeon (meeting hall) was built in AD 150.

Baths of Varius

Colonnaded Street
Lined with Ionic and Corinthian columns, the street runs from the Baths of Varius to the Temple of Domitian.

DESIGN AND DEVELOPMENT

The city of Aphrodisias was laid out in grid form in the 1st century BC, with only the ▷ *Temple of Aphrodite* and the ▷ *Theater* at odds to this plan, possibly because they pre-dated it. From the 1st century AD, as Roman influence continued to grow, the major public buildings, south of the temple, took shape. These included the ▷ *Bouleuterion* (Council House), which could seat 1,750 people, the ▷ *Sebasteion* (a temple complex), and the ▷ *Civil Basilica,* all surrounding two colonnaded squares, the ▷ *North and South Agora.* Ionic and Corinthian columns prevailed (▷ *Classical style p231)* and the buildings, some of which were three stories high, were adorned with sculptures of local dignitaries, Roman officials, and emperors, as well as detailed friezes glorifying the empire and depicting scenes from mythology. The demand for such artifacts kept a permanent sculptors' workshop in business from the 2nd to the late 4th century. The site is entered through a massive eastern gateway known as the ▷ *Tetrapylon* (AD 200).

CULT OF APHRODITE

Aphrodite, daughter of Zeus, was the goddess of love and beauty and was worshiped by the ancient Greeks. Sites devoted to her developed around the Mediterranean and from the 5th century BC Greek sculptors began producing statues of her. The statue at the center of the temple in Aphrodisias had distinctive characteristics. Her hands were outstretched and she was clothed in a heavy over-garment. This was divided into sections filled with motifs relating to her mythological powers.

Statue of Aphrodite, goddess of love

Aphrodisias

Marble frieze in the museum

THE REMOTE SITE OF APHRODISIAS is one of the most important archaeological sites in Turkey, with an impressive stadium, a theater and exquisite marble sculptures. As early as 5800 BC the site was a shrine and Neolithic farmers came here to worship the Mother Goddess of fertility and crops. At some point, the site was dedicated to Aphrodite, Greek goddess of love, and during the 2nd century BC it was given the name Aphrodisias. For centuries it remained little more than a shrine but from 74 BC, when the city came under Roman patronage, it grew and prospered as a cultural and artistic hub. During the Byzantine era, the Temple of Aphrodite was converted to a Christian church. Gradually, the city faded into obscurity, later becoming the Turkish village of Geyre.

★ Stadium
The stadium is one of the best-preserved structures of its kind from the Classical era. Spectators would have sat under awnings.

★ Temple of Aphrodite
Fourteen columns of the temple have been re-erected. The lateral colonnades became the nave of the Christian church.

Gable ends were surmounted by statues, called *akroteria.*

The stepped platform was built on a stone foundation.

The west cella was used as a treasury.

PLAN OF APHRODISIAS

North Temenos Complex

Temple of Aphrodite

Odeon

Tetrapylon

Bouleuterion

Museum

Hadrianic Baths

North Agora

Sebasteion

South Agora

Civil Basilica

Theater

Theater Baths

0 meters　　50
0 yards　　50

KEY

Building

STAR FEATURES

★ **Stadium**

★ **Temple of Aphrodite**

★ **Tetrapylon**

★ Tetrapylon
One of the jewels of Aphrodisias, this 2nd-century gateway was reconstructed with four groups of Corinthian columns.

HADRIANIC BATHS

Archaeologists have found the remains of a Roman bath house at Aphrodisias. It comprised five barrel-vaulted chambers with tiled floors. Citizens entered from the ▷ *South Agora* through a colonnaded courtyard. This is rich in sculptures and contains a statue of an old fisherman.

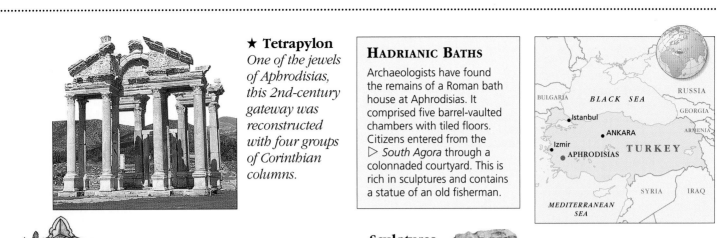

Sculptures
Works produced by the city's famous school of sculpture were exported as far afield as North Africa and Rome. Some are exhibited in the museum.

Decorated friezes

Fluted columns
were constructed from high-quality marble brought from nearby quarries.

RECONSTRUCTION OF THE TEMPLE OF APHRODITE

Completed in the 1st century AD, the temple formed the religious heart of Aphrodisias. Dedicated to Aphrodite, the goddess of love, it housed a cult statue of Aphrodite to which votive offerings were made.

The cult statue
of Aphrodite, with arms outstretched, stood in the cella.

Theater
Constructed in 27 BC, structural changes were made in AD 200 to make it suitable for gladiatorial spectacles.

KEY DATES

1st century BC Aphrodisias develops as a town.

AD 500 The temple is converted into a Christian basilica, columns are moved and a nave created.

14th century Aphrodisias declines in importance.

1961 Archaeologists from New York University start excavating the site.

THE STADIUM, THEATER, AND MUSEUM

Two exceptionally well-preserved auditoria have been uncovered at Aphrodisias, the ▷ *Stadium* to the north of the city and the ▷ *Theater*. As many as 30,000 spectators could be seated in the 1st-century BC stadium, in 30 tiers shaded by awnings. The names of regular visitors can still be seen inscribed on the seats they reserved. Built of marble, the stadium was the venue for Greek-style athletics competitions, music, drama, and Roman gladiatorial games. The theater, with its 27 tiers of seating, also hosted gladiatorial events after the arrival of the Romans. Statues of Apollo, Demos, and the Muses decorated the three-story stage built in 28 BC. A wealth of sculpture has been discovered among the ruins of Aphrodisias, much of which is on display in the museum. The Aphrodite Hall, containing statues of the goddess, is particularly interesting.

Aphrodisias

INSIDE THE MEDERSA

No expense was spared in the lavish decoration of the Bou Inania Medersa. Sultan Abou Inan wanted a building to rival that of Fès's illustrious Karaouiyine Mosque built in 859. The medersa's ▷ *main entrance* is through a hall beneath a domed roof with a stalactite design. An exquisite carved cedar screen featuring knots and stars surrounds the central ▷ *courtyard* and pool, off which open two lecture halls and a ▷ *prayer hall*. Beautiful ▷ *zellij tilework*, ornamental stuccowork, calligraphy, ▷ *stained-glass windows*, and a green-tiled roof complete the decorations. To his glory, an inscription describes Abou Inan as "caliph" (a successor to the Prophet Mohammed).

Calligraphic frieze in cursive script from the Bou Inania

ARABIC CALLIGRAPHY

Islam traditionally forbids all figurative representation and since the 8th century this prohibition has encouraged the use of calligraphy. Decorative writing became an art form that was used not only for manuscripts, but also to embellish buildings such as the Bou Inania Medersa. Writing in an especially fine script the words of the Koran and the 99 names of Allah are considered to be a very pious undertaking. The importance of this art form in Islamic civilization is shown by the carved, painted and tiled friezes that decorate the walls of domes, mosques, and medersas, as well as private homes. A rounded cursive script was used until the 12th century when the angular Maghrebi script from Andalusia became fashionable.

Bou Inania Medersa, Fès

Glazed tiles on the medersa's roof

THIS IS THE LARGEST and most sumptuously decorated medersa ever built by the Merinid dynasty (r.1248–1465). Constructed between 1350 and 1355 by the sultan Abou Inan, it is the only medersa in Morocco that has a *minbar* (pulpit) and a minaret. A mosque, students' residence, and school combined, its functions have determined its architectural complexity. The one-story building, on a rectangular plan, is arranged around a square Moorish courtyard paved with marble and onyx, and surrounded on three sides by a cloister. It is one of the few Islamic religious buildings in Morocco that is open to non-Muslims.

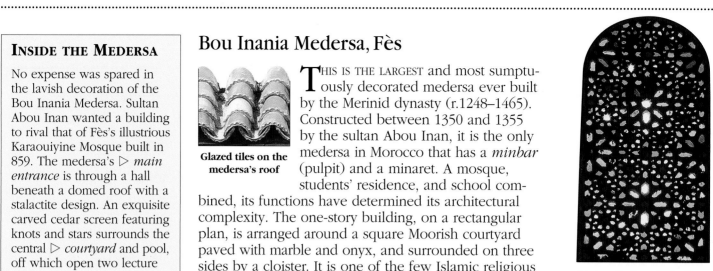

Stained-glass Windows
The windows of the prayer hall feature beautiful stained-glass panels.

Capitals
The carved motifs on the capitals in the medersa show Moorish influence.

Pitched roofs over the mosque

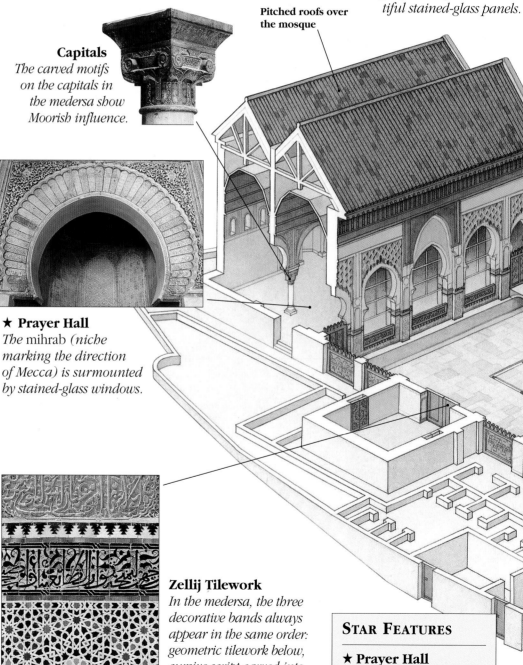

★ Prayer Hall
The mihrab *(niche marking the direction of Mecca) is surmounted by stained-glass windows.*

Zellij Tilework
In the medersa, the three decorative bands always appear in the same order: geometric tilework below, cursive script carved into tiles in the center, and stuccowork above.

STAR FEATURES

★ Prayer Hall

★ Façade

THE MOROCCAN MEDERSA

Student at a medersa

The medersa was both a cultural and a religious establishment. It was primarily a residential college, designed for local students from the town or city and especially for those from the immediate or more distant rural areas, but also for anyone who came in search of learning. It was an extension of the great university-mosque, an institution once dedicated to the study of religion, law, science, and even the arts. It was finally a place of prayer and reflection. The medersas of Fès, home to the greatest scholars in Morocco, were the most highly esteemed in the country.

THE WATER CLOCK

Outside Bou Inania's entrance is a curious water clock (1357), once used to sound the hour of prayer. Now in disrepair, the clock's workings remain a mystery to scholars of today.

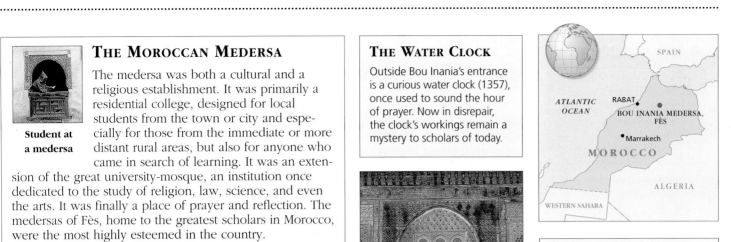

Windows
The upper floor windows of the students' rooms are framed by stuccowork crowned by three-dimensional muqarnas.

★ Façade
Richly decorated with zellij tilework, stuccowork and sculpted wood, the façade runs the gamut of the Moorish decorative repertoire.

The minaret, one of the finest in Fès, is decorated with typical latticework motifs, a frieze crowned by merlons and a splendid lantern.

Shops

Beggars' Gate

Main entrance

Student's cell

Courtyard paved with marble and onyx

Wooden Screen
The magnificent carved wooden screen of the main entrance is framed by sturdy pillars. A nearby door, of much plainer design, is known as Beggars' Gate.

Bou Inania Medersa

KEY DATES

9th century The Berber town of Fès prospers from an influx of 8,000 Arab families from Andalusia bringing skills and learning.

1250 The Merinids choose Fès as their imperial capital.

1666 Conquering Alaouites move the capital to Meknès.

1981 The Medina (old town) of Fès is declared a UNESCO World Heritage Site.

SULTAN ABOU INAN

Born a Merinid, Sultan Abou Inan (r.1349–58) was, like his predecessors, an inspired builder. The Merinids were rulers of Morocco from the mid-13th to the late 15th centuries after capturing Fès in 1248. They went on to capture Marrakech in 1269. Fès was their capital but they also had the fortified Fès el-Jedid (New Fès, now part of the Medina) constructed near the city. Fès el-Jedid housed the army government, administration, and the beautiful Dar el Makzhen palace built for the Merinid rulers. Abou Inan's dynasty reached its peak under his father, Abou el-Hassan, the Black Sultan (r.1331–49). The city was a leading intellectual center with a university, mosques, and medersas. Abou Inan also invited the revered historian, Ibn Khaldun, to his court. Abroad, campaigns in Spain and Tunisia weakened the Merinids. Abou Inan's reign was cut short when he was strangled by a vizier.

The *Decumanus maximus* leading to the Triumphal Arch

THE EXCAVATIONS

Volubilis had lain abandoned for 800 years when, it is said, two diplomats came across the ruins in the late 19th century and interest in its existence was kindled. A team of French archaeologists began the painstaking work of excavating Volubilis in 1915. To date, nearly half the site has been uncovered. With the exception of the Triumphal Arch, the archaeologists found little standing. The powerful Sultan Moulay Ismail (r.1672–1727) had caused enormous destruction when he plundered the site for stone to build his new capital, Meknès. Then a severe earthquake in 1755 toppled many of the remaining structures.

HOUSE OF ORPHEUS

Of the many villas found around the city, the ▷ *House of Orpheus* is remarkable not only for its size, but for the rooms that it contains. Opposite the entrance is a large peristyle courtyard, with a sunken square pool that is decorated with a mosaic of cuttlefish, dolphins, and other sea creatures. The main reception room, looking onto the courtyard, is paved with the Orpheus Mosaic, the largest of the circular mosaics that have been discovered in Volubilis. A richly dressed Orpheus is depicted charming a lion, an elephant, and other animals with his lyre. The house also has an olive oil press with purification tanks, as well as further rooms paved with mosaics in geometric patterns, and bath suites warmed by hypocausts (underfloor heating).

Volubilis

ONCE AN IMPORTANT OUTPOST of the Roman empire, the impressive Classical ruins of Volubilis (▷ *Classical Style p231*) are Morocco's best-preserved Roman site. It was settled and began to prosper under the Mauretanian kings, from the 3rd century BC to AD 40. Temples from this period, as well as a tumulus, have been uncovered. When Mauretania was annexed by Emperor Claudius in AD 45, Volubilis was raised to the status of *municipia* (free town), becoming one of the most important cities in Mauretania Tingitana (Morocco). Buildings in the northeastern quarter date from the 1st century AD, and those around the forum from the 2nd century. After Rome withdrew in the 3rd century, the city declined. It was inhabited by Christians but had been Islamicized when the Berber ruler Idris I came to power in 788.

House of the Columns
This house is arranged around a huge peristyle courtyard with a circular pool. Columns with twisted fluting and composite capitals front the grand reception room.

★ Triumphal Arch
Bestriding the Decumanus maximus, *the triumphal arch overlooks plantations of cereals and olive trees. The fertile plain to the west of Volubilis has provided the area with grain and oil since antiquity.*

Mosaic from the House of Dionysus and the Four Seasons

Gordian Palace

House of the Bathing Nymphs

House of Dionysus and the Four Seasons

Decumanus maximus

The House of the Labors of Hercules is named after a mosaic depicting the Greek hero's 12 labors.

Knight's House

House of the Dog

House of the Athlete

Macellum (market)

STAR FEATURES

★ **Triumphal Arch**

★ **Diana and the Bathing Nymphs**

★ **Basilica**

Tangier Gate

THE SITE OF VOLUBILIS TODAY

The forum, basilica and capitol were
built in the 2nd century, under the Severi
dynasty. Richly appointed residences
paved with mosaics also graced the city.
Each of these buildings is still easily
identifiable on the site today.

House of the Golden Coins

Aqueduct

ARCH OF HONOR

The ▷ *Triumphal Arch* was
erected in AD 217 by governor
Marcus Aurelius Sebastenus in
honor of Emperor Caracalla
and his mother Julia Domna.
It was originally crowned by a
chariot drawn by six horses.

SPAIN

ATLANTIC
OCEAN

RABAT
VOLUBILIS

• Marrakech

MOROCCO

ALGERIA

WESTERN SAHARA

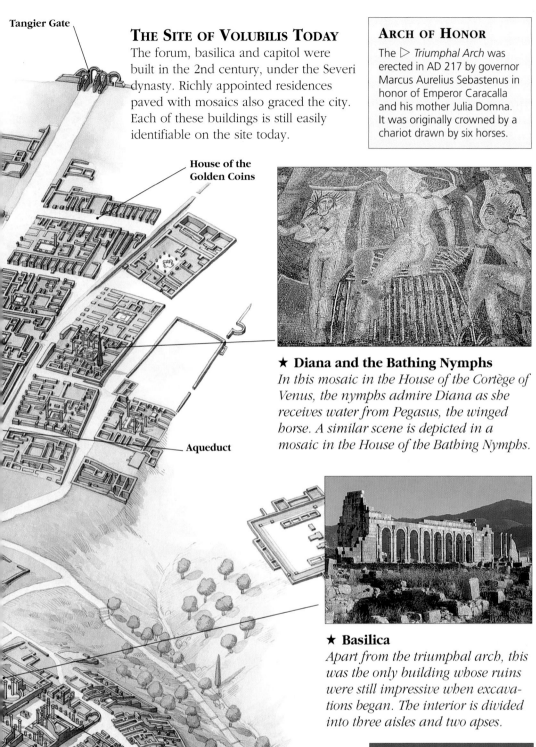

★ Diana and the Bathing Nymphs

*In this mosaic in the House of the Cortège of
Venus, the nymphs admire Diana as she
receives water from Pegasus, the winged
horse. A similar scene is depicted in a
mosaic in the House of the Bathing Nymphs.*

★ Basilica

*Apart from the triumphal arch, this
was the only building whose ruins
were still impressive when excavations began. The interior is divided
into three aisles and two apses.*

Visitors' entrance

The Capitol

*Of the original
building (dating
from the early
3rd century) only
the foundations
remain. The
sacrificial altar,
identifiable by its
molded base, stood
in front of the steps.*

Forum

House of Orpheus

KEY DATES

1st century BC Juba II of
Mauretania makes Volubilis
his capital.

AD 45 The city becomes an
outpost of the Roman Empire.

788 Idris I, founder of the
Idrissid dynasty, adopts
Volubilis as his capital. His
successor prefers Fès and
Volubilis fades from glory.

1997 Volubilis is declared a
UNESCO World Heritage Site.

THE FORUM, BASILICA AND CAPITOL

Like the other major public
buildings in the heart of the
city, the ▷ *Forum* dates
from the early 2nd century. It
was the focal point of public
life and administration, as
well as a meeting place where
business was done. At its
entrance stands the stele of
Marcus Valerius Servus, which
lists the territory that the
citizens of Volubilis possessed
in the hinterland. On the
forum's northern side is the
▷ *Macellum*, a market that
was originally covered. To
the east, a short flight of
steps and three semicircular
arches leads into the
▷ *Basilica*. This was the
meeting place of the curia
(senate), as well as the
commercial exchange and
tribunal, and somewhere for
the people to take a stroll.
On the ▷ *Capitol*, a raised
temple south of the basilica,
public rites were performed
in honor of the divine
protectors of the province,
Jupiter, Juno, and Minerva.

Volubilis

THE ART OF *ZELLIJ*

A highlight of Moroccan architecture is the intricate tilework known as ▷ *zellij*. Throughout the country, and particularly in the great imperial cities of Meknès, Fès, and Marrakech, the otherwise stark walls and floors of palaces, mosques, and mausoleums – such as those of the Mausoleum of Moulay Ismaïl – are adorned with lively patterns and colors. Since Islam forbids the portrayal of living things, Moroccan craftsmen developed their own distinctive art form based on a repertoire of complex geometric designs in vibrant hues. *Zellij* reached its peak in the 14th century but tilemakers today are still in business decorating modern buildings.

MOULAY ISMAÏL

For 55 years Moulay Ismaïl (r.1672–1727) ruled Morocco with an iron hand. A member of the Alaouite dynasty, which still rules the country today, he was utterly ruthless. It is said that he marked his accession by displaying the severed heads of his enemies on the walls of Fès and Marrakech. Order was maintained by his fearsome army, the Black Guard. Moulay Ismaïl moved his capital from Fès to Meknès, transforming it into a glorious imperial city, described as the Versailles of Morocco. He was a contemporary of Louis XIV of France, with whom he was keen to foster relations against Spain, which he thought was a threat.

Sultan Moulay Ismaïl, the great ruler of the Alaouite dynasty

Mausoleum of Moulay Ismaïl, Meknès

ONE OF THE FINEST and grandest buildings in the royal city of Meknès is the Mausoleum of Moulay Ismaïl. It was raised in the 17th century by the great Sultan Moulay Ismaïl, who was fond of large-scale building projects and whose ambition was to transform the small city of Meknès into a capital city. A superb example of Islamic architecture, it was restored and remodeled in the 18th and 20th centuries. The wife of Moulay Ismaïl and his sons, as well as the Sultan Moulay Abder Rahman (1822–59), are laid to rest in the burial chamber, which is decorated with stuccowork and mosaics.

Far-stretching view of Meknès and the mausoleum

Mihrab
The mausoleum's mihrab, *indicating the direction of Mecca, is located in the open courtyard. This is an unusual position.*

Finials
The roof of the mausoleum is topped with five brass spheres identifying the building as a shrine or sacred place.

Prayer Hall
The floor of the prayer hall is covered with mats on which worshipers kneel to pray or to reflect before going into the burial chamber.

Cemetery

Clock presented by Louis XIV

Tomb of Moulay Ismaïl

Decorated Door
This carved and painted wooden door between the ablutions room and the second room of the burial chamber is similar to those of the palaces and fine town houses of Meknès.

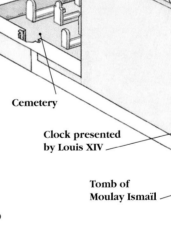

★ Burial Chamber
This consists of a suite of three rooms, including the ablutions room with central fountain (above) and the room containing the tomb of Moulay Ismaïl, and those of his wife and sons.

Mausoleum of Moulay Ismaïl

Entrance to Mausoleum

This imposing carved stone doorway, surmounted by an awning and pyramidal roof, indicates the importance of the royal building.

Empty courtyard

Walls with no windows

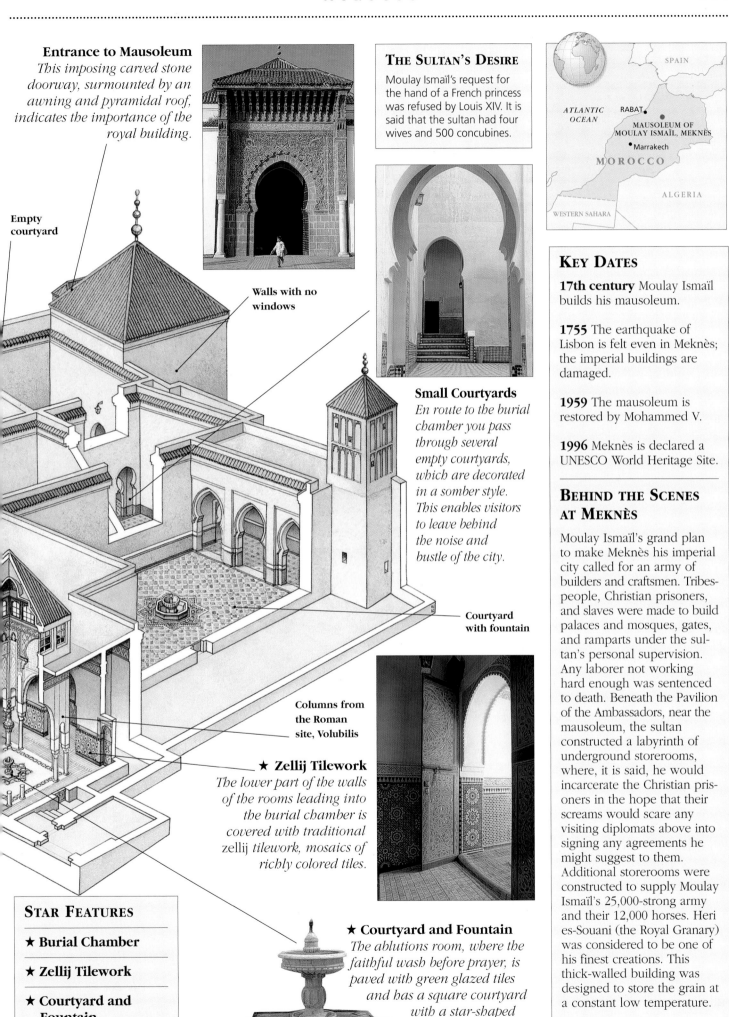

THE SULTAN'S DESIRE

Moulay Ismaïl's request for the hand of a French princess was refused by Louis XIV. It is said that the sultan had four wives and 500 concubines.

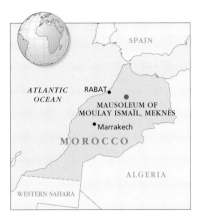

Small Courtyards

En route to the burial chamber you pass through several empty courtyards, which are decorated in a somber style. This enables visitors to leave behind the noise and bustle of the city.

Courtyard with fountain

Columns from the Roman site, Volubilis

★ Zellij Tilework

The lower part of the walls of the rooms leading into the burial chamber is covered with traditional zellij tilework, mosaics of richly colored tiles.

STAR FEATURES

- ★ **Burial Chamber**
- ★ **Zellij Tilework**
- ★ **Courtyard and Fountain**

★ Courtyard and Fountain

The ablutions room, where the faithful wash before prayer, is paved with green glazed tiles and has a square courtyard with a star-shaped fountain and bowl.

KEY DATES

17th century Moulay Ismaïl builds his mausoleum.

1755 The earthquake of Lisbon is felt even in Meknès; the imperial buildings are damaged.

1959 The mausoleum is restored by Mohammed V.

1996 Meknès is declared a UNESCO World Heritage Site.

BEHIND THE SCENES AT MEKNÈS

Moulay Ismaïl's grand plan to make Meknès his imperial city called for an army of builders and craftsmen. Tribes-people, Christian prisoners, and slaves were made to build palaces and mosques, gates, and ramparts under the sultan's personal supervision. Any laborer not working hard enough was sentenced to death. Beneath the Pavilion of the Ambassadors, near the mausoleum, the sultan constructed a labyrinth of underground storerooms, where, it is said, he would incarcerate the Christian prisoners in the hope that their screams would scare any visiting diplomats above into signing any agreements he might suggest to them. Additional storerooms were constructed to supply Moulay Ismaïl's 25,000-strong army and their 12,000 horses. Heri es-Souani (the Royal Granary) was considered to be one of his finest creations. This thick-walled building was designed to store the grain at a constant low temperature.

HASSAN II

Moulay Hassan succeeded to the throne of Morocco on the death of his father, Mohammed V, in 1961. A skillful politician, he alternated liberalizing policies with repression. He introduced the country's first constitution (1962) and parliamentary elections (1963), but the road to reform was rocky. Hassan also successfully defended bids to overthrow him as leader. Abroad, war raged with Algeria over border disputes (1963). When Spain withdrew from the mineral-rich Western Sahara in 1975, Hassan initiated the Green March of 350,000 civilians who crossed the border to assert Morocco's claim to the region. Spain agreed to the transfer of power, but Algerian-backed Polisario Front guerrillas began a violent campaign for independence. A ceasefire was agreed in 1991. Hassan II died in 1999. He was succeeded by Mohammed VI.

INSIDE THE MOSQUE

The waterfront Mosque of Hassan II in Casablanca is the crowning glory of the king's reign. Built for his 60th birthday, the mosque was mainly financed by donations from the Moroccan people. Inside, the massive marble-floored ▷ *prayer hall* sparkles in the glow of Venetian chandeliers. It is said that the hall is large enough to accommodate St Peter's in Rome. Cedar from Morocco's Middle Atlas has been shaped and carved to form ▷ *doors* and screens and the paneling of 70 cupolas. Even the sliding roof is painted and gilded. The ▷ *hammam* (traditional bathhouse) is below the prayer hall.

Mosque viewed from the sea

Mosque of Hassan II, Casablanca

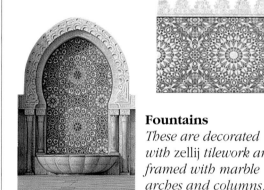

Mosque door, interior view

WITH A PRAYER HALL that can accommodate 25,000, the Mosque of Hassan II is the second-largest religious building in the world after the mosque in Mecca. The complex covers 9,000 sq m (96,840 sq ft), with two-thirds of it built over the sea. The minaret, the lighthouse of Islam, is 200 m (656 ft) high, and two laser beams reaching over a distance of 30 km (18.5 miles) shine in the direction of Mecca. The building was designed by Michel Pinseau and it took 35,000 craftsmen to build it. With carved stucco, *zellij* tilework, a painted cedar ceiling and marble, onyx and travertine cladding, it is a monument to Moroccan architectural virtuosity.

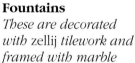

★ Minaret
Its vast size and exquisite decoration make this minaret an exceptional building.

Fountains
These are decorated with zellij *tilework and framed with marble arches and columns.*

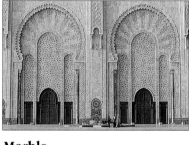

Marble
Used throughout the building on the columns of the prayer hall, doorways, fountains, and stairs, marble is everywhere. It is also sometimes combined with granite and onyx.

Minbar
The minbar, *or pulpit, located at the western end of the prayer hall, is particularly ornate. It is decorated with verses from the Koran.*

STAR FEATURES

★ **Minaret**

★ **Prayer Hall**

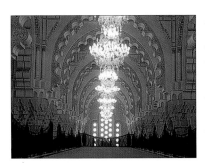

Women's Gallery
Above two mezzanines and hidden from view, this gallery extends over 5,300 sq m (57,000 sq ft) and can hold up to 5,000 women.

VISITING A MOSQUE

Unusually in Morocco, the Mosque of Hassan II is open to non-Muslims. Shoes should be removed, shoulders and knees covered. Men must take off their hats and women are asked to cover their hair.

Dome
The cedar-paneled interior of the dome, over the prayer hall, glistens with carved and painted decoration.

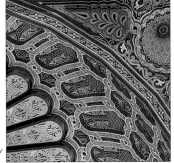

Royal Door
This is decorated with traditional motifs engraved on brass and titanium.

Columns

KEY DATES

1986 Construction begins on the Mosque of Hassan II.

1993 The mosque is completed.

MUSLIM BELIEFS AND PRACTISES

Muslims believe in one God (Allah), and their holy book, the Koran, shares many stories and prophets with the Christian Bible. However, whereas Christians believe that Jesus is the son of God, Muslims hold that he was just one in a line of prophets, the last being Mohammed, who brought the final revelation of God's truth to humankind. Muslims believe that Allah communicated the sacred texts of the Koran to Mohammed through the archangel Gabriel. In their belief in Allah, Muslims pray five times a day wherever they might happen to be. The calls to prayer are broadcast from the mosque. Worshipers who visit a mosque to pray remove their shoes and wash their feet, head, and hands outside before entering the prayer hall. Once inside, depending on the size of the mosque, women and men pray in separate areas. When praying, Muslims face Mecca in Saudi Arabia, the birthplace of Mohammed and also the site of the Kaaba, a sacred shrine built by Abraham. In a prayer hall the direction is indicated by the *mihrab* (a niche in the wall). Kneeling and lowering the head to the ground are gestures of humility and respect for Allah.

Doors
Seen from the exterior, these are double doors in the shape of pointed arches framed by columns. Many are clad in incised bronze.

Mashrabiyya screenwork at the windows protects those within from prying eyes.

Hammam

Stairway to the Women's Gallery
The stairway features decorative woodcarving, multiple arches and marble, granite, and onyx columns, arranged in a harmonious ensemble.

★ Prayer Hall
Able to hold 25,000 believers, the prayer hall measures 200 m (656 ft) by 100 m (328 ft). The central part of the roof can be opened to the sky.

Mosque of Hassan II

Soaring above Koutoubia Mosque, the glorious 12th-century minaret

A MODEL MINARET

The Almohads left their architectural mark not only on Morocco but also on the Iberian peninsula, part of which (known as Al-Andalus) they controlled. Inspired by Koutoubia, Sultan Yacoub el-Mansour (r.1184–99) commissioned a similar but higher tower, the Giralda, for the Great Mosque in Seville (1172–98). In Rabat, Morocco, he initiated another grand project based on Koutoubia: the Hassan Tower (1196), the crowning glory of his massive new mosque. It was intended to surpass Koutoubia and reach a height of 80 m (262 ft) but was unfinished at 44 m (144 ft). Its decorative arches are similar to those of the Giralda.

INSIDE KOUTOUBIA

The great ▷ *prayer hall* covers an area of 5,400 sq m (58,000 sq ft), divided into 16 aisles by 112 columns. Five domes are aligned over the main aisle, directing the eye towards the niche, known as the *mihrab*, which faces Mecca. At one end of the prayer hall is an exquisitely carved *minbar*. This pulpit is one of the few items saved from the former Almoravid mosque that stood on the site, and is thought to have come from Córdoba, Spain, in the early 12th century.

Koutoubia Mosque, Marrakech

IN ABOUT 1147, to mark his victory over the Almoravids, the Almohad sultan Abd el-Moumen set about building one of the largest mosques in the western Muslim world. The mosque and the minaret, a masterpiece of Islamic architecture, were completed during the reign of Yacoub el-Mansour, grandson of Abd el-Moumen. The minaret later served as the model for the Giralda in Seville, as well as for the Hassan Tower in Rabat. The "Booksellers' Mosque" takes its name from the books and manuscripts for sale in the souk that used to surround it. The interior of the minaret contains a gently sloping ramp, which was used by donkeys to carry building materials to the top.

Four gilt-bronze spheres surmount the lantern.

Denticulate merlons

★ Minaret
This splendid tower in pink Gueliz stone stands like a sentinel above the city. It is 70 m (230 ft) high and its proportions obey the canons of Almohad architecture: its height equals five times its width.

The minaret's interior
has six rooms, each above the other.

Entrance to the Koutoubia Courtyard
This restrained and simple entrance follows the design of most gateways to important Moroccan buildings: a horseshoe arch with molded arcature.

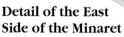

Detail of the East Side of the Minaret
Each side of the minaret has a different decorative scheme. Common to all, with variations, are floral motifs, calligraphic inscriptions, molded terracotta bands, and, as here, windows with festooned arches.

West View of the Minaret
The minaret is the highest building in the city and it stands as a landmark for many miles around. Only Muslims may enjoy the unforgettable view from the top of the building.

Roof of green tiles

Eastern Entrance to the Prayer Hall
This is the main entrance for the faithful. The design of the doorway is relatively plain, with minimal ornamentation.

Courtyard and pool

The interior of the mosque consists of 16 parallel aisles of equal width bisected by a wider nave.

The original mosque was demolished because the *qibla* (direction to be faced during prayer) wall of the mosque was not accurately oriented towards Mecca. It was superseded by the construction that can be seen today.

KEY DATES

1147 Almohad sultan Abd el-Moumen begins construction of the Koutoubia Mosque.

1158 Abd el-Moumen's original mosque is demolished.

1199 Construction of the present-day mosque is completed under the rule of el-Moumen's grandson, Yacoub el-Mansour.

ABD EL-MOUMEN

Morocco flourished under the Almohad dynasty, of which Sultan Abd el-Moumen (r.1130–63) was the founding father. Under his leadership, the Almohads conquered the empire of their Berber rivals, the once powerful but now somewhat decadent Almor-avids (1062–1147), gaining control of Marrakech, Fès, and the great cities of Al-Andalus: Seville, Granada, and Córdoba. As leader of the greatest empire that ever existed in the Muslim west – stretching from Libya in the east to the Iberian peninsula in the north – Abd el-Moumen reorganized its army, administration, and economy. He imposed taxes, created a navy and founded universities. Intellectual life blossomed. In 1162, he proclaimed himself caliph (a successor of the Prophet Mohammed). His passion for splendid architecture was inherited by his grandson, Yacoub el-Mansour. How-ever, under el-Mansour's successors, Spanish strong-holds were lost and the empire declined. In 1248 the Merinids seized power.

STAR FEATURES

★ **Minaret**

★ **Prayer Hall**

★ Prayer Hall
This can accommodate some 20,000 faithful. The white columns supporting horseshoe arches and the braided pattern of the floor create a striking perspective.

Koutoubia Mosque

UQBA IBN NAFI AND KAIROUAN

At the time of the Prophet Mohammed's death in AD 632, Muslims only ruled Arabia. However, by 750 the Arab Muslims had achieved one of the most spectacular conquests in history, ruling over the Middle East, Central Asia, and North Africa. In AD 670 the Muslim leader Uqba ibn Nafi crossed the desert from Egypt as part of the conquest of North Africa. Establishing military posts along the way, he stopped to camp at the location of present-day Kairouan (the word *Qayrawan* means "military camp" in Arabic). Legend tells of a golden cup being discovered in the sand, which was recognized as one that had previously disappeared from Mecca several years before. When the cup was picked up, a spring emerged from the earth which, it was declared, was supplied by the same source as that of the holy Zem-Zem well in Mecca. Uqba founded his capital and swept on to conquer Morocco. Returning home in 683, he was defeated and killed in battle by the Berbers.

ISLAM'S FOURTH HOLIEST CITY

Kairouan grew in importance to become the capital of the Aghlabid dynasty in the 9th century. When the Fatimids took power in AD 909 they moved their capital elsewhere. By the 11th century the city's political and economic power had been surpassed by other cities but it never lost its holy status. As a religious center it continued to grow in prominence with the mosque proving a powerful magnet for Muslim pilgrims. Today, Kairouan is Islam's holiest city in North Africa and its fourth holiest city in the world after Mecca, Medina, and Jerusalem. Pilgrims come to drink the waters of the holy spring and to visit the mosque built by the city's founder.

Great Mosque, Kairouan

Ornately decorated capital

THE MOSQUE OF SIDI UQBA is considered the first mosque to have been built in North Africa, and the city of Kairouan owes its fame as Islam's fourth holiest city to the Great Mosque. The founder of the city, Uqba ibn Nafi, built a small mosque on the site as long ago as AD 670. As the city thrived, the mosque was rebuilt and enlarged several times, in 703, again in 774, in 836 and 863, reaching its current dimensions by the end of the 9th century. Its design and ornamentation continued to evolve through to the 19th century.

Columns
Most of the arched colonnades and columns were salvaged from Roman and Byzantine buildings elsewhere. Some however, were carved by local craftsmen.

★ Minaret
Built between AD 724 and 728, the imposing square minaret is one of the oldest surviving towers of its kind, and is the oldest part of the Mosque. It rises in three sections, each diminishing in size, and is topped by a dome. The lower stories are built of blocks taken from Roman buildings. There are 129 steps leading to its highest point.

Wells provide water for ritual ablutions. They contain water collected from the cistern.

The sundial in the courtyard shows the times of prayer.

Cistern
The courtyard slopes down towards its center where there is a latticed plate shielding a cistern. The plate has a decorative function but also prevents the water, which drains into the cistern, from being polluted.

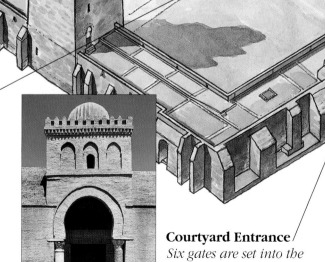

Courtyard Entrance
Six gates are set into the wall surrounding the courtyard. The main entrance is through a gate surmounted by a dome.

Cloisters
Surrounding the courtyard on three sides are cloisters giving shade and protection from the elements.

KAIROUAN CARPETS

Kairouan is a carpet-making center, a tradition going back hundreds of years, and it is renowned for the quality of its rugs. However, the large rug in the ▷ *prayer hall* was a gift from Saudi Arabia.

MEDITERRANEAN SEA

TUNIS

GREAT MOSQUE, KAIROUAN

TUNISIA

ALGERIA

LIBYA

Dome
The exterior of the mosque's dome shows the position of the mihrab, *which indicates the direction of Mecca. It is more richly decorated than the other domes.*

KEY DATES

670 Kairouan is founded by Uqba ibn Nafi who constructs a small mosque.

836 The Great Mosque is renovated and enlarged under the Aghlabids and takes the appearance of what can be seen today.

Mid-9th century The Great Mosque becomes a site for Islamic pilgrimage.

1988 Kairouan is declared a UNESCO World Heritage Site.

INSIDE THE PRAYER HALL

Entrance to the ▷ *prayer hall* at the southern end of the courtyard is through a set of beautiful, finely carved, wooden doors dating from the 19th century. Inside is a rectangular, domed chamber with arched aisles. Most of the stunning 400-odd marble and granite pillars that support the roof were taken from Roman and Byzantine sites, many from Carthage and Sousse. The *imam* leads the prayers from the ▷ *minbar*, a marvelous pulpit sculpted out of wood from Baghdad and thought to be one of the oldest in the Arab world. Behind the *mihrab* (▷ *dome*) at the end of the central aisle are 9th-century tiles also from Baghdad, surrounding carved marble panels. A carved wooden screen, the *maqsura*, dating from the 11th century stands nearby and many Kairouan carpets cover the floor.

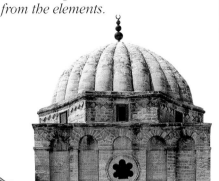

★ Prayer Hall
This hall is divided into seventeen long naves divided by arcades. The two wider naves form a "T" shape.

The *minbar* (pulpit), made out of teak, was built around AD 863 and commissioned by the Aghlabid emir, Abu Ibrahim.

Entrance to the Mosque
There are two entrances to the prayer hall from the road. Non-Muslims are not permitted to enter but they may look in the open doors.

Decoration
The richly decorated mosque contains some rare examples of ceramic decorative features. Plant motifs and geometric forms are popular.

STAR FEATURES

★ Minaret

★ Prayer Hall

Sbeïtla

Main Sights

Sbeïtla is laid out on a grid plan, like a typical ancient Roman town, with a large paved ▷ *forum* (still well preserved) and ▷ *market* at its heart. Traces can still be seen of ▷ *baths* and ▷ *theaters*. The Antonine arch at the Forum entrance bears an inscription naming Emperor Antoninus Pius, which dates it back to AD 139. Sbeïtla's most striking sight, however, is the large group of temples of the ▷ *Capitol*, thought to be dedicated to the Roman god Jupiter and the goddesses Minerva and Juno. The largest buildings at the site are those of the ▷ *St Vitalis Basilica*, with its five, mosaic-covered aisles. Byzantine additions to the town include several small, 7th-century houses.

The striking temples of Juno, Minerva, and Jupiter

Gregory, Byzantine Governor

Sbeïtla experienced its most dramatic episodes in the middle of the 7th century AD. The Byzantines of Constantinople took over the province, subsequently known as Numidia, in 533, with little resistance. By 641 the threat of Arab invasion had begun to grow and in late 646 Gregory, the governor of the city of Carthage, declared his independence from the Byzantine emperor. He moved his residence to Sbeïtla and the town briefly became the capital. However, shortly after, in 647, the Arabs led by Abdullah Ibn Saad invaded and Gregory and many of his men were killed. By the 8th century Byzantine North Africa – Libya, Tunisia, Algeria, and Morocco – was under Arab control.

Sbeïtla

Arch of Diocletian at the entrance

The SMALL TOWN OF Sbeïtla, once known as Sufetula, was a thriving Roman colony. Today it is surrounded by olive groves and fields and boasts fine examples of well-preserved Roman temples, built in the 2nd century AD. The town is also known for its numerous basilicas dating back to the 3rd century AD when Christians settled here. Sbeïtla was a Byzantine focus of resistance against the Arabs until AD 647 when the Arabs defeated the Byzantine army. Under them, Byzantine North Africa became known as Ifriqiya.

These small baths are among several built in Sbeïtla.

★ St Vitalis Basilica
The basilica was built toward the end of the 5th century on the site of a large villa. The building, which had five naves, was 50 m (164 ft) wide and 25 m (82 ft) long. Its oval font is decorated with colorful mosaics.

Star Features

★ St Vitalis Basilica

★ Capitol

★ Forum

Plan of Sbeïtla

Amphitheatre
Roman bridge
Basilica
Arch of Septimius Severus
KASSERINE
• Temple
House of the Four Seasons
Baths
Fountain
Baths
St Vitalis Basilica
Bellator Basilica
Baths
Church of St Servus
Forum
• Fountain
Reservoir
Great Baths
Theater
Byzantine church
Baths
Baths
• Byzantine fort
Olive press
• Byzantine fort
Entrance
Byzantine fort
Museum
Arch of Diocletian

0 meters 250
0 yards 250

Key
■ Building
— Road
= Footpath

★ Capitol
Situated in the northwestern part of the Forum, the capitol contains three temples dedicated to Juno, Jupiter, and Minerva. The rostrum used to stand in front of the Temple of Jupiter.

Bellator Basilica

The basilica was probably built at the start of the 4th century AD and expanded in the 5th century AD.

ROMAN LIFE

Sbeïtla was once a prosperous town in Roman North Africa. Its fertile land and forests of olive trees ensured a thriving economy based on olive oil production and cereal crops, which it exported to Rome. High revenues allowed the city to invest in the construction of grand public buildings.

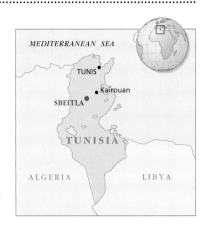

★ Forum

The Forum of Sbeïtla is one of the best preserved in Northern Africa. Entered through the Arch of Antonius Pius, which was never completed, the Forum was surrounded by a 4-m (13-ft) high wall in Byzantine times.

KEY DATES

2nd century AD Sbeïtla becomes a flourishing city under the Romans.

3rd century AD With the spread of Christianity, the city becomes the head-quarters of a diocese.

533 Byzantine Emperor Justinian retakes Sbeïtla from the Vandals, who occupy the city from 439–533.

646 Governor Gregory declares the independence of the province, and transfers his headquarters to Sbeïtla.

647 Arabs invade Sbeïtla and Gregory is killed in battle. The town gradually falls into decline.

ROMAN NORTH AFRICA

Numerous sites remain in North Africa as testament to Roman rule, ancient Roman Carthage being the most famous. At El Djem (between Sousse and Sfax), there is a large well-preserved amphitheater similar in style to the Colosseum in Rome, which was also used for gladiatorial fights and spectacles. The most extensive Roman ruins are at Dougga while Sbeïtla is the most southerly of all the ancient Roman sites in Tunisia. Excavations at Sbeïtla have unearthed a variety of objects including coins and altars used for religious ceremonies as well as mosaics. A small ▷ *museum* on the site contains an interesting display of excavated artifacts.

Church of St Servus

Built in the 4th century on the site of a pagan temple, the church may have been a Donatist cathedral or that of another non-Catholic sect. The Donatists, a staunch Christian sect active in Africa during the 4th and 5th centuries, protested fiercely against any lapse in the reverence paid to martyrs.

The reservoir was a huge cistern that was used for water storage.

Market

Sbeïtla's plan consisted of rectangular blocks divided by streets set at right-angles. Their stone plates have survived in excellent condition to the present day. The market close by the Forum has not fared so well. Many items were traded here, principally olive oil.

Sbeïtla

THE CITY'S PORT

A promontory protects the harbor at the mouth of the Wadi Lebdah at Leptis Magna, and it is here that the Phoenicians settled in the 7th century BC. They exploited the fertile hinterland and traded olive oil, ivory, and animal skins throughout the Carthaginian Empire and around the Mediterranean. During the early 3rd century AD, under the Roman emperor Septimius Severus, the harbor was rebuilt and enlarged. New quays, 1-km (half-a-mile) long, were constructed with warehouses, a temple, and a watchtower; a ▷ lighthouse was built on the promontory. Awnings were installed around the port to provide protection from the sweltering sun. The mooring blocks on the quay, which were covered in sand soon after completion, have been well preserved.

EMPEROR SEPTIMIUS SEVERUS

The Roman ruler Lucius Septimius Severus was born in Leptis Magna in Roman North Africa in AD 146. Regarded as an outstanding soldier, Severus rose to the rank of consul and by 190 was in command of the legions in Pannonia. Soon after the murder of Emperor Pertinax in 193, Severus was proclaimed emperor, but he had to fight off two rivals to secure his position. He was a strong but popular ruler, who was known for his lavish entertaining. He marked his victory over the Parthians in 199 with a triumphal arch in Rome (203), which still stands today. His final campaign was to England in 208 to secure the empire's northern border at Hadrian's Wall. Severus died in York in 211 while preparing to invade Scotland.

Bust of Emperor Septimius Severus

Leptis Magna

Column detail, Severan Basilica

ONE OF THE WORLD's greatest ruined cities, Leptis Magna attests to the prosperity and status of the Roman empire in North Africa. Leptis was particularly fortunate in AD 193 when Septimius Severus, a native of the city, became emperor of Rome. During his reign the population grew to some 70,000, and buildings were raised to glorify his name. Attacks by nomadic tribes led eventually to the city's abandonment, at which point sand dunes engulfed it, preserving the site that is still being excavated by archaeologists.

Market
Once surrounded by arcades and centred on two beautiful kiosks, this grand trading place was endowed by one wealthy citizen, Annobal Rufus, in 9–8 BC.

←— To Hunters' quarters   Arch of Septimius Severus   Arch of Trajan

Arch of Tiberius

★ Theater
Like the market, this vast structure was given to the city by Annobal Rufus. The lowest, wider stone steps would have held chairs for distinguished visitors. From the top, the panoramic view of the ancient city is magnificent.

★ Severan Basilica

Begun during the reign of Septimius to house the law courts, this massive double-apsed building was converted into a church by Justinian in the 6th century AD, though part of it seems to have served as a synagogue from the 5th century AD.

HUNTERS' QUARTERS

To the west of the city lies a group of well-preserved, small domed buildings. Wall paintings indicate they belonged to hunters who supplied the amphitheaters of the Roman Empire with wild animals.

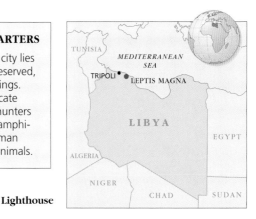

Leptis Magna

Lighthouse

0 metres   100

0 yards   100

Severan Forum
A series of vast reliefs of Medusa's head once adorned the arcade of the Severan Forum.

RECONSTRUCTION OF LEPTIS MAGNA

This shows the many magnificent buildings erected during the reigns of successive emperors up to and including Septimius Severus.

STAR FEATURES

★ **Theater**

★ **Severan Basilica**

Hadrian's Baths

This baths complex includes an outdoor sports ground (palaestra), *hot and warm baths* (caldarium *and* tepidarium), *once heated by underfloor fires, and a huge cold bath* (frigidarium) *with two plunge pools, one still containing water.*

KEY DATES

600 BC A Phoenician trading post is founded on the site.

23 BC Leptis Magna forms part of the new Roman province of Africa.

523 The city is sacked by Berbers and abandoned.

1982 Leptis Magna becomes a UNESCO World Heritage Site.

1994 A new archaeological program begins at Leptis Magna.

THE EMPEROR'S NEW BUILDING

Leptis Magna prospered under Roman rule as a major commercial center, but at the beginning of the 3rd century, after the appointment of Septimius Severus as Roman emperor, the city underwent a transformation. Marble was imported from Asia Minor, Greece, and Italy, granite columns from Egypt, and the limestone buildings took on a grand appearance (▷ *Classical Style p231*). In AD 200, Severus built a fine new ▷ *Severan Forum*, surrounded by colonnades topped with arches. At the northeastern end he constructed the three-aisled ▷ *Severan Basilica*. Its marble pilasters were carved with scenes from the lives of Hercules and Dionysus, his family's patron gods. The mighty four-sided ▷ *Arch of Septimius Severus*, constructed in white marble, was raised for his visit to the city in 203.

The Sphinx and Pyramid of Khafre viewed from the plateau

THE SPHINX

Dating back to 2500 BC, and positioned at the entrance to the Pyramid of Khafre, the Sphinx is the earliest known ancient Egyptian sculpture. It stands 20-m (66-ft) high with an elongated body, a royal headdress and outstretched paws. It is carved from an outcrop of natural rock, augmented by shaped blocks around the base, added during several renovations. It was once thought that the nose of the Sphinx was shot off by Napoleon's French army, but in reality it was lost before the 15th century.

THE GIZA PLATEAU

During the 4th Dynasty (2613–2498 BC), Giza became the royal burial ground for Memphis, capital of Egypt. In less than 100 years, the ancient Egyptians built three pyramid complexes to serve as tombs for their dead kings. These consisted of the Great Pyramid, the Pyramid of Khafre (r.2558–2532) and the Pyramid of Menkaure (r.2532–2530). The Sphinx was also added to guard the pyramids, while each king's close family and royal court were buried in satellite pyramids and ▷ *mastaba* tombs nearby. Of important note is the 6th-Dynasty (2345–2181 BC) tomb of Qar, a high-ranking official in charge of maintaining the Giza pyramids. His tomb is decorated with fine reliefs.

The Great Pyramid, Giza

THE FACTS OF KHUFU'S PYRAMID, commonly referred to as the Great Pyramid, are staggering. Until the 19th century it was the tallest building in the world. Yet for such a vast structure the precision is amazing – the greatest difference in length between the four 230-m (756-ft) sides is only 4 cm (2 inches). The construction methods and exact purpose of some of the chambers and shafts are unknown, but the fantastic architectural achievement is clear. It is estimated to contain over two million blocks of stone weighing on average around 2.5 tonnes, with some weighing as much as 15 tonnes.

Statue of Khufu (Cheops)
Khufu's only surviving statue is this 7.5-cm (3-inch) high ivory figure from Abydos, now kept in the Egyptian Museum in Cairo.

The Queen's Chamber probably held a statue representing the *ka* or life-force of the king.

Queens' Pyramids
These three small pyramids were built for members of the king's family, although the actual identity of the occupants is unknown.

Underlying bedrock

The "air shafts" may have been symbolic paths for the king's soul to ascend to the stars.

★ **King's Chamber**
Probably emptied 600 years after being built, the chamber, despite holding only a lidless sarcophagus, was often broken into by treasure seekers.

Unfinished underground chamber

★ **Great Gallery**
Soaring nearly 9 m (30 ft) high, this is thought to have been used as a slipway for the huge blocks that sealed the passageway.

STAR FEATURES

★ **King's Chamber**

★ **Great Gallery**

RECONSTRUCTION OF THE KING'S CHAMBER

Built to protect the chamber, the stress-relieving rooms also hold the only reference to Khufu in the Great Pyramid – gangs who built the pyramid left graffiti stating "How powerful is the great White Crown of Khufu".

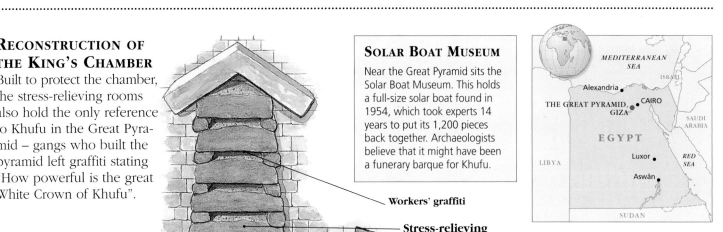

King's Chamber

The "air shaft" would have been closed off by the outer casing.

Workers' graffiti

Stress-relieving chambers were built out of huge blocks of granite weighing up to 80 tonnes.

Counterbalanced slabs of granite were lowered to seal the tomb.

SOLAR BOAT MUSEUM

Near the Great Pyramid sits the Solar Boat Museum. This holds a full-size solar boat found in 1954, which took experts 14 years to put its 1,200 pieces back together. Archaeologists believe that it might have been a funerary barque for Khufu.

This vertical shaft probably served as an escape route for the workers.

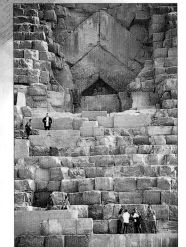

Entrance
The original entrance is blocked and a lower opening made by the Caliph Maamun in AD 820 is now used.

THE DEVELOPMENT OF PYRAMIDS

It took the ancient Egyptians around 400 years to progress from mudbrick *mastaba* to smooth-sided pyramid. The last stage, from stepped to "true" or smooth-sided pyramid took only 65 years. In this time each pyramid was a brave venture into the unknown. Rarely in the history of mankind has technology developed at such a rate.

The Red or North Pyramid, at Dahshur (c.2600 BC)

Mastaba

Around 3000 BC the sandy mounds of the graves of the upper echelons of society were formalized into low, box-like mastabas.

Stepped Pyramid (c.2665 BC)

A more impressive memorial was made by putting six stone mastabas on top of each other.

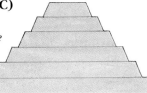

Prototype Pyramid (c.2605 BC)

The first smooth-sided pyramid was achieved by filling in the steps of a pyramid. This was followed by purpose-built, smooth-sided pyramids.

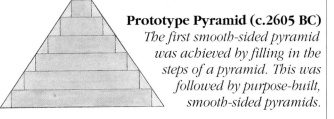

KEY DATES

2589–2566 BC King Khufu builds the Great Pyramid during his reign.

2555–2532 BC Construction of the Pyramid of Khafre.

1550–1295 BC The Sphinx is restored for the first time.

1979 The Giza Plateau is inscribed a UNESCO World Heritage Site.

KHUFU

Reigning for approximately 24 years, this 4th-Dynasty pharaoh (r.2589–2566 BC) is also known as Cheops or Suphis due to the late Greek influence on Egypt. His real name, Khnum-Khufwy, meaning "the god of Khnum protect me", was often shortened to Khufu. He built the most famous tomb in the ancient world, the Great Pyramid, one of the world's seven ancient wonders. His tomb was robbed long before archaeologists discovered it and all that remains is his modest statue (▷ *statue of Khufu*). He is believed to have been a wealthy ruler of a highly structured society. He led and coordinated his people in the building of the Great Pyramid which, contrary to popular belief, was not achieved through slave labor, but by a conscripted workforce. Despite his benevolent parentage, Khufu was reputedly both ruthless and cruel. He also enjoyed stories about the reigns of his predecessors and tales about magic and mystery.

The Great Pyramid

Chapel of the Burning Bush, viewable only by special dispensation

THE MONASTERY'S LIBRARY

The ▷ *library's* collection of over 3,000 manuscripts, in Greek and other ancient languages, is second in importance only to that held by the Vatican. The collection also includes around 5,000 early printed books and 2,000 scrolls. The remarkable condition of many of these artifacts owes much to the arid mountain climate that preserves the objects far better than if they were located in a damper climate. A small museum inside the monastery walls, known as the Sacred Sacristy, displays some of the finest items. One of the highlights is the *Codex Syriacus*, a 5th-century version of the New Testament, which is one of the world's oldest surviving bibles.

MOUNT SINAI

Rising to a height of 2,286 m (7,500 ft), Mount Sinai is considered to be the Biblical Mount Horeb where, in the Book of Exodus, Moses discovered a burning bush and heard the voice of God. The voice commanded Moses to lead his fellow Hebrew people out of slavery in Egypt to the Promised Land. Having done this, Moses returned to the mountain to commune with God. He spent 40 days and nights here, before receiving the Ten Commandments. Elijah's Basin, a sandy plain at the base of Mount Sinai, is marked as the place where the Israelites camped while Moses climbed the mountain, and where he later built the first Tabernacle.

St Catherine's Monastery

AT THE FOOT OF MOUNT SINAI, this Greek Orthodox monastery is thought to be the oldest continuously inhabited Christian monastery in the world. Founded in AD 527 by Emperor Justinian, it replaced a chapel built by Empress Helena in the 4th century on the site where, it is believed, Moses saw the Burning Bush. The monastery was renamed St Catherine's in the 9th or 10th century after monks claimed to have found the intact body of the saint on a nearby mountain.

Library
The collection of priceless early Christian manuscripts is one of the most important in the world.

★ Icon Collection
The monastery holds 2,000 icons, including this of St Peter. A selection is kept on view in the basilica.

The Walls of Justinian, dating from the 6th century, are part of the complex's original structure.

The Burning Bush
This evergreen is said to be from the same stock as the bush through which God instructed Moses to lead his people out of Egypt to the Promised Land.

STAR FEATURES

★ **Icon Collection**

★ **Basilica of the Transfiguration**

The Chapel of the Burning Bush lies beyond the altar in the Basilica of the Transfiguration.

★ Basilica of the Transfiguration
This richly decorated church owes its name to a rare 6th-century mosaic of the Transfiguration in the apse. The mosaic is located behind the gilded 17th-century iconostasis.

St Catherine's Monastery

Bell Tower
Built in 1871, the tower houses nine bells donated by Tsar Alexander II of Russia. They are only rung on religious festivals.

The Mosque was built in 1106 by converting a chapel originally dedicated to St Basil. Its creation was an attempt to placate local Muslim rulers.

CHARNEL HOUSE
Bones of monks who died at St Catherine's Monastery over the centuries are stored in the ▷ *Charnel House*, located in the Chapel of St Triphonius' crypt. The remains include the robed skeleton of Stephanos, a 6th-century guardian of the path to Mount Sinai.

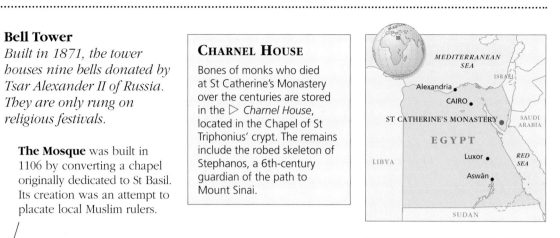

St Catherine's Monastery (side margin)

KEY DATES

337 AD The Chapel of the Burning Bush is constructed.

565 AD The Basilica of the Transfiguration is completed.

2002 The area of St Catherine's Monastery and Mount Sinai is inscribed a UNESCO World Heritage Site.

THE INTERIOR OF THE BASILICA

The monastery's main church is known as the ▷ *Basilica of the Transfiguration*. It was built by Emperor Justinian's architect Stephanos Ailisios in the 6th century. Massive 11th-century wooden doors open onto the narthex (porch). Beyond this, another door carved with reliefs of animals, birds, and flowers is believed to be an original door from Justinian's church. The central nave is flanked by six pillars bearing Byzantine icons of saints worshiped throughout the year. The marble floor and coffered ceiling of the basilica dates from the 18th century. The roof of the apse is decorated with a superb mosaic of the Transfiguration of Jesus. Shaped in a half moon, the mosaic shows Jesus in the presence of Moses and Elijah on the sacred Mount Tabor. A gilded iconostasis, painted in the early 17th century, separates the nave from the altar. Suspended above this, in the central aisle, is the figure of Christ on the Cross. Beyond the altar lies the ▷ *Chapel of the Burning Bush*, the holiest place in the monastery.

Monks' quarters

St Stephen's Well

Dispensary

Guest house

Monastery Gardens
A cemetery is located in the orchard, from where monks' bones are periodically exhumed and taken to the Charnel House.

Charnel House

The elevated entrance, reached by a pulley system, used to be the only access.

The underground cistern was dug to store fresh water from the monastery's springs.

Visitors' entrance

Well of Moses
Inside the outer wall lies the monastery's main water source, where Moses is said to have met his future wife, Zipporah, Jethro's daughter.

ST CATHERINE OF ALEXANDRIA

St Catherine was one of the most popular early Christian saints. Supposedly born into a wealthy Alexandrian family in the early 4th century, she was tortured for her criticism of pagan worship. First spun on a spiked wheel (hence the Catherine wheel), she was then beheaded by the pagan Roman emperor, Maximus. A marble sarcophagus in the basilica contains two silver caskets said to hold part of her remains, found by monks 600 years after her death.

Detail of St Catherine from clerical vestments

THE ROYAL BUILDERS

The 11th-Dynasty pharaoh Montuhotep II (r.2055–2004 BC) was the first ruler to build a temple at Deir al-Bahri. A Theban warlord, he conquered the north to reunite the country after a period of civil war. Queen Hatshepsut (r.1473–1458 BC) was the daughter of Tuthmosis I. On his death she married her half-brother, Tuthmosis II. He died three years later and was succeeded by the three-year-old Tuthmosis III. Hatshepsut ruled as regent, then in 1473 BC crowned herself pharaoh. After her death, Tuthmosis III (r.1458–1425 BC), a cunning military strategist, succeeded her and expanded the Egyptian empire into Asia Minor.

A LIFE IN PICTURES

Frescoes of Hatshepsut's achievements in the course of her reign decorate the temple. They may appear faded today, but 3,500 years ago the walls were a riot of brilliant colors. The ▷ *Birth Colonnade* and chapels to the gods are rich in mythology. There is a relief of the ▷ *Punt Expedition*, Hatshepsut's trip to Somalia where goods such as incense, cinnamon, ▷ *myrrh trees,* and even exotic animals were bought. Hatshepsut is often portrayed with a false beard, a symbol of the pharaoh's power (▷ *statues of Hatshepsut)*. However, her face and name were erased from many reliefs by her successors.

Artist's impression of Queen Hatshepsut in full regalia

Hatshepsut Temple, Thebes

Head of Hatshepsut

AGAINST ITS STARK mountainous backdrop, the partly rock-hewn Mortuary Temple of Hatshepsut at Deir al-Bahri is a breathtaking sight. It was designed by Queen Hatshepsut's architect Senenmut in the 18th Dynasty and is an extraordinary monument which rises from the desert plain in a series of imposing terraces. The temple was damaged by Ramses II and his successors, and Christians later turned it into a monastery (hence the name Deir al-Bahri, which means "Northern Monastery"). However, the ongoing excavation of the site continues to reveal much exquisite decoration. Adjacent to the main temple are the ruins of the much older Temple of Montuhotep II, the ruler of the 11th Dynasty who managed to unite Egypt, and the 18th-Dynasty Temple of Tuthmosis III.

The imposing Hatshepsut Temple, in its stunning setting at the foot of a sheer limestone cliff-face

RECONSTRUCTION OF THE TEMPLES AT DEIR AL-BAHRI

This reconstruction shows the Temples of Montuhotep II, Tuthmosis III, and Hatshepsut as they would have looked during the reign of Tuthmosis III in the 18th Dynasty. Partly rock-cut and partly free-standing, the three temples are set into a natural amphitheater and are given added majesty by the dramatic cliffs behind them.

STAR FEATURES

★ **Chapel of Hathor**

★ **Statues of Hatshepsut**

★ **Reliefs of Punt Expedition**

Temple of Montuhotep II
The prototype for Hatshepsut's Temple, the older Temple of Montuhotep II now lies in ruins.

Temple of Tuthmosis III

★ **Chapel of Hathor**
This chapel is noted for its columns, each of which is crowned with the head of Hathor, goddess of love. Reliefs here include this one of the ankh *and* djed *pillar, symbols of life and stability.*

★ Statues of Hatshepsut

The columns of the portico around the upper terrace were decorated with Osiride statues of Hatshepsut, characteristically represented as a male king with a beard. Although many statues were destroyed by later pharaohs, such as Tuthmosis III, several have recently been reconstructed from their fragments.

The Shrine of Amun was dug into the cliff behind the temple.

Sanctuary of the Sun

Chapel of Anubis

This chapel contains brightly colored murals, including a relief of Tuthmosis III making offerings to the sun god Ra-Harakhty.

Myrrh trees planted in the gardens yielded a gum that was burnt as incense.

Avenue of sphinxes led off in the direction of the temple complex at Karnak.

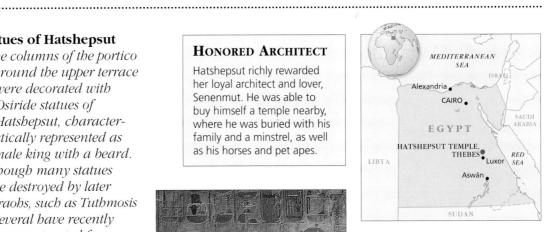

HONORED ARCHITECT

Hatshepsut richly rewarded her loyal architect and lover, Senenmut. He was able to buy himself a temple nearby, where he was buried with his family and a minstrel, as well as his horses and pet apes.

KEY DATES

2004 BC Montuhotep II dies and is buried in his temple at Deir al-Bahri.

1473 BC Hatshepsut becomes Queen of Egypt and builds her temple at Deir al-Bahri.

1479–1425 BC Reign of Tuthmosis III, who builds his temple next to Hatshepsut's.

1979 Thebes is declared a UNESCO World Heritage Site.

GODS OF THE TEMPLE

The Hatshepsut Temple contains shrines to three of the most important gods in the queen's life: Amun-Re (▷ *the Shrine of Amun*), her divine father; Hathor (▷ *Chapel of Hathor*), goddess of love and pleasure; and Anubis (▷ *Chapel of Anubis*), the jackal-headed god of embalmers. Amun-Re had been worshiped at Thebes since the 11th Dynasty. He was the creator god of Egypt and the father of the king, through whom he ruled the country. Scenes in the ▷ *Birth Colonnade* tell of how Amun-Re created Hatshepsut and how, when she was born, Hathor presented the child to the delighted god. In early mythology, Hathor was the wetnurse and lover of Horus and mother of his son. It is said that Horus's father, the king Osiris, was brutally murdered and his body scattered in pieces over Egypt. Anubis helped to put together his body and embalm it as a mummy. For this Anubis was worshiped as the god of embalmers.

Birth Colonnade

Scenes along the Birth Colonnade portray the divine birth of Hatshepsut, designed to legitimize the queen's claim to the throne. On the right, the young queen is shown in the arms of the goddess Neith.

★ Reliefs of Punt Expedition

Stunning reliefs relate Hatshepsut's journey to the Land of Punt (Somalia). The king of Punt is seen here with his wife Ati (left), who is depicted suffering from obesity.

Hatshepsut Temple

RAMSES II

Also known as Ramses the Great, Ramses II (r.1279–1213 BC) was the 19th Dynasty's third king. He had a large number of wives and concubines and reputedly fathered over 100 children. During his long reign there was a proliferation in the construction of royal buildings. Majestic temples, huge monuments, and colossal statues of him, erected in every major Egyptian city of the period, were a deliberate attempt to impress his subjects and preserve his reputation for posterity (▷ *Colossus of Ramses II*). Ramses II is responsible for completing Karnak's ▷ *Great Hypostyle Hall*, begun under Ramses I (r.1295–1294 BC). Known as a great warrior, he defeated the invading Hittites at the Battle of Qadesh (c.1275 BC).

TEMPLES AND RELIGIOUS LIFE

For the ancient Egyptians, the universe was composed of dualities – fertile and barren, life and death, order and chaos – held in equilibrium by the goddess of cosmic order and harmony, Maat. To maintain this balance, they built enormous temples dedicated to the gods. At the center of every settlement and devoted to a particular god or set of gods, the "cult" temple served as a storehouse of divine power, maintained by the priesthood for the benefit of all. The temple was also an economic and political centre employing large numbers of the local community and serving as a town hall, medical center, and college.

Statues of the lioness-goddess Sekhmet in the Precinct of Mut

Temple of Amun, Karnak

Statue of a scarab beetle

WITH ITS ENDLESS courts, halls, colossi and sacred lake, the scale and complexity of this sprawling temple is overwhelming. Lying at the heart of the immense Karnak complex, the Temple of Amun is dedicated to the king of the gods. From its modest 11th-Dynasty beginnings, pharaoh after pharaoh added to and changed the existing buildings, seeking to make their mark on the country's most important temple. No expense was spared and during the 19th Dynasty some 80,000 men worked in the temple as laborers, guards, priests, and servants. The temple lay buried under sand for more than 1,000 years before excavation work began in the mid-19th century. Today, the huge task of restoration continues.

★ **Great Hypostyle Hall**
The glorious highlight of Karnak, this cavernous hall was supported by 134 gigantic columns.

★ **Colossus of Ramses II**
An imposing granite statue of Ramses II, with one of his daughters at his feet, stands in front of the entrance to the Great Hypostyle Hall.

Tomb of Seti II
dedicated to the Theban Triad.

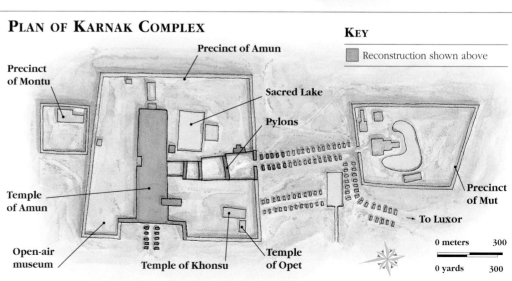

RECONSTRUCTION OF THE TEMPLE OF AMUN
The temple's brightly colored exterior is visible in this reconstruction, which shows how the temple would have looked in around 1000 BC.

A row of sphinxes led to the Nile.

Temple of Ramses III

PLAN OF KARNAK COMPLEX

KEY

⬛ Reconstruction shown above

Precinct of Montu

Precinct of Amun

Sacred Lake

Pylons

Precinct of Mut

Temple of Amun

Open-air museum

Temple of Khonsu

Temple of Opet

→ **To Luxor**

| 0 meters | 300 |
| 0 yards | 300 |

Botanic Gardens

Part of the temple built by Tuthmosis III (r.1479–1425 BC), this garden enclosure lies behind the Great Festival Temple. It is decorated with reliefs of exotic flora and fauna, brought back to Egypt by the 18th-Dynasty pharaoh during his campaign in Syria.

THE THEBAN TRIAD

Amun was the principal god of Thebes who, with his consort Mut and their son Khonsu, was worshiped as part of the Theban Triad. Accompanied by priests and revellers in the riotous Festival of Opet, images of the Triad were carried from Karnak on decorated barques each year to celebrate the king's rebirth as the son of Amun.

KEY DATES

2055–1985 BC Construction of the Temple of Amun starts.

1295–1294 BC Work begins on the Great Hypostyle Hall.

663 BC Karnak and the Temple of Amun are plundered by Assyrian armies.

1979 Ancient Thebes, including Karnak, is named a UNESCO World Heritage Site.

EXPLORING KARNAK

Excavations in Karnak have uncovered a fantastic array of temples, chapels, pylons, and obelisks. Dedicated to the son of Amun and Mut, the well-preserved ▷ *Temple of Khonsu* was built largely during the reigns of Ramses III (r.1184–1153 BC) and Ramses IV (r.1153–1147 BC). The ▷ *Open-air Museum* displays a fine collection of monuments. These include the restored 18th-Dynasty Red Chapel of Hatshepsut and the reconstructed 12th-Dynasty White Chapel of Senusret I, which has delicate carvings of Senusret I (r.1965–1920 BC) making offerings to Amun. Within the ▷ *Precinct of Mut*, built by Amenhotep III (r.1427–1400 BC), are the ruins of a temple dedicated to Amun's consort Mut. Black granite statues of the lioness-goddess Sekhmet line the temple courts. The ▷ *Precinct of Montu* is north of the Temple of Amun. Montu the warrior god was the original deity of Thebes who was still worshiped after Amun rose to pre-eminence.

★ **Great Festival Temple**
The central hall of this temple built by Tuthmosis III was supposedly designed to resemble the tent in which he lived while on campaign.

The Ninth Pylon was built by Horemheb using blocks from the demolished Aten temple.

Flagpoles

Eighth Pylon

To Precinct of Mut →

Row of Sphinxes

Sacred Lake

Priests purified themselves in the holy water of the Sacred Lake before performing rituals in the temple. North of the lake is a huge stone scarab of Khepri, built by Amenhotep III.

STAR FEATURES

★ **Great Hypostyle Hall**

★ **Colossus of Ramses II**

★ **Great Festival Temple**

Temple of Amun

A NEW LOCATION

When the Aswan Dam proved too small to control the floodwaters of the Nile, the Egyptian government embarked on a project to build the High Dam and create Lake Nasser as a reservoir. But the rising waters of the lake threatened to submerge Abu Simbel. Concern over losing the temples led UNESCO to back an international relief scheme and in 1964 an ambitious four-year operation began to move the two monuments to safety. The temples, complete with their artifacts, were cut into 950 blocks and transferred to a higher site against the backdrop of a purpose-built mountain (▷ *Relocated Temples*). Care was taken to ensure that the ▷ *Inner Sanctuary* remained aligned with the sun.

The Aswan Dam, built in 1902 to regulate the flow of the Nile

THE GREAT STATUES

Three of the four 20-m (65-ft) high statues, the ▷ *Ramses II Colossi*, gaze southwards to deter even the most determined of the pharaoh's enemies. Their enormous size is thought to illustrate Ramses' divinity as a supreme god. The gods and Ramses' family feature prominently among the other statues. At the feet of the colossi stand figures of the pharaoh's mother, his wife Queen Nefertari, and the royal children. Above the entrance to the Great Temple is the falcon-headed statue of the sun god ▷ *Ra-Harakhty*. Hapi, the god of the Nile flood, associated with fertility, is featured holding lotus and papyrus, symbols of Upper and Lower Egypt respectively.

Abu Simbel

Carved baboon at Abu Simbel

HEWN OUT OF a solid cliff in the 13th century BC, the Great Temple of Abu Simbel and the smaller Temple of Hathor are a breathtaking sight. Although dedicated to the patron deities of Egypt's great cities – Amun of Thebes, Ptah of Memphis, and Ra-Harakhty of Heliopolis – the Great Temple was built to honor Ramses II. Its 33-m (108-ft) high façade, with four colossal enthroned statues of Ramses II wearing the double crown of Upper and Lower Egypt, was intended to impress and frighten, while the interior revealed the union of god and king.

Relocated Temples at Abu Simbel
In the 1960s, as Lake Nasser threatened to engulf the temples, UNESCO cut them from the mountain and moved them to an artificial cliff 210 m (688 ft) back from and 65 m (213 ft) above their original position.

Ramses II Colossi
Accompanied by carved images of captives from the north and south, the four colossi on the temple façade boast of a unified Egypt. Ramses' names adorn the thrones in cartouche form.

STAR FEATURES

★ **Temple Façade**

★ **Inner Sanctuary**

★ **Hypostyle Hall**

★ **Temple Façade**
Buried in sand for centuries, this façade was discovered in 1813 by Swiss explorer Jean-Louis Burckhardt.

Store rooms held offerings to the gods and ritual items.

Baboons greeting the rising sun

Statue of Ra-Harakhty

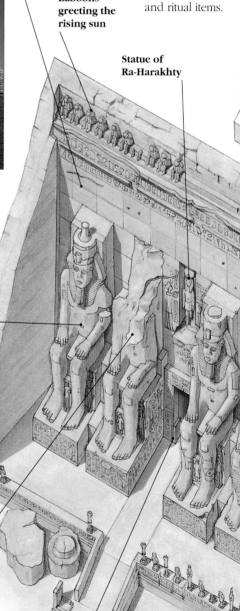

The broken colossus lost its head in an earthquake in 27 BC.

Entrance to temple

The vestibule is adorned with scenes of Ramses and Nefertari making offerings to Amun and Ra-Harakhty.

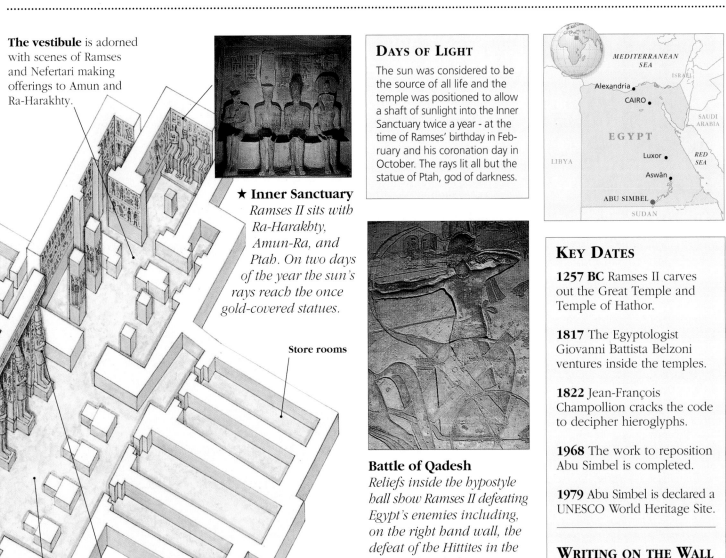

★ **Inner Sanctuary**
Ramses II sits with Ra-Harakhty, Amun-Ra, and Ptah. On two days of the year the sun's rays reach the once gold-covered statues.

Store rooms

10-m (33-ft) high statue of Ramses as Osiris

DAYS OF LIGHT

The sun was considered to be the source of all life and the temple was positioned to allow a shaft of sunlight into the Inner Sanctuary twice a year - at the time of Ramses' birthday in February and his coronation day in October. The rays lit all but the statue of Ptah, god of darkness.

Battle of Qadesh
Reliefs inside the hypostyle hall show Ramses II defeating Egypt's enemies including, on the right hand wall, the defeat of the Hittites in the Battle of Qadesh c.1275 BC.

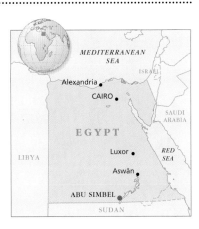

KEY DATES

1257 BC Ramses II carves out the Great Temple and Temple of Hathor.

1817 The Egyptologist Giovanni Battista Belzoni ventures inside the temples.

1822 Jean-François Champollion cracks the code to decipher hieroglyphs.

1968 The work to reposition Abu Simbel is completed.

1979 Abu Simbel is declared a UNESCO World Heritage Site.

WRITING ON THE WALL

Graphic wall paintings and reliefs found in the Great Temple of Abu Simbel and the ▷ *Temple of Hathor* glorify Ramses II as a divine pharaoh. They tell of his victories and show him fighting his enemies. In the Temple of Hathor Nefertari's consecration as divine queen is illustrated. Surrounding the paintings and reliefs are detailed rows of hieroglyphs. This pictorial script, thought to have developed around 3200 BC, is the world's oldest known form of writing. The word "hieroglyph" means "sacred carved letter" and a complex system of 6,000 symbols was used by the ancient Egyptians to write their names and express their religious beliefs. Stories of the life of Ramses and Nefertari have been engraved in this way on the walls. This painstaking work, undertaken by highly-trained scribes, fell from use in the 4th century AD.

TEMPLE OF HATHOR

Dedicated to the goddess Hathor, deity of love, pleasure, and beauty, the smaller temple at Abu Simbel was built by Ramses II to honor his favorite wife, Nefertari. The hypostyle hall has Hathor-headed pillars and is decorated with scenes of Ramses slaying Egypt's enemies, watched by Nefertari. The vestibule shows the royal couple making offerings to the gods.

★ **Hypostyle Hall**
In this hall the roof is supported by pillars with colossi in Osiride form – carrying crook and flail. Those on the southern pillars wear the Upper Egypt crown, while the northern ones wear the double crown of Upper and Lower Egypt.

Statues of Nefertari as goddess Hathor alternating with Ramses II on the façade of Queen Nefertari's Temple

Abu Simbel

Djenné Mosque, Mali

WITH ITS STRIKING façade and unique architectural style, the Djenné Mosque ranks among the most unusual and beautiful buildings in the world. This large mud-brick structure is typical of the special African-Islamic "marriage" found on the continent – in which African societies have molded Islam to fit their own traditional beliefs, values, and concerns. Usually a mosque is made of the finest materials available, but the Djenné Mosque is made with the modest, humble material of sun-baked mud (also known as *adobe* or *pisé*), which in the skilled hands of the Mali master masons has resulted in one of the most remarkable expressions of faith in Africa.

Mosque Interior
Inside the mosque the impressive prayer hall with its sandy floor is covered by a wooden roof supported by nearly 100 pillars.

The mosque's imposing mud-brick façade

THE HISTORY OF DJENNÉ MOSQUE

Djenné's present-day mosque was constructed in 1907 on the foundations of the town's first mosque. This was built in 1280 by Koi Konboro, the 26th king of Djenné, following his conversion to Islam. As a demonstration of his allegiance to the new faith, he had his royal palace knocked down and the mosque constructed on its site. His mosque survived until the early 19th century when the fundamentalist Islamic king, Cheikou Amadou, keen to reinforce local Islamic religious practises, allowed it to fall into ruin. Instead, a more austere mosque was built close by (now the site of a *medresa*).

MOSQUE DESIGN

With its thick, battlemented walls and towers, and the peculiar "spiky" appearance of the projecting ▷ *wooden beams*, the mosque seems more like a fortress than a religious building. Its imposing exterior is made up of ▷ *three sloping minarets*, which stand over 10 m (33 ft) high, some ▷ *towers*, and a large ▷ *base*, accessible via a number of ▷ *stepped entrances*. The interior is not accessible to non-Muslims, but views of it can be had from the roofs of nearby houses. The art and skill of the masons have been handed down from generation to generation since the 15th century. The master masons still mix the mud mortar by foot, and shape the mud bricks by hand. A simple iron trowel is their only tool, and is used for cutting the bricks and levelling the walls.

The Market
A colorful market is set up in front of the Djenné Mosque every Monday, attracting traders from the surrounding area. Djenné and its region are famous for the mud cloth sold here, known as bogolan.

Three sloping minarets
are used by the *muezzin* (mosque official) to call the faithful to prayer. Staircases inside each minaret lead directly to the roof.

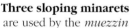

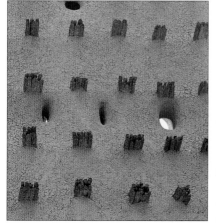

★ Wooden Beams
Giving the mosque its distinctive "spiky" appearance, the palm beams not only support the mud walls, but also serve as a kind of permanent scaffolding for the annual repairs, as well as esthetically relieving the solidity of the structure.

The Spring Renovation
The annual restoration of the mosque is a communal concern, with up to 4,000 towns-people taking part in the work. Specialist masons, bareys (a kind of builder-magician caste dating back to the 15th century), carefully oversee the work.

WIND, SUN, AND RAIN

The elements cause damage to the Djenné Mosque. Rain-water erodes the walls and damp can weaken the structure. Extreme temperature and humidity also cause stress to the building. However, the yearly replastering helps keep the building in good shape.

★ **Base**
The large base on which the mosque sits raises it some 3 m (10 ft) above the market area, and separates it both physically and symbolically from the pedestrian and profane activities of the market place.

Stepped entrance

Tower

★ **Pillars and Roof**
A forest of 90 wooden pillars supports the roof, which is perforated with small vents to allow light and air to penetrate. In the rainy season, the holes are covered with ceramic caps.

STAR FEATURES

★ Wooden Beams

★ Base

★ Pillars and Roof

Djenné Mosque

KEY DATES

c.1250–1300 Djenné town is founded and the first mosque is built.

1300–1468 Djenné forms part of the Mali Empire.

1468 The Songhay Empire captures and annexes the city.

1591 Moroccans take over the city.

1819 Cheikou Amadou abandons the old mosque and builds a new one on a different site.

1907 A third mosque is constructed on the foundations of the 13th-century original.

1988 Djenné is declared a UNESCO World Heritage Site.

DJENNÉ TOWN

Djenné is one of the oldest trading towns in the region. Founded in 1250 on the ancient trans-Saharan trade routes, Djenné quickly grew into a thriving center of commerce, attracting merchants from north, east, west, and central Africa. Textiles, brass, ceramics, and copperware were exchanged for Sahel gold, ivory, and precious Saharan salt. By the end of the 13th century, Islam had also arrived, brought to Djenné by Muslim merchants from North Africa, and the first mosque was built. By the 14th century, Djenné had not only become an important center of Islamic learning, but also one of the wealthiest and most cosmopolitan towns of sub-Saharan Africa.

The Royal Enclosure, Gonder

WITH ITS COLLECTION of castles and palaces, and once the site of a legendary court, Gonder has been called "Africa's Camelot." At the end of the 17th century, Gonder boasted magnificent buildings, beautiful gardens, orchards, and plantations, and a thriving market which attracted merchants from all over the area. Flourishing for more than 200 years, the city became one of the largest in this part of Africa. Gonder's court, the setting for extravagant pageantry and sumptuous feasts, became widely renowned and visitors from around the world came to visit the city. It has been suggested that Portuguese craftsmen, left behind after the expulsion of the Jesuits from Ethiopia in 1632, were probably responsible for building the castles.

The imposing façade of Fasiladas' Castle, Gonder

THE HISTORY OF GONDER

When the Emperor Fasiladas founded Gonder in 1636, he was following an ancient Ethiopian custom. According to the imperial tradition, new rulers were expected to establish new capital cities. Fasiladas' choice was a wise one. Gonder lay at the crossroads of three major caravan routes and was surrounded on all sides by fertile land. Sources of gold, ivory, and slaves existed to the southwest; access to the Red Sea could be found to the northeast; and to the northwest lay the lucrative markets of Egypt. As trade boomed, the city grew and by the time of the emperor's death in 1667, Gonder's population numbered more than 65,000.

FASILADAS' CASTLE

The oldest and arguably the most impressive of the castles in Gonder is ▷ *Fasiladas' Castle*. With its thick, roughly hewn, basalt stone walls the castle's distinguishing features are its crenelated parapet, flat ▷ *roof*, and four, small domed towers. Allegedly the work of an Indian architect, the construction embodies an unusual synthesis of Indian, Portuguese, and Moorish influences, as well as Aksumite (the old, indigenous Ethiopian style). From the tower in the southwest corner of the castle, there are excellent views over the Royal Enclosure all the way to Lake Tana in the south (Ethiopia's largest lake).

★ Banqueting Hall and Stables
Emperor Bakaffa (r.1721–30) built the huge banqueting hall, which was the scene of elaborate feasts and extravagant entertainment. He also built the nearby stables to house the legions of imperial horses.

View from Fasiladas' Castle
The view over the Royal Enclosure shows the quadrangular library in the foreground, built by Fasiladas' son, Yohannes I (r.1667–82). Yellow stucco covers the exterior and steps lead up to the crenelated third floor.

STAR FEATURES
★ Banqueting Hall and Stables
★ Iyasu's Palace
★ Fasiladas' Castle

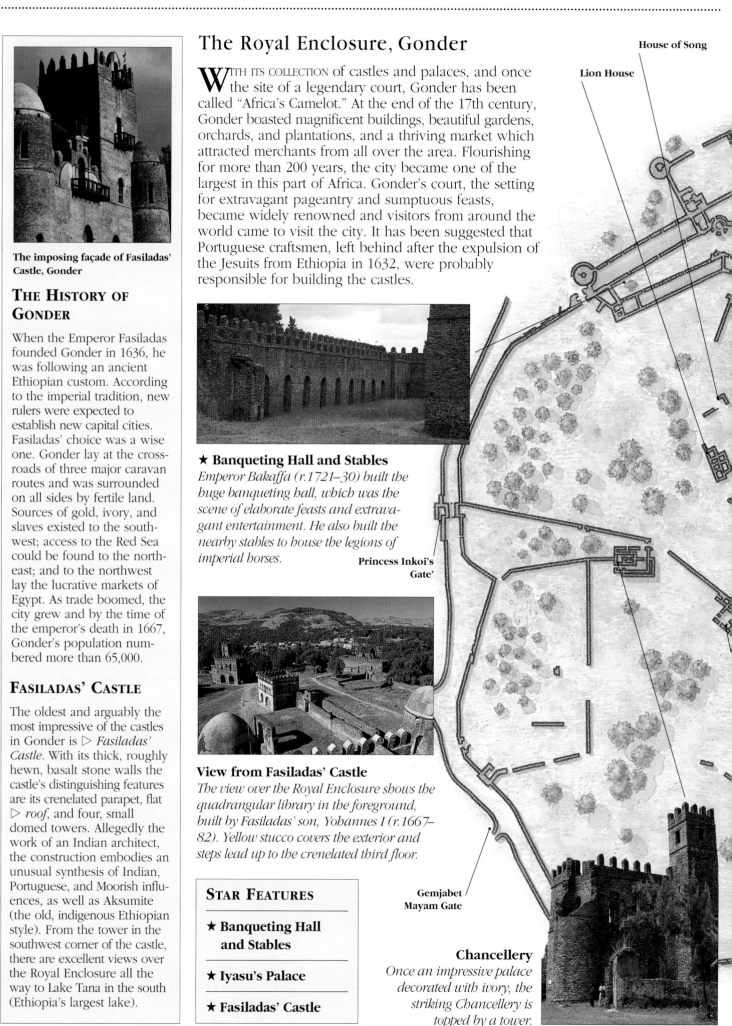

House of Song

Lion House

Princess Inkoi's Gate'

Gemjabet Mayam Gate

Chancellery
Once an impressive palace decorated with ivory, the striking Chancellery is topped by a tower.

Atatami Mikael Church

DEBRE BERHAN SELASSIE

About 2km (1.24 miles) from the Royal Enclosure is the Debre Berhan Selassie church. Its plain exterior belies a fabulous interior containing a painted ceiling covered with over 80 different angels' faces gazing down.

Mentewab's Castle

Built by Emperor Bakaffa's consort, this elegant two-storied castle is decorated with red tuff crosses on the façade.

★ Iyasu's Palace

Grandson of Fasiladas, Iyasu (r.1682–1706) is considered the greatest of the Gonderine rulers. His palace was sumptuously decorated with gold leaf, ivory, and beautiful paintings.

Bathing Pool

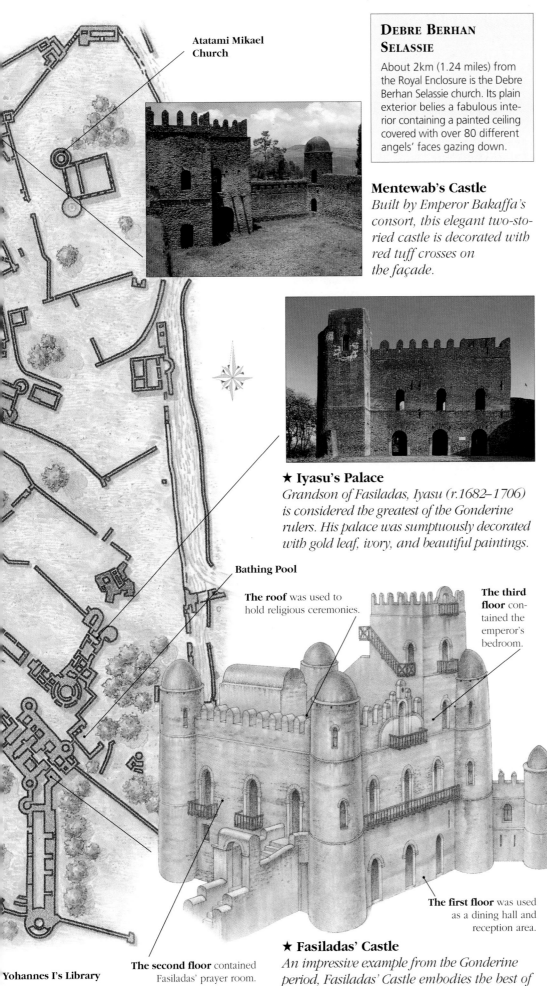

The roof was used to hold religious ceremonies.

The third floor contained the emperor's bedroom.

The first floor was used as a dining hall and reception area.

Yohannes I's Library

The second floor contained Fasiladas' prayer room.

★ Fasiladas' Castle

An impressive example from the Gonderine period, Fasiladas' Castle embodies the best of Portuguese, Indian, and Ethiopian influences.

KEY DATES

1636 Emperor Fasiladas founds Gonder and builds his castle.

1667 Yohannes I builds the quadrangular library.

1682 Iyasu I begins work on his palace.

1716 Dawit I constructs the House of Song.

1721 Bakaffa builds the banqueting hall and stables; Mentewab builds her castle.

c.1755 Gonder's importance declines as the city is riven by internal power struggles.

1979 The Royal Enclosure is declared a UNESCO World Heritage Site.

OTHER BUILDINGS

Surrounded by high stone walls, the Royal Enclosure covers an area of over 75,000 sq m (18.53 acres). In addition to the castles and palaces, other buildings included a ▷ *bathing pool*, the two-storied ▷ *Yohannes I library*, and a ▷ *chancellery*. Religious and secular ceremonies, as well as lavish entertainment, were staged in the ▷ *House of Song*, while the royal Abyssinian lions, a symbol of imperial power, were kept in the ▷ *Lion House*. Though looted in the 1880s by the Sudanese Dervishes, and damaged by British bombs in the 1941 campaign to liberate Ethiopia from the Italians, most of the Royal Enclosure remains remarkably well preserved.

RED SEA
ERITREA YEMEN
THE ROYAL ENCLOSURE, GONDER
SUDAN
ADDIS ABABA · Diré Dawa
ETHIOPIA
SOMALIA
KENYA

The Royal Enclosure

THE WILLIAM FEHR COLLECTION

The Castle of Good Hope houses the famous ▷ *William Fehr Collection* of historical paintings and furnishings. Dr Fehr (1892–1968) was a local businessman who started collecting colonial pictures and objects at a time when the practise was unusual. His collection now forms an invaluable record of many aspects of social and political life in the Cape, from the early days of the Dutch East India Company (VOC in Dutch) to the end of the 19th century. As well as landscape paintings by English artists Thomas Baines and William Huggins, there are also exhibits of 17th-century Japanese porcelain and 18th-century Indonesian furniture.

COMMANDER JAN VAN RIEBEECK

In April 1652, the Dutchman Jan van Riebeeck arrived at the Cape with about 80 men and women to establish a staging post for the Dutch East India Company. This was needed to provision Dutch ships plying the lucrative trade route between Europe and Asia. Despite setbacks (20 men died during that first winter), the station flourished and began to provide ships with meat, milk, and vegetables. Rivalry with the indigenous Khoina over water and grazing, however, soon turned into open hostility, escalating into bitter wars.

Commander Jan van Riebeeck, founder of Cape Town

Castle of Good Hope, Cape Town

Dutch East India (VOC) monogram, 17th century

Sᴏᴜᴛʜ ᴀғʀɪᴄᴀ's ᴏʟᴅᴇsᴛ sᴜʀᴠɪᴠɪɴɢ structure, the Castle of Good Hope, was built between 1666–79, replacing an earlier clay-and-timber fort erected by Commander Jan van Riebeeck in 1652. The castle overlooks the Grand Parade and is now home to a military museum, an art collection, a banqueting hall, and is the headquarters for Cape Army regiments.

Dolphin Pool
Descriptions and sketches made by Lady Anne Barnard in the 1790s enabled the reconstruction of the dolphin pool over two hundred years later.

The Castle Moat
Sections of the moat were rebuilt as part of an extensive restoration program launched in the 1980s.

Old Slates
Slate, taken from a quarry on Robben Island in the 17th century, was used as the paving material inside the castle.

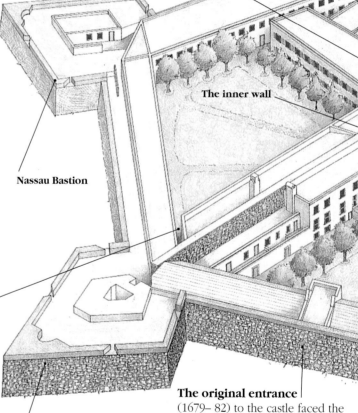

Bakery

The inner wall

Nassau Bastion

Catzenellenbogen Bastion

The original entrance
(1679– 82) to the castle faced the sea, but has since been closed.

STAR FEATURES

★ **The Castle Military Museum**

★ **William Fehr Collection**

★ **De Kat Staircase**

★ **The Castle Military Museum**
On display is an array of military artifacts, including weapons and uniforms from the VOC and British periods in the Cape.

★ William Fehr Collection

Exhibits include paintings by artists such as Thomas Baines, as well as period furniture, glass, ceramics, and metalware.

DUTCH TRADERS

In 1602 the Dutch East India Company (Verenigde Oost-indische Compagnie, or VOC) was founded to trade with Asia mainly for its prized spices. Successful and powerful, by 1669 the VOC fleet numbered 150 merchant ships and 40 warships.

Oranje Bastion

Entrance Gable
A teak copy of the original VOC gable reflects martial symbols: a banner, flags, drums, and cannon balls.

Leerdam Bastion
Each bastion was named after titles held by Prince William of Orange – Leerdam, Oranje, Nassau, Catzenellenbogen, and Buuren.

Colonnaded veranda

Moat

The Castle Entrance
The original bell, cast in Amsterdam in 1697, still hangs in the belfry. The coat of arms of the United Netherlands can be seen on the pediment above the gate.

Buuren Bastion

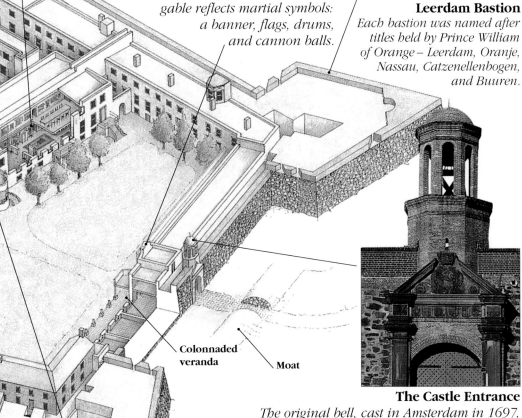

★ De Kat Staircase
The original staircase, built in 1695 as part of a defensive crosswall, divided the square into an inner and outer court, and was remodeled between 1786 and 1790.

KEY DATES

1652 First Dutch settlers, under the command of Jan van Riebeeck, land on the Cape.

1666–79 Settlers build a stone castle to replace van Riebeeck's earlier timber fort.

1795 Rule by the Dutch East India Company (VOC) ends and British forces occupy the Cape.

1952 The William Fehr art collection moves to the Castle.

THE CASTLE

The design of the castle was influenced by the work of the French military engineer Vauban, employed at the court of Louis XIV. The castle was built in the shape of a pentagon with five defensive bastions, from which the out-side walls could be defended by cross-fire. The ▷ *original entrance* faced the sea but it was moved to its present position in 1684. From the beginning the castle was intended as a base for the Dutch East India Company in the Cape. In 1691 a line of rooms known as De Kat was added across the center of the castle courtyard and this became the Governor's resi-dence. Today this area houses the ▷ *William Fehr Collection*. In the past the Castle of Good Hope housed facilities to support a community, with living quarters, a church, a bakery, offices, and a jail with a torture chamber. In the 1930s a new banqueting hall was created from a series of rooms on an upper floor.

Castle of Good Hope

Krak des Chevaliers

O NE OF THE GREATEST castles in the world, Krak des Chevaliers was built in the middle of the 12th century by the Crusaders. Having captured Jerusalem and the Holy Land from the Muslims, they required strong bases from which to defend their newly won territories. The largest of a string of such fortresses, Krak des Chevaliers withstood countless attacks and sieges, but the Crusaders abandoned it after their defeat at the hands of the Arabs in 1271. Villagers settled within the walls and remained there until the 1930s, when the castle was cleared and restored.

Krak des Chevaliers, the Crusaders' magnificent fortress

INSIDE THE CASTLE

Krak des Chevaliers (Castle of the Knights) crowns a 650-m (2,133-ft) high hill at Homs Gap, commanding the route from Antioch to Beirut. The crusading Knights Hospitalers undertook a massive expansion program in the mid-12th century, adding a 30-m (98-ft) thick outer wall, seven guard towers, and ▷ *stables* for 500 horses. An inner reservoir filled by water from an ▷ *aqueduct* supplied the needs of the 4,000-strong garrison. Storerooms were stocked with food produced by local villagers. The castle had its own olive presses and a bakery. The later Muslim occupants converted the Crusaders' ▷ *Chapel* of St George into a mosque and also added refinements, such as ▷ *baths* and pools.

THE FINAL CONQUEST

While the Crusaders continued their campaigns in the Middle East throughout the 12th and into the 13th centuries, Krak des Chevaliers remained secure. In 1163, the knights successfully fought off the army of Nuradin, sultan of Damascus, in the valley below. Then in 1188, the Muslim leader, Saladin, attempted to lay siege to the castle, but finding it impenetrable, withdrew his forces. Finally, in 1271, the Mameluk sultan, Baibars I, devised a scheme. He forged a letter, said to be from the Crusader commander in Tripoli, instructing the army at Krak to surrender. Baibars' forces succeeded in taking the Crusaders' bastion without so much as a fight.

General view of Krak des Chevaliers

RECONSTRUCTION OF KRAK DES CHEVALIERS

This shows how the castle would have looked over 800 years ago. In its heyday the castle would have housed a garrison of 4,000.

Inner Wall

An aqueduct fed the castle's reservoirs with rainwater from the hills.

Stables

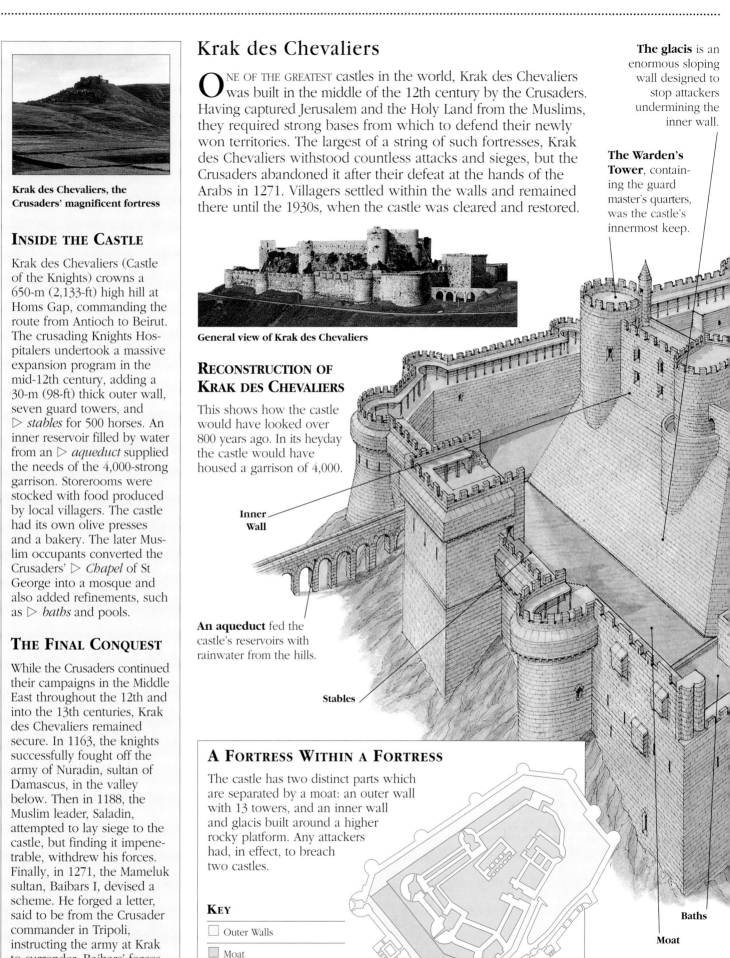

The glacis is an enormous sloping wall designed to stop attackers undermining the inner wall.

The Warden's Tower, containing the guard master's quarters, was the castle's innermost keep.

Baths

Moat

A FORTRESS WITHIN A FORTRESS

The castle has two distinct parts which are separated by a moat: an outer wall with 13 towers, and an inner wall and glacis built around a higher rocky platform. Any attackers had, in effect, to breach two castles.

KEY

☐ Outer Walls

▨ Moat

▨ Inner Walls

▨ Baths

0 metres   100

0 yards   100

★ Tower of the King's Daughter

The northern face of this tower has a large projecting gallery from which rocks could be hurled if the outer wall was breached. At ground level the tower is decorated with three blind arches.

Outer wall

THE PERFECT CASTLE

The author T E Lawrence ("Lawrence of Arabia") described Krak des Chevaliers as "the most wholly admirable castle in the world". Indeed, it served as an inspiration to the English king, Edward I, who passed by on the ninth Crusade in 1272 and returned home to build his own castles across England and Wales.

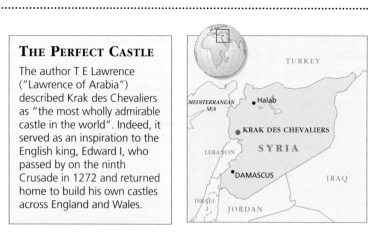

KEY DATES

1031 The Emir of Aleppo builds the original fortress.

1110 Crusaders under Tancred take the bastion.

1142 The Knights Hospitalers occupy the castle and construct the outer wall.

1271 Baibars I, the Mameluk sultan, captures the castle and adds further fortifications.

1934 Restoration begins.

TANCRED, PRINCE OF ANTIOCH

In 1096 a young Norman lord from southern Italy, Tancred of Hauteville (1078–1112), set out with his uncle, Bohemund, and fellow Norman lords on the first Crusade to the Holy Land. Their object was to halt the advance of the Seljuk Turks, who were threatening the Byzantine Empire, and to claim Jerusalem for the Christians. Tancred soon made a name for himself when he captured Tarsus from the Turks. He played a major role in the siege of Antioch and led the march on Jerusalem (1099) and its occupation. A year later, when Bohemund was taken prisoner by the Turks, Tancred took control of the Principality of Antioch. As Prince of Antioch, he ruled supreme in northern Syria, mounting attacks on both the Turks and Byzantines. In 1110 he occupied the hilltop fortress, which the Crusaders were to transform into the mighty Krak des Chevaliers.

★ Main Entranceway

A long, stepped passage leads from the site of the former drawbridge to the upper castle. Small ceiling apertures throw light into the corridor, though they were also designed for pouring boiling oil over invaders. The passageways are high and wide enough to allow for mounted riders.

The chapel was built by the Crusaders and later converted into a mosque after the Muslim conquest. Its Islamic *minbar* (pulpit) can still be seen.

The entrance passage doubled back on itself to confuse any invaders who managed to get this far.

★ Loggia

Running along one side of the castle's innermost courtyard, the loggia is a graceful Gothic arcade with a vaulted ceiling (▷ Gothic Style p73). It is decorated with carved floral motifs and animals. Beyond the loggia is the Great Hall, which functioned as a refectory.

Inner Fortress

STAR FEATURES

★ **Tower of the King's Daughter**

★ **Main Entranceway**

★ **Loggia**

THE CULT OF BAAL

The Phoenician word *Baal* is thought to mean "god" and *Baalbek*, "the god of the Bekaa valley". According to legend, Baalbek was the birthplace of the Phoenician sun god Baal-Hadad, one of three deities worshiped here before Roman times. In the Old Testament of the Bible, Baal is believed to have been the pagan god of nature and fertility. The idolatrous worship of Baal was derided for its practice of sacrificing children, its lasciviousness, and because believers were seen to prostrate themselves and kiss its image. According to 1 Kings 18:19–40, the fraud of the many priests of Baal was exposed in a contest with the prophet Elijah on Mount Carmel.

TEMPLE OF VENUS

Standing apart from the main complex are the ruins of the pentagonal Temple of Venus. Built in the 3rd century AD, it is smaller and more intimate than the other temples and exquisitely decorated. Sea-shells, doves, and other motifs relating to the goddess of love adorned the interior. The remains of an arch perch precariously at the end of a row of columns, having survived the rumblings of earthquakes and pillaging by later architects. After the region's conversion to Christianity, the Byzantines converted the temple into a church dedicated to the martyr St Barbara, who remains the patron saint of modern-day Baalbek. Nearby are the ruins of the 1st-century Temple of the Muses.

The ruins of Baalbek, the Roman Empire's largest religious site

Baalbek

Rainwater spout, Temple of Jupiter

ONE OF THE best preserved Classical architectural ensembles in the Middle East (▷ *Classical Style p231*) is in Baalbek. Although Phoenician in origin, the site seen today is Roman, begun during the reign of Augustus (27 BC–AD 14). Such was the scale of the project that it took ten generations to complete. Ultimately, however, Christianity triumphed over the pagan gods and most of Baalbek's temples were knocked down. The temples were used as a fortress by the Arabs from 634, raided by Mongol hordes in the 13th and 14th centuries and left abandoned by the Ottomans in the 16th century. Numerous earthquakes also damaged the structures. Excavation of the site began in 1898.

Temple of Bacchus, the Arab Fortification and Mosque ruin, Baalbek

★ Temple of Jupiter
Only six columns remain to convey the massive scale of this building. Each is 2.5 m (8 ft) in diameter and 20 m (67 ft) high, the equivalent of a six-story apartment block.

The Corinthian columns of the peristyle (colonnade) still support the enormous cornice stones and huge triangular pediment.

The interior was lavishly decorated with fluted columns supporting two tiers of niches for statuary.

The monumental portal was set in walls decorated with reliefs of vines, grapes and other Bacchanalian motifs.

STAR FEATURES

★ Temple of Jupiter

★ Hexagonal Court

★ Temple of Bacchus

★ Great Court

★ Hexagonal Court
Acting as a vestibule to the Temple of Jupiter, this court's central area was open to the sky and decorated with a mosaic floor. It was surrounded by a covered arcade.

Temple of Bacchus

is is the best preserved of all the buildings in Baalbek. It is generally assumed to have been dedicated to the man god of wine and revelry because of its vine decorations.

BAALBEK FESTIVAL

In July and August each year Baalbek is the venue for a prestigious festival of drama and music. Against the awesome backdrop of the temple ruins, international artists from companies such as the Berlin Philharmonic Orchestra, the Bolshoy Ballet and the Old Vic Theatre have performed here.

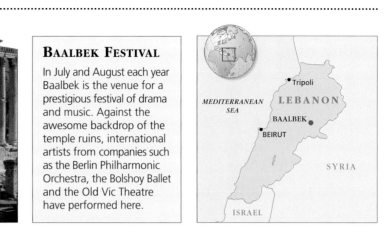

The statue of the dedicatory god would have stood here, at the temple's western end, approached by a flight of stairs.

★ Great Court

This huge, colonnaded area is where sacrifices and dances took place to the fertility god, Baal, the Semitic forerunner of Jupiter. At the centre is a large sacrificial altar flanked by decorated ablution pools.

Cella (inner hall)

RECONSTRUCTION OF THE TEMPLE OF BACCHUS

This shows the temple as it would have been after its completion in the middle of the 2nd century AD. Although a huge structure in its own right, it was known as the "small temple" because it was dwarfed by the adjacent Temple of Jupiter.

PLAN OF BAALBEK

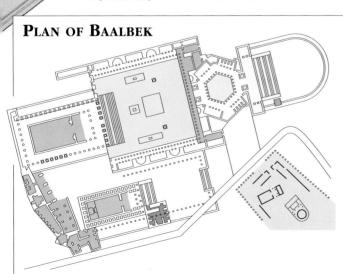

KEY

- Temple of Jupiter
- Great Court
- Hexagonal Court
- Forecourt & Propylaeum
- Ticket Office
- Museum Entrance
- Temple of Venus
- Arab Tower & Museum
- Temple of Bacchus
- Arab Fortification & Mosque

KEY DATES

15 BC Julius Caesar makes Baalbek a Roman colony.

c.244–9 Emperor Philip the Arab builds the Hexagonal Court; the last monument on the Baalbek site.

1984 Baalbek is declared a UNESCO World Heritage Site.

THE ROMAN SUN CITY

Baalbek was known as Heliopolis – the City of the Sun – after the Romans arrived in 15 BC and transformed the site into the largest place of worship in the empire. One of the first and greatest structures to be built was for their sun God Jupiter (▷ *Temple of Jupiter)*. Its base was a vast stone podium that had been constructed by the Phoenicians. The large sanctuary of Jupiter was surrounded by 104 granite columns from Aswan and the inner temple itself had a further 50 columns. It was completed in AD 60, during the reign of Nero (r.54–68). Beyond the temple, altars and other religious buildings filled the colonnaded ▷ *Great Court*, which was begun during Trajan's reign (r.98–117), but was never finished. Only a few of its original columns remain, as most of them were stolen or destroyed. In the 6th century, Justinian (r.527–65) used eight columns from the Great Court in the construction of the Haghia Sophia basilica in Turkey. Successive Roman emperors constructed further temples on the Baalbek site, which included the ▷ *Temple of Bacchus* and the ▷ *Temple of Venus*.

GOLGOTHA

Inside the church, two stair-cases lead up to Golgotha, meaning "Place of the Skull" in Hebrew. On the left is a Greek Orthodox chapel with its altar placed directly over the rocky outcrop on which the cross of Christ's Crucifixion is believed to have stood (▷ *Rock of Golgotha*). The crack in Golgotha, visible from the apse of the ▷ *Chapel of Adam* below, is believed to have been caused by the earthquake that followed Christ's death (*Matthew* 27:51). To the right is a Roman Catholic chapel containing a silver and bronze altar made in 1558 and donated by Cardinal Ferdinand de Medici. In between the two altars is the Stabat Mater, an altar commemorating Mary's sorrow at the foot of the cross.

The Holy Sepulcher seen from the roof of St Helena's chapel

THE STATUS QUO

No fewer than 17 churches are represented in Jerusalem, a result of many historical schisms. Fierce disputes, lasting centuries, between Christian creeds over ownership of the Church of the Holy Sepulcher were largely resolved by an Ottoman decree issued in 1852. Still in force and known as the Status Quo, it divides custody of the church among Armenians, Greeks, Copts, Roman Catholics, Ethiopians, and Syrians. Some areas are administered communally. Every day, the church is unlocked by a Muslim keyholder acting as a "neutral" intermediary. This ceremonial task has been performed by a member of the same family for generations.

Church of the Holy Sepulcher, Jerusalem

BUILT AROUND WHAT IS BELIEVED to be the site of Christ's crucifixion, burial, and resurrection, this complex church is the most important in Christendom. The first basilica here was built by Roman emperor Constantine between AD 326 and 335 at the suggestion of his mother, St Helena. It was rebuilt on a smaller scale by Byzantine emperor Constantine Monomachus in the 1040s following its destruction by Fatimid sultan Hakim in 1009, but was much enlarged again by the Crusaders between 1114 and 1170. A disastrous fire in 1808 and an earthquake in 1927 necessitated extensive repairs.

The mosaic of roofs and domes of the Church of the Holy Sepulcher°

The Rotunda, heavily rebuilt after the 1808 fire, is the most majestic part of the church.

★ Christ's Tomb

For Christians, this is the most sacred site of all. Inside the 1810 monument, a marble slab covers the rock on which Christ's body is believed to have been laid.

The Crusader bell tower was reduced by two stories in 1719.

Stone of Unction

This is where the anointing and wrapping of Christ's body after his death has been commemorated since medieval times. The present stone dates from 1810.

Chapel of the Franks

The main entrance is early 12th-century. The right-hand door was blocked up late in the same century.

Courtyard

The main entrance courtyard is flanked by chapels. The disused steps opposite the bell tower once led to the Chapel of the Franks, the Crusaders' ceremonial entrance to Golgotha.

THE HOLY FIRE

On the Saturday of Orthodox Easter, all the church's lamps are put out and the faithful stand in the dark, a symbol of the darkness at the Crucifixion. A candle is lit at Christ's Tomb, then another and another, until the entire basilica and courtyard are ablaze with light, symbolizing the Resurrection. Legend says the fire comes from heaven.

The Easter ceremony of the Holy Fire

THE FIRST CHURCHES

Christian churches did not appear in the Holy Land until AD 200. Roman suspicion of unauthorized sects kept these churches underground until the 4th century AD when Christianity became the dominant religion.

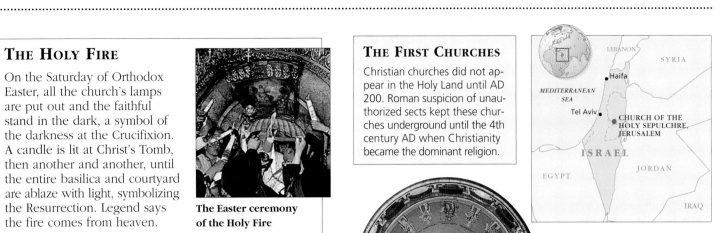

The Seven Arches of the Virgin are the remains of an 11th-century colonnaded courtyard.

Catholikon Dome
Rebuilt after the 1927 earthquake and decorated with an image of Christ, this dome covers the central nave of the Crusader church. This part of the building is now used for Greek Orthodox services.

KEY DATES

326–35 Emperor Constantine and St Helena have the first basilica built.

1114–70 Crusaders enlarge the building.

1981 Old City of Jerusalem joins the list of UNESCO World Heritage Sites.

CHRIST'S TOMB

For the construction of the first church, in the 4th century, Emperor Constantine's builders dug away the hillside to leave the presumed rock-hewn tomb of Christ (▷ *Christ's Tomb*) isolated, with enough room to build a church around it. To achieve this end, an old temple had to be cleared from the site and in the process the ▷ *Rock of Golgotha*, believed to be the site where Christ was nailed to the cross, was found. A succession of shrines replaced the original 4th-century one. In 1555, a shrine was commissioned by the Franciscan friar Bonifacio da Ragusa. The present shrine was rebuilt in 1809–10, after a severe fire in 1808. The shrine contains two chapels. The outer Chapel of the Angel has a low pilaster with a piece of the stone said to have been rolled from the mouth of Christ's tomb by angels. It serves as a Greek Orthodox altar. A low door leads to the inner Chapel of the Holy Sepulcher which houses the place where Christ's body was said to have been laid.

The Centre of the World, according to ancient map-makers, is marked here by a stone basin.

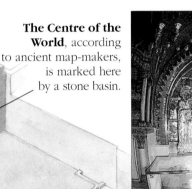

★ Rock of Golgotha
Through the glass around the Greek Orthodox altar can be seen the outcrop of rock venerated as the site of the Crucifixion.

Chapel of Adam

Rock of Golgotha

The Chapel of St Helena is now dedicated to St Gregory the Illuminator, patron saint of the Armenians.

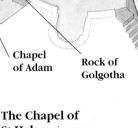

Ethiopian Monastery
Living in the cluster of small buildings on the roof of the Chapel of St Helena is a community of Ethiopian monks.

STAR FEATURES

★ **Christ's Tomb**

★ **Rock of Golgotha**

Stairs to the Inventio Crucis Chapel

Dome of the Rock, Jerusalem

Tile above the south entrance

CONSIDERED ONE of the first and greatest achievements of Islamic architecture, the Dome of the Rock was built in AD 688–91 by the Omayyad caliph Abd el-Malik. Built to proclaim the superiority of Islam and provide an Islamic focal point in the Holy City, the majestic structure now dominates Jerusalem and has become a symbol of the city. More a shrine than a mosque, the mathematically harmonious structure echoes elements of Classical and Byzantine styles of architecture (▷ *Classical style p231* and ▷ *Byzantine style p247*).

View of the Dome of the Rock with the Muslim Quarter in the background

The drum is decorated with tiles and verses from the Koran which tell of Mohammed's Night Journey.

★ Tile Work
The multicolored tiles that adorn the exterior are faithful copies of Persian tiles that Suleyman the Magnificent added in 1545 to replace the damaged original mosaics.

Koranic verses

The octagonal arcade is adorned with original mosaics (AD 692) and an inscription inviting Christians to recognize the truth of Islam.

Marble panel

Inner Corridor
The space between the inner and outer arcades forms a corridor around the Rock. The shrine's two corridors recall the ritual circular movement of pilgrims around the Qaaba in Mecca.

STAR FEATURES

★ **Tile Work**

★ **Interior of Dome**

Crescent Finial and Dome

The dome was originally made of copper but is now covered with gold leaf, thanks to the financial support of the late King Hussein of Jordan.

HOLY SITE

One of the oldest and most beautiful of all mosques, the Dome of the Rock is the third most holy site of Islam after Mecca and Medina. The mosque is also important for Judaism as it stands on the site of the two temples of the Jews - the first built by King Solomon and the second by Herod.

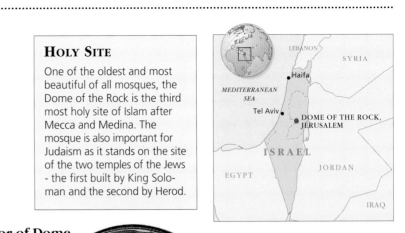

★ Interior of Dome

The dazzling interior of the cupola has elaborate floral decoration as well as various inscriptions. The large text commemorates Saladin, who sponsored restoration work on the building.

Green and gold mosaics

create a scintillating effect on the walls below the dome.

Outer corridor

KEY DATES

691 Building work on the Dome of the Rock is completed.

16th century Suleyman the Magnificent commissions the dazzling tile work on the exterior.

1981 The Dome of the Rock joins the UNESCO list of World Heritage Sites.

THE DOME OF THE CHAIN AND THE GOLDEN GATE

Just east of the Dome of the Rock stands the small Dome of the Chain, set at the approximate center of the *Haram ash-Sharif*. The reasons given for its construction are varied. According to one theory it sits at the site of the Holy of Holies (the most sacred and inaccessible place in Herod's Temple), which is thought of in Jewish tradition as the *omphalos*, the navel of the universe. The Dome of the Chain is a simple structure with a domed roof supported by 17 columns. It is famous for its marvelous 13th-century interior tiling which surpasses even that of the Dome of the Rock. Its name derives from the legend that a chain once hung from the roof and whoever told a lie while holding it would be struck dead by lightning. Further east is the Golden Gate, one of the original Herodian city gates. Jews believe the Messiah will enter Jerusalem through this gate, which is said to be the reason why the Muslims walled it up in the 7th century.

Well of Souls

This staircase leads down to a chamber under the Rock known as the Well of Souls. The dead are said to meet here twice a month to pray.

Stained-glass window

The Rock

The Rock is variously believed to be where Abraham was asked to sacrifice Isaac, where Mohammed left the Earth on his Night Journey, and the site of the Holy of Holies of Herod's Temple.

Each outer wall is 20.4 m (67 ft) long. This exactly matches the dome's diameter and its height from the base of the drum.

South entrance

The cliff-top plateau of Masada is surrounded by two walls 1,400 m (4,593 ft) long and 4 m (13 ft) wide. Within, King Herod built palaces, barracks, and storehouses. His private retreat, the splendid northern ▷ *Hanging Palace*, extended over three terraces cut into the cliff-face and connected by steep staircases. The rooms were lavishly decorated with mosaic floors. Walls and ceilings were painted to resemble stone and marble, and elegant columns surrounded balconies and courtyards. His other palace, the larger ▷ *Western Palace*, served as the administrative center and contained Herod's throne room and royal apartments. In the ruins of a stone-built storehouse complex, the remains of storage jars used for keeping wine, oil, and grain were found.

THE ZEALOTS

Around the time of Herod's death in 4 BC, the inhabitants of Masada became embroiled in a rebellion against Rome. The uprising was led by Judas of Galilee, founder of the Zealots, a militant Jewish sect which vehemently opposed the Romans because of their pagan beliefs. The Romans crushed the rebellion and took Masada. In AD 66, at the start of the First Jewish Revolt, the Zealots regained the mountain-top. They lived among the palaces using the fortress as a base to conduct raids against the Romans. At the time of the ▷ *Roman siege of Masada*, there were 1,000 inhabitants.

The desert fort of Masada, site of the Zealots' last stand

Masada

Tᴴɪꜱ ɪꜱᴏʟᴀᴛᴇᴅ ᴍᴏᴜɴᴛᴀɪɴ-ᴛᴏᴘ ꜰᴏʀᴛʀᴇꜱꜱ about 440 m (1,300 ft) above the banks of the Dead Sea, known as Masada, is believed to be the location of the oldest synagogue in the world. It was fortified as early as the 1st or 2nd century BC and then enlarged and reinforced by Herod the Great, who added two luxurious palace complexes. On Herod's death the fortress passed into Roman hands but it was captured in AD 66 during the First Revolt by Jews of the Zealot sect. After the Romans crushed the rebels in Jerusalem, Masada remained the last Jewish stronghold. It remained defended for over two years before the walls were breached by the Romans in AD 73.

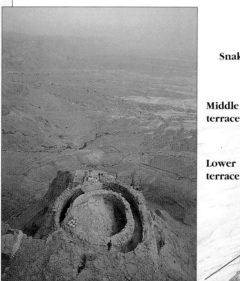

★ Hanging Palace
Part of the large Northern Palace complex, the Hanging Palace was Herod's private residence. It was built on three levels; the middle terrace had a circular hall used for entertaining, the lower had a bathhouse.

Calidarium
Masada's hot baths are one of the best preserved parts of the fortress. The columns remain, on which the original floor was raised to allow hot air to circulate underneath and heat the room.

Cable Car
A large number of pilgrims visit this rocky mountain citadel every year. The cable car was installed to help with their tiring journey.

Upper terrace

Snake Path

Storerooms

Middle terrace

Lower terrace

The Water Gate is at the head of a winding path leading to reservoirs below.

Synagogue
Possibly built by Herod, this synagogue is thought to be the oldest in the world. The stone seats were added by the Zealots.

STAR FEATURES

★ **Hanging Palace**

★ **Western Palace**

Cistern

At the foot of the mountain Herod built dams and canals that collected the seasonal rainwater to fill cisterns on the northeast side of the fortress. This water was then carried by donkey to the cisterns on top of the rock, such as this one in the southern part of the plateau.

THE SURVIVORS

The story of the Roman siege of Masada and the mass suicide of the Jewish inhabitants was told by two women survivors. They had escaped the killings and the devastating fire lit by the last man before he, too, took his life, by hiding with their children in a cave.

Southern Citadel

Columbarium

This is a small building with niches for funerary urns; it is thought the urns held the ashes of non-Jewish members of Herod's court.

Western Wall

West Gate

The Roman ramp is now the western entrance to the site.

★ Western Palace

Used for receptions and the accommodation of Herod's guests, the Western Palace was richly decorated with mosaic floors and frescoes adorning the walls.

KEY DATES

37–31 BC Herod starts his grandiose building projects.

1963 Excavations of the Masada stronghold begin.

2001 UNESCO declares Masada a World Heritage Site.

HEROD THE GREAT

Herod was born in 73 BC, the son of a Jewish father, Antipater, and an Arab mother, Cyprus. Herod, like his father, was a practicing Jew. Antipater was the right-hand man of Hyrcanus, king of Judea (r.76–30 BC) – a vassal state of Rome – and instrumental in Herod's first appointment at the age of 16 as governor of Galilee. With cunning and ruthlessness, Herod moved up the political ladder, married the king's daughter, found favor with his Roman overlords and was ultimately crowned king of Judea himself in 37 BC. He embarked on a massive building programme, which included a modern port, Caesarea, fortresses such as Masada, and the grand reconstruction of the Temple in Jerusalem. Orthodox Jews however, considered him racially impure and were incensed by his tyrannical rule and his excessive taxes. They despised the presence of the golden eagle – a symbol of Roman power – on the Temple gate. When he died in 4 BC his kingdom was divided among four of his sons – he had had two sons executed just before dying to prevent them from succeeding him.

THE ROMAN SIEGE OF MASADA (AD 70–73)

Roman catapult missiles

According to a 1st-century account by historian Flavius Josephus, the Roman legions laying siege to Masada numbered about 10,000 men. To prevent the Jewish rebels from escaping, the Romans surrounded the mountain with a ring of eight camps, linked by walls; an arrangement that can still be seen today. To make their attack, the Romans built a huge earthen ramp up the mountainside. Once this was finished, a tower was constructed against the walls. From the shelter of this tower the Romans set to work with a battering ram. The defenders hastily erected an inner defensive wall, but this proved little obstacle and Masada fell when it was breached. Rather than submit to the Romans the Jews inside chose to commit mass suicide. Josephus relates how each man was responsible for killing his own family. "Masada shall not fall again" is a swearing-in oath of the modern Israeli army.

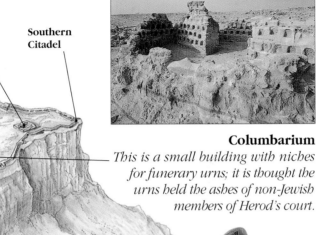

Remains of one of the Roman base camps viewed from the fortress top

THE SIQ

Access to Petra is through a deep ravine called the Siq, preceded by a wide valley called the Bab el-Siq. The entrance to the Siq is marked by the remains of a monumental arch and is the start of a gallery of intriguing insights into the Nabataeans' past. These include rock-cut water channels, Nabataean graffiti, carved niches with worn outlines of ancient deities, Nabataean paving stones, and flights of steps leading nowhere. As the Siq descends it becomes almost imperceptibly deeper and narrower (at its narrowest the walls are only 1 m (3 ft) apart). At its deepest, darkest point the Siq opens out before Petra's most thrilling monument, the ▷ *Treasury*. From here the path leads into the ▷ *Outer Siq*.

The Palace Tomb, a three-storey imitation of a Roman palace

THE ROYAL TOMBS

Carved into the base of El-Khubtha mountain, where the ▷ *Outer Siq* opens out onto Petra's central plain, are the Urn, Palace, and Corinthian Tombs. Together they are known as the Royal Tombs. Their monumental size suggests they were built for wealthy or important people, possibly Petran kings or queens. These tombs and their neighbors are also remarkable for the vivid striations of color rippling through their sandstone walls, an effect heightened in the warm glow of late afternoon sun. Particularly striking are the Silk Tomb and the ceiling in the Urn Tomb.

Petra

S ET DEEP IN THE ROCK and protected by the valley walls is one of the world's most marvellously preserved and impressive archaeological sites, Petra. There has been human settlement here since prehistoric times, but before the Nabataeans came, Petra was just another watering hole. Between the 3rd century BC and the 1st century AD they built a superb city, the center of a vast trading empire. In AD 106 Petra was annexed by Rome. Christianity arrived in the 4th century, the Muslims in the 7th and the Crusaders in the 12th. Petra then lay forgotten until the early 19th century.

The Outer Siq Designs
A range of intermediate design styles are displayed throughout, including on the Treasury and Theater tombs. One, freestanding, uniquely combines Classical features with a crowstep used as a battlement.

Treasury Tholos
The central figure may be the Petran fertility goddess El-Uzza. Bullet marks in the tholos and urn have been made over the years by Bedouins attempting to release hidden treasure.

Eagle, Nabataean male deity symbol

"Attic" burial chambers were a device to protect the dead from animals and tomb robbers.

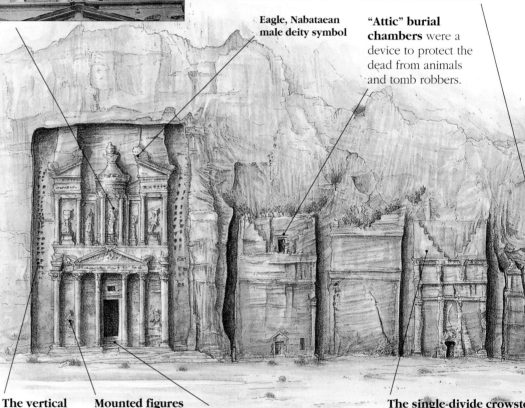

The vertical footholds may have been to aid the sculptors.

Mounted figures of Castor and Pollux, sons of Zeus, flank the portico.

THE OUTER SIQ

The artwork above shows some of the major constructions on the left-hand side of the Outer Siq leading from the Treasury to the Theater. In reality, of course, the route bends and twists and on both the left and right sides are a great number of other tombs and features of architectural interest.

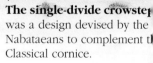

The single-divide crowstep was a design devised by the Nabataeans to complement the Classical cornice.

Treasury Interior
A colossal doorway dominates the outer court (left) and leads to an inner chamber of 12 sq m (129 sq ft). At the back of the chamber is a sanctuary with an ablution basin, suggesting that the Treasury was in fact a temple.

THE ARCHITECTURE OF PETRA

The Nabataeans were adventurous architects, inspired by other cultures but always creating a distinctive look. The multiple crowstep can be seen as a design of the first settlers, whereas complex Nabataean Classical buildings reflect a later period. The dating of façades is very difficult, as many examples of the "early" style appear to have been built during the Classical period (▷ *Classical style p231*) or even later.

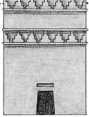
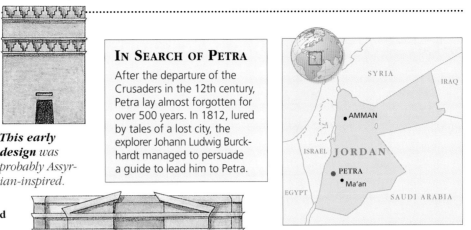

This early design was probably Assyrian-inspired.

IN SEARCH OF PETRA

After the departure of the Crusaders in the 12th century, Petra lay almost forgotten for over 500 years. In 1812, lured by tales of a lost city, the explorer Johann Ludwig Burckhardt managed to persuade a guide to lead him to Petra.

Stacked look, favored by Nabataeans

Single-divide crowstep, lending height

This intermediate style, *seen frequently in Petra, placed multiple crowsteps with a single-divide crowstep, adding Classical cornices and pillars and Hellenistic doorways. This style continued well into the 1st century AD.*

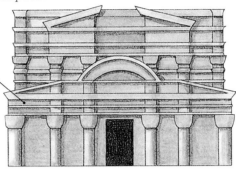

Nabataean Classical designs, such as the Bab el-Siq Triclinium (above), are complex, possibly experimental fusions of Classical and native styles.

KEY DATES

3rd century BC Nabataeans settle in Petra.

12th century AD Petra falls into decline after the Crusaders depart.

1812 The explorer Johann Burckhardt rediscovers Petra.

1985 Petra joins UNESCO's World Heritage list.

THE NABATAEANS

The Nabataeans' original homeland lay in northeastern Arabia but they migrated west in the 6th century BC, settling eventually in Petra. As merchants and entrepreneurs, they grasped the lucrative potential of Petra's position on the spice and incense trade routes from East Asia and Arabia to the Mediterranean. By the 1st century BC they had made Petra the center of a rich, powerful kingdom extending from Damascus in the north to the Red Sea in the south and had built a city large enough to support 20–30,000 people. Key to their success was their ability to control and conserve water. Conduits and old terracotta piping can be seen along the walls of the ▷ *Siq* – part of an elaborate city water system. The Romans felt threatened by their achievements and took over the city in AD 106. Petra continued to thrive culturally for a time. In the end, changes in trade routes and two devastating earthquakes eventually brought about the city's demise.

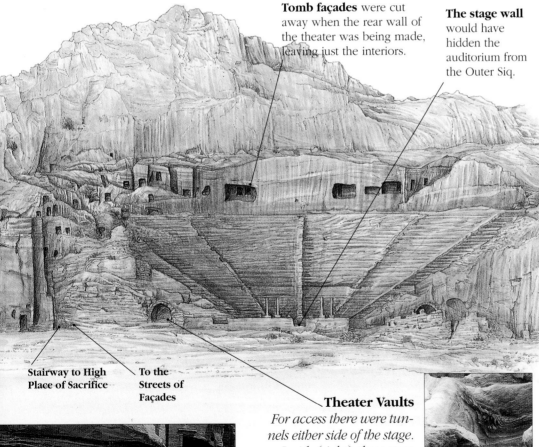

Tomb façades were cut away when the rear wall of the theater was being made, leaving just the interiors.

The stage wall would have hidden the auditorium from the Outer Siq.

Stairway to High Place of Sacrifice

To the Streets of Façades

Theater Vaults
For access there were tunnels either side of the stage. Inside (right) these were dressed with painted plaster or marble.

Streets of Façades
Carved on four levels, these tightly packed tombs may include some of Petra's oldest façades. Most are crowned with multiple crowsteps.

POOLS AND CHANNELS

Isfahan is a desert settlement where water is of paramount importance. Shah Abbas had his builders construct channels from the Zayandeh-Rud river to irrigate his palace gardens. The use of water was integral to Persian architecture. In the Imam Mosque the central courtyard is dominated by a large rectangular pool (▷ *ablutions pool*), used for the ritual washing required of Muslims before prayers. The pool perfectly reflects the ▷ *iwans* and the great ▷ *dome* creating an almost mystical impression of the real building blending with its otherworldly double. The two flanking ▷ *medresas* each have a trio of smaller ablutions basins connected by a narrow channel.

PERSIAN TILING

The Koranic prohibition of depicting humans and animals led Persian artisans to find alternative forms of expression in geometric and floral patterns. This is seen to greatest effect in the ceramic tiling and mosaics used to cover the façades, domes, and minarets of Iran's royal and public buildings. The art of ceramics was first imported from China and refined in Central Asia between the 10th and 13th centuries. The predominant use of turquoise and cobalt blue represents the heavens, while the luxuriant flower and leaf motifs suggest paradise or the Garden of Eden. Borders and bands of white script bear verses from the Koran so that mosques, in particular, can be read like one big, open holy book.

Decorative Persian tiling adorning the Imam Mosque

Imam Mosque, Isfahan

FORMERLY THE ROYAL MOSQUE (Masjid-i Shah), the Imam Mosque was the climax of Shah Abbas' (r.1586–1628) reconstruction of Isfahan. While not the largest mosque in Iran, it is considered to be the most architecturally perfect. The entrance sits at the centre of the south side of the city's main square, the Meydan-i Imam, but the architects skilfully switched the axis so that the mosque itself is angled to face Mecca, as all mosques must be. Despite the skewed axis, the ground plan is almost perfectly symmetrical, with four great *iwans* (arched portals) around a central courtyard. Either side of the main dome chamber are two smaller courtyards with colorfully tiled arcades and small pools. These serve as *medresas*, places in which the Koran and Islamic law are taught to students.

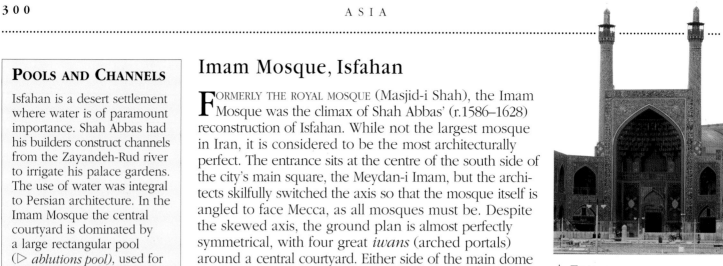

Meydan-i Imam Façade
The four minarets and great dome of the dominating Imam Mosque rise high above Isfahan's main square. The skewed axis that the mosque sits upon is barely discernable.

Shops lining the Meydan-i Imam paid rent which was used for the upkeep of the mosque.

Ablutions fountain

★ **Entrance**
The arched recess of the great entrance is lined with stalactite-like muqarnas *(three-dimensional Islamic decoration).*

Minaret

The entrance portal addresses the vast Meydan-i Imam, the central square of Isfahan.

Vaulted *iwan*

Ablutions pool

STAR FEATURES

★ **Entrance**

★ **Domed Prayer Chamber**

★ **Vaulted Interiors**

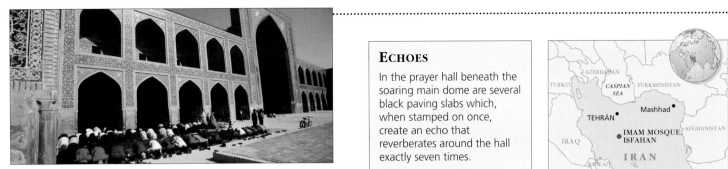

Prayer Courtyard
*Supplicants pray facing towards Mecca, the
direction of which is indicated by the* mihrab
(niche) in the prayer chamber.

ECHOES
In the prayer hall beneath the
soaring main dome are several
black paving slabs which,
when stamped on once,
create an echo that
reverberates around the hall
exactly seven times.

**A double
shell** reduces
the internal
height of
the prayer
chamber.

★ Domed Prayer Chamber
*The roof of the prayer hall
consists of a bulbous dome
sitting on a high drum. Its
exterior is covered in the
most fantastic blue and
gold tiling.*

Medresa

Domed side halls
connect the main
courtyard with the
twin *medresas*.

★ Vaulted Interiors
*Two hypostyle halls flank the main prayer
chamber. They are roofed by shallow domed
vaults, carried on broad Persian arches
supported on octagonal stone columns.*

KEY DATES

1586 Abbas I assumes
power in Persia.

1612 Construction of Imam
Mosque begins.

1628 Shah Abbas I dies.

1637 Imam Mosque is
finished.

1930–60 Restoration work
carried out by André Godard.

1979 Imam Mosque is
inscribed as a UNESCO
World Heritage Site.

SHAH ABBAS I AND ISFAHAN

The city of Isfahan has existed
for more than 2,500 years,
since it was first settled by the
Achaemenid kings (600–330
BC). However, its fame and
renown were only ensured
during the 17th century due to
the efforts of the Safavid Shah
Abbas I, who ruled Persia
from the late 16th to the early
17th century. Although a cruel
despot, Abbas was also cosmopolitan and far sighted. He
invited architects and craftsmen from Europe, the Middle
East, India, and as far afield as
China to come to Isfahan and
build. They created a magnificent palace quarter and, as its
centerpiece, a grand square
(▷ *Meydan-i Imam Façade*)
surrounded by regal pavilions,
arcades, and mosques. The
Imam Mosque was to have
been the crowning glory but
Abbas died before seeing it
completed. Following his
death it was said, "When this
great prince ceased to live,
Persia ceased to prosper."

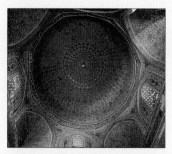

Stunning interior of the Tilla Kari Medresa

BUILDING THE REGISTAN

The three *medresas* were built over a period of 230 years. The first was the ▷ *Ulug Beg*, begun in 1417. Directly opposite, the ▷ *Sher Dor* ("Lion Bearer"), modeled on the Ulug Beg, was added two centuries later. Its unconventional façade depicts live animals and human faces (an interpretation of the Koran forbids this). The combined mosque and *medresa* of ▷ *Tilla Kari* ("Gold Decorated") was added in the mid-17th century. Its ceiling appears domed but is in fact flat – an effect created by the decreasing pattern size toward the center. The two later buildings were the work of the architect Abd al-Jabbar, who drew his inspiration from the earlier Timurid style, hence the harmonious relationship between the three.

A CENTER OF SCIENCE AND LEARNING

With room for over 100 students and teachers lodged in 52 cells around the courtyard, the ▷ *Ulug Beg* was effectively a university. Unlike the traditional *medresa*, which was wholly devoted to Islamic studies, students here also received an education in mathematics and the sciences. This was a reflection of Ulug Beg's own personal passions. Known as the "astronomer king" he also endowed Samarkand with one of the world's earliest observatories, a two-story structure built on a hill and meant to serve as a giant astronomical instrument pointing at the heavens. Only its circular foundations survive today.

The Registan, Samarkand

T HE THREE BUILDINGS SURROUNDING Samarkand's Registan square comprise one of the world's most spectacular architectural ensembles. In the 15th century Ulug Beg, grandson of the Mongol warlord Tamerlane, built a group of mosques, *caravanserais* (merchants' inns), and the Ulug Beg, a *medresa* (Koranic school), around the city's sandy market square. With the exception of the Ulug Beg, the other buildings were later destroyed and replaced in the 17th century by two more *medresas*, the Sher Dor and Tilla Kari.

★ Tilla Kari Medresa
Lavish gold-leaf gilding covers the Mecca-facing mihrab *beneath the dome chamber.*

★ Ulug Beg Medresa
The façade consists of a central arched pishtaq *(porch) flanked by two minarets. The elaborate tiling of stars is in keeping with Ulug Beg's passion for astronomy.*

STAR FEATURES

★ Tilla Kari Medresa

★ Ulug Beg Medresa

★ Sher Dor Medresa

Ornamental gardens today replace the former single-story buildings that stood in this area.

Prayer hall

The Courtyard has two arcaded tiers of cells for students and professors.

Arched Portals

The Sher Dor Medresa's marvelous courtyard contains large iwans *(arched portals) that are covered with spectacular tiling.*

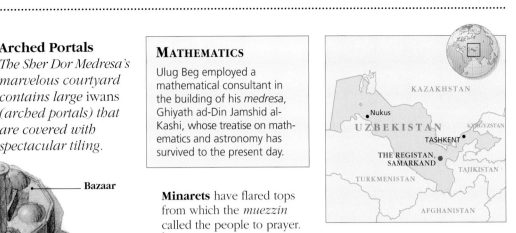

Bazaar

Minarets have flared tops from which the *muezzin* called the people to prayer.

Ablutions pool

★ **Sher Dor Medresa**

The impressive tiling on the pishtaq *(porch) depicts two lions stalking gazelles. Behind each lion is a sun portrayed with a human face.*

Ulug Beg Medresa Tiling

The brilliant glazed tiles of vine scrolls and flowers in a polychromy of gold leaf and lapis lazuli is typical of Timurid decoration.

Registan Square

A vast space at the heart of the city, the Registan, meaning a "sandy place", is the most famous site in Samarkand.

KEY DATES

c.1417–20 Construction of the Ulug Beg Medresa.

1619 Completion of the Sher Dor Medresa.

1647 The Tilla Kari is finished.

1932–52 Restoration of the Ulug Beg Medresa.

2001 The Registan is designated a UNESCO World Heritage Site.

GOLDEN SAMARKAND

Until recently isolated and largely forgotten, what is now known as Central Asia (formerly Turkestan and before that Transoxiana) was once the glittering center of the Islamic world. Its cities, which included Bukhara and Khiva, boasted magnificent palaces, mosques, and mausoleums. Most magnificent of all was Samarkand. The city was already renowned at the time of Alexander the Great but it owes its legendary reputation to Tamerlane (1336–1405), a distant relative of Genghis Khan. Brutal and despotic, Tamerlane was responsible for an estimated 17 million deaths as a result of his military campaigns. He is reported to have had walls and towers built with the skulls of his enemies. However, with the riches he accrued and the artisans he captured and sent back to Samarkand, he built a city that became a political, religious, commercial, and cultural capital whose influence extended widely into all corners of the known world.

Potala Palace, Lhasa

Perched on Lhasa's highest point, the Potala Palace is the greatest monumental structure in Tibet. Thirteen stories high, with over a thousand rooms, it was once the residence of Tibet's chief monk and leader, the 14th Dalai Lama, and therefore the center for both spiritual and temporal power. These days, after his escape to India in 1959, it is a vast museum, serving as a reminder of Tibet's rich and devoutly religious culture. The first palace on the site was built by Songtsen Gampo in 641, and this was incorporated into the larger building which stands today. There are two main sections – the White Palace, built by the fifth Dalai Lama in 1645, and the Red Palace which was completed in 1694.

★ Golden Roofs
Seemingly floating above the huge structure, the gilded roofs (actually copper) cover the funerary chapels dedicated to previous Dalai Lamas.

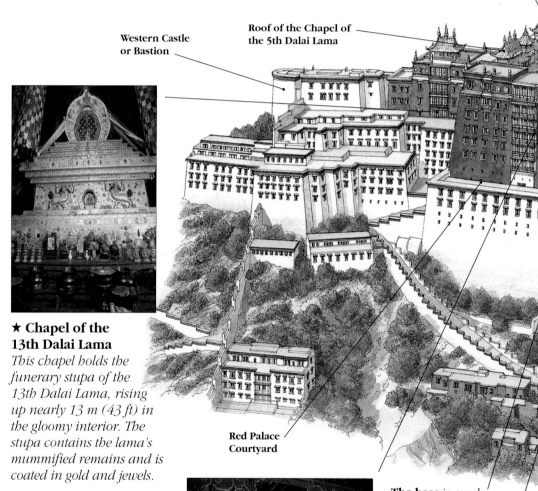

Western Castle or Bastion

Roof of the Chapel of the 5th Dalai Lama

★ Chapel of the 13th Dalai Lama
This chapel holds the funerary stupa of the 13th Dalai Lama, rising up nearly 13 m (43 ft) in the gloomy interior. The stupa contains the lama's mummified remains and is coated in gold and jewels.

Red Palace Courtyard

The base is purely structural, holding the palaces onto the steep hill.

Thangka Storehouse

★ 3D Mandala
This intricate mandala of a palace, covered in precious metals and jewels, embodies aspects of the path to enlightenment.

STAR FEATURES

★ Golden Roofs

★ Chapel of the 13th Dalai Lama

★ 3D Mandala

The Western Hall
The largest hall inside the Potala, the Western Hall is located on the second floor of the Red Palace and contains the holy throne of the 6th Dalai Lama.

Maitreya Chapel

East Sunshine Apartment

White Palace
The entrance to the main part of the building has a triple-stairway – the middle one is reserved for the sole use of the Dalai Lama.

The Eastern Courtyard is a huge open space used for important religious celebrations.

School of Religious Officials

The Eastern Bastion shows that the palace also had a defensive function.

View from the Roof
On a clear day the view of the valley and mountains is unequaled, although the newer parts of Lhasa are less impressive.

Heavenly King Murals
The East Entrance has sumptuous images of the Four Heavenly Kings, Buddhist guardian figures.

PRINCESS WENCHENG

Offered as a wife to Songtsen Gampo to broker peace, the Tang Dynasty (618–907) bride apparently converted the king and thus Tibet to Buddhism. She also instigated building many of Tibet's finest temples.

KEY DATES

AD 641 The first Potala Palace is built.

9th century The Tubo kingdom collapses and the Potala Palace is almost completely destroyed in the struggle for power.

1642 After the 5th Dalai Lama unites Tibet and becomes its spiritual and political leader, he decides to reconstruct the Potala Palace.

1922 The 13th Dalai Lama renovates much of the White Palace and adds two stories to the Red Palace.

1994 UNESCO adds the Potala Palace to its World Heritage List.

SONGTSEN GAMPO

The warrior king and founder of the Tubo kingdom, Songtsen Gampo, was born in AD 617 and built the original Potala Palace for his wife, Princess Wencheng. Most of it has long since burned down – only the Dharma Cave, set almost into the mountain, and the Saints' Chapel remain from the 7th century. They are both in the northern part of the Red Palace. The Dharma Cave is said to be the place where King Songtsen Gampo meditated. Inside, statues of the king, Princess Wencheng and his chief ministers are venerated. In the Saints' Chapel on the floor above, several important Buddhist figures and the 7th, 8th, and 9th Dalai Lamas are enshrined and worshiped.

Puning Temple, Chengde

Incense burner

ONE OF THE GREAT OUTER TEMPLES at the Imperial Summer Retreat at Chengde, Puning Si (Puning Temple) was built in 1755 by the emperor Qianlong to commemorate the defeat of Mongol rebels. The temple complex is a harmonious synthesis of Chinese and Tibetan architectural styles. As part of a series of halls ascending a mountain slope, the temple's climax is the Mayahana Hall, in which towers the world's largest wooden statue, a vast multi-armed 22-m (73-ft) high representation of Guanyin, the Buddhist goddess of compassion.

EMPEROR KANGXI

Kangxi (1654–1722) was the second Qing Emperor, and held on to power for 61 years, the longest reign in China's history. His rule was, in comparison with other emperors, frugal, practical, and conscientious. During his reign the empire increased in size and wealth, and most of the time enjoyed peace and prosperity. In 1703 he started to build a resort at Chengde, with gardens and temples, to shelter from the oppressive summer heat of Beijing, and also so that he could have a place to entertain his allies. An exceptional militarist, he was also a patron of the arts and sciences. His rule was followed by that of his son, Yongzheng (r.1723–35), and then his grandson, Qianlong (r.1736–96) who idolized his grandfather so much that he resigned after sixty years' rule so as not to outdo him.

Emperor Kangxi, the longest ruling emperor of China

THE SUMMER RETREAT

The second seat of rule for the Qing dynasty, the Imperial Summer Retreat fulfilled another important political function as nobles from all over China were invited to Chengde to forge alliances and be entertained by the traditional outdoor sports of wrestling, horse racing, and hunting. It was also common for the hardy Qing emperors and their entourages to forgo the palaces and camp out in the grounds of the Imperial Summer Retreat in the traditional round tents (yurts) of their Manchu homeland.

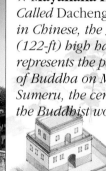

Buddhist Symbols
Guanyin's hands hold an array of Buddhist symbolic instruments – the pure sound of the bell is said to drive away evil spirits.

STAR FEATURES

★ **Mayahana Hall**

★ **Guanyin**

The Five Roofs of the Mahayana Hall are modeled on the roof of the main temple at Samye Monastery, the oldest in Tibet.

Viewing gallery

Attendant statue

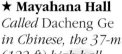

★ **Mayahana Hall**
Called Dacheng Ge in Chinese, the 37-m (122-ft) high hall represents the palace of Buddha on Mount Sumeru, the center of the Buddhist world.

Temple buildings appear to be randomly dotted around the complex but actually form a physical representation of Buddhist cosmology.

★ **Guanyin**
This huge effigy of Guanyin, also known to Buddhists as Avalokitesvara, is made of five types of wood and weighs 110 tons. On her head sits a statue of her teacher Amitabha.

Prayer Wheels

In Tibetan Buddhism, sacred mantras and prayers are inserted into the decorated cylinders and activated by spinning the wheel clockwise.

Stupas *(chortens)* traditionally hold sacred Buddhist relics (▷ *Buddhist Style p334*).

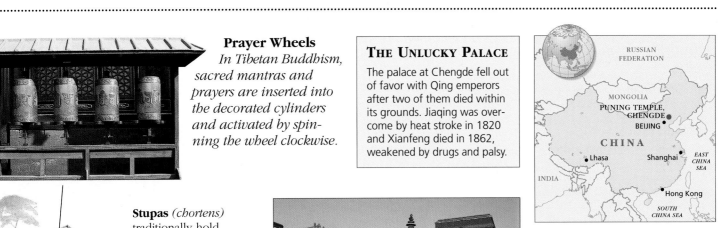

Terrace

The various small buildings on the terrace emphasize the monumental aspect of the main hall. The walls are painted to look as though they have windows in them showing the largely symbolic nature of the buildings.

PUNING TEMPLE

This illustration shows the Tibetan-styled rear section of the temple complex. This uses terraces to emphasize the differences of height and scale whereas the traditional Chinese part of the complex is a symmetrical series of buildings built on a single axis.

The defensive wall also symbolizes the limits of the Buddhist universe.

Gatehouse

THE IMPERIAL SUMMER RETREAT

Ringed by a wall over 10 km (6 miles) long the Summer Retreat contains over 100 halls and pavilions. Most of the outlying temples face the main palace complex, the center of authority.

① Main Palace Complex
② Puren Si
③ Pule Si
④ Anyuan Miao
⑤ Xumifushou Zhi Miao
⑥ Putuozongcheng Zhi Miao
⑦ Shuxiang Si
⑧ Puyou Si
⑨ Puning Si

0 meters   750
0 yards   750

TIMELINE

1703 Building work starts on the palace at Chengde.

1759 Puning Temple is completed.

1994 The Summer Retreat at Chengde is added to the UNESCO World Heritage List.

THE EIGHT OUTER TEMPLES AT CHENGDE

Eight temples out of a total of twelve originally constructed between 1713 and 1780 are still to be found set in a large semi-circle in the foothills outside the grounds of the ▷ *Imperial Summer Retreat*. Many of the temples at Chengde were built during the rule of Kangxi's grandson Qianlong who added Tibet and Xinjiang to the empire. To make his new allies feel at home, he built several temples with obvious Tibetan characteristics such as the Temple of Sumeru Happiness and Longevity (▷ *Xumifushou Zhi Miao*), built in 1780 for a visit by the Panchen Lama (second to the leader of Tibet, the Dalai Lama). Qianlong also built the huge Putuozongcheng Temple (▷ *Putuozongcheng Zhi Miao*), an imitation of the even bigger Potala Palace in Lhasa. Other ethnic groups such as the Han – the Chinese majority conquered by the Qing – were also represented. For example, Pule Temple (▷ *Pule Si*) features a hall with a conical roof similar to that of the Hall of Prayer for Good Harvests in Beijing's Temple of Heaven.

THE EXPANDING WALL

Sections of the bastion called the Great Wall were first built during the Warring States period (475–221 BC) by individual states to thwart incursions by northern tribes and to defend against aggressive neighbors. Simple and unconnected earthen ramparts, they were not joined together until the Qin dynasty (221–207 BC) first unified China under Shi Huangdi, the First Emperor. The maintenance and expansion of the wall reflected each succeeding dynasty's feelings of insecurity. Enlarged under the expansionist Han (206 BC–AD 220), the wall was neglected by the cosmopolitan Tang (AD 618–907), only to be heavily fortified by the more inward-looking Ming.

Qin Emperor Shi Huangdi, the so-called First Emperor

BUILDING ON SAND

The Qin wall was a simple tamped earth affair but the later Han dynasty adopted a more advanced technology that enabled them to build walls even in the bleak expanses of the Gobi desert. They would line wooden frames with a layer of willow reeds and twigs and then fill the frame with a mixture of mud, fine gravel, and water. This would then be pressed firmly into place. When the mix dried, the frame could be removed, leaving behind a large slab of hard brick-like mud that could be built upon again in the same manner. This is much like modern construction when steel rods are use to reinforce concrete.

The Great Wall of China

SYMBOL OF CHINA'S HISTORIC DETACHMENT and sense of vulnerability, the Great Wall snakes through the Chinese landscape over deserts, hills, and plains for over 4,000 km (2,500 miles). Yet despite its seemingly impregnable battlements the wall was ultimately an ineffective barricade. In the 13th century it was breached by the ferocious onslaught of the Mongols and then in the 17th century by the Manchu, helped by the decline of the Ming dynasty. Today, its dilapidated remains crumble across the rugged terrain of north China and only select sections have been restored.

★ **Panoramic Views**
Because the wall took advantage of the natural terrain for defensive purposes, following the highest points and clinging to ridges, it now offers some superb panoramic views.

Surface of stone slabs and bricks

Tamped layer of earth and rubble

Bigger rocks and stones

Kiln-fired bricks, cemented with a mortar of lime and glutinous rice

Large, locally quarried rocks

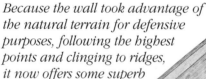

Crumbling Ruin
Away from Beijing, most of the wall is unrestored and has crumbled away with only the core remaining.

Ramparts enabled the soldiers to fire down on their attackers with relative impunity.

STAR FEATURES

★ **Panoramic Views**

★ **Watchtowers**

RECONSTRUCTION OF THE GREAT WALL

This shows a section of the wall as built by the most prolific wall builders of them all, the Ming dynasty (1368–1644). The section at Badaling, built around 1505, is similar to this and was restored in 1950s and 1980s.

★ **Watchtowers**
A Ming addition, these served as signal towers, forts, living quarters, and storerooms for provisions, gunpowder, and weapons.

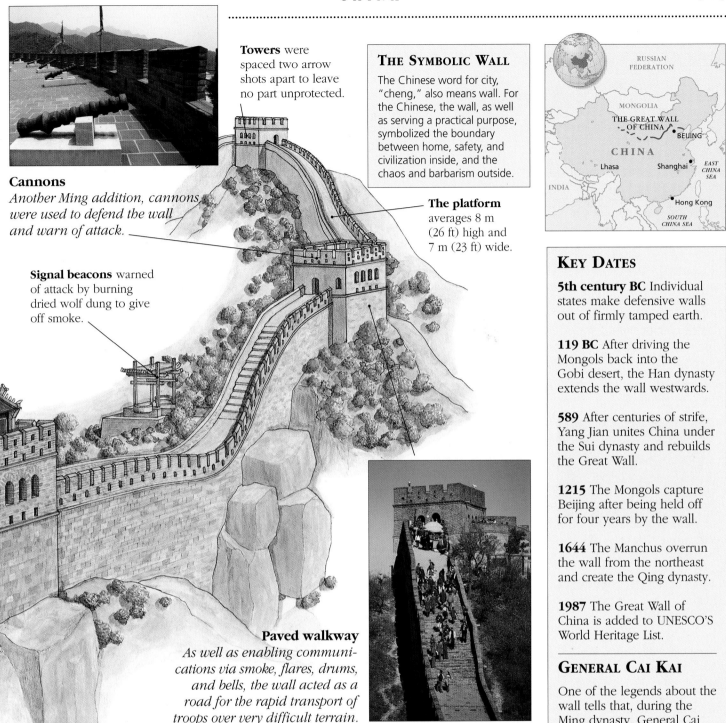

Towers were spaced two arrow shots apart to leave no part unprotected.

THE SYMBOLIC WALL

The Chinese word for city, "cheng," also means wall. For the Chinese, the wall, as well as serving a practical purpose, symbolized the boundary between home, safety, and civilization inside, and the chaos and barbarism outside.

Cannons

Another Ming addition, cannons were used to defend the wall and warn of attack.

Signal beacons warned of attack by burning dried wolf dung to give off smoke.

The platform averages 8 m (26 ft) high and 7 m (23 ft) wide.

Paved walkway

As well as enabling communications via smoke, flares, drums, and bells, the wall acted as a road for the rapid transport of troops over very difficult terrain.

KEY DATES

5th century BC Individual states make defensive walls out of firmly tamped earth.

119 BC After driving the Mongols back into the Gobi desert, the Han dynasty extends the wall westwards.

589 After centuries of strife, Yang Jian unites China under the Sui dynasty and rebuilds the Great Wall.

1215 The Mongols capture Beijing after being held off for four years by the wall.

1644 The Manchus overrun the wall from the northeast and create the Qing dynasty.

1987 The Great Wall of China is added to UNESCO'S World Heritage List.

GENERAL CAI KAI

One of the legends about the wall tells that, during the Ming dynasty, General Cai Kai was put in charge of building the section of wall at Huanghua. Rumor got back to the emperor that the general was taking too long over the task and wasting too much money. The unfortunate general was therefore summarily executed. Later when the Mongols mounted a concerted attack, General Cai Kai's efforts paid off; Huanghua was the only fortress that successfully warded off the enemy. Realising his mistake the emperor exhumed General Cai Kai's body and it was reburied with full honors near the part of the wall that he built.

THE GREAT WALL OF CHINA (MING DYNASTY)

0 kilometres 500

0 miles 400

Inner Mongolia

Yellow River

Datong

② ③ ④

Beijing

⑤

Taiyuan

Tianjin

Bo Hai

Qinghai Lake

Lanzhou

Yellow Sea

THE GREAT MYTH

The story that the Great Wall is the only man-made object visible to the naked eye from the moon is obviously false – it is far too thin.

PLACES TO VISIT THE WALL

① Jiayuguan
② Juyongguan and Badaling
③ Huanghua
④ Simatai
⑤ Shanhaiguan

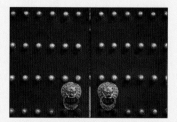
Forbidden City, Beijing

Glazed decorative wall relief

FORMING THE HEART OF BEIJING, the Forbidden City is China's most magnificent architectural complex. Completed in 1420, the palace is a comprehensive compendium of Chinese imperial architecture and a lasting monument of dynastic China where 24 emperors ruled over 500 years, ending with the pitiful Last Emperor, Puyi. As the symbolic center of the Chinese universe, the palace was the exclusive domain of the imperial court and dignitaries on royal business, but was opened to the public in 1949.

Chinese Lions
Lions symbolized sovereign power and the splendor of the imperial palace. Males are portrayed with a ball under their paw, while females have a lion cub.

Golden Water
Five marble bridges, symbolizing the five cardinal virtues of Confucianism, cross the Golden Water, which flows from west to east in a course designed to resemble the jade belt worn by officials.

OUTER COURT
Despite its name, this forms the very core of the complex. The surrounding buildings, originally built to service this series of halls, now house a variety of interesting displays.

★ Meridian Gate
From the balcony overlooking the courtyard the emperor would review his armies and perform ceremonies marking the start of a new calendar.

Gate of Supreme Harmony
Originally used for receiving visitors, the 24-m (78-ft) high, double-eaved hall was later used for banquets during the Qing dynasty (1644–1912).

★ Marble Carriageway
The central ramp carved with dragons chasing pearls among clouds was reserved for the emperor.

FALL OF THE MING

In 1644, as peasant rebels were storming the capital, the last Ming emperor, Chong Zhen, killed his daughter and concubines before fleeing the Forbidden Palace to hang himself on nearby Coal Hill.

The Hall of Preserving Harmony held the Civil Service Exams.

The Gate of Heavenly Purity leads to the Inner Court – reserved for the Imperial family only.

Bronze cauldrons filled with water were a practical precaution against fire.

The Hall of Middle Harmony was a place of preparation for the emperor when on official business.

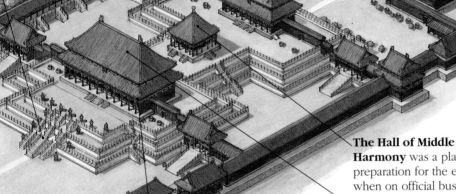

★ Hall of Supreme Harmony
The largest hall in the palace, this was used for major occasions such as the enthronement of an emperor. Inside the hall, the ornate throne sits beneath a fabulously colored ceiling.

Roof Guardians
These figures, associated with water, were supposed to protect the building from fire.

THE LAST EMPEROR

Henry (Aixinjueluo) Puyi ascended the Qing throne in 1908 aged three. His brief reign ended on 12 February 1912, when he abdicated in favor of the Republic of China. Puyi remained a virtual prisoner in the palace until 1924, before fleeing to the Japanese concession in Tianjin. Puyi never returned to the Forbidden City and died childless and anonymous in 1967 after working for seven years as a gardener at the Beijing Botanical Gardens.

Henry Puyi, the boy emperor

KEY DATES

1407 Construction of the Forbidden City starts.

1557 Fire destroys the main halls in the palace.

1925 The palace is renamed the Palace Museum.

1987 The Forbidden City is Listed by UNESCO as a World Heritage Site.

THE INNER COURT

The structure of the Inner Court mirrors that of the Outer Court but on a smaller scale. There are three main inner court palaces – the double-eaved Palace of Heavenly Purity was originally used as the imperial sleeping quarters and later for the reception of imperial officials. Banquets were held here for New Year and other important occasions. Beyond this palace lies the Hall of Union, which was used as a throne room by the empress as well as a depository for the imperial seals used to sign official documents. Still further on, the Palace of Earthly Tranquility served as living quarters for the Ming empresses. During the Qing dynasty, the hall was used for Manchurian shaman rites, including the sacrifice of animals. Behind the inner court is the Imperial Garden, a typical Chinese recreation of nature in all its guises. On either side of the state apartments were the private residences of the whole imperial family and their attendants – reputed to number as many as 9,000 by the 18th century.

LAYOUT OF THE TEMPLE OF HEAVEN

The design of the Temple of Heaven is replete with cosmological significance. All the major structures lie on the favored north-south axis. The ancient Chinese saying "sky round, earth square" is represented here by the interplay of squares and circles. Heaven is suggested in the round, conical roofing and the blue tiles of both the ▷ *Hall of Prayer for Good Harvests* and the ▷ *Imperial Vault of Heaven*. The ▷ *Round Altar* symbolizes Heaven, while Earth is there in its square enclosure. Numerology is also important, with odd numbers being the most fortunate, hence the triple eaves of the Hall of Prayer for Good Harvests and the Round Altar's three tiers. Nine is the most important of the single-digit odd numbers and the uppermost tier of the altar is designed with nine rings of stones, each ring itself a multiple of nine stones. The significance of numbers finds further refrain throughout the structure (▷ *Dragon Well Pillars*).

CEREMONIES & RITES

The emperor would perform the ceremonies at the Temple of Heaven to pray for rain and good harvests or in the event of natural disasters that required the appeasement of Heaven. After fasting for three days, he would be conveyed in a spectacular procession from the Forbidden City to spend the night before the sacrifice in the Palace of Abstinence just inside the Temple of Heaven compound. The emperor would rise before dawn the next day and be ceremonially robed. Then proceeding north to south, with sacred music and dance, he would ascend the ▷ *Round Altar* to burn a freshly killed ox and bundles of silk before an array of wooden spirit tablets (*shenpai*), including those of his ancestors who were thus also "participating."

Temple of Heaven, Beijing

Gate to the Round Altar

BUILT DURING THE MING Dynasty, Tiantan, commonly called the Temple of Heaven, is one of the largest temple complexes in China and a paradigm of Chinese architectural balance and symbolism. It was here that the emperor, after a ceremonial procession from the Forbidden City, would make sacrifices and pray to heaven at the winter solstice. As the Son of Heaven, the emperor could intercede with the gods on behalf of his people and ensure a good harvest. Off-limits to the common people during the Ming and Qing dynasties, the Temple of Heaven is situated in a large park that now attracts early-morning practitioners of Tai Chi.

The Hall of Prayer where the emperor prayed for a good harvest for his people

TEMPLE OF HEAVEN COMPLEX

The main parts of the complex are all connected by the Red Step Bridge (an elevated ceremonial path) to form the focal point of the park. The doorways at each triple gate are for the emperor (east), the gods (center) and the officials (west). The circular Echo Wall is famed for its supposed ability to carry a whisper from one end of the wall to the other.

① Hall of Prayer for Good Harvests
② Red Step Bridge
③ Echo Wall
④ Imperial Vault of Heaven
⑤ Round Altar

KEY
☐ Area illustrated

Three door gates to the Imperial Vault of Heaven

Imperial Vault of Heaven with the spirit tablets of the gods

The Center of Heaven Stone at the heart of the Round Altar

Name plaques often copied the calligraphy of an emperor.

The circular roof symbolizes the sky.

Red is the emperor's color.

Dragon and phoenix motifs, inside and out, represent the emperor and empress.

STAR FEATURES

★ **Caisson Ceiling**

★ **Dragon Well Pillars**

The golden finial is 38 m (125 ft) high and prone to lightning strikes.

★ Caisson Ceiling

The splendidly decorated circular caisson ceiling has a beautiful gilded dragon and phoenix at its center. The hall is entirely built of wood without using a single nail.

Blue represents the color of heaven.

★ Dragon Well Pillars

The roofs of the hall are supported on 28 highly-decorated pillars. At the centre, the four colossal columns, known as Dragon Well Pillars, represent the seasons, while the outer 12 pillars represent the months of the year and the inner circle of 12 pillars represent the 12 two-hour periods into which the Chinese divided the day.

Emperor's throne

Central "Dragon and Phoenix Stone"

Symbolic offerings

KEY DATES

1420 Qinian Dian is built – originally called the "Temple of Earth and Heaven".

1530 Round Altar is constructed by Emperor Shizong.

1889 Qinian Dian burns down after a lightning strike.

1918 The Temple of Heaven is opened to the public.

1998 UNESCO inscribes the Temple of Heaven onto the World Heritage List.

THE LAST CEREMONY

Observed by China's emperors since the Zhou dynasty (1100–771 BC), the winter solstice rites at the Temple of Heaven were last performed by the first president of the Republic of China, the former Qing general Yuan Shikai (1859–1916). The general had helped modernize the Chinese army and, as the head of such a force, could easily ask for positions of influence in return for his and the army's support. Once he was made president, he aimed to install himself as emperor and re-establish an imperial dynasty. Therefore Yuan performed the ceremony at the Temple of Heaven on the occasion of the winter solstice in 1914, clearly asserting his imperial ambitions. However, despite dressing in the appropriate robes, he failed to recreate the traditional majesty of the occasion, arriving in an armored car. Yuan Shikai died in 1916, before he could ascend the throne.

HALL OF PRAYER FOR GOOD HARVESTS

The Qinian Dian or Hall of Prayer for Good Harvests is the most famous structure at the complex and is often thought to be the "Temple of Heaven." Tiantan refers not to one building but to the whole complex.

Marble Platform

Three tiers of marble form a circle 90-m (300-ft) in diameter and 6-m (20-ft) high. The balusters on the upper tier are carved with dragons to signify the imperial nature of the structure.

Extravagant carving by the Yomeimon Gate

FEATURES OF THE TOSHU-GU SHRINE

The magnificent design of the Toshu-gu shrine is not at all in keeping with the sense of duty and simplicity that is normally central to Shintoism. This incongruity highlights the transformation that Shintoism has undergone, following the introduction of Buddhism to Japan in the 6th century. Many of the buildings in the shrine share elements from Buddhist architecture. The 5-story temple (▷ *Pagoda*) and the gate guarded by the Nio figures (▷ *The Niomon*) are just two examples of how both Buddhism and Shintoism co-exist at Tosho-gu Shrine. The shrine is famous for its ornate carvings that decorate entire buildings both inside and out. The most exquisite is the Twilight Gate (▷ *Yomeimon Gate*) whose name implies that it can take all day to view the carvings.

Tosho-gu Shrine, Nikko

NIKKO WAS a renowned Buddhist-Shinto religious center, and the warlord Tokugawa Ieyasu chose this area specifically for his mausoleum. Tokugawa Iemitsu set out to dazzle with this mausoleum-shrine for his grandfather, and his elaborately decorated result is magnificent. Some 15,000 artisans worked on the shrine, building, carving, gilding, painting, and lacquering. Although designated a shrine in the late 17th century, it retains many Buddhist elements. The *sugi-namiki* (Japanese cedar avenue) leading to the shrine was planted by a 17th-century lord, in lieu of a more opulent offering.

Honden *(inner sanctuary)*

Haiden *(sanctuary)*

The Karamon gate is the smallest at Tosho-gu.

The Honji-do's ceiling is painted with the "crying dragon," which echoes resoundingly if you clap your hands beneath it.

Drum tower

The Rinzo contains a sutra library of Buddhist scriptures in a revolving structure.

★ **Yomeimon Gate**
Lavishly decorated with beasts and flowers, this gate has one of its 12 columns carved upside-down, a deliberate imperfection to avoid angering jealous spirits. Statues of imperial ministers occupy the niches.

Sleeping Cat Carving
Over an entrance in the east corridor, this tiny, exquisite carving of a sleeping cat is attributed to Hidari Jingoro (Hidari the Left-handed).

Bell tower

STAR FEATURES
★ **Yomeimon Gate**
★ **Pagoda**
★ **Sacred Stable**

Sacred Fountain
The granite basin (1618), for ritual purification, is covered with an ornate Chinese-style roof.

TOKUGAWA IEYASU

Ieyasu (1543–1616) was a wily strategist and master politician who founded the dynasty that would rule Japan for over 260 years. Born the son of a minor lord, Ieyasu spent his life accumulating power, not becoming shogun until 1603, when he was 60. He built his capital at the swampy village of Edo (now Tokyo), and his rule saw the start of the flowering of Edo culture. He ensured that, after his death, he would be enshrined as a god and *gongen* (incarnation of the Buddha). His posthumous name was Tosho-Daigongen (the great incarnation illuminating the East).

CELEBRATIONS

Tosho-gu Festivals are held on 17 and 18 May and on 17 October. Over 1,200 participants, dressed in clothes from the Edo period, take part in processions in which relics from the shrine are displayed.

KEY DATES

1603–1867 The Tokugawa Shogunate brings about a prolonged period of peace.

1616 Death of Tokugawa Ieyasu.

1617 Construction begins on the Tosho-gu Shrine as a mausoleum for Tokugawa Ieyasu.

1636 The mausoleum and shrine are completed.

1999 The shrines and temples in Nikko are designated a World Heritage Site.

THREE WISE MONKEYS

Introduced to Japan by a Buddhist monk from China in the 8th century AD, the proverb of the Three Wise Monkeys represents the three truths of Tendai Buddhism. The names of the monkeys are *Mizaru* meaning "see no evil," *Kikazaru* meaning "hear no evil," and *Iwazaru* meaning "speak no evil". In Japan, monkeys are traditionally thought to keep horses healthy. At Tosho-gu, these monkeys are the guardians of the sacred horse, an animal long dedicated to the Shinto gods (▷ *Sacred Stable*). Their well-known gestures of covering their eyes, ears, and mouth are a dramatic representation of the commands of the blue-faced deity Vadjra: if we do not see, hear, or speak evil, we will be spared from all evil. As their names not only express their gestures but also the three truths, anyone referring to them will also proclaim their message.

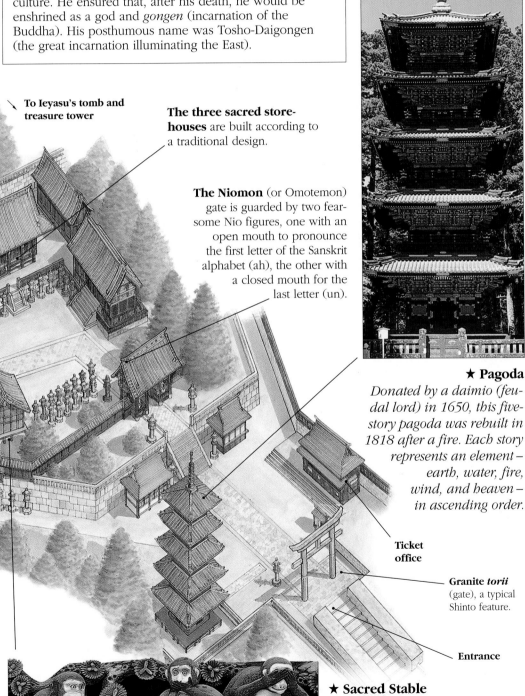

To Ieyasu's tomb and treasure tower

The three sacred storehouses are built according to a traditional design.

The Niomon (or Omotemon) gate is guarded by two fearsome Nio figures, one with an open mouth to pronounce the first letter of the Sanskrit alphabet (ah), the other with a closed mouth for the last letter (un).

★ Pagoda
Donated by a daimio (feudal lord) in 1650, this five-story pagoda was rebuilt in 1818 after a fire. Each story represents an element – earth, water, fire, wind, and heaven – in ascending order.

Ticket office

Granite *torii* (gate), a typical Shinto feature.

Entrance

★ Sacred Stable
A carving of the three wise monkeys decorates this wooden building. A horse given by the New Zealand government is kept here a few hours a day.

Ancient Japanese warriors in battledress

THE SAMURAI & THEIR WEAPONRY

The samurai came into being in the 9th century, when the emperor made constables and farmer-warriors responsible for the defense of far-flung holdings. Affiliated to *daimyo* (lords), they formed their own clans and became more powerful than the emperor; establishing the shogunates (military dictatorships), of the 12th–19th centuries. Strict codes of behavior included intense study and spiritual discipline. Each warrior took a musket, spear, or bow, and a pair of swords into battle. They also wore remarkably ornate armor. The Museum of Weaponry at Himeji-jo has a fine collection of samurai arms, guns, and gunpowder.

HISTORY OF THE CASTLE

Originally built as a fortress by Norimura Akamatsu in the early 14th century, Himeji-jo was presented to Ikeda Terumasa, the son-in-law of shogun Tokugawa Ieyasu, in 1600, in thanks for his loyal support. Terumasa spent nine years reconstructing the fortress, until it reached its current form and appearance. Although built as a military compound, it was never used in battle. After Terumasa, it was inhabited by several different families, until it was designated a national treasure in 1931.

Himeji Castle

Built on a high bluff, Himeji-jo, the grandest of Japan's 12 remaining feudal castles, dominates the city of Himeji. The building is better known among the Japanese as Shirasagi-jo, the "white egret castle," because of the supposed resemblance of its plastered walls, stretched either side of the main donjon, to the image of a bird taking flight. For many people, its military architecture, ameliorated by graceful aesthetic lines, qualifies Himeji-jo as the ultimate samurai castle. Its cinematic potential was exploited by Akira Kurosawa who used the castle's stunning exterior for his 1985 movie epic, *Ran*.

View from lower floor of donjon to the modern city of Himeji

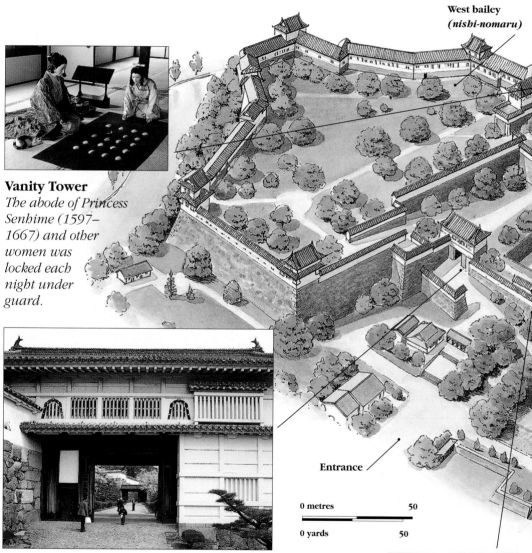

West bailey (nishi-nomaru)

Vanity Tower
The abode of Princess Senhime (1597–1667) and other women was locked each night under guard.

Entrance

0 metres		50

0 yards		50

Gates and Passageways
Though never put to the test, the castle's labyrinth of passageways and gateways in the outer zones were designed to confuse enemies.

★ Fan Walls
Samurai castles are notable for their graceful fan-shaped stone walls, which were very difficult for enemies to scale.

★ **Main Tower**
*The current five-story
donjon was developed
by Ikeda Terumasa in
1609, transforming a
modest military strong-
hold into a symbol of
the Tokugawa
shogunate's newly
consolidated power.*

CASTLE GARDENS

The grounds at Himeji are
very attractive during April,
when the cherry trees are in
bloom. The garden, Koko-en,
created in 1992, consists of
nine separate Edo-style
gardens. Traditional plantings,
covered walkways built of
cypress, and delicate water
features convey the atmo-
sphere of the period.

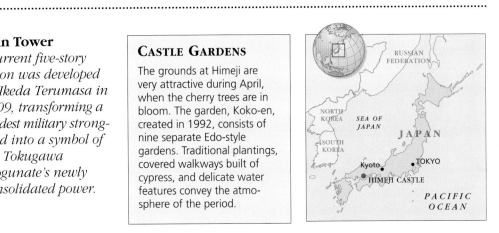

KEY DATES

1333 Norimura Akamatsu
builds a fortress at Himeji.

1618 Tabamasa Honda adds
buildings in the west bailey.

1993 Himeji-jo is declared a
UNESCO World Heritage Site.

PRINCESS SENHIME &
THE KESHO YAGURA

One of the most interesting
sections of Himeji Castle is
the ▷ *Vanity Tower* or *Kesho
Yagura*, the former chamber
of Princess Senhime (or Sen).
The granddaughter of
Shogun Tokugawa Ieyasu,
Senhime was only seven
when she was married to
Toyotomi Hideyori, the son
of Hideyoshi, who unified
Japan. When she was 19,
her husband was forced to
commit suicide after losing a
battle. Senhime then married
Tadatoki Honda, and came to
live at Himeji-jo. The two-
story Vanity Tower was built
with her considerable dowry
of 100,000 *koku* (a measure of
rice), and was used by her as
a resting place while on her
way to a shrine located in the
castle grounds. The tower's
rooms are lavishly decorated.
Its ceilings are made of cedar
and delicate paper screens,
framed in black lacquered
wood, hang from the walls.
It is one of the few surviving
17th-century buildings in
Japan, and a significant
example of Japanese culture
at that time. The shrine at
which Senhime is said to
have prayed each morning
can also still be seen in the
grounds of the castle.

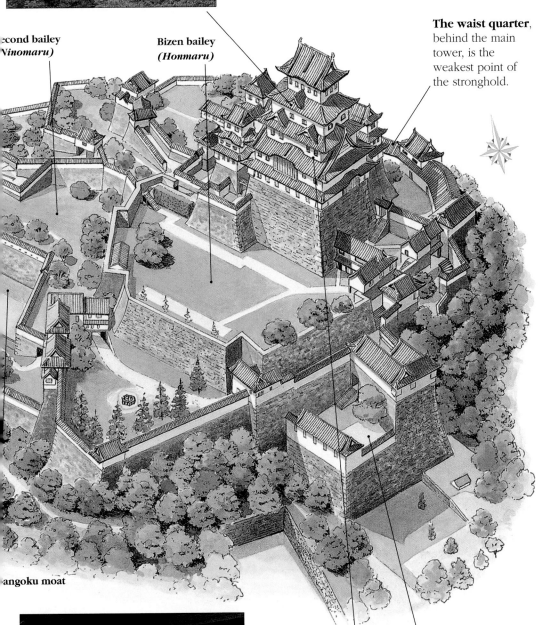

**Second bailey
(Ninomaru)**

**Bizen bailey
(Honmaru)**

The waist quarter,
behind the main
tower, is the
weakest point of
the stronghold.

angoku moat

Interior of Keep
*Situated on the 5th
floor of the tower,
the keep was
originally an
armaments store.
It remains largely
unadorned and
houses exhibits
on castle life.*

The suicide quarter
may have been
intended as a place for
ritual suicide when it
was built. However, it
was probably used only
for its water supply.

EMPEROR SHOMYO

The imperial court at Nara embraced Buddhism in the 8th century, during the reign of Emperor Shomyo (r.724–49). Shomyo (or Shomu) built temples in every province, and used this vast network to strengthen the administration and to consolidate control of his empire. He is, however, best known for commissioning the Todai-ji Temple and its ▷ *Great Buddha Vairocana* statue in 743. This phenomenal endeavor took seven years to complete and was so expensive it almost drained Japan's economy as well as its reserves of precious metals. When the temple finally opened in 752, Shomyo personally painted the statue's eyes and declared himself the Buddha's servant. By this time his daughter Koken (r.749–758) had been declared the new ruler of Japan. Shomyo died in 756.

Temple of Kofuku-ji, one of the many temples built by Shomyo

THE CONSTRUCTION OF TODAI-JI TEMPLE

Wood has long been the basis of Japanese architecture, particularly temples, mainly because of its ability to endure weathering in winter. It has, however, also meant that such structures are highly susceptible to devastating fires. Todai-ji's ▷ *Great Buddha Hall* is constructed in the traditional post-and-lintel style. The base of the hall has posts anchored along a rectangular perimeter. This rigid geometric shape marks the boundary between the material and divine world. There are 62 pillars supporting the grand sloping roof. A unique roof construction (▷ *Wooden Hall*) is effective in resisting minor earthquakes.

Todai-ji Temple, Nara

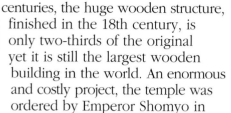

Stone lantern at Todai-ji Temple

THERE ARE MANY REASONS to visit the impressive Todai-ji Temple in Nara but sheer size must be its main attraction. After alterations and fires over the centuries, the huge wooden structure, finished in the 18th century, is only two-thirds of the original yet it is still the largest wooden building in the world. An enormous and costly project, the temple was ordered by Emperor Shomyo in the mid-8th century to highlight the position of the city as a powerful Buddhist site and Japan's capital. Inside, the magnificent seated figure at 16 m (53 ft) is Japan's largest bronze image of the Buddha.

The 19-m (62-ft) high Nandaimon (great southern gate) of Todai-ji

Koumokuten, a heavenly guardian, dates from the mid-Edo period (1603–1868).

Kokuzo Bosatsu
This bosatsu, *or* bodhisattva, *"Enlightened Being," was completed in 1709.*

Entrance

★ Great Buddha Vairocana
The casting of this vast statue required hundreds of tons of molten bronze, mercury, and vegetable wax. Fires and earthquakes have destroyed the head several times; the current head dates from 1692.

GREAT BUDDHA HALL

The main hall of Todai-ji was rebuilt several times after natural disasters in the 12th and 16th centuries. The enormous figure inside is a jaw-dropping sight. Occasionally it is possible to see several monks standing in the upturned palm — dusting.

Sacred Site
Above Nara, the ancient city that was once Japan's capital, sits Todai-ji Temple. The curved roof is almost hidden by surrounding trees.

OMIZU-TORI FESTIVAL

The Omizu-tori or water-drawing festival has been celebrated at Todai-ji Temple since the 8th century to signal the arrival of spring. During the festival, held from March 1–14, water is ritually drawn from a sacred well to the sound of music in the early hours on the 13th day. Enormous torches are used to purify the water.

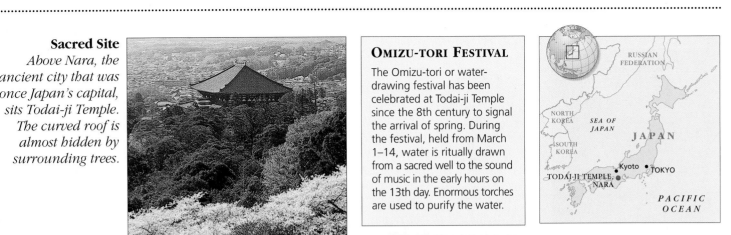

KEY DATES

752 The temple is completed.

1180, 1567 Great Buddha's head melts in raging fires.

1998 The Todai-ji complex at Nara is declared a UNESCO World Heritage Site.

BUDDHISM IN JAPAN

Buddhism was founded in India and arrived in Japan via China and Korea in the 6th century AD. Prince Shotoku (573–621) promoted Buddhism in its early days. Initially, despite incorporating parts of the native belief system, Buddhism had an uneasy relationship with Japan's oldest religion, Shinto. Buddhism lost official support after Shinto was declared Japan's national religion in 1868, but it flowered again after World War II. Today, the beliefs and morality of Buddhism permeate modern Japanese life, especially the Zen Buddhist emphasis on simplicity and mental control. The religion's cornerstone is meditation, which is also believed to be the road to Enlightenment. Pilgrimages to sacred sites are still popular, and devotees, dressed in white, sometimes make journeys lasting several weeks. Festivals take place to honor events in the Buddha's life and the return of spirits *(bon)* to Earth, and often incorporate Shinto elements. Buddhist temples in Japan include a main hall *(hondo)*, with its stark interior, a cemetery, and often a tiered pagoda, housing a relic of the Buddha, and a small Shinto shrine.

Todai-ji Temple

Ornamental roof decoration

★ Wooden Hall
The unusual bracketing and beam-frame construction of this vast wooden hall, built in 1688–1709, were possibly the work of craftsmen from southern China.

Interior of Daibutsuden (Buddha hall)

Roofline
The striking roofline, with its golden "horns" and curved lintel, was an 18th-century embellishment.

Tamonten, another heavenly guardian, dates from the same period as Koumokuten on the other side of the hall.

Niyorin Kannon Bosatsu, like the Kokuzo Bosatsu to the left of the Great Buddha, is an Enlightened Being and dates from 1709.

Behind the Buddha is a small hole bored into a large wooden pillar. A popular belief holds that those who can squeeze through the hole will attain Nirvana.

Covered walkway in compound

STAR FEATURES

★ **Great Buddha Vairocana**

★ **Wooden Hall**

One of the many prayer rooms in Alchi monastery

DUKHANG & SUMTSEK

Renowned as a great center of Buddhist art, Alchi was built as a monument to the Second Spreading, the revival of Buddhism in Tibet in the 11th century. The oldest of the five temples, the ▷ *Dukhang* or assembly hall, holds some of Alchi's greatest treasures. The beautiful central image of Vairocana, the main Buddha of Meditation, is surrounded by exuberant carvings of dancers and mythical animals. It is flanked by four other Buddhas of Meditation. Even more impressive are the six mandalas painted on the walls. The second-oldest temple is the three-storied ▷ *Sumtsek*, with its gigantic images of ▷ *Avalokiteshvara*, (the Bodhisattva of Compassion), Manjushri (the Bodhisattva of Wisdom), and Maitreya (the Future Buddha), standing in alcoves in three of its walls. Only their torsos are visible from ground level, while their heads protrude into the upper story.

RINCHEN ZANGPO

The legendary 11th-century Tibetan scholar ▷ *Rinchen Zangpo* is highly venerated in Tibetan Buddhism. He is best known for the mammoth task of translating Indian Buddhist texts into Tibetan, thus initiating the revival of Buddhism in Tibet. He was also the main force behind a great temple building movement (▷ *Buddhist style pp334–5*) and stories claim he once constructed 108 monasteries in one night.

Alchi Monastery

Dancing deity in the Sumtsek

FOUNDED IN THE early 12th century AD, Alchi is a jewel among the monasteries of this culturally Tibetan part of India. Because Alchi was abandoned as a site of active worship, for reasons unknown, as early as the 16th century, the 12th- and 13th-century paintings in its temples have remained remarkably well preserved, undimmed by the soot from butter lamps and incense sticks. Of the five temples in the enclave, the finest murals are in the two oldest, the Dukhang and the Sumtsek. These have been executed with great delicacy and skill by master painters who were probably from Kashmir.

Avalokiteshvara
The legs of this gigantic statue in the Sumtsek are covered with exquisite miniature paintings of palaces and Buddhist pilgrimage sites.

Lhakhang Soma
This painting of a Guardian Deity and his female counterpart symbolizes the union of opposites.

★ Sumtsek
The carved wooden façade of this temple is in the style of Kashmiri temple architecture.

Green Tara or Prajnaparamita

GREEN TARA

There are several exquisite images of this goddess, variously identified as Green Tara, the Savior, and Prajnaparamita (the Perfection of Wisdom) in the Sumtsek. Five of them are to the left of the gigantic Avalokiteshvara statue, opposite his leg. The Green Tara seems to have held a special place in Alchi, since the goddess is not given such importance in other monasteries.

STAR FEATURES

★ Sumstek

★ Dukhang

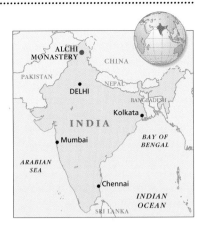

View of Alchi
Idyllically located on a bend in the Indus river, Alchi's simple white-washed buildings with their band of deep red trim stand out against an impressive backdrop of barren mountains.

THE BODHISATTVAS
Among the various Buddhist divinities are the Bodhisattvas – supremely compassionate almost-Buddhas, who are willing to forgo nirvana to help others obtain liberation. They include Avalokitesvara, Tara, his female form, and Manjushri.

Chortens containing holy relics are dotted around the complex. They are often built in memory of a great lama.

★ Dukhang
The serene image of the Vairocana Buddha is surrounded by elaborate woodwork, decorative friezes and superb mandalas.

Lotsawa Lhakhang

King and Queen
This mural in the Dukhang shows details of royal dress and hairstyles.

Rinchen Zangpo
This rare portrait of Rinchen Zangpo, an influential Tibetan saint known as the Great Translator, is in the 12th-century Lotsawa ("Translator") Lhakhang.

Manjushri Lhakhang, one of the five temples, contains a large image of Manjushri.

Entrance

KEY DATES

Early 12th century Alchi monastery is founded.

Late 12th–early 13th century The temples Manjushri Lhakhang, Lotsawa Lhakhang and Lhakhang Soma are built.

16th century Alchi monastery is abandoned as a center of worship.

Mid-16th century Minor restoration done on paintings in the Sumtsek during the reign of King Tashi Namgyal.

THE FIVE BUDDHAS OF MEDITATION

Tibetan Buddhism lays great emphasis on the Five Dhyani Buddhas, or the Buddhas of Meditation. Each of these Buddhas is associated with a direction, a color, and a symbolic attribute: Vairocana (the Resplendent) is associated with the center, the color white, and the wheel of law (*dharma-cakra*); Amitabha (the Boundless Light) with the west, the color red, and the lotus flower (*padma*); Akshobhya (the Imperturbable) with the east, the color blue, and the thunderbolt of wisdom (*vajra*); Amoghasiddhi (Infallible Success) with the north, the color green, and the double crossed thunderbolt (*visvavajra*); and Ratnasambhava (the Jewel-Born) with the south, the color yellow, and the gem (*ratna*). They symbolize the Buddha's different aspects, and Alchi's several mandalas help devotees meditate on them.

THE HOLIEST SHRINE

The Sikh community's holiest shrine, the Golden Temple complex is actually a city within a city, with a maze of lanes protected by 18 fortified gates. The main entrance is through the northern gateway, the Darshani Darwaza, which also houses the Central Sikh Museum and its collections of paintings, manuscripts, and weapons. From here, steps lead down to the Parikrama (marble pathway), encircling the ▷ *Amrit Sarovar* ("Pool of Nectar," after which Amritsar is named) and ▷ *Hari Mandir* ("Temple of God"), the golden-domed main shrine. Several holy sites line the Parikrama, including the Dukh Bhanjani Ber, a tree shrine said to have healing powers, and the Athsath Tirath, representing 68 pilgrim shrines. The Parikrama continues to the ▷ *Akal Takht*. The complex includes the Guru ka Langar, a free kitchen symbolizing the caste-free, egalitarian society the Sikh gurus sought to create.

MAHARAJA RANJIT SINGH

One of North India's most remarkable rulers, Maharaja Ranjit Singh (r.1790–1839) established Punjab's first Sikh kingdom by persuading rival chieftains to unite. A military genius, his strong army kept both the British forces and Afghan invaders at bay, by making Punjab a prosperous center of trade and industry. A devout Sikh, the one-eyed Ranjit Singh was an enlightened ruler who liked to say "God intended me to look at all religions with one eye."

The Golden Temple, with its central shrine and main entrance

The Golden Temple, Amritsar

***Pietra dura* detail**

THE SPIRITUAL CENTER of the Sikh religion, the Golden Temple was built between 1589 and 1601, and is a superb synthesis of Islamic and Hindu styles of architecture. In keeping with the syncretic tradition of those times, its foundation stone was laid by a Muslim saint, Mian Mir. The temple was virtually destroyed in 1761 by an Afghan invader, Ahmed Shah Abdali, but was rebuilt some years later. Maharaja Ranjit Singh, ruler of Punjab, covered the dome in gold and embellished its interiors with lavish decoration during his reign.

First Floor
The marble walls have pietra dura *inlay and decorative plasterwork, bearing animal and flower motifs covered in gold leaf.*

★ Sheesh Mahal
The Hall of Mirrors on the top floor has a curved bangaldar *roof, and its floors are swept with a special broom made of peacock feathers.*

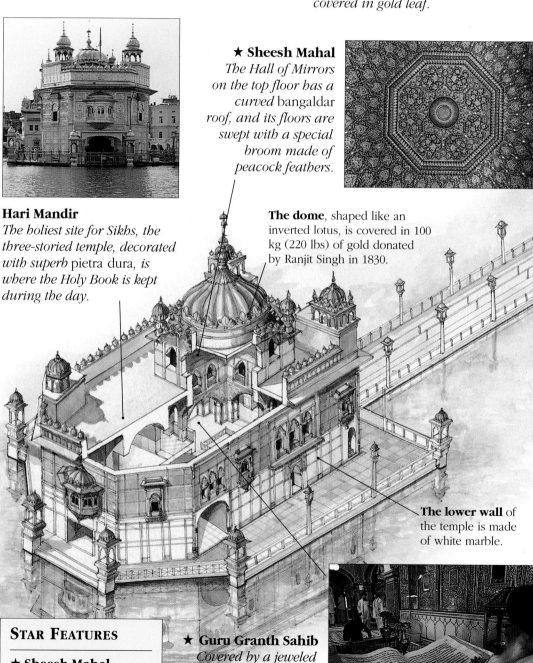

Hari Mandir
The holiest site for Sikhs, the three-storied temple, decorated with superb pietra dura, *is where the Holy Book is kept during the day.*

The dome, shaped like an inverted lotus, is covered in 100 kg (220 lbs) of gold donated by Ranjit Singh in 1830.

The lower wall of the temple is made of white marble.

STAR FEATURES

★ Sheesh Mahal

★ Guru Granth Sahib

★ Guru Granth Sahib
Covered by a jeweled canopy, the Holy Book lies in the Durbar Sahib ("Court of the Lord").

Darshani Deorhi
This gateway provides the first glimpse of the temple's inner sanctum. It has two splendid silver doors and sacred verses carved on its walls.

GURU PARAB

The festival of Guru Parab celebrates Guru Nanak's birthday on a full moon night in late Oct–early Nov (date varies). It is particularly spectacular at the Golden Temple, which is illuminated by thousands of lamps.

Akal Takht

Akal Takht
The seat of the supreme governing body of the Sikhs, it houses the gurus' swords and flagstaffs, as well as the Holy Book at night.

Amrit Sarovar, the pool where Sikhs are baptized, was built in 1577 by Ram Das, the fourth guru.

The Causeway
The 60-m (197-ft) long marble causeway is flanked by nine gilded lamps on each side, and leads to the temple across the Amrit Sarovar.

KEY DATES

1589–1601 Golden Temple is constructed.

1757, 1761, 1762 Afghans demolish Golden Temple.

1776 Golden Temple rebuilt.

1830 Maharaja Ranjit Singh adorns the dome with gold.

1984 Golden Temple damaged during Operation Blue Star, undertaken by the army to flush out extremists.

2003 Punjabi government funds an extensive beautification project of the area surrounding the Golden Temple.

SIKHISM

With their characteristic turbans and full beards, the Sikhs are easy to identify. Sikhism is a reformist faith, founded in the 15th century by Guru Nanak. It believes in a formless God. It is also called the Gurmat or the "Guru's Doctrine," and Sikh temples are known as *gurdwaras*, literally "doors to the guru." Nanak, the first of a series of 10 gurus, chose his most devout disciple as his successor. The tenth and last guru, Guru Gobind Singh (1666–1708) reorganized the community as a military order, the Khalsa, to combat religious persecution by the Mughals. He gave the Sikhs their distinctive identity as well as the Khalsa's five symbols – *kesh* (long hair), *kachha* (underwear), *kirpan* (small sword), *kangha* (comb), and *kara* (bracelet) – that all Sikhs are obligated to wear.

GOLDEN TEMPLE COMPLEX

1. Temple Office
2. Cloakrooms
3. Darshani Darwaza and Clocktower
4. Hari Mandir (Temple of God)
5. Athsath Tirath (68 Shrines)
6. Guru ka Langar (Dining Hall)
7. Baba Karak Singh's Residence
8. Assembly Hall
9. Baba Deep Singh's Shrine
10. Darshani Deorhi (Gateway to Sanctum)
11. Arjun Dev's Tree
12. Akal Takht (Seat of Sikh religious authority)
13. Nishan Sahibs (Flagstaffs)
14. Gobind Singh's Shrine
15. Dukh Bhanjani Ber (Tree Shrine)

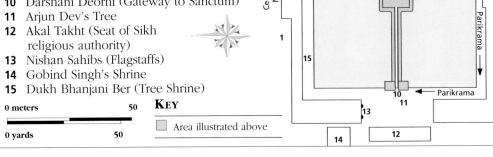

0 meters 50

0 yards 50

KEY

Area illustrated above

INDO-ISLAMIC ARCHITECTURE

The Muslim rulers introduced several new technologies and customs that had a significant impact on the cultural and urban milieu of the subcontinent. Of these the most visible influence was on architecture. The dome and the true arch as well as the use of mortar, which made it possible to build high structures, were essentially Islamic contributions. Traditional Hindu carving skills, a legacy of temple sculpture, added a new element to the austere Islamic architectural lexicon. Mosques, with their domed prayer halls at one end of an open courtyard, and tombs represent the imported tradition.

QUWWAT-UL-ISLAM MOSQUE

Built by Qutbuddin Aibak soon after his conquest of Delhi, the ▷ *Quwwat-ul-Islam Mosque* was the first congregational mosque in Delhi. The large, rectangular courtyard and galleries were initially constructed with carved pillars and ceilings taken from 27 Hindu and Jain temples. The western portion of its courtyard occupies the original site of one of the temples. Later Qutbuddin added a huge, free-standing, sandstone screen, punctuated by five giant arches. The screen has been embellished with typically Islamic patterns, such as bands of calligraphy and flowing arabesques. Standing in the center of the open courtyard is the 4th-century ▷ *Iron Pillar*, said to have been brought from a Vishnu temple and installed here. The mosque was later enlarged by Iltutmish and Alauddin Khilji.

Qutb Minar, focus of the Islamic Qutb Complex

The Qutb Complex, Delhi

Floral motif, Qutb Minar

INDIA'S HIGHEST SINGLE tower, the Qutb Minar (Arabic for pole or axis), looms over the historic area of the Mehrauli Archaeological Park, where Qutbuddin Aibak laid the foundation of the Delhi Sultanate, the first Islamic kingdom in North India. In 1193, he began building the Quwwat-ul-Islam ("Might of Islam") Mosque and the Qutb Minar to announce the advent of the Muslim sultans. The mosque is a patchwork fusion of decorative Hindu panels, salvaged from razed temples around the site, and Islamic domes and arches. Later, Iltutmish, Alauddin Khilji, and Feroze Shah Tughluq added more structures, heralding a new architectural style that mingled aspects of both the Hindu and the Islamic cultures.

Alauddin Khilji's Tomb

Alai Darwaza
This gateway to the complex, erected in 1311 by Alauddin Khilji, is one of the earliest buildings in India to employ the Islamic principles of arched construction.

STAR FEATURES

★ **Iron Pillar**

★ **Quwwat-ul-Islam Mosque**

★ **Qutb Minar**

Carved Panels
Ornate calligraphy panels carved with inscriptions from the holy Koran embellish the gateway to the Qutb.

Imam Zamin's Tomb
This small sandstone structure with a dome contains fine perforated jalis (screens). Zamin, a holy man from Turkestan, was buried here in 1538.

Iltutmish's
Tomb

Iltutmish's Tomb
*Built in 1235 by
Iltutmish himself, the
interior has geometric
and calligraphic
patterns.*

★ **Iron Pillar**
*This 4th-century pillar, orig-
inally made as a flagstaff in
Vishnu's honor, is a tribute to
ancient Indian metallurgy.*

★ **Quwwat-ul-
Islam Mosque**
*Hindu motifs,
such as bells and
garlands, are
clearly
visible on the
pillars of this
mosque.*

★ **Qutb Minar**
*The five-storied,
72.5-m (238-ft) high
Victory Tower started by Qutbuddin Aibak was completed by his
son-in-law and successor Iltutmish
around AD 1200.*

QUTB MINAR STAIRCASE REOPENS

The spiral staircase leading to
the top of the Qutb reopened
in 2003 after 22 years. It was
closed in 1981, after a group
of schoolchildren died tragi-
cally in a stampede. The long
climb to the top reveals an
unparalleled view of Delhi.

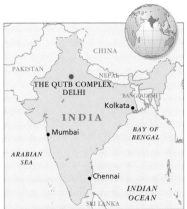

KEY DATES

1198 Quwwat-ul-Islam
Mosque is built.

1200 Qutb Minar is
completed by Iltutmish.

1230 Quwwat-ul-Islam
Mosque is enlarged.

1311 Alauddin Khilji begins
a second tower, but he dies
leaving it incomplete.

1368 Feroze Shah Tughluq
adds two stories to the Qutb
Minar and a pavilion on top.

1794 British engineer Major
Smith repairs the Qutb Minar
for the third time.

1993 The Qutb Complex is
declared a UNESCO World
Heritage Site.

QUTBUDDIN AIBAK & THE COMING OF ISLAM

Between the 11th and 12th
centuries, waves of Arab
invaders from Central Asia
swept across North India,
lured by tales of fabulous
wealth. The first, Mahmud of
Ghazni, repeatedly raided
India 17 times, carrying back
large quantities of loot from
its temples. He was followed,
almost a century later, by
Muhammad of Ghor, who
established control of Punjab
and Delhi after defeating the
Rajput ruler, Prithviraj
Chauhan in 1192. He was
succeeded by his slave
general Qutbuddin Aibak
(r.1206–10), who founded
the first of the many Muslim
dynasties, collectively known
as the Delhi Sultanate.

MUGHAL STYLE

Mughal buildings, whether built of red sandstone or marble, assert their exalted, imperial status. The emperors were great patrons of the arts, literature, and architecture and their rule established a rich pluralistic culture, blending the best of Islamic and Hindu traditions. Their greatest contribution was the garden tomb, raised on a high plinth in the center of a ▷ *charbagh*. Decorative elements such as perforated *jalis* or screens, used extensively for privacy and ventilation, refined inlay work, and cusped arches gave Mughal buildings an ethereal grace that offset their massive size. Other features include *chhatris* (domed rooftop pavilions) that were adapted from Rajput architecture, and minarets that gave symmetry to the buildings.

Marble inlay above the mosque's central arch, Taj Mahal

THE PARADISE GARDEN

The hallmark of Mughal landscape design, the Paradise Garden was introduced by Babur (1483–1530), the first Great Mughal, who yearned for the beauty of Ferghana, his homeland in Central Asia. Based on Islamic geometric and metaphysical concepts of design, the ▷ *charbagh* was an enclosed garden divided by raised walkways, water channels, and sunken groves, into four quarters, representing the four quarters of life. Water, the source of life in Central Asian desert kingdoms, was the central element and the intersecting channels met at a focal point which contained a pavilion for the emperor, seen as a representative of God on Earth.

Taj Mahal, Agra

Carved dado on outer niches

ONE OF THE WORLD'S most famous buildings, the Taj Mahal was built by the Mughal emperor Shah Jahan in memory of his favourite wife, Mumtaz Mahal, who died in 1631. Its perfect proportions and exquisite craftsmanship have been described as "a vision, a dream, a poem, a wonder." This sublime garden-tomb, an image of the Islamic garden of paradise, cost nearly 41 million rupees and 500 kg (1,102 lb) of gold. About 20,000 workers labored for 12 years to complete it in 1643.

★ Marble Screen
The filigree screen, daintily carved from a single block of marble, was meant to veil the area around the royal tombs.

Four minarets, each 40 m (131 ft) high and crowned by an open octagonal pavilion or *chhatri*, frame the tomb, highlighting the perfect symmetry of the complex.

Plinth

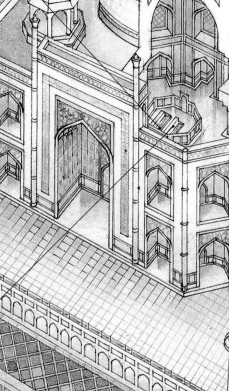

The Dome
The 44-m (144-ft) double dome is capped with a finial.

Yamuna river

★ Tomb Chamber
Mumtaz Mahal's cenotaph, raised on a platform, is placed next to Shah Jahan's. The actual graves, in a dark crypt below, are closed to the public.

STAR FEATURES

- ★ Marble Screen
- ★ Tomb Chamber
- ★ Pietra Dura

The *charbagh* was irrigated with water from the Yamuna river.

Main entrance

MUMTAZ MAHAL

Arjumand Banu (later Mumtaz Mahal) was the emperor's favorite wife. She accompanied him on all his campaigns and died in 1631, while giving birth to their 14th child. They were married 19 years.

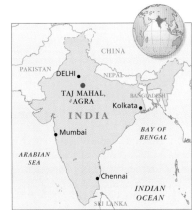

The Lotus Pool

Named after its lotus-shaped fountain spouts, the pool reflects the tomb. Almost every visitor is photographed sitting on the marble bench here.

Pishtaq

Recessed arches provide depth while their inlaid panels reflect the changing light to give the tomb a mystical aura.

★ Pietra Dura

Inspired by the paradise garden, intricately carved floral designs inlaid with precious stones embellish the austere white marble surface to give it the look of a bejeweled casket.

Calligraphic Panels

The size of the Koranic verses increases as the arch gets higher, creating the subtle optical illusion of a uniformly flowing script.

TAJ MAHAL

1 Main Tomb
2 *Masjid* (mosque)
3 *Mehmankhana* (guesthouse)
4 *Charbagh* (quadrified garden)
5 Gateway

KEY

☐ Area illustrated

☐ *Charbagh*

KEY DATES

1632 Following the death of Mumtaz Mahal in 1631, construction of the Taj Mahal begins.

1643 Taj Mahal completed.

1666 Shah Jahan dies and is laid to rest beside his queen.

1983 Taj Mahal declared a UNESCO World Heritage Site.

2001 Taj Mahal Conservation Collaborative begins restoration of Taj grounds, and improvement of visitors' facilities.

DECORATIVE ELEMENTS OF THE TAJ MAHAL

It is widely believed that the Taj Mahal was designed to be an earthly replica of one of the houses of paradise. Its impeccable marble facing, embellished by a remarkable use of surface design, is a showcase for the refined esthetic that reached its zenith during Shah Jahan's reign (r.1627–1658). The Taj manifests the wealth of Mughal art as seen in architecture, garden design, painting, jewelry, calligraphy, and textiles. Decorative elements include ornamental *jalis* (screens), carved panels of flowering plants, inlaid calligraphy, as well as floral motifs in ▷ *pietra dura*. The Florentine technique of *pietra dura* is said to have been imported by Emperor Jahangir. Even today, artisans in Agra's old quarter maintain pattern books on the fine motifs used on the Taj to recreate 17th-century designs in contemporary pieces.

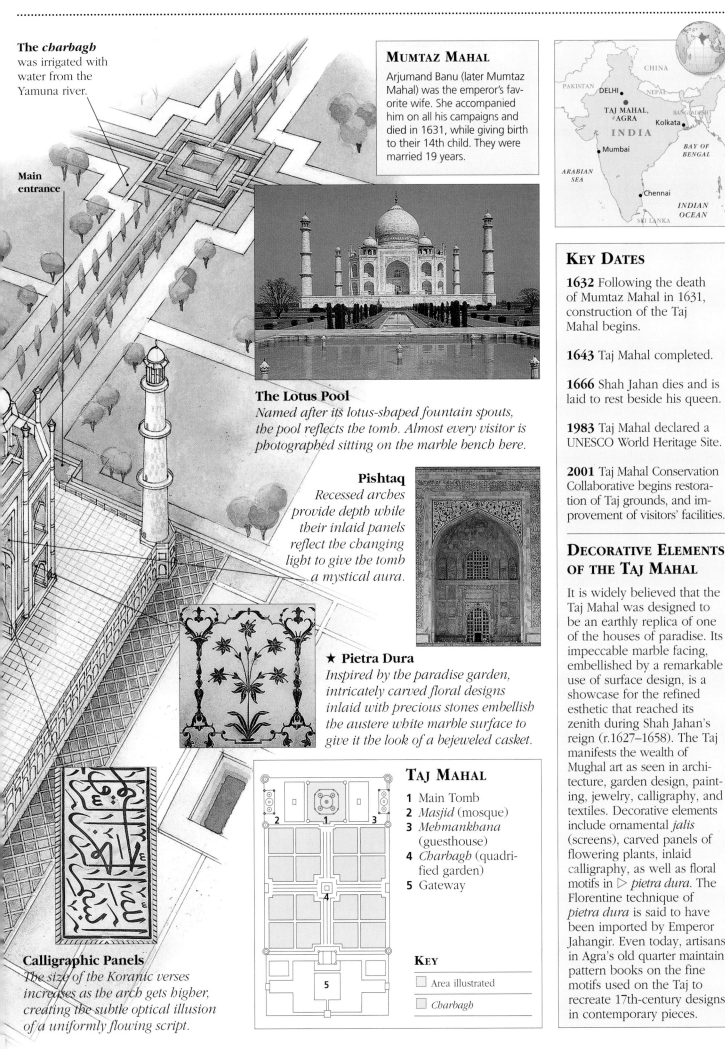

The Jami Masjid & Salim Chishti

Towering over Fatehpur Sikri is the grand open mosque ▷ *Jami Masjid*. Its vast congregational area has monumental gateways to the east and south. The 54 m (177 ft) high Buland Darwaza, a triumphal arch, was erected by Akbar to mark his 1573 conquest of Gujarat. The spiritual focus of the complex is the tomb of Sufi mystic Salim Chishti. Ever since Akbar's childlessness was ended after the saint's prediction in 1568, his tomb has attracted thousands, particularly childless women in search of a miracle. Visitors make a wish, tie a thread on the screen around the tomb, and return home confident that their wish will come true.

The exquisite, white marble tomb of Salim Chishti

Akbar the Great

The greatest Mughal emperor, Akbar (r.1556–1605) was a brilliant administrator and enlightened ruler. He was only 14 years old when he ascended the throne and his first task was to consolidate and expand his fledgling empire. His most significant moves were the political and matrimonial alliances he formed with the neighboring Rajput king of Amber (now Jaipur). However, it was his policy of religious tolerance that truly set him apart. Akbar was fascinated by the study of comparative religion and built a special "House of Worship" in Fatehpur Sikri where he often met leaders of all faiths. The outcome was *Din-i-Ilahi* (Religion of God), that tried to bring together all religions.

Fatehpur Sikri

Fretwork *jali*

BUILT BY EMPEROR AKBAR between 1571 and 1585 in honor of Salim Chishti, a famous Sufi saint of the Chishti order, Fatehpur Sikri was the capital of the Mughal empire for 14 years. One of the best examples of a Mughal walled city with defined areas and imposing gateways, its architecture, a blend of Hindu and Islamic styles (▷ *Mughal Style p326*), reflects Akbar's secular vision as well as his type of governance. After the city was abandoned, some say for lack of water, many of its treasures were plundered. It owes its present state of preservation to the efforts of the viceroy, Lord Curzon, a legendary conservationist.

Pillar in the Diwan-i-Khas
The central axis of Akbar's court, supported by carved brackets, was inspired by Gujarati buildings.

Haram comp

\ **Jami Masjid**

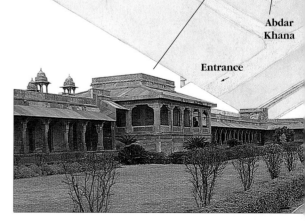

Khwabgah
The emperor's private sleeping quarters, with an ingenious ventilating shaft near his bed, lie within this lavishly decorated "Chamber of Dreams."

Anoop Talao is a pool associated with Akbar's renowned court musician Tansen who, as legend says, could light oil lamps with his magical singing.

Abdar Khana

Entrance

★ Turkish Sultana's House
The fine dado panels and delicately sculpted walls of this ornate sandstone pavilion make the stone seem like wood. It is topped with an unusual stone roof of imitation clay tiles.

Diwan-i-Aam
This large courtyard with an elaborate pavilion was originally draped with rich tapestries and was used for public hearings and celebrations.

★ Panch Mahal

This five-storied open sandstone pavilion, overlooking the Pachisi Court, is where Akbar's queens and their attendants savored the cool evening breezes. Its decorative screens were probably stolen after the city was abandoned.

TANSEN

A musical genius, the legendary Tansen was Emperor Akbar's Master of Music and one of the "nine jewels" in his court. He developed an exciting new range of *ragas* or melodic modes.

★ Diwan-i-Khas

This hall for private audience and debate is a unique fusion of different architectural styles and religious motifs.

Jodha Bai's Palace   Sunehra Makan   Birbal's House

Ankh Michauli

Sometimes identified as the treasury, this building has mythical guardian beasts carved on its stone struts. Its name means "blind man's buff".

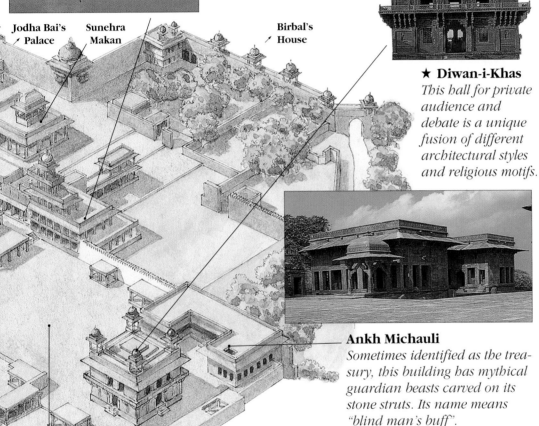

Pachisi Court is named after a ludo-like game played here by the ladies of the court.

PLAN OF FATEHPUR SIKRI

Fatehpur Sikri's royal complex contains the private and public spaces of Akbar's court, which included the harem and the treasury. The adjoining sacred area with the Jami Masjid (great mosque), Salim Chishti's Tomb, and the Buland Darwaza, are separated from the royal quarters by the Badshahi Darwaza, an exclusive royal gateway.

KEY

☐ Area illustrated

☐ Other buildings

☐ Sacred complex (Jami Masjid)

STAR FEATURES

★ Turkish Sultana's House

★ Panch Mahal

★ Diwan-i-Khas

KEY DATES

1571 Construction begins on Akbar's new capital at Fatehpur Sikri.

1576 Buland Darwaza is erected by Akbar.

1585 Fatehpur Sikri is abandoned by Akbar.

1986 Fatehpur Sikri becomes a UNESCO World Heritage Site.

LORD CURZON, VICEROY & CONSERVATIONIST

One of British India's most flamboyant viceroys, Lord Curzon (1859–1925), believed British rule was necessary to civilize "backward" India. He introduced sweeping changes in the education system. Paradoxically, the western-style institutions set up helped make Indians more aware of the injustices of colonial rule. Remembered for his role as conservator of Indian monuments, Curzon was responsible for the restoration of a vast number of Hindu, Islamic, and Mughal buildings. Among them are the gateway to Akbar's tomb at Sikandra, Agra Fort, buildings at Fatehpur Sikri, the Jain temples at Mt Abu, and the Taj Mahal. In 1905, due to differences with the British military commander-in-chief, Lord Kitchener, Curzon returned to England. By the time he left, he had achieved sufficient legislation to protect historic buildings, and set up an organization to conserve them.

THE IMPORTANCE OF ASTROLOGY

Indian astrology, believed to be one of the oldest systems in the world (its origins date back 4,000 years), used the position of constellations in the sky to reveal an individual's past and future. The practice of astrology was the driving force for the advancement of astronomy as a science. It is likely that Indian astronomy and astrology originated from the Greeks, but India integrated this science into its own culture and made significant advances in Platonic and Aristotleian astronomy. In fact, in the 5th century, the Indian astronomer Aryabhatta believed that the sun was the source of moonlight, and that the earth rotated on its own axis.

The astronomical instruments at Jantar Mantar, New Delhi

THE INSTRUMENTS

Jai Singh II named his observatory Jantar Mantar after *yantra* (instrument) and *mantra* (formula). His huge instruments allowed for minute gradations in scale, which facilitated great accuracy of measurement. Perfectly stable, they were resistant to vibration and are thus accurate even today. Jai Singh designed three of these *yantras* himself. The most striking, the gigantic sundial ▷ *Samrat Yantra*, had many uses, including measuring the time of day and annual crop prospects. It is in such good condition that it is still used to predict the onset of the monsoon. The instrument consists of a right-angled triangle with finely calibrated quadrants on either side.

Jantar Mantar, Jaipur

Kantivrita Yantra

O F THE FIVE OBSERVATORIES built by Sawai Jai Singh II, the one in Jaipur is the largest and best preserved; the others are in Delhi, Ujjain, Mathura, and Varanasi. A keen astronomer himself, Jai Singh kept abreast of the latest astronomical studies in the world, and was most inspired by the work of Mirza Ulugh Beg, the astronomer-king of Samarkand. Built between 1728 and 1734, the observatory has been described as "the most realistic and logical landscape in stone," its 16 instruments resembling a giant sculptural composition. Some of the instruments are still used to forecast how hot the summer months will be, the expected date of arrival, duration, and intensity of the monsoon, and the possibility of floods and famine.

Narivalaya Yantra
Inclined at 27°, these sundials represent the two hemispheres and calculate time by following the solar cycle.

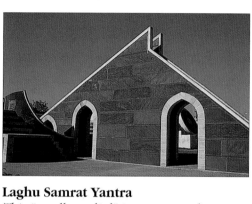

Laghu Samrat Yantra
This "small sundial" is constructed on Latitude 27° North (Jaipur's latitude) and calculates Jaipur's local time up to an accuracy of 20 seconds.

Unnatansha Yantra was used to determine the positions of stars and planets at any time of day or night.

`City Palace Museum`

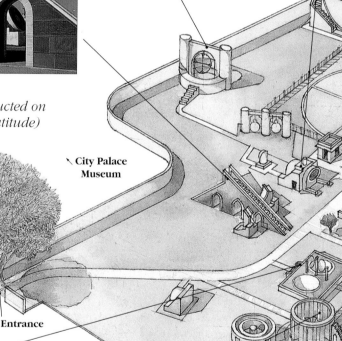

Chakra Yantra
A brass tube passes through the center of these two circular metal instruments. They can be used to calculate the angles of stars and planets from the equator.

Entrance

★ Ram Yantra
Vertical columns support an equal number of horizontal slabs in the two identical stone structures that comprise this instrument. Its readings determine the celestial arc from horizon to zenith, as well as the altitude of the sun.

A view of Jantar Mantar
The complex of stone and metal instruments was repaired with the addition of marble inlay comissioned by Madho Singh II in 1901.

★ Samrat Yantra
Jai Singh believed that gigantic instruments would give more accurate results. This 23-m (75-ft) high sundial forecasts the crop prospects for the year.

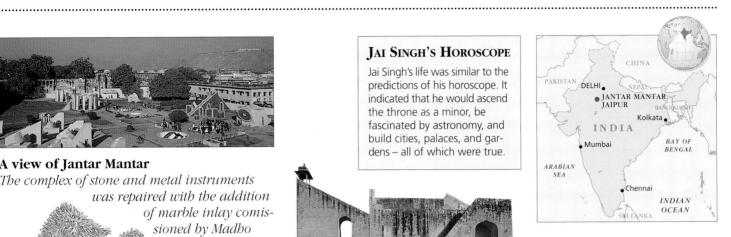

Hawa Mahal

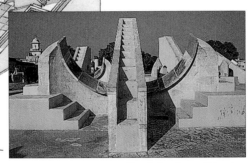

Rashivalaya Yantra
This is composed of 12 pieces, each of which represents a sign of the zodiac and therefore faces a different constellation. This yantra (instrument), used by astrologers to draw up horoscopes, is the only one of its kind.

★ Jai Prakash Yantra
These two sunken hemispheres map out the heavens. Some historians believe that Jai Singh invented this instrument himself, to verify the accuracy of all the other instruments in the observatory.

KEY DATES

1724 Jai Singh's first observatory is built in Delhi.

1728–34 Jai Singh builds his largest observatory, the Jantar Mantar in Jaipur.

1901 Jantar Mantar in Jaipur is restored.

1948 Jantar Mantar complex is declared a National Monument.

SAWAI JAI SINGH II

Jai Singh II, king and astronomer, came to the throne of Amber in 1699 when he was barely 11 years old. Impressed by the young Jai Singh, Mughal emperor Aurangzeb rewarded him with the title "Sawai," meaning "one-and-one quarter" or "he who is extraordinary." Jai Singh proved to be an able ruler and statesman, and a keen builder who, with the help of a gifted Bengali engineer, Vidyadhar Chakravarty, built a scientifically planned capital to the south of Amber and named it Jaipur ("the City of Victory"). He was well versed in Sanskrit and Persian, and passionately interested in the sciences, especially astronomy. He sent an ambassador to Central Asia to bring back details of Mirza Ulugh Beg's works. Jai Singh also studied the earlier observatory built by Persian astronomer Nasir-ud-din Al Tusi, and also managed to procure the latest European astronomical texts and instruments. His observatories constitute an integral part of India's scientific legacy.

STAR FEATURES

★ **Ram Yantra**

★ **Samrat Yantra**

★ **Jai Prakash Yantra**

RAO JODHA SINGH

A chieftain of the martial Rathore clan, Rao Jodha Singh (r.1458–88) chose this site, 9 km (6 miles) south of his capital at Mandore, due to its strategic location on the overland trade routes. He built the formidable Mehrangarh Fort high on the rocky outcrop, and established the new capital city of Jodhpur, nestling beneath its ramparts. During his reign the desert kingdom of Marwar ("The Land of Death") entered a period of stability, flourishing as a center of trade and commerce. His descendants expanded the city and also added palaces, pavilions, and gardens within the fort, laying the foundation for Jodhpur's status as the second largest city in Rajasthan.

Maharaja's cradle with a mechanical rocking system, Jhanki Mahal

PHOOL MAHAL

Built by Maharaja Abhaya Singh (r.1724–1749), the ▷ *Phool Mahal* ("Flower Palace") is an exquisite example of the fusion between Rajput and Mughal architecture. This splendid chamber was once the Hall of Public Audiences, where royal celebrations were held. The king watched musicians and dancers perform while seated on his throne which is surmounted by a ceremonial umbrella. The ornate, gold filigree ceiling has been painted with portraits of earlier kings. Other decorative elements include stained-glass windows, perforated screens, and a collection of miniatures, including a set of 36 *Ragamala* paintings that depict the moods of various musical *ragas* (melodic modes).

Mehrangarh Fort, Jodhpur

Sati **handprints on Loha Pol**

RISING SHEER out of a 125-m (410-ft) high rock, Mehrangarh is perhaps the most majestic of India's forts. Described by an awe-struck Rudyard Kipling as "the creation of angels, fairies, and giants," Mehrangarh's forbidding ramparts are in sharp contrast to the flamboyantly decorated palaces within. Founded by Rao Jodha in 1459, the sandstone fort was added to by later rulers, mostly between the mid-17th and mid-19th centuries. The royal apartments within the fort now form part of an outstanding museum.

The Ramparts
The bastioned walls, parts of which are hewn out of the rock itself, are in places 24 m (79 ft) thick and 40 m (131 ft) high. Perched on them are old cannons.

Nagnechiaji Mandir
has a 14th-century image of the goddess Kuldevi, the family deity of the rulers.

Zenana Chowk

★ Phool Mahal
Built between 1730 and 1750, this is the fort's most opulent chamber, richly gilded and painted. It was used for royal celebrations.

Suraj Pol is the entrance to the museum.

Shringar Chowk
This courtyard has the coronation throne of the Jodhpur rulers, made of white marble. Every ruler after Rao Jodha was crowned on it.

Chamundi Devi Mandir
is dedicated to the goddess Durga in her wrathful aspect.

Palki Khana

Shringar Chowk

Fateh Mahal's carved balconies crown the towering bastions.

STAR FEATURES

★ **Phool Mahal**

★ **Moti Mahal**

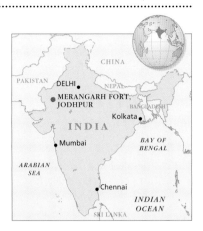

The blue-washed houses of Brahmapuri village, clustered below the ramparts of Mehrangarh Fort

Chokelao Palace, now under restoration, was a pleasure palace built around a sunken garden.

★ Moti Mahal

Built between 1581 and 1595, this magnificent room was the Hall of Private Audience. Its ceiling is decorated with mirrors and gold leaf, and crushed seashells were mixed with plaster to give its walls a lustrous sheen.

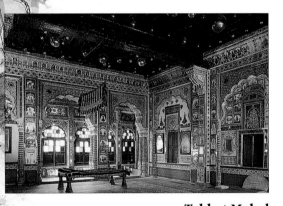

Takhat Mahal

This exuberantly painted room with a wooden ceiling was the favourite retreat of Maharaja Takhat Singh (r.1843–73), who had 30 queens and numerous concubines.

Jhanki Mahal is a long gallery with exquisite latticed stone screens.

Phool Mahal

Sileh Khana's exceptional collection of weapons includes damascened Mughal daggers, gem-studded shields, and special armor for war elephants.

Jai Pol

One of the seven fortified gates to the fort, it is now the main entrance. It was built in 1806 by Maharaja Man Singh to commemorate a victory in battle.

KEY DATES

1459 Construction of Mehrangarh Fort and Jodhpur begins.

1460 Jasmade, Jodha's queen, builds Rani Sar (the Queen's Lake) as a source of water.

1707 Fateh Mahal (the Palace of Victory), is built by Maharaja Ajit Singh.

1974 Mehrangarh Fort Museum opens.

MEHRANGARH FORT MUSEUM

Regarded as the best of Rajasthan's many palace museums, the Mehrangarh Fort Museum has a rich and varied collection that encompasses a gold throne, miniature paintings, royal costumes, and turbans housed in finely restored chambers. Near the entrance is the ▷ *Palki Khana* with its collection of gilded palanquins and the Howdah Gallery, displaying the ceremonial seats placed on elephants during grand processions. The Armory (▷ *Sileh Khana*) houses the weapons. Miniature paintings from the Jodhpur School depicting courtly life are the focus of Umaid Mahal. Other paintings, particularly murals, can be seen in the 19th-century ▷ *Takhat Mahal*. Next door is the ▷ *Jhanki Mahal* ("Peeping Palace"), so called because its latticed stone screens gave the women of the royal harem (*zenna*) a view of the courtyard below. It now houses a collection of royal cradles.

The Buddha was born in 566 BC as Siddhartha Gautama, prince of Kapilavastu. Renouncing his princely life, he left his palace at the age of 30 to search for answers to the meaning of human existence and suffering. He spent six years living with hermits, undertaking severe fasts and penances, only to find that self-mortification gave him no answers. Enlightenment finally came at Bodh Gaya where, after meditating for 49 days under the Bodhi Tree, he discovered that the cause of suffering is desire; and that desire can be conquered by following the Eightfold Path of Righteousness: Right Thought, Understanding, Speech, Action, Livelihood, Effort, Concentration, and Contemplation. The essence of his teachings is non-violence and peace.

BUDDHIST STYLE

India's earliest Buddhist monuments were stupas, large reliquaries in which the ashes of the Buddha and other great teachers were interred. Solid throughout, the stupa itself is undecorated, designed to stimulate prayer and represent the path to divine understanding. As Indian traditions spread throughout southeast Asia, the Buddhist stupa reached new heights of complex Buddhist symbolism. Borobodur Temple in Java, with its design and sculpture of the highest order, is probably the greatest monument of this architectural style.

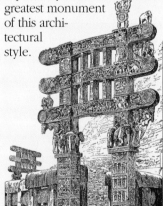

Buddhist *tope* (sculpture) on the East Gateway, Sanchi

The Great Stupa, Sanchi

Animals on the *torana* (gateway)

DOMINATING THE HILL at Sanchi, one of India's best preserved and most extensive Buddhist sites, is the Great Stupa. Its hemispherical shape is believed to symbolize the upturned alms bowl of a Buddhist monk, or an umbrella of protection for followers of the Buddhist dharma. The stupa's main glory lies in its four stone *toranas* (gateways), added in the 1st century BC. Their superb sculptures replicate the techniques of wood and ivory carving, and cover a rich variety of Buddhist themes.

West Gateway
This animated scene from the Jataka Tales *shows monkeys scrambling across a bridge to escape from soldiers.*

Circumambulatory Paths
The paths have balustrades carved with medallions of flowers, birds, and animals, and the names of donors who funded them.

South Gateway
The Wheel of Law, being worshiped by devotees, symbolizes the Buddha.

The four gateways show scenes from the Buddha's life, and episodes from the *Jataka Tales*. The Buddha is not depicted in human form, but only through symbols such as a Bodhi Tree, footprints, or a wheel.

Detail of Architrave
The intricate carving on the architraves is the work of wood and ivory craftsmen hired to carve the stone.

★ North Gateway

Sujata, the village chief's daughter, offers the Buddha (represented by the Bodhi Tree) kheer (rice pudding), as the demon Mara sends the temptress to seduce him.

The *vedika* (railings) are an impressive recreation in stone of a typical wooden railing design. They were the inspiration for the stone railings around Sansad Bhavan or the Parliament House in New Delhi.

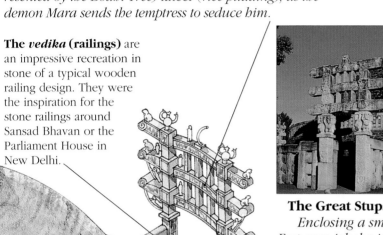

THE JATAKA TALES

The Buddha's past lives are retold in this large collection of fables, where an animal or bird often took the part of the Buddha. These tales had great religious, moral, social, and cultural significance.

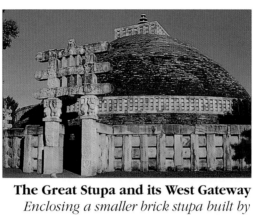

The Great Stupa and its West Gateway
Enclosing a smaller brick stupa built by Emperor Ashoka in the 3rd century BC, the Great Stupa is capped by a three-tiered stone umbrella, symbolizing the layers of heaven.

Statues of the Buddha meditating, added in the 5th century AD, face each of the gateways.

East Gateway
This scene shows a royal retinue at the palace of Kapilavastu, the Buddha's home before he renounced his princely life.

★ Salabhanjika

Supporting the lowest architrave of the East Gateway is this sensuous, voluptuous tree nymph, gracefully positioned under a mango tree.

STAR FEATURES

★ **North Gateway**

★ **Salabhanjika**

KEY DATES

2nd century BC The Great Stupa is built at Sanchi.

14th century AD The Great Stupa is deserted.

1818 General Taylor of the Bengal Cavalry "rediscovers" the Great Stupa.

1912–19 Director General of Archaeology in India, Sir John Marshall, excavates and restores the site.

1989 The Great Stupa is declared a UNESCO World Heritage Site.

EMPEROR ASHOKA

One of India's greatest rulers, Ashoka (r.269–232 BC) was the grandson of Chandragupta Maurya, who founded the country's first empire. The carnage and misery brought about by Ashoka's bloody conquest of Kalinga (now Orissa) in 260 BC filled him with remorse. He gave up *digvijaya* (military conquest) for *dharmavijaya* (spiritual conquest), and became a great patron of Buddhism instead, building many stupas including the original brick stupa at Sanchi. Ashoka was a humane ruler, whose edicts on rocks and pillars all over his vast empire record his ethical code of righteousness and non-violence *(ahimsa)*. His decree at Dhauli (site of the Kalinga battle) declares, "All men are my children." He asked his officials to be impartial, just, and compassionate; and his subjects to respect others' religions, give to charity, and avoid the killing of animals.

HINDU MYTHOLOGY

The vast pantheon of Hindu gods and goddesses range from anthropomorphic symbols to half-human, half-animal forms. Brahma the Creator, Vishnu the Preserver, and Shiva the Destroyer form the holy Trinity. Their consorts respectively are Saraswati the Goddess of Learning, Lakshmi the Goddess of Wealth, and Parvati, whose many manifestations as the Devi (goddess) include Durga (slayer of the buffalo demon) and Kali (destroyer of evil). Shiva's sons are Ganesha, the beloved elephant-headed god of auspicious beginnings, and Karttikeya, the warrior god. Other popular gods are Rama and Krishna, both incarnations of Vishnu. Each god has a personal vehicle (vahana) and symbols of divinity.

Sculpture of Shiva and Parvati, Ellora

THE MAHABHARATA & THE RAMAYANA

These two great epic poems have had an abiding impact on Indian culture and philosophy. The *Mahabharata* recounts the rivalry between the five Pandava brothers – Yudishthira, Bhima, Arjuna, Nakul, and Sahdeva – and 100 members of the Kaurava clan, headed by Duryodhana, and culminates in a great battle. In the ▷ *Ramayana,* Rama, the ideal hero, was sent into a 14-year exile with his wife Sita and brother Lakshman. Sita is abducted in the forest by Ravana, the demon-king of Lanka. Hanuman, the monkey god, helps rescue Sita and defeat Ravana. Rama's triumphant return to Ayodhya is celebrated in the festival of lights, Diwali.

Rock Sites of Ellora: Kailasanatha Temple

Detail, roof of the entrance gateway

THE 34 CAVES AT Ellora, hewn from a 2-km (1.3-mile) long escarpment, are the most splendid examples of rock-cut architecture in India. The Kailasanatha Temple (Cave 16) was commissioned by the Rashtrakuta king Krishna I in the 8th century. This huge complex, spanning 81 m (266 ft) by 47 m (154 ft), was carved out of a vast rocky cliff face. Sculptors chiseled through 85,000 cubic m (approximately 3 million cubic ft) of rock, beginning at the top of the cliff and working their way down. The result, embellished with huge sculptural panels, was meant to depict Mount Kailasa, the sacred abode of Lord Shiva.

★ **The Roof**
The mandapa (assembly hall) *roof is embellished by a lotus carved in concentric rings, topped by four stone lions.*

Courtyard
On either side of the courtyard are two life-size elephants.

The Nandi Pavilion

Obelisks
Flanking the Nandi Pavilion are two monolithic pillars, 17 m (56 ft) high, with carvings of lotus friezes and garlands.

★ **Lakshmi with Elephants**
Facing the entrance, the ornate Gaja-lakshmi panel in the Nandi Pavilion depicts Lakshmi seated in a lotus pond and being bathed by elephants bearing upturned pots in their trunks.

The tower rises 32.6 m (107 ft), and was once covered in white plaster, to replicate Mount Kailasa's snowy peaks.

VISHNU'S AVATARS

Vishnu descends to earth periodically to redress the balance between good and evil. He is said to have ten main incarnations or *avatars*, of which nine have already appeared; the tenth is yet to come.

Supporting Elephants

Elephants with lotuses in their trunks are carved all along the lower story, and appear to support the structure.

0 meters   10

0 yards   10

Rock-cut monasteries

★ **Ravana Shaking Mount Kailasa**
A large panel depicts Ravana (the demon king in the Ramayana*) shaking Mount Kailasa in order to disturb Shiva and Parvati in their mountain home.*

Ramayana **panels** flank the south wall, while the north wall has *Mahabharata* and Krishna legends.

STAR FEATURES

★ **The Roof**

★ **Lakshmi with Elephants**

★ **Ravana Shaking Mount Kailasa**

Three Goddesses

The Hall of Sacrifice contains life-size images of Durga, Chamunda, and Kali, as well as of Ganesha, Parvati, and the seven mother goddesses.

KEY DATES

AD 757–73 Building of the Kailasanatha Temple.

1983 Ellora Caves declared a UNESCO World Heritage Site.

BUDDHIST, HINDU AND JAIN CAVES AT ELLORA

Situated on an important trade route, Ellora was excavated and occupied by three distinct religious communities – Buddhist, Hindu and Jain – over a period of 500 years. The excavation of the Buddhist Caves (1 to 12), coincided with a Buddhist Revival in the 5th–7th centuries. The first nine caves are variations of *viharas* (monasteries) and are filled with Buddha figures and Bodhisattvas. The most splendid is Cave 10 or Vishwakarma, a striking *chaitya* (shrine) which is dominated by a figure of a Teaching Buddha in front of a votive stupa. The gradual decline of Buddhism was followed by a Hindu Renaissance under the Chalukya and Rashtrakuta dynasties (7th–9th centuries). The Hindu Caves (13 to 29), were carved during this period and represent the peak of Ellora's development. Cave 14, or Ravana ki Khai, has sculptures of Hindu deities such as Durga slaying the buffalo demon, and Vishnu as the boar-headed Varaha. The Jain Caves (30 to 34) date from Ellora's final stage (9th–10th centuries), and are simpler than the Hindu ones. The finest, Cave 32 or Indra Sabha, is a monolithic shrine with carvings of elephants, lions, and *tirthankaras* (beings who guide souls into the next life) on the courtyard walls.

Padmanabhapuram Palace

Detail from a carved rosewood door

S ET AMID LUSH HILLS, verdant paddy fields, and perennial rivers, Padmanabhapuram Palace is the finest example of Kerala's distinctive wooden architecture. Laid out in a sequence of four adjoining walled compounds, comprising public and private zones, the palace has richly carved wooden ceilings, sculpted pillars, slatted windows, and pagoda-like tiled roofs. From 1590 onwards, Padmanabhapuram was the capital of the former princely state of Travancore, which straddled parts of present-day Tamil Nadu as well as Kerala. In 1750, Travancore's most powerful maharaja, Marthanda Varma, shifted his capital to Thiruvananthapuram, 55km (34 miles) to the northwest, which remains the capital of Kerala today.

Padmanabha, the national deity of Travancore

THE ROYAL FAMILY OF TRAVANCORE

Kerala's southernmost kingdom, Travancore, came into existence by the end of the 10th century. Its most significant ruler was Marthanda Varma (1729–58), who dedicated his kingdom to his family's patron deity Padmanabha, and renamed the capital in his honor. Marthanda Varma and his successor, Rama Varma, initiated several public works projects that developed the network of irrigation systems, thus improving agriculture and ensuring widespread prosperity. The 19th-century ruler, Swathi Tirunal Rama Varma, was a great scholar and musician under whose reign Travancore became a center of arts and culture. The rulers strengthened ties with the British East India Company, while maintaining their status as an independent kingdom. In 1956, after India's independence, Travancore became a part of Kerala state.

VAASTU SHASTRA

The ancient Indian treatise (*shastra*) on architecture (*vaastu* or dwelling place) is based on the *vaastu purush mandala*, a diagram representing the cosmos in the form of a man lying with his head towards the northeast. By following its rules, the five elements of Sky, Earth, Water, Fire, and Wind fall into perfect accord. The Padmanabhapuram Palace follows the local version of this science, which combines architectural and mathematical principles, astronomy, astrology, and mysticism as well as social and religious conventions.

The Lady's Chamber houses two large swings, a pair of enormous Belgian mirrors and a royal bed.

★ Prayer Hall
The prayer hall, on the fourth floor of the King's Palace, has exquisite murals on its walls. The four-poster bed, carved from 64 different types of wood, was a gift from the Dutch.

The clock tower's chimes could be heard from a distance of 3 km (2 miles).

Entrance Hall
The entrance hall has a profusely carved wooden ceiling with 90 different inverted flowers, a polished granite bed, and an ornate Chinese throne.

Main Gate
The main entrance to the palace complex is reached after crossing a large courtyard. This gate has a decorated gabled roof.

Entrance

```
0 meters                    20
0 yards                     20
```

Carved bay window for watching processions

Guest house

The Bath House is a small airy room, where the male members of the royal family were given a massage before they descended, down covered steps, to a private tank to bathe.

PADMANABHA

In a Hindu myth of creation, Vishnu reclines on the cosmic serpent, Anantha, whose hood shelters him from the churning of the ocean. In this form he is known as Padmanabha.

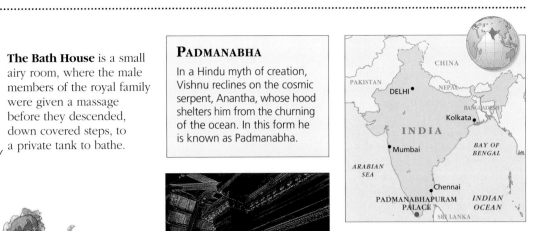

CHINA
PAKISTAN
DELHI
NEPAL
BANGLADESH
Kolkata
INDIA
BAY OF BENGAL
Mumbai
ARABIAN SEA
Chennai
INDIAN OCEAN
PADMANABHAPURAM PALACE
SRI LANKA

KEY DATES

1550 Construction begins on Mother's Palace.

1590 The site becomes the residence and capital of the royal family of Travancore.

1744 Marthanda Varma renames the capital after his patron deity, Padmanabha.

1750 The capital moves to Thiruvananthapuram.

★ Mother's Palace

Built in 1550, this is the oldest building in the complex. It contains intricately carved wooden pillars fashioned from the wood of the jackfruit tree. The floor was polished to a red gloss with hibiscus flowers.

Lamp

A horse lamp (the horse is a symbol of valor) in the entrance hall hangs suspended from a special chain that keeps the lamp perfectly balanced.

The dining hall, laid out over two stories, could seat 2,000 guests.

The palace museum houses artifacts including furniture, wooden and granite statues, coins, weapons, and utensils.

STAR FEATURES

★ **Prayer Hall**

★ **Mother's Palace**

★ **Council Chamber**

★ Council Chamber

The king's council chamber has wooden louvers to let in light and air. The gloss on the floor was achieved with a mixture of lime, sand, egg white, coconut water, charcoal, and jaggery.

WOODEN ARCHITECTURE IN KERALA

The importance of wooden architecture in Kerala is evident in legends that glorify the master carpenter, Perunthachhan. Palaces, temples, mosques, and homes all have characteristic sloping tiled roofs to drain away the heavy rains during the monsoon. Roofs are generally hipped, often with decorated gables, topped by brass pot finials. To achieve height, they rise in two or more superimposed tiers to create steeply pyramidal profiles. Joints and wooden pegs, instead of nails, are used. Other typical features are the ornate wooden pillars, which are decorative as well as functional as they support the roof, and brackets that are often carved as *yalis* (mythical leonine creatures) or figures of gods and goddesses. The richly embellished ceilings are divided into panels carved with lotus designs or Hindu deities, such as Brahma, surrounded by numerous *dikpalas* or guardian figures.

KHMER ARCHITECTURE

Thailand's northeast stone temple complexes, or *prasats*, were built by the Khmers, who ruled much of modern Cambodia and northeast Thailand in the 9th–13th centuries. Khmer *prasats* were built to symbolize kingship and the universe, and are awesome in their scale and beauty. Most have staircases or bridges lined with *nagas* (a seven-headed serpent thought to be the keeper of life's force), leading to a ▷ *central sanctuary*. This is usually decorated with carved stone reliefs depicting Hindu myths, and topped by a *prang* (tower). *Prangs* symbolize Mount Meru, the mythical abode of the gods. Lintels and pediments over the sanctuary entrances depict Hindu and Buddhist deities.

SYMBOLISM

Khmer *prasats* were heavily influenced by Hindu culture and religion. The main object of worship was the *lingam*, a phallus representing the creative force of the Hindu god Shiva. The *prasats'* surrounding moats depict the cosmic ocean dividing heaven from earth. The concentric walls symbolize the mountains, while the central *prang* represents both Mount Meru and the axis of the world. In the late 12th century, the Khmers embraced Buddhism, and many *lingams* were replaced with images of Buddha.

Naga* antefix on the central sanctuary's *prang

Prasat Hin Khao Phnom Rung

Carved stone elephants

Crowning the extinct volcano of Khao Phnom Rung is Prasat Hin Khao Phnom Rung, one of Thailand's finest examples of Khmer architecture. A Hindu temple, it was built here to glorify the deity Shiva. The temple's construction began in the early 10th century and, like other Khmer sites, it lies on a route to the old Khmer capital of Angkor in Cambodia. The buildings are aligned so that at the Songkran festival, the rising sun can be seen through the western *gopura's* (entrance pavilion) 15 doors. Its three *naga* bridges, extending for 200 m (655 ft) in total, are the only ones remaining in Thailand.

Western Porch Pediment
This carving shows monkeys rescuing Sita in a chariot that is itself a model of the temple.

★ **Central Sanctuary**
The corncob-shaped prang *of the central sanctuary is the cosmological summit of the processional way.*

Brick Sanctuary
Located just southeast of the central sanctuary, this 13th-century structure, a late addition to the compound, was built as a library.

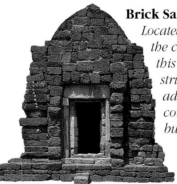

STAR FEATURES
★ Central Sanctuary
★ Naga Bridge
★ Ornamental Ponds
★ Processional Way

★ **Naga Bridge**
This naga *bridge, which is located inside the main temple compound, links the east-facing* gopura *to the central sanctuary. The body of the* naga *forms the bridge's balustrade.*

Pediment over Porch of Mandapa

The carving on this pediment represents Shiva Nataraja, the dancing Shiva, his ten arms splayed out in a dance of death and destruction.

KEY DATES

11th century The central sanctuary is built.

1988 Art Institute of Chicago returns a prized Vishnu relief that had been in its collection since the 1960s.

Nandin the Bull

This image of Nandin the bull, the mythical mount of the Hindu deity Shiva, is located in the first, eastern chamber of the central sanctuary.

Main temple compound

Gopura

SCULPTURAL DECORATIONS

The most outstanding feature of this Khmer temple is the intricate carvings that ornament almost every surface, from the ▷ *central sanctuary* and *prang* to the lintels and pediments. They usually depict Hindu deities; one of the most interesting reliefs shows Vishnu reclining on the back of the 100-hooded serpent. There is also a relief of Brahma, the god of creation and Shiva Nataraja, the cosmic dancer, who represents nature's cycle of evolution and destruction. Scenes from ancient Hindu myths and epic texts, particularly the *Ramayana*, are also portrayed. The central characters are Rama, an incarnation of Vishnu; Sita, his wife; and Lakshman, his loyal younger brother. Other motifs include mythical and sacred creatures, such as ▷ *Nandin the Bull*, and especially the serpents that flank either side of the ▷ *naga bridges*. Stone inscriptions and bas-reliefs of battle scenes also embellish the surfaces, providing invaluable historical insights into the period. After Buddhism replaced Hinduism as the state religion, Buddhist divinities were added to the pantheon of gods.

★ Ornamental Ponds

Located at the front of the entrance to the main temple compound are four ponds. They supposedly represent the four sacred rivers of the Indian subcontinent. In the background, a naga *bridge leads into the complex.*

★ Processional Way

This processional walkway was built to symbolize the spiritual journey from earth to Hindu heaven.

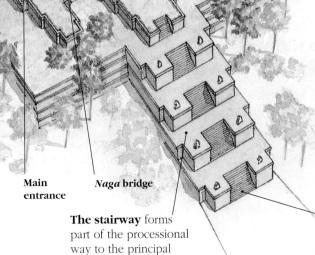

Main entrance

Naga **bridge**

The stairway forms part of the processional way to the principal temple compound.

Wat Mahathat, Sukhothai

Oᴺᴄᴇ ᴛʜᴇ sᴘɪʀɪᴛᴜᴀʟ center of the Sukhothai Kingdom, Wat Mahathat is one of the most important temples in central Thailand. The central *chedi* was founded by Si Intharathit (c.1240–70), first king of Sukhothai, and rebuilt in the 1340s by Lo Thai (1298–1346) to house relics of the Buddha. Buildings were added to the complex by successive kings, in the Buddhist architectural style (▷ *Buddhist Style p334*). By the time it was abandoned in the 16th century it had some 200 *chedis* as well as numerous *wihans* and *mondops*.

A Buddha image in the meditation posture (dhyana mudra)

BUDDHA GESTURES

Buddha images in Thailand follow strict rules laid down in the 3rd century AD. There are four basic postures: sitting, standing, walking, and reclining. The first three are associated with the Buddha's daily activities, the last with his final passing or *parinirvana*. When combined with hand and feet positions these create a variety of attitudes (*mudras*), representing key Buddhist themes. Exposition (*vitarkha mudra*) symbolizes his first public discourse. The thumb and forefinger form a circle that signifies the perpetuity of life and the law of cause and effect called *karma*. Meditation (*dhyana mudra*) is a sitting posture with both hands positioned palms up, the right over the left. Reassurance (*abhaya mudra*), with the right hand raised, implies the Buddha's offer of protection to his followers.

THE SUKHOTHAI HISTORICAL PARK

This site is a potent reminder of the 13th-century Sukhothai kingdom. It spreads over 70 sq km (27 sq miles). At its center is the walled Royal City containing the most important ruins. The Ramkamhaeng National Museum, near the east gate, houses a collection of artifacts and old photographs. Wat Mahathat lies at the heart of the city. Other significant *wats* are Wat Si Sawai, with three 12th–14th-century Khmer-style *prangs*, and Wat Sorasak, a 15th-century bell-shaped *chedi*, with a square base supported by 24 stucco elephants.

Arch on central *chedi*

Bell-sha...

Ornamental pond

★ **Lotus-Bud Chedi**
At the epicenter of the wat *complex is this classic Sukhothai lotus-bud chedi. The remains of beautiful stucco decoration can be seen in patches.*

Multi-layered Chedi
At the western end of a minor wihan *are the crumbling remnants of a large, square-based, multi-layered chedi. It is built out of brick.*

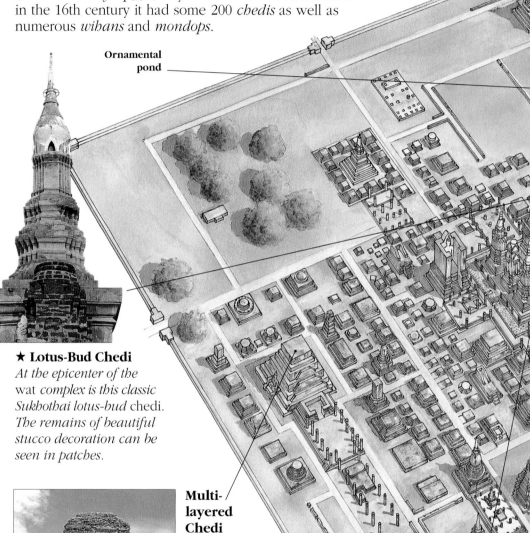

Octagon... *chedi*

★ **Frieze of Walking Monks**
A stone frieze runs around the square base of the central group of chedis. *It depicts monks processing around the shrine – a ritual called* pradaksina.

Remains of Bot

To the north of the central chedi *are the remains of a* bot, *with a large, seated Buddha. Like all major Buddha images in Thailand, it faces east.*

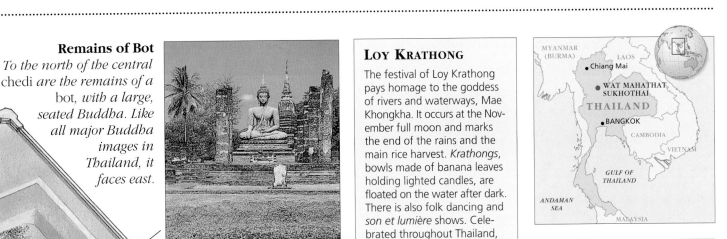

LOY KRATHONG

The festival of Loy Krathong pays homage to the goddess of rivers and waterways, Mae Khongkha. It occurs at the November full moon and marks the end of the rains and the main rice harvest. *Krathongs*, bowls made of banana leaves holding lighted candles, are floated on the water after dark. There is also folk dancing and *son et lumière* shows. Celebrated throughout Thailand, the most exuberant festivities, however, are at Sukhothai.

The perimeter wall is adorned with headless Buddha images. They were decapitated by souvenir hunters; many heads are in private homes or museums.

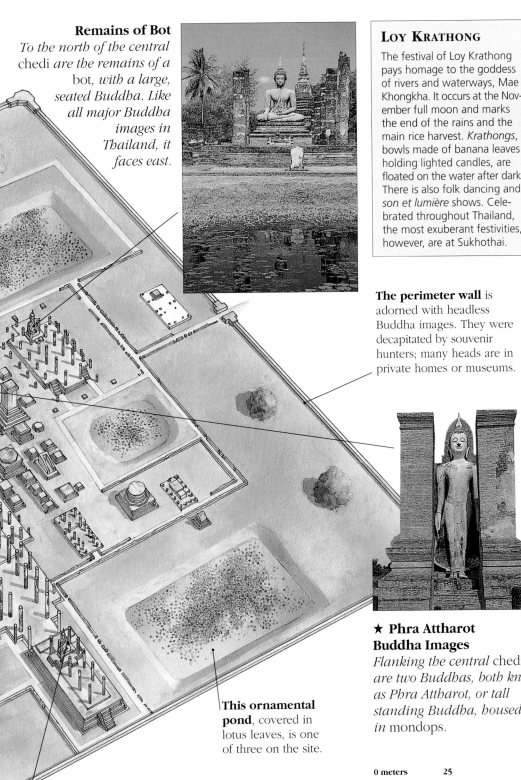

This ornamental pond, covered in lotus leaves, is one of three on the site.

★ Phra Attharot Buddha Images

Flanking the central chedis *are two Buddhas, both known as Phra Attharot, or tall standing Buddha, housed in* mondops.

0 meters   25

0 yards   25

Remains of Main Wihan

Aligned on an east-west axis with the central group of chedis *is the main* wihan. *The only remains today are columns that once supported a roof and a seated Buddha image.*

STAR FEATURES

★ **Lotus-Bud Chedi**

★ **Frieze of Walking Monks**

★ **Phra Attharot Buddha Images**

KEY DATES

c.1240–70 The central lotus-bud *chedi* is raised.

1345 The central *chedi* is pulled down and rebuilt during the reign of King Lo Thai (1298–1346).

Mid-19th century King Rama III (r.1824–51) renovates the temples on the Wat Mahathat site.

1956 Excavation work is carried out on the Wat Mahathat complex by Thailand's Fine Arts Department.

1991 Sukhothai Historical Park is declared a UNESCO World Heritage Site.

FEATURES OF A WAT COMPLEX

A wat is a collection of buildings serving various purposes: Buddhist monastery, temple, and community center. The most important structure is the *bot* or ordination hall, containing the main Buddha image (▷ *Remains of Bot*). Nearby, the *ho rakang* or bell tower summons monks to prayer. The *wihan* or assembly hall is similar to the *bot*, while the *mondop* is a square-based structure topped by a spire, housing an object of worship. Wats are often built expressly to surround a *chedi*, a conical structure that encases a relic of the Buddha or the ashes of a king. Other features include monks' quarters, *salas* or meeting halls for pilgrims, ▷ *ornamental ponds*, and the sacred Bodhi tree.

THE LEGEND OF THE EMERALD BUDDHA

In 1434, lightning struck Wat Phra Kaeo in Chiang Rai, revealing a simple stucco image, encasing a jadeite image, the ▷ *Emerald Buddha*. Chiang Mai's king sent an army of elephants to bring the image to him, but as the animal bearing it refused to take the road to Chiang Mai, it was enshrined at Lampang. After several moves, the image was taken to Laos in 1552, where it remained until Rama I brought the Buddha back to Thailand in 1778. For several years it was kept in Wat Arun, until it was brought to its current resting place in 1785.

Ramakien figure outside the Phra Si Rattana Chedi

THE RAMAKIEN

The *Ramakien* is an allegory of the triumph of good over evil. Rama, heir to the throne of Ayodhya, is sent into a 14-year exile with his wife Sita and brother Lakshman. Tosakan, the demon-king of Longka, abducts Sita from the forest. Hanuman, the monkey god, helps rescue Sita and defeat Tosakan, and Rama returns triumphantly to Ayodhya. This epic tale was probably established after the Thais occupied Angkor in the 15th century. All the Chakri kings adopted Rama as one of their names, and the 14th-century kingdom of Ayutthaya was named after the fictional Ayodhya. The legend has also been a great inspiration for Thai painting, classical drama, and puppetry.

Grand Palace and Wat Phra Kaeo, Bangkok

Detail on Phra Mondop Library

CONSTRUCTION of this remarkable site began in the late 18th century to mark the founding of the new capital and to provided a resting place for the sacred Emerald Buddha (Phra Kaeo), and a residence for the king. Surrounded by walls stretching for 1.9 km (1.18 miles), the complex was once a self-sufficient city within a city. The Royal Family now lives in Dusit, but Wat Phra Kaeo is still Thailand's holiest temple and a stunning piece of Buddhist architecture (▷ *Buddhist Style p334*).

Wat Phra Kaeo's skyline, as seen from Sanam Luang

The Emerald Buddha, displayed in the temple, is carved from a single piece of jade.

The Chapel of the Gandharara Buddha, adorned with glazed ceramic tiles, was constructed in the 19th century.

Hor Phra Rajphongsanusorn

★ **Bot of the Emerald Buddha**
Devotees make offerings to the Emerald Buddha at the entrance to the bot, *the most important building in the* wat.

Eight *prangs* border the east side of the *wat*.

★ **Ramakien Gallery**
Extending clockwise all the way around the cloisters are 178 panels depicting the complete story of the Ramakien.

STAR FEATURES

★ **Bot of the Emerald Buddha**

★ **Ramakien Gallery**

Decorative Gilt Figures

Encircling the exterior of the bot are 112 garudas (mythical beasts that are half-man, half-bird). They are shown holding nagas *(serpents) and are typical of the* wat's *dazzling decorative details.*

Phra Mondop (library)

The Phra Si Rattana Chedi contains a piece of the Buddha's breastbone.

Upper Terrace

Apsonsi

A mythical creature (half-woman, half-lion), Apsonsi is one of the beautiful gilded figures on the upper terrace of Wat Phra Kaeo.

Ho Phra Nak (royal mausoleum)

Northern Terrace

Wihan Yot

WAT PHRA KAEO

Wat Phra Kaeo (shown here) is a sub-complex within the greater Grand Palace complex. The temple is Thailand's most important shrine, but unlike other Thai *wats*, has no resident monks.

Model of Cambodia's Angkor Wat

The Hor Phra

rasat Phra Thep Royal Pantheon) was ilt by King Rama IV house the Emerald ddha, but the building as considered too small.

GRAND PALACE AND WAT PHRA KAEO

1 Entrance
2 Wat Phra Kaeo complex
3 Dusit Throne Hall
4 Aphonphimok Pavilion
5 Chakri Throne Hall
6 Inner Palace
7 Phra Maha Monthien Buildings
8 Siwalai Gardens
9 Rama IV Chapel
10 Boromphiman Mansion
11 Audience Chamber

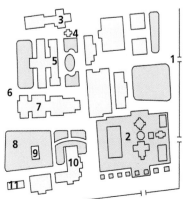

KEY

▢	Wat Phra Kaeo complex
▢	Buildings
▢	Lawns

KEY DATES

1783 Work begins on Wat Phra Kaeo, Dusit Throne Hall, and Phra Maha Monthien.

1809 Rama II remodels the building and introduces new Chinese details.

1932 The Chakri Dynasty's 150th year in power is celebrated at the palace.

1982 The Grand Palace and Wat Phra Kaeo is restored.

EXPLORING WAT PHRA KAEO

When Rama I established his new capital, he envisioned a temple that would surpass its Sukhothai and Ayutthaya predecessors. The result was the splendid Wat Phra Kaeo. The ▷ *bot* houses the surprisingly small image of the Emerald Buddha, seated in a glass case high above a gilded altar. Opposite, the ▷ *Upper Terrace* has several structures; the most striking is the ▷ *Phra Si Rattana Chedi*, built by King Mongkut (Rama IV) in 1855 to house sacred Buddha relics. The adjacent ▷ *Phra Mondop* was initially used as a library. Its exterior has Javanese Buddha images on the four outer corners. To its north is a ▷ *model of Cambodia's Angkor Wat*, commissioned by Rama I. On the ▷ *Northern Terrace*, the ▷ *Ho Phra Nak* or royal mausoleum enshrines the ashes of minor royals, while the ▷ *Wihan Yot* contains the Nak Buddha (an alloy of gold, silver, and copper) rescued from Ayutthaya.

THE CHAKRI DYNASTY

In 1782, Chao Phraya Chakri (later King Rama I) established the Chakri dynasty in Krung Thep (Bangkok). The reigns of Rama I, II and III signaled an era of stability. Rama II was a literary man, while Rama III was a staunch traditionalist. King Mongkut (Rama IV) modernized Siam (Thailand), and opened it up to foreign trade and influence. His son, King Chulalongkorn or Rama V (r.1868–1910), perhaps the greatest Chakri king, furthered modernization by introducing financial reforms and abolishing slavery. He was idealized by his subjects, and his cremation was a grand state affair. Even today, his death is commemorated on Chulalongkorn Day (23 October).

COMMON BUDDHIST RITUALS

Merit-making is an essential part of Buddhist life. It emphasizes that good deeds lead to good outcomes, such as happiness, in this life or the next. Becoming a monk or sponsoring a monk's ordination is a way to achieve merit. Rituals for monks include shaving the head. The alms round takes place at dawn and is where lay people give food to monks as a way of earning merit and to practice generosity. Temple rituals focus on offerings of lotus buds, representing the purity of the Buddha's thoughts, applying gold leaf to Buddha images, lighting candles and incense sticks, and listening to the monks' chanting.

Gold leaf honoring the Buddha

Wat Arun, Bangkok

Ceramic flower on main *prang*

NAMED AFTER ARUNA, the Indian god of dawn, Wat Arun temple is one of Bangkok's best-known landmarks. Legend says that King Taksin arrived here from the sacked capital, Ayutthaya, in 1767. He then enlarged the temple that stood on the site into a Royal Chapel to house the most revered image of the Buddha in Thailand, the Emerald Buddha. Rama I and Rama II were responsible for the size of the current temple: the main *prang* is 79 m (260 ft) high and the circumference of its base is 234 m (768 ft). In the late 19th century, Rama IV added ornamentation created with broken pieces of porcelain. The style of the monument derives mainly from Khmer architecture (▷ *Khmer Style p340*).

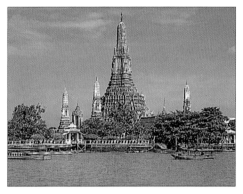

★ River View of Temple
This popular image of Wat Arun, seen from the Chao Phraya river, appears on the 10-baht coin and in the Tourism Authority of Thailand (TAT) logo.

Minor *prangs* at each corner of the *wat*

Chinese Guards
These figures, at the entrances to the terrace, complement the Chinese-style porcelain decorating the prangs.

STAR FEATURES

★ River View of Temple

★ Ceramic Details

Multicolored Tiers
Rows of demons, decorated with pieces of porcelain, line the exterior walls of the main prang.

CENTRAL MONUMENT OF WAT ARUN

The monument's design symbolizes Hindu-Buddhist cosmology. The central *prang* (tower) is the mythical Mount Meru, and its ornamental tiers are worlds within worlds. The layout of four minor *prangs* around a central one is a symbolic mandala shape.

Top terrace

One of the eight entrances

Gallery of the Bot
Elsewhere in the temple complex are the usual buildings found in a wat. *This image of the Buddha in the main ordination hall or* bot *sits above the ashes of devotees.*

Indra's weapon, the *vajra* or thunderbolt, at the crest

SYMBOLIC LEVELS

The Devaphum (top) is the peak of Mount Meru, rising above four subsidiary peaks. It denotes six heavens within seven realms of happiness.

The Tavatimsa Heaven (central section), where all desires are fulfilled, is guarded at the four cardinal points by the Hindu god Indra.

The Traiphum (base) represents 31 realms of existence across the three worlds (Desire, Form, and Formless) of the Buddhist universe.

ROYAL BARGE PROCESSION

Every 5 or 10 years, the King of Thailand takes robes and gifts to the monks at Wat Arun inside a splendid royal barge on the Chao Phraya River.

Stairs on the Central Prang
The steep steps represent the difficulties of reaching higher levels of existence.

Small Cove
On the third level of the central prang *are many small coves, inside which are* kinnari, *mythological creatures, half-bird, half-human.*

KEY DATES

18th century King Taksin re-models the Wat Arun temple.

Early 19th century Rama II restores the temple and extends the central *prang's* height.

1971 Wat Arun undergoes minor repairs after lightning splits a section of the spire.

ARUNA, INDRA & NAYU

Worshiped in India from the early Vedic age (1500 BC), the Hindu deities Aruna, Indra, and Nayu personify nature and the elements. Aruna, the beautiful god of dawn, is the charioteer of Surya, the sun god. Red-skinned, he stands on the chariot in front of the sun, sheltering the world with his body from the sun's fury. Indra, the god of the sky and the heavens, rides a golden chariot drawn by horses and is armed with a *vajra* or thunderbolt. Indra sends the rain and rules the weather, and is often depicted sitting on Airavatta, the four-trunked white elephant who represents a rain-cloud. Nayu (or Vayu) is the god of the winds and messenger of the gods. He is also the regent of the northwest quarter of the heavens and is depicted as white-skinned sitting on an antelope. His other names are "Pavana" (the purifier), "Gandha-vaha" (carrier of perfumes), and "Satata-ga" (always moving). Illustrations from the *Ramayana* (an ancient Indian epic text dating from 500 BC) portray him carrying his baby son Hanuman, the monkey god.

Decoration of the Four Minor Prangs
Inside the niches of each minor prang *are statues of Nayu, the god of wind, on horse-back.*

Square-based structures topped by spires, *mondops*, at the cardinal points

★ Ceramic Details
Much of the colorful porcelain used to decorate the prangs *was donated by local people. The flowers depicted are said to evoke the vegetation of Mount Meru, home of the gods.*

BAS-RELIEFS

Angkor Wat is covered with 1,200 sq m (12,917 sq ft) of intricately carved scenes depicting Khmer myths, Angkorian warfare, and tales from the great Hindu epics the *Ramayana* and the *Mahabharata*. Divided into eight sections, some of the most celebrated panels include the *Battle of Kuruk-setra* in the ▷ West Gallery, the *Churning of the Ocean of Milk* in the east gallery, and the *Heavens and Hells* in the ▷ South Gallery. Angkor Wat is also covered with 1,850 carved ▷ apsaras, Sanskrit for celestial dancers. These sensuous goddesses, naked except for ornate jewelry and elaborate head-dresses, have enigmatic smiles, known as the "Khmer Smile," and are the glory of Angkor.

Battle of Kuruksetra from the Hindu epic the *Mahabharata*

THE FALL OF ANGKOR

The last great king of Angkor was Jayavarman VII (1181–1220) who built the temple of the Bayon at Angkor Thom amongst many others. His ambitious temple building programs probably depleted the kingdom's coffers, as did wars with neighboring Siam (present-day Thailand) and Champa (Vietnam). Succeeding kings are little known but in 1432, the Siamese sacked Angkor and the last king, Ponhea Yat, was forced to move south toward Phnom Penh, the present capital of Cambodia. Although Angkor Wat remained a holy place, the empire subsequently went into decline and most of the temples were deserted, gradually becoming covered in jungle.

Angkor Wat

ONE OF THE LARGEST RELIGIOUS monuments in the world, the 12th-century temple of Angkor Wat is covered with exquisite carvings, forming the longest bas-relief in existence. Part of a vast complex of sacred monuments spread over 400 sq km (154 sq miles), it was constructed between the 9th and 14th centuries, when the Khmer Empire spanned half of Southeast Asia. The temple is an earthly representation of the Hindu cosmos. Its five towers, shaped like lotus buds, form a pyramidal structure symbolizing the mythical Mount Meru, home of the gods. The outer walls represent the edge of the world, and the moat the cosmic ocean. Dedicated to Vishnu, it was built for the god-king Suryavarman II (r.1113–50), probably as a funerary monument. It faces west, towards the setting sun, a symbol of death.

Meditating Buddhist Monk
Angkor was originally Hindu but subsequently became a Buddhist site. Today, the monks live in a pagoda by the side of the temple.

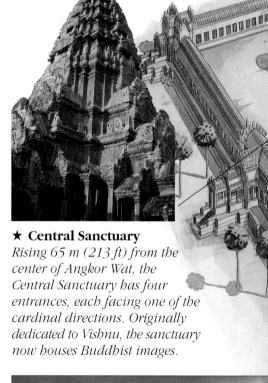

★ **Central Sanctuary**
Rising 65 m (213 ft) from the center of Angkor Wat, the Central Sanctuary has four entrances, each facing one of the cardinal directions. Originally dedicated to Vishnu, the sanctuary now houses Buddhist images.

★ **Gallery of the Bas-Reliefs**
The walkway is framed by balustrades terminating with the body of the naga, the seven-headed serpent. Beyond is the Gallery of the Bas-Reliefs – the outer side comprising 60 columns, while the inner wall is carved with beautiful bas-reliefs of epic events.

Spring Equinox

Khmer architects aligned Angkor Wat with the sun and moon. At the spring equinox, it has a spectacular solar alignment with the causeway as the sun rises over the exact center of the ▷ central sanctuary.

View of Towers

The well-preserved monument of Angkor Wat rises on a series of colonnaded platforms and is surrounded by a moat. The view of the five towers of the temple when reflected in water makes for a stunning spectacle.

South Gallery

★ Apsaras

Numerous celestial dancers are carved onto the walls, each slightly different in gesture and detail. The variety of hairstyles and headdresses is extraordinary.

The West Gallery bas-reliefs depict a battle scene from the *Mahabharata* epic.

The Causeway

Angkor Wat's majestic façade can be seen from the causeway at its west entrance. Balustrades in the form of nagas border the causeway on either side and extend all around the temple.

STAR FEATURES

★ Central Sanctuary

★ Gallery of the Bas-Reliefs

★ Apsaras

KEY DATES

1113–50 Construction of Angkor Wat during the rule of the Khmer Empire.

1432 The Siamese sack Angkor Wat.

1860 Angkor Wat is rediscovered by Henri Mouhot.

1898 The French *École Française d'Extrême Orient* starts to clear the site.

1992 Angkor Wat is declared a UNESCO World Heritage Site.

1993 International conservation project begins to preserve the temples of Angkor Wat.

REDISCOVERY OF ANGKOR

Although the ruins of Angkor Wat had been chronicled by a number of foreigners, it was the Frenchman Henri Mouhot, traveling under the auspices of the Royal Geographical Society in 1860, who is attributed with the rediscovery of Angkor Wat. A naturalist and botanist, he spent three weeks among the ruins, drawing and surveying the temples and writing a detailed and lyrical account in his diaries. They were published after his death in Laos a year later from malaria. His descriptions inspired numerous travelers, including the Scottish photographer John Thomson who took the first black and white photos of Angkor in 1866.

THE BAS-RELIEFS

There are 1,460 superbly carved ▷ *bas-reliefs* extending for 5 km (3 miles) round the five lower levels of Borobudur. As visitors walk clockwise, keeping the monument to the right, the reliefs on the lowest sphere show daily life, earthly pleasures, the punishments of hell, and the laws of cause and effect, *karma*. This vivid evocation of daily life in ancient Javanese society was later covered with stone to support the temple's weight. The second level depicts the Buddha, Siddhartha Gautama and his life, showing him leaving his father's palace and going out into the world. These reliefs feature graceful figures with serene expressions wearing jewels and headdresses. Images on the other levels follow texts such as the *Lalitavistara*, and the *Jataka* tales, Buddha's earlier incarnations, and search for enlightenment.

A graceful, bejeweled king and queen holding court at Borobudur

THE SAILENDRA DYNASTY

Between AD 730–930, the Sailendra dynasty ruled most of Java in Indonesia. Their name is Sanskrit for "Lords of the Mountain" and they were heavily influenced by Indian culture through the maritime trade routes of the region. Java was one of the world's leading civilizations during this period, enriched by trade and the sale of rice, and the Sailendras created the greatest monuments in Asia at the time. Borobudur Temple, arguably their finest accomplishment, took 75 years to complete. The balance of power shifted in the late 9th century, and the Sailendras were forced to leave Java.

Borobodur Temple, Java

THE WORLD'S LARGEST Buddhist stupa (▷ *Buddhist Style p334*), Borobodur Temple is made from 1.6 million blocks of volcanic andesite and is constructed over nine levels. Five square terraces are surmounted by three circular ones and culminate with another stupa at the top. The powerful image of this structure is enhanced by five levels of sublime carvings depicting the lives of the Buddha, expounding the meaning of his doctrine. These images form the most comprehensive ensemble of Buddhist reliefs ever carved. As pilgrims circumambulate, praying before each image, they ascend from the terrestrial to the divine world. Abandoned in the 10th century, and later buried under ash from a volcanic eruption, the temple was not discovered again until 1815.

View of Borobudur Temple
The name of this colossal structure probably came from the Sanskrit Vihara Buddha Uhr, *meaning High Buddhist monastery. It is the earthly manifestion of the Buddhist vision of the universe.*

Temple Roof
The view from the top of Borobudur Temple shows the volcanic plain with its palm trees and groves.

STAR FEATURES

★ **Rupadatu Bas-Reliefs**

★ **Meditating Buddhas**

★ **Kamadhatu Bas-Reliefs**

★ **Rupadatu Bas-Reliefs**
These carvings depict the life of Siddhartha Gautama, the Buddha.

CONSTRUCTION

Borobodur is square in plan, rising to 34.5 m (113.19 ft). Originally, five square diminishing terraces were built, leading to a sixth terrace from which three circular terraces arose, with a stupa at the summit. The original intention seems to have been to construct a pyramid but the weight was so immense that a stone buttress was constructed around the base to prevent it collapsing. The geometrical precision and complex imagery of Borobodur continue to fascinate scholars.

★ Meditating Buddhas

Most of the Buddhas on the temple roof are enclosed in individual stupas but several are exposed. They are remarkable for their serenity and poise.

RESTORATION

In 1973, a $21 million restoration project began. The terraces were dismantled, catalogued, cleaned, and reconstructed on a concrete foundation. This Buddhist site is now a national monument in a Muslim country.

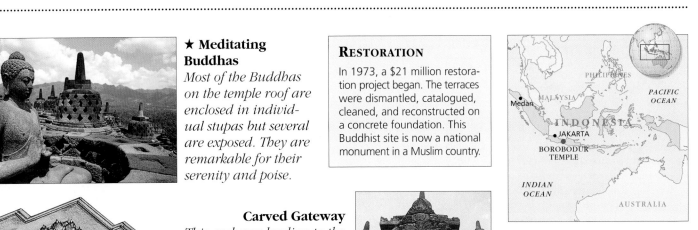

Carved Gateway

This archway leading to the roof is guarded by Kala, a protective deity and a mythical monster who swallowed his own body.

Seated Buddha

Sitting within an arched niche in the temple, this Buddha is thought to represent a hermit in a mountain cave.

★ Kamadhatu Bas-Reliefs

Illustrating ancient Javanese society, the finesse and quality of the carvings on the first level of the temple are superb. This bas-relief depicts a group of musicians.

KEY DATES

AD 770 Construction begins on Borobodur Temple.

AD 845 Borobodur Temple is completed.

c.900 The balance of power shifts to East Java and the temple is abandoned.

c.900 Heavy volcanic activity submerges the temple in ash.

1815 Borobodur is rediscovered by Sir Stamford Raffles.

1991 Borobodur is declared a UNESCO World Heritage Site.

THE MEANING OF BOROBODUR

Initially built as a Hindu temple, Borobodur is a recreation of Mount Meru, the mythical mountain abode of Hindu gods. Symbolically the temple is a *mandala*, an aid to meditation, and a meeting place of heaven and earth. It represents the transition from the lowest manifestations of reality through to the highest spiritual awareness at the summit. The base represents the lowest sphere of consciousness, (▷ *Kamadhatu Bas-Reliefs*). The next level (▷ *Rupadatu Bas-Reliefs*), is the intermediate period of consciousness. The upper levels, with 72 small, perforated stupas, each containing a seated ▷ *meditating Buddha*, represent the sphere of formlessness, *Arupadhatu*. At the top, the empty central stupa suggests *nirvana* (Sanskrit for extinction), and symbolizes enlightenment, the ultimate state of supreme awareness.

TRADITIONAL BELIEFS

Animism, ancestor worship, and a sense of the supernatural permeate Balinese life. The term *sekala niskala* (visible-invisible) sums up the idea that the physical world is permeated by a spirit world. Loosely described as "gods" and "demons," the spirits are believed to dwell in natural objects such as stones or trees. Shrines are built for them and they are honored with offerings of flowers and other materials. The invisible world is represented in many vivid symbols. Ancestors are deified in complex rituals and venerated at temples. Guardian effigies such as the dragon-like Barong and his demonic counterpart Rangda are periodically awakened to restore a village's spiritual balance.

***Canang* or daily flower offerings made to the spirits**

THE BALE GONG & THE GAMELAN ORCHESTRA

In Bali and Lombok, traditional music is performed by a *gamelan* orchestra, a percussion ensemble consisting largely of bronze metallophones (instruments with tuned metal keys), led by drums *(kendang)*. Bronze gongs of various sizes form the heart of the orchestra. Struck with mallets, they produce resonant sounds which punctuate the keyed instruments' melodies. There are a few wind and stringed instruments, including bamboo flutes *(suling)*. Most villages own a set of *gamelan* instruments for ritual occasions; some are sacred and played only at religious ceremonies. Temples have pavilions known as ▷ *bale gong* to house the instruments.

Pura Ulun Danu Batur, Bali

Stone sculpture

O NE OF BALI'S MOST popular and spiritually significant temples, the Pura Ulun Danu Batur has a vital association with Lake *(danu)* Batur, however it is uncertain when the temple was built. It is the country's guardian temple of water supplies as it controls the irrigation system of much of the island. From a distance the temple's silhouette can be seen on the rim of the vast Batur caldera.

Inner Courtyard
The inner courtyard is the most sacred. Three gateways lead from one courtyard to the next.

Garuda
The figure of Garuda, a bird from Hindu mythology, is depicted in this stone relief on the courtyard wall.

Temple Flags
Deities and mythical beasts are often depicted in rich colors on temple flags and sculptures.

★ **Central Courtyard**
The great quadrangle, shown here occupied by a festive structure of bamboo and straw, is the occasional setting for ritual dances.

OFFERINGS TO THE LAKE GODDESS

Offerings of fruits and flowers

Devotees from all over Bali present elaborate offerings at this temple, which is dedicated to Ida Betari Dewi Ulun Danu, the goddess of Lake Batur. The respect accorded to the goddess is reinforced by events in the temple's history. At its former location closer to the lake, the temple was miraculously saved from destruction in the volcanic eruption of 1917, when the lava flow stopped just short of its walls. Another eruption, in 1926, prompted the villagers to move the temple to its present location.

TEMPLE FESTIVALS

Odalan (temple festivals) are anniversary ceremonies where deities are honored with offerings, prayers, and entertainment, creating a carnival atmosphere that generally lasts for three days.

★ Gold-painted Doors

The great timber doors of the main temple gateway are reserved for the use of priests on important occasions.

Side Gate

This tall, slender gate, built in a combination of brickwork and paras *stone decoration, leads to another temple.*

KEY DATES

1917 Pura Ulun Danu Batur is miraculously unharmed during a volcanic eruption.

1926 Another eruption almost entirely covers the temple.

1927 The temple is rebuilt at its current location.

BALINESE TEMPLE ARCHITECTURE

A Balinese *pura* (public temple) is a holy enclosure where Hindu deities are periodically invited to descend into *pratima* (effigies) kept in shrines. The arrangement of Balinese temples follows a consistent pattern, with individual structures oriented along a mountain-sea axis. Degrees of sacredness are reflected in proximity to the mountain. Of the three temple courtyards, the outer and ▷ *central courtyards* have a variety of secondary shrines and pavilions including the *kulkul* (watchtower), which houses a drum that is sounded when deities are thought to descend. It also traditionally serves as a general alarm bell. The *jeroan* (▷ *inner courtyard*) contains shrines to the temple's core deities and often to deities of the mountains, lakes, and sea. The *padmasana,* or lotus throne shrine, in the temple's most sacred corner, has an empty seat on top signifying the Supreme God. The *meru* shrine with a number of tiers, depending on its deity's importance, symbolizes the mythical Hindu peak, Mount Meru.

The *bale gong* is a pavilion housing the temple's set of *gamelan* instruments, including a great gong believed to have a magical history.

Entrance

STAR FEATURES

★ **Central Courtyard**

★ **Gold-painted Doors**

View of Gunung Agung from the base camp at Pura Pasar Agung

INDIVIDUAL SHRINES AT BESAKIH TEMPLE

The Besakih complex contains 22 temples, of which the three main ones honor the Hindu trinity of Brahma, Vishnu, and Shiva. Penataran Agung, dedicated to Shiva, is the pilgrimage site for the Indonesian royal family. The other two, Kiduling Batu Madeg (honoring Vishnu) and Kreteg (devoted to Brahma) are associated with a cardinal direction and color, as are Gelap and Ulun Kulkul. On the lower slopes of Gunung Agung is Dalem Puri, the Temple of Palace Ancestors, dedicated to Batari Durga, the goddess of death. Other temples include ones to Basuki, the guardian dragon who is said to dwell on Gunung Agung, and to Rsi Markandya, as well as several belonging to different clans and caste groups.

Besakih Temple Complex, Bali

Stone wall carving

KNOWN AS THE parent of all Balinese temples, Pura Besakih is a grand complex of 22 temples on the slopes of the active volcano Gunung Agung, where the Balinese believe the spirits of their ancestors live. Said to have been founded in the late 8th century by the Javanese sage Rsi Markandya, it later came under the jurisdiction of the Klungkung kingdom. All but two shrines were destroyed in the earthquake of 1917, and the complex underwent several major renovations in the 20th century, escaping damage in the 1963 eruption of Gunung Agung. Now it is an important focus of Indonesian Hinduism.

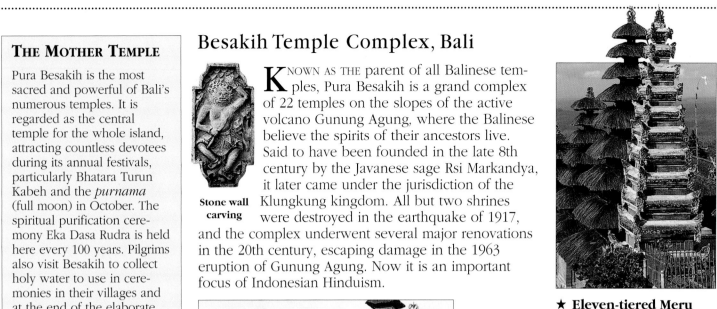

Terraced Entrance
The terraces at the entrance to Pura Penataran Agung are an echo of the stepped pyramids of Indonesian prehistory.

Stairs
Only worshipers are allowed to use the entrance stairway.

★ **Eleven-tiered Meru**
The tall meru *(pagodas) are shrines for deified kings, ancestral spirits, and nature gods.*

★ **Main Courtyard**
This is the main focus of worship at the temple. A padmasana tiga *(triple lotus shrine) is dedicated to Brahma, Shiva, and Vishnu.*

Footpaths connect the temples in the complex.

Pura Ratu Pande
The roofs of this clan temple beside Pura Penataran Agung have been restored with black palm fiber and gilded roof caps.

BHATARA TURUN KABEH

Besakih's great festival, meaning "Gods Descend Together," falls on a full moon in the 10th lunar month *(kadasa)* in Mar/Apr. At this time, the gods of all Bali's temples are believed to visit Besakih's main shrine and devotees flock here from across the country.

In the inner courtyards of the temple there may have been *meru* towers since the 14th century.

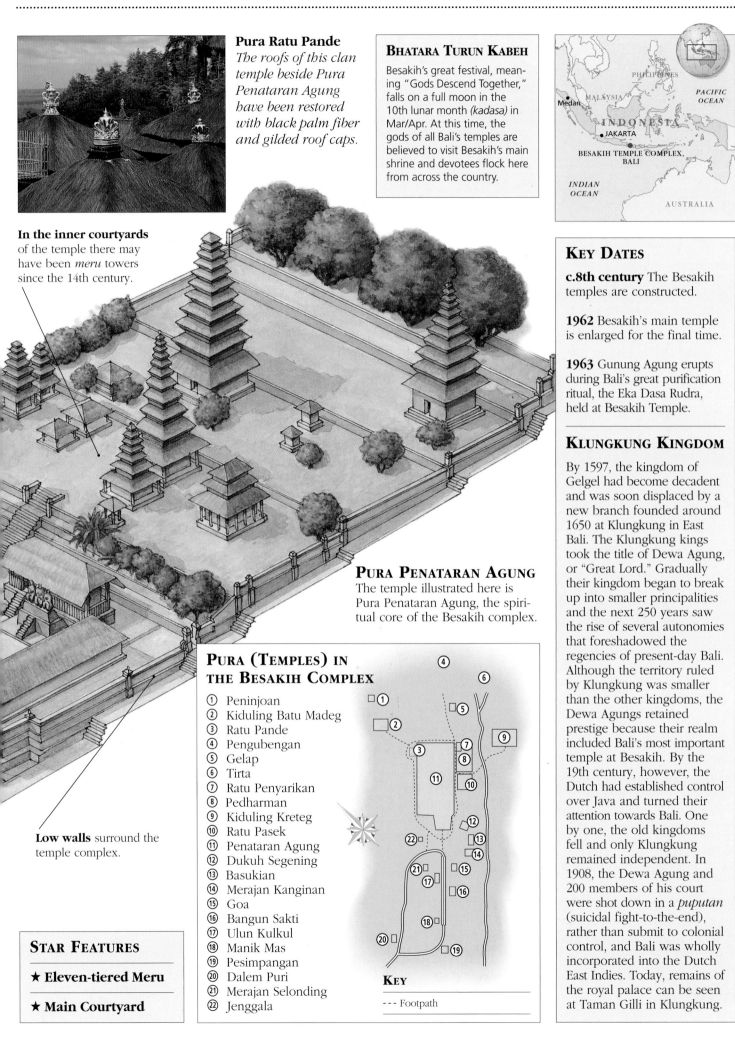

PURA PENATARAN AGUNG
The temple illustrated here is Pura Penataran Agung, the spiritual core of the Besakih complex.

Low walls surround the temple complex.

PURA (TEMPLES) IN THE BESAKIH COMPLEX

1. Peninjoan
2. Kiduling Batu Madeg
3. Ratu Pande
4. Pengubengan
5. Gelap
6. Tirta
7. Ratu Penyarikan
8. Pedharman
9. Kiduling Kreteg
10. Ratu Pasek
11. Penataran Agung
12. Dukuh Segening
13. Basukian
14. Merajan Kanginan
15. Goa
16. Bangun Sakti
17. Ulun Kulkul
18. Manik Mas
19. Pesimpangan
20. Dalem Puri
21. Merajan Selonding
22. Jenggala

KEY

--- Footpath

STAR FEATURES

★ **Eleven-tiered Meru**

★ **Main Courtyard**

KEY DATES

c.8th century The Besakih temples are constructed.

1962 Besakih's main temple is enlarged for the final time.

1963 Gunung Agung erupts during Bali's great purification ritual, the Eka Dasa Rudra, held at Besakih Temple.

KLUNGKUNG KINGDOM

By 1597, the kingdom of Gelgel had become decadent and was soon displaced by a new branch founded around 1650 at Klungkung in East Bali. The Klungkung kings took the title of Dewa Agung, or "Great Lord." Gradually their kingdom began to break up into smaller principalities and the next 250 years saw the rise of several autonomies that foreshadowed the regencies of present-day Bali. Although the territory ruled by Klungkung was smaller than the other kingdoms, the Dewa Agungs retained prestige because their realm included Bali's most important temple at Besakih. By the 19th century, however, the Dutch had established control over Java and turned their attention towards Bali. One by one, the old kingdoms fell and only Klungkung remained independent. In 1908, the Dewa Agung and 200 members of his court were shot down in a *puputan* (suicidal fight-to-the-end), rather than submit to colonial control, and Bali was wholly incorporated into the Dutch East Indies. Today, remains of the royal palace can be seen at Taman Gilli in Klungkung.

Aerial view of the Opera House

Sydney Opera House

Advertising poster

NO OTHER BUILDING ON EARTH looks like the Sydney Opera House. Popularly known as the "Opera House" long before the building was complete, it is, in fact, a complex of theaters and halls linked beneath its famous shells. Its birth was long and complicated. Many of the construction problems had not been faced before, resulting in an architectural adventure which lasted 14 years. An appeal fund was set up, eventually raising A$900,000, while the Opera House Lottery raised the balance of the A$102 million final cost. Today it is the city's most popular tourist attraction, as well as one of the world's busiest performing arts centers.

★ Opera Theater
Mainly used for opera and ballet, this 1,547-seat theater is big enough to stage grand operas such as Verdi's Aïda.

The Opera Theater's ceiling and walls are painted black to focus attention on the stage.

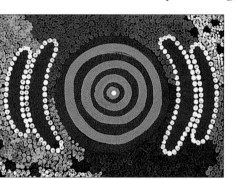

Detail of The Possum Dreaming *(1988)*
The mural in the Opera Theater foyer is by Michael Tjakamarra Nelson, an artist from the central Australian desert.

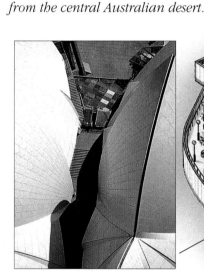

Opera House Walkway
Extensive public walkways around the building offer the visitor views from many different vantage points.

STAR FEATURES

★ **Opera Theater**

★ **Concert Hall**

★ **Roofs**

Northern Foyers
The Reception Hall and the large northern foyers of the Opera Theater and Concert Hall have spectacular views over Sydney harbor.

★ Concert Hall

This is the largest hall, with seating for 2,690. It is used for symphony, choral, jazz, folk, and pop concerts, chamber music, opera, dance, and everything from body building to fashion parades.

BACKSTAGE

Artists performing at the Opera House have the use of five rehearsal studios, 60 dressing rooms, suites, and a green room complete with restaurant, bar, and lounge. The scene-changing machinery works on well-oiled wheels; crucially in the Opera Theater where there is regularly a nightly change of performances.

The Monumental Steps and forecourt are used for outdoor movies and free entertainment.

Bennelong Restaurant
This is one of the finest restaurants in Sydney.

The Playhouse, seating almost 400, is ideal for intimate productions, while also able to present plays with larger casts.

★ Roofs

Although apocryphal, the theory that Jørn Utzon's arched roof design came to him while peeling an orange is enchanting. The highest point is 67 m (221 ft) above sea level.

Curtain of the Moon *(1972)*
Designed by John Coburn, this and its fellow Curtain of the Sun *were originally used in the Drama and Opera theaters. Both have been removed for preservation.*

KEY DATES

1957 Jørn Utzon wins the Opera House design competition.

1959–73 The Sydney Opera House is constructed.

1973 Prokofiev's opera *War and Peace* is the first public performance in the Opera House.

THE THEATER AND HALLS

Underneath the ten spectacular ▷ *roofs* of varying planes and textures lies a complex maze of more than 1,000 rooms of all shapes and sizes showcasing different events. The ▷ *Concert Hall* is decked out in native white birch and brush box (hardwood timber). A Grand Organ, built by Ronald Sharp from 1969–79, is the centerpiece of the hall. The Drama Theater stage is 15 m (49 ft) square, and can be clearly viewed from every seat in the auditorium. Refrigerated aluminum panels in the ceiling control the temperature. Fine Australian art hangs in the ▷ *Playhouse* foyer, notably Sidney Nolan's *Little Shark* (1973) and a fresco by Salvatore Zofrea (1992–3). The ▷ *Opera Theater* is the second largest venue in the building. It hosts both spectacular opera and dance performances. The proscenium opening is 12 m (39 ft) wide, and the stage extends back 21 m (69 ft), while the orchestra pit accommodates up to 70–80 musicians.

Sydney Opera House

THE TRANSPORTATION OF CONVICTS

Between the late 18th and mid-19th centuries, many British convicts were transported abroad to places like Australia, where they provided forced labor for Britain's colonies. This was deemed a humane alternative to the death penalty which was in place at the time, and also provided a solution to the overcrowded prisons back home. In the 1830s, the government began to reform the English judicial system and by the 1850s prisoner transportation to Australia ended. Convicts who earned their ticket-of-leave were absorbed back into society, often preferring a colonial life rather than a return to 19th-century England.

Port Arthur's church built by convicts in the 1830s

PORT ARTHUR MUSEUM

Inside the late 19th-century ▷ *asylum* is the fascinating Port Arthur ▷ *museum*. Original artifacts from the Port Arthur site are displayed throughout the building. These include leg irons and handcuffs worn by convicts who were imprisoned here. The museum holds a fully modeled British criminal court scene, where a judge's sentencing can be heard. A flight of stairs inside leads down to a careful recreation of a full-size ship bound for transportation to the Australian colonies. The museum also displays an exact model of Port Arthur's buildings, as well as its beautiful gardens and grounds, as it would have looked in the 1870s.

Port Arthur, Tasmania

Handcuffs from Port Arthur museum

ESTABLISHED AS a timber station and prison settlement for repeat offenders, Port Arthur is a nationally recognized symbol of Australia's convict past. While transportation to the island colony from Britain ceased in 1853, the prison remained in operation for a further twenty-four years, by which time some 12,000 men had passed through the institution. Punishments included incarceration in the Separate Prison where, away from the main penitentiary, inmates were subjected to sensory deprivation and extreme isolation in the belief that such methods promoted "moral reform." Between 1979 and 1986, a major redevelopment and conservation project was undertaken to restore the prison ruins. The 40-ha (100-acre) site is now Tasmania's most popular tourist attraction.

Commandant's House
One of the first houses at Port Arthur, this cottage has now been restored and furnished in early 19th-century style.

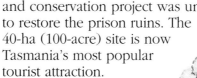

The Semaphore was a series of flat, mounted planks that could be arranged in different configurations, in order to send messages to Hobart and across the Tasman peninsula.

The Guard Tower was constructed in 1835 in order to prevent escapes from the prison and pilfering from the Commissariat Store, which the tower overlooked.

| 0 meters | 50 |
| 0 yards | 50 |

★ Penitentiary
This building was thought to be the largest in Australia at the time of its construction in 1842. Originally a flour mill, it was converted into a penitentiary in 1857 and housed over 600 prisoners in dormitories and cells.

STAR FEATURES

★ **Penitentiary**

★ **Hospital**

★ **Hospital**
This sandstone building was completed in 1842 with four wards of 18 beds each. The basement housed the kitchen with its own oven, and a morgue, known as the "dead room."

The Paupers' Mess was the dining area for poor prisoners.

Museum

Asylum
By 1872, Port Arthur's asylum housed more than 100 mentally ill or senile convicts. When the settlement closed, it became the town hall, but now serves as a museum.

The Separate Prison was influenced by Pentonville Prison in London. Completed in 1849, the prison was thought to provide "humane" punishment. Convicts lived in 50 separate cells in silence and anonymity, referred to by number not by name.

Trentham Cottage was owned by the Trentham family who lived in Port Arthur after the site closed. The refurbished interior is decorated with early 19th-century furnishings.

St David's Church

Government Cottage was built in 1853 and was used by visiting dignitaries and government officials.

Church
Built in 1836, Port Arthur's church was never consecrated because it was used by all denominations. The building was gutted by fire in 1884, but the ruins are now fully preserved.

KEY DATES

1830 The prison settlement is established.

1877 The prison closes.

Late 20th century Restoration of the Port Arthur site begins.

PORT ARTHUR'S BUILDINGS

In addition to the prison structures, Port Arthur also includes restored buildings which were inhabited by civilians who lived in the area. These include the Junior Medical Officer's House and the Accountant's House, which now holds the Convict Research Centre. Much of the food for the settlement was grown in orchards and vegetable gardens that surrounded ▷ *Trentham Cottage*. The Anglican parson would have lived in the Parsonage which later became the Post Office. The military precinct located around the ▷ *guard tower* was the place where the soldiers lived, played sports, and held parades. Their barracks were partly demolished at the settlement's closure, with others lost in bushfires in 1895 and 1897. The Commandant was the most senior official at Port Arthur and it was at the ▷ *Commandant's house* that convicts lined up to hear the rules of the settlement. The house grew from a simple cottage to a many-roomed complex that extended up the hill.

Port Arthur

BEGINNING OF DUNEDIN'S RAILROAD

In the early 1860s gold was discovered in Dunedin and gold-miners from other parts of the country poured into the region. The money gold brought into the area ensured, for a time, that Dunedin became the commercial capital of New Zealand. Railroads were therefore constructed to transport the growing population. The first journey, with the new "Josephine" trains, was from Dunedin to Port Chalmers, on 10 September 1872. In 1875 a second station was built in Dunedin to ease the busy station; a third followed four years later. As the number of passengers on the railroad increased further, Dunedin Railway Station was commissioned.

Front view of Dunedin Railway Station

AN ARCHITECTURAL CHALLENGE

For its day, the construction of Dunedin Railway Station was an engineering challenge. Built on the foundations of the old harbor, iron-bark piles had to be driven deep into the reclaimed land to prevent flooding. George Troup used a number of railroad staff, who he had trained in the art of stonemasonry, to help build the station. Machinery, including cranes, was also loaned by New Zealand Railways for use during building works to reduce cost. It is believed that New Zealand's first electrically driven concrete mixer was used in the station's construction. Costing £120,500, the station is seven times larger than its predecessor, Dunedin's third station, built in the late 1800s.

Dunedin Railway Station

Frieze with cherub and foliage

ONE OF NEW ZEALAND'S finest historic buildings, Dunedin Railway Station is also one of the best examples of railroad architecture in the southern hemisphere. Although not large by international standards, the station's delightful proportions lend it an air of grandeur. It was designed in the Flemish Renaissance style (▷ *Renaissance Style p211*) by New Zealand Railways architect George Troup, whose detailing on the outside of the building earned him the nickname "Gingerbread George."

★ Exterior Stonework
Beige Oamaru limestone detailing provides a striking contrast to the darker Central Otago bluestone on the walls and the finely polished Aberdeen granite of the columns.

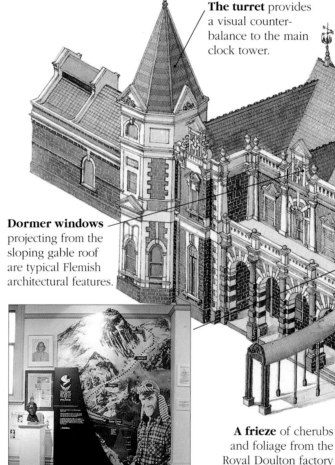

The turret provides a visual counterbalance to the main clock tower.

The roof is covered with clay Marseille tiles from France.

Dormer windows projecting from the sloping gable roof are typical Flemish architectural features.

A frieze of cherubs and foliage from the Royal Doulton factory in England encircles the ticket hall below the wrought-iron bordered balcony.

Main entrance

New Zealand Sports Hall of Fame
This features imaginative displays recounting the exploits and achievements of famous New Zealanders.

Ticket Windows
The ticket windows are ornately decorated with white tiles and a crest featuring the old New Zealand Railways logo.

STAR FEATURES

★ Exterior Stonework

★ Stained-glass Windows

★ Mosaic Floor

★ Stained-glass Windows

Two imposing stained-glass windows on the mezzanine balcony depict approaching steam engines, lights blazing, facing each other across the ticket hall.

FLOOR RESTORATION

By 1956 the original floor had subsided dramatically. Exact replica mosaics had to be laid on a new concrete foundation in order to alleviate the problem.

Staircase

Complete with wrought-iron balustrades and mosaic tiled steps, a staircase sweeps up from the ticket hall to the balcony above.

Finely carved sandstone lions on each corner of the clock tower guard the cupola behind them.

The clock tower rises 37 m (120 ft) above street level.

The platform behind the station is still a departure and arrival point for travelers.

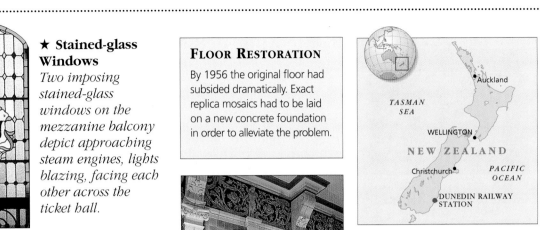

TASMAN SEA

Auckland

WELLINGTON

NEW ZEALAND

Christchurch

PACIFIC OCEAN

DUNEDIN RAILWAY STATION

KEY DATES

1906 Dunedin Station is opened.

1956 The clock tower is restored.

1994 The station is sold to Dunedin City Council for a nominal sum.

1996–98 The exterior stonework is cleaned.

TROUP & THE DESIGN OF DUNEDIN STATION

In 1884 the 20-year-old George Troup (1863–1941) arrived in New Zealand, after emigrating from his home in Scotland with an apprenticeship in architectural design. He quickly secured a job with New Zealand Railways in Dunedin, where he was employed to design bridges and stations all over the country. He was soon promoted to Head of the Architectural branch and while working in this new role he designed the renowned Dunedin Railway Station. No expense was spared to create this magnificent station. The ▷ *roof* was adorned with red Marseille tiles, while the ▷ *exterior stonework* featured lavish ornate detailing – referred to as "Gingerbread style". Inside, Troup covered the floor with rich mosaic tiles (▷ *mosaic floor)*, some embellished with images of railroad engines, wheels, signals, and wagons. After retiring from the railroad, Troup became a patron of the arts and Mayor of Wellington. He was knighted in 1937.

★ Mosaic Floor

More than 725,000 Royal Doulton porcelain squares form images of steam engines, rolling stock, and the New Zealand Railways logo.

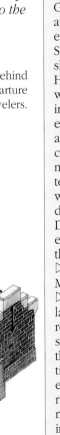

Dunedin Railway Station

Sacred vessels in the museum attest to the pilgrims' devotion

St Anne Museum

Many works of art that describe earlier pilgrims' devotion to St Anne are on view in the museum at the shrine. There are also displays dedicated to the heritage of French Canada, from the 17th century to the present, with wax figures, paintings, and educational artifacts illustrating the life of St Anne. One of the most important pieces is an 18th-century ▷ *sailor painting*, which depicts the story of shipwrecked sailors.

In and Around the Basilica

The lower level has two chapels: the ▷ *Immaculate Conception Chapel* and the Blessed Sacrament Chapel. Also on the lower level is a copy of Michelangelo's ▷ *Pietà* and the tomb of Venerable Father Alfred Pampalon (1867–96), patron saint of alcoholics and drug addicts. The main church is on the upper level, where hundreds of crutches, braces, and artificial limbs attest to miraculous cures. The earliest healing here, in 1658, is said to have been that of Louis Guimond, a crippled man who insisted on carrying stones for the construction of the first church despite his affliction, and who was cured before the other workers' eyes. Pilgrims gather on the hillside to follow the Way of the Cross and to go up the Holy Stairs, representing Christ's climb to meet Pontius Pilate. A model of the original church stands next to the Holy Stairs. Nearby, a building showcases the world's largest cyclorama depicting Jerusalem at the time of the Crucifixion.

Sainte-Anne-de-Beaupré

THE SHRINE TO ST ANNE, mother of the Virgin Mary, is the oldest pilgrimage site in North America. In 1620 a group of sailors who had survived a shipwreck established the shrine and dedicated it to St Anne. In 1658 a chapel was erected and since then several churches have been built on this site. The fifth and present one, dating from the 1920s, receives 1.5 million visitors every year, including those who come for the annual pilgrimage on St Anne's Feastday on 26 July. The collection of crutches in the entrance bears witness to the basilica's reputation for miraculous cures. Inside, the dome-vaulted ceiling is decorated with gold mosaics portraying the life of St Anne. She is represented in a large gilt statue in the transept, cradling the Virgin Mary.

Plan of the Shrine

1 Basilica
2 Monastery
3 Church store
4 Museum
5 Blessing Office

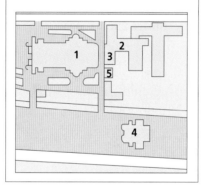

The Basilica

In 1876, St Anne was proclaimed patron saint of Quebec, and in 1887 the existing church was granted basilica status. The Redemptorist order became the guardians of the shrine in 1878.

Façade
The present basilica was built by the Canadian architect Napoleon Bourassa. He based the design on a mix of Gothic and Romanesque ideals.

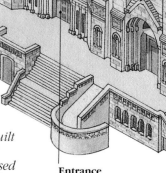

★ The Great Rose Window
This beautiful stained-glass window was designed by the French artist Auguste Labouret (1950).

The spire

Entrance to the basilica's upper floor

Interior

Lit by sun streaming through the stained-glass windows, the cream and gold interior is divided into a nave and four aisles by large pillars topped with sculpted capitals.

The Statue of St Anne is on the upper floor. It sits in front of the relic of St Anne, presented to the shrine by Pope John XXII in 1960.

Basilicas

Originally, a basilica was simply any public building modeled on Roman structures with a nave, aisles, and an apse. The Roman Catholic church has given special, honorary significance to the term. A basilica is entitled to display certain papal emblems, and it is also expected to celebrate the liturgy solemnly and maintain choirs whose repertory includes great church music of the past.

★ Pietà

A faithful copy of Michelangelo's original in St Peter's, Rome, this shows Christ at his death being held by a seated Madonna.

Key Dates

1876–1922 The first basilica, built in honor of St Anne, is used for worship.

1922 A fire on 29 March destroys the basilica.

1923 Work on the present basilica begins.

1976 The basilica is consecrated by Cardinal Maurice Roy.

The Life of St Anne

Although the Bible makes no mention of the mother of the Virgin Mary, Christians from the earliest times had an interest in knowing more about Jesus' family, especially his mother and grandmother. A 3rd-century Greek manuscript called the *Revelation of James* tells the story of Jesus' grandparents, naming them Anne (from Hannah) and Joachim. According to this account, Anne of Bethlehem and Joachim of Nazareth, a shepherd, were childless after 20 years of marriage. Each cried out separately to God, asking why they were childless, and vowing to dedicate any offspring to His work. An angel came to Joachim and Anne, and they learned that they were to have a child, Mary, who became the mother of Christ. There is no mention of Anne and Joachim's death in this record, but a later one claims that Jesus was with his grandparents when they died. In Canada, Anne is the patron saint of Quebec and her feast day is celebrated on 26 July.

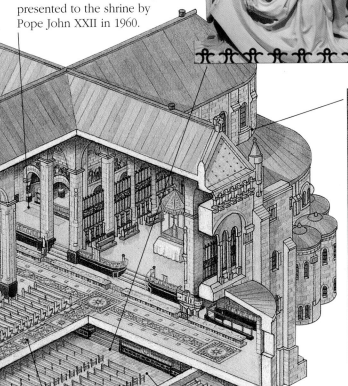

Immaculate Conception Chapel

Bright mosaic floor tiles echo the ceiling patterns.

Sanctuary Mosaic

This splendid mosaic was created by the artists Auguste Labouret and Jean Gaudin (1940–41). God is shown overlooking an infant Jesus, flanked by Mary and St Anne.

Sailor Painting

The Ex-voto of the Three Shipwrecked Sailors from Lévis (1754) is an oil on wood painting. It is on display in the St Anne Museum.

Star Features

★ The Great Rose Window

★ Pietà

FORTRESS DESIGN

Fortress Louisbourg was built to general fortification principles of the 17th and 18th centuries as perfected by S bastien Le Prestre de Vauban, chief engineer to Louis XIV. Louisbourg's walls completely surrounded the town, together with seven bastions, projections from the main wall with two faces and two flanks. This design allowed concentration of fire and the mutual protection of one bastion by another. For harbor defense, two batteries were placed in the town and two at the harbor entrance. Elaborate works were proposed to help protect the main wall, however a shortage of funds prevented their construction.

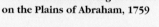

Medal commemorating the battle on the Plains of Abraham, 1759

A LIVING MUSEUM

A small museum displays a scale model of the fortress and military and civilian artifacts found during the reconstruction. In summer, the fortress springs to life as men, women, and children reenact 1744 society from the leisurely pastimes of the rich to the demanding physical labor of the poor. Special exhibits explore history and culture: the Carrerot House explores period building techniques, and at the ▷ *Ordonnateur's Residence* paintings portray the Louisbourg of 1744. At the DuHaget House there is a 15-minute video about the life of a soldier. Guided tours start at the costume photo studio.

Fortress Louisbourg

Costumed interpreter

BUILT BETWEEN 1713 AND 1744, the magnificent Fortress Louisbourg in Nova Scotia was France's bastion of military strength in the New World. Today, it is the largest military reconstruction in North America, taking visitors back to the year 1744, when war had just been declared between France and England. Inside, historically costumed guides bring the excitement of an 18th-century French trading town to life, offering information about the fortress, its history, and the lives of people they portray. The streets and buildings are peopled with merchants, soldiers, fishmongers, and washerwomen, all going about the daily business of the 1700s. From the lowliest fisherman's cottage to the elegant home of the Chief Military Engineer, attention to detail throughout is superb.

Overview of the Fortress
Popular with French fishermen and a haven for French privateers who preyed on New England shipping, the Fortress was home to a town of some 3,000 inhabitants.

0 meters 50

0 yards 50

The Ordonnateur's Residence

The Quay and Frederic Gate
The Quay was the center of commercial activity in the flourishing town. The Frederic Gate features Baroque elements (▷ Baroque Style p111).

STAR FEATURES

★ **Engineer's Residence**

★ **King's Bastion**

★ **Engineer's Residence**
Responsible for all public construction projects at the fortress, the engineer was one of the most important and powerful men in the community.

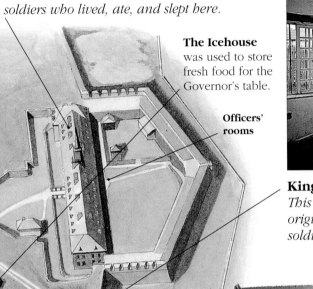

Feast of St Louis

At the end of August, King Louis IX, once the patron saint of France, is fêted with an 18th-century celebration that includes cannon salutes, musket firing, dancing, gambling, games, music, and a bonfire.

★ King's Bastion

The largest building in the Citadel, the King's Bastion Barracks was home to the 500 French soldiers who lived, ate, and slept here.

The Icehouse
was used to store fresh food for the Governor's table.

Officers' rooms

King's Bakery

This working garrison bakery was originally established to supply the soldiers' daily rations of warm bread.

The Forge

Tools such as chisels, nails, hammers, and hinges were made here for the construction and maintenance of the fortress.

The Guardhouse held the vital human line of defense; guards were stationed here while on duty.

The Dauphin Gate

Soldiers in historic uniforms stand guard at this gate, the main entrance to the fortress by land. The gate's artistic details are based on archaeological relics from the original gate recovered in the 1960s.

Key Dates

1713 First settlement at Port St Louis, later Louisbourg.

1718 Louisbourg selected as capital of Île Royale (Cape Breton Island).

1760 British destroy Louisbourg's fortifications.

1961 Reconstruction begins.

Control of the Land

Ever since the 17th century, France and England had struggled to control North America's lucrative trade in fur and fish. Queen Anne's War (1702–13) almost resulted in the total English conquest of Canada, but the Treaty of Utrecht (1713) granted France Cape Breton and Prince Edward islands. To protect their fisheries and the mouth of the St Lawrence River, the French built the Louisbourg fortress. In 1744, the rivals were at war again. An army of New Englanders captured Louisbourg in only 46 days, but the town was returned to France in 1748. In 1758 Louisbourg was retaken by the British and General Wolfe was able to sail up the St Lawrence River and launch a surprise assault on Quebec City. General Montcalm, the French commander, was defeated by Wolfe and his army on the Plains of Abraham in 1759. Both generals were killed and Quebec fell to the British. The war finally ended in 1763 with the Treaty of Paris, which ceded all French Canadian territory to the British.

Fortress Louisbourg

CN Tower, Toronto

A T NO LESS THAN 553 m (1,815 ft) high, the CN Tower is the world's tallest building, acclaimed as one of the wonders of the modern world. In the 1970s Canadian National Railway (CN), the railroad conglomerate, in consultation with local broadcasters, decided to build a new transmission mast in Toronto on its land, to meet the telecommunications needs of the growing city and to demonstrate its pride in Toronto. Upon opening, it so overwhelmed the city's visitors that it soon became one of Canada's prime tourist attractions. Its revolving restaurant is also renowned for both its food and wine.

View of the CN Tower from Centre Island's gardens

OBSERVATION DECKS

The ▷ *Lookout Level* enables visitors to look out and over Toronto. Actually built over several levels, the upper tier has a café and a photo shop. Below, visitors can feel the wind at 113 stories up, peer straight down through the ▷ *glass floor* or dine in the revolving ▷ *restaurant*. Thirty-three stories above the Lookout Level, the ▷ *Sky Pod* is higher than most of the world's tallest skyscrapers, even though it is not at the top of the Tower. With an impressive 360-degree view of Toronto and Lake Ontario, on a clear day visitors can see as far as Niagara Falls.

FASCINATING FACTS

Construction of the CN Tower began in 1973, took about 40 months and cost around $63 million to build. A 6,968 sq m (75,000 sq ft) entertainment expansion and renovation was completed in 1998 at a further cost of $26 million. The tower has six ▷ *lifts*, which travel at 24 km/h (15 mph) and reach the ▷ *Lookout Level* at 346 m (1,136 ft) in 58 seconds; a separate lift takes visitors 101 m (329 ft) higher to the ▷ *Sky Pod*. The tower is flexible, and in winds of 195 km/h (120 mph), the Sky Pod can sway as much as 0.48 m (1.5 ft) from the center. Every year, about two million people visit the tower.

Foundations for the single-shaft structure were sunk 17 m (55 ft) and required the removal of over 56,000 tonnes of earth and shale.

★ **The Sky Pod**
The world's highest observation platform at 447 m (1,465 ft), the Sky Pod offers fantastic views in every direction. It is reached by its own lift.

★ **Exterior Lookout**
Open to the elements, this outdoor terrace is secured with steel safety grills. Air temperatures at this height can be up to 10°C (50°F) cooler than at ground level.

The CN Tower from Lake Ontario
The tower's height is highlighted by the comparison with the SkyDome stadium (left) and the buildings of the Harbourfront.

The interior staircase is the longest metal staircase in the world with 1,776 steps. The stairwell is only open to the public twice a year for fundraising stair climbs which attract almost 20,000 climbers.

The exterior lifts are high-speed and glass-fronted, shooting visitors up the outside of the building to the upper levels. Traveling at high speeds, they reach the Lookout Level in under a minute.

CN Tower

The CN Tower at Night

Lit up against the night-time skyline, the majestic and elegant CN Tower soars above the city. Toronto is home to about 2,000 high-rise buildings but they are all at least 250 m (820 ft) lower than the CN Tower.

TALLEST STRUCTURES

The world's ten tallest structures are all television and/or radio broadcast masts, and all are in the US. Supported by guy wires, these structures do not qualify for inclusion in the tallest-building category. The tallest is a 629 m (2,063 ft) television mast near Fargo, North Dakota. The Warszawa Radio Mast in Flock, Poland, was the world's tallest-ever man-made structure, at 647 m (2,120 ft) before it collapsed in 1991.

KEY DATES

1973 Construction begins.

1976 The CN Tower opens to the public.

1977 The first annual stair-climb is held for charity.

1995 The CN Tower is declared a Wonder of the Modern World by the American Society of Civil Engineers.

360 The Restaurant at the CN Tower

At a height of 350 m (1,148 ft), the revolving restaurant turns a full circle every 72 minutes, and boasts the world's highest wine cellar with more than 500 labels.

A bar and disco

are located on the rotating restaurant level.

View of the City from the Lookout Level

At 346 m (1,136 ft) above the city, the Lookout Level provides panoramas of Toronto, Lake Ontario, and the surrounding area. Visibility can stretch to just under 160 km (100 miles).

TALL BUILDINGS

The CN Tower's claim as "World's Tallest Building" at 553 m (1,815 ft) does not go undisputed. To sort out these claims, it is helpful to define three categories: tallest *supported* structure (such as radio masts), tallest *freestanding* structure and tallest *habitable* building. By these criteria, the CN Tower is clearly the tallest free-standing structure, even since the 2004 completion of Taipei's 101 skyscraper (509 m/1,669 ft). Other tall structures include the Ostankino Tower in Moscow (537 m/1,762 ft); the Shanghai World Financial Centre (460 m/1,509 ft); Petronas Towers in Kuala Lumpur (452 m/1,483 ft); Sears Tower in Chicago (442 m/1450 ft); and the Menara Kuala Lumpur Tower (421 m/1,381 ft). The Oriental Pearl Tower in Shanghai, at 468m/1,535 ft, yields fifth place to Union Square Phase 7 in Hong Kong at 474 m/ 1,555 ft completed in 2004. The new World Trade Center in New York will have a tower with an antenna reaching 541 m/1,776 ft, just under the CN Tower height.

★ Glass Floor

The ground is over 342 m (1,122 ft) below this thick layer of reinforced glass. It is made from 24 sq m (256 sq ft) of solid glass that is five times stronger than the weight-bearing standard for commercial floors.

STAR FEATURES

★ Sky Pod

★ Exterior Lookout

★ Glass Floor

CN Tower

EARLY HISTORY

Old State House spire

Constructed in 1713 to replace the original Town House, the Old State House is Boston's oldest surviving public building. During its period as the seat of the colonial government, it was also the Boston center for the political activity that led up to the American Revolution (1775–81). From the first-floor gallery (1766), Boston's citizens could – for the first time in the English-speaking world – watch their elected legislators debate the issues of the day. The west end housed the county and colony law courts. Wealthy merchant and patriot John Hancock, active opponent of the Stamp Act (1765) which imposed a tax on all paper goods and the first signatory of the Declaration of Independence, had warehouse space in the basement.

THE BOSTONIAN SOCIETY

The Bostonian Society, which maintains the Old State House, also runs the museum in the State House and a library across the street. Changing and permanent exhibitions depict the history of the city from the settlement of the town through the American Revolution to the 21st century. Permanent exhibitions also include a sound-and-light show on the Boston Massacre of 1770, "From Colony to Commonwealth," interpreting the role of Boston in the Revolution, "Treasures from the Bostonian Society's Collections" in the ▷ *Council Chamber*, which includes Revolutionary icons and militia equipment, and "Preservation of the Old State House," tracing progress from 1881–1981.

Old State House, Boston

DWARFED BY THE TOWERS of the Financial District, this historic building is typical of the modest and unique architectural style of New England in the 18th century. It was the seat of British colonial government between 1713 and 1776. A replica royal lion and unicorn decorate each corner of the eastern façade. After independence, the Massachusetts legislature took possession of the building, and it has since had many uses, including being a produce market, merchants' exchange, Masonic lodge and Boston City Hall. Its wine cellars now function as a downtown subway station, and it also houses Bostonian Society memorabilia.

Old State House amid the sky-scrapers of the Financial District

A gold sculpture of an eagle, symbol of America, can be seen on the west façade.

West Façade
A Latin inscription, relating to the first Massachusetts Bay colony, runs around the outside of this crest. The relief in the center depicts a local Native American.

Keayne Hall
This is named for Robert Keayne who, in 1658, gave £300 to the city so that the Town House, predating the Old State House, could be built. Exhibits in the room depict events from the Revolution.

Entrance

★ Central Staircase
A fine example of 18th-century workmanship, the central spiral staircase has two beautifully crafted wooden handrails. It is one of the few such staircases still in existence in the US.

SITE OF THE BOSTON MASSACRE

Cobbled circle: site of the Boston Massacre

A circle of cobblestones below the balcony on the eastern façade marks the site of the Boston Massacre. After the Boston Tea Party (where Boston patriots, in protest at taxation, boarded three British East India Company ships and threw their cargoes of tea into Boston Harbor), this was one of the most inflammatory events leading up to the American Revolution. On 5 March 1770, an unruly mob of colonists taunted British guardsmen with insults, rocks, and snowballs. The soldiers opened fire, killing five colonists. A number of articles relating to the Boston Massacre are exhibited inside the Old State House.

The tower is a classic example of Colonial style. In 18th-century paintings and engravings it can be seen clearly above the Boston skyline.

British Lion and Unicorn
A royal symbol of Britain, the original lion and unicorn were pulled down when news of the Declaration of Independence reached Boston in 1776.

The Declaration of Independence was read from this balcony in 1776. In the 1830s, when the building was the City Hall, the balcony was enlarged to two tiers.

THE FREEDOM TRAIL

Boston's sites relating to the Revolution have been linked together as "The Freedom Trail". This 4-km (2.5-m) walking route, marked in red on the pavement, begins at the Boston Common.

★ East Façade
This façade has seen many changes. An earlier clock from the 1820s was removed in 1957 and replaced with an 18th-century replica of the sundial that once hung here. The clock has now been reinstated.

Council Chamber
Once the chambers for the British governors, and from 1780 chambers for the first US governor of Massachusetts (John Hancock), this room has hosted many key events. Among them were numerous impassioned speeches made by Boston patriots.

CANADA

USA

OLD STATE HOUSE, BOSTON

WASHINGTON DC

Los Angeles

MEXICO

GULF OF MEXICO

KEY DATES

1667 Boston Town House is constructed of wood.

1711 Fire destroys the building which is rebuilt in 1713.

1780–98 Serves as Massachusetts State House.

1798 Renovated for private retail tenants.

1830–40 Becomes the Boston City Hall.

1840–80 The building falls into disrepair.

1881 The Old State House is completely restored by the city.

1976 Queen Elizabeth II addresses Bostonians from the balcony.

LIFE IN COLONIAL BOSTON

First settled by Puritans in 1630, Boston became one of North America's leading colonial cities. Its life and its wealth centered around its role as a busy seaport, but its streets were crooked, dirty, and crowded with people and livestock. Other problems included waste disposal, fire fighting, and caring for the numerous poor. Unlike the other major American cities outside of New England, Boston had a "town meeting" form of government. This was unusually democratic for the times and helps to explain why Boston became such a center of colonial resistance prior to the American Revolution.

STAR FEATURES

★ **East Façade**

★ **Central Staircase**

The Solomon R Guggenheim museum floodlit at dusk

GUGGENHEIM AND WRIGHT

Guggenheim amassed his wealth through his family's mining and metal businesses, which he ran from New York. He collected modernist paintings and in 1942, Frank Lloyd Wright was asked to design a permanent home for the collection. Wright disagreed with the choice of New York for the project. He felt the city was overbuilt, overpopulated, and lacking in architectural merit, but he acquiesced and designed a structure to challenge these shortcomings. He wished to disregard Manhattan's rectilinear grid system and to bring a fresh notion of exhibition areas to the city using curving, continuous spaces.

THE OTHER MUSEUMS

The Guggenheim Foundation runs three other museums. In Bilbao, Spain, a building designed by US architect Frank O Gehry houses a permanent collection of modern art with exhibitions from ancient China to Jasper Johns. Solomon's niece, Peggy Guggenheim, donated her collection of post-1910 masterworks of surrealist and abstract painting and sculpture to the Foundation. Opened in 1951, this collection is housed in her villa on the Grand Canal in Venice. In cooperation with Deutsche Bank, the Deutsche Guggenheim Berlin has four exhibitions a year, including performance art and music. The Foundation is also considering plans for new museums in Rio de Janeiro, Vienna, and St Petersburg.

Solomon R Guggenheim Museum, New York

HOME TO ONE of the world's finest collections of modern and contemporary art, the building itself is perhaps the museum's greatest masterwork. Designed by architect Frank Lloyd Wright, the shell-like façade is a New York landmark. It takes its inspiration from nature, attempting to render the fluidity of organic forms. The spiral ramp curves down and inward from the dome, passing works by major 19th- and 20th-century artists. The imaginative layout of the Great Rotunda affords visitors the opportunity of simultaneously viewing works located on different levels.

Fifth Avenue façade

Paris Through the Window
The vibrant colors of Marc Chagall's 1913 masterwork illuminate the canvas, conjuring up images of a magical and mysterious city where nothing is quite what it appears to be.

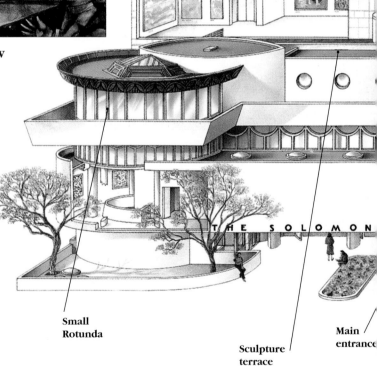

Small
Rotunda

Sculpture
terrace

Main
entrance

Woman Ironing (1904)
A work from Pablo Picasso's Blue Period, this painting is his quintessential image of hard work and fatigue.

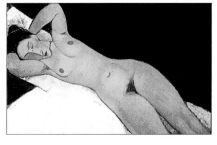

Nude (1917)
This sleeping figure is typical of Amedeo Modigliani's stylized work. His simplified faces are reminiscent of African masks.

MUSEUM GUIDE

The Great Rotunda puts on special exhibitions. The Small Rotunda shows some of the museum's celebrated Impressionist and Post-Impressionist holdings. The Tower galleries feature exhibitions of work from the permanent collection as well as contemporary pieces. A sculpture terrace on the sixth floor overlooks Central Park.

Tower galleries

Great Rotunda

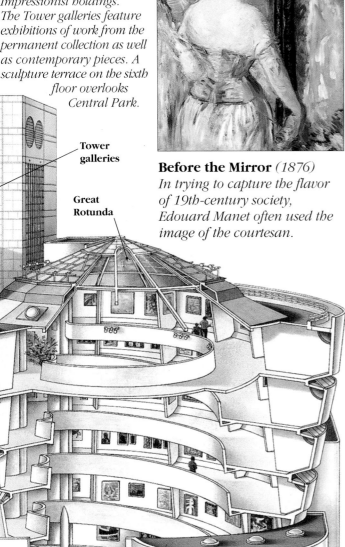

Before the Mirror *(1876)*
In trying to capture the flavor of 19th-century society, Edouard Manet often used the image of the courtesan.

Woman Holding a Vase
Fernand Léger incorporated elements of Cubism into this work from 1927.

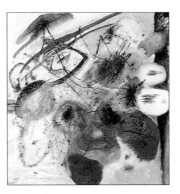

Black Lines *(1913) This is one of Vasily Kandinsky's earliest examples of his work in "non-objective" art.*

Woman with Yellow Hair
(1931) Marie-Thérèse Walter, Picasso's mistress, is shown as a gentle, voluptuous figure.

GUGGENHEIM ONLINE

Encompassing highlights from the Guggenheim holdings worldwide, the excellent online site (www.guggenheimcollec tion.org) includes conceptual definitions, artist biographies, and suggested further reading.

KEY DATES

1946 Construction begins.

1949 Solomon Guggenheim dies.

1959 Guggenheim Museum opens on Fifth Avenue.

1992 The Frank Wright building is restored and supplemented by a new tower.

THE COLLECTION

At first a collector of mediocre Old Masters, Guggenheim began, after meeting artist Hilla Rebay, to amass a superb stock of works by modernists such as Delaunay, Léger, and Kandinsky. The Guggenheim Foundation was founded in 1937 and established the Museum of Non-Objective Art, as it was known until 1959, in a temporary residence. Design of the new building began in 1943, but it was not until after Guggenheim's death in 1949 that the collection was expanded, through purchases and bequests, to include such artists as Picasso, Cézanne, Klee, and Mangold. Other highlights include works by Modigliani, Chagall, Braque, and Rousseau. Thannhauser's collection of Impressionist, Post-Impressionist, and early Modern art, donated from 1978 to 1991 by collector Justin Thannhauser and his widow, is hung in the ▷ *Tower galleries*. This collection includes masterpieces by innovators such as Cézanne, Degas, Manet, Pissarro, van Gogh, and an exceptional number of works by Picasso. The Guggenheim's exhibits change on a regular basis.

FRANK LLOYD WRIGHT

During his lifetime, Wright was considered the great innovator of American architecture. Characteristic of his work are Prairie-style homes and office buildings of concrete slabs, glass bricks, and tubing. Wright received the Guggenheim commission in 1942 and it was completed after his death in 1959, his only New York building.

Interior of the Guggenheim's Great Rotunda

Solomon R Guggenheim Museum

THE SKYSCRAPER RACE

With the construction of the Eiffel Tower in 1889, American architects were challenged to build ever higher, so at the beginning of the 20th century the skyscraper race began. By 1929, New York's Bank of Manhattan Building, at 283 m (972 ft), was the tallest skyscraper but Walter Chrysler, the famous automobile manufacturer, was planning to top that height. John Jakob Raskob, of rival General Motors, decided to join the race and, with Pierre S Du Pont, was a major investor in the Empire State project. Since Chrysler was keeping the height of his building a secret, Raskob had to be flexible in his planning. He first aimed at building 85 floors but, unsure of Chrysler's goal, he kept going until the building reached 102 floors, and by adding a spire beat Chrysler by 62 m (204 ft).

WHO DESIGNED IT?

The Shreve, Lamb & Harmon company has designed some of the most notable skyscrapers in Manhattan. By the time work on the Empire State Building began, they had designed seven buildings, including 40 Wall Street (now the Trump Building), at 70 floors, which was completed in only 11 months. With a team of top engineers and contractors, using up to 3,000 workers, the Empire State Building, too, was completed under budget and in record time.

Al Smith, former governor of NY State, with a model of the ESB

Empire State Building, New York

Empire State Building

ONE OF THE WORLD'S most famous buildings, the Empire State broke all height records when it was finished. Construction began in March 1930, not long after the Wall Street Crash, but by the time it opened in 1931, it was so hard to find anyone to fill it that it was nicknamed "the Empty State Building." Only the popularity of its observatories saved it from bankruptcy. However, the building was soon seen as a symbol of New York throughout the world.

Art Deco Medallions
Displayed throughout the lobby, these depict symbols of the modern age.

CONSTRUCTION
The building was designed to be erected easily and speedily with everything possible prefabricated and slotted into place at a rate of about four stories per week.

The framework is made from 60,000 tons of steel and was built in 23 weeks.

Aluminum panels were used instead of stone around the 6,500 windows. The steel trim masks rough edges on the facing.

Ten million bricks were used to line the whole building.

Sandwich space between the floors houses the wiring, pipes, and cables.

Over 200 steel and concrete piles support the 365,000-ton building.

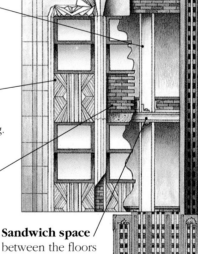

STAR FEATURES

★ **Views from the Observatories**

★ **Fifth Avenue Entrance Lobby**

102nd-floor observatory

The Empire State has 102 floors, but only 85 have office space. A 46 m (150 ft) mooring mast for Zeppelins was added. Now 62 m (204 ft), the mast transmits TV and radio to the city and four states.

Colored floodlighting of the top 30 floors marks special and seasonal events.

High-speed elevators travel at up to 366 m (1,200 ft) a minute.

Ten minutes is all it takes for fit runners to race up the 1,576 steps from the lobby to the 86th floor, in the annual Empire State Run-Up.

★ **Views from the Observatories**

The 86th floor has outdoor observation decks for bird's-eye views of Manhattan. On a clear day, visitors can see more than 80 miles (125 km) in all directions. The observatory on the 102nd floor closed in 1994.

ART DECO DESIGN

The Empire State Building is considered New York City's last Art Deco masterpiece. The movement flourished from the 1920s to the 1940s and was noted for its use of crisp, graphic lines, geometric shapes, and vertical setbacks evocative of Aztec ziggurats.

KEY DATES

1930 Building work begins.

1931 Empire State Building is tallest building in the world.

1977 The first annual Empire State Run-Up takes place.

2002 Donald Trump sells the Empire State Building to a real estate consortium.

BUILDING SKYSCRAPERS

The modern skyscraper would not have been possible without several building developments. Elevators had been in use for some time, but it was not until Elisha Otis's 1854 demonstration of his safety brake that the public began to trust them. The second necessary innovation was the use of the structural steel skeleton, seen in the world's first skyscraper in 1885. With this kind of construction, the walls became merely a sheathing, not a load-bearing element, and enormously tall, heavy buildings could now rise ever higher. Building in the heart of Manhattan presented a further problem; large amounts of essential construction materials could not be kept in the street. To solve this, the aluminum elements were prefabricated and only three days' worth of structural steel was kept on site, creating an extremely complicated organization job. Although no longer the world's tallest, the Empire State Building is arguably still the most famous.

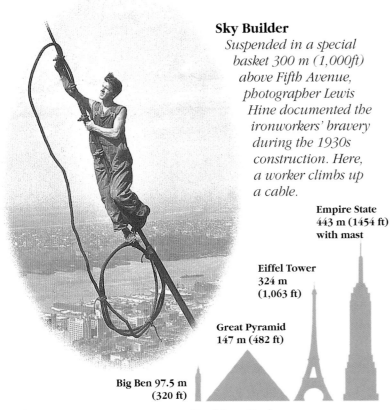

Sky Builder

Suspended in a special basket 300 m (1,000ft) above Fifth Avenue, photographer Lewis Hine documented the ironworkers' bravery during the 1930s construction. Here, a worker climbs up a cable.

Empire State 443 m (1454 ft) with mast

Eiffel Tower 324 m (1,063 ft)

Great Pyramid 147 m (482 ft)

Big Ben 97.5 m (320 ft)

Pecking Order

New Yorkers are justly proud of their city's symbol, which towers above the icons of other countries.

Lightning Strikes

A natural lightning conductor, the building is struck up to 100 times a year. The observation decks are closed during inclement weather.

★ **Fifth Avenue Entrance Lobby**

A relief image of the skyscraper is superimposed on a map of New York State in the marble-lined lobby.

STARRING ROLE

The Empire State Building has been seen in many movies. However, the finale from the 1933 classic *King Kong* is easily its most famous guest appearance, as the giant ape straddles the spire to do battle with army aircraft. In 1945 a real bomber flew too low over Manhattan in fog and struck the building just above the 78th floor. The luckiest escape was that of a young elevator operator whose cabin plunged 79 floors. The emergency brakes saved her life.

Empire State Building

Building the Lady

In his Parisian workshop, the sculptor Bartholdi began by creating four scale models, the largest at one-fourth the actual size. This was divided into 300 plaster sections, and each section was then enlarged to full size. A mold of laminated wood was made from each of these sections, and sheets of copper were pounded into the molds to a thickness of only 2.5 mm (0.1 in). In all, 350 sheets were connected with 50 mm- (2 in-) wide iron straps. The straps acted like springs, which allowed the surface to flex in high winds or extremes of temperature. The statue arrived in New York packed in over 200 crates and was attached to the frame using some 300,000 copper rivets.

Statue construction workshop in France, c.1882

Fund-Raising

Although the French contributed to the cost of the statue, early on in the plan it was decided that funds for the pedestal would come from the US. As fund-raising was going slowly, media baron Joseph Pulitzer used the editorial clout of his newspaper *The World* to criticize the wealthy for withholding their financial support and the middle class for relying on the wealthy. He pointed out that the statue was a gift to the entire US and attacked those who were not supporting it on the grounds that it was a New York project. Soon the whole nation was involved. When the crated statue arrived on 19 June 1885, fund-raising rose to fever pitch. It reached its target in just two months.

Statue of Liberty, New York

A GIFT FROM THE FRENCH to the American people, the statue was a celebration of a century of independence. The brainchild of French politician Edouard-René Lefebvre de Laboulaye, it has become a symbol of freedom to many since it was unveiled by President Grover Cleveland on 28 October 1886. Its spirit is encapsulated in the poem engraved on the base "Give me your tired, your poor, /Your huddled masses yearning to breathe free." After decades of wear and tear, the statue needed restoration work and was given an expensive facelift in time for its 100th anniversary in 1986.

From Her Toes to Her Torch
Three hundred molded copper sheets riveted together make up Lady Liberty.

★ **Statue of Liberty Museum**
Posters featuring the statue are among the items on display.

The Golden Torch is a 1986 replacement for the original, which became corroded over the years. The replica's flame is coated in 24-carat gold leaf.

The frame was designed by Gustave Eiffel, who also built the Eiffel Tower. He realized that the copper shell would react to the iron frame and put a barrier between them.

A central pylon anchors the 225-tonne statue to its base.

354 steps lead from the entrance to the crown.

Observation deck and museum

The Statue
With a height of 93 m (305 ft) from ground to torch, the Statue of Liberty dominates New York Harbor.

The pedestal is set within the walls of an army fort. It was the largest concrete mass ever poured.

The original torch now stands in the main lobby.

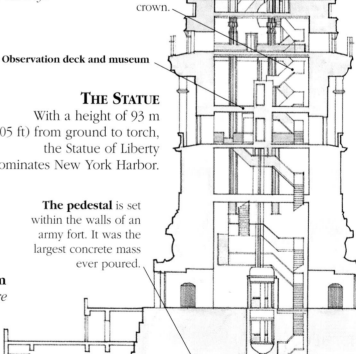

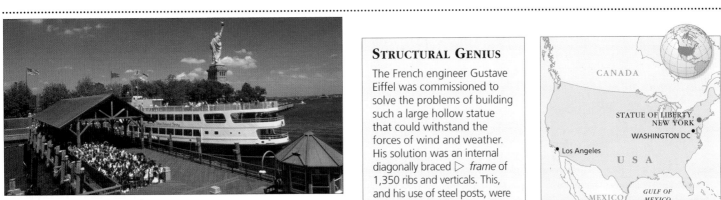

★ Ferries to Liberty Island

Ferries cross New York Harbor to Liberty Island, which was originally known as Bedloe's Island.

STRUCTURAL GENIUS

The French engineer Gustave Eiffel was commissioned to solve the problems of building such a large hollow statue that could withstand the forces of wind and weather. His solution was an internal diagonally braced ▷ *frame* of 1,350 ribs and verticals. This, and his use of steel posts, were seen as structural innovations.

KEY DATES

1865 Bartholdi has the idea of building a tribute to Liberty in America.

1876 Bartholdi is given the commission to create the Statue of Liberty.

1886 The Statue of Liberty is unveiled.

1986 The Statue of Liberty is reopened after extensive restoration.

Face of Liberty
The sculptor's mother was the model for Liberty's face. The seven rays of her crown represent the seven seas and seven continents.

Making the Hand
To make the copper shell, the hand was made first in plaster, then in wood. The scale of the project can be seen by the figures around it.

THE MUSEUM

The ▷ *Statue of Liberty Museum* is located in the base of the structure. The Torch Exhibit in the lobby holds the much-altered flame and the ▷ *original 1886 torch*. Overlooking the lobby is a display covering the history of the torch and flame. The Statue of Liberty Exhibit, on the pedestal's second level, is a biography of Lady Liberty and an examination of the ideals for which she stands. Through artifacts, prints, photographs, videos, and oral histories, seven sections with topics such as "From Image to Ideal" and "Stretching Technology" focus on her history. Another area has five sections on her symbolism, exploring ideas such as "Mother of Exiles," and "The Statue in Popular Culture." There is also a display of full-scale models of Liberty's face and left foot (▷ *A Model Figure*). A plaque dedicated to Emma Lazarus's famous sonnet *The New Colossus* was added to the pedestal in the early 1900s.

A Model Figure
A series of graduated scale models enabled Bartholdi to build the largest metal statue ever constructed.

FRÉDÉRIC-AUGUSTE BARTHOLDI (1834–1904)

Initially called "Liberty Enlightening the World", the Statue of Liberty was intended by its designer the French sculptor Bartholdi as a monument to the freedom he thought was lacking in his own country. He said "I will try to glorify the Republic and Liberty over there, in the hope that some day I will find it again here." He devoted 21 years of his life to the project, travelling to the US in 1871 to persuade President Ulysses S Grant and others to help to fund the pedestal.

Restoration Celebration
On 4 July 1986, after a $100 million clean-up, the statue was revealed. The $2 million fireworks display was the largest ever seen in America.

STAR FEATURES

★ Statue of Liberty Museum

★ Ferries to Liberty Island

Statue of Liberty

Ellis Island

Immigrants being transferred to Ellis Island for processing

TRAVEL IN STEERAGE

By the end of the 19th century, steam-powered ocean liners had cut the Atlantic passage time to two weeks. The poorest passengers traveled in "steerage," the lowest decks that also housed the ship's steering mechanism. Here, narrow compartments were divided into separate dormitories for single men, single women, and families. The air was rank with the odors of communal living and many were seasick. The food was poor, consisting, at best, of potatoes, soup, eggs, and unrefrigerated food brought from home. Arrival in New York did not bring better conditions, as immigrants sometimes had to wait on board for days before being ferried to Ellis Island.

THE ADMISSION PROCESS

Immigrants landing on Ellis Island joined a queue for the ▷ Great Hall, a wait that could last five hours. During this time, doctors checked them for a variety of diseases including cholera and tuberculosis, as well as insanity and trachoma, a contagious eye infection that could cause blindness and death. Immigrants who did not pass were sent either to the island's hospital to recover or, if incurable, back to their country of origin. In the Registry Room, the immigrants' socio-economic background was established to ensure that they would not become a burden on society. Unescorted women were detained until their safety could be assured, through the arrival of a telegram or letter.

Ellis Island, New York

NO OTHER PLACE EXPLAINS so well the "melting pot" that formed the character of the United States of America as Ellis Island in New York Harbor. Over one-third of Americans can trace their point of arrival here, the country's immigration depot from 1890 until 1954. Nearly 17 million people passed through its gates and were dispersed across the country in the greatest wave of migration ever known. Outside, the American Immigrant Wall of Honor is the largest wall of names in the world. Abandoned for over 35 years, the restored site now centers on the Great Hall or Registry Room, and houses a three-story museum with permanent exhibits and an electronic database for Americans to trace their ancestors.

Main building

Rail Ticket
A special fare for immigrants led many on to California.

★ **Dormitory**
There were separate sleeping quarters for male and female detainees.

The train station office sold tickets onward to the final destination.

THE RESTORATION

In 1990 a $189 million project, by a company called the Statue of Liberty-Ellis Island Foundation, rebuilt the ruined buildings, replaced the copper domes, and restored the interior with surviving original fixtures.

The ferry office sold tickets to New Jersey.

★ **Baggage Room** *The immigrants' meager possessions were checked here on arrival.*

★ **Great Hall**
Immigrants were made to wait for "processing" in the Registry Room. The old metal railings were replaced with wooden benches in 1911.

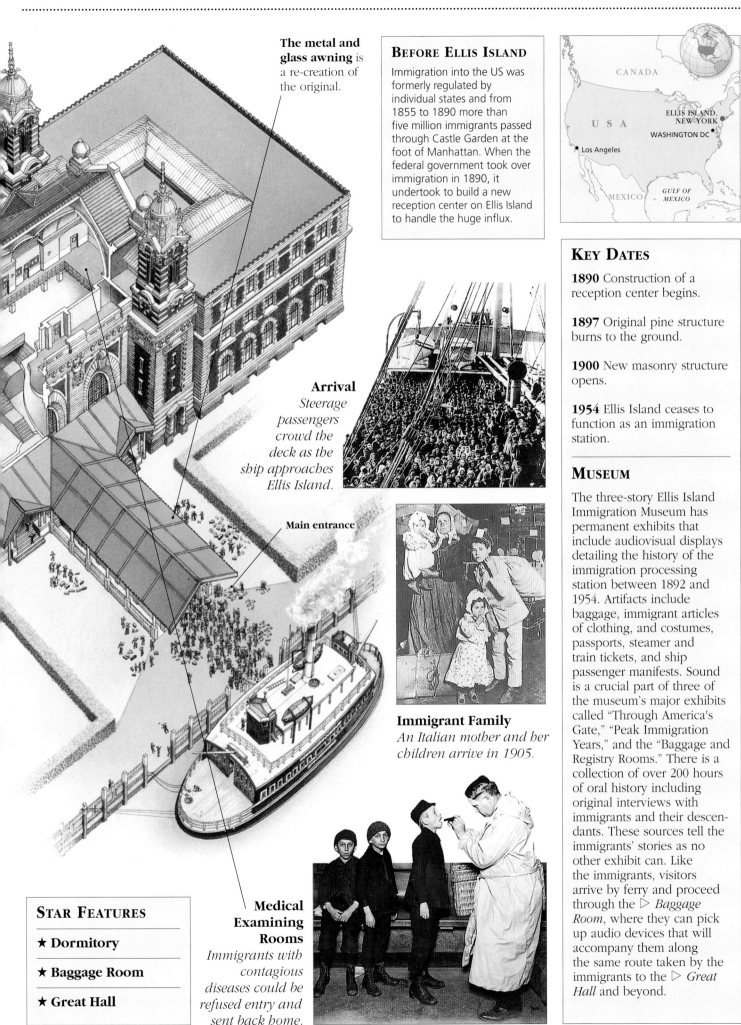

The metal and glass awning is a re-creation of the original.

Ellis Island

BEFORE ELLIS ISLAND

Immigration into the US was formerly regulated by individual states and from 1855 to 1890 more than five million immigrants passed through Castle Garden at the foot of Manhattan. When the federal government took over immigration in 1890, it undertook to build a new reception center on Ellis Island to handle the huge influx.

KEY DATES

1890 Construction of a reception center begins.

1897 Original pine structure burns to the ground.

1900 New masonry structure opens.

1954 Ellis Island ceases to function as an immigration station.

MUSEUM

The three-story Ellis Island Immigration Museum has permanent exhibits that include audiovisual displays detailing the history of the immigration processing station between 1892 and 1954. Artifacts include baggage, immigrant articles of clothing, and costumes, passports, steamer and train tickets, and ship passenger manifests. Sound is a crucial part of three of the museum's major exhibits called "Through America's Gate," "Peak Immigration Years," and the "Baggage and Registry Rooms." There is a collection of over 200 hours of oral history including original interviews with immigrants and their descendants. These sources tell the immigrants' stories as no other exhibit can. Like the immigrants, visitors arrive by ferry and proceed through the ▷ *Baggage Room*, where they can pick up audio devices that will accompany them along the same route taken by the immigrants to the ▷ *Great Hall* and beyond.

Arrival
Steerage passengers crowd the deck as the ship approaches Ellis Island.

Main entrance

Immigrant Family
An Italian mother and her children arrive in 1905.

STAR FEATURES

★ **Dormitory**

★ **Baggage Room**

★ **Great Hall**

Medical Examining Rooms
Immigrants with contagious diseases could be refused entry and sent back home.

THE WAR OF 1812

Tensions with Britain over restrictions on trade and freedom of the seas began to escalate during James Madison's administration. On 18 June 1812, the US declared war on Britain. In August 1814, British troops reached Washington and officers of the Capitol fled, taking the Declaration of Independence and the Constitution with them. On 24 August, the British defeated the Americans at Bladensburg, a suburb of Washington. They set fire to the War Department, the Treasury, the Capitol, and the White House, but a night of heavy rain prevented the city's destruction. The Treaty of Ghent, which finally ended the war, was signed on 17 February 1815.

Façade of the White House Visitor Center

THE WEST WING

In 1902, the West Wing of the White House was built by the architectural firm McKim, Mead, and White for a total cost of $65,196. This wing (▷ *The West Terrace*) houses the Cabinet Room, where government officials convene with the president, and the Oval Office, where the president meets visiting heads of state. Many presidents have personalized this room in some way: President Clinton chose as his desk a table given to President Rutherford B Hayes by Queen Victoria in 1880.

The White House, Washington DC

THE OFFICIAL RESIDENCE of United States presidents for over 200 years, the White House is one of the most distinguished buildings in America and was built on a location chosen by George Washington in 1790. Irish-born architect James Hoban designed the original building in a Palladian style (▷ *Neo-Classical Style p79*) and when it was nearing completion, President and Mrs John Adams became the first occupants. It has survived two fires, in 1814 and 1929, and the interior was completely gutted and renovated throughout President Harry S Truman's presidency, 1945–53. In 1901, President Theodore Roosevelt officially gave the White House its current name.

★ **State Dining Room**
Able to seat as many as 140 people, the State Dining Room was enlarged in 1902. A portrait of President Abraham Lincoln, by George P A Healy, hangs above the mantel.

The West Terrace
leads to the West Wing, the Cabinet Room, and the Oval Office, the president's official office.

STAR ROOMS

★ **State Dining Room**

★ **Red Room**

★ **Vermeil Room**

The North Façade
The Palladian-style façade of the White House is familiar to millions of people around the world.

The stonework
has been painted over and over to maintain the building's white façade.

★ **Red Room**
One of four reception rooms, the Red Room is furnished in red in the Empire style (1810–30). The fabrics were woven in the US from French designs.

Lincoln Bedroom

President Lincoln used this room as his Cabinet Room, and it was turned into a bedroom by President Truman who filled it with furnishings from the Lincoln era.

THE WHITE HOUSE VISITOR CENTER

Interesting exhibits about the history of the White House, its décor, and its inhabitants are on display in the White House Visitor Center. Guided tours of the presidential official residence are extremely limited and can only be booked by special arrangement through a Member of Congress or an embassy.

The East Terrace leads to the East Wing.

The East Room is used for large gatherings, such as dances and concerts.

Treaty Room

The Green Room was first used as a guest room before Thomas Jefferson turned it into a dining room.

Blue Room

★ Vermeil Room

This yellow room houses seven paintings of first ladies, including this portrait of Eleanor Roosevelt by Douglas Chandor.

Diplomatic Reception

This room is used to welcome friends and ambassadors. It is elegantly furnished in the Federal Period style (1790–1820).

WHITE HOUSE ARCHITECTS

After selecting the site, George Washington held a design competition to find an architect to build the residence where the US president would live. In 1792 James Hoban, an Irish-born architect, was chosen for the task. It is from Hoban's original drawings that the White House was initially built and all subsequent changes grew. In 1902 President Theodore Roosevelt hired the New York architectural firm of McKim, Mead, and White to check the structural condition of the building and refurbish areas as necessary. The White House underwent further renovations and refurbishments during the administrations of Truman and Kennedy.

James Hoban, architect of the White House

KEY DATES

1792 Construction begins on the Executive Mansion (renamed the White House in 1901).

1800 President Adams and his wife are the first to move into the White House.

1814 The British set fire to the White House during the war of 1812–15.

1902 The West Wing, including the Oval Office, is built.

1942 The East Wing of the White House is added, on the instructions of Franklin D Roosevelt, completing the final structure.

THE WHITE HOUSE INTERIOR

The rooms in the White House are decorated in period styles and filled with valuable antique furniture, china, and silverware. Hanging on its walls are some of America's most treasured paintings including portraits of past presidents and first ladies. The room that served as the Cabinet Room from 1865 for ten presidential administrations (▷ *Treaty Room*), was restored in 1961 and contains Victorian pieces bought by President Grant. The most central room on the State Floor (▷ *Blue Room*) was decorated in 1817 in the French Empire style by President Monroe. The same style was later used by First Lady Jackie Kennedy to redecorate one of the reception rooms (▷ *Red Room*) in 1962.

The White House

THE DOME

By the 1850s, the original Charles Bulfinch ▷ *Dome* was too small for the enlarged Capitol. Moreover, it leaked and was deemed a fire hazard. In 1854, the first $100,000 was appropriated for Thomas U Walter's new dome to be constructed of cast iron. Walter's double-dome design recalls the Panthéon in Paris. Thomas Crawford designed and executed a 6-m (19.5-ft) sculpture to crown the dome, and in 1863, during the American Civil War (1861–5), the Statue of Freedom was raised atop the 87.5-m (287-ft) high dome – a Classical female figure standing on a globe with the national motto, *E Pluribus Unum* (Out of many, one). The statue was restored in 1993.

View of the US Capitol in Washington DC

THE ROTUNDA FRIEZE

Thomas U Walter's 1859 drawings showed a recessed, bas-relief sculpture in the ▷ *Rotunda*. Plans changed, and by 1877, a fresco 2.5 m (8.3 ft) high and 91 m (300 ft) in circumference was being painted. The *Frieze of American History* has 19 panels. The first contains the only allegorical figures in the frieze: America, an American Indian maiden, History, and an American eagle. The second panel represents Columbus's landing, and the next six show well-known events from early New World history. Panel ten represents the founding of Georgia and is followed by scenes from US history. The first flight in 1903 is featured in the final panel, *The Birth of Aviation*, completed in 1953.

United States Capitol, Washington DC

THE US CAPITOL IS ONE of the world's best-known symbols of democracy. The center of America's legislative process for 200 years, its Neo-Classical architecture (▷ *Neo-Classical Style p79*) reflects the principles of Ancient Greece and Rome that developed America's political system. The cornerstone was laid by George Washington in 1793 and by 1800, although unfinished, the Capitol was occupied. With more funding, construction resumed under architect Benjamin Latrobe; however the British burned the Capitol in the War of 1812. Restoration began in 1815. Many features, such as the Statue of Freedom and Brumidi's murals, were added later.

Dome
Originally ma[de] of wood and copper, the dome was designed by Thomas Walter.

★ **Rotunda**
Completed in 1865, the 55-m (180-ft) high Rotunda is capped by The Apotheosis of Washington, *a fresco by Constantino Brumidi.*

The Hall of Columns is lined with statues of notable Americans.

The House Chamber

The Rotunda Frieze

The Crypt

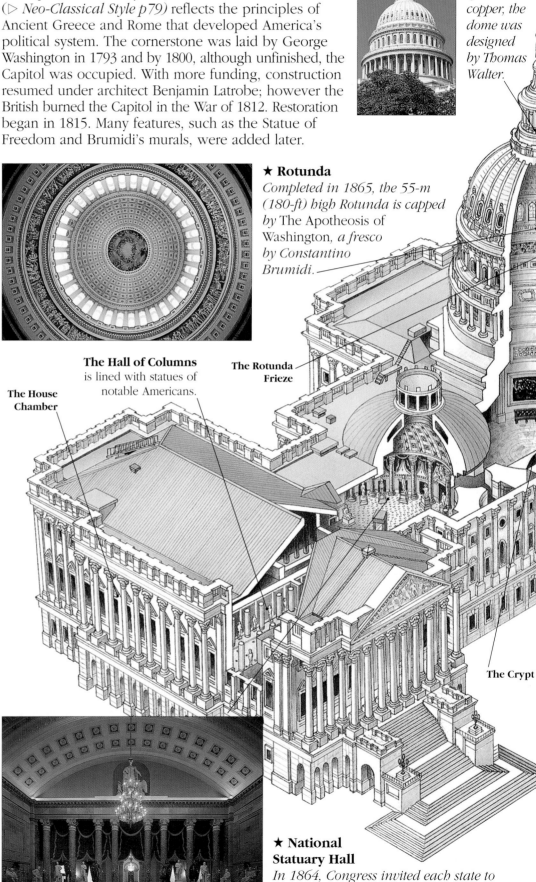

★ **National Statuary Hall**
In 1864, Congress invited each state to contribute two statues of prominent citizens to stand in this hall.

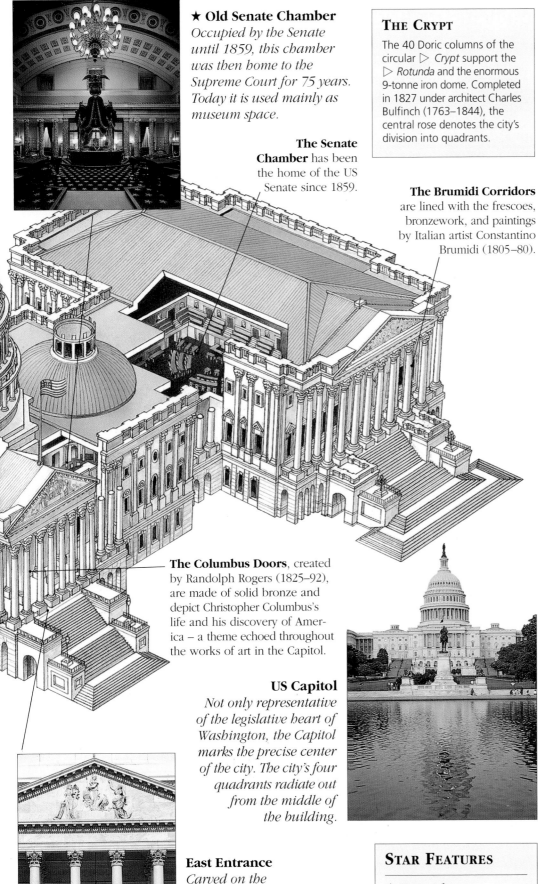

★ Old Senate Chamber
Occupied by the Senate until 1859, this chamber was then home to the Supreme Court for 75 years. Today it is used mainly as museum space.

The Senate Chamber has been the home of the US Senate since 1859.

The Brumidi Corridors are lined with the frescoes, bronzework, and paintings by Italian artist Constantino Brumidi (1805–80).

THE CRYPT

The 40 Doric columns of the circular ▷ *Crypt* support the ▷ *Rotunda* and the enormous 9-tonne iron dome. Completed in 1827 under architect Charles Bulfinch (1763–1844), the central rose denotes the city's division into quadrants.

The Columbus Doors, created by Randolph Rogers (1825–92), are made of solid bronze and depict Christopher Columbus's life and his discovery of America – a theme echoed throughout the works of art in the Capitol.

US Capitol
Not only representative of the legislative heart of Washington, the Capitol marks the precise center of the city. The city's four quadrants radiate out from the middle of the building.

East Entrance
Carved on the pediment are striking Classical female representations of America. These are flanked by figures of Justice and Hope.

KEY DATES

1791–92 Site is chosen for new national capital; city of Washington DC is designed and mapped.

1829 Original Capitol building is completed.

1851 Cornerstones are laid for new wings.

1983–93 West front and terrace are restored.

STATUARY

In 1864, Congress invited each state to contribute two statues of notable citizens to stand in the ▷ *National Statuary Hall*. Soon the collection grew too large, and much of it can now be seen in the ▷ *Hall of Columns* and the various corridors of the Capitol. Four statues of former US Presidents Washington, Jackson, Garfield, and Eisenhower can be found in the ▷ *Rotunda*. Also here is a statue of Sacajawea, Native American translator for the Lewis and Clark Expedition (1803–1806) into the new Louisiana Territory, pending selection of a permanent location. In the Statuary Hall itself, visitors can see Confederate General Robert E Lee and President Jefferson Davis; King Kamehameha I, unifier of Hawaii; Robert Fulton, inventor of the first commercially successful steamboat; Huey P Long, Depression-era demagogue from Louisiana; Sam Houston, president of the Republic of Texas; and Sequoyah, inventor of the Cherokee alphabet.

STAR FEATURES

★ **Rotunda**

★ **National Statuary Hall**

★ **Old Senate Chamber**

United States Capitol

Golden Gate Bridge

BUILDING THE BRIDGE

The Golden Gate Bridge is a classic suspension bridge of the kind first built in the mid-19th century. Its main elements are the anchorages, towers (pylons), cables, and road. Enormous concrete anchorages were poured at either end to hold the cables. The steel for the towers was fabricated in Pennsylvania and shipped through the Panama Canal. Engineer Joseph B Strauss chose John A Roebling and Sons, builders of the Brooklyn Bridge, to make the cables. Since no derrick of the time could lift cables as heavy as these would be, they were spun in place, the machines passing back and forth continuously for six months. Rejecting steel grey, architect Irving Morrow chose "International Orange" for the bridge's paint color, believing it better suited the natural light of the area.

BRIDGE PARTY

The Golden Gate Bridge opened to pedestrian traffic on 27 May 1937, on schedule and under budget. On a typically foggy and windy day, over 18,000 people took part in the grand opening by walking its total length (including the approaches) of 2,737 m (8,981 ft). The next day, President Franklin D Roosevelt pressed a telegraph key in the White House that opened the bridge to vehicular traffic. Every siren and church bell in San Francisco and Marin County sounded simultaneously. A week-long celebration followed the event.

The Golden Gate in "International Orange" paint

Golden Gate Bridge, San Francisco

One of the builders in a protective mask

SUPERLATIVES FLOW WHEN describing this world-famous landmark. It is the third-largest single-span bridge ever built and, when it was erected, was the longest and tallest suspension structure. Named after the part of San Francisco Bay dubbed "Golden Gate" in the mid-19th century, the bridge opened in 1937. There are breathtaking views of the bay from this spectacular structure, which has six lanes for vehicles as well as a free pedestrian walkway.

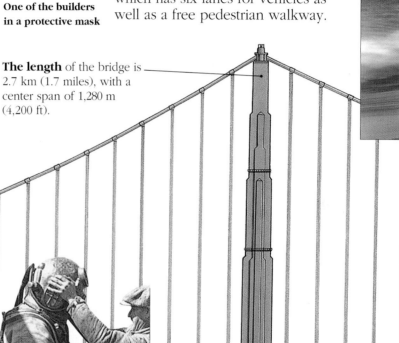

The length of the bridge is 2.7 km (1.7 miles), with a center span of 1,280 m (4,200 ft).

The Foundations

The foundations of the twin towers are a remarkable feat of engineering. The south pier, 345 m (1,125 ft) off-shore, was sunk 30 m (100 ft) below the surface in open water.

20-m (65-ft) thick pier base

47-m (155-ft) high fender

The road is 67 m (220 ft) above water 97 m (318 ft) deep.

Reinforcing iron frame

Divers

To reach the bedrock, divers were employed to dynamite 6-m (20-ft) deep holes in the ocean floor.

The Concrete Fender

During construction, the south pier base was protected from the force of the tides by a fender of concrete. Water was pumped out to create a vast watertight locker.

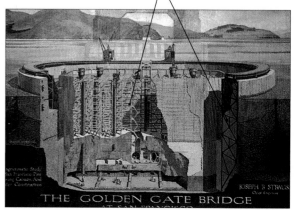

THE GOLDEN GATE BRIDGE

The Roadway

The steel-supported concrete roadway was constructed from the towers in both directions, so that the weight on the cables was evenly distributed.

THE FERRIES' RETURN

Originally built in the main to relieve ferry congestion in San Francisco Bay, in recent times the bridge has become so busy that thousands of car commuters have abandoned their cars for reliable water travel – there are now 18 ferries serving the area.

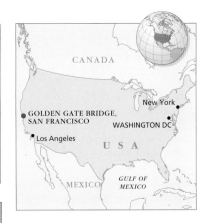

KEY DATES

c.1872 Earliest discussion of building a bridge across the entrance of San Francisco Bay.

1923 California legislature passes a bill to explore the feasibility of building the bridge.

1933 Construction begins in January.

1937 Bridge opens on time to great celebrations.

1985 The one-billionth car passes over the bridge.

DESIGNER SQUABBLES

Conceived as early as 1872 by railway tycoon Charles Crocker, building a bridge across the Golden Gate was not considered feasible until architect Joseph B Strauss stepped forward with a plan in 1921. Nine years of bureaucratic wrangling passed before Strauss was named chief engineer, but it was assistant chief engineer Clifford Paine and architect Irving Morrow who actually deserve credit for the design and construction of the bridge that stands today. By all accounts, Strauss seems to have been a difficult individual; he fired his first assistant chief engineer, Charles Ellis, for attracting too much publicity. Strauss even kept Ellis's name from appearing on any official documents. Ellis had his supporters however, who blocked a proposal to erect a statue of Strauss on the bridge until 1941.

Construction of the Towers

The twin steel towers rise to a height of 227 m (746 ft) above the water. The towers are hollow.

Man with a Plan

Chicago engineering titan Joseph Strauss is officially credited as the bridge's designer. He was assisted by Leon Moisseiff, Charles Ellis, and Clifford Paine. Irving F Morrow acted as consulting architect.

THE BRIDGE IN FIGURES

- Every day about 118,000 vehicles cross the bridge; this means that every year more than 40 million cars use it.
- The original coat of orange paint lasted for 27 years, needing only touch-ups. But since 1965, a crew has been stripping off the old paint and applying a more durable coating.
- The two great 2,332-m (7,650-ft) cables are more than 1 m (3 ft) thick, and contain 128,744 km (80,000 miles) of steel wire, enough to circle the earth at the equator three times.
- The volume of concrete poured into the piers and anchorages during the bridge's construction would be enough to lay a 1.5-m (5-ft) wide pavement from New York to San Francisco, a distance of more than 4,000 km (2,500 miles).
- The bridge can stand firm in the face of 160 km/h (100 mph) winds.
- Each pier has to withstand a tidal flow of more than 97 km/h (60 mph), while supporting a 44,000-ton steel tower above.

View towards Marin County

Alcatraz Island

ESCAPE FROM ALCATRAZ

Some of the 36 men who attempted to escape from Alcatraz really did use files or hacksaws to remove or bend window bars, but most attempts involved taking guards hostage. The majority of the attempts took place in the various work areas. Of the 36 prisoners in 14 separate escape attempts, none is known to have succeeded: six were shot and killed, two drowned, six were never seen again (and probably drowned), and the rest returned. Two were later executed for killing the only guards murdered during an escape attempt (▷ *Famous Inmates*). Although Alcatraz is only 3 km (2 miles) from the mainland, the strong currents and cold water probably account for the loss of life by drowning.

NATIVE AMERICAN OCCUPATION

In November 1969, a group of Native Americans, led by Mohawk Richard Oakes, occupied Alcatraz Island, claiming it in the name of all Native tribes. They soon established a civil administration and jobs were assigned to all of the estimated 100 occupiers. In negotiations with the federal government, the Native Americans wanted a deed to the island, their own university, and a cultural center. But negotiations broke down, the community became disaffected, electricity was cut off, and on 10 June 1971 federal agents removed the 15 remaining occupiers.

Native American Indians seizing Alcatraz Island

Alcatraz Island, San Francisco

ALCATRAZ MEANS "pelican" in Spanish and refers to the first inhabitants of this rocky, steep-sided island. Lying in San Francisco Bay 5 km (3 miles) east of the Golden Gate Bridge, its location is strategic, yet exposed to harsh ocean winds. In 1859, the US army established a fort here that guarded the Bay until 1907, when it became a military prison. From 1934 to 1963, it served as a maximum-security Federal Penitentiary. Unoccupied until 1969, it was seized by members of the Native American Movement claiming it as their land. They were expelled in 1971, and Alcatraz is now part of the Golden Gate National Recreation area.

Badge on entrance to cell house

★ Cell Block
The cell house contains four cell blocks. No cell has an outside wall or ceiling. The dungeon-like foundation of the prison block shares the original foundation of the old military fortress.

Alcatraz Island from the Ferry
"The Rock" has no natural soil. Soil was shipped from nearby Angel Island to make garden plots.

The officers' apartments stood here.

Military parade ground

The Warden's House was fire damaged during the 1969–71 siege.

Barracks buildings

0 meters   75

0 yards   75

STAR FEATURES

★ Cell Block

★ Exercise Yard

Alcatraz Pier
Most prisoners took their first steps ashore here; no other wharf served the steep-sided island. Now visitors alight at this pier.

★ Exercise Yard
Meals and a walk around the exercise yard were the highlights of a prisoner's day. The walled yard featured in movies set in the prison.

ALCATRAZ IN THE MOVIES

Alcatraz has been a popular topic for several films since 1938. Better-known movies include: *Escape from Alcatraz* (1979), *Birdman of Alcatraz* (1962), and *The Rock* (1997).

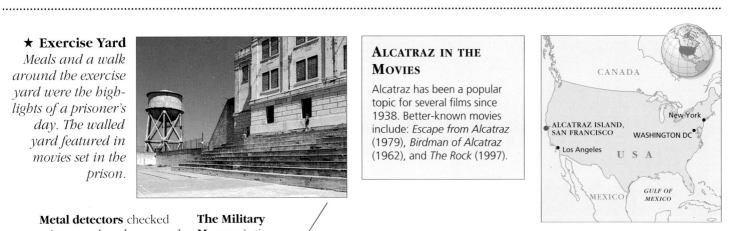

CANADA

New York

ALCATRAZ ISLAND, SAN FRANCISCO
WASHINGTON DC

Los Angeles
USA

MEXICO
GULF OF MEXICO

Metal detectors checked prisoners when they passed to and from the dining hall and exercise yards.

The Military Morgue is tiny and cramped, and is not open to the public.

Water tower

Prison workshops

The Visitors' Center is in the old barracks.

The Military Dorm was built in 1933.

Alcatraz Island

KEY DATES

1775 Spanish explorer Juan de Ayala charts the Bay, naming the island Alcatraz.

1847 US Army starts a geological survey.

1861 Fortress is used to house Civil War prisoners.

1973 Alcatraz is acquired by the National Park Service.

PRISON ROUTINE

Life on "The Rock" seldom varied. Awakened in their windowless cells (▷ *Cell Block*) at 7am, inmates were given 20 minutes before the ten-minute count of all inmates. Breakfast lasted 20 minutes with another head-count, then inmates reported to the ▷ *Prison Workshops*. The workday lasted until 4.10pm, with two eight-minute breaks and 20 minutes for lunch. Supper followed at 4.40pm; inmates were locked in their cells for the night at 5pm, with lights-out at 5.30pm. Two classes of prisoner did not follow this routine. Some were held in their cells all day until supper, either as punishment or for protection. Prisoners guilty of serious offenses could be placed in solitary confinement. These cells contained only one small window in the door (which could be closed by guards), a hole in the floor for a toilet, and no bed. The single light was often turned off by the guards to intimidate the prisoner. Long-term solitary confinement often led to serious psychological deterioration.

The officers' club, dating from the days of Fort Alcatraz, was a military store that also served as a recreation center.

FAMOUS INMATES

Al Capone

The Prohibition gangster Al "Scarface" Capone, was actually convicted in 1934 for income tax evasion. He spent much of his five-year sentence on Alcatraz in an isolation cell.

Robert Stroud

The original *"Birdman of Alcatraz"* was a murderer allowed to study birds in his cell before his transfer to Alcatraz. He spent 6 of his 17 years here in solitary confinement.

Carnes, Thompson, and Shockley

In May 1946, prisoners led by Clarence Carnes, Marion Thompson, and Sam Shockley overpowered guards and captured their guns. The prisoners failed to break out of the cell house, but three inmates and two officers were killed in what became known as the "Battle of Alcatraz." Carnes received an additional life sentence, and Shockley and Thompson were executed at San Quentin prison for their part in the insurrection.

Anglin Brothers

John and Clarence Anglin, with Frank Morris, chipped through the walls of their cells. Leaving dummy heads in their beds, they made a raft to enable their escape and were never caught, but the FBI officially listed them as presumed drowned. Their story was dramatized in the movie *Escape from Alcatraz* (1979).

Santa Barbara Mission

MISSION HISTORY

As part of the Mexican struggle for independence from Spain in the 19th century, Santa Barbara Mission was secularized in 1834 and the native Chumash people placed under civil rather than church authority. Although its lands were confiscated, then sold in 1846, Franciscans continued to work at the Mission. In 1848, California became part of the United States and following this, the mission was returned to the Church in 1865 by Abraham Lincoln. From 1868 to 1877 the Franciscans ran a school and junior college, and from 1896 to 1968 a seminary and school of theology were located in the Mission buildings. Since 1968, St Barbara Parish has used the Mission church. Friars from the whole Franciscan community, including Santa Barbara Mission, continue to work with Native Americans in Arizona and New Mexico.

THE MISSION MUSEUM

The ▷ *church* and living quarters of the Mission have now been converted into a small museum which houses artifacts of former residents and 18th- and 19th-century Mexican art. The sacristy holds the only known remaining Chumash-built altar. Each room in the mission museum has a central theme. The music room contains an extensive collection of instruments and music belonging both to the friars and to the native Chumash. From the 16th century, Spanish galleons sailed from the Philippines to California, transporting the riches of the Orient such as silks, porcelain, and spices. A Philippine crucifix and Chinese silk vestments in the museum chapel room reflect this Asian cultural influence. The ▷ *kitchen* has china displays from both Europe and Asia alongside Mexican majolica and California native basketry.

Santa Barbara Mission

L ABELED THE "Queen of the Missions," Santa Barbara is the only California mission to have been in continuous use since it was founded. It was the tenth mission built by the Spanish in the 18th century, founded on the feast day of St Barbara. After the third adobe church on the site was destroyed by an earthquake, the present structure took shape. Its twin towers and mix of replicated Classical (▷ *Classical Style p231*), Moorish, and Spanish styles served as the main inspiration for what came to be known as Mission Style – the distinctive features of which are massive walls covered with white lime cement, small window openings, rounded gables, and tiered bell towers. An earthquake in 1925 damaged the towers and the church façade. These were repaired but, because of a chemical reaction between the alkalis and aggregates in the cement, the entire front had to be rebuilt in 1953, following the original design.

Franciscan monk

A missionary's bedroom has been furnished as it would have been in the early 1800s.

Entrance

Central Fountain
Palm trees tower above a central fountain in the Sacred Gardens.

Arcaded Corridor
An open corridor fronts the museum rooms. Originally the living quarters, these now display a rich collection of mission artifacts.

Kitchen
The kitchen has been restored to show the typical cooking facilities of the early 1800s. Most of the food eaten was produced on the mission, which had fields and livestock.

STAR FEATURES

★ **Sacred Gardens**

★ **Church**

★ **Main Façade**

★ Sacred Gardens
The beautifully landscaped Sacred Gardens were once a working area for Native Americans to learn Western trades. Workshops and some missionary living quarters were located in the surrounding buildings.

HERITAGE

Early settlers in Santa Barbara included Mexican Indians, Jews, Africans, and Spanish. These ethnic groups inter-married with each other and with the native Chumash, creating a rich ancestry represented by those buried in the Mission cemetery.

★ Church
The church's interior is Neo-Classical (▷ Neo-Classical Style p79). Imitation marble columns and detailing have been painted on the walls and doors. The reredos has a painted canvas backdrop and carved wooden statues.

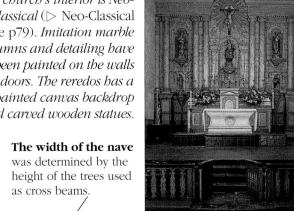

The side chapel, next to the altar, is dedicated to the Blessed Sacrament.

The width of the nave was determined by the height of the trees used as cross beams.

The cemetery garden contains the graves of some 4,000 Native Americans as well as friars.

★ Main Façade
The church's façade was designed by Padre Antonio Ripoll. Ripoll admired the Roman architect Vitruvius Pollio (working around 27 BC) and drew heavily on his ideas when building the church.

KEY DATES

1786 Mission is founded.

1812 Earthquake destroys the mission. Rebuilt 1815–20.

1834 Mission is secularized.

1865 Mission is returned to Church by Abraham Lincoln.

THE FRANCISCANS AND THE CHUMASH

In 1768 the Spanish king Carlos III gave responsibility for California missions to the Franciscans. A missionary cross was raised in Santa Barbara in 1782. Prior to the arrival of the Spanish, the native Chumash inhabiting the area were hunters and gatherers. They founded autonomous settlements, under the guidance of hereditary leaders. After a number of Chumash leaders were converted to Christianity, many villagers followed, and the Franciscans introduced them to agriculture and husbandry and employed them as artisans and laborers. Their skilled handiwork greatly contributed to the Mission's success. The Chumash did most of the reconstruction of the mission from 1815–20 and built a reservoir that still serves the city of Santa Barbara. Many descendants of the Chumash still live in the city of Santa Barbara today and community groups have been established to increase cultural awareness, to implement preservation programs, and to ensure that traditions continue to flourish.

Santa Barbara Mission

THE KIVAS

Usually a pueblo had a number of adjoining ▷ *kivas* (pit-houses), as well as one great *kiva*. Early smaller *kivas* seem to have been dwellings, but most scholars today agree that the great *kivas* were ceremonial places, barred to women and children, not merely community gathering sites. The first Chaco Canyon *kivas* appeared around AD 700 and while most were round, some were D-shaped. *Kivas* were entered through a hole in the roof and there was also a hole in the floor called a *sipapu*, which possibly symbolized the people's connection from birth with Mother Earth. Near the center was a fireplace and air shafts on the sides of the *kivas* made them more livable.

Elaborate cliff dwellings built into the walls of Mesa Verde

OTHER ANASAZI SITES

The Aztec Ruins National Monument was built by Puebloans in the 12th century. This important archaeological site is situated 111 km (69 miles) north of Chaco Canyon. There is a reconstructed great *kiva* here, as well as a pueblo consisting of 450 interconnecting rooms built of stone and mud. Further to the north is Mesa Verde, Spanish for "green table," which was inhabited by Puebloan people between AD 550 and 1300. The Navajo National Monument, located 358 km (223 miles) northwest of Chaco Canyon, was also occupied by the Puebloan people in the late 13th century. Three of their best preserved cliff dwellings, including the splendid Keet Steel, are located here.

Chaco Culture National Historical Park

Arrowhead at Chaco Museum

ONE OF THE MOST IMPRESSIVE cultural sites in the American Southwest, Chaco Culture National Historical Park at Chaco Canyon reflects the sophistication of the Ancestral Puebloan civilization (also known as the Anasazi) that existed here. With its six "great houses" (pueblos containing hundreds of rooms) and many lesser sites, the canyon was once the political, religious, and cultural center for this people. Despite the size of the pueblos, it is thought that Chaco's population was small because the land could not have supported a larger community. Archaeologists believe that the city was mainly used as a ceremonial gathering place, with a year-round population of less than 3,000. The inhabitants sustained themselves largely by growing their own crops and trading.

Stone Doorway
Chaco's skilled builders had only stone tools to work with to create this finely wrought stonework.

Kivas are round pit-like rooms dug into the ground and roofed with beams and earth.

PUEBLO BONITO
Pueblo Bonito is an example of a "great house". Begun around AD 850, it was built in stages over the course of 300 years. This reconstruction shows how it might have looked, with its D-shaped four-story structure that contained more than 650 rooms.

Chetro Ketl
A short trail from Pueblo Bonito leads to another great house, Chetro Ketl. Almost as large as Pueblo Bonito, Chetro Ketl has more than 500 rooms. The masonry used to build the later portions of this structure is among the most sophisticated found in any Puebloan site.

Casa Rinconada
The great kiva of Casa Rinconada is the largest religious chamber at Chaco, measuring 19 m (62 ft) in diameter. It was used for spiritual gatherings.

Pueblo Alto

Located on top of the mesa at the junction of several Chacoan roads is Pueblo Alto. In the 1860s W H Jackson discovered an ancient stairway carved into the cliff wall.

CHACO POTTERY

Archaeologists believe that the inhabitants of Chaco Canyon replaced baskets with ceramics for culinary usage between AD 400 and AD 750. Pieces of ceramics found so far are decorated with geometric designs and painted with minerals and carbons.

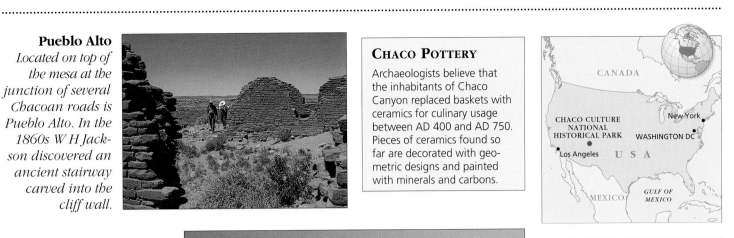

This great house was four stories high.

Hundreds of rooms within Pueblo Bonito show little sign of use and are thought to have been kept for storage or for guests arriving to take part in ceremonial events.

Early Astronomers at Fajada Butte

Measurement of time was vital to the Puebloans for crop planting and the timing of ceremonies. A spiral petroglyph, carved on Fajada Butte, is designed to indicate the changing seasons through the shadows it casts on the rock.

KEY DATES

AD 700–900 Domestic and ceremonial *kivas* are built in Chaco Canyon.

AD 850–1250 Chaco Canyon serves as a religious, trade, and administration center for the Anasazi people.

1896–1900 Archaeologist George H Pepper and his team excavate Pueblo Bonito.

1920 Edgar L Hewitt excavates Chetro Ketl.

1987 Chaco Culture National Historical Park is named a UNESCO World Heritage Site.

THE ANASAZI

Around AD 400, the Chaco Canyon people began to settle in well-defined groups with a common culture known as "Anasazi," a Navajo name said to mean "Ancient Enemy Ancestor." For centuries their villages stayed small, but a population explosion beginning in the 11th century led to the construction of elaborate cliff dwellings and the building of a road system connecting some 400 settlements. Agriculture thrived with the building of dams and irrigation systems. Better strains of corn (maize) that could reach deep into the ground for scarce water were also planted to support the growing population. However, by AD 1130, the towns began to empty, perhaps because of drought. People migrated east, south and west, and by the 13th century the canyon was completely deserted.

EXPLORING CHACO

The area around Chaco Canyon is full of hauntingly beautiful ruins left behind by the Ancestral Puebloan people. As well as the sites described here, they include Una Vida, the fifth largest great house with intriguing petroglyphs, Wijiji, Pueblo del Arroyo, and Kin Kletso, a two-story pueblo.

KEY

≡	Highway
=	Unpaved road
--	Hiking route
⛺	Campground/RV
⛱	Picnic area
ℹ	Visitor information

Kin Kletso

Pueblo Alto

Pueblo del Arroyo

Chetro Ketl

Una Vida

Pueblo Bonito

7950

Casa Rinconada

Wijiji

57

0 km   2

0 miles   2

Chaco Canyon

Chaco Culture National Historical Park

Kennedy Space Center

THE VISITOR COMPLEX

Offering a wealth of exhibits, the Visitor Complex can easily take a whole day to explore. ▷ *Exploration in the New Millennium* offers a movie, lecture, and exhibits on the future of space exploration with the chance to touch a piece of a Mars meteorite. In the ▷ *Shuttle Plaza,* visitors can board and enjoy a close-up view of a full-sized replica of the space shuttle *Explorer.* The ▷ *Robot Scouts* display reveals the latest planetary explorer robots and the ▷ *Astronaut Encounter* show presents a chance to meet real astronauts. The ▷ *Astronaut Memorial* honors astronauts who have died in the service of space exploration.

APOLLO/SATURN V CENTER

North of the Visitor Complex, the ▷ *Apollo/Saturn V Center* offers a close look at the program and the rocket that sent men to the moon. In the Firing Room Theater, three screens recreate the 1968 launch of Apollo 8, the first manned mission to the moon. The theater is an authentic representation of the firing room, with original equipment on display. The Saturn V Rocket Plaza features an actual 111-m (363-ft) Saturn V moon rocket. The Lunar Surface Theater shows footage of the first lunar landing, and the New Frontiers Gallery features works representing NASA's bold vision of the future.

A shuttle lifting off from the launch tower

Kennedy Space Center

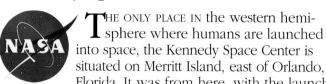

NASA insignia

The ONLY PLACE IN the western hemisphere where humans are launched into space, the Kennedy Space Center is situated on Merritt Island, east of Orlando, Florida. It was from here, with the launch of Apollo 11 in July 1969, that President Kennedy's dream of landing a man on the moon was realized. The center is the home of NASA (National Aeronautics and Space Administration), whose Space Shuttles can regularly be seen lifting off from one of the launch pads. With a scale and popularity comparable to Orlando's other theme parks, the Visitor Complex is both informative and entertaining.

Spacemen
Staff dressed up as astronauts wander throughout the center, allowing visitors to see a variety of NASA's space suit designs.

★ **Rocket Garden**
Among the towering rockets is an incredible Mercury Atlas, identical to the rocket that first launched John Glenn into space in 1962 for America's first orbit.

STAR FEATURES

★ **Apollo/Saturn V Center**

★ **Rocket Garden**

★ **KSC Bus Tour**

★ **IMAX® Films**

★ **Apollo/Saturn V Center**
A Saturn V rocket, of the kind used by the Apollo missions, is the showpiece here. There is also a reconstructed control room where visitors can experience a simulated rocket launch.

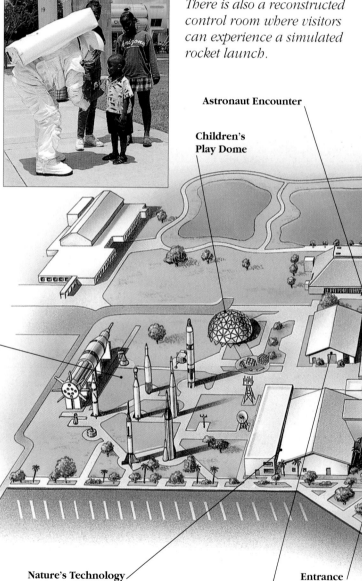

Astronaut Encounter

Children's Play Dome

Nature's Technology Universe Theater

Entrance

Exploration in the New Millennium

VISITOR COMPLEX

All visitors to the Kennedy Space Center must stop at the Visitor Complex, which was established in 1966 to offer bus tours of the area. It is now an extensive attraction with comprehensive movies, exhibitions, lectures, and galleries.

★ KSC Bus Tour

A bus tour makes a circuit of the center's launch pads, passing the Vehicle Assembly Building and the "crawlerway," along which the shuttle is slowly maneuvered into position.

SECURITY MEASURES

Any objects which could potentially be used as a weapon are not allowed to be carried into the space center. Visitors pass through metal detectors where bags are routinely inspected. On launch days, rucksacks are forbidden.

★ IMAX® Movies

At the Galaxy Center, huge IMAX® theaters run movies about space exploration. Footage from the shuttle missions offers some breathtaking views of Earth from space.

KEY DATES

1958 NASA is founded.

1961 Allan Shepard is the first American in space.

1969 The first men land on the Moon.

2003 The *Columbia* re-entry disintegration.

THE SPACE SHUTTLE PROGRAM

By the late 1970s, the cost of launching astronauts into space had become too much for the national budget. In response, NASA developed reusable orbital vehicles that could help build and supply a space station, and possibly prepare the way for manned exploration of the solar system. The shuttle *Columbia* lifted off in 1981. *Challenger* was the next shuttle added to the fleet, in 1982, and was followed by *Discovery*, *Atlantis*, and *Endeavor*. The fleet has had some remarkable accomplishments, including the launch and subsequent repair of the Hubble space telescope and the ongoing construction of the International Space Station. In 1998, *Discovery* carried John Glenn, the first American to orbit the Earth, back into space; Glenn was 77 years of age, the oldest man ever in space. The shuttle program has faced two disasters: the 1986 explosion on lift-off of *Challenger*, and the 2003 re-entry disintegration of *Columbia*. Following the latter, shuttle launches were suspended pending investigations.

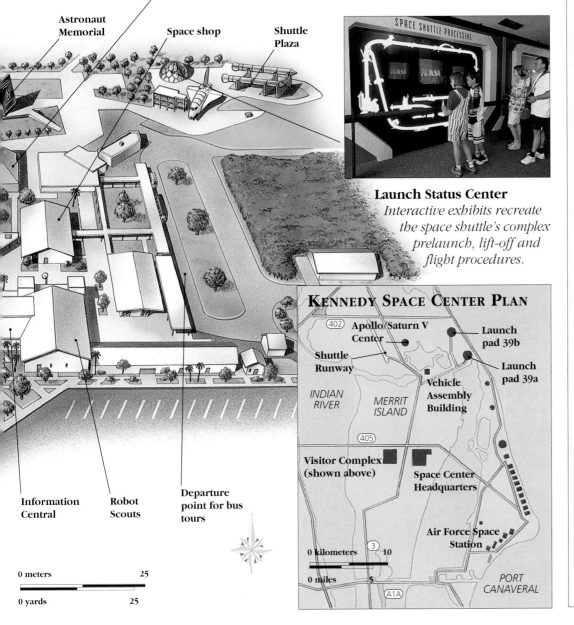

Astronaut Memorial

Space shop

Shuttle Plaza

Launch Status Center

Interactive exhibits recreate the space shuttle's complex prelaunch, lift-off and flight procedures.

Information Central

Robot Scouts

Departure point for bus tours

0 meters 25

0 yards 25

KENNEDY SPACE CENTER PLAN

402

Apollo/Saturn V Center

Launch pad 39b

Shuttle Runway

INDIAN RIVER

MERRIT ISLAND

Vehicle Assembly Building

Launch pad 39a

405

Visitor Complex (shown above)

Space Center Headquarters

3

Air Force Space Station

0 kilometers 10

0 miles 5

A1A

PORT CANAVERAL

MAYAN DEITIES

A vast array of gods and goddesses were worshiped by the Maya. Some of them related to celestial bodies, such as the stars, sun, and moon. Some had calendrical significance, while others held sway over creation, death, and aspects of daily life. Deities were feared as much as revered so it was essential to appease them as much as possible, often through human sacrifice. Kukulcan, a feathered serpent, was an important deity. Chac, the Mayan god of rain and lightning, was venerated as abundant rainfall was vital to farming communities. Also worshiped was Kinich Ahau, the "great sun" or "sun-eyed" lord. This deity was associated with the jaguar, an animal that evoked the vigor and power of the rising sun.

EL CASTILLO PYRAMID

Built around AD 800, the incredible ▷ El Castillo pyramid has a perfect astronomical design. The four staircases face the cardinal points, with various features corresponding to aspects of the Mayan calendar. At the two yearly equinoxes a fascinating optical illusion occurs whereby a serpent appears to crawl down the north staircase due to the play of light and shadow. The temple at the top of the inner pyramid contains a *chacmool*, a carved reclining figure, with a stone dish on its stomach thought to have held sacrificial offerings. There is also a beautiful, bright-red throne carved as a jaguar and encrusted with jade. The entrance to the temple is divided by snake-shaped columns.

A serpent's head representing the god Kukulcan, El Castillo

Chichén Itzá

Carved figure, Temple of the Warriors

THE BEST-PRESERVED Mayan site on the Yucatán peninsula, Chichén Itzá continues to confound archaeologists. The date of first settlement in the older, southern part of the site is uncertain, but the northern section was built during a Mayan renaissance in the 11th century AD. Similarities with Tula, the ancient capital of the Toltec empire, and myths of exiled Toltec god-king Quetzalcoatl (Kukulcan) settling at Chichén Itzá, suggest that the renaissance was due to a Toltec invasion. However, other theories hold that Tula was influenced by the Maya, not vice versa. In its heyday as a commercial, religious, and military center, which lasted until about the 13th century, Chichén Itzá supported over 35,000 people.

★ Ballcourt
At 168 m (550 ft) in length, this is the largest ballcourt in Mesoamerica. Still in place are the two engraved rings that the ball had to pass through.

Main entrance

Tomb of the High Priest

★ Observatory
Also called El Caracol (The Snail) for its spiral staircase, this building was an astronomical observatory. The various slits in the walls correspond to the positions of certain celestial bodies on key dates in the Mayan calendar.

Nunnery
So named because its small rooms reminded the Spaniards of nuns' cells, this large structure, built in three stages, was probably a palace. This façade of the east annex has particularly beautiful stone fretwork and carvings.

Chichén Viejo

The building known as "La Iglesia" is decorated with fretwork, masks of the rain god Chac, and the *bacabs* – four animals who, in Mayan myth, held up the sky.

| 0 meters | 150 |
| 0 yards | 150 |

The Tzompantli is a low platform whose perimeter is carved with grinning skulls. Archaeologists believe that it was used to display the heads of victims of human sacrifice, practised during Chichén Itzá's late period.

OFFERINGS

Incense, statues, jade, metal disks, and humans were cast into the ▷ *Sacred Cenote* in offering. Surviving sacrificial victims supposedly emerged with the power of prophesy, having conversed with deities.

Sacred Cenote

A sacbe (Mayan road) leads to this huge natural well, thought to have been revered as the home of rain god Chac, and used for human sacrifice.

KEY DATES

c.750 The Sacred Cenote is used for ritual offering.

c.900 Chichén Itzá becomes the center of Mayan culture.

1960–1 The Sacred Cenote is thoroughly dredged.

1988 Chichén Itzá is added to UNESCO's World Heritage Site list.

MAYAN CULTURE

Unlike the other peoples of Mesoamerica, the Maya did not develop a large, centralized empire. Instead they lived in independent city-states. Once thought to have been a peaceful people, the Maya are now known to have shared the lust for war and human sacrifice of other ancient civilizations. Immensely talented, they also cultivated a remarkable understanding of astronomy and developed sophisticated systems of writing, counting, and recording the passing of time (▷ *Observatory*). They observed and predicted the phases of the moon, equinoxes and solstices, and solar and lunar eclipses. They knew that the Morning and Evening Star were the same planet, Venus, and calculated its "year" to 584 days, within a fraction of the true figure (583.92 days). It is almost certain that they calculated the orbit of Mars as well. Remarkably, they achieved all this without the use of lenses for observing distant objects, instruments for calculating angles, or clocks to measure the passing of seconds, minutes, and hours.

Platform of the Jaguars and Eagles

★ El Castillo

Built on top of an older structure that can also be visited, this 24-m (79-ft) high pyramid was dedicated to Kukulcan, the Mayan representation of the god Quetzalcoatl. Its height and striking geometric design dominate the whole site.

The Group of a Thousand Columns, made up of carved stone colonnades on two sides of a huge plaza, may have been used as a market.

Entrance

Temple of the Warriors

Set on a small pyramid, this temple is decorated with sculptures of the rain god Chac and the plumed serpent Kukulcan. A chacmool and two columns, carved to represent snakes, guard the entrance.

STAR FEATURES

★ **Ballcourt**

★ **Observatory**

★ **El Castillo**

Carving showing the god Quetzalcoatl

THE GOD QUETZALCOATL

The most famous Mexican god was Quetzalcoatl, (called Kukulcan by the Maya). He was believed to be the son of Camaxtli and Chimalma. The first carvings of him were made by the Olmecs, who often portrayed him as a plumed or feathered serpent. He is sometimes depicted holding a thorn used for bloodletting, which was thought to give life to the dead. He was worshiped as the God of wind and the creator of heaven and earth by the Aztecs, who appeased him with human sacrifices. Slaves captured during wars were often killed by priests as offerings. Legend says that Quetzalcoatl was driven from Mexico by a superior God but that he promised to return in the future.

LOS VOLADORES RITUAL

During this ancient Nahua and Totonac ritual, five men known as ▷ *los voladores* climb to the top of a pole often as high as 30 m (100 ft). While one plays a drum and a reed-pipe on a tiny platform at the top, the other four "fly" to the ground, suspended on ropes. Each *volador* circles the pole 13 times before reaching the ground, making a total of 52 turns. This symbolizes the 52-year cycles of the Mesoamerican calendar. The central pole represents a vertical connection between the Earth, the heaven above, and the underworld below.

El Tajín

O NE OF MEXICO's best-preserved pre-Hispanic cities, El Tajín was a political and religious center for the Totonac civilization. Many of its buildings date from between AD 900 and 1150. Decorated with relief panels and sculptures, they would have been painted in strong colors such as red, blue, and black. The excavated nucleus of this spectacular ancient city covers about 1 sq km (0.4 sq miles), but the entire urban area once spread over 10 sq km (4 sq miles) and had a population of 25,000.

★ Pyramid of the Niches
Originally crowned by a temple, this pyramid has 365 niches, representing the days of the year. Each niche may have held an offering.

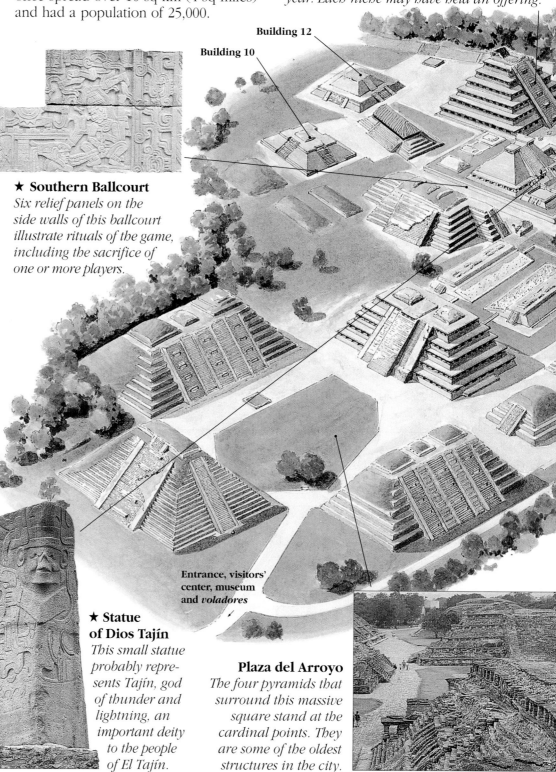

Building 12

Building 10

★ Southern Ballcourt
Six relief panels on the side walls of this ballcourt illustrate rituals of the game, including the sacrifice of one or more players.

Entrance, visitors' center, museum and *voladores*

★ Statue of Dios Tajín
This small statue probably represents Tajín, god of thunder and lightning, an important deity to the people of El Tajín.

Plaza del Arroyo
The four pyramids that surround this massive square stand at the cardinal points. They are some of the oldest structures in the city.

Los Voladores

This ancient ritual of the Totonac people takes place near the site entrance. The voladores wear brightly colored velvet panels decorated with sequins and beads. Their headdresses are adorned with mirrors and plastic flowers.

THE TOTONACS

Totonac Indians settled near the Mexican state of Veracruz. In the 13th century they were overthrown by the Aztecs, but when the Spanish arrived in 1519 the Totonacs assisted them in conquering the Aztecs.

KEY DATES

9th–13th century The El Tajín site is occupied by the Totonacs.

1992 El Tajín is inscribed a UNESCO World Heritage Site.

THE BALL GAME

More than a sport or a form of entertainment, the ball game that was played throughout Mesoamerica had a ritual significance. Two teams would compete against each other to manipulate a large rubber ball through a stone ring set high on the wall on each side of the court. The ball had to be kept off the ground using only knees, elbows, or hips, never the hands or feet. The I-shaped ballcourt varied in size, but early examples were usually aligned north-south and later ones east-west. Ballcourts have been found at all the main pre-Columbian sites, the largest being at Chichén Itzá. The cities of Cantona and El Tajín also had a number of ballcourts. It is thought that the losers of the game were subsequently sacrificed after a match. This was considered an honorable way to die. Carved panels in the ▷ *Southern Ballcourt* show two victors killing one of the losing team with an obsidian knife, while a third player looks on from the right. A savage-looking death god descends from the skyband at the top of the panel to receive the human offering. Today a less-lethal version of the ball game, called *hulama*, is still played by Mexicans in the northern state of Sinaloa.

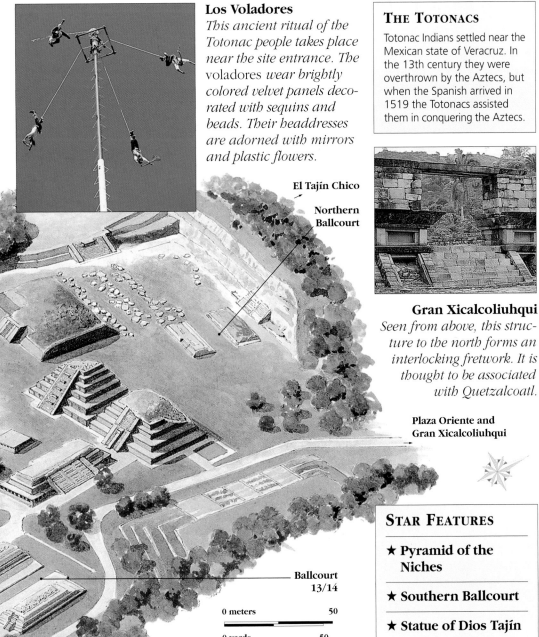

El Tajín Chico

Northern Ballcourt

Gran Xicalcoliuhqui
Seen from above, this structure to the north forms an interlocking fretwork. It is thought to be associated with Quetzalcoatl.

Plaza Oriente and Gran Xicalcoliuhqui

Ballcourt 13/14

| 0 meters | 50 |
| 0 yards | 50 |

STAR FEATURES

★ **Pyramid of the Niches**

★ **Southern Ballcourt**

★ **Statue of Dios Tajín**

El Tajín

PLAN OF SITE

The buildings in the lower part of the site were used for ceremonial or religious purposes only.

The Building of the Columns, on the highest part of the site, was the home of the ruler known as 13 Rabbit.

El Tajín Chico, the middle level of the site, was the residential area for the elite ruling class.

Entrance, museum and *voladores*

Pyramid of the Niches

| 0 meters | 100 |
| 0 yards | 100 |

PLAZA DEL ARROYO

PLAZA ORIENTE

Gran Xicalcoliuhqui

PLAZA DE HURAKAN

KEY

▢ Illustrated area

Quetzalpapalotl Palace Complex, Teotihuacán

Iᴛs ɴᴀᴍᴇ ᴍᴇᴀɴɪɴɢ "the place where men become gods," Teotihuacán is one of the most impressive cities of the ancient world. The maze of residential and temple structures of the Quetzalpapalotl Palace Complex grew over several centuries. Probably the last part to be built was the elegant Palace of Quetzalpapalotl itself which sits atop the now buried Temple of the Feathered Conches (2nd century AD).

Pyramid of the Sun, one of the biggest pyramids in the world

Pʏʀᴀᴍɪᴅs & Tᴇᴍᴘʟᴇs

Teotihuacán was an urban and ceremonial center with temples, palaces, and pyramids. The two edifices which dominate the site are the ▷ *Pyramid of the Moon* and the Pyramid of the Sun. The latter is the larger of the two, and was constructed during the 2nd century AD. It contained chambers and a tunnel beneath the structure. Made of adobe bricks and earth, and covered with gravel and stone, it would have been coated with painted stucco. Towards the south, along the Avenue of the Dead, is the Temple of Quetzalcoatl. This was decorated with masks of the plumed serpent and was later covered by a pyramid.

Tʜᴇ Mʏᴛʜ ᴏғ ᴛʜᴇ Bɪʀᴅ-Bᴜᴛᴛᴇʀғʟʏ

The word *quetzalpapalotl* derives from the Nahuatl word *quetzal* for bird and *papalotl* for butterfly. The myth sprung from the belief that butterflies and hummingbirds were the same. It was thought that with the onset of winter hummingbirds would drive their beaks into a branch, leaving their lifeless bodies hanging from the tree. Their feathers would fall, leaving behind a sack from which a new bird-butterfly would emerge the following spring. The sacks were in fact caterpillar cocoons. It was also believed that on occasions the bird-butterflies would metamorphose into gods.

The Palace of Quetzalpapalotl
This building is so named because of the mythological creatures carved into its courtyard pillars. These bird-butterflies with obsidian eyes are flanked by water and fire symbols.

Murals in the Jaguar Palace
Plumed jaguars playing musical instruments made from feathered shells decorate this palace.

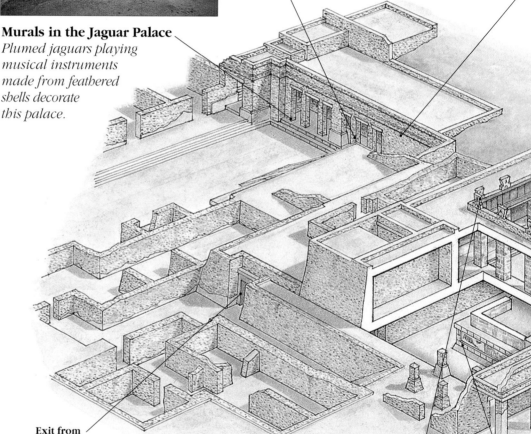

Entrance to lower level

Exit from lower level

Decorative merlons
symbolizing the calendar crown the courtyard.

The Temple of the Feathered Conches
This temple is an older structure that archaeologists discovered buried beneath the Palace of Quetzalpapalotl. It sits on a platform adorned with brilliantly colored murals such as this one, which depict green parrot-like birds spewing water from their beaks. Reliefs of feathered conches and four-petaled flowers decorate the temple façade.

Pyramid of the Moon

Although smaller than the Pyramid of the Sun, this four-tiered structure rises just as high, due to a difference in ground level.

FALL OF THE CITY

Although no records explain the city's demise, it is thought that the concentration of such a large population led to ecological ruin. Deforestation, soil erosion, and water crises, combined with poor governance, may have led to its downfall.

Stone Serpent's Head

Guarding the porticoed entrance to the Palace of Quetzalpapalotl is this stone serpent's head. The sculpture juts out from the top of a steep staircase and is of enormous proportions.

Carving of Quetzalcoatl

Throughout Teotihuacán, carvings of the plumed serpent Quetzalcoatl, a combination of the quetzal bird and rattlesnake, decorate the walls of the temples.

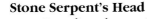

Temple platform

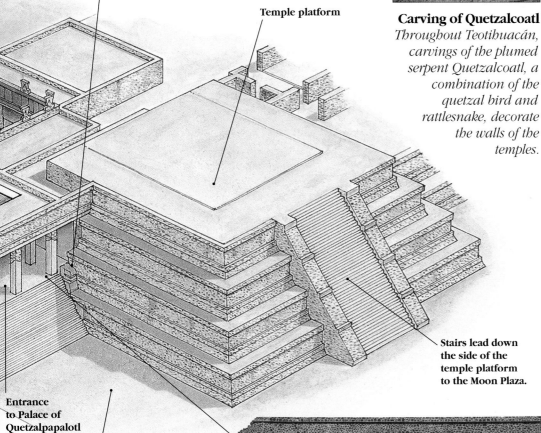

Stairs lead down the side of the temple platform to the Moon Plaza.

Entrance to Palace of Quetzalpapalotl

Moon Plaza

Priests' Residence

The square pillars indicate that the priests, the elite of Teotihuacán and the custodians of the Temple of the Moon, lived here.

KEY DATES

AD 100–200 Intensive building work at Teotihuacán.

500 Teotihuacán reaches the height of its power, influencing much of the Meso-American region.

c.750 Quetzalpapalotl Palace is ritually destroyed and burned along with the other major palaces and temples of the city.

c.850 The city collapses; only local peasants remain in the surrounding area.

1962 Palace of Quetzalpapalotl is excavated and reconstruction of the building begins.

1987 Teotihuacán becomes a UNESCO World Heritage Site.

THE JAGUAR AND FEATHERED CONCH

The importance of the jaguar in Mexican mythology dates back hundreds of years before Teotihuacán was founded. Cults relating to it have also been identified throughout pre-Columbian Latin America. Contemporary popular belief held that the big cat represented the earth and was one of the three animals that the god Quetzalcoatl embodied. In the ▷ *Jaguar Palace* the murals depict the jaguar playing a conch trumpet and taking on human characteristics. These shells were valuable items for the city. Their association with water, and its vitality, may be the reason for their prominence.

Metropolitan Cathedral

THE INTERIOR

Like the exterior, the interior decoration reflects a blend of the prevalent colonial period styles. Its Baroque altars and side chapels are particularly ornate. A highlight is the richly carved ▷ *Altar de los Reyes*. A statue of Christ, the *Señor del Cacao*, probably dating from the 16th century, is worshiped in the ▷ *Capilla de San José*. Its name derives from the donations made in cocoa beans by the indigenous people toward the construction of the cathedral – a common currency during the pre-colonial era. An urn containing the remains of Emperor Agustín de Iturbide (1783–1824), the champion of Mexican Independence, is located in the chapel of San Felipe de Jesús.

The southern façade of the Metropolitan Cathedral

THE CONQUISTADORS AND CHRISTIANITY

When the Spanish conquistadors arrived in the New World in the 1500s, they encountered flourishing indigenous settlements. In addition to their desire for conquest and greed for gold, silver, copper, and land, the conquistadors also saw themselves as missionaries, attempting to convert the established civilizations from paganism to Christianity. Franciscan and Dominican friars tirelessly preached to, converted, and baptized the Mesoamericans. Although the New World was ultimately conquered, elements of the indigenous cultures survived and were absorbed into the developing Christian society.

Metropolitan Cathedral, Mexico City

Hymn book on view in the choir

THE BIGGEST CHURCH in Latin America, Mexico City's cathedral is also at the heart of the world's largest Catholic diocese. Its towers rise 67 m (220 ft) above one of the largest public squares in the world, and it took almost three centuries – from 1525 to 1813 – to complete. This long period is reflected in the multiple styles of its architecture, ranging from Classical through Baroque (▷ *Baroque Style p111*) to Neo-Classical (▷ *Neo-Classical Style p79*). It has five principal altars and 16 side chapels containing a valuable collection of paintings, sculpture, and church furniture.

Sacristy
The sacristy contains 17th-century paintings and items of carved furniture such as this decorated cabinet.

Kings and Queens
The sculptures adorning the Altar de los Reyes are of kings and queens who have been canonized.

The high altar is a block of white marble carved with images of saints.

Side entrance

★ **Altar de los Reyes**
The two oil paintings on this Baroque masterpiece are the Adoration of the Kings *and the* Assumption of the Virgin, *both by Juan Rodríguez Juárez.*

STAR FEATURES
★ **Altar de los Reyes**
★ **Choir**

Capilla de San José
This side chapel is one of 16 dedicated to saints and manifestations of the Virgin, all exquisitely decorated with statues and oil paintings.

The Sinking Cathedral
The cathedral is sinking into the soft clay of what was once the bed of Lake Texcoco. Scaffolding has been installed in the interior in an attempt to stabilize the building.

ALTAR OF PARDON
A figure of the Virgin, by Simón Pereyns, was replaced after the 1967 fire with a black Christ which, legend says, absorbed the poison from a devout man who kissed it on his deathbed.

Sagrario Metropolitano
Built in the mid-18th century as the parish church attached to the cathedral, the Sagrario has a sumptuous high Baroque façade adorned with sculpted saints.

KEY DATES

1521 Construction starts on the cathedral.

1667 The cathedral is consecrated.

1967 Fire causes damage to parts of the cathedral.

1985 A powerful earthquake damages the cathedral.

1987 The Historic Center of Mexico City is inscribed a UNESCO World Heritage Site.

THE SINKING OF MEXICO CITY

When Spanish conquistador Hernán Cortés led his army into the Aztec capital of Tenochtitlán in 1521, it stood on an island in Lake Texcoco. After conquering the city the Spanish razed it to the ground, reusing much of the stonework in their own constructions and gradually filling in the lake. The cathedral was built on the ruins of the main Aztec temple of worship whose stones were used in the building's walls. Like so many of Mexico City's buildings, the cathedral has been sinking, almost since its initial construction, into the ground beneath – the slant is quite visible despite extensive work to stabilize the structure in recent years (▷ *The Sinking Cathedral*). This is due to the large amount of water pumped from the aquifer beneath the city which supplies the needs of the rapidly-growing city.

The clocktower is decorated with statues of Faith, Hope, and Charity.

The façade is divided into three parts and flanked by monumental bell towers.

Main entrance

★ Choir
With its gold-alloy choir-rail imported from Macao, superbly carved stalls, and two magnificent organs, the choir is a highlight of the cathedral.

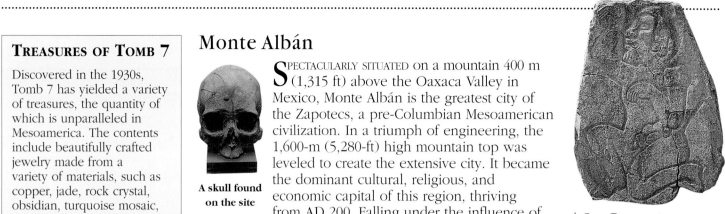

Treasures of Tomb 7

Discovered in the 1930s, Tomb 7 has yielded a variety of treasures, the quantity of which is unparalleled in Mesoamerica. The contents include beautifully crafted jewelry made from a variety of materials, such as copper, jade, rock crystal, obsidian, turquoise mosaic, amber, and coral. The finds also reveal how skilled craftsmen used the bones and teeth of jaguars, a symbolic animal, to produce delicately carved objects and beads made of finely incised molars. A wealth of silverware, including bracelets, tweezers, plaques, rings, and bells, was also buried along with the dignitary in the tomb. Although the owner and his goods date to the post-Classic period (1350–1521), the tomb is much older. First constructed in period I (650–200 BC), the burial chamber was reused several times.

Mesoamerican Terraced Pyramids

Like the Zapotecs, many other Mesoamerican cultures created massive stepped pyramids, which they used for ceremonial purposes. These evolved from thatched-roof, perishable buildings that were the focus of village life. The terraced pyramids that remain today are typically crowned with a temple. For the Aztecs they were the site of human sacrifices, while for the Maya they were usually funerary buildings. Mayan ceremonial pyramids provided the core around which the rest of the city was built, and the temples' levels or stories represented the planes of the underworld. Most pyramids were built on top of earlier temples.

Pottery urn for ashes of the dead, Oaxaca Valley

Monte Albán

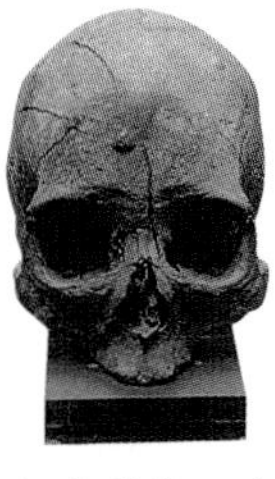

A skull found on the site

Spectacularly situated on a mountain 400 m (1,315 ft) above the Oaxaca Valley in Mexico, Monte Albán is the greatest city of the Zapotecs, a pre-Columbian Mesoamerican civilization. In a triumph of engineering, the 1,600-m (5,280-ft) high mountain top was leveled to create the extensive city. It became the dominant cultural, religious, and economic capital of this region, thriving from AD 200. Falling under the influence of the city of Teotihuacán during the height of its power, Monte Albán declined in later years and by AD 800 was largely abandoned. In the 13th century, it was adopted by the Mixtecs as a ceremonial center, primarily as the site for some magnificent gold-laden burials.

★ Los Danzantes
This gallery of carvings shows humans in strange, tortured positions. Once identified as dancers, they are now thought to be prisoners of war.

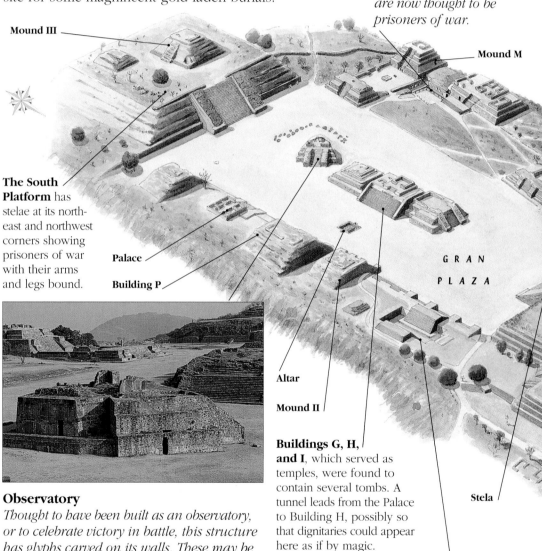

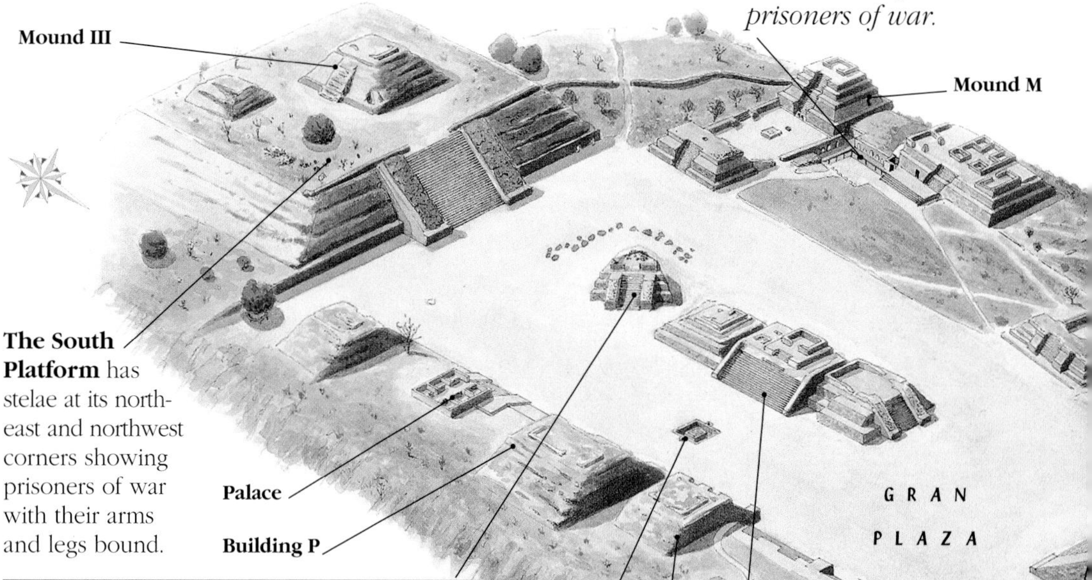
Mound III
Mound M
Palace
Building P
Altar
Mound II
GRAN PLAZA
Stela

The South Platform has stelae at its northeast and northwest corners showing prisoners of war with their arms and legs bound.

Buildings G, H, and I, which served as temples, were found to contain several tombs. A tunnel leads from the Palace to Building H, possibly so that dignitaries could appear here as if by magic.

Observatory
Thought to have been built as an observatory, or to celebrate victory in battle, this structure has glyphs carved on its walls. These may be the names of conquered tribes.

Ballcourt
A typical ballcourt, this I-shaped structure was used for playing the ceremonial ballgame. There would originally have been a stone ring at the top of each sloping side to act as a "goal".

The enormous Gran Plaza, aligned on a north-south axis

EARLY CALENDARS

The Zapotecs produced the first written calendars in Mesoamerica. In Monte Albán, two were created, one based on the agricultural cycle and one on the solar year. Both calendars included systems of naming for the days and months.

System IV is almost identical to Mound M. Both are well-preserved pyramids that would once have been surmounted by one-room wooden temples.

The Sunken Patio has an altar at its center.

Building B

★ **Tomb 104**
Above the entrance to Tomb 104 is this ceramic urn in the form of a figure seated on a jaguar throne. An image of Cocijo, the Zapotec rain god, is in the center of the head-dress. When the tomb was opened in 1937 a vaulted burial chamber containing a single skeleton, surrounded by urns, perfume pots, and other offerings, was discovered.

KEY DATES

c.800 BC The Olmecs build simple structures on the site of Monte Albán.

c.600 BC First Zapotec settlement begins.

c.AD 600 Monte Albán reaches its zenith.

c.900 After 200 years of decline, the Zapotecs abandon the city.

1931 Excavation begins by Mexican archaeologist Alfonso Caso.

1987 Monte Albán becomes a UNESCO World Heritage Site.

EARLY CIVILIZATIONS

The Olmecs emerged around 1200 BC and were the first to settle in the area around Monte Albán. Often called the *cultura madre* (mother culture) because of their influence on later civilizations, the Olmecs constructed ceremonial centers rather than cities. They traded widely, spreading their influence throughout Central America until their gradual decline around 800 BC. The Zapotecs settled in the Oaxaca Valley around 600 BC. They adopted and developed Monte Albán dominating the entire region for over 1,000 years. Influenced by the Olmecs, they developed the Mesoamerican calendar, and the hieroglyphs found in the city (▷ *Observatory*) are examples of the earliest writing known in the Americas. Eventually control of Monte Albán passed to the Mixtecs, in AD 800.

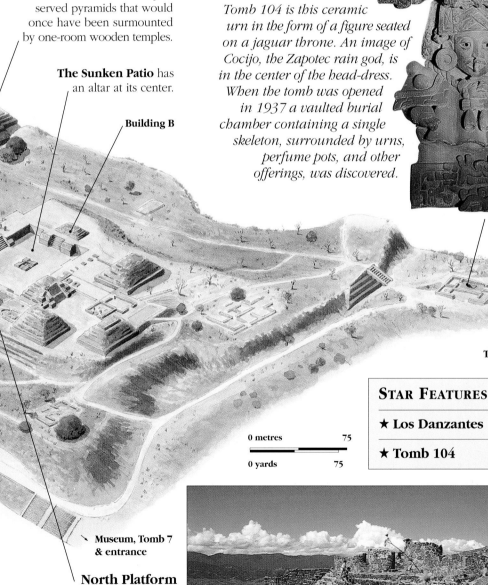

Tomb 103

STAR FEATURES

★ **Los Danzantes**

★ **Tomb 104**

0 metres 75

0 yards 75

Museum, Tomb 7 & entrance

North Platform
A broad staircase leads up to the North Platform, the largest structure at Monte Albán. At the top of the steps are two rows of broken columns that would once have supported a flat roof.

Palace of the Captain Generals

CUBAN BAROQUE ARCHITECTURE

The 18th century was a golden age of civic architecture in Cuba, characterized by Baroque ideals (▷ *Baroque Style p111*) imported at a late stage from Europe. Designs were adapted to the tropical climate to maximize shade and ventilation, maintaining typical Spanish elements such as a central courtyard. Colonial mansions typically had two floors, with spacious rooms and shallow staircases. The Palace of the Captain Generals has thick stone walls, arches, columns, porticoes, and balconies. Other Baroque gems in Havana are the Palace of the Second Cabo (1776), once the residence of the Spanish lieutenant governor, and Havana Cathedral (begun in 1748). More 18th-century colonial buildings are in the town of Trinidad, on Cuba's south coast.

CUBA'S CULTURAL EVOLUTION

The explorer Christopher Columbus first landed in Cuba in 1492 on his first voyage of discovery to the New World. From 1510–16 Diego Velázquez de Cuellar, commissioned by Columbus' son, set about annexing the island to Spain and in time the Spanish began to use the island as a base. In the 17th century the population increased with the arrival of Spanish settlers and African slaves. The 18th century marked the birth of a Creole aristocracy. These people, Cuban-born of Spanish descent, commissioned buildings which can still be seen today, and led a colonial lifestyle based on a combination of Indian, Spanish, and African traditions.

The richly decorated entrance, added in 1835

Palace of the Captain Generals, Havana

Early 19th-century marble bathtub in the bathroom

A SPLENDID EXAMPLE OF Cuban Baroque, this imposing palace was constructed between 1776 and 1792. It was commissioned by the governor Felipe Fondesviela and designed by engineer Antonio Fernández de Trebejos y Zaldívar. The palace originally housed the Chapter House and the governor's residence as well as a house of detention, which until 1834 occupied the west wing. The seat of the Cuban Republic in 1902, the building became the Museo de la Ciudad (City Museum) in 1967, but the original structure of the sumptuous residence and political center has not been altered. The complex as a whole offers an overview of the history of Havana, from the remains of the old Espada cemetery and Parroquial Mayor church to mementos from the wars of independence in the 19th century.

Hall of Heroic Cuba
This hall contains various objects and memorabilia from the independence wars.

The Cabildo Maces
Considered the first major example of Cuban goldsmithery, these maces, by Juan Díaz (1631), are on display in the Sala del Cabildo, the room where local town council meetings were held in the governor's palace.

★ **Cenotaph from the Parroquial Mayor Church**
In 1557 the oldest Colonial monument in Cuba was placed in the old Parroquial Mayor (parish church), which then stood on this site. It commemorates the death of a young woman who was killed by accident while she was praying.

STAR FEATURES

★ **Cenotaph from the Parroquial Mayor Church**

★ **La Giraldilla**

★ **Salón de los Espejos**

★ **La Giraldilla**
At the foot of the steps leading to the mezzanine is the oldest bronze statue in Cuba. It was commissioned by the governor, Juan Bitrián de Viamonte, for the lookout tower of the Real Fuerza fortress.

Gallery

The monumental gallery, which overlooks a large, leafy courtyard, features a collection of busts of illustrious figures, the work of the Italian sculptor Luigi Pietrasanta in the early 1900s.

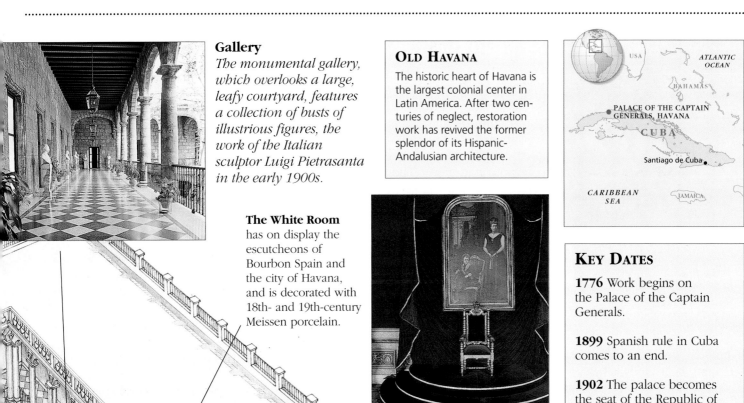

Old Havana

The historic heart of Havana is the largest colonial center in Latin America. After two centuries of neglect, restoration work has revived the former splendor of its Hispanic-Andalusian architecture.

The White Room

has on display the escutcheons of Bourbon Spain and the city of Havana, and is decorated with 18th- and 19th-century Meissen porcelain.

Throne Room

Modeled on the large salon in the Palace of Orient in Madrid, this room was originally built for a Spanish monarch, but never used. It was restored in 1893 for the visit of Princess Eulalia of Bourbon.

The stained-glass windows brighten the grey of the *piedra marina*, a limestone encrusted with coral fossils.

The Espada Cemetery Room

has relics from the first city cemetery, founded by Bishop Juan José Díaz de Espada in 1806. They include the tomb of the French artist Vermay.

★ Salón de los Espejos

The end of Spanish rule was proclaimed in 1899 in this light-filled salon with its 19th-century Venetian mirrors, and in 1902 the first president of the Republic of Cuba took office here.

The portico pavement, made of *china pelona*, a hard, shiny stone, dates from the 18th century.

Key Dates

1776 Work begins on the Palace of the Captain Generals.

1899 Spanish rule in Cuba comes to an end.

1902 The palace becomes the seat of the Republic of Cuba.

1967 The Museo de la Ciudad (City Museum) opens in the palace.

1982 Old Havana, which includes the Palace of the Captain Generals, joins the UNESCO World Heritage Sites list.

Governing Cuba

Pope Alexander VI granted control of the island of Cuba to Spain in 1493. Later, dissatisfied with the lack of gold in Cuba, the Spanish began to use the island both as a base from which they set out to conquer other American territory, as well as a port of call for ships taking the riches of the New World back to Spain. Spanish rule was enforced from the Palace of the Captain Generals. During this period, trade in sugar and slaves was booming and Havana prospered. Between 1791 and 1898 the palace was home to 65 Captain Generals, or colonial rulers, and was the seat of national and city government. Slavery was abolished in 1886 and Spanish rule came to an end in 1899. Post-independence, the palace became the official residence of the president of Cuba.

Palace of the Captain Generals

El Morro Castle, Santiago de Cuba

A T THE ENTRANCE TO THE BAY OF SANTIAGO, 10 km (6 miles) southwest of Santiago city, stands the imposing Castillo del Morro, the finest fortress in Cuba. The Castillo seen today was designed in the 1630s by Giovan Battista Antonelli for the governor Pedro de la Roca, with the aim of defending the city against constant pirate raids. The structure has medieval and Renaissance elements (▷ *Renaissance Style p211*) and is large enough to house 400 soldiers. Construction and reconstruction of this huge citadel continued until 1693. In 1662, it was damaged by the British. Converted into a prison in 1775, it became a fortress once again in 1898 during the Wars of Independence, when the US fleet attacked the Spanish in Santiago Bay. The fortress was restored to its present state in the 1960s.

British privateer Sir Henry Morgan (1635–88)

CARIBBEAN PIRATES

In the 16th century the battle for the spoils of South America meant that Spanish galleons loaded with treasure and Spanish ports in the Caribbean were a target for looting pirates. Indeed, it is recorded that Santiago de Cuba was subjected to pirate attacks for 24 successive years from 1538. Later, in the 17th century, the French, followed by the Dutch and the British, sent out ships to attack their enemy, Spain, and to protect their colonies. Two of the most notorious English privateers who sailed under the British flag were Christopher Myngs (1625–66) and Henry Morgan. These men fought like pirates but were acting as representatives of the British government, and later were knighted for their services.

GIOVAN BATTISTA ANTONELLI

An Italian military engineer and architect, Giovan Battista Antonelli designed the Castillo del Morro fortress to repel pirates. He was also responsible for other innovative defense devices and fortifications in the Caribbean, including an ingenious floating chain linking Castillo de San Salvador de la Punta and Castillo de los Tres Reyes, on either side of Havana bay, that kept ships from entering.

A cannon, part of the old battery used to defend the bay

In the casemates a display of prints illustrates the history of Santiago's forts.

Artillery area

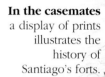

★ **View of the Bay**
The parapets and lookouts on the upper parts of the fortress were used by the sentries to keep watch.

Underground passageways link the various parts of the castle. This one leads to the artillery area.

The stone stairway on the side of the castle facing the sea is part of an open-air network of steps leading to the upper levels.

STAR FEATURES
★ View of the Bay
★ Central Square

Plataforma de la Punta (*morrillo*, or bluff)

Triangular Lunette
Built in 1590–1610 as the protection for the fortress gate, this structure was originally separate from the castle. It was later incorporated into the main structure.

KEY DATES

1633–1639 Castillo del Morro is constructed.

1662 British attack Castillo.

1667 Castillo is rebuilt.

1960s Restoration work commences.

1978 Museo de la Piratería opens to the public.

1997 Castillo joins UNESCO's World Heritage Site list.

Drawbridge
This bridge passes over a dry moat that runs alongside the fortification on the inland side. It is well preserved, and still has the original winch that was used to raise and lower the bridge.

Dry moat

★ **Central Square**
This square, the nerve center of the castle, was used as an area for organizing daily activities. The square provides access to the chapel, barracks, garrison, and underground rooms.

SUGAR AND SLAVES

Slaves were brought to the Caribbean from Africa in great numbers from the late 18th to the early 19th centuries. About one million men and women were brought to Cuba, and by around 1830 black Africans, including slaves and legally freed slaves, made up more than half of the country's population. At the beginning of the 19th century the Cuban sugar industry was booming, thanks to the growing demand for sugar in Europe and America. This was made possible by the labor of Cuba's large slave population. The island became the world's leading sugar manufacturer, and the industry continued to thrive after the abolition of slavery. Life on the sugar plantations therefore became a key feature of the island's history and society. Because of its location, Santiago was the first city in Cuba where African slaves were landed. Many were held in transit in cells within Castillo del Morro.

SANTIAGO'S FOUNDER

Founded in 1515, Santiago de Cuba was one of seven cities established in the 16th century by a small group of Spaniards led by Diego Velázquez de Cuéllar, who named the port Santiago (St James) after the patron saint of Spain. Santiago was the island's capital until 1607 and is now its second city historically. Velázquez's house in the city center, which is a fine example of the Cuban Mudéjar Style (▷ *Mudéjar Style p194*) is considered by some to be the oldest private house in Cuba and has been declared a national monument because of its historic value.

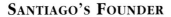
The courtyard in a wing of Diego Velázquez's house

Three separate main structures, built on five different levels, form the skeleton of the castle. This unusual construction is due to the uneven terrain of the headland.

El Morro Castle

Inca terraces and irrigation channels preventing soil erosion

INCA ARCHITECTURE

The people who built this most famous of Inca sites displayed incredibly advanced construction methods. Despite some of the building blocks weighing more than 50 tons, they are meticulously designed and fit together so exactly that the thinnest knife cannot be inserted between the mortarless joints. The ruins are roughly divided into two areas: the agricultural sector, consisting of terraces for cultivation; and the urban sector, with different sized structures, canals, and steps. The design of the site emphasizes the esthetic creativity of the builders. The enormous walls, delicate terracing, and steep ramps could almost have been sculpted by the elements into the rock.

HIRAM BINGHAM

When this major Inca site buried in undergrowth was discovered, it was one of the most significant archaeological discoveries of the 20th century. American explorer Hiram Bingham had set out to find Vilcabamba, the legendary last refuge of the defeated Inca Empire, but instead he came across Machu Picchu. It took Bingham and his team several years to clear the massive growth of jungle that had covered the ruins. Underneath were houses, temples, canals, and thousands of steps and terraces. What made his discovery so exciting was not only the fact that the Spanish conquistadors had never discovered Machu Picchu, but also that the site had been completely untouched by treasure hunters.

Machu Picchu

THIS LOST CITY of the Incas is one of the most spectacular archaeological sites in the world. Perched high on a saddle between two peaks, surrounded by thick jungle and often shrouded in clouds, it is almost invisible from below. A compact site of just 13 sq km (5 sq miles), it was built in AD 1460 by the Inca ruler Pachacuti Inca Yupanqui. Although frequently referred to as a city, it was more of a royal retreat for the Inca aristocracy. About 1,000 people inhabited the area and they were completely self-sufficient, being surrounded by agricultural terraces and watered by natural springs. Even at the time, few people outside the closed Inca community were even aware of Machu Picchu's existence.

★ **Intihuatana**
This sundial, the size of a grand piano, was extremely sacred and one of the most important features of the whole site. Winter solstice festivals would take place here.

★ **Sacred Plaza**
With huge windows, the Temple of the Three Windows adjoins the Sacred Plaza, along with the Main Temple, which contains a wall almost flawlessly constructed.

STAR FEATURES

★ **Intihuatana**

★ **Sacred Plaza**

★ **Temple of the Sun**

0 meters   25

0 yards   25

The Sacred Rock is a large rock which is believed to have been used by the Incas for their sacrificial rituals.

View of Machu Picchu
Made up of around 200 buildings and connected by more than 100 stairways, the ruined palaces, temples and residences were built around large central squares.

Residential and industrial areas within the urban sector

Agricultural terraces

MACHU PICCHU TRAIN

A train for the site leaves the town of Cusco on a regular basis. It makes the scenic 5-hour journey through the valley to Aguas Calientes, a town just below Machu Picchu. From here a local bus zig-zags up the mountain to this historical Inca site.

Preserved Brick Work
The Incas are admired today for their stone constructions, although it is unknown how they managed to make the blocks fit so closely together.

★ Temple of the Sun
The only circular building on the site, this temple contains two windows positioned precisely to catch the first rays of the winter and summer solstices.

THE INCA TRAIL

The legendary Inca Trail climbs and descends a number of steep valleys and crosses three mountain passes of more than 3,658 m (12,000 ft). The breathtaking scenery includes snow-capped mountains, dense cloud forest and delicate flowers. Cobblestones laid by the Incas, as well as the tunnels that they constructed, can still be seen. It takes about four or five days before hikers are rewarded with the unforgettable sight of Machu Picchu through the sun gate (Intipunku).

Majestic view of Machu Picchu at the end of the Inca Trail

KEY DATES

c.1200 Rise of the Inca Empire.

1460 Machu Picchu is constructed by the Incas.

Mid-1500s Machu Picchu is abandoned, possibly due to civil war over succession.

1911 Site is discovered by Hiram Bingham.

1983 Declared a World Heritage Site by UNESCO.

INCA CULTURE

Although at its peak the Inca Empire only lasted a century, it ruled around 12 million people and reached from Chile to Colombia. This incredibly organized civilization had a sophisticated economy and social system and an efficient road network of nearly 32,200 km (20,000 miles). The Incas ruled with fierce military might and had a strict social hierarchy, yet also managed to learn from the cultures they conquered. Worshiping the natural world, they saw the sun as the ultimate giver of life, believing their leader to be its direct descendant and that the mountain peaks, where they made human sacrifices, were the home of spirits. Celestial events were monitored so they knew when to plant and harvest crops and when to hold religious ceremonies. Machu Picchu stands as testimony to the sophistication of the Inca society, demonstrating what the New World had already achieved prior to Spanish arrival.

Machu Picchu

THE LAYOUT OF THE CITY

The city's unique design is referred to as the ▷ *Pilot Plan*. Urban planner Lucio Costa said he simply used a shape that followed the lie of the land. He wanted to form a centralized, geometric city plan to create an ideal city and therefore an ideal society. The design is based on two axes (▷ *Monumental Axis* and ▷ *Residential Axis*). Six wide avenues were intended to provide the grandeur of a capital city, with the ▷ *Supreme Court*, ▷ *Congress Complex*, and Presidential Palace (▷ *Planalto Palace*) representing the balance of the three powers. The residential area is made up of large six-story "super-blocks", each grouped to form a neighborhood.

Statues of apostles by Alfredo Ceschiatti, Brasília Cathedral

THE COMPETITION

In 1957 Lucio Costa and Oscar Niemeyer were announced as the winners of the competition launched to choose the urban design of Brasília. Costa was responsible for the general design of Brasília, but Niemeyer created the main buildings. Both were students of the modernist Le Corbusier, the father of functional, box-like buildings. Costa has been criticized for not providing for public transport and for designing a city for 500,000 people which today accommodates two million residents, many living in slums. However, it is generally agreed that Niemeyer achieved his aim of creating a city with "harmony and a sense of occasion" with his powerful public buildings.

Brasília

A 20TH-CENTURY CITY of pure invention, Brasília is the realization of a seemingly impossible dream. President Juscelino Kubitschek de Oliveira (1956–60) was elected partly on the basis of his highly ambitious pledge to move the capital of Brazil 1,200 km (746 miles) inland, from Rio de Janeiro into the country's empty center, before the end of his first term. This was miraculously achieved by tens of thousands of workers who created the purpose-built city from an area of scrubland. The principal public buildings, which include the cathedral, are each strikingly designed. Brasília fulfilled Kubitschek's ambition to develop the interior and to create a monument both to modern architecture and the country's economic potential.

JK Memorial
Inaugurated in 1981, this monument was built to honor the former Brazilian President Juscelino Kubitschek, whose tomb is housed here.

Monumental Axis
Light gilds the row of rectangular buildings standing sentry-like along the Esplanade of the Ministries. Each one is home to a different government department. In the distance is the Congress Complex.

The Baptistry is an unusual egg-shaped building said to be a representation of the Host. It is connected to the cathedral by a tunnel.

⌐ **The cathedral's entrance**

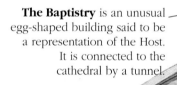

Interior of the Cathedral
Through colored panes designed by Antonia Marianne Peretti, daylight falls on the seating area for hundreds of worshippers. Suspended from the ceiling are three floating angels made by the Brazilian sculptor Alfredo Ceschiatti.

BRASÍLIA CATHEDRAL

The striking yet simplistic form of the cathedral provides Brasília with an instant and recognizable identity. An illusion of space is created in the interior by the circular floor being set below ground level and therefore lower than the entrance.

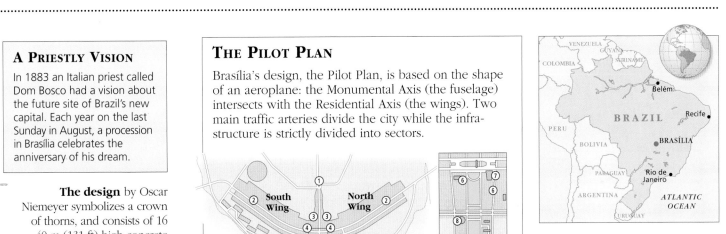

Brasília

A PRIESTLY VISION

In 1883 an Italian priest called Dom Bosco had a vision about the future site of Brazil's new capital. Each year on the last Sunday in August, a procession in Brasília celebrates the anniversary of his dream.

The design by Oscar Niemeyer symbolizes a crown of thorns, and consists of 16 40-m (131-ft) high concrete columns which appear as arms reaching to the sky.

THE PILOT PLAN

Brasília's design, the Pilot Plan, is based on the shape of an aeroplane: the Monumental Axis (the fuselage) intersects with the Residential Axis (the wings). Two main traffic arteries divide the city while the infrastructure is strictly divided into sectors.

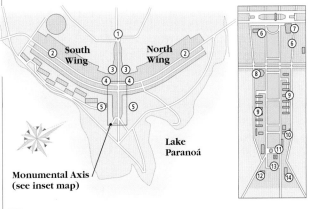

South Wing

North Wing

Lake Paranoá

Monumental Axis (see inset map)

KEY

① JK Memorial
② Residential Axis
③ Hotel sectors
④ Commercial sectors
⑤ Embassy sectors
⑥ Cultural sectors
⑦ National Theater
⑧ Brasília Cathedral
⑨ Esplanade of the Ministries
⑩ Palace of Justice
⑪ Congress Complex
⑫ Supreme Court
⑬ Plaza of the Three Powers
⑭ Planalto Palace

Water is a recurring theme in Brasília. Here it surrounds the cathedral.

KEY DATES

1956 Kubitschek is inaugurated as President of Brazil. A competition is launched for the design of the city.

1957 Construction of the city based on the Pilot Plan begins.

1959 Building work starts on the cathedral.

1960 Brasília is inaugurated on 21 April and becomes the capital city of Brazil.

1987 Brasília is designated a World Heritage Site by UNESCO.

OSCAR NIEMEYER

The vision of Oscar Niemeyer has become synonymous with the rise of modern Brazil. Born in Brazil in 1907, Niemeyer graduated from Rio de Janeiro's National School of Fine Arts in 1934 and collaborated with Lucio Costa and Le Corbusier on the new Ministry of Education and Health in Rio. In 1947 he designed the Brazilian pavilion at the New York World's Fair. His architectural style became more daring as he adapted reinforced concrete into a modern style of architecture. He is probably best known for his designs for the main public buildings in Brasília such as the concave and convex domes of the ▷ *National Congress,* the ▷ *Palace of Justice,* and the simple yet evocative ▷ *Cathedral.* Recognized as a pioneer of modern architecture, he has won numerous prizes for his work.

Palace of Justice
The low-rise, unimposing Palace of Justice features water cascading between its delicate white arches. Nearby is a stone sculpture of the head of President Juscelino Kubitschek.

National Congress
The juxtaposition of the dishes and twin towers provides a dramatic, space-age silhouette that is a symbol of the city.

Estancia de Alta Gracia, one of the five *estancias* of Córdoba

JESUITS IN SOUTH AMERICA

The city of Córdoba became the center of the Jesuit movement in northern and western Argentina, Paraguay, southern Brazil, and Uruguay. Sanctioned by the Spanish crown, Jesuit missions were founded on egalitarian principles and promoted the autonomy of the indigenous people as an innovative and powerful example of religious colonization. Assisted by the Jesuits, the Indians developed a sophisticated social system with a strong community base. However, after about 160 years of work, the Jesuits were expelled from the area by Carlos III of Spain for reasons not entirely clear. Their holdings were subsequently sold.

SOCIAL AND AGRICULTURAL ROLE

Santa Catalina and the other *estancias* were hives of activity and had a twin role – acting as both church and farm. Thousands of cows, sheep, and horses roamed the paddocks, huge swathes of wheat and corn were grown in the fields, and vegetables cultivated in the gardens. The ranches had their own water reservoirs and sophisticated irrigation systems, carpentry workshops for producing exquisite furniture, and enormous flour mills. In addition, they were centers of intellectual activity and spawned esteemed philosophers, musicians, and architects. The Jesuits were responsible for the first printing press in South America and the cartographers here made the very first maps of the region.

Estancias of Córdoba: Santa Catalina

THE FIVE ESTANCIAS (large farming estates) and Jesuit buildings of Córdoba in Argentina are among the most important examples of colonial architecture in South America. The *estancias* were built or acquired in the 17th and 18th centuries to finance the Jesuit mission to Christianize the region, and they formed part of a successful religious and social experiment. These unique, organized communities, where the native population acquired new knowledge and skills, made impressive contributions to the arts and science, forming an extraordinary fusion of indigenous and European architecture and culture. The largest of the *estancias*, Santa Catalina, was an important center for cattle breeding. Eventually the Jesuit order was expelled and the lands auctioned off, although their legacy has remained to this day.

★ Patio Principal
The architects of Santa Catalina are unknown and the different buildings vary in style. The Patio Principal had not been completed by the time the Jesuits left the estancia.

Entrance to Patio de las Higueras.

Patio de las Higueras
This patio contained carpentry and blacksmith workshops and was the most important courtyard despite its modest architecture.

STAR FEATURES

★ **Patio Principal**

★ **Altar**

★ **Church Façade**

Patio Bajo
The entrance courtyard for the estancia, *Patio Bajo was a less important service area for general use.*

★ Altar

The entire altar is made of wood, gilded in gold leaf and adorned with wooden sculptures. At the top of the altar sits a carving of Santa Catalina (St Catherine). She is also depicted in the central painting. Other religious sculptures adorn the single nave.

CATTLE BREEDING

The Jesuits' construction of irrigation channels enabled Estancia de Santa Catalina to become a major center for cattle and sheep breeding. Workshops containing looms were built to manufacture the wool.

The fruit garden contained hundreds of fruit trees, many of which were grape vines. Within the complex, the Patio de la Torre contained a smaller fruit and vegetable garden. →

Patio de la Torre contains a corridor of rooms where the Jesuits slept.

The cemetery is thought to be where the Jesuit clergy were buried.

A network of cloisters runs throughout the *estancia*. The beautiful cloisters of the Patio Principal were constructed in an Italian Mannerist style.

★ Church Façade

The high, domed towers on either side of the church doorway and the curved pediments are examples of the "colonial" Baroque style (▷ Baroque Style p111) of this magnificent church.

KEY DATES

1616 The building of the Jesuit *estancias* begins.

1622 Estancia de Santa Catalina is founded.

1767 Carlos III of Spain signs a decree to expel the Jesuit Order from the Spanish Americas.

2000 The Jesuit Block and Estancias of Cordoba are inscribed on the UNESCO World Heritage List.

OTHER ESTANCIAS OF CÓRDOBA

Estancia de Caroya was Córdoba's first Jesuit ranch, founded in 1616. From 1814 to 1816 it was used to manufacture weapons in the War of Independence. Built with local materials and set around a large courtyard and cloister, the architectural design is characteristic of the region. Estancia Jesús María (1618) was devoted to wine production, an activity which has continued to this day. The residence is noted for its two-tiered cloister and the National Jesuit Museum that it now accommodates. The well-preserved Estancia de Alta Gracia (1643) is Córdoba's most active settlement today. It is the local parish church and houses a museum, and the workshops that once specialized in textile manufacture are now home to a secondary school. The area's most remote settlement is Estancia de La Candelaria (1683). Located in the middle of the sierras, it was once a center for cattle breeding.

General Index

Page numbers in **bold** type refer to main entries

ACKNOWLEDGMENTS

DORLING KINDERSLEY would like to thank the following people whose contributions and assistance have made the preparation of this book possible:

ADDITIONAL CONTRIBUTORS: Jane Egginton, Frances Linzee Gordon, Denise Heywood, Andrew Humphries, Roger Williams.

ILLUSTRATORS: Richard Almazan, Studios Arcana, Modi Artistici, Robert Ashby, William Band, Gilles Beauchemin, Dipankar Bhattacarga, Anuar Bin Abdul Rahim, Richard Bonson, François Brosse, Michal Burkiewicz, Cabezas/Acanto Arquitectura y Urbanismo S.L., Jo Cameron, Danny Cherian, Yeapkok Chien, ChrisOrr.com, Stephen Conlin, Garry Cross, Bruno de Robillard, Brian Delf, Donati Giudici Associati srl, Richard Draper, Dean Entwhistle, Steven Felmore, Marta Fincato, Eugene Fleury, Chris Forsey, Martin Gagnon, Vincent Gagnon, Nick Gibbard, Isidoro González-Adalid, Kevin Goold, Paul Guest, Stephen Gyapay, Toni Hargreaves, Trevor Hill, Chang Huai-Yan, Roger Hutchins, Kamalahasan R, Kevin Jones Assocs., John Lawrence, Wai Leong Koon, Yoke Ling Lee, Nick Lipscombe, Ian Lusted, Andrew MacDonald, Maltings Partnership, Lena Maminajszwili, Kumar Mantoo Stuart, Pawel Marczak, Lee Ming Poo, Pawel Mistewicz, John Mullaney, Jill Munford, Gillie Newman, Luc Normandin, Arun P, Lee Peters, Otakar Pok, Robbie Polley, David Pulvermacher, Avinash Ramscurrun, Kevin Robinson, Peter Ross, Simon Roulstone, Suman Saha, Fook San Choong, Ajay Sethi, Derrick Slone, Jaroslav Staněk, Thomas Sui, Ashok Sukumaran, Peggy Tan, Pat Thorne, Gautam Trivedi, Frank Urban, Mark Warner, Paul Weston, Andrzej Wielgosz, Ann Winterbotham, Martin Woodward, Bohdan Wróblewski, Hong Yew Tan, Kah Yune Denis Chai, Magdalena Zmadzinska, Piotr Zubrzycki.

PROOFREADER AND RESEARCHER: Stewart J Wild.

INDEXER: Hilary Bird.

SPECIAL ASSISTANCE
www.santacatalina.info; Maire ni Bhain at Trinity College, Dublin; Chartres Cathedral; Château de Chambord; San Zeno Maggiore, Verona; Procurate di San Marco (Basilica San Marco); Campo Dei Miracoli, Pisa; Hayley Smith and Romaine Werblow from DK Picture Library; Duomo, Siena; Mrs Marjorie Weeke at St. Peter's; Le Soprintendenze Archeologiche di Agrigento e di Pompei; Topkapi Palace, Istanbul; M. Oulhaj (Mosque of Hassan II); The Castle of Good Hope; Port Arthur Historic Site.

ADDITIONAL PHOTOGRAPHY
Shaen Adey, Max Alexander, Fredrik & Laurence Arvidsson, Gábor Barka, Philip Blenkinsop, Maciej Bronarski, Demetrio Carrasco, Tina Chambers, Joe Cornish, Andy Crawford, Ian Cumming, Tim Daly, Geoff Dann, Robert O'Dea, Barbara Deer, Vladimír Dobrovodský, Jiři Doležal, Alistair Duncan, Heidi Grassley, Paul Harris, Adam Hajder, John Heseltine, Nigel Hicks, Ed Ironside, Stuart Isett, Dorota & Mariusz Jarymowicz, Alan Keohane, Dinesh Khanna, Dave King, Paul Kenward, Andrew McKinney, Jiři Kopřiva, Neil Lukas, Pawel Marczac, Eric Meacher, Wojciech Mędrzak, Michael Moran, Roger Moss, Tomasz Myśluk, Stephen Oliver, Vincent Oliver, Lloyd Park, John Parker, Amit Pasricha, Aditya Patankar, Artur Pawłowski, František Přeučil, Ram Rahman, Bharath Ramamruthum, Rob Reichenfeld, Magnes Rew, Lucio Rossi, Jean-Michel Ruiz, Kim Sayer, Jürgen Scheunemann, Colin Sinclair, Toby Sinclair, Frits Solvang, Tony Souter, Jon Spaull, Eric Svensson, Cécile Tréal, Lübbe Verlag, BPS Walia, Mathew Ward, Richard Watson, Linda Whitwam, Jeppe Wikström, Alan Williams, Peter Wilson, Paweł Wójcik, Stephen Wooster, Francesca Yorke.

PHOTOGRAPHY PERMISSIONS
Dorling Kindersley would like to thank all the churches, temples, mosques, castles, museums, and other sights too numerous to list individually for their assistance and kind permission to photograph their establishments.

PICTURE CREDITS
t=top; tl=top left; tlc=top left center; tc=top center; trc=top right center; tr=top right; cla=center left above; ca=center above; cra=center right above; cl=center left; c=center; cr=center right; clb=center left below; cb=center below; crb=center right below; bl=bottom left; b=bottom; bc=bottom center; bcl=bottom center left; bcr=bottom center right; br=bottom right; d=detail.

Every effort has been made to trace the copyright holders and we apologize in advance for any unintentional omissions. We would be pleased to insert the appropriate acknowledgments in any subsequent edition of this publication.

DORLING KINDERSLEY would like to thank the following for their assistance: Høymagasinet 12tl; Instituto du Biblioteca Nacional E Do Livro Lisboa 169bc; Instituto Portugues do Patrimonio Arquetectonico e Arqueologico (IPPAR), Lisbon 168 -9 all except 169br; © Provost and Scholars of Kings College, Cambridge/English Heritage 36–7all except 36br; National Archaeological Museum, Naples: 221bcr; © Patrimonio Nacional 188–9; Private Collection 34bl, 50cl, 56clb, 68tl, 72tl, 80cl, 84bl, 88tl, 144cl, 198cl, 210cl, 214tl, 218tl, 264tl, 286bl, 290bl, 316tl, 334bl, 336cl, 338tl; Österreich Werbung 128bc, 128br; Royal Green Jackets Museum 364c; Toledo Museum 190–1; University Museum of Archaeology and Anthropology, Cambridge 400bl; Establissement public du musée et du domaine national de Versailles 80tl/80tr/80b/81t/81cra/81cla/81b.

Works of art have been reproduced with the permission of the following copyright holders: *Paris through the Window* (1913), Marc Chagall © ADAGP, Paris, 2003 370c; *Mosaics in the Golden Hall Stockholm Stadhus* Einer Forseth © BUS 2004 16tr; *Black Lines* (1913) Vasily Kandinsky © ADAGP, Paris, 2003 371crb; *Woman Holding a Vase* (1927), Fernand Léger © ADAGP, Paris, 2003 371cra; *Woman Ironing* (1904) Pablo Picasso © Succession Picasso/DACS 2004 370clb; *Woman with Yellow Hair* (1931) Pablo Picasso © Succession Picasso/DACS 2004 371bl; *The Snake* (1904) Richard Serra © ARS, NY and DACS London 2004 180br.

The Publishers thank the following individuals, companies, and picture libraries for permission to reproduce their photographs:

A1 PIX: Mati 302cb.

ACCADEMIA ITALIANA: Sue Bond 221c.

AGENZIA FOTOGRAFICA MARIA PIA STRADELLA: 210clb.

IDRIS AHMED: 324bc.

ARCHIVO ICONOGRAFICO S.A. (AISA) : 174bc, 245bl.

AKG: 144c, 145crb, 277bl, 289r, 292cla.

ALAMY IMAGES: Goodshoot Royalty Free 7b; Robert Harding World Imagery 303c.

ANCIENT ART & ARCHITECTURE COLLECTION: 272br.

ARCAID: Paul Rafferty 180bcl.

ARCHIVIO DELL'ARTE: Luciano Pedicini 220cl, 222bc.

FABRIZIO ARDITO: 298tr.

THE ART ARCHIVE: 223bc, 281cra; Devizes Musem/Eileen Tweedy 53c.

ART DIRECTORS: Eric Smith 303t.

FREDRIK & LAURENCE ARVIDSSON: 321tl.

AUSTRALIAN PICTURE LIBRARY: R. Eastwood 358tr; JP & ES Baker 359cra.

AUSTRIAN TOURIST BOARD: 131bc.

AVERY ARCHITECTURAL & FINE ART LIBRARY, COLUMBIA UNIVERSITY: 373cl.

AXIOM: Heidi Grassley 281bcl; Jim Holmes 159bl; James Morris 281tc.

TAHSIN AYDOGMUS: 246tr, 248tr.

M. BALAN: 338tr, 338cla, 339tl.

JAUME BALANYA: 186br.

© CH BASTIN & J EVRARD: 59br, 59t, 60cr, 60b.

BENOY BEHL: 320tr, 320tc, 320ca, 320c, 320b, 321ca, 321c, 321bc, 336tr, 336bc, 337cra, 337crb.

BERLIN CATHEDRAL (BERLINER DOM): 102br.

SUBHASH BHARGAVA: 330clb.

BLACKSTAR: 377ca.

OSVALDO BÖHM:201tc.

BOLSHOY THEATER: 162tr, 162bc, 163tc, 163cra.

BORD FÁILTE/IRISH TOURIST BOARD: Brian Lynch 22tc, 22tr.

GERARD BOULLAY: 73bl; 73cra.

BRAZIL STOCK PHOTOS: Fabio Pili 408tr.
BRIDGEMAN ART LIBRARY, LONDON/NEW YORK: 159c; British Library *Historia Anglorum* 48tc(d); Guildhall Art Library Clytemnestra, John Collier 233cr; Private Collection 54bc; Royal Holloway & Bedford New College, *The Princes Edward and Richard in the Tower* Sir John Everett Millais 47bc; Basilica San Francesco, Assisi 215br; Smith Art Gallery and Museum, Stirling 30bc; Stapleton Collection 272cb, 280tr.

CAMERA PRESS: 39bl; P. Abbey 41crb; Cecil Beaton 42clb.

DEMETRIO CARRASCO: 154bc, 157cra, 157bc.

CEPHAS PICTURE LIBRARY: Herve Champollion 90tl.

CHINAPIX: Zhang Chaoyin 304c, 304b.

Photos Editions Combier, Macon: 69tc.

CORBIS: Paul Almasy 290c, 291tc; Archivo Iconografico, S.A. 160ca, 161tl, 344b; Yann Arthus-Bertrand 408cr; Bettmann Archive 30cl, 227t, 372bl, 374c, 376c, 377crb, 377bc, 384bl; Dave Bartruff 101c, 253tc; Marilyn Bridges 52c; Chromo Sohm Inc./Jospeh Sohm 308b; Elio Ciol 4tr, 289cra; Dean Conger 310cr; Bernard and Catherine Desjeux 269bc; Eye Ubiquitous/Thelma Sanders 283b; Todd Gipstein 375t; Lowell Georgia 310cr; John and Dallas Heaton 9b, 9t; Angelo Hornak 35tl, 54tr; Wolfgang Kaehler 133c, 282tl, 303bl; Kelly-Mooney Photography 313t; Danny Lehman 8b; Charles Lenars 308cl; Charles & Josette Lenars 4tl, 58tr; Massimo Listri 132tr; Craig Lovell 4b, 305br; Gail Mooney 94cl; Diego Lezama Orezzdi 300tr, 301tl; Michael Nicholson 27t, 290c, 300c; Abu'l Qasim 300b; Carmen Redondo 9c; David Samuel Robbins 305tl; Galen Rowell 6; Sakamoto Photo Research Lab 319ca; Kevin Schafer 53b; Paul A Souders 5c; Ruggero Vanni 227b; Sandro Vannini 228ca, 283c; Vanni Archive 236tl; Nik Wheeler 282c; Roger Wood 290br, 290tr CORBIS SYGMA: Thierry Prat 92c.

JOE CORNISH: 182tr.

CRESCENT PRESS AGENCY: David Henley 345ca.

GERALD CUBITT: 345tl.

CULVER PICTURES INC.: 373cr, 374cb, 375cra, 375crb, 376crb.

DAS FOTOARCHIV: Henning Christoph 282tr.

PHOTO DASPET, AVIGNON: 96bc.

DEUTSCHE APOTHEKENMUSEUM: 120tr.

DIAF (AGENCE D'ILLUSTRATION PHOTOGRAPHIQUE): Camille Moirenc 94cl.

DIATOTALE: Château de Chenonceau 86cr.

ASHOK DILWALI: 328tc.

THOMAS DIX: 336tc, 336ca, 336br, 337bc.

DOMBAUVERWALTUNG DES METROPOLITANKAPITELS KÖLN: Brigit Lambert 112tc, 112c, 112bc, 113tl, 113cra, 113cb, 113bc, 113bl.

DOM MUSEUM (HILDESHEIM): 106cla, 106tl.

JURJEN DRENTH: 64tr.

DTV: 114bl.

D.N. DUBE: 326ca, 327cr, 328tr, 329tl.
DUBLIN CASTLE: Courtesy of the Garda Museum 26cl.

EISENACH-WARTBURG (Photographs by Ulrich Kneise): 114ca, 114br, 114cb, 115ca.

EKDOTIKE ATHENON S.A.: 236bc, 239b.

MARY EVANS PICTURE LIBRARY: 27crb, 40clb, 41bc, 52bl, 55ca, 58bl, 76cr, 77crb, 78br, 173bc, 216bc. ROBERT EVERTS: 194ca.

EYE UBIQUITOUS: Hugh Rooney 58tc; Julia Waterlow 408b.

FESTUNG HOHENSALZBURG: 135cra.

FORTIDSMINNEFORENINGEN: Kjersheim/Lindstad, NIKU 15b.
JOHN FREEMAN: 160c.

MICHAEL FREEMAN: 380bc, 381tl.

CHRISTINA GAMBARO: 293bc.

GEHRY PARTNERS LLP: 180tl.

EVA GERUM: 118c, 119tl, 119cra, 119c, 119bc, 122tr, 122cla, 122clb, 122bc.

GETTY IMAGES: Anne Frank Fonds-Basel/Anne Frank House 64c, 64bc, 65c, 65bc; Hulton-Deutsch 24bc, 311b; Image Bank/Peter Adams 5b, /Peter Hendrie 344tr, /A. Setterwhite 375bc; Photographer's Choice/John Warden 309t; Stone/Jerry Alexander 407cb; Taxi/Chris Rawlings 10–1.

EDUARDO GIL: 410tl, 411t.

GIRAUDON, PARIS: 89bcr.

EVA GLEASON: 398tr, 398tc, 398bc, 398br, 399bc.

LA GOÉLETTE: *The Three Graces* Charles-André Van Loo photo JJ Derennes 86br.

GOLDEN GATE BRIDGE HIGHWAY & TRANSPORTATION DISTRICT (GGBHTD): 382tc, 382–383tc,

382br, 383clb, 383cra, 382cl.

GOLDEN GATE NATIONAL RECREATIONAL AREA: 385bl, 385c.

FRANCES LINZEE GORDON: 284tl, 284ca, 284cb, 284b, 285t.

GUGGENHEIM BILBAO MUSEO: 180tr, 180br, 181tc, 181bc.

PHOTOTHEQUE HACHETTE LIVRE: Bibliothèque Nationale, Paris 260bl.

SONIA HALLIDAY: Laura Lushington 83ca.

ROBERT HARDING PICTURE LIBRARY: 93cr, 219bc; R.Francis 72clb; R. Frerck 407b; Sylvain Grandadam 408cl; Michael Jenner 245bc; Eitan Simmnor 289bc; James Strachan 302ca; A Wolf 75tl, 75b; Explorer/P. Tetrel 81crb.

DENISE HEYWOOD: 348cl, 348cr, 348b, 348t, 349tl, 349tr, 349b, 350tl, 350car, 350cl, 350cbr, 351tr, 351bl, 351br.

JULIET HIGHET: 351tl.

HISTORIC ROYAL PALACES (Crown Copyright): 50tc, 50tr, 50c, 50bc, 51bc, 51tl, 51ca, 51cb.

HISTORIC SCOTLAND (Crown Copyright): 31cra, 32tr, 32c, 33bl.

MICHAEL HOLFORD: 277bc.
ANGELO HORNAK LIBRARY: 34tlc, 34bc.

DAVE G. HOUSER: 401bc.

IDEAL PHOTO SA.: C. Vergas 232bc.

IMAGES OF AFRICA: Shaen Adey 286cb; Hein von Horsten 286ca; Lanz von Horsten 287tl.

IMAGE STATE: Pictor International 155t.

IMAGINECHINA: 306cl, 311cr, 313c.

IMPACT PHOTOS: Y Goldstein 302tl.

INSIGHT GUIDES: APA/Jim Holmes 157tl.

HANAN ISACHAR: 253bc, 292clb, 293cra, 296tr.

ISRAEL MUSEUM: 297c.

PAUL JACKSON: 299br.

JARROLD COLOUR PUBLICATIONS: 24br.

MICHAEL JENNER PHOTOGRAPHY: 288ca.

WUBBE DE JONG: 65tl.

KATZ: Mansell Collection 96tc.

KEA PUBLISHING SERVICES LTD.: Francesco Venturi 156cla, 156bc, 156br.

KOSTOS KONTOS: 234tr, 236cla.

KSC VISITOR CENTER, CAPE CANAVERAL: 390tr, 391ca, 391cr.

KUNGLIGA HUSGERÅDSKAMMAREN: Alexis Daflos 20cla, 20bc, 21tc, 21bc; Håkan Lind 21cr.
KUNSTHISTORISCHES MUSEUM, VIENNA: *Italienische Berglandschaft mit Hirt und Herde* (GG 7465) (*Italian Landscape with Shepherd and Herd*), Joseph Rosa 131cra.

BERND LASDIN: 100cla, 100c, 101cra.

HÅKON LI: 14c, 14bc, 15c.

JÜRGEN LIEPE: 272tc.

EADEN LILLEY PHOTOGRAPHERS: 36br.

ROMILLY LOCKYER: 38bc, 40b.

LÜBBE VERLAG: 130tl.

AGENCIA LUSA: Tiago Petinga 176tr, 177ca, 177br.

MAGNUM: Topkapı Palace Museum/Ara Guler 245tl.

MANDER & MITCHENSEN COLLECTION: 163bc.

FRED MAWER: 390cb.

MEHRANGARH FORT TRUST: 332bc, 333bc.

FOTO MODERNA: Mozzati 211cra.

MONDADORI CENTRO DI DOCUMENTAZIONE: 227cra.

NARODNÍ GALERIE V PRAZE: 146br.

NASA: Kennedy Space Center 390b.

NATIONAL PARK SERVICE (CHACO CULTURE NATIONAL HISTORICAL PARK): Dave Six 388tc.

NATIONAL PARK SERVICE (ELLIS ISLAND IMMIGRATION MUSEUM): 376tl, 376ca, 376br.

NATIONAL PARK SERVICE (STATUE OF LIBERTY NATIONAL MONUMENT): 374cl, 375clb.

© THE NOBEL FOUNDATION: 16cl.

JÜRGEN NOGAI: 100tr, 101bc.

NORWEGIAN TOURIST BOARD: Per Eide 14tl.

RICHARD NOWITZ: 292bc, 293tc, 293cr, 295cr, 296br, 297bl, 297bc, 299bl.

© THE OFFICE OF PUBLIC WORKS, IRELAND: 22c, 23tl, 23c.

MARCO OLIVA, MILAN: 404c.

ORLETA AGENCY: Jerzy Bronarski 142ca, 142cb, 143c, 143bl, 143br.

ARCHIVO FOTOGRAFICO ORONOZ: 171bc, 192c, 195bl.

GÜNGÖR ÖZSOY: 243tl, 243cr.

PALEIS HET LOO: 66tr, 66ca, 66cb, 66bc, 67tl.

PANOS PICTURES: Christien Jaspars 283t.

PHOTOS 12: Panorama Stock 308cr.

PHOTOBANK: Peter Baker 252c, 252bc.

ANDREA PISTOLESI: 380c.

PRAGUE CITY ARCHIVES (ARCHIV HLAVNIKO MESTA PRAHA): 148cr.

PRIVATE COLLECTION: 228tc, 229tc, 229bc.

NATASHA RAZINA: 158br, 159tl.
RIHA-FWTG GMBH: 127tl.

REUNION DES MUSEES NATIONAUX (RMN): 75bl.

REX FEATURES LTD: 48c, 49bc.

ROCAMADOUR: 93ca.

ROWOHLT VERLAG: 104tl.

THE ROYAL COLLECTION © 2004, Her Majesty Queen Elizabeth II: 38tr, 38ca, 39tl, 39cra, 39bcr, 46br, 46bc, 47tl, 48tr, 49tlc, 49tr, 49bl, 50br; photo A.C. Cooper Ltd *Rome: The Pantheon* Canaletto 38bcl.

ROYAL GEOGRAPHICAL SOCIETY PICTURE LIBRARY: Chris Caldicott 282b, 406tl; Eric Lawrie 5t, 407t; Sassoom 406cb.

SALVATORE SPAGNUOLO: 291cra.

SAN FRANCISCO PUBLIC LIBRARY: 385clb.

FOTOGRAFIE GREGOR M. SCHMID: 161cr.

SHALINI SARAN: 334tr, 334cla, 334clb, 335tl, 335crb, 335bl.

SCALA GROUP SPA: 198c, 204bc, 205tc, 206cla, 210tr, 210br, 211tl, 211b, 214ca, 214cb, 215bl, 217b, 218br, 219tl, 222tr.

SCHLOSS SCHÖNBRUNN: 130tr, 130ca, 130c, 130bc, 131tc.

AJAY SETHI: 339cra.

SHRINE OF SAINTE-ANNE-DE-BEAUPRÉ: 362tl, 362tr, 363cb, 363ca, 363b.

SKYSCAN: 53t.

SOLOMON R. GUGGENHEIM MUSEUM: photo by D Heald 370c, 370bcl, 370bc, 371tc, 371ca, 371crb, 371bl.

SOUTH AMERICAN PICTURES: Tony Morrison 397cr, 401tl, 409br; Chris Sharp 395tl, 397b;

STAATLICHES MUSEUM SCHWERIN: 98tr, 98br, 99tl.

STAATLICHE KUNSTSAMMLUNGEN DRESDEN: 110tr, 110cb, 111cb, 111bc.

STATE RUSSIAN MUSEUM: 156bl.

STIFT MELK: 132ca, 132cb, 133tl, 132br, 133bl, 133bc.

STIFTUNG PREUSSISCHE SCHLÖSSER UND GÄRTEN BERLIN: 104c, 104br, 105tc, 105c, 105bl, 105bc.

STOCKHOLMS STADHUS: 16tr; Jan Asplund 16tr, 16br.

SUPERSTOCK LTD.: 346ca.

SYDNEY OPERA HOUSE TRUST: 356tr, 356ca,

357bc, 357bl, 357tc.

SUZIE THOMAS PUBLICITY: 356bc.

TIPS IMAGES: Guido Alberto Rossi 404tr, 405c.

TOURISM TASMANIA: 358cl.

TRAVEL INK: Allan Hatley 347tc; Pauline Thorton 346cb.

TRIZECHAHN TOWER LIMITED PARTNERSHIP: 366c, 367bl, 367tl.

TRINITY COLLEGE, Dublin: 25cr.

TURNER ENTERTAINMENT CO.: 373bc

UNIVERSITY MUSEUM OF CULTURAL HERITAGE – UNIVERSITY OF OSLO, NORWAY: 15t.

O.VAERING: *Akershus Slott* Jacob Croning 13tl.

VASAMUSEET: Hans Hammarskiöld 18tr, 18cla, 18clb, 18br, 19tc, 19cra, 19crb, 19bc.

MIREILLE VAUTIER: 406ca, 407ca, 409bl.

VERKEHRSVEREIN HILDESHEIM e.V: 106clb.

ROGER VIOLLET: 76bc(d), 79tl, 95b.

VISIONS OF THE LAND: Garo Nalbandian 298bc, 298cla; Basilio Rodella 292tr, 296cl, 296bc, 297tl, 297cra.

B.P.S. WALIA: 322tc, 322tr, 322cla, 322cra, 322br, 323tl, 323ca, 323clb.

EMMY WERNER: 410tr, 410c, 410b, 411b.

Reproduced by kind permission of the DEAN & CHAPTER OF WESTMINSTER: 43bl.

WHITE HOUSE HISTORICAL ASSOCIATION: 378cla, 378bc, 379tl, 379c, 379bl, 379bc.

PETER WILSON: 228c, 230ca, 249tl.

WOODMANSTERNE: Jeremy Marks 44tr, 45ca.

WORLD PICTURES: 285c, 301tr, 301b, 303br.

Reproduced by kind permission of the DEAN & CHAPTER OF YORK: Alan Curtis 35tr; Jim Korshaw 34tr; Newbury Smith Photography 34c.

ZEFA: 359tl.

JACKET – Front – CORBIS: Tibor Bognar cr; Aaron Horowitz tl; Jose Fusta Raga tr; Royalty Free cl, cb, tc, tlc; Phil Schermeister cla; Sandro Vannini cra; DK IMAGES: Linda Whitwam trc; GETTY IMAGES: Image Bank/Cosmo Condina br; /Harald Sund clb; /Paul Trummer crb; Stone/Dale Boyer bc; /Stephen Studd bl; Taxi/VCL ca.
Back – ALAMY IMAGES: Carol Dixon tr; Christopher Wyatt tr; CORBIS:Patrick Ward trc; DK IMAGES: Mike Dunning tlc; Ken Robertson tl.
Spine – PHOTOS12.com: Panorama Stock.

All other images © Dorling Kindersley. For further information see: www.dkimages.com

LONDON, NEW YORK, MELBOURNE, MUNICH AND DELHI
www.dk.com

PUBLISHER Douglas Amrine
PUBLISHING MANAGER Kate Poole
MANAGING EDITOR Anna Streiffert
PROJECT EDITOR Lucinda Cooke
SENIOR ART EDITOR Marisa Renzullo

SENIOR DESIGNER Tessa Bindloss
DESIGNER Maite Lantaron
SENIOR DTP DESIGNER Jason Little
DTP DESIGNER Conrad Van Dyk
SENIOR MAP-COORDINATOR Casper Morris
SENIOR CARTOGRAPHER Uma Bhattacharya
CARTOGRAPHIC RESEARCHER Suresh Kumar
EDITORS Sherry Collins, Stephanie Driver, Jane Hutchings, Jacky Jackson, Vandana Mohindra, Marianne Petrou, Mani Ramaswamy, Mary Sutherland, Karen Villabona, Fiona Wild
PRODUCTION Joanna Bull, Sarah Dodd
PICTURE RESEARCH Taiyaba Khatoon, Ellen Root

Reproduced by Colourscan (Singapore)

Printed and bound by L. Rex Printing Company Ltd. (China)

Copyright 2006 © Dorling Kindersley Limited, London
A Penguin Company

LIBRARY AND ARCHIVES CANADA CATALOGUING IN PUBLICATION

THE WORLD'S 200 MUST-SEE PLACES. – CANADIAN ED.

Includes index.
ISBN 1-55363-065-3

1. TRAVEL–GUIDEBOOKS. I. TITLE: WORLD'S TWO HUNDRED MUST-SEE PLACES.
G153.4.W675 2006 910'.2'02 C2005-906593-1

FLOORS ARE REFERRED TO THROUGHOUT IN ACCORDANCE WITH EUROPEAN USAGE; IE THE "FIRST FLOOR" IS THE FLOOR AT GROUND LEVEL.